PEOPLE OF THE EARTH

Virginia Indians fishing from canoes, with a weir at the left. Painting by
Elizabethan artist John White.

PEOPLE OF THE EARTH

AN INTRODUCTION TO WORLD PREHISTORY

ELEVENTH EDITION

BRIAN M. FAGAN
UNIVERSITY OF CALIFORNIA, SANTA BARBARA

PEARSON

Prentice
Hall

Upper Saddle River
New Jersey 07458

Library of Congress Cataloging-in-Publication Data

FAGAN, BRIAN M.
  People of the earth : an introduction to world prehistory/Brian Fagan.—11th ed.
    p. cm.
  Includes bibliographical references and index.
  ISBN   0-13-111316-X (pbk)
  1. Prehistoric peoples.   2. Civilization, Ancient.   I. Title.

GN740F33 2004
930—dc21

                                                    2003045612

AVP, Publisher: Nancy Roberts
Editorial assistant: Lee Peterson
VP, Director of production and manufacturing: Barbara Kittle
Project manager: Joan Stone
Copy editor: M. L. Byrd
Manufacturing manager: Nick Sklitsis
Prepress and manufacturing buyer: Ben Smith
Manager, production/formatting and art: Guy Ruggiero
Creative design director: Leslie Osher
Senior art director: Anne Bonanno Nieglos
Interior design: Susan Walrath, Anne Bonanno Nieglos
Cover design: Susan Walrath
Director of marketing: Beth Mejia
Marketing assistant: Adam Laitman
Director, image resource center: Melinda Reo
Manager, rights and permissions: Zina Arabia
Interior image specialist: Beth Boyd-Brenzel
Image permission coordinator: Michelina Viscusi
Photo researcher: Francelle Carapetyan
Media project manager: Kate Ramunda
Electronic artist: Mirella Signoretto
Cover photo: Thera, fresco of boxing children
Cover image: R. Sheridan/Ancient Art & Architecture Collection

Credits may be found on p. 577, which constitutes an extension of this copyright page.

This book was set in 10/11.5 New Baskerville by Interactive Composition Corporation and was printed and bound by Courier Companies, Inc.
The cover was printed by Coral Graphics.

© 2004, 2001 by The Lindbriar Corp.
Pearson Education, Inc.
Upper Saddle River, NJ 07458

Printed in the United States of America

10 9 8 7 6 5 4 3 2 1

ISBN 0-13-111316-X

PEARSON EDUCATION LTD., *London*
PEARSON EDUCATION AUSTRALIA PTY, LIMITED, *Sydney*
PEARSON EDUCATION SINGAPORE, PTE. LTD
PEARSON EDUCATION NORTH ASIA LTD, *Hong Kong*
PEARSON EDUCATION CANADA, LTD., *Toronto*
PEARSON EDUCACIÓN DE MEXICO, S.A. *de C.V.*
PEARSON EDUCATION—JAPAN, *Tokyo*
PEARSON EDUCATION MALAYSIA, PTE. LTD
PEARSON EDUCATION, UPPER SADDLE RIVER, *New Jersey*

To William Frucht, because of El Niño and many other things.

And to all the dozens of archaeologists and students who have read and used this book in its various editions and sent me their comments and criticisms. This is the only way I can thank them all and expose them for what they are: honest and unmerciful critics. I am deeply grateful.

And as usual to our cats, who disapprove of authors in general and my writing efforts in particular. Their contribution was to tread on the manuscript—with muddy paws, of course.

BRIEF CONTENTS

CONTENTS

CHAPTER
3

HOMO ERECTUS AND HOMO SAPIENS SAPIENS 70
1.9 MILLION TO 40,000 YEARS AGO

PART

II

THE GREAT DIASPORA: THE SPREAD OF MODERN HUMANS 111

45,000 YEARS AGO TO MODERN TIMES

CHAPTER

4

EUROPE AND EURASIA 112

c. 40,000 TO 8000 B.C.

CHAPTER
13

THE STORY OF MAIZE: EARLY FARMERS IN THE AMERICAS   300

PART
IV

OLD WORLD CIVILIZATIONS   333

c. 3000 B.C. TO MODERN TIMES

CHAPTER
14

THE DEVELOPMENT OF CIVILIZATION   334

CHAPTER
17

EARLY STATES IN SOUTH AND SOUTHEAST ASIA   408

CHAPTER
18

EARLY CHINESE CIVILIZATION   430

PREFACE

GOLDEN PHARAOHS, LOST CITIES, GRINNING HUMAN skeletons—archaeology is the stuff of romance and legend. Many people still think of archaeologists as adventurers and treasure hunters, like Indiana Jones of Hollywood movie fame seeking the elusive Holy Grail. This enduring image goes back to the late nineteenth century, when archaeologists like Heinrich Schliemann of Troy fame could still find lost civilizations and excavate three royal palaces in a week. Today, few, if any, archaeologists behave like Indiana Jones. They are scientists, not adventurers, as comfortable in an air-conditioned laboratory as they are on a remote excavation.

The development of scientific archaeology from its Victorian beginnings ranks among the greatest triumphs of twentieth-century science. Archaeology has changed our perceptions of ourselves in profound ways, giving us a better understanding of our biological and cultural diversity. Welcome to the fascinating world of archaeology!

The eleventh edition of *People of the Earth* comes at a time when new discoveries and archaeological methodologies are deeply affecting our understanding of the human past. This edition continues a more-than-30-year tradition of clear, jargon-free writing for the beginning student, the incorporation of the latest scholarship, and an accessible (five-part) organization of the story of world prehistory. This time, I have added both valuable new content and effective new pedagogy to what has always been a straightforward narrative. But the basic objective remains the same: to provide an interesting journey through the 7-million-year-old landscape of the human past. At the same time, the book attempts to achieve geographic balance, giving equal time to both well-trodden and less-well-known parts of the world. Any world prehistory that does otherwise is presenting a skewed picture of the human past. *People of the Earth* is an adventure in archaeology. I hope you enjoy your sojourn in its pages.

Writing a straightforward narrative of human prehistory is a mammoth task, especially at a time when a torrent of new literature about archaeological discoveries around the world is revolutionizing our knowledge of the remote past. We are well beyond the point where a single author can possibly hope to keep up with every new find and intellectual development in world archaeology, but I have done my best, while trying to keep the narrative as simple and uncluttered as possible. The past five years alone have witnessed remarkable discoveries, among them new early fossil hominids from East Africa, major changes in our understanding of the evolution of modern humans, new perceptions of the beginnings of farming, and a revolution in our knowledge of short-term climatic change in the past.

Changes in the Eleventh Edition

Our knowledge of world prehistory increases constantly, mostly in fits and starts, but occasionally in a dramatic way, when new fossil discoveries in Chad, in the Sahara Desert, rewrite an entire chapter of early human evolution, or the decipherment of Maya script adds a new dimension to our understanding of an early civilization. For the most part, however, the changes are relatively small and undramatic.

The eleventh edition reflects a combination of a few major discoveries, like the 7-million-year-old mysterious primate *Sahelanthropus tchadensis* in Chad, with numerous less spectacular, but nevertheless important, advances like new data on the origins of wheat in Turkey, new insights into the date of the famous Ice Man in the Italian Alps, and so on.

Following reviewer suggestions, I have retained the same basic organization of the book for this edition. Chapter 1 introduces world prehistory and discusses new perceptions of the subject derived from new perspectives on the past. We survey alternative perspectives on the past and outline some of the important theoretical frameworks that influence our thinking about prehistory. *People of the Earth* has always been designed as a straightforward narrative, which is why the book is not written with a specific theoretical view. Judging from reviewer and user comments, this is a wise decision, as this allows instructors to add their own biases and viewpoints to the basic narrative material. I have, of course, paid careful attention to such major controversies as the origins of modern humans and the first settlement of the Americas, where an even-handed perspective is essential. The eleventh edition includes Site Boxes in each chapter, which discuss key locations and discoveries where more detailed information is valuable. Examples include the spectacular Grotte de Chauvet cave paintings in France and the Lords of Sipán from coastal Peru, one of the most important archaeological discoveries of the twentieth century. A series of boxes in the early chapters of the book describes key dating methods at appropriate places in the text.

This narrative of world prehistory is divided into five parts. Part I (Chapters 2 and 3) discusses human beginnings, what is sometimes called "archaic prehistory," the human past from the earliest times up to the appearance of *Homo sapiens sapiens*, ourselves. Here we cover important new fossil discoveries of recent years and such fascinating sites as Boxgrove in southern England. We also continue to take account of new theoretical advances in cognitive, or "postprocessual," archaeology, especially of the emerging synthesis of evolutionary psychology and archaeology. Part II (Chapters 4 to 7) discusses what I call the "Great Diaspora," the spread of anatomically modern humans through the world during and immediately after the late Ice Age. We go from Southwest Asia to Europe and Eurasia, then straight into the Americas, a logical order preferred by many users. Part II includes coverage of the new AMS radiocarbon chronology for first settlement made possible by extended calibration curves. From the Americas, we move on to Africa and Australia, with Chapter 7, "Intensification and Complexity," immediately preceding the chapters on the first farmers.

Part III describes the origins of food production, with Chapter 8 devoted to the theoretical background and the following five chapters discussing the earliest farming in different areas of the world. New discussions in this edition include the increasing impact of refined AMS chronologies, genetic fingerprinting of potentially domesticable animals and plants, and a fresh generation of research into the origins of rice cultivation. Important new perceptions of the Mississippian and other, more complex farming societies in eastern North America also receive more extended treatment.

Parts IV and V cover the early civilizations of the Old World and the Americas, with Chapter 14 describing the major theories of the origins and collapse of states. The ferment of theorizing has diminished somewhat in recent years, as fieldworkers wrestle to document their theories with new data from the field. At the same time, a new emphasis on ideology and the archaeology of the intangible is throwing fresh light on preindustrial civilization. There is expanded coverage of the origins of Egyptian civilization, as well as of South and Southeast Asian states. Maya archaeology has been revolutionized in recent years by the decipherment of ancient glyphs and by our new understandings of the turbulent political history of Maya states. We take account of some of these advances here, but, alas, do not have space for extended coverage.

Much of this edition consists of small changes, which come from reading hundreds of books and scientific papers and from discussions with colleagues in all parts of the world. Revision and updating occur throughout. Individually, the modifications are inconspicuous, but taken together, they represent a considerable change from the tenth edition. The number of illustrations has increased, although one suffers from the inevitable frustration of writing about a visual subject and being restricted by space and budget as to the number of pictures one can include. As in earlier editions, I suggest a brief list of further readings after each chapter and cross-reference the text to an updated "Bibliography of World Prehistory" for those who wish to delve more closely into topics treated briefly in the book.

As always, the book is designed for easy accessibility and effective learning. *People of the Earth* is free of distracting features that draw the reader away from the main narrative. High-interest chapter-opening vignettes, which describe a moment of discovery or reconstruct life in the past, grab the student's interest from the outset. Chronological tables at the beginning of each chapter, as well as chapter summaries, clearly defined key terms, and updated "Guides to Further Reading" at the end of each chapter, also add to the effectiveness of the book as a learning tool.

Other pedagogical features include the following:

- Special time-line columns at the opening of each part of the book. By means of varied shading, each time line tells at a glance which period of time the part covers, as well as which periods have already been covered and are yet to be covered in the text.

- Expanded picture captions that augment the visual information.

- A unique innovation in this eleventh edition of *People of the Earth:* a stand-alone *Study Companion*. This paperback, written by Brian Fagan, contains commentary on the narrative, tables, and line drawings and is intended as a study aid to be taken to class. If your instructor does not assign the *Companion* as part of your text package for your course, you can easily and quickly order it on-line from the publisher (see the box at the end of the Preface).

〰〰 A Note on the World Wide Web

The World Wide Web has become an important medium of communication for archaeologists, like everyone else. This is a confusing universe for those unfamiliar with the Web, especially since so much is changing all the time. However, the major Web sites are here to stay and offer links to other important locations. Everything operates with Uniform Resource Locators (URLs), some of which we list here.

The Virtual Library for archaeology worldwide is ArchNet: http://www.archnet.asu. edu. This is both geographically and subject-matter based, covering everything from the archaeology of Australia to method and theory and site tours. There are also listings of academic departments, museums, and other archaeological organizations, even of journals. ArchNet is an extraordinary resource; it does not claim to be comprehensive, but it covers a huge range of topics. The European equivalent is ARGE, the Archaeological Resource Guide for Europe: http://www.odur.let.rug.nl/~arge/. This site also lists areas and subjects and is multilingual. Both ArchNet and ARGE have links to virtually any kind of archaeology you are looking for.

Realize that Web pages and addresses change all the time, so this information may already be out of date. Many departments of anthropology and archaeology and dozens of excavations and sites have Web sites, which you can access through ArchNet. For example, for information on archaeology in Southwest Asia and the eastern Mediterranean, go to http://www.argonet.co.uk/education/diggings.

〰〰 Ancillary Materials

The ancillary materials that accompany this textbook are carefully created to enhance the topics being discussed.

Instructor's Manual with Tests.   For each chapter in the text, this manual provides a detailed outline, list of objectives, discussion questions, classroom activities, and additional resources. The test bank includes multiple-choice, true/false, and essay questions for each chapter.

TestGen.   This dual-platform CD-ROM is a test generator designed to allow the creation of personalized exams.

CD-ROM. In the back of every new copy of *People of the Earth, Eleventh Edition*, is an exciting CD-ROM that allows students to review key topics and study important concepts in more depth. Interactive simulations, text-specific study questions, and an extensive map and table reference section will help to make the learning experience more enjoyable.

Companion Website™. In tandem with the text, students can now take full advantage of the World Wide Web to enrich their study of prehistory through the Fagan Companion Website™. This resource correlates the text with related material available on the Internet. Features include chapter objectives, study questions, research projects, and links to additional material that can reinforce and enhance the content of each chapter. Address: www.prenhall.com/fagan

Research Navigator™. Research Navigator™ is the easiest way for students to start a research assignment or research paper. Complete with extensive help on the research process and three exclusive databases of credible and reliable source material, it includes EBSCO's ContentSelect™ Academic Journal Database, *The New York Times* Search-by-Subject Archive, and "Best of the Web" Link Library. Research Navigator™ helps students quickly and efficiently make the most of their research time.

Evaluating Online Resources, Anthropology 2004. This guide encourages students to be critical consumers of online resources. References related specifically to the discipline of anthropology are included. Also included with the guide is an access code for Research Navigator™. This guide is free when packaged with *People of the Earth, Eleventh Edition.*

〽 Acknowledgments

This eleventh edition has benefited greatly from the willing comments of many colleagues—alas, too many to name individually. I would like to thank the following archaeologists for their help with this revision: Richard E. W. Adams, University of Texas at San Antonio; Randall McGuire, Binghamton University; Mary Pohl, Florida State University; Brian Siegel, Furman University; and James E. Snead, George Mason University.

I appreciate their frank comments. I also want to thank the many instructors and users who have contacted me to correct errors, provide references, or make other useful suggestions—including the anonymous correspondent who sent me a photocopy of page 61 of the tenth edition, with a line marked against a paragraph and the word "wrong." I am still trying to figure out how I sinned.

Lastly, my thanks to my much beloved editor, Nancy Roberts, her assistant, Lee Petersen, and to the editorial and production staff at Prentice Hall. Without them, this revision would never have been completed and I would have even more gray hairs. As always, I would be most grateful for criticisms, comments, or details of new work, sent to me at brian@brianfagan.com.

Brian Fagan

To order the *People of the Earth Study Companion* for yourself, please log on to: www.prenhall.com/anthropology, which will take you right to the catalog and order page. You should receive the book in a few days.

AUTHOR'S NOTE

Conventions for Dates and Measurements

The following conventions are used for dates in this book:

B.P.　　　Years before present. In general, years before 40,000 B.P. are given in years before present, while dates after 12,000 B.P. are invariably expressed as A.D./B.C., unless the context is obvious.

mya　　　Million years ago.

kya　　　Thousand years ago.

B.C./A.D.　To avoid confusion, I use the common B.C./A.D. usage. Another common convention is B.C.E./C.E. (Before the Common Era/Common Era), which is not used in this book.

"Present"　By scientific convention, "present" is A.D. 1950.

For clarity, all radiocarbon and potassium argon dates are quoted here without their statistical errors. However, readers should be aware that such calculations exist for every chronometric date in this book.

All measurements are given in metric, with miles, yards, feet, and inch equivalents, as this is now common scientific convention.

Calibration of Radiocarbon Dates

The calibration of radiocarbon dates has now reached a high degree of refinement, as scientists develop ever more accurate time scales for the past 15,000 years, using tree-ring, coral, and ice-core data. Here is the latest calibration table (Stuiver et al., 1998):

Tree-ring calibrations	
Radiocarbon calibrated age (Years A.D./B.C.)	Age in years
A.D. 1760	A.D. 1945
1505	1435
1000	1105
500	635
1	15
505 B.C.	767 B.C.
1007	1267
1507	1867
2007	2477
3005	3795
4005	4935
5005	5876
6050	7056
7001	8247
8007	9368
9062	9968

Barbados coral calibrations using uranium-thorium and AMS Carbon-14	
AMS radiocarbon dates	Uranium-thorium calibration
7760 B.C.	9140 B.C.
8270	10,310
9320	11,150
10,250	12,285
13,220	16,300
14,410	17,050
15,280	18,660
23,920	28,280

Increasing differences after 25,000 B.C. [calibrated]

It should be stressed that these calibrations are provisional, statistically based, and subject to modification, especially before 7000 B.C.

ABOUT THE AUTHOR

Brian Fagan is one of the leading archaeological writers in the world and an internationally recognized authority on world prehistory. He studied archaeology and anthropology at Pembroke College, Cambridge University, and then spent seven years in sub-Saharan Africa working in museums and in monument conservation and excavating early farming sites in Zambia and East Africa. He was one of the pioneers of multidisciplinary African history in the 1960s. Since 1967, he has been Professor of Anthropology at the University of California, Santa Barbara, where he has specialized in lecturing and writing about archaeology to wide audiences.

Professor Fagan has written six best-selling textbooks: *Ancient Lives: An Introduction to Archaeology and Prehistory; In the Beginning; Archaeology: A Brief Introduction; World Prehistory; Ancient Civilizations* (with Chris Scarre); and this volume—all published by Prentice Hall—which are used around the world. His general books include *The Rape of the Nile,* a classic history of Egyptology; *The Adventure of Archaeology; Time Detectives; Ancient North America; The Little Ice Age;* and *Before California: An Archaeologist Looks at Our Earliest Inhabitants.* He was also General Editor of the *Oxford Companion to Archaeology.* In addition, he has published several scholarly monographs on African archaeology and numerous specialized articles in national and international journals. He is also an expert on multimedia teaching and the recipient of the Society for American Archaeology's first Public Education Award for his indefatigable efforts on behalf of archaeology and education.

Brian Fagan's other interests include bicycling, sailing, kayaking, and good food. He is married and lives in Santa Barbara with his wife and daughter, four cats (who supervise his writing), and last but not least, a minimum of four rabbits.

PEOPLE OF THE EARTH

INTRODUCING WORLD PREHISTORY

The Avebury earthworks and stone circles, viewed from the air. The site, in southern England, was an important shrine, c. 2500 B.C.

The two men paused in front of the doorway that bore the seals of the long-dead pharaoh. They had waited six long years, from 1917 to 1922, for this moment. Silently, Howard Carter pried a hole through the ancient plaster. Hot air rushed out of the small cavity and massaged his face. Carter shone a flashlight through the hole and peered into the tomb. Gold objects swam in front of his eyes, and he was struck dumb with amazement.

Lord Carnarvon moved impatiently behind him as Carter remained silent.

"What do you see?" he asked, hoarse with excitement.

"Wonderful things," whispered Carter as he stepped back from the doorway.

They soon broke down the door. In a daze of wonderment, Carter and Carnarvon wandered through the antechamber of Tutankhamun's tomb. They fingered golden funerary beds, admired beautifully inlaid chests, and examined the pharaoh's chariots stacked against the wall. Gold was everywhere—on wooden statues, inlaid on thrones and boxes, in jewelry, even on children's stools (Reeves, 1990). Soon Tutankhamun was known as the golden pharaoh, and archaeology as the domain of buried treasure and royal sepulchers (Figure 1.1).

Gold, silver, lost civilizations, unsolved mysteries, grinning skeletons—all are part of the romantic world of archaeology in most people's minds. Archaeologists seem like adventurers, digging into pyramids and finding long-forgotten inscriptions in remote places. Like Indiana Jones of movie fame, we seem to be students of sunken continents and great migrations, experts on epic journeys and powerful civilizations. A century ago, many archaeologists were indeed adventurers. Even as late as the 1870s, you could go out digging in Southwest Asia and find a long-lost civilization. German businessman-turned-archaeologist Heinrich Schliemann was convinced that Homer's Troy had actually existed. Armed with a copy of the *Iliad,* he went to Turkey and cut great trenches into the ancient mounds at Hissarlik in northwest Turkey. Schliemann found the remains of nine cities stratified one above the other and announced that the seventh was Homer's Troy (Traill, 1995). His discoveries caused an international sensation. So did Frenchman Emil de Sarzec when he unearthed Sumer in desolate southern Mesopotamia, a civilization that soon turned out to be one of the earliest in the world and the society where the Flood legend in Genesis probably originated (Fagan, 1979) (Figure 1.2).

Today, however, the fascination of great adventure has been replaced by all the excitement of the detective story. Fictional detectives take a handful of clues and solve apparently insoluble murders. Archaeologists take a multitude of small and apparently trivial archaeological finds and use them to answer basic questions about past human behavior.

FIGURE 1.1 Howard Carter peers with bright lights into the inner shrines of the pharaoh Tutankhamun's tomb. (Egyptian, Dynasty XVIII; Thebes; Valley of the Kings, Tomb of Tut-ankh-amun. Opening the door of the second [237] shrine. Photography by Egyptian Expedition, The Metropolitan Museum of Art.)

FIGURE 1.2 The famous "Flood Tablet" from the Assyrian king Assurbanipal's library at Nineveh. The tablet, found by epigrapher George Smith in 1873, records the story of a flood that bears a remarkable resemblance to the one described in Genesis. This was a copy of a much earlier Sumerian legend, which dates from long before the writing down of the Old Testament. (Copyright The British Museum.)

The twentieth century saw archaeology turn from a casual treasure hunt into a complex and demanding science (Fagan, 1985). There have been dramatic discoveries by the dozens: Tutankhamun's tomb in 1922; the royal cemetery at Ur in Iraq in 1928; the spectacular early human fossils discovered by the Leakey family in East Africa during the last quarter of the century; and the magnificent royal burials in China, Guatemala, and Peru in the 1980s. Although these finds have stirred the popular imagination, archaeologists have been engaged in a less conspicuous but just as fascinating adventure of discovery—through 2.6 million years of the human past.

People of the Earth takes you on a journey through these 2.6 million years, from the origins of the first humans through the evolution of modern humanity—ourselves—to the last 5000 years, when literate civilizations appeared on earth. This is a book about the prehistory of humankind.

𓂃 Archaeology and Prehistory

Contrary to popular belief, archaeologists do not study dinosaurs, for ancient fossil animals are the scholarly province of paleontologists. Archaeologists are anthropologists. **Anthropology** is the biological and cultural study of all humanity, ancient and modern. Anthropologists are concerned with living societies, whereas archaeologists study the human cultures and societies of the past. (No attempt is made to describe the basic principles, methods, and theoretical approaches of archaeology in this book. For information, the reader should consult one of the following widely available college texts: Fagan, 2000a; Renfrew and Bahn, 2000; Sharer and Ashmore, 2001; Thomas, 2003.)

A British archaeologist once described archaeology as "the science of rubbish," a somewhat apt description, for archaeologists do indeed spend much of their time delving into the garbage heaps and **middens** of long-vanished human societies. **Archaeology** is the study of ancient human behavior based on surviving material finds. These material remains come in many forms: as crude or finely made stone artifacts tens of thousands, even millions, of years old; as durable pot fragments from clay vessels used by early farmers; as house foundations; as seeds and broken food bones; in the form of cave paintings; and, when preservation conditions permit, as wooden artifacts, textiles, or human corpses. All these finds constitute the **archaeological record**, the archives of the past made up of surviving finds resulting from ancient human behavior. Reconstructing such behavior from such fragmentary records requires great scientific skill, insight, and creativity. Imagine trying to reconstruct twentieth-century life from a handful of artifacts, including two broken plates, a spark plug, a computer keyboard, three cow bones, and an aluminum beer can tab, and you will realize the challenge facing students of the remote past (Figure 1.3).

I use the word *remote* deliberately because most of the archaeological research described in this book deals with biological and cultural developments thousands of years back in the past, with long-vanished environments and societies that lived on earth when it was very different. Few people realize just how much the world has changed during the past 2 million years, and especially during the past 750,000 years, when the constant climatic fluctuations of the Ice Age have kept global climate in a state of transition from extreme cold to warmer conditions (see Chapters 2, 3, and 4). Only 15,000 years ago, the world was in the grip of a major glacial episode that covered much of northern Europe and North America with vast ice sheets, lowered sea levels everywhere by about 91 m (300 feet), and resulted in open, treeless plains from western France to Siberia. England was part of the European continent; Siberia was joined to Alaska; and Borneo was part of mainland Southeast Asia. The human inhabitants of this late Ice Age world lived on a planet unimaginably different from our own, which makes it doubly hard for us to reconstruct and explain their societies.

For the past 5000 years, humans have used writing as a means of recording business transactions, making inventories of commodities, and measuring the passage of time (Robinson, 1995). From these simple records developed far more sophisticated writings: primordial epics and poems; king lists; histories and literature itself; written archives preserved on clay tablets and papyrus reed documents or as inscriptions on stone and eventually on parchment and paper. Such archives are the realm of historians, scholars who study the written records of the past.

FIGURE 1.3 Archaeology is the study of the material remains of the past. An excavation of a prehistoric settlement in the central median of Interstate 10 near Tucson, Arizona. Much archaeological excavation is cultural resource management, such as this dig.

History is very different from archaeology. While eclectic in their interests, historians work with documents, which are sometimes chronicles of individual deeds, of great kings and lords anxious to trumpet their triumphs or justify their doings. They also study more prosaic archives: the records of royal palaces and governments, the day-to-day transactions of officialdom, to gain wider perspectives on every aspect of society from religious beliefs to food supplies, trade, and social interactions.

In contrast, archaeology is, most of the time, entirely anonymous. Its chronologies are not the years, even hours and minutes, found in history books but are much larger chunks of time, rarely shorter than a half century or a generation. The archaeologist's past is usually without written records to fill in vital gaps. Even when documents are available to amplify historical records on, say, the Egypt of Pharaoh Rameses II or the rituals celebrated by a Maya lord, archaeology brings a unique quality to the past. Only a few people in ancient societies were literate, so the scope of written records is immediately limited. But archaeologists study artifacts and food remains, a dispassionate record of all ancient human behavior, whether that of a monarch or an anonymous sea captain and his crew wrecked on the cliffs of southern Turkey. By excavating the humble dwellings of common folk or the middens of imposing palaces, archaeologists add new dimensions to the study even of societies that are well documented with written records of all kinds.

Archaeologists make a clear distinction between two major types of archaeology:

- **Text-aided archaeology** is archaeology practiced with the aid of historical documents. Many of the civilizations described in Parts IV and V of this book involve specialist archaeologists, such as Assyriologists, Egyptologists, or Mayanists, who have at least some expertise in ancient scripts. Text-aided archaeology is confined to societies that have flourished during the past 5000 years and sometimes provides fascinating insights into the people of the past, as it did at Vindolanda (see Site box).

- **Prehistoric archaeology** is the archaeology of ancient societies that were nonliterate. The term *période anti-historique* was coined by French archaeologist Paul Tournal in 1833 for the period of human history extending back before the time of written documents (Grayson, 1983). In time, this phrase shrank to **prehistory,** and it now encompasses the enormous span of human cultural evolution that extends back at least 2.6 million years.

People of the Earth is a book about both prehistoric and text-aided archaeology. We draw on archaeology, geological evidence, linguistic and biological data, oral traditions, historical records, and many other sources of information about 2.6 million years of the human past, sometimes called **world prehistory.**

Some people, notably Native Americans, object to the word *prehistoric.* They feel it implies racial inferiority and also expresses the belief that people without written documents have no worthwhile history. These objections are part of a wider debate about the ownership of the past and about archaeology's role in modern society (see the section "Who Needs the Past?" in this chapter).

Prehistory and prehistoric are convenient, and long-established, scientific terms without any pejorative implications. While it is true that many scholars of a century ago classified human societies in racist terms, those days are long gone. Modern archaeologists study both literate and nonliterate societies and how they changed without making any value judgments as to their superiority or inferiority to the archaeologists' own society. Their concern is the broad sweep of the human past, for scientific archaeology is a unique way of studying cultural change in human societies over enormously long periods of time. From about 3000 B.C., written records and oral histories provide useful perspectives on the past. But in most areas of the world, these sources have but a limited chronological span. And earlier than that, the past is a blank, featureless landscape that can be filled in only by archaeological research.

🐾 The Beginnings of World Prehistory

For generations, archaeology was largely a phenomenon of European and North American scholarship (Bahn, 1996). The first archaeologists were amateurs, often men and women with private means. Even 50 years ago, the community of professional archaeologists throughout the world was no more than a few thousand people, many of them trained in Europe or the United States. The spread of archaeological research into other parts of the world began in the 1920s and 1930s, as Belgian, British, and French colonial governments established museums and research institutes in their colonies. Sub-Saharan Africa saw much archaeological research between the 1930s and 1950s conducted by a handful of prehistoric archaeologists like Louis and Mary Leakey and J. Desmond Clark. In the Americas, the Carnegie Institution of Washington, D.C., was active in Maya archaeology for many years; and other academic institutions, like Harvard University, organized expeditions to Southeast Asia, China, the Andes, and other archaeologically little-known regions. But right up to the late 1950s, most archaeology was decidedly provincial, focusing on relatively few areas of the world.

World prehistory developed as a result of two major changes in archaeology. The first was the development of **radiocarbon (C-14) dating** by University of Chicago physicists Willard Libby and J. R. Arnold in 1949. For the first time, archaeologists had at their disposal a dating method of potential global application that enabled them not only to date sites in all corners of the world but also to compare the chronology of, say, the first agriculture in Southwest Asia with that in the Americas (see the box "Radiocarbon Dating" in Chapter 3). Until then, no one could make easy, direct chronological comparisons between widely separated regions, nor was there a way of measuring the rate of culture change through time. Within 15 years of Libby and Arnold's remarkable discovery, radiocarbon dates from hundreds of sites allowed the construction of the first reliable global chronologies (see Science box on page 12).

The second change resulted from an explosion in the number of professional archaeologists during the 1950s and 1960s. This rapid expansion resulted from increased funding for higher education after World War II and from the establishment of many more archaeological organizations outside the narrow confines of Europe and North America.

For years, Cambridge University had trained archaeologists and anthropologists, many of whom went into the British colonial service. From the late 1950s, Cambridge actively encouraged its archaeological graduates to emigrate to tropical Africa, Australia, the Pacific, and other archaeologically little-known parts of the world. These researchers took with them a new, multidisciplinary approach to archaeology, one that stressed environmental change and the importance of explaining as well as describing

SITE

A Roman Garrison at Vindolanda, England

In A.D. 122, the Roman Emperor Hadrian ordered the building of a massive wall 117 km (73 miles) long across northern England "to separate Romans from the barbarians." For ten years, hundreds of soldiers and civilians labored on a classic Roman defense work, which linked the river Tyne in the east with the Solway Firth in the west. Hadrian's Wall was one of the wonders of the ancient world, a fortification up to 6 m (20 feet) high and 3 m (10 feet) thick. Forts, towers, and garrisons punctuated the wall at regular intervals. Only the 6437-km (4000-mile) -long Great Wall of China built three centuries later dwarfs this stupendous undertaking.

For more than three centuries, Hadrian's Wall served as the northernmost frontier of the Roman Empire, garrisoned by as many as 5000 troops. Thanks to a remarkable archaeological discovery in the shadow of the wall, we know something of the men and women who served in this remote garrison. The Vindolanda frontier garrison lies 3 km (2 miles) south of the wall and the Roman road that ran from east to west behind it (Figure 1.4) (Birley, 1977). Archaeologists Eric and Robin Birley, father and son, have excavated Vindolanda since the 1930s, uncovering a series of well-organized forts and settlements, stratified one above the other and occupied for more than two centuries.

Vindolanda was home to a cohort of Tungrians, a regiment originally recruited on the river Rhine but largely manned by local recruits. The soldiers had money to spend, so civilian settlements arose around the fort on poorly drained ground. Robin Birley identified the location of these settlements with aerial photographs, then excavated the disorganized timber buildings and workshops. To his astonishment, he unearthed hundreds of wooden slivers covered with crabbed script, official records and correspondence of A.D. 95 to 105 abandoned when the cohort was suddenly transferred to the Danube Valley in southeastern Europe.

The deciphered letters, written on bark slivers and read with the aid of infrared photography, provide insights into life on a cold and unsettled frontier of the Roman Empire. The commander, Flavius Ceralis, lived in chilly quarters, burdened down with administrative detail. Some of his documents were military strength reports. We learn that only 265 men, including one centurion, were at Vindolanda itself and "fit and well." The rest were serving elsewhere. Store inventories reveal allocations to soldiers and punishments. Occasionally, the correspondence takes a more personal note. "Why have you not written back to me for such a long time about our parents?" laments a soldier

the past. Since the 1960s, **cultural resource management (CRM)** has assumed increasing importance in many countries, especially Canada and the United States, with a resulting explosion in the number of archaeologists. Archaeological activity has expanded greatly in many other nations, too. In 1959, for example, there were just nine professional archaeologists in the whole of sub-Saharan Africa. In 1996, there were over 70 in South Africa alone.

In 1961, the Cambridge archaeologist Grahame Clark published his classic *World Prehistory* (third edition published in 1977), the first global synthesis of archaeology, which took full account of radiocarbon chronology and archaeological research. This groundbreaking volume became a modern classic and helped turn archaeology intellectually from a somewhat provincial discipline into the global enterprise it is today. All subsequent attempts to synthesize world prehistory, of which *People of the Earth* is one, have built on Grahame Clark's pioneering work.

Today, archaeological expeditions are at work in every corner of the world and in every environment imaginable: in the remote wilds of Siberia, in tropical rain forests along the Amazon River in South America, on Easter Island in the Pacific, in the depths of the arid Sahara, and under the world's oceans (Figure 1.5). The heaviest concentrations of research are still in Europe, Southwest Asia, and North America, but knowledge is accumulating rapidly in areas like Africa and Asia, from which the most spectacular discoveries of the twenty-first century will come.

FIGURE 1.4   Aerial view of the Vindolanda frontier fort and settlement, England.

named Chrautius to an old messmate in distant London. "I have sent you . . . woolen socks . . . two pairs of sandals and two pairs of underpants," writes a friend of a Vindolanda officer, who was thankful for the gift. There are even fragments of school tablets, one a copy of a passage from Virgil's *Aeneid,* with the notation in another hand: "sloppy work." Thanks to the Birleys' discovery, we now know by name more than 140 Roman Britons of the late first century A.D.

FIGURE 1.5   The ancient port of Suakin on the East African coast, one of many little investigated sites, which will tell us much about ancient Indian Ocean trade more than 1000 years ago. The most spectacular archaeological discoveries of the twenty-first century will most likely come from outside Europe, Southwest Asia, and North America, where the heaviest concentration of research has been carried out.

༝ Who Needs the Past?

"There is not yet one person, one animal, bird, fish, crab, tree, rock, hollow, canyon, meadow, forest. Only the sky alone is there; the face of the earth is not clear. Only the sea alone is pooled under all the sky; there is nothing whatsoever gathered together. . . . Whatever is that might be is simply not there: only the pooled water, only the calm sea, kept at rest under the sky" (Tedlock, 1996, p. 64).

The Maya *Popol Vuh,* a book of counsel sometimes called the Maya Bible, tells the story of the creation and recounts the deeds of gods and kings in a brilliant celebration of the Quiché Maya past. The impact of its creation myth is as powerful as that in the Book of Genesis (Figure 1.6). All societies have an interest in the past. It is always around them, haunting, mystifying, tantalizing, sometimes offering potential lessons for the present and future. The past is important because social life unfolds through time, embedded within a framework of cultural expectations and values. In the high Arctic, Inuit preserve their traditional attitudes, skills, and coping mechanisms in one of the harshest environments on earth. They do this by incorporating the lessons of the past into the present (Anawak, 1994). In many societies, the ancestors are the guardians of the land, which symbolizes present, past, and future. Westerners have an intense scientific interest in the past, partly born of curiosity but also out of a need for historical identity. There are many reasons to attempt to preserve an accurate record of the past, and no people, least of all archaeologists, should assume that they are uniquely privileged in their interest in the remains of that past (Layton, 1994).

We may all share an interest in the past, but we think of it, and use it, in different ways, just as we have different perspectives on time.

Cyclical and Linear Time

Archaeologists tend to claim that only they are qualified to reconstruct the early human past. While it is true that archaeology is the only method Western science has of studying culture change through time, that fact does not give archaeologists unique authority over the past. In many societies, the past is a valued cultural commodity in ways that are fundamentally different from those of the archaeologist. The transmission of knowledge about the past lies in the hands of respected elders, who take pains to preserve the accuracy of oral traditions. Such traditions are of vital importance and are carefully controlled, for they define and preserve a group's identity from one generation to the next. The past is vested not in science but in household, community, kin groups, and territory. Among the Yolngu Aborigines of Australia's Northern Territory, for example, only the oldest clan members are repositories for the most important historical knowledge (Williams and Mununggurr, 1994).

As both Australian Aborigines and Native Americans have pointed out, Western science and its perspectives on the past are fundamentally incompatible with those of

FIGURE 1.6 Maya history. Two monkey scribes sit on either side of a thick screen-fold book, discussing a page they have opened. The scribe on the left holds a writing instrument in his hand.

other societies. This incompatibility revolves around the notion of linear time. Westerners think of the passage of the human past along a straight, if branching, highway of time. The great nineteenth-century German statesman Otto von Bismarck called this the "stream of time" upon which all human societies ride for a while. The analogy is apt if you think of time in a linear fashion, as archaeologists do. They use a variety of chronological methods to date the long millennia of human prehistory (see Science box) and provide the chronological framework for world prehistory (Fagan, 2000a).

An unfolding linear past is not the only way of conceptualizing ancient times. Many non-Western societies, ancient and modern, think of time as a cyclical phenomenon, or sometimes as a combination of the linear and the cyclical. The cyclical perspective stems from the passage of seasons and of heavenly bodies and from the close relationships between foragers and village farmers and their natural environments. It is also based on the eternal verities of human life: fertility and birth, life, growth, and death. The endlessly repeating seasons of planting and harvest, of game movements or salmon runs, and of ripening wild foods have governed human existence in deeply significant ways. The ancient Maya developed an elaborate cyclical calendar of interlocking secular and religious cycles to measure the passage of the seasons and to regulate religious ceremonies (see Chapter 21).

But we should not assume that societies with a cyclical view of time did not have linear chronologies as well. The celebrated Maya "Long Count" was a linear sacred calendar that formed an integral part of the close relationship between Maya rulers and the cosmos. The ancient Egyptians developed a linear chronology for administrative purposes. But, in general, societies develop linear chronologies only when they need them. For example, Western societies use linear time to regulate times of prayer, to control the working day, and to schedule airline flights. It is hard to generalize, but societies with centralized political systems tend to use the reigns of chiefs or kings as signposts along a linear timescale. For instance, the history of the rulers of the state of Benin in West Africa shows a significant shift in the interpretation of time. Before the fourteenth century A.D., Benin history is essentially mythological, with inaccurate chronology and a variable number of kings. But with the founding of the Yoruba dynasty, the deeds and reigns of every *oba* (king) are remembered in detail with chronological accuracy right down to modern times (Ben-Amos, 1980) (Figure 1.7).

Robert Layton points out (1994) that many non-Western societies do not perceive themselves as living in a changeless world. They make a fundamental distinction

FIGURE 1.7 Art as history. A brass plaque from Benin City, West Africa, showing a heavily armed *oba* (king) with his attendants. These artifacts, which served as important history records of royal reigns and genealogy, were stored in the royal palace. (National Museum of African Art, Smithsonian Institution, Washington, D.C., U.S.A. Aldo Tutino/Art Resource, NY.)

SCIENCE

Dating the Past

How do archaeologists date the past? Prehistoric chronologies cover long periods of time, millennia or centuries in most cases. Some idea of the scale of prehistoric time can be gained by piling up 100 quarters. If the whole pile represents the entire time that humans and their culture have been on earth, the length of time covered by historical records would equal considerably less than the thickness of one quarter.

Archaeologists are constantly experimenting with new methods of dating the past (Fagan, 2000a; Renfrew and Bahn, 2000). However, four major chronological methods date the 2.6 million years of the human past (Table 1.1):

1. *Historical records* (present day to c. 3000 B.C.). Historical records can be used to date the past only as far back as the beginnings of writing and written records, which first appeared in Southwest Asia at about 3000 B.C. and much later in many other parts of the world.

2. *Dendrochronology* (tree-ring dating) (present day to 8000 B.C.). The annual growth rings of long-lived trees such as sequoias, bristlecone pines, and European oaks, whose wood was used for beams, posts, and other purposes by ancient people, can be used to date sites in some areas such as the southwestern United States, the Mediterranean, and western Europe. Originally used on southwestern pueblos, **dendrochronology,** or tree-ring dating, using sequences of growth rings, is also used to calibrate radiocarbon dates and is a useful source of information on ancient climatic change.

3. *Radiocarbon dating* (c. A.D. 1500 to 40,000 years ago). Radiocarbon dating is based on the measurement of the decay rates of carbon-14 atoms in organic samples like charcoal, shell, wood, hair, and other materials. When combined with accelerator mass spectrometry, it can produce dates from tiny samples, which are then calibrated, if possible, against tree-ring dates to provide a date in calendar years. Radiocarbon chronologies date most of prehistory after about 40,000 years ago, well after modern humans appeared in Africa for the first time (see the box "Radiocarbon Dating" in Chapter 3).

4. *Potassium-argon dating* (250,000 years ago to the origins of life). **Potassium-argon dating** is a chronological method, used to date early prehistory, which measures the decay rate of K40 atoms in volcanic rocks (see the box "Potassium-Argon Dating" in Chapter 2). This method is an excellent way of dating East African hominid fossils, many of which are found in volcanic levels.

Other dating methods include obsidian hydration, paleomagnetic dating, thermoluminescence, and uranium-thorium dating. However, none of these methods is of universal application.

• •

between the recent past, which lies within living memory, and the more remote past, which came before it. For instance, the Australian Aborigine groups living in northeast Queensland distinguish among *kuma*, the span of events witnessed by living people; *anthantnama*, a long time ago; and *yilamu*, the period of the creation. Furthermore, the existence of culture change in the past has also been accepted by many societies, among them the Hindus, whose traditions of history speak of early people who lived without domesticated animals and plants, and the Hazda hunter-gatherers of East Africa, who speak of their homeland's first inhabitants as being giants without fire or tools. These paradigms of the past take many forms, with mythic creators of culture, usually primordial ancestors, deities, or animals, establishing contemporary social customs and the familiar landscape, or with a more remote, discontinuous heroic era like that of the Greeks, which allowed writers like the playwright Aeschylus to evaluate contemporary behavior (Sparkes, 1994).

Written Records, Oral Traditions, and Archaeology

Most human societies of the past were nonliterate, which meant that they transmitted knowledge and history by word of mouth. Written records are the most comprehensive source of information about the past, but they usually follow a strictly linear chronology.

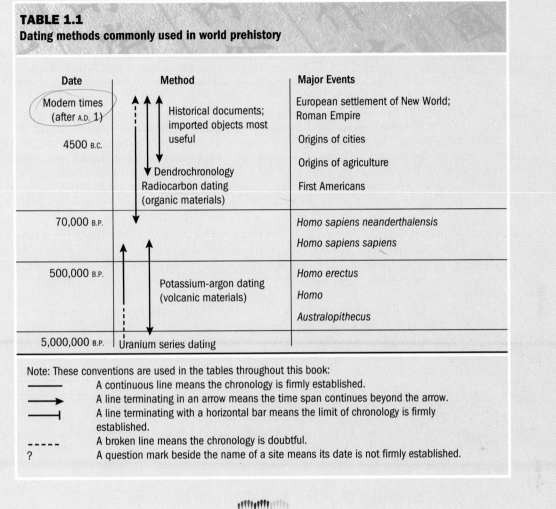

TABLE 1.1
Dating methods commonly used in world prehistory

Date	Method	Major Events
Modern times (after A.D. 1)	Historical documents; imported objects most useful	European settlement of New World; Roman Empire
4500 B.C.		Origins of cities
		Origins of agriculture
	Dendrochronology Radiocarbon dating (organic materials)	First Americans
70,000 B.P.		*Homo sapiens neanderthalensis*
		Homo sapiens sapiens
500,000 B.P.		*Homo erectus*
	Potassium-argon dating (volcanic materials)	*Homo*
		Australopithecus
5,000,000 B.P.	Uranium series dating	

Note: These conventions are used in the tables throughout this book:
——— A continuous line means the chronology is firmly established.
———▶ A line terminating in an arrow means the time span continues beyond the arrow.
———⊣ A line terminating with a horizontal bar means the limit of chronology is firmly established.
– – – – A broken line means the chronology is doubtful.
? A question mark beside the name of a site means its date is not firmly established.

They also served as educational tools. Apart from anything else, written documents were useful as cues for people to memorize standardized historical, ritual, or mythical information.

The Aztec **oral histories,** partially set down after the Spanish Conquest of the fifteenth century A.D., are an excellent example of history transmitted by word of mouth. These oral histories were recited according to a well-defined narrative plot that focused on charismatic figures in Aztec history; key events, like the dedication of the sun god Huitzilopochtli's temple in the Aztec capital in 1487; and the histories of favored groups. In these, as in other oral histories, there were formulas and themes that formed the central ingredients of a story that varied considerably from one speaker to the next, even if the essential content was the same. Many oral histories are mixtures of factual data and parables that communicate moral and political values. But to those who hear them, they are publically sanctioned history, performed before and subject to the critical evaluation of an audience who may have heard the same stories before (M. Smith, 1996).

Both written records and oral histories are subject to all kinds of bias. Neither can claim to be totally objective, any more than archaeology is. The problem for the archaeologist is to correlate data from excavations with that from oral traditions and to establish critically what is factual history and what is myth or moral exhortation. Oral traditions are hard to use, as their antiquity is very difficult to establish. In some cases—in Australia, for example—there are instances where oral histories and archaeology coincide in general terms. For example, the traditions speak of the arrival of the first people from overseas, of the flooding of coastal areas after the Ice Age, and of the hunting of giant marsupials (pouched animals like the kangaroo). So Australia's past can be said to come from two sources: archaeological data and oral traditions (Flood, 1983). In some instances, the archaeologists and the indigenous people have shared interests and come together to identify sacred and historic places, often to ensure that they are preserved. However, the two groups may differ greatly on the significance of a particular location, such as a place where archaeologists find no buildings or artifacts, yet which the local people consider sacred.

But all too often the archaeologist and a local community have different interests in the past. To the archaeologist, the past is scientific data to be studied with all the rigor of modern science. To local people, the past is often highly personalized and the property of the ancestors. Such accounts are valid alternative versions of history that deserve respect and understanding, for they play a vital role in the creation and reaffirmation of cultural identity. And they raise a fundamental question that lies behind many Native Americans' objections to archaeological research: What do archaeologists, usually outsiders, have to offer to a cultural group that already has a valid version of its history? Why should they be permitted to dig up the burials of the ancestors or other settlements and sacred places under the guise of studying what is, to the people, a known history? It is a question that archaeologists have barely begun to address (Layton, 1994).

Archaeologists are not alone in considering the past of value, nor are they immune to the politics that sometimes surrounds the interpretation of aspects of the past. Many Westerners may consider "world prehistory" written from archaeological and many other sources the most reliable account of the human past. But we should never forget that alternative, and often compelling, accounts of ancient times exist that play an important role in helping minority groups and others to maintain their traditional heritage as it existed before the arrival of the Westerner. *People of the Earth* offers an account of 2.6 million years of human history based on the latest scientific archaeological research, but it does so with a profound respect for the cultures and histories of others with different historical perspectives. At the core of our story is the concept of culture.

🐾 Studying Culture and Culture Change

As anthropologists, archaeologists study human cultures and how they have changed through time.

Culture is a concept developed by anthropologists to describe the distinctive adaptive system used by human beings. Culture can be called a society's traditional systems of belief and behavior, as understood by individuals and the members of social groups and as manifested in individual or collective behavior. It is also part of our way of adapting to our environment. Humans are the only animals to manufacture tools for this purpose (for an extended discussion, see Fagan, 2000a; Sharer and Ashmore, 2001). Thus tools and dwellings are also part of our culture.

Ordinarily, when animals die, their experience dies with them. However, human beings use the symbolic system of language to transmit their ideas and their culture, their feelings and experiences, from one generation to the next (Figure 1.8). This is why language as communication is so important in many societies. Culture is learned by intentional teaching as well as by trial and error and simple imitation. People can share ideas, which in turn become behavior patterns that are repeated again and again—witness the long-lived stone hand ax, a multipurpose tool that remained in use for more than 1 million years of early prehistory (see Chapter 4). All archaeological research is based on the principle that culture is an ongoing phenomenon that changes gradually over time, although change can be abrupt as well.

Culture is nongenetic and provides a much quicker way than biological adaptation to share ideas that enable people to cope with their environment. It is the adaptiveness

FIGURE 1.8 !Kung San women foraging for mongongo nuts in the Kalahari Desert. Like all humans, they benefit from cultural knowledge and experience transmitted from one generation to the next.

of culture that allows archaeologists to assume that artifacts found in archaeological sites are patterned adaptations to the environment. Many archaeologists think of cultures as ever-adjusting cultural systems adapting to changing natural environments and other stimuli.

A **cultural system** is a complex system comprising a set of interacting variables—tools, burial customs, ways of getting food, religious beliefs, social organization, and so on—that function to maintain a community in a state of equilibrium with its environment. When one element in the system changes—say, hunting practices as the result of a prolonged drought—then reacting adjustments will occur in many other elements. It follows that no cultural system is ever static. It is always changing, and these processes of culture change are a primary focus of archaeological research.

Cultural process refers to the processes by which human societies changed in the past. Culture changes take place through time, most, but by no means all, being gradual and cumulative. Inventions and design improvements result in dozens of minor alterations in the ways people live. Generally, cultural evolution was gradual in prehistoric times, although there are cases of sudden change, such as the Roman conquest of Gaul in the first century B.C. Dramatic cultural modification can also result from the spread from neighboring areas of a new idea or invention, such as the plow or maize agriculture.

The cumulative effects of long-term culture change are easily seen. A comparison of the simple flaked stone tools of the earliest humans and the sophisticated contents of the Egyptian pharaoh Tutankhamun's tomb will help one to understand the power of cumulative change over thousands of years.

Primary Cultural Processes

The term **process** is used in archaeology to refer to mechanisms by which cultures change. Archaeologists generally agree on three primary cultural processes that figured importantly in world prehistory:

- **Invention** involves creating a new idea and transforming it—in archaeological contexts—into an artifact or other tangible innovation that has survived. Inventions are adopted by others if they are useful; if sufficiently important, they spread rapidly. The microchip, for example, is in almost universal use because it is an effective advance in electronic technology. Most inventions in prehistory were the result of prolonged experimentation, a logical extension of the use and refinement of an existing technology, or a response to changes in the surrounding environment.

- **Diffusion** is the label for those processes by which new ideas or cultural traits spread from one person to another or from one group to another, often over long distances. These ideas are socially transmitted from individual to individual and ultimately from group to group, but the physical movement of many people is not involved. A classic modern example of diffusion is tobacco smoking, a favorite pleasure of North American Indians that was adopted by Elizabethan colonists in the sixteenth century. Within a few generations, tens of thousands of Europeans were smoking pipes and enjoying the narcotic effect of American tobacco.

- **Migration** involves the movement of a people and is based on a deliberate decision to enter new areas and leave old ones. The classic instance of migration in prehistory is that of the Polynesians; they settled the remote islands of the Pacific in consequence of deliberate explorations of the open ocean by their skilled navigators (Finney, 1994).

Theoretical Approaches: Culture as Adaptation

World prehistory is the story of an emerging and increasingly complex human biological and cultural diversity that unfolded over millions of years. We have made giant steps in describing the archaeological record in many parts of the world, but attempts to explain such major developments as the spread of modern humans, the origins of food production, or civilization are still at an early stage (Trigger, 1989). The very diversity and local nature of most ancient human society make it well-nigh impossible to develop comprehensive, all-embracing theoretical frameworks for world prehistory; indeed, it is rash to attempt it. Nor does a single approach like, for example, the popular notion of culture as adaptation provide sufficient theoretical background. Several perspectives, taken together or used separately, provide significant insights, so a diversity of theoretical approaches is valuable.

Climatic Change

In recent years, we have begun to understand the enormous impact of short- and long-term climatic shifts as agents for culture change. The long cycles of cold and warm associated with the Ice Age occur on a millennial scale and have long-term effects on human existence (see descriptions in Chapters 3 and 4). For example, the existence of a low-lying land bridge between Siberia and Alaska during much of the late Ice Age may have allowed humans to make their way from Asia into the Americas before 15,000 years ago, but the actual formation of the shelf that linked the two continents would have taken many centuries and human generations (see Chapter 5). Short-term climatic changes, such as the floods or droughts caused by El Niño episodes or the volcanic eruptions that dump ash into the atmosphere, are another matter. Memories of catastrophic famines and other results associated with such events would have endured for generations, for they had immediate impact on hundreds, if not thousands, of people.

We look back at the past through shadowed mirrors, which become less blurred as we approach recent times. Our knowledge of Ice Age climatic change is necessarily on a grand scale, for, until recently, even ice cores did not attain the year-by-year resolution that is needed to track short-term shifts. Yet, such sudden changes are the most important of all to human populations, who have to adjust constantly to unusual weather conditions—droughts and floods, extreme heat and cold. It is only now that we are beginning to understand their profound impact on ancient societies. As research into these and other centuries-long events has intensified, so more scholars have paid increasing attention to violent, year-long episodes such as monsoon failures, volcanic eruptions, and, most important of all, El Niños (Fagan, 1999; Keys, 1999).

Identifying ancient short-term climatic change requires extremely precise and sophisticated environmental and climatic evidence, much of it obtained from ice cores, **pollen analysis,** and tree rings. Ice cores, in particular, are revolutionizing our knowledge of ancient climatic shifts, for they are now achieving a resolution of five years or less, which readily allows one to study drought cycles and major El Niño events of the past. From the archaeologist's point of view, El Niños are of compelling interest, for they had drastic effects on many early civilizations living in normally dry environments but where flooding may have wiped out years of irrigation agriculture in hours. Humanity was not so vulnerable to El Niños until people settled in permanent villages, then cities, and the realities of farming and growing population densities made it harder for them to move away from drought or flood. A classic example of such vulnerability comes from the north coast of Peru. Droughts and strong El Niños had a catastrophic effect on the Moche civilization of the first millennium A.D. (see Chapter 22).

It is very easy to attribute major cultural developments like the origins of food production or the collapse of a civilization to climatic change alone. But such straightforward environmental determinism is long outdated by realizations that climate was but one factor that came into play.

Culture as Adaptation

Most archaeologists believe that human cultures are best interpreted as adaptations to the subsistence and ecological requirements of a locality. This is the **culture as adaptation** approach, which places considerable emphasis on cultural systems and ecology. Under this approach, culture is the result of human beings' unique ability to infuse events and objects with meaning that can be appreciated, decoded, and understood (Gamble, 1999). This means that culture is participated in as well as shared by human beings. However, this process of participation and sharing differs greatly from place to place and from time to time, resulting in variations in prehistoric material culture—the data for studying prehistory. The widely used culture as adaptation approach employs a complex, multidimensional model to investigate the significance of patterning and variation in archaeological finds (Binford, 2001a).

Under the culture as adaptation approach, human behavior, both today and in the remote past, is an adaptation not to a single site but to environmental regions. Thus, to understand individual sites and artifact patternings, archaeologists have to study regions, as we do in this book. And they usually do so within a framework of evolutionary theory and cultural ecology.

Cultural Evolution and Cultural Ecology

Charles Darwin's theory of biological and natural selection has influenced theories of culture change since the mid-nineteenth century. Today, the archaeologist studies human culture change over long periods of time within a sophisticated framework of cultural evolutionary theory that has developed over more than a hundred years.

Following a theory of **unilinear cultural evolution,** early Victorian social scientists believed human societies evolved in a simple, linear fashion, slowly ascending an evolutionary ladder of human progress toward that ultimate pinnacle, industrial civilization. Under this rubric, humanity passed from a state of barbarism (hunting and foraging) through a stage of savagery (subsistence farming) to civilization. Such unilinear frameworks are not only too simplistic but also smack of assumptions of racial superiority and notions of universal human progress.

Multilinear cultural evolution is now widely accepted as a very general framework for studying the cultural evolution of human societies. Unlike early unilinear theories, multilinear evolution assumes that each human society pursues its own evolutionary course, determined by the long-term success of its adaptation, via technology and social institutions, to its natural environment (Steward, 1970).

Cultural ecology, the total way in which human populations adapt to and transform their environments, is at the core of multilinear evolutionary theory. Some societies achieve a broad measure of equilibrium with their environment, in which adaptive changes consist of little more than some refinements in technology and the fine-tuning of organizational structures. Other societies become involved in cycles of growth that are triggered by environmental change or from within society. If these changes involve either greater food supplies or population growth, accelerated culture change may result from the need to feed more people or the deployment of an enlarged food surplus. Continued growth may place additional strains on the society, triggering technological changes, adjustments in social organization, or alterations in the belief system that provides the society's integrative force.

Multilinear cultural evolution combines the notion of cultural systems and cultural ecology into a closely knit, highly flexible way of studying and explaining cultural processes. Under this approach, there is no one primary agent of cultural evolution but, rather, a series of important variables, all with complex interrelationships. When we seek to explain the major and minor developments of prehistory, we must consider the ways in which change took place, the processes and mechanisms of change (cultural evolution, experimentation), and the socioeconomic stresses (population pressure, game scarcity, and so on) that triggered those mechanisms.

Multilinear Evolution: Prestate and State-Organized Societies

The sophisticated concept of multilinear evolution has led to the (often controversial) classification of human societies into two broad groups that do not necessarily evolve into one another: prestate and state-organized societies (Service, 1962). We use these general groupings in these pages purely for convenience.

Prestate societies are societies on a small scale, based on the community, band, or village. They vary greatly in their degree of political integration and are sometimes divided into three loosely defined categories (Figure 1.9):

- **Bands** are associations of families that may not exceed 25 to 60 people. Knit together by close social ties, bands were the dominant form of social organization for most hunter-gatherers from the earliest times up to the origins of food production.

- **Tribes** are clusters of bands that are linked by clans. A clan is a group of people linked by common ancestral ties that serve as connections between widely scattered communities. Clans are important because they are a form of social linkage that gives people a sense of common identity with a wider world than their own immediate family and relatives.

- **Chiefdoms** are still kin-based but more hierarchical, with power concentrated in the hands of kin leaders. These leaders are usually individuals with unusual ritual, political, or entrepreneurial skills. Chiefdoms tend to have higher population densities (generally between 5000 and 20,000 people) and display clear signs of social ranking. Often there is local specialization in craft products. Frequently, surpluses of food and craft products are paid to the chief, who redistributes them to his followers. Most chiefdoms have permanent ritual and ceremonial centers, which act as the central focus of the chiefdom, where the chief and his or her retainers live. Chiefdoms vary greatly in elaboration (Earle, 1978). The chiefdom is not necessarily a precursor of a state, although some were (see Chapter 14), but another form of more complex society, bound by different environmental and social constraints (Yoffee, 1990).

State-organized societies (civilizations) operate on a large scale with centralized political and social organization, class stratification, and intensive agriculture. They have complex political structures and many permanent government institutions, and they are based on notions of social inequality. Such societies are ruled by a tiny elite, who

	Prestate			
	Band	**Tribe**	**Chiefdom**	**State-Organized Societies**
Total Numbers	Less than 100	Up to a few thousand	5,000 – 20,000+	Generally 20,000+
Social Organization	Egalitarian Informal leadership	Segmentary society Pan-tribal associations Raids by small groups	Kinship-based ranking under hereditary leader High-ranking warriors	Class-based hierarchy under king or emperor Armies
Economic Organization	Mobile hunter-gatherers	Settled farmers Pastoralist herders	Central accumulation and redistribution Some craft specialization	Centralized bureaucracy Tribute-based Taxation Laws
Settlement Pattern	Temporary camps	Permanent villages	Fortified centers Ritual centers	Urban: cities, towns Frontier defenses Roads
Religious Organization	Shamans	Religious elders Calendrical rituals	Hereditary chief with religious duties	Priestly class Pantheistic or monotheistic religion
Architecture	Temporary shelters	Permanent huts Burial mounds Shrines	Large–scale monuments	Palaces, temples, and other public buildings
	Paleolithic skin tents, Ukraine	*Neolithic shrine Çatalhöyük, Turkey*	*Stonehenge, England — final form*	*Pyramids at Giza* / *Castillo Chichén Itzá, Mexico*
Archaeological Examples	All Paleolithic societies, including Paleo-Indians	All early farmers (Neolithic/Archaic)	Many early metalworking and Formative societies Mississippian, USA Smaller African kingdoms	All ancient civilizations, e.g., in Mesoamerica, Peru, Near East, Southwest Asia, India and China, Greece and Rome
Modern Examples	Eskimos !Kung San Australian Aborigines	Pueblos, Southwest USA New Guinea Highlanders Nuer and Dinka in East Africa	Northwest Coast Indians, USA 18th-century Polynesian chiefdoms in Tonga, Tahiti, Hawaii	All modern states

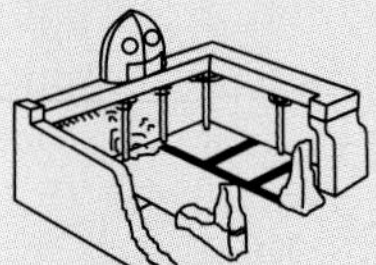

FIGURE 1.9   General categories of ancient human societies. (Modified from Renfrew and Bahn, 2000.)

hold monopolies over strategic resources and use coercion to enforce their authority. State-organized societies of the past were first ruled by priest-bureaucrats, then gradually came under the rule of secular kings, who sometimes became despotic monarchs, often with alleged divine powers. This type of social organization was typical of the early literate civilizations and was the forerunner of the classical civilizations of Greece and Rome.

We describe the prestate societies of prehistory in Chapters 2 to 13; state-organized societies in Chapters 14 to 22.

🐾 Theoretical Approaches: Evolutionary Ecology and Hunter-Gatherers

Inevitably, biological evolution has had an important influence on contemporary thinking about prehistory, especially hunter-gatherer societies. Humans are animals, and, as such, are subject to the same evolutionary mechanisms such as natural selection. This assumption, which has generated sharp controversy, forms the basis of an important approach to explaining culture change, known loosely as evolutionary ecology.

Evolutionary Ecology and Optimal Foraging Strategy

Evolutionary ecology is based on the proposition that variation in the behavior of individual organisms is shaped by natural selection (Broughton and O'Connell, 1999). Thus, it identifies a single goal, the maximization of potential reproductive success, toward which all behavior is directed and in terms of which it can be predicted. Evolutionary ecology does not require rational choice on the part of its subjects, nor does it deny the existence of intentional behavior. All it assumes is that natural selection has designed organisms (including people) to behave in ways that tend to enhance fitness. In other words, the process of selection will tend to favor the best strategy among various alternatives available at the time. Evolutionary ecology has the advantage of being comprehensive, so that it can generate predictions about any aspect of fitness-related behavior. At the same time, it allows integration and provides a basis for predicting linkages between variation in one aspect of behavior and that in others. Above all, evolutionary ecology's predictions are testable.

Most evolutionary ecology in archaeology has been applied to settlement and subsistence, using optimal foraging models. **Optimal foraging strategy** argues that the most efficient **foraging** strategies adopted by human groups are those that produce the greatest return in energy relative to time and effort expended. From the archaeological perspective, optimal foraging theory assumes that, under certain well-defined circumstances, human decisions are made to maximize the net rate of energy gain. These decisions can revolve around diet or breadth of diet, where to forage, the amount of time spent on different activities, or settlement location or group size. The hunter-gatherer would logically not choose to pass over a higher-ranked resource, like abundantly available pecan nuts, to exploit one with fewer benefits—there is no benefit in doing so. Therein lies the nub of optimal foraging theory—the implication that the hunter-gatherer uses higher-ranked resources when available.

This is fine in a world where everything is infinitely abundant. In practice, resources vary greatly in distribution and abundance and, thus, in the time needed to search for them. A new twist to optimal foraging theory now enters the picture. When a hunter in the Midwest's Illinois River valley hunted, say, a deer, a highly valued prey, he might have encountered a rabbit warren on the way, rabbits being the second or third highest ranked food resource on his mental list. He stops and takes six rabbits, and forgets about deer, deciding on a new course of action based on anticipated energy consumption and immediate food needs at the time he encountered the warren. In this case, exploitation of the food resource is independent of its abundance, what optimal foraging theorists call a **contingency model.** Such models are important, for they imply a basic reality that repeats itself again and again in human prehistory: As food resources decline in abundance, the time required to search for them increases, and the breadth of the hunter-gatherer diet widens to compensate for this reality. Conversely, as resources become more abundant, so does selectivity increase.

A **prey model** has also come into wide use; it assumes that foragers will try and maximize the net rate of energy capture. The model predicts that foragers will exploit the highest-ranked prey should they encounter it, whereas lower-ranked items move in and out of the diet as rates of foraging return rise and fall within an area. In North America, acorns are a classic example of a resource that was extremely expensive to process relative to their caloric return, yet they assumed increasing importance to ancient foragers over the millennia and especially in late pre-Columbian times (Basgall, 1987). This suggests that overall foraging return rates declined after the Ice Age as populations rose and food resources became harder to find, reflected by an increase in acorn exploitation. In many areas such as the Midwest and parts of California, smaller terrestrial animals and acorns assumed ever greater importance through time, as they also did in Southwest Asia immediately after the Ice Age. It is probably no coincidence that the technology used for processing such foods as acorns and small animals became more sophisticated as time went on, reflecting a far greater energy expenditure on such activities in environments where high-yielding prey were rare.

∰ Theoretical Approaches: People as Agents of Change

The first known Egyptian ruler, Narmer, is at best a shadowy figure, but there seems little doubt that he lived in about 3100 B.C. This little-known king must have been a remarkably able man, for he unified a patchwork of competing chiefdoms along the Nile River into a single civilization that endured for nearly 3000 years. Narmer lived at a time of political unrest, warfare, and intense rivalry, where different chiefdoms rose to prominence in the hands of able leaders, then vanished into obscurity after their deaths. This process of what is sometimes called "chiefly cycling" went on for centuries before Narmer rose to power and embarked on the military and diplomatic campaigns that joined narrow, valley-bound Upper Egypt with the flat delta country of Lower Egypt to form the "Two Lands." Narmer and his successors wore regalia that symbolized the unification of Egypt, the creation of order out of chaos. Unification was surrounded with powerful myth and religious symbolism and was a foundation of Egyptian life (see Chapter 16). Even if the process of forging a single state took many generations, one can easily imagine the powerful effect of having a single, exceptionally able general and statesman who conquered his neighbors, then created a well-organized state from his new domains. To some degree, the processes of culture change that led to ancient Egyptian civilization came from long-term adaptations to changing conditions. But they also resulted from the deeds of exceptionally able leaders, among them Narmer.

People are agents of culture change, even if most of them remain anonymous, unseen figures in the obscurity of a preliterate past. We just happen to know something of Narmer because he appears on Egyptian king lists. Many of the most recent theoretical approaches to world prehistory are now taking account of humans as agents (Flannery, 1999).

External and Internal Constraints

Computers, radiocarbon dating, pollen analysis, statistical methods, **zooarchaeology**—the list of scientific innovations in archaeology over the past half century is almost unending. The culture as adaptation approach to world prehistory developed out of an increasingly "scientific" perspective on the past during the 1960s and 1970s. It has focused on explanations of culture change, and on the relationships between people and their environments, to the point where many archaeologists complained that this perspective is more concerned with the processes of culture change than with the people behind the changes. They pointed out that all human societies are made up of individuals—men and women, children and adults, members of families and entire communities, and their neighbors near and far. They spend their lives interacting with one another: agreeing, disagreeing, negotiating, quarreling, and living in peace. From these interactions stem cultural traditions that provide guidance for coping with the environment. The same traditions can be a powerful conservative force that inhibits change or one that encourages innovation in times of stress.

Ecological and other external constraints can be culturally mediated, but they operate independently of human actions, so they are susceptible to being understood in terms of evolutionary theory and other such generalizations. Cultural traditions are far more idiosyncratic and haphazard. Therefore, it is difficult to impose evolutionary order on human history, for despite external constraints, much culture change is contingent on ever-changing circumstances and cultural traditions, on ideologies and changing political realities, which may even depend on the whims of individuals. This has led to a new generation of archaeological theory, loosely called **post-processual archaeology,** which places a much greater focus on individual and group behavior, the cultural biases that archaeologists use in interpreting their data, and on the intangibles of human behavior, such as social organization, religious beliefs, and worldviews.

Post-processual archaeology is complex, contradictory, and often highly abstract. But it has been enormously valuable in drawing attention to the critical importance of individual and group human behavior in such major developments as the origins of food production and state formation. As a leading post-processualist, Ian Hodder, has pointed out (1999), processual and post-processual archaeology complement one another. Processual archaeology is concerned with external constraints such as environmental change, whereas post-processual archaeology concentrates on internal constraints such as social and political change, religious beliefs, and individual and group behavior (for constraints, see Trigger, 1991). These internal constraints include ethnic diversity, gender roles, knowledge, beliefs, values, and other culturally conditioned habits, all of them different in every culture. Yet some of them are shared by cultures flourishing thousands of miles apart. For instance, two widely separated cultures may develop bronze metallurgy, which is based on a common body of technological know-how, but the cultural context of that knowledge may be radically different, as it was, say, in the Shang civilization of China (see Chapter 18) and the Moche culture in coastal Peru (see Chapter 22). Some symbols, like associations between rulers and the sun or the common practice of elevating chiefs or kings on a dais, have developed in many places. That does not mean, of course, that they are connected.

It would be foolish to describe one overarching theoretical approach that embraces all the internal constraints that have affected ancient human societies. We can but describe some of the different factors that were important in shaping human prehistory.

Interactions

In the final analysis, it is people who share culture and groups and individuals who make decisions about daily life: Men interact with women, children with adults; a kin group quarrels within itself, pitting small faction against small faction; ethnic groups compete for access to wealth or political power; or foreigners have their own enclave within a vast city. Such dealings between individuals, between individuals and groups, and between groups are the forces that constrain or encourage cultural change. By its very nature, the archaeological record tends to be impersonal, its artifacts and food remains chronicling the dealings of blurred groups rather than individuals, or even categories of people—say, women at a given moment in time.

Only rarely can the archaeologist go beyond artifacts and food remains to study the roles of groups or individuals, the work they undertook, and the subtle ways in which they influenced the course of events. The great city of Teotihuacán on the edge of the Valley of Mexico housed tightly packed communities of foreigners from the Valley of Oaxaca and lowland Vera Cruz, identified by distinctive pottery and architecture quite unlike that of the Teotihuacanos. At the early farming village of Abu Hureyra in Syria, dating to 7000 B.C., biological anthropologist Theya Molleson (1994) observed malformations of the toes, knees, and lower vertebrae in the skeletons of all the adult women, a condition due, almost certainly, to hours of grinding grain. Male skeletons did not display the same impairments (see the box "Men's and Women's Work at Abu Hureyra" in Chapter 9). Molleson's discovery is some of the earliest evidence in human history for a division of labor between men and women. Such research requires very complete field data and fine-grained laboratory and recovery methods.

Gender: Men and Women

Archaeologists have long studied people and households, but only recently have they turned their attention to the complex issue of gender and gender relations, a promising avenue of new research. Gender is not the same as sex, which refers to the biological male or female. Gender is socially and culturally constructed. Gender roles and relations acquire meaning in culturally and historically meaningful ways. This means that gender is a vital part of human social relations and a central issue in the study of ancient human societies.

The expression of gender varies, and has always varied, from society to society and through time. Some archaeologists, such as Margaret Conkey and Joan Gero (1991), write of "engendering archaeology," an attempt to reclaim men and women in nonsexist ways in the past. This goes much further than merely demonstrating that pots were made by women and stone projectile points by men or trying to identify women's activities in the archaeological record. The archaeology of gender deals with the ideology of gender, with roles and gender relations—the ways in which gender intersects with all aspects of human social life. How are roles and social relationships constructed? What contributions did men and women make to ancient societies? An engendered archaeology uses a wide diversity of archaeological methods and approaches to find out how gender "works" in ancient societies, to unravel its cultural meanings.

To "engender the past" means to focus not only on major material achievements such as metallurgy or pot making or on ancient environments but also on interpersonal relations and the social dynamics of everyday activity. These are the activities that take up most of people's daily lives—hunting, gardening, preparing meals, building houses, and so on. But gender also impacts on trade, craft specialization, state formation, religion, and ritual—to mention only a few major human activities.

Gender research in archaeology is concerned not just with women but with people as individuals and their contributions to society. Archaeologist Elizabeth Brumfiel (1991) has studied Aztec women, who were expert weavers; indeed, weaving was a fundamental skill for an Aztec noblewoman. However, she points out that to characterize them merely as weavers ignores the vital links between weaving, child rearing, and cooking (to mention only a few of women's tasks) and the wider society in which the women lived. For instance, the population of the Valley of Mexico rose tenfold during the four centuries before the conquest, a striking testimony to the success of the Aztec household economy. Women wove textiles and the capes that were the badges of social status in Aztec society. Their woven products were vital to the enormous tribute system on which Aztec civilization depended. Cotton mantles even served as a form of currency. Cloth was a primary way of organizing the ebb and flow of goods and services that sustained the state.

Brumfiel shows that the Aztec household and the roles of women were much more varied than those attributed to them by early Spanish observers. Furthermore, the skills of cooking and weaving were important political tools, ways of maintaining social and political control. Thus, she argues, the idealization of these skills in both Aztec folklore and schooling developed because women were makers of both valuable goods and of people. It was they who assured the continuity of Aztec kin groups.

What, then, is an "engendered past"? Scientific reporting tends to obliterate the actors whose deeds created the past. An engendered archaeology ventures into new territory, using innovative approaches to present the multiple voices of the past in order to report both data and stories of the past. Such research requires exceptionally complete data and meticulously excavated sites.

Trade and Exchange

Exchange systems were part of human life long before the Sumerians and ancient Egyptians. Shells from the Black Sea appear in late Ice Age hunting encampments deep in Ukraine from at least 18,000 years ago. The Paleo-Indians of the Great Plains exchanged fine-grained toolmaking stone over long distances as early as 11,000 B.C. Few human societies are completely self-sufficient, for they depend on others for resources outside their own territories. And, as the need for raw materials or for prestigious ornaments increased, so did the tentacles of exchange and trade between neighbors near and far. This trade often had powerful political or symbolic overtones, conducted under the guise of formal gift-giving or as part of complex exchange rituals.

People make trade connections and set up the exchange systems that handle trade goods when they need to acquire goods and services that are not available to them within their own local area. The movement of goods need not be over any great distance, and it can operate internally, within a society, or externally, across cultural boundaries—within interaction spheres. Both exchange and trade always involve two elements: the goods and commodities being exchanged and the people doing the exchanging. Thus any form of trading activity implies both procurement and handling of tools and raw materials and some form of social system that provides the people-to-people relationships within which the trade flourishes. Not only raw materials and finished objects but also ideas and information passed along trade routes.

Conventionally, exchange and trade are recognized in the archaeological record by the discovery of objects exotic to the material culture or economy of the host society. For instance, glass was never manufactured in sub-Saharan Africa, yet imported glass beads are widespread in archaeological sites of the first millennium A.D. Until recently, such objects were recognized almost entirely on the basis of style and design—the appearance of distinctive pottery forms far from their known points of origin, and so on. Sometimes exotics such as gold, amber, turquoise, or marine shells, commodities whose general area of origin was known, provided evidence of long-distance exchanges. Between 3000 B.C. and the Christian Era, Late Archaic and Woodland peoples in the North American Southeast used native copper from outcrops near Lake Superior and conch shells from the Gulf Coast, both commodities of known origin (see Figure 5.12).

In the early days of archaeology, such exotica were deemed sufficient to identify trade, what were loosely called "influences" or even "invasions." The assumptions made about the nature of human interactions were very limited and never precise. Today, however, studies of prehistoric exchange are far more sophisticated, owing to two major developments. The first is a new focus throughout archaeology on cultural process and on regional studies. The second is the development of a wide range of scientific techniques that are capable of describing the composition of certain types of raw material and even of identifying their sources with great precision. As we shall see in Chapter 9, fine-grained obsidian, a volcanic rock used for toolmaking and ornaments, has distinctive trace elements that have allowed archaeologists to identify at least nine zones of obsidian exchange in the eastern Mediterranean region alone.

The Uluburun ship, wrecked off southern Turkey in the fourteenth century B.C., is a fine example of the importance of trade and exchange in the ancient world. Its cargo came from at least nine different areas (see Chapter 19). The study of prehistoric trade is a vital source of information on social organization and the ways in which societies became more complex. Trade itself developed a great complexity, in both goods traded and in the interactions of people involved. Such contacts ranged from simple interactions between individuals to exchanges by professional traders, such as the Aztec *pochteca* (merchants), who sometimes acted as spies.

Ideologies and Beliefs

Nothing informs one more about an ancient society than its worldview and religious beliefs. Unfortunately, the intangible ideologies and beliefs of ancient times are extremely difficult to reconstruct from material remains such as artifacts, art, and architecture. We can only guess at the beliefs and motivations behind late Ice Age cave art (see Chapter 4) or the celebrated plastered human portraits from the early farming settlement at Jericho, Jordan (see Chapter 9). But the study of ancient ideology and beliefs offers great potential when written records such as Egyptian documents or Maya glyphs can be combined with excavations (Figure 1.10). Intensive research combining deciphered hieroglyphs and archaeology are throwing new light on ancient Maya religious beliefs (summary in Sharer, 1995) (see Chapter 21), on what are often called "ideologies of domination."

Elites have used many tactics to exercise power over others, everything from gentle persuasion to divine kingship, precedent, economic monopolies, and naked force. The ancient Maya lords built great ceremonial centers with towering pyramids and vast plazas that were symbolic models of the sacred landscape—the Maya universe. Their pyramids were sacred mountains, the sites of sacred openings that were the threshold to the spiritual world of the ancestors. It was here that the ruler went into a shamanistic trance, communicating with the gods and ancestors in lavish public ceremonies. Everything validated the complex relationship between the living and the dead, and between the ruler and the commoner, displayed in lavish, pointed metaphors that confirmed the divine power of the supreme lords. Linda Schele and David Freidel write: "The Maya believed in a past which always returned . . . in endless cycles repeating patterns already set into the fabric of time and space. Our challenge . . . is to interpret this history, recorded in their words, images, and ruins, in a manner comprehensible to the modern mind, yet true to the Mayas' perception of themselves" (1990, p. 18).

Studying ancient beliefs, the intangibles of the past, can be likened to studying a series of pictures without the captions. Herein lies one of the great frustrations of archaeology. In looking at a giant bull from the 15,000-year-old frieze painted by Stone Age

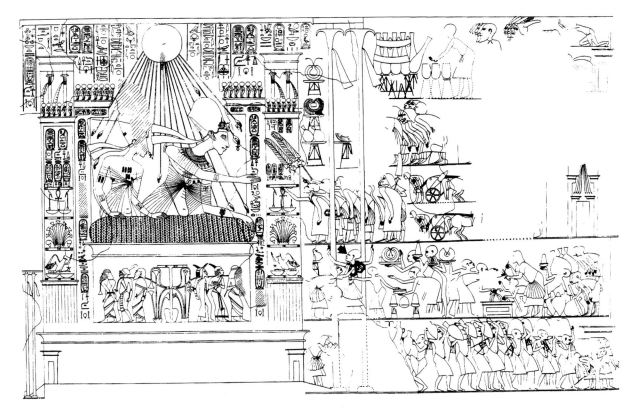

FIGURE 1.10   The New Kingdom pharaoh Akhenaten, who reigned from 1353 to 1335 B.C., appears at the Window of Appearance, rewarding one of his loyal officials, Pannefer. Pannefer receives gold necklaces and other gifts, as well as provisions, being carried off at the lower right. Scenes such as this, from Pannefer's tomb, are an important amplification of the archaeological data from Akhenaten's capital, El-Amarna (Chapter 16). (After N. de G. Davies, *The Rock Tombs of El-Amarna*, vol. 6, Pl. IV [London: Egypt Exploration Society, 1908].)

artists on the walls of Lascaux Cave in southwestern France (see Figure 4.10) or tracing the intricate engraving on a freshwater shell from the Mississippian culture of the southeastern United States (see Chapter 13), we can admire the artistry behind the image, but we can only rarely discern the complex beliefs and motives behind these magnificent achievements. We cannot speak to the ancients; we can only seek to understand some of the brilliant, and often frustrating, complexity of their diverse societies.

The most powerful new explanations of major developments in human prehistory will undoubtedly come from a combination of both processual and post-processual approaches, such as those being used with success with Mississippian chiefdoms in North America, with Maya civilization, and in Southeast Asia.

World prehistory is, in the final analysis, the study of unfolding human diversity in the context of four major developments: the origins and early evolution of Archaic humans, the emergence and spread of anatomically modern humans (ourselves after about 150,000 years ago), the beginnings of agriculture and animal domestication (food production), and the appearance of literate civilization. Steven Mithen (1996) has likened the long millennia of human existence to an archaeological play with several acts that reaches a climax with the appearance of farming a mere 10,000 years ago. In ten short millennia, humanity has moved from a simple village existence into a world of automobiles, aircraft, vast industrial cities, and an emerging global computerized society. *People of the Earth* performs most of this play, ending with the Spanish Conquest of Mexico and Peru, the climactic encounter between Westerners and the last of the preindustrial civilizations in the early sixteenth century A.D.

The actors are in the wings, the curtain is about to rise, and the inexorable stream of time is already flowing. Let the play commence!

Summary

Archaeology is the study of the cultural evolution of humankind, using the material remains of past human behavior. These material remains make up the archaeological record, the archives of the human past. While historians study written records, archaeologists deal with an anonymous past. Archaeology is unique among the sciences in its ability to study culture change over long periods of time. Text-aided archaeology combines the evidence of archaeology with documentary sources, whereas prehistoric archaeology is the study of prehistory, the period of the human past before the advent of written records. The study of world prehistory, which developed in the 1950s, is the study of human prehistory from a global perspective using archaeological data and other sources.

All human societies are interested in the past, but they think of it in different terms and use it for different purposes. Archaeologists, Westerners generally, conceive of time in a linear way, whereas many non-Western groups measure time by the cycles of the seasons and the movements of heavenly bodies. They use linear time only when it is of use to them. Archaeology is not the only way of approaching history, for many societies have oral histories, alternative perspectives on the past that are of vital importance in preserving traditional culture and values. Theoretical approaches to human prehistory abound, but they can be divided, in general terms, into processual and post-processual approaches. The processual (culture as adaptation) approach uses multilinear cultural evolution and cultural ecology to provide a viable general framework for studying world prehistory, based on the assumption that human societies evolved in many diverse ways. Archaeologists conventionally make a distinction between prestate and state-organized societies as part of this framework. Evolutionary ecology makes use of the mechanism of natural selection and optimal foraging strategy to interpret hunter-gatherer societies in terms of energy costs and risk management. In recent years, archaeologists have distinguished between external constraints on cultural change, such as environmental factors, and internal constraints, created by the actions of individuals and groups. A new generation of research is focusing on ideologies, human interactions, gender relations, and other topics, combining processual and post-processual approaches to study both types of constraints and their influences on the past.

Key Terms

Anthropology The study of humanity in the broadest possible sense, ancient and modern, from both biological and cultural perspectives.

Archaeological record Artifacts, sites, and other manufactured features or results of ancient human behavior and their matrices.

Archaeology The study of the material remains of ancient human societies to reconstruct human behavior in the past.

Band A simple form of human social organization that flourished for most of prehistory. A band consists of a family or series of families, normally with 20 to 50 people.

Chiefdom A form of social organization, more complex than a tribal society, that has evolved some form of leadership structure and some mechanisms for distributing goods and services throughout the society. The chief who heads such a society and the specialists who work for the chief are supported by the voluntary contributions of the people.

Contingency model In optimal foraging strategy, exploitation of foods as opportunity arises, independent of their abundance.

Cultural ecology The study of the dynamic interactions between human societies and their environments. Under this approach, culture is the primary adaptive mechanism used by human societies.

Cultural process A deductive approach to archaeological research that is designed to study the changes and interactions in cultural systems and the processes by which human cultures change throughout time. Processual archaeologists use both descriptive and explanatory models.

Cultural resource management (CRM) The conservation and management of archaeological sites and artifacts as a means of protecting the past.

Cultural system A perspective on culture that views culture and its environment as a number of linked systems in which change occurs through a series of minor, linked variations in one or more of these systems.

Culture A set of designs for living that help mold human responses to different situations. Culture is our primary means of adapting to our environment. In archaeology, culture is an arbitrary unit applied to similar assemblages of artifacts found at several sites, defined in a precise context of time and space.

Culture as adaptation approach An approach to human prehistory that uses cultural systems and ecology to study culture change over time.

Dendrochronology From the Greek *dendros*, "tree," and *chronos*, "time"; a term for tree-ring dating.

Diffusion The spread of a cultural trait from one area to another by means of contact between people.

Elite In archaeology, a class of nobility or relatives of a chief or ruler.

Evolutionary ecology An approach to prehistory that is based on natural selection as a way of predicting variations in human behavior.

Exchange system A system for exchanging goods and services between individuals and communities.

Foraging Commonly used to refer to plant gathering, also generically (in this book) to hunting and plant gathering.

History The study of the past using written records.

Invention Some kind of innovation, material or otherwise, produced by a person or group at one place at a single moment in time.

Midden Trash heaps containing food remains, often applied to piles of sea shells and freshwater shells.

Migration The movement of an entire population from one area to another.

Multilinear cultural evolution A theory of cultural evolution that sees each human culture as evolving in its own way through adaptation to its particular environment.

Optimal foraging strategy An approach to studying hunter-gatherer societies that is based in the assumption that people will use the most efficient foraging strategies relative to considerations of energy and time expended.

Oral history Historical traditions, often genealogies, passed from generation to generation by word of mouth.

Pollen analysis (palynology) The study of fossil plant pollens to reconstruct ancient vegetation through time.

Post-processual archaeology A wide variety of theoretical approaches that search for the meaning of the archaeological record, for the ideology and structure of ancient societies. A reaction to processual archaeology.

Potassium-argon dating A chronometric dating method based on the decay rate of potassium-40, which becomes argon-40. Applicable to the earliest millennia of human prehistory.

Prehistoric archaeology The study of nonliterate ancient societies.

Prehistory The millennia of human history preceding written records.

Prestate society A small scale egalitarian society without stratified social classes or centralized government.

Prey model In optimal foraging strategy theory, an assumption that people will maximize their exploitation of highest-ranked prey.

Process In archaeology, the culture change that takes place as a result of interactions between a cultural system's elements and the system's environment.

Radiocarbon (C-14) dating A chronometric dating method based on measuring the decay rate of the carbon isotope carbon-14 to stable nitrogen. The resulting dates are calibrated with tree-ring chronologies to convert radiocarbon ages into dates in calendar years.

State-organized society (civilization) A socially stratified society with a strongly centralized government, social complexity, and writing.

Text-aided archaeology The study of the past using both archaeology and historical documents.

Tribe A group of bands unified by sodalities (age-sets or secret societies) and governed by a council of representatives from the bands, kin groups, or sodalities within it.

Unilinear cultural evolution A late nineteenth-century evolutionary theory envisaging all human societies as evolving, or being capable of evolving, along one track of cultural evolution from simple hunting and gathering to literate civilization.

World prehistory The prehistory of humankind studied from a global perspective.

Zooarchaeology The study of animal bones in archaeology.

Guide to Further Reading 🐾

General books on archaeology are legion, but the following are good basic sources.

Bahn, Paul, ed. 1996. *The Cambridge Illustrated History of Archaeology.* Cambridge: Cambridge University Press.
  A history of world archaeology written by regional specialists and aimed at a general audience. Many illustrations.

_____, ed. 2001. *The Penguin Archaeology Guide.* London: Penguin.
  An up-to-date dictionary of archaeology that includes invaluable entries on many sites in this book, as well as others more obscure.

Fagan, Brian M., ed. 1996. *The Oxford Companion to Archaeology.* New York: Oxford University Press.
  All you have ever wanted to know about archaeology within the covers of one reference book.

_____, ed. 1997. *Eyewitness to Discovery.* New York: Oxford University Press.
  An anthology of eyewitness accounts of great archaeological discoveries.

_____. 2000. *In the Beginning,* 10th ed. Upper Saddle River, NJ: Prentice Hall.
  A widely used college text on basic method and theory in archaeology.

Feder, Kenneth L. 1998. *Frauds, Myths, and Mysteries,* 2nd ed. Mountain View, CA: Mayfield.
  Feder tells the story of pseudo-archaeology and the many myths that surround the human past.

Layton, Robert, ed. 1994. *Who Needs the Past?* 2nd ed. London: Routledge.
  Essays on the relationship between indigenous peoples' values and archaeology. Perceptive and essential for any serious student of archaeology.

Renfrew, Colin, and Paul Bahn. 2000. *Archaeology: Theories, Methods, Practice,* 3rd ed. London and New York: Thames & Hudson.
  Comprehensive survey of archaeological method and theory for interested readers and students. Lavishly illustrated with many examples.

Thomas, David H. 2003. *Archaeology: Down to Earth,* 3rd ed. New York: Harcourt Brace.
  Thomas's short textbook is an excellent introduction, especially to North American archaeology.

Wenke, R. J. 1991. *Patterns in Prehistory.* New York: Oxford University Press.
  An excellent advanced text on world prehistory.

BEGINNINGS

7 MILLION TO 40,000 YEARS AGO

Six million years is a vast span of time. In order to begin to comprehend it, to grasp its salient pattern of events, it helps to think of those events as constituting a play, a drama of our past. A very special play, for no one wrote the script: 6 million years of improvisation. Our ancestors are the actors, their tools are the props and the incessant changes of environment through which they lived the changes of scenery. But as a play do not think of it as a "whodunit," in which action and ending are all. For we already know the ending—we are living it. The . . . Stone Age actors all died out leaving just one single survivor, Homo sapiens sapiens.

Steven Mithen, *Prehistory of the Mind* (1996)

Part I comprises two chapters. Chapter 2 describes the earliest stages of human evolution and the emergence of the first toolmaking hominids in tropical Africa some 2.6 million years ago. Chapter 3 begins with the appearance of *Homo erectus,* an archaic but true human, and traces the spread of these people throughout the Old World. The chapter ends with the evolution of the first modern humans, *Homo sapiens sapiens,* south of the Sahara and their spread into Southwest Asia as the last glaciation of the Ice Age began.

| period already covered | period covered in this part | partial coverage |

| 5 mya | 2.5 mya | 1 mya | 100,000 B.P. | 10,000 B.C. | A.D. 1 | A.D. 1500 |

HUMAN ORIGINS

7 MILLION TO 1.9 MILLION YEARS AGO

Artist's reconstruction of *Australopithecus afarensis* walking on soft volcanic ash at Laetoli, Tanzania, c. 3.6 million years ago.

t was a blazing hot day at Olduvai Gorge, East Africa, in 1959. Back in camp, Louis Leakey lay in his tent, suffering from a bout of influenza. Meanwhile, Mary Leakey, sheltered by a beach umbrella, was excavating the small scatter of broken bones and crude artifacts deep in the gorge. For hours she brushed and pried away dry soil. Suddenly, she unearthed part of an upper jaw with teeth so human-like that she took a closer look. Moments later, she jumped into her Land Rover and sped up the track to camp. "Louis, Louis!" she cried, as she burst into their tent, "I've found Dear Boy at last." Louis leapt out of bed, his flu forgotten. Together, they excavated the fragmentary remains of a magnificent robust hominid skull. The Leakeys named it *Zinjanthropus boisei*[1] ("African human of Boise"), a Mr. Boise being one of their benefactors. With this dramatic discovery, they changed the study of human evolution from a part-time science into an international detective story.

Not that the search for human origins began with the Leakeys. As long ago as 1863, the great Victorian naturalist Thomas Huxley called it the "question of questions," the nature of the exact relationship between humans and their closest living relatives such as the chimpanzee and the gorilla. Ever since his day, scientists have been locked in controversy as they trace the complex evolutionary history of humanity back to its very beginnings (Figure 2.1; Table 2.1).

!!!!! The Great Ice Age

The story of humanity begins deep in geologic time, during the later part of the Cenozoic era—the age of mammals (Table 2.2). For most of geologic time, the world's climate was warmer and more homogeneous than it is today. During the Oligocene epoch, some 35 million years ago (mya), the first signs of glacial cooling appeared with the formation of a belt of pack ice around Antarctica (Butzer, 1974). World temperatures dropped considerably between 14 and 11 mya. As temperatures lowered, glaciers formed on high ground in high latitudes. About 3.2 mya, large ice sheets formed on the northern continents, locking up enough water to lower world sea levels by about 40 m (130 feet). Then, about 2.5 mya, glaciation intensified still more and the earth entered its present period of a constantly fluctuating climate. These changes culminated during the **Pleistocene** epoch, the most recent interval of earth history, which began about 1.6 mya. This epoch is sometimes called the Age of Humanity, for it was during this

---

[1]Now known as *Australopithecus boisei*.

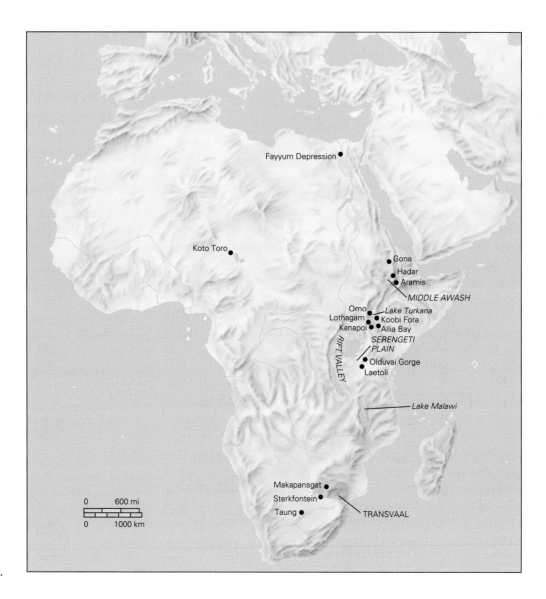

FIGURE 2.1
Archaeological sites mentioned in Chapter 2.

time that human beings first populated most of the globe (Table 2.3). The major climate and environmental changes that took place during the Pleistocene were the backdrop for some of the most important stages in human evolution.

The Pleistocene epoch had constant fluctuations between warm and intensely cold global climates. For long stretches of time, the northern parts of Europe and North America were mantled with great ice sheets, the last retreating only some 15,000 years ago. There have been at least nine of these glacial periods during the last 700,000 years, which is why the Pleistocene is sometimes called the Great Ice Age. Interglacials, with climates as warm as or warmer than that of today, were rare, and the constant changes repeatedly displaced plants and animals from their original habitats (Kurtén, 1968; Kurtén and Anderson, 1980). During colder cycles, plants and animals usually fared better at lower altitudes and in warmer latitudes. Populations of animals spread slowly toward more hospitable areas, mixing with populations that already lived there and creating new communities with new combinations of organisms. This repeated mixing surely affected the direction of evolution in many ways. No one knows how many mammal species emerged during the Pleistocene, although paleontologist Björn Kurtén once estimated that no fewer than 113 of the mammal species now living in Europe and adjacent Asia have appeared during the past 3 million years.

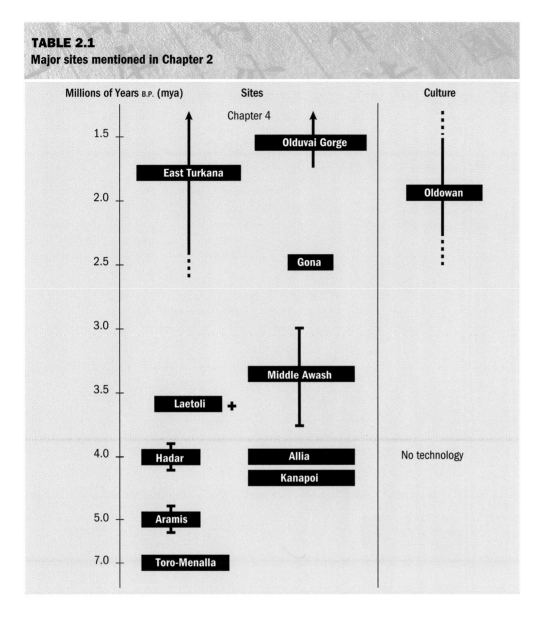

TABLE 2.1
Major sites mentioned in Chapter 2

Deep-sea cores lifted from the depths of the world's oceans and glacial ice cores from the Antarctic and Greenland ice sheets have revealed a complex picture of Pleistocene climate. These cores have shown that climatic fluctuations between warm and cold were relatively minor until about 800,000 years ago. Since then, periods of intense cold have recurred about every 100,000 years, with minor oscillations about 20,000 and 40,000 years apart (Petit and others, 1999). Many scientists believe that these changes are triggered by long-term astronomical changes, especially in the earth's orbit around the sun (Covey, 1984), which affect the seasonal and north-south variations of solar radiation received by the earth.

The earliest chapter of human evolution unfolded during a period of relatively minor climatic change—indeed, before the Pleistocene truly began. Between 4 million and 2 million years ago, the world climate was somewhat warmer and more stable than it was in later times, and the African savanna, the probable homeland of humankind, contained many species of mammals, large and small, including a great variety of the order of primates, of which we humans are a part. (Details of later Pleistocene climatic change are discussed in Chapters 3, 4, and 5; see also Table 2.3.)

TABLE 2.2
Geological epochs from more than 60 million years ago

The curve demonstrates relative temperature changes on earth since the late Miocene.
Notice that the general trend is toward cooler temperatures with more frequent fluctuations.
(Pleistocene temperatures are shown in Table 2.3.)

Millions of Years B.P.	Geological Epochs	Global Temperatures (Lower ← → Higher)	Developments
2 3	Holocene Pleistocene Pliocene		Human evolution Hominoid radiation
10	Miocene		Many new mammal species
20			
30	Oligocene Eocene		Expansion of mammals
40			
50			
60	Paleocene		

CENOZOIC ERA

🐾 The Origins of the Human Line

All of us are members of the order **Primates,** which includes most tree-living placental mammals. There are two suborders: **anthropoids** (apes, humans, and monkeys) and **prosimians** (lemurs, tarsiers, and other "premonkeys"). The research of more than a century has shown that the many similarities in behavior and physical characteristics between the **hominids** (primates of the family **Hominidae,** which includes modern humans, earlier human subspecies, and their direct ancestors) and the **pongids** (our closest living primate relatives) can be explained by identical characteristics that each group inherited millions of years ago from a common ancestor. (For an overview of human development covered in Parts II and III, see Table 2.4.)

The questions are: When did humankind separate from the nonhuman primates, and how do we define the genus *Homo* (Klein, 1999)?

Aegyptopithecus

During the Oligocene, some 35 million to 30 million years ago, large bands of small fruit-eating primates, known to paleontologists as *Aegyptopithecus,* trooped through the

TABLE 2.3
Geological events, climatic changes, and chronology during the Pleistocene (highly simplified), with approximate dates

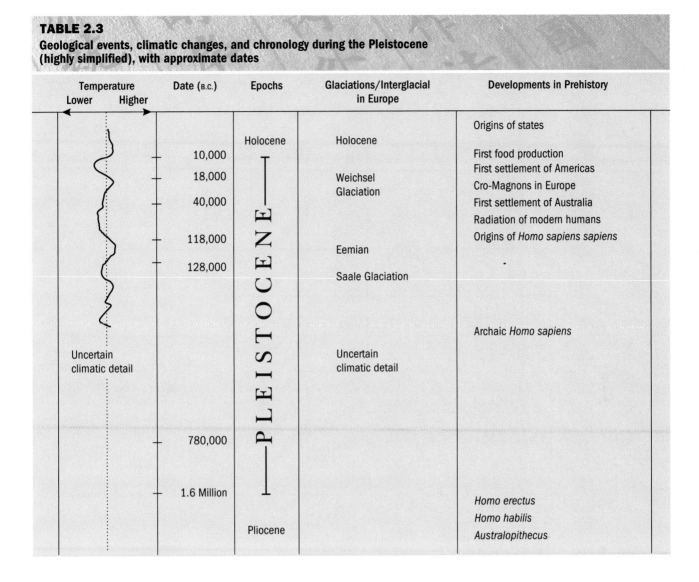

Temperature Lower Higher	Date (B.C.)	Epochs	Glaciations/Interglacial in Europe	Developments in Prehistory
		Holocene	Holocene	Origins of states
	10,000			First food production
	18,000		Weichsel Glaciation	First settlement of Americas
	40,000			Cro-Magnons in Europe
				First settlement of Australia
		PLEISTOCENE		Radiation of modern humans
	118,000			Origins of *Homo sapiens sapiens*
	128,000		Eemian	
			Saale Glaciation	
				Archaic *Homo sapiens*
Uncertain climatic detail			Uncertain climatic detail	
	780,000			
	1.6 Million			*Homo erectus*
		Pliocene		*Homo habilis*
				Australopithecus

lush, wet forests of the Nile Valley. These creatures were no larger than a fox and weighed no more than 4 to 4.5 kg (9 to 10 pounds). Elwyn Simons (1992) has found their jawbones and skulls near the Fayyum Depression west of the Nile. The bones bear some resemblance to those of later primates in East Africa dating to the Miocene epoch, which lasted from 23.5 to 5.2 mya. It was in Africa that apes and humans diverged from the monkeys, but no one knows when this divergence took place.

Seventeen million years ago the world looked very different from what it is today. New mountain ranges like the Alps formed, and the climate became cooler as atmospheric and oceanic circulation patterns changed. Continental drift linked Africa and Arabia with Europe and Asia. Hitherto, they had been separated by sea. As a result, previously separated animal species came into contact via the new land bridges, which led them into new habitats.

Miocene Primates

During the initial stages of their evolution apes were apparently restricted to the African continent. The oldest known African apes date to about 26 million years ago. Between 26 and 16 mya, apes were abundant and diverse in East Africa, ranging in size from small forms weighing as little as 3 kg (7 pounds) to species that were about as

TABLE 2.4
Human development: 10 million to 5000 years ago

Date (B.P.)	Technology	Economy	Brain Changes	Body Changes
5,000	Writing, metals ↑	Food production ↑	↑	↑
10,000	Bows and arrows ↑	↑		
20,000				
31,000	Art in Europe		↑	
37,000	Mounted tools ↑		Fully developed brain and speech	Modern humanity
200,000	↑			First *Homo*
250,000	Fire in use ↑		Premodern speech	*sapiens* forms
500,000			Rapid brain expansion	
2,000,000	Stone toolmaking ┊	Hunting and gathering ┊	Reorganization of brain and slow expansion	Bipedalism is perfected— change in forelimbs ┊ Bipedalism begins (?)
7,000,000				┊

heavy as a modern-day female gorilla (Benefit and McCrossin, 1995). The best known is *Proconsul* from Kenya (Figure 2.2). They were predominantly arboreal and walked on four feet. Between 15 and 12 mya, many apes that subsisted on soft foods became extinct, but hard-fruit- and grass-seed-eating species like *Kenyapithecus,* an ape with large molars, flourished throughout eastern Africa. Unfortunately, the fossil record for the critical period between 11 and 5 mya, when the ancestors of chimpanzees split off from the human line, is virtually nonexistent.

These Miocene hominoids (**Hominoidia**) appear not to have been members of the modern ape and human branch of the evolutionary tree. *Kenyapithecus* walked on four feet and was semiterrestrial. These characteristics suggest that a transition from life in the trees to life on the ground had begun long before open savanna spread throughout eastern Africa in later times. Unfortunately, the lack of fossils between 11 million and 5 million years ago means that we have no transitional forms between the quadrupedal *Kenyapithecus* and **bipedal** humans and knuckle-walking apes like gorillas and chimpanzees.

The basic anatomical pattern of the large hominoids appeared in the Middle Miocene, 18 to 12 mya. One lineage of these hominoids has survived in modified form as the modern orang (Pilbeam, 1986). A second radiation began in the Late Miocene, between 8 and 5 mya. This radiation eventually produced four lineages, at least one of which, human beings, has been modified considerably. These evolutionary patterns have resulted from changing climates and habitats—from warmer, less seasonal, more forested environments to colder, more seasonal, and less forested conditions. Such

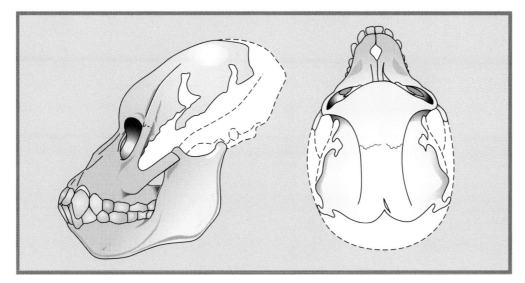

FIGURE 2.2 Side and top views of a reconstructed skull of an early Miocene ape, *Proconsul africanus,* dating to about 21 million years ago (two-thirds actual size).

changes have occurred throughout the past 25 million years, but there were major, pulselike shifts between 17 and 14 mya and again between 8 and 5 mya. These reflected changes in the configuration of continents, mountain systems, and Antarctic ice (Foley, 1995). Everyone agrees that the critical evolutionary radiation that produced the hominid line occurred in Africa.

In the absence of key fossils, we can only speculate about the nature of the apelike animals that formed the hominoid segment during these millennia (Benefit and McCrossin, 1995).

David Pilbeam (1986) has used existing fossils and evolutionary theory as well as molecular biology to guess—he can do no more—that these animals were mostly tree-living, with long arms and legs and a broad chest. They would have used all four limbs in the trees, occasionally scrambling on the ground and even standing on their rear limbs at times. There was a marked difference in size between males and females, females perhaps weighing around 20 kg (44 pounds), males about double. At least one of the Late Miocene hominoid lineages led to the gorilla, a much larger, more terrestrial form.

Pilbeam goes on to speculate that a later hominoid lineage divided into western and eastern parts in Africa at least 5 million years ago. The western segment, the "protochimpanzees," remained dependent on fruit and other tree foods, scattered resources that required a flexible social organization. To the ancestors of modern chimpanzees, which enjoyed a specialized adaptation to the forest, tree-living behaviors remained essential (Figure 2.3 on page 38). Long arms and hands as well as grasping feet were still vital for climbing (Stanford, 1998). In contrast, today's humans are the descendants of the generalized common hominoid ancestor who underwent an adaptive shift to a different ecological zone, the savanna.

Early hominids became *bipedal* (walking on two feet) over a long period of time, perhaps as a result of spending more and more time feeding on food resources on the ground. Bipedalism is a way of moving that is configured for endurance rather than power or speed. Walking is highly effective for wide-ranging foraging or running a marathon. It might have had social advantages, too, allowing males to monitor females more efficiently when they were dispersed over larger areas (Foley, 1995).

༔ Molecular Biology and Human Evolution

In the 1960s, two biochemists, Vincent Sarich and Alan Wilson, developed a means of dating primate evolution. They assumed that the albumin protein substances found in primate blood had evolved at a constant rate (Sarich, 1983). Thus, the difference between the albumins of any pair of primates could be used to calculate the time that had elapsed since they had separated. Sarich and Wilson showed that the albumins of

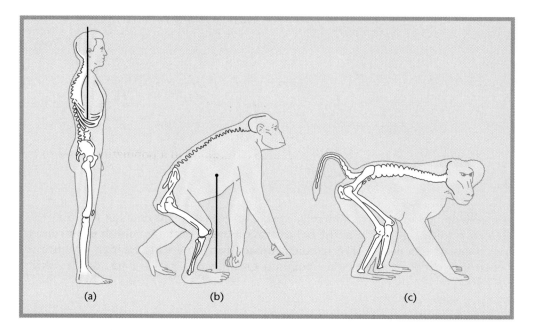

FIGURE 2.3 Bipedalism and four-footed posture. (a) Human bipedal posture. The center of gravity of the body lies just behind the midpoint of the hip joint and in front of the knee joint, so that the extension of both the hip and the knee in a standing posture conserve energy. (b) A knuckle-walking chimpanzee. The body's center of gravity lies in the middle of the area bounded by legs and arms. When the ape walks bipedally, its center of gravity moves from side to side and up and down. The human center of gravity is displaced much less, so that walking is much more efficient. (c) A baboon. Baboons are **quadrupedal** and adapted to living on the ground.

apes and humans are more similar than those of monkeys and humans. Thus, they argued, apes and humans have a more recent common ancestry. They estimated that apes and Old World monkeys diverged approximately 23 million years ago and the gibbon and humankind only 8 million or so years ago, and that the chimpanzee and humans last shared a common ancestor about 5 million to 6 million years ago (see Figure 2.4 on p. 42). The apparent separation of apes and humans is so recent that statistically reliable numbers of albumin differences have not yet accumulated.

Newer ways of comparing proteins and DNA are now refining the original "time clock" of evolutionary change and strongly imply some regular pattern of change along independent lineages. The new studies confirm that African apes and humans are similar, orangs roughly twice as distant, and gibbons a bit more dissimilar than orangs. Chimpanzees share more than 99 percent of their genetic material with humans, even though it is packaged in their chromosomes in a different way. The precise relationships between any genetic differences and the geologic timescale are still uncertain and are the subject of much discussion (Avise, 1994; Cavalli-Sforza and Cavalli-Sforza, 1995).

We are unlikely to achieve a greater understanding of very early human evolution unless we discover hominoid fossils dating to between 10 and 5 mya. These 5 million years were a period of major environmental change. As recently as 5.5 million years ago, the Mediterranean basin dried up when it became separated from the Atlantic. This development must have had major effects on the climate and ecology of Africa as well as on the evolution of many species. That such an evolution took place seems certain. During this critical period, many mammal species as well as specialized tree-dwellers and other primates inhabited the African savanna, with its residual forests and extensive grassland plains (Vrba et al., 1995). Both the chimpanzee and the gorilla evolved in the forests, surviving from earlier times. On savanna plains, other primates were flourishing in small bands, probably walking upright and conceivably making tools. No fossil remains of these creatures have been found, so we do not know when primates first achieved the bipedal posture that is the outstanding hominid physical feature. We can, however, provide models of some of the ecological problems our earliest ancestors encountered.

🐾 The Ecological Problems Faced by Early Hominids

The evolutionary process is based on selection and other processes (Foley, 1984a, 1987a, 1995). For example, one can consider the emergence of the first humans in terms of adaptive evolutionary change. Organisms are mostly in balance with their environment. Mutations are the original source of variation in a population. They occur constantly and consistently, providing a reservoir of new variation. It is this variation, always present in a population, that occasionally provides significant advantages to some individuals, especially during ecological transitions. Thus, a minority of the members of a population may increase their numbers through time because they have a selective advantage. As far as the behavioral evolution of the hominids is concerned, this process gives a model of terrestrial primates living in the increasingly dry environments of tropical Africa. In one hominid group, mutations led to adaptive shifts: bipedalism, toolmaking, meat eating, and so on. These shifts put the group at an advantage over other terrestrial primates.

New adaptations are selected if they solve problems effectively. The selective agent is the organism's environmental problems. In this scenario, the characteristics of a hunter-gatherer adaptation would persist among hominids if these characteristics were solutions to problems faced in the environment. One viewpoint sees a species' problems as the other species it eats, those with which it competes, and those that eat it. In other words, an evolutionary advance made by one species in an ecosystem can be seen as a deterioration of the environment for another. Thus, environmental problems are not inanimate forces but dynamic, evolving processes. Early hominid populations, like other animal populations, underwent adaptive changes through natural selection to solve environmental problems caused by the broader ecological community.

Adaptive Problems

Early hominids faced three major adaptive problems: They were large mammals; they were terrestrial primates; and they lived in an open, tropical savanna environment.

Being Large Mammals.   Human beings are large relative to most warm-blooded animals. Hominids have become larger through their evolutionary history, a change that has led to additional food requirements because of higher metabolic rates. Thus, every individual has to range efficiently over a larger area to obtain food. Population densities must fall because the **carrying capacity** of any territory is finite. An increase in dietary breadth results. Hunter-gatherers use a wider range of foods, many of lower quality, than do some smaller nonhuman primates, often because these people are living close to the carrying capacity of the land.

Larger mammals are more mobile than their smaller relatives. They cover more ground, so they can subsist off resources that are unevenly distributed not only in space but also at different seasons. Mobility allows larger-bodied animals to incorporate unpredictable, often seasonal, resources in their diets. Larger mammals can also tolerate extremes of heat and cold, a capacity that may have contributed to the expansion of humans out of tropical latitudes later in prehistory. Humans have sweat glands and are heavily dependent on water supplies. These glands are a direct adjunct to bipedalism, for they enhance endurance for long-distance foraging. Efficient sweating aided early hominids because both large and small animals are at a disadvantage if attacked at high noon (Tattersall, 1996).

These and several other factors, such as increased longevity and brain enlargement, created adaptive problems for emerging humans. These problems resulted in a variety of solutions: wider territorial ranges, the need to schedule food gathering, broadening of the diet, a high degree of mobility, and much greater behavioral flexibility. This flexibility included enhanced intelligence and learning capacity, parental care, and new levels of social interaction (Potts, 1996).

Being Terrestrial Primates.   An upright posture and a bipedal gait are the most characteristic hominid physical features. Upright posture is vital because it frees the hands for other actions, like toolmaking. **Knuckle walking**—used, for instance, by chimpanzees—is a specialized way of walking in which the backs of the fingers are placed on the ground and act as main weight-bearing surfaces (Goodall, 1986). Human arms are too short for us to be comfortable with this posture, used by football linemen and runners at the starting block. However, this posture is highly adaptive in forest environments, where apes jump into trees and need the power of a fast, short sprint. In contrast, bipedalism favors endurance and the covering of long distances, important considerations on the open savanna. Bipedalism was a critical antecedent of both hunting and gathering and toolmaking (Aiello and Dean, 1990) (see Figure 2.3).

The fall in temperatures during the Late Miocene resulted in increasingly open environments in tropical latitudes. With this reduction in forested environments there probably came a trend toward terrestrially adapted species. The main constraint on arboreal primates is body size. Thus, to be part of the general trend toward larger body size among mammals, such primates would have to be at least partially terrestrial in their habits. Some 40 or more extinct and living primates, including the hominids, have adapted to a terrestrial existence. This secondary adaptation among tree-living forms may have occurred some time after 10 million years ago; expressed in the simplest terms, primates "came down from the trees" (Foley, 1995; Tattersall, 1996).

Coming down from the trees created three immediate problems: Locomotion difficulties arise for animals with limbs that are adapted for moving through forests and thus are less efficient for moving on the ground. All terrestrial primates underwent some modification of their way of getting about—in the case of hominids, a shift to bipedalism. We know that this selection was a powerful one. It was in existence over 4.5 million years ago.

Shelter becomes an acute problem in open country, where predators abound. Arboreal primates have special sleeping areas and are safe in the trees. Those adapted to living in open country return to trees at night or use cliff faces or caves, even if they have to disperse. Large hominids, which were safer from predators, made ground nests, where they slept and also sought shade on hot days—"home bases." Exactly what form these home bases took is a matter of constant scientific debate.

Competition for food was another pressing problem for primates that required high-quality plant food, abundant in the forests. Such foods were dispersed widely in open country. There were two possible solutions: to specialize in a small spectrum of plant foods and become an effective competitor, or to maintain a broad dietary niche and expand the range of foods consumed. It is striking that such a broad-based niche is characteristic of later hunter-gatherers in tropical environments. And as part of human evolution, hominids expanded their food range to include meat.

Living in a Savanna Environment.   Although there are hints that the earliest hominids evolved in environments more wooded than the dry grasslands of East Africa today, the increase in drier grasslands and woodland presented another set of challenging problems. Water supplies are certain to be restricted in distribution and by season, a critical environmental reality for hominids, who need regular access to liquids. The distributions of water and of hominid populations are closely connected. Further, plant foods in a savanna are of lower quality, and early hominids had to compete for them with other animals.

Most plant species were seasonal and of low productivity, so a great deal of time would have been expended in searching for them. A whole range of species would have been needed to ensure year-round food supplies. Most plant species that do occur in the savanna are grasses, which are largely unsuitable for primates but not for a diverse population of herbivores. This secondary biomass of animals could have been

DATING THE PAST

Potassium-Argon Dating

The world's first archaeological sites are so ancient that they lie far beyond the chronological range of radiocarbon dating (see Chapter 1). We are fortunate that a radioactive counting technique known as potassium-argon dating allows the dating of volcanic rocks between 2 billion and 100,000 years old. Many of the earliest hominid sites are in volcanically active areas. Human tools are found in direct association with cooled lava fragments or ash from contemporary eruptions, allowing the dating of the East Turkana locations: Olduvai Gorge and other famous early sites.

This well-established dating method is based on potassium (K), an abundant element in the earth's crust present in nearly every mineral. Potassium in its natural form contains only a small proportion of radioactive potassium-40 (^{40}K) atoms. For every 100 ^{40}K atoms that decay, 11 percent become argon-40, an inert gas that can easily escape from its material by diffusion when lava and other igneous rocks are formed. As volcanic rock forms by crystallization, the argon-40 concentration drops to almost nothing, but the process of ^{40}K decay continues. Thus, it is possible, using a spectrometer, to measure the concentration of argon-40 that has accumulated since the volcanic rock formed.

Potassium-argon dates come from many igneous minerals, among them biotite and muscovite. The rocks are crusted, concentrated, and treated with hydrofluoric acid to remove atmospheric argon from the sample. The various gases are then removed, and the argon gas is isolated and subjected to mass spectrographic analysis. The age of the sample is then calculated by use of the argon-40 and potassium-40 content and a standard formula. The resulting dates have large standard deviations—for early human sites, on the order of a quarter million years.

Recent advances in potassium-argon dating involve computerized laser fusion, a variant of the method that uses a laser beam to analyze irradiated grains of volcanic ash that give off a gas that is purified; this gas's constituent argon atoms are then measured in a spectrometer. The new method—somewhat akin to accelerator mass spectrometry (AMS) radiocarbon dating (see the box "Accelerator Mass Spectrometry (AMS) Radiocarbon Dating" in Chapter 8)—uses crystals of volcanic materials from layers associated with hominid fossils to produce much more accurate dates, like recent readings of about 3.18 million years for Lucy, *Australopithecus afarensis*. Computerized laser fusion has also produced controversial dates for the first human settlement of Southeast Asia of about 1.8 million years ago (see Chapter 3).

Potassium-argon dating has provided the first relatively reliable method of establishing the chronology of the earliest stages of human evolution and for the first human cultures on earth.

---

a valuable walking food source if the hominids found a way of tapping it. But there were competitors—a great diversity of predators—that would also have eaten an occasional hominid if the opportunity arose.

The long-term solutions to living in the savanna centered on an adaptation that involved exploiting a broad but patchy subsistence base. The lifeway was highly mobile, the range dependent on restricted water supplies. Meat became a larger part of the diet as a way of coping with long periods of plant scarcity. Among mammal species, these characteristics are associated with a trend toward larger brain size (Eisenberg, 1981; Fleagle, 1988). The earliest hominids lived at relatively low population densities. Their home ranges were larger than those of equivalent-sized mammals and primates. They were highly mobile and omnivorous. This very general description coincides, in general terms, with that of human subsistence throughout most of prehistory.

If the ecological model is on track in assuming that this lifeway evolved in response to selective pressures in the open savanna more than 2 million years ago, were the hominids of 2 million years ago true hunters and gatherers? Or were they far more apelike in behavior than their successors? Before exploring this question, we must examine the fossil evidence (see Dating the Past box).

~~ Fossil Evidence: 7 to 3 MYA

After 6 million years ago, molecular biology tells us, the last common ancestral hominoid stock split into two main lineages: the ancestors of chimpanzees and the ancestors of humans (Figure 2.4). The details of this split remain a complete mystery, largely because fossil beds dating to this critical period are very rare in Africa.

A generation ago, people conceived of early human evolution as a simple ladder. Such simple schemes have now given way to highly tentative studies of early human evolution completed by reconstructing precise evolutionary relationships from fossil specimens, a process fraught with difficulty when bone fragments are the raw materials. It is a matter of fine and careful judgment, the weighing of anatomical details, the weighing of different characteristics, and the assessment of chronology and **stratigraphy** (Foley, 1995). The problem is complicated by an extremely thin fossil record between 7 and 1 mya, representing less than 1500 individuals. Most of these are single teeth found in fossil-rich South African caves. Very few are skull or jaw fragments, the most valuable of all fossil finds.

During this long period, our ancestors went through dramatic transformations, visible only through an incomplete paleontological lens. We know that many hominid forms flourished in tropical Africa during this period. Which of them, however, were direct human ancestors? We can only achieve an understanding of human evolution by getting to know as many species as we can, and this task has hardly begun. The summary of fossil hominids that follows is certain to be outdated within a few years. (For a guide through the many taxonomic labels and a basic chronology, see Table 2.5.)

Toumaï: *Sahelanthropus tchadensis*

**Toro-Menalla
? 6–7 mya**

*Sahelanthropus
tchadensis*

The Toro-Menalla region of the Djurab Desert in Chad, Central Africa, is a brutal place for paleoanthropological research. But French scholars Michel Brunet, Patrick Vignaud, and their colleagues have found a chimpanzee-sized skull of a hominid dated (albeit very loosely) to between 6 million and 7 million years old (Brunet et al., 2002). The cranium is confusing. From the back, the skull looks like that of a chimpanzee. From the front, the facial structure and tooth layout look like those of a hominid of about 1.75 mya, an Australopithecine (for a discussion of *Australopithecus*, see below). The point at the base of the skull where the neck muscles attach suggests that this creature walked upright. Brunet and his team have named this remarkable fossil *Sahelanthropus tchadensis* ("hominid of the Sahel, of Chad").

FIGURE 2.4 A much-simplified version of how Old World monkeys, apes, and humans evolved. For later human evolution, see Figure 2.10.

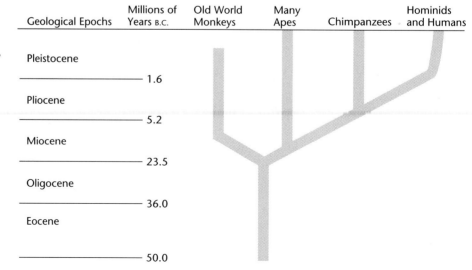

TABLE 2.5
Five tentative groups of East and South African hominids, much simplified for this book

Variables	Aramis/Allia Group	Hadar/Laetoli Group	Gracile Group	Robust Group	Homo Group
Brain size	Comparable to that of a chimpanzee	Comparable to that of a chimpanzee	450–550 cc	500–550 cc	650–775 cc
Teeth	Small back teeth; large front teeth	Small back teeth; large front teeth	Large front and back teeth	Very large back teeth; relatively small front teeth	Variable; generally smaller than those of robust and gracile forms
Limbs	Bipedal; long arms	Bipedal; arms slightly longer than those of *Homo sapiens*		Some elements of limb bones differ from those of modern humans	Bipedal, but lower limbs still partially adapted to arboreal life
Species and sites	*Ardipithecus ramidus* *Australopithecus anamensis* East Africa: Allia Bay, Kanapoi, Aramis	*Australopithecus afarensis* East Africa: Hadar and Laetoli	*Australopithecus africanus* South Africa: Taung, Sterkfontein, Makapansgat East Africa: Omo? East Turkana	*Australopithecus robustus* South Africa: Swarkrans, Kromdraai *Australopithecus boisei* East Africa: Olduvai, East Turkana, Omo *Australopithecus aethiopicus* East Turkana	*Homo* East Africa: Olduvai and East Turkana South Africa: Sterkfontein
Dates	East Africa: c. 5 million to c. 4 million B.P.	East Africa: c. 4 million to c. 3 million B.P.	East Africa: c. 3 million to c. 1.5 million B.P. South Africa: no reliable dates	East Africa: c. 2.6 million to c. 1 million B.P. South Africa: no reliable dates	East Africa: c. 2 million to c. 1.5 million B.P.

Sahelanthropus tchadensis confirms what many people have long believed. Hominid evolution was much more complicated than was suspected a generation ago. In all probability, a wide variety of apes, some with larger brains, flourished in tropical Africa between 8 and 5 mya, of which the Chad find is but one. At this early stage in research, paleoanthropologists are uncertain whether *S. tchadensis*, usually called Toumaï, is a hominid or an ape. Most believe it may be a very early hominid, perhaps even an ancestor of *Ardipithecus ramidus*, hominids known from Ethiopia after 5 mya (see below). It is also possible that the date when the ancestors of humans split off from apes may have to be pushed back somewhat earlier. The finders of Toumaï readily admit that they still have not dated their find accurately, so this remarkable discovery may prove to be of somewhat different antiquity in the future.

Whatever the ultimate status of Toumaï, the new find shows that very early human evolution took many branches, and was not a matter of simple linear development.

Many paleoanthropologists believe that East Africa was the main crucible of early human evolution, largely because this is the area that has yielded the greatest diversity of primordial hominids. Five million to four million years ago, the now-desertic regions of Ethiopia and northern Kenya were open savanna grassland, teeming with herds of antelope and other mammals that were hunted by both predators and our remote hominid ancestors. And it is here that some of the earliest known hominids have been found, among them *Orrorin tugenensis*, a still little known hominid, which lived about 6 mya, about the time when humans and apes split from one another. Its relationships to later forms are still unknown.

Orrorin tugenensis
? 6 mya

Ardipithecus ramidus

Ardipithecus ramidus was a small creature. It stood upright and had thin-enameled teeth and a skull closer to those of apes, suggesting close links with ancestral chimpanzees. We know little of this remote, small-brained ancestor, one example of which dates to about 5.8 mya. Better known specimens were found by paleoanthropologist Tim White in a 4.5-million-year-old layer at Aramis in the arid Awash region of Ethiopia (Figure 2.5) (White, Suwa, and Asfaw, 1994). White and his colleagues named their find *Ardipithecus ramidus*, to distinguish it from later, and different, australopithecines. Fragments of about 17 individuals are known.

Aramis
4.5 mya

Ardipithecus ramidus apparently lived in more wooded terrain than many of its successors and must lie close to the first hominids to diverge from the African apes. This still little known, probably bipedal, hominid was related to, or even ancestral to, two later East African forms: *Australopithecus anamensis* and *Australopithecus afarensis*.

Ardipithecus ramidus

FIGURE 2.5 A small jaw fragment of *Ardipithecus ramidus*.

At the time of this writing, there are unconfirmed reports of hominid discoveries dating to earlier than 5 million years ago, but they are still being analyzed.

Australopithecus anamensis

Australopithecus anamensis (*anam* is "lake" in Turkana) is the name given to complete upper and lower hominid jaws, some teeth, and limb fragments of almost 80 individuals from Allia Bay and Kanapoi on Lake Turkana, Kenya. These fossil finds date to about 4 to 4.17 mya (M. G. Leakey et al., 1995). The jaws display parallel sides, like those of apes, in contrast to human mandibles, which are wider in the back. The ear holes are smaller and also more apelike. *Australopithecus anamensis* is a mosaic of apelike and humanlike anatomy, for the limbs are far more human-looking. The hind limbs are thick enough to support the extra weight of walking on two feet. Measurements of the hind limb suggest the hominid weighed between 47 and 55 kg (104 and 121 pounds).

Australopithecus anamensis was notably primitive anatomically, with less mobile hands than the later *Australopithecus afarensis*, but was fully bipedal. However, this hominid had short legs and was not as efficient a walker as modern humans.

Allia Bay
4.10 mya

Australopithecus anamensis

Australopithecus afarensis

Australopithecus afarensis is best known from the Hadar region of Ethiopia and from the Laetoli site in Tanzania (Johanson and Edey, 1981; Johanson and White, 1979). When Maurice Taieb and Donald Johanson discovered a remarkably complete skeleton of a small primate at Hadar, on the Awash River, they named it "Lucy." Lucy was only 1.0 to 1.2 m (3.5 to 4.0 feet) tall and 19 to 21 years old. Nearby, they found the remains of at least 13 males, females, and children. Lucy herself has recently been dated to 3.18 million years ago by means of a variant of potassium-argon dating that uses computerized argon laser fusion. A nearly intact *A. afarensis* skull and arm bones from several other males have come from another Awash location about 1.5 km (1 mile) upstream; they date to about 3 million years ago, some 200,000 years later than Lucy (Kimball et al., 1994) (Figure 2.6). This important find hints that all the *A. afarensis* fragments found over the past 20 years are from a single australopithecine species, although some authorities challenge this assumption.

Australopithecus afarensis displays considerable variation in size. Some individuals stood 1.5 m (5 feet) tall and probably weighed approximately 68 kg (150 pounds), a far cry from the small, slender Lucy. These creatures, however, were powerful, heavily muscled individuals, thought to be as strong as chimpanzees. *Australopithecus afarensis* was an anatomical mosaic, bipedal from the waist down, arboreal in the upper part of the body. All were fully bipedal, with the robust, curved arms associated with tree

Hadar
3.5 to 3.0 mya

Australopithecus afarensis

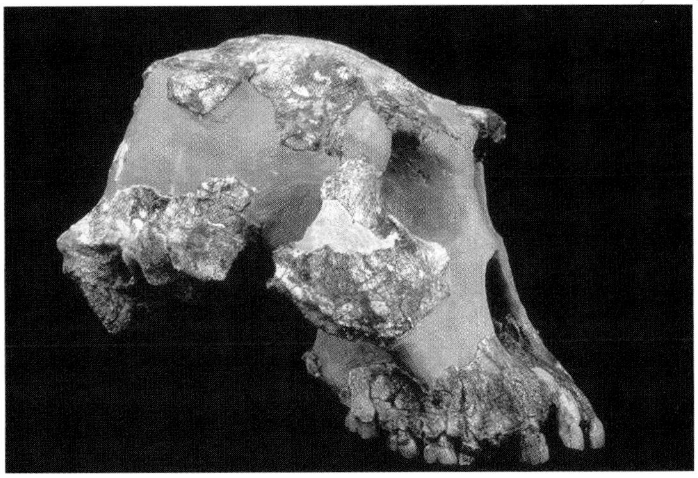

FIGURE 2.6 Reconstructed male cranium of *Australopithecus afarensis*.

climbers. The arms were slightly longer for their size than are the arms of humans. They had humanlike hands, except that their fingers were slightly more curved. The Hadar hominids had brains approximating the size of chimpanzee brains, ape-shaped heads, and forward-thrusting jaws. There is no evidence that they made tools.

The Hadar finds confirm that the fundamental human adaptation of bipedalism predates the first evidence of toolmaking and the expansion of the brain beyond the level found in our nearest living relatives, the African apes. Bipedalism also implies that later hominids were preadapted (had evolved sufficiently) to utilize their hands for toolmaking.

Originally, experts thought *A. afarensis* was confined to East Africa. However, French paleontologist Michel Brunet has discovered a 3.0-million- to 3.5-million-year-old fossilized hominid jaw with seven teeth at Koto Toro in Chad, in the southern reaches of the Sahara. The Koto Toro hominid teeth bear a strong resemblance to those of *A. afarensis*. The Chad hominid flourished in a savanna-woodland environment, much wetter than the arid landscape of today (Brunet et al., 1995).

Koto Toro
3.5 to 3.0 mya

Koto Toro is the first australopithecine find west of East Africa's Rift Valley and debunks a long-held theory that the great valley formed a barrier separating ape populations and causing those in more open country to move from the trees onto the ground. The evolutionary picture was much more complex than that, witness a recent discovery of a complete Australopithecine skeleton that may also be *A. afarensis* at Sterkfontein in South Africa.

Many scientists consider *A. afarensis* a primitive form of the australopithecines, which displayed considerable anatomical variation yet was hardy enough to adapt to harsh, changing savanna environments and survive for nearly a million years.

Laetoli: Footprints of *A. afarensis*

Laetoli
3.75 to 3.59 mya

Dramatic confirmation of *A. afarensis* bipedalism comes from fossil-bearing beds at Laetoli in northern Tanzania, excavated by Mary Leakey and potassium-argon–dated to 3.75 million to 3.59 million years ago. They have yielded not only the bones of extinct animals but also the incomplete jaws and teeth of at least 13 hominids, classified as *A. afarensis* (M. D. Leakey and Harris, 1990). The footprints came from the buried bed of a seasonal river, where thin layers of fine volcanic ash once formed a pathway for animals traveling to water holes. The hardened surface of the ash, dated to more than 3.59 mya, bore the footprints of elephants, rhinoceroses, giraffes, a saber-toothed tiger, and many species of antelope. Mary Leakey also identified trails of prints of two hominids (Figure 2.7). "The tracks," she wrote, "indicate a rolling and probably slow-moving gait, with the hips swiveling at each step, as opposed to the free-striding gait of modern man" (p. 74). The two hominid trails lay about 25 cm (10 inches) apart and probably had been laid down at different times. The feet display well-defined arches and distinctive heel and toe prints made by upright-walking individuals about 1.4 m (4 feet 7 inches) and 1.49 m (4 feet 11 inches) tall.

Without question, however, there were several as-yet largely unknown hominid forms that flourished in eastern Africa before 3 million years ago, perhaps the most widespread being *A. afarensis*.

⏜ Fossil Evidence: 3 to 2.5 MYA

Somewhere around 3 million years ago, the descendants of *afarensis* split into lines. At this point, the evolutionary plot really thickens. One line comprises the more gracile *Australopithecus africanus*, first identified by Raymond Dart in 1925 and known entirely from South Africa, far from the putative East African cradle of humankind. The second line held at least three species of robustly built australopithecines, somewhat later than *africanus*, which became extinct about 1 million years ago. There are probably other, still undescribed lines. With this diversification, we emerge into a more complex

FIGURE 2.7 Hominid footprints from Laetoli, Tanzania.

chapter in human evolution, marked by geographic and biological diversification and many competing theories. As British physical anthropologist Chris Stringer once put it: "The field is littered with abandoned ancestors and the theories that went with them" (1984, p. 486).

Gracile Australopithecines: *Australopithecus africanus*

Australopithecus africanus was a gracile, highly mobile hominid, marked in fossil form by small, almost delicate skulls and prognathous (jutting-out) faces (Figure 2.8, back). Found entirely in South Africa, *africanus* is an evolutionary mystery, for no one has yet found this form in East Africa, where *A. afarensis* flourished, even if it ultimately evolved from this widely distributed ancestor. It could be an evolutionary experiment that went nowhere, or even have been among the first of a doomed line of robust hominids.

Australopithecus africanus
3 mya

Robust Australopithecines: *A. aethiopicus, A. boisei,* and *A. robustus*

The robust australopithecines, known by several taxonomic labels, lived between 3 million and 1 million years ago. Found in both eastern and southern Africa, they are remarkable for their heavy build (Figure 2.8, front). These hominids had small brains and large teeth that were specialized for chewing coarse, fibrous plant foods (McCollum, 1999). As a group, these squat, heavily built hominids were very diverse.

Robust australopithecines
3 to 1 mya

Australopithecus garhi

A recently discovered large-toothed, small-brained hominid with an apelike face defies classification within either the gracile or robust australopithecine lines.

Working the arid washes of Ethiopia's Awash Desert, a team of 40 researchers from 13 countries recently unearthed teeth and skull fragments from yet another hominid

FIGURE 2.8 Hominid skulls compared. In back, a gracile *Australopithecus africanus;* in front, the massive cranium of *Australopithecus robustus.*

Australopithecus garhi
2.5 mya

form, dating to about 2.5 million years ago (Asfaw et al., 1999; de Heinzelin et al., 1999). The new hominid, named *Australopithecus garhi* (*garhi* means "surprise" in the local dialect), stood about 1.46 m (4 feet 10 inches) tall and had protruding features, not unlike those of a chimpanzee. The lower molars are three times the size of those of modern humans, the canines almost as large. *Australopithecus garhi*'s brain was only a third the size of that of a modern human. The legs are long and humanlike, while the arms are long and more like an ape's. The hominid was an efficient scavenger. Bones of antelope and other large animals found only a few feet away display cut marks from stone tools, the earliest known instance of hominid butchery of animals. Unfortunately, no stone tools were found close to the fossil remains, but surface finds of crude stone flakes and cobbles have come from a nearby lake-bed level dating to about 2.5 mya.

Australopithecus garhi is a remarkable find and will renew debate over the identity of the very first human toolmaker. That this hominid was eating meat suggests that a switch to a high-energy, high-fat meat diet was under way. This, in turn, may have led to an increase in brain size among some hominids, which occurred only a few hundred thousand years later.

The latest player on the evolutionary field is an enigma. With its apparent toolmaking and meat-eating propensities, *A. garhi* could conceivably be the exclusive ancestor of the *Homo* family tree and technically the first human. No one, least of all Tim White, arguably the leading human paleontologist in the world, is prepared to make such a claim on so little fossil evidence. What we do know is that a far from robust australopithecine derived from *A. afarensis* survived until at least 2.5 mya. But whether this form participated in a rapid evolutionary transition or a series of transitions into an early form of *Homo* remains a complete mystery (Asfaw et al., 1999). We do know that major changes to the hominid skull and face occurred after 2.5 million years ago, many of them as a direct consequence of brain enlargement. New behavior patterns connected with obtaining more meat and marrow using stone tools may have played a highly important role during what may have been a short, and highly critical, period of human evolution.

⁝⁝⁝⁝ Early *Homo:* 2.5 to 2.0 MYA

Homo habilis

Louis and Mary Leakey were the first to identify the first hominid that was classified as early *Homo*—at Olduvai Gorge in 1960. They named their fragmentary discovery *Homo habilis*, "Handy Person," a label that commemorated the assumed toolmaking abilities of these hominids. Then Richard Leakey found the famous Skull 1470 in East Turkana, a large-brained, round-headed cranium that confirmed the existence of *H. habilis* in no uncertain terms (Lewin, 1993) (Figure 2.9).

If you had encountered *H. habilis* 2 million years ago, you would have seen little to distinguish the new hominid from *Australopithecus.* Both were of similar height and weight, about 1.3 m (4 feet 3 inches) tall and about 40 kg (88 pounds). Both were bipedal, but *H. habilis* would have looked less apelike around the face and skull. The head was higher and rounder, the face less protruding, the jaw smaller. Some of the most significant anatomical differences involved the more even and less specialized teeth. The molars were narrower, the premolars smaller, and the incisors larger and more spadelike, as if they were used for slicing. However, microscopic wear studies of the teeth have shown that both *Australopithecus* and *H. habilis* were predominantly fruit eaters, so there does not seem to have been a major shift in diet between the two (Tobias, 1991). *Homo habilis* had a larger brain, with a larger cranial capacity between 600 and over 700 cc, in contrast with that of australopithecines, which ranged between 400 and 500 cc.

Thigh and limb bones from Koobi Fora and from Olduvai confirm that *H. habilis* walked upright. The hand bones are somewhat more curved and robust than those of modern humans. Theirs was a powerful grasping hand, more like that of chimpanzees and gorillas than of humans, a hand ideal for climbing trees. An opposable thumb allowed both powerful gripping and the precise manipulation of fine objects. With the

Homo habilis
2.0 mya

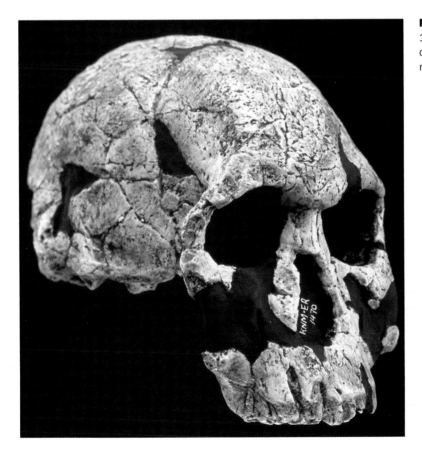

FIGURE 2.9 A tentative reconstruction of Skull 1470 from East Turkana, Kenya. This early *Homo* cranium is remarkable for its large capacity and rounded back.

latter capacity, *H. habilis* could have made complex tools. There was probably considerable difference in size between males and females (Johanson et al., 1987).

The skeletal anatomy of *H. habilis* gives a mosaic picture of both primitive and more advanced features, of a hominid that both walked bipedally and retained the generalized hominoid ability to climb trees. A telling clue comes from one Olduvai specimen's upper arm bones, which, like Lucy's, are within 95 percent of the length of the thigh bone. The chimpanzee has upper arm and upper leg bones of almost equal length, whereas modern human upper arms are only 70 percent of the length of the upper leg bones. Almost certainly *H. habilis* spent a great deal of time climbing trees, an adaptation that would make them much less human in their behavior, and presumably in their social structure, than had been assumed even a few years ago.

Homo habilis, like many taxonomic labels, accommodates what may actually be two or more early human species. The resulting proliferation of hominid names reflects a concern with documenting an anatomical variation that far exceeded possible differences between males and females. For example, *H. habilis* may have lived alongside another East African form, *Homo rudolfensis* (see Table 2.5). For clarity, we retain the generic term *H. habilis* here, but we stress that it disguises considerable morphological variation, especially after 2 million years ago, when new human forms were evolving in Africa and perhaps in Asia, too.

A Burst of Rapid Change?

Our scientific predecessors thought of evolution as a gradual and progressive mechanism. The early East African fossils suggest a very different scenario, coinciding with that of the current view of evolution as *punctuated equilibrium*—long periods of relative stability punctuated with bursts of rapid change caused by new, selective pressures resulting from altered conditions, perhaps environmental change or alterations in the organism itself.

Such a burst of rapid change could have taken hold during the brief 500,000 years that separate *A. garhi* from *H. habilis*. Whoever was the first toolmaker, the development of stone tool technology gave its inventors a major advantage over other hominid species. Stone hammers and flakes let them exploit predator kills, shift to an energy-rich, high-fat diet, which could lead to all manner of evolutionary consequences. Brain size increased from about 450 cc in *A. afarensis* to 1000 cc in the much more advanced *Homo erectus* (see Chapter 3). There were further modifications in hips and limbs for bipedal locomotion and a reduction in **sexual dimorphism.** The primitive body form and sexual dimorphism characteristic of earlier hominids vanished only with the emergence of *H. erectus.* But what caused this change of evolutionary pace remains a mystery. Some authorities suspect that climate change, especially cooler temperatures, played a role (Vrba et al., 1995).

〰 Who Was the First Human?

A generation ago, human evolution was thought of as a ladder through time, with an apelike ancestor at the base and modern humans at the top. As for humans, they first appeared when toolmaking began. This was the reasoning that caused the great controversies of the 1960s as to who was the earliest toolmaker. Was it *Australopithecus* or some closely related hominid form, like the hopefully named *Homo habilis?* As the pace of discovery accelerated, it soon became apparent that several hominid forms were around at the time when toolmaking began, making identification of the first "human" an even more challenging task.

In recent years, four criteria have been generally used to assign a fossil to the genus *Homo:*

- An absolute brain size of 600 cc
- The possession of language, identified from casts of the brain patterns on the inside of the braincase

- The possession of a modern, humanlike precision grip and an opposable thumb
- The ability to manufacture stone tools

As Bernard Wood and Mark Collard (1999) have pointed out, there are serious problems with all of these criteria. Absolute brain capacity is of dubious biological importance. We now know that evidence of language cannot be inferred from a braincase. Furthermore, we still do not know much about the range of precision grips found among early hominids. Stone tools are an inconclusive criterion to use, simply because 2.6 million years ago both early *Homo* and robust australopithecines flourished in the same area where the earliest artifacts are found.

Hominid evolution involves a far greater level of species diversity than was previously thought (Foley, 1995). Human evolution can be seen as one or more **adaptive radiations** rather than a simple, one-way evolution of successive species. This view stems from *cladistics,* an analytic system for reconstructing evolutionary relationships, first proposed in the 1950s. Classical evolutionary analysis is based on morphological similarities between organisms. So is cladistics, but with a difference: Cladistic analysis concentrates not only on features that identify common ancestry but also on those that are derived independently and are unique to specific lineages. Inevitably, cladistics tends to emphasize diversity over homogeneity.

A cladistic definition considers the human genus a group of species that are more closely related to one another than to species assigned to another genus. This interpretation insists that the human genus is monophyletic, that is, with all its members ultimately descended from a common ancestor. Wood and Collard define the human genus "as a species, or monophylum, whose members occupy a single adaptive zone" (1999, p. 66). Using this definition, they carried out a cladistic analysis of all the known fossil *Homo* species and devised a cladogram that separates all the australopithecine forms, *Homo habilis* into one genus and later humans, starting with *Homo erectus,* into another (Figure 2.10). Their intricate statistical analysis suggests that enough is known of body size and shape, locomotion, development, and relative size of chewing apparatus to divide fossil hominid adaptive strategies into two broad groups:

- The australopithecines and *Homo habilis* (also *H. rudolfensis*) belong in a group of hominids with a relatively low body mass, a body shape better suited to a relatively closed environment, and a postcranial skeleton that combines terrestrial bipedalism with expert climbing. The teeth and jaws of these hominids are well adapted to chewing and biting a varied and mechanically demanding diet. *Australopithecus* teeth and upper leg bone studies show that the rate of development (and dependence) of young hominids in this group was closer to that of modern African apes. The tooth development of *H. habilis* and *H. rudolfensis* also appears to have been closer to that of African apes, as if their development period was also shorter than that of modern humans.

- *Homo erectus* and contemporary and later human forms belong in a second group, marked by a larger body mass, a modern, humanlike physique that was adaptive

FIGURE 2.10 A highly simplified diagram showing the chronology and evolutionary status of early hominids and humans.

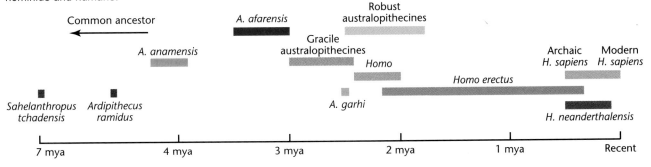

SITE

Olduvai Gorge, Tanzania, East Africa

Olduvai Gorge is a vast gash in the game-rich Serengeti Plains of northern Tanzania, formed by an earthquake more than 100,000 years ago and called a miniature Grand Canyon by many visitors (Figure 2.11). The earth movement exposed a long series of ancient lake beds, extending back as far as 2 mya, stratified in the walls of the gorge. Geologists have identified four major series of lake beds, labeled Bed I (at the base) to Bed IV, which formed in a semi-arid environment much like that of today. Olduvai was discovered by German butterfly hunter Wilhelm Kattwinkel before World

FIGURE 2.11   Olduvai Gorge, Tanzania.

in more open terrain, and a postcranial skeleton consistent with terrestrial bipedalism. The ability to move around in trees was very limited; teeth and jaws had similar mechanical properties to those of modern humans. Development rates were the same as our own.

This definition of *Homo* makes a clear distinction between the hominids of earlier than 1.9 million years ago and *Homo erectus* and its successors who evolved after that date. It implies that a behavioral and evolutionary chasm separates true humans from the many other hominids who flourished in Africa before 2 million years ago. What caused this adaptive shift in human evolution is unknown. Did it correspond with significant climatic and environmental change, with equivalent evolutionary changes in other large mammal groups, or with specific changes in hominid culture? The answers will have to come from a new generation of research.

Hominid evolution can be thought of as a series of adaptive radiations that unfolded over at least 5 million years. The first radiation was of bipedal apes, which lived, for the most part, in the drier parts of Africa. Two later radiations gave rise to what is still called early *Homo* and the robust australopithecines, each with their own adaptive theme. In the case of early *Homo,* expanded brain size played a key role, while the robust australopithecines developed specialized teeth. Although the latter varied greatly

War I and was investigated by paleontologist Hans Reck in the 1920s. He found numerous fossil animal bones, including a long-extinct elephant that he named after himself. Today, more than 150 species of extinct animals ranging in size from elephants to birds and rodents are known from Olduvai.

The gorge will always be associated with Louis and Mary Leakey, who realized the great potential of Olduvai for documenting early human evolution. Louis Leakey first found stone axes in the gorge in 1931. Between 1935 and 1959, the Leakeys surveyed and excavated numerous sites and published an important monograph on the Olduvai stone tools (Leakey, 1951) in which they traced the evolution of stone artifacts from a simple technology based on lava lumps, which they named the Oldowan, to progressively more complex and better made hand axes and flake tools (the Acheulian). Then, in 1959, they discovered *Zinjanthropus boisei* and changed the chronicle of human evolution forever. Subsequently, large-scale excavations by the Leakeys unearthed other hominid fossils, including *Homo habilis,* whom they considered the first toolmaker. Don Johanson of Lucy fame has also worked in the gorge and has recovered more *Homo habilis* fragments.

The most important Olduvai hominid fossils come from Beds I and II. Bed I lies on a volcanic bedrock, known as a tuff, which has been potassium-argon–dated to about 2 mya, an excellent baseline for the lake bed sequence above. The beds themselves were close to the shore of an extensive, shallow lake that expanded and contracted from one season to the next. The waters covered places where hominids had paused to process and eat animal parts they had scavenged from nearby predator kills, preserving both stone tool fragments and broken animal bones, as well as the occasional hominid fossil in situ. Excavating these land surfaces requires great patience and skill. Once a location is identified, the investigators sift the ground surrounding the original find through fine screens, looking for significant fossils. Then they excavate into the lake bed to establish the stratigraphic relationship of the ancient land surface to the surrounding lake bed layers before exposing the scatter of artifacts and bones in the horizontal plane. This process is slow-moving and calls for meticulous excavation and recording, with each fragment, even those as small as snake fangs, being exposed in place, then its precise location recorded, before removal. The end product after months of work is a precise three-dimensional plan of the artifact and bone scatter, so that the relationships between stone fragments and other finds, including (hopefully) hominid fossils, are established with the greatest possible precision.

The pioneer excavation methods used by the Leakeys at Olduvai have been adopted and refined in both the Lake Turkana and Hadar regions, where archaeologists work alongside human paleontologists, geologists, geomorphologists, and other specialists in a multidisciplinary investigation of the earliest human behavior (see Figure 2.12, page 55).

---

in morphological terms, later humans radiated not so much morphologically as ecologically, spreading from Africa and creating distinct geographic populations.

This flowering of hominid types is exactly what evolution is about: "an endless production of novel ways of doing things, exploring alternatives, trying out new strategies as conditions themselves shift and change all driven by natural selection" (Foley, 1995, p. 103). Hominids were no different from other mammals, which began as a slim stem and radiated into distinct branches. We still do not know much about the relationships between such branches.

🐾 Archaeological Evidence for Early Human Behavior

Studying early hominid behavior is complicated both by poor preservation conditions and by the vast time chasm that separates us from our remotest ancestors. In general terms, three lines of evidence offer opportunities for testing hypotheses about early hominid behavior:

1. *Scatters of artifacts.* Scatters of artifacts and food remains form the archaeological record for hominid activities, perhaps at predator kills, home bases, or meat caches.

2. *Manufactured artifacts.* Because of preservation conditions, manufactured artifacts are mainly objects made of stone. The transport of the raw materials used to make these tools is also an important consideration.

3. *Surviving food remains.* Finds of food remains, almost entirely fragmentary animal bones, reveal valuable information about our remote forebears.

Evidence for "Central Places"?

Later hunter-gatherers made habitual use of **central places,** sites where they returned to sleep, fabricate tools, cook food, and engage in a wide variety of social activities. Did hominids have similar central places?

The only archaeological evidence comes from East Turkana and Olduvai Gorge (see Site box), where a number of concentrations of bones and stone tools dating to around 2 million years ago and later have been excavated and studied with meticulous care. No such concentrations have been found with the earlier Laetoli or Hadar hominids.

For years, Louis Leakey and other pioneer paleoanthropologists believed that these scatters were "living floors," places where our ancestors slept, made tools, and butchered game. These were home bases, they argued, on the assumption that the hominids who created the artifact concentrations were hunters and gatherers behaving like primitive versions of living bands.

Recent thinking on the subject regards such assumptions as dangerous. First, the archaeological record is very ancient, so ancient that the only way one can hope to interpret it is with a thorough knowledge of the geologic and other processes that have affected the bone and tool scatter since its makers abandoned it. Second, we now know much more about living hunters and nonhuman primates, enough to undermine confidence that direct analogies with such populations have any validity when we are dealing with 2-million-year-old hominid behavior. Third, a whole new generation of research involving controlled experimentation, edge-wear studies (microscopic examination of tool-working surfaces), and other sophisticated approaches has thrown doubt on the notion that *Homo habilis* (or any other hominid of the day) was a hunter at all.

Gona
2.6 mya
Koobi Fora
1.8 mya

If the earliest artifact scatters are not central places, what behavior do they represent? Some of the earliest manufactured tools in the world come from Gona, Ethiopia (c. 2.6 mya) (Semaw et al., 1997). Others, often in association with animal bones, come from the Koobi Fora area of East Turkana and from west of the lake (Isaac and Harris, 1978; Roche and others, 1999). Several localities have been excavated, among them a dry streambed where a group of hominids apparently found the carcass of a hippopotamus about 1.8 mya. They gathered around and removed bones and meat from the dead animal with small stone flakes. The deposits in which the stones and flaked debris were found are so fine-grained that they contain natural pebbles no larger than a pea. Thus, every lump of rock at the site was carried in by the hominids to make tools nearby the carcass. Some of the cores came from nearly 14 km (9 miles) away, presumably so the people could strike off sharp flakes to butcher the carcass. This site provides clear evidence of toolmaking, raw material transport, and butchering. We simply do not know whether the hominids themselves killed the hippopotamus. The site may represent a place where they paused briefly to scavenge meat from a predator kill or an animal that had died of natural causes. (Archaeologists identify the uses of sites by their artifact content and other finds, for example, traces of brush shelters that suggest a site was a "central place" or a settlement. Judging from the finds, this location was certainly not a central place.)

Site FxJj50, also at Koobi Fora, is in an ancient watercourse, a place where the hominids could find shade from the blazing sun, located close to water and abundant supplies of stone for toolmaking (Figure 2.12) (Bunn, 1994; Bunn et al., 1980). The site consists of a cluster of stone artifacts: choppers, crude scrapers, battered cobbles, and sharp-edged flakes. Approximately 2100 bones representing at least 20 vertebrates,

FIGURE 2.12 Excavations at site FxJj50, Koobi Fora, Kenya.

mainly antelope, are associated with the tools, some of them bearing carnivore chewing marks. There are clear signs that the bones were smashed and cut by hominids, for reconstructed fragments show signs of hammer blows and fine linear grooves that can have resulted only from cutting bone with stoneworking edges. The excavators noted the lack of articular ends of bones, a characteristic of bone accumulations resulting from carnivore kills. Perhaps the hominids simply chased away lions and other predators, then moved in on a fresh kill; we cannot be sure. There is a strong possibility that successful hunting played a relatively limited role in hominid life at this early time.

Another site consists of a scatter of stone tools and broken animal bones, these from several antelope and larger mammals. The scatter lay on the surface of a dry streambed where water could still be easily obtained by digging in the sand. The banks of the watercourse were probably shaded by dense stands of trees that provided both shelter and plant foods. Perhaps the people who left the tools and bones climbed into these trees at night. The site was so sheltered that even minuscule stone chips were still in place, unaffected by the strong winds that sweep over the area; the leaves, too, left impressions in the deposits. The nearest source of toolmaking stone is 3.2 km (2 miles) from the site, so the inhabitants must have carried in their tools and, in all probability, portions of the several animals whose bones accumulated at the site. This type of behavior—the carrying in of food to a fixed location—is fundamentally different from that of the nonhuman primates.

Much of our present knowledge about the lifeways of the earliest hominids comes from Olduvai Gorge, where Mary Leakey plotted and recorded sites in Bed I at the base of the gorge (M. D. Leakey, 1971). The *Zinjanthropus* floor at Olduvai was found to be 115 sq m (1239 square feet), consisting of more than 4000 artifacts and bones. Many artifacts and bones were concentrated in an area some 4.5 m (15 feet) across. A pile of shattered bones and rocks lay a short distance away, the bones perhaps piled in heaps as the marrow was extracted. A bare, arc-shaped area between these bone heaps and the pile of more complete fragments remains unexplained. Leakey wondered whether it was the site of a crude windbreak of branches, since the area lies in the path of today's prevailing winds.

Recent researchers have approached the Olduvai locations from several angles (Bunn and Kroll, 1986; Potts, 1984a). Careful examination of the bones has revealed that many of them had lain on the surface for considerable periods of time, perhaps as long as four to six, even ten, years, to judge from weathering patterns on modern East

Olduvai Gorge
1.75 mya

African bones. The bones of many different animals are found in the assemblages, and the remains of carcasses are from a very ecologically diverse set of animals. Limb bones predominate on the "floors," as if these isolated bones were repeatedly carried to the site. Furthermore, the stone tools found on the Olduvai surfaces were all imported from raw material sources some distance away.

What is one to make of this pattern of meat and marrow-rich bones concentrated in a small area with stone tools? The percentage of carnivore bones is somewhat higher than the natural environment would suggest, about 3 percent in the Olduvai assemblages, as opposed to 1 percent in the local environment today (in one case, the figure was as high as 21 percent). Was there, then, intense ecological competition for game between hominids and other carnivores? It seems possible that the presence of carnivores restricted the activities of hominids at Olduvai. They may have grabbed meaty bones from carnivore kills, then taken them to a place where they had a collection of stone tools. There they could have hastily cut off meat and extracted marrow before abandoning the fresh bones to the carnivores hovering nearby. The Olduvai sites may not have been safe from carnivores, and without fire or domesticated dogs, *H. habilis* probably had to rely on opportunistic foraging. As we have already noted, many of the Olduvai bones bear both carnivore teeth marks and stone tool cuts, perhaps a reflection of competition for game. It is also worth noting that one hominid bone found at Olduvai had been gnawed by carnivores.

Whatever their actual purpose, we can be sure that the Olduvai bone and artifact accumulation sites were places that were used only on a very transitory basis. Were they locations to which hominids returned to sleep, feed their dependents, and carry out other activities, or were they merely used occasionally for breaking up bones and eating meat? We know that the hominids transported toolmaking stone and portions of animal carcasses from one place to another. We cannot be certain that they actually lived at the places where these objects were abandoned, in the way that later hunter-gatherers did. Several experts believe that the accumulations were useful caches of stone artifacts to which bones and other food resources were taken for processing (Potts, 1984b). Perhaps these caches lay near water supplies or predictable food resources. Perhaps, too, they were maintained throughout a group's range, so the hominids did not have to carry meat or stone very far. However, a consistent pattern of caches spread throughout a territory requires a level of forethought, planning, and memory that may have been beyond the intellectual capacities of the Olduvai hominids.

All archaeology currently tells us is that the early Olduvai sites were places to which stone and food resources were carried. These may have been the remote predecessors of hunter-gatherer central places, which were to come into being in later times, conceivably with the regular use of fire for heat and protection.

Hunting and Scavenging

Were these hominids full-fledged hunter-gatherers, or did they scavenge predator kills for meat? Or both? Therein lie some of the fundamental controversies of paleoanthropology. **Taphonomy, microwear studies,** and other highly sophisticated approaches to the archaeological record of 2 million years ago have shown again and again the sheer folly of basing theories about early hominid behavior on crude analogies with modern hunting societies. Just for a start, the hominids belonged to a quite different species. Furthermore, no living apes display their behaviors. Nor, indeed, did all early hominids, some of whom never accumulated bones.

Diverse carnivore and **ungulate** communities had developed in eastern and southern Africa by 4 million years ago, with a wide diversity of hominids as part of the mammalian community. Some scientists believe that new ways of adapting to a heterogeneous environment like that of the East African savanna developed opportunistically. Under some ecological conditions, they argue, an opportunistic shift in the use of a food source such as meat could have led to a breakthrough in human behavior that had long-term significance. With a wide diversity of predators in the savanna, hominids consuming meat would have to have competed successfully with carnivores to obtain it. This competitive ability was selected because meat eating became vital to survival and reproductive success, and the dangers of competing with carnivores were more than outweighed by the advantages of more available food supplies and increased reproductive success because of better nutrition and easily transportable meat for social feeding. At present, it is difficult to choose between these very general ecological models.

The Olduvai sites contain bones of smaller animals for the most part, species that were less powerful than hominids. Rather than scavenging, hunters may have run down their quarry and thrown it to the ground before killing it. This is more of an apelike form of behavior, although apes have been observed scavenging meat from predator kills. Some microscopic evidence from very early archaeological sites at Olduvai Gorge suggests that scavenging may have been much more important than hunting. Pat Shipman (1984) and others have examined dozens of broken animal bones from Olduvai, peering at minute but distinctive cut marks resulting from such activities as butchery, disarticulation of carcasses, and skin removal. They made high-fidelity replicas of bone marks and then examined them under a scanning electron microscope, comparing the results with those obtained from a 2300-year-old agricultural settlement in Kenya, where the inhabitants were actively engaged in disarticulation, butchery, and other activities. They found that 90 percent of the 2300-year-old bones showed cut marks resulting from the disjointing of carcasses, but only 45 percent of those from Olduvai showed the same marks. This was also true of butchery marks, those made when removing meat from bones. In contrast, about 75 percent of both the Olduvai and the 2300-year-old bones show the characteristic marks left by skin and tendon removal, which are especially visible on the lower limb bones since they had little meat on them.

Both disarticulation and butchery were, surprisingly, uncommon at Olduvai, so it seems doubtful the hominids were butchering and disjointing large animals and carrying them back to base. They seem to have obtained meat without cutting up very many carcasses. It is possible that they scavenged it from predator kills. A tantalizing clue came from 13 Olduvai bones on which both carnivore and human-made markings were present. In eight instances, the human marks overlay carnivore tooth marks, as if the humans had scavenged the bones from carcasses that had already been killed by lions or other predators (see Potts, 1984a).

The diversity of animals, including nonmigratory species, represented in the Olduvai bone accumulations is striking. Richard Potts (1984b) believes that it represents the variety of animals found in a resident rather than a migratory ungulate population, where only a few species are represented. He argues that the hominids depended at least partially on resident animals in a situation in which the generalization about large carnivores being hunters and scavengers might apply. Thus, the Olduvai hominids were hunting resident mammals as well as competing with other carnivores in scavenging activity.

By studying body part frequencies in Olduvai accumulations, Potts (1984b) has shown that carnivore bone assemblages contain a high proportion of forelimbs, the body part usually removed first from a carcass by a scavenger. In accumulations where hominid activity took place, higher forelimbs are also common, but hind limbs are relatively abundant as well, as if the hominids were obtaining meat both early and later in the sequence of carcass disarticulation.

What do these new archaeological findings mean in behavioral terms? Robert Blumenschine has spent long field seasons studying animal predators on the game-rich Serengeti Plain of northern Tanzania (Blumenschine and Cavallo, 1992). This semi-arid grassland environment, intersected by occasional watercourses lined by trees, is the closest we can come to the open landscape exploited by our remotest ancestors. The Serengeti abounds in game animals of all kinds, and in predators that hunt them. It is an environment of plenty, yet of danger, where bipedal hominids would compete with lions and hyenas and were potential prey themselves. The treeless savanna offered little refuge to hominids armed not with sharp teeth and claws but with sticks and stones, yet they acquired game meat successfully, either by being expert hunters or by opportunistic scavenging. Blumenschine observed dozens of predator kills and examined the surviving carcasses and shattered bones, comparing them to those from Olduvai and other hominid sites. At the same time, he identified two distinctive scavenging opportunities where hominids would have been at an advantage over their competitors.

The first lay in streamside woodlands, places where lions kill close to water in the dry season, feeding on a carcass under a canopy of trees and hidden from roaming vultures high above. In many cases, Blumenschine found that a day would elapse before even hyenas would find the abandoned kill, ample time for observant hominids to move in for their share. It is here, too, that leopards hide small antelope kills in trees, high above the ground. Two million years ago saber-toothed tigers may have killed much larger animals in similar riparian (riverside) environments. During the dry months, large animals sometimes starved to death or died of disease near streams, another potentially important source of fresh meat.

Blumenschine believes that scavenging would have been most important in the dry season, when plant foods were in shortest supply. During these months, the best food-getting strategy was to scavenge from kills by many predators near permanent water supplies. The rainy season found the same predators ranging over the open plains, killing in places where hyenas and vultures would make quick work of the remaining carcass—far away from the trees that were so vital to puny hominids. But our ancestors then relied more heavily on plant foods, which came into season at different times. Thus, scavenging and foraging went hand in hand, each complementing the other at different times of the year.

The Blumenschine scavenging theory is highly plausible, for it is based on assumptions that hominids were subject to the same pressures as other animals and on a rapidly growing body of scientific data from many sources. He notes that scavenging was not easy for slow-moving animals like hominids. Careful observation was all-important—of the purposeful early-morning flights of vultures toward new kills, of the telltale antelope fur tufts at the foot of a tree where a leopard had stashed its kill, of the triumphant laughs of a feeding hyena at a fresh kill. Blumenschine theorizes that early hominids made "mental maps" of their territories, which enabled them to predict where carcasses might be found and where clumps of fruit ripened in different months (for a review and disagreement, see Dominguez-Rodrigo, 2002).

Archaeologist Glynn Isaac (1984) believes that opportunism—a restless process, like mutation and natural selection—is a hallmark of humankind. The normal pressures of ecological competition were able to transform the versatile behavior of ancestral primates into the new and distinctive early hominid pattern. The change required feedback between cultural subsystems, such as hunting and sharing food. Weapons and tools made possible new ways of getting and processing foods, even with entirely new forms of diet: not only plant foods but meat as well. Foraging provided stability, making the savanna an ideal and vacant ecological niche for hominids, who lived on scavenging, hunting, and foraging combined. The microwear patterns on the tooth surfaces of *Australopithecus* and *H. habilis* show that both creatures flourished on a diet very similar to that of chimpanzees. But *H. habilis* had a much larger brain, a development that was probably associated with an increase in economic and social complexity, and perhaps in food sharing as well.

Maybe our earliest ancestors shared food, dividing the labor of scavenging and foraging and of processing food between males and females. Such social cooperation and advanced planning were necessary, especially since the stone used for flakes and hammers was often found in one place, with animal carcasses far away. To bring the two together required planning and social cooperation to the point where some groups carried stone as far as 10 km (6 miles) from its source. And scavenging may have begun as a way of supplementing plant foraging as global cooling brought more open environments to tropical Africa. Thus, *Australopithecus* and *H. habilis*, with their flaked-stone toolkits, took not only marrow but fresh meat, using sharp-edged stones as the equivalent of hyena teeth.

Plant Foraging and the Early Hominids

Beyond some microscopic wear traces from plant tissues on early stone artifacts, there is as yet no archaeological evidence that plant foods were consumed by early hominids, because this kind of data does not preserve well (Sept, 1994). Yet a scanning electron microscope focused on tooth microwear has shown that some Lower Pleistocene hominids had diets very similar to those of modern nonhuman primates (Walker, 1981). The recent discovery of *H. habilis* limb bones revealed an unexpected inconsistency, for their anatomy was far more arboreal than that previously assumed for a terrestrial bipedal primate of 2 mya. Such adept tree climbers are certain to have relied on fruit and other plant foods, perhaps enjoying a diet closer to that of modern apes than to that of hunter-gatherers. Clearly, plant foods were a major element in a broadly based early hominid diet, even if the archaeological evidence tends to stress meat eating over foraging.

〰 Toolmaking

Other animals, such as chimpanzees, use tools (Figure 2.13), but human beings manufacture tools regularly and habitually and with much more complexity (Boesch and Tomasello, 1998). In other words, we have gone much farther in the toolmaking direction than other primates (Gowlett, 1984). One reason is that our brains allow us to plan our actions much more in advance. Prehistoric tools, in all their simplicity and sometimes extraordinary complexity, provide a record of ancient decision-making processes. By analyzing the ways in which prehistoric stone artifacts—the most enduring of all technologies—were made, we can gain insights into the mind processes of the people who created them.

All studies of stone artifacts are based on the assumption that a sequence of removing flakes ultimately produced a finished artifact, whether simple or complex, to be used for a specific purpose. Many details of the world's earliest stone technology are debated, but there is no doubt that it was the work of individuals with an impressive knowledge of the properties of stone (Figure 2.14). They knew how to select the right rock, could

FIGURE 2.13 Chimpanzee using a stick as a tool to fish for insects. Chimpanzees also use objects for play and display and carry them in their hands. Sometimes, they improve their sticks slightly with their teeth. They use leaves for cleaning the body and sipping water. Chimpanzees have inherited behavior patterns far closer to our own than to those of any monkey.

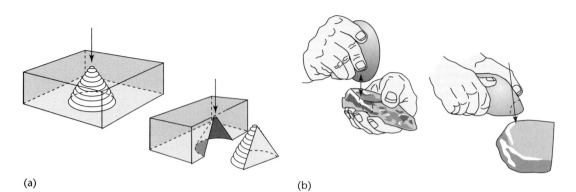

(a)

(b)

FIGURE 2.14 Early stone technology. The principles of fracturing stone were fully understood by early stoneworkers, who used them to make simple but very effective artifacts. Certain types of flinty rock will fracture in a distinctive way, as illustrated in (a). Early stoneworkers used a heavy hammerstone to remove edge flakes, or they struck lumps of rock against anvils to produce the same effect, as shown in (b). Oldowan tools were frequently made by removing a few flakes from lava lumps to form jagged working edges. Such flakes have been shown by experiment to be remarkably effective for dismembering and butchering game animals. Perhaps it is small wonder that this simple stone technology was so long-lasting. (a) When a blow is struck on flinty rock, a cone of percussion is formed by shock waves rippling through the stone (left). A flake is formed (right) when the block (or core) is hit at the edge, and the stone fractures along the edge of the ripple. (b) Using a hammerstone (left) and an anvil (right).

visualize in three dimensions how to put it to use and flake it, had mastered the routine steps needed to create a tool, and were capable of passing this knowledge on to others.

The Oldowan Industry

Everyone has always assumed that the earliest stone technology would be very simple (Schick and Toth, 2001). When the Leakeys found crudely chipped stones in the long-buried lake beds at Olduvai Gorge, the artifacts were indeed nothing much to look at. (The Leakeys called their early tool assemblages Oldowan, after the gorge where they were first identified.) Most were broken cobbles and flakes, flakes being in the majority. Some Oldowan tools were so crude that only an expert can tell them from a naturally fractured rock, and experts often disagree. All the Oldowan choppers and flakes strike one as extremely practical implements; many are so individual in design that they seem haphazard artifacts, not standardized in the way later Stone Age tools were. Classifying them is very difficult, for they do not fall into distinct types. The tools cannot be described as primitive since many display a sophisticated understanding of stone's potential uses in toolmaking. We now know that the Olduvai hominids were adept stone toolmakers, using angular flakes and lumps of lava to make weapons, scrapers, and cutting tools. The tools themselves were probably used to cut meat and perhaps wood. Most likely, the hominids made extensive use of simple and untrimmed flakes for many purposes.

Oldowan industries occur at several sites in East Africa dating to between about 2.6 and 1.5 mya. There appears to be relatively little variability among toolkits, and the artifacts show certain common technological features. All of them were made from cobbles, often struck from lumps, with edges flaked from both sides (Figure 2.15). Some of these cores may have served as crude choppers, for the toolkit consisted of both heavy- and light-duty tool forms, some modified into crude scrapers. This seems like a very simple technology, but the artifacts show a skilled appreciation of basic stone-flaking techniques and flaking sequences that were envisaged in the mind's eye.

For years, archaeologists have thought of the Oldowan as a static technological stage without any perceptible change. As more sites come to light and analytic techniques are refined, though, the Oldowan appears in a different light—as a simple, highly effective technology that grew more complex over time with the appearance of crude bifacial working, in which cores were flaked on both sides (Figure 2.16) (Gowlett, 1984).

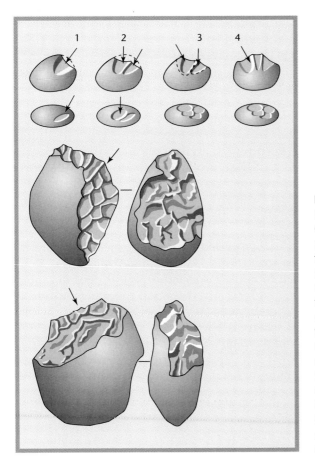

FIGURE 2.15 Oldowan technology. Many cobbles at Koobi Fora and Olduvai Gorge were used as cores to produce sharp-edged flakes. The technology was simple in the extreme. First, sharp blows were struck near the natural edge of a pebble to remove flakes. The pebble was then turned over, and more blows were struck on the ridges formed by the scars of the earlier flakes. A core with a jagged edge, perhaps used as a chopper, resulted. Many cores were "mined" for as many flakes as possible before being discarded. The figure shows Oldowan cores from Olduvai Gorge. Arrows show flake edges. Front and side views (two-fifths actual size).

Mary Leakey (1971) studied the Oldowan choppers and flakes from the early hominid levels at Olduvai and divided the artifacts into different morphological forms. Her classification remained unchallenged until Nicholas Toth and a new generation of scholars approached early stone technology from a more holistic perspective (Schick and Toth, 2001; Toth, 1985). The objective of their studies has been to learn as much

FIGURE 2.16 A modern hand grasps an Oldowan chopper.

as possible about early hominid behavior from the stone artifacts left behind. Such research is founded on every aspect of technology, from raw material acquisition through artifact manufacture and use to the discarding and incorporation of the tools into the geological record. As part of his work, Toth became an expert stone toolmaker and carried out edge-wear and taphonomic studies on sites in East Turkana.

Toth emerged from his work with a very different view of the Oldowan. He points out that conventional approaches to the stone artifacts are based on the idea that the makers had premeditated artifact forms in mind. His experiments replicated thousands of Oldowan cores and flakes and led him to argue that much of the variety in Oldowan artifacts was, in fact, the result of flake production. Many of the choppers from Olduvai and Koobi Fora are actually "waste," cores discarded when as many flakes as possible had been removed from them. Toth also observes that the size of the available raw material can profoundly affect the size and variety of choppers and flakes at an Oldowan site (Schick and Toth, 2001).

Toth's experiments with replicated tools revealed that sharp-edged flakes are far more effective for butchering animal carcasses, especially for slitting skin. Flakes, then, were of much greater importance than hitherto suspected—but this does not mean that all choppers were just waste. Some may have served as wood-chopping and adzing tools or for breaking open bones for their marrow. Microwear studies of the few Oldowan flakes made of fine-grained materials have hinted at three possible uses: butchering and cutting meat, sawing and scraping wood, and cutting soft plant matter.

Lokalalei
2.34 mya

The Lokalalei sites on the west shore of Lake Turkana date to around 2.34 mya and have yielded lava cobbles, which hominids knapped to make sharp-edged flakes (Roche and others, 1999). By retrofitting flakes to cobbles, Roche and his colleagues have demonstrated that the hominids exercised a high degree of control over the force and direction of the blows to the stone. They believe that the toolmakers had a good understanding of their raw material and argue that clues as to toolmaking abilities can come from biomechanical studies of finger and hand bones.

What are the implications of these researches for our knowledge of early hominid cognitive skills? Nicholas Toth believes the early hominids had a good sense of the mechanics of stone tool manufacture and of the geometry of core manipulation. They were able to find the correct acute angle needed to remove flakes by percussion. Not even modern beginners have this ability; it takes several hours of intensive practice to acquire the skill. Although chimpanzees use sticks and crack nuts with unflaked stones, they rarely carry their "artifacts" more than a few yards. In contrast, the Koobi Fora and Olduvai hominids carried flakes and cores over considerable distances, up to 13 km (8 miles). This behavior represents a simple form of curation, retaining tools for future use rather than just utilizing convenient stones, as chimpanzees do. Toth hypothesizes that the hominids tested materials in streambeds and other locations, transported the best pieces to activity areas, and sometimes dropped them there, carrying the rest off with them. He also points out that they must have relied heavily on other raw materials, like wood and bone, and that stone artifacts do not necessarily give an accurate picture of early hominid cognitive abilities.

The archaeologists' traditional view of the Oldowan considers it a "protohuman culture," its simple stone artifacts being a first step on the long evolutionary trail to modern humanity. Perhaps this view has been colored by analogies with modern hunter-gatherers and by overoptimistic interpretations claiming that early hominids aimed and threw stone missiles, shared food, and so on. Another viewpoint argues that the Oldowan hominids were at an apelike grade of behavior, on the grounds that all the conceptual abilities and perceptions needed to manufacture Oldowan tools also appear in ape-manufactured tools like termite-fishing tools and sleeping platforms (Wynn, 1991). Furthermore, like the Oldowan hominids, chimpanzees also scavenge and hunt for game, chasing down small animals, carrying meat over considerable distances, and using "extractive technology" to break open animal bones and nuts.

Chimpanzees, like early hominids, use the same places again and again, pounding nuts at the same locations and carrying food to their favorite eating sites. Western

African chimpanzees use stone "tools" to crack open hard-shell nuts and obtain more than 3000 calories a day from them. Some of these nuts are very hard-shelled indeed, especially those of the *panda* tree. A single chimpanzee cracks as many as 100 nuts a day, forming heaps of discarded shells around immovable stone anvils. Females tend to crack more nuts than males, using a technique employing stone hammers up to 15 kg (33 pounds) in weight that can take as many as seven years for a young chimpanzee to master. Both the hammerstones and anvils display a characteristic pitting resulting from the pounding.

Julio Mercader and his colleagues (2002) used the same methods used to excavate early hominid sites to investigate such a location in the Taï National Park in Ivory Coast, West Africa. The site lies near a stream in dense rain forest, away from human habitation. Six hardwood anvils lay around a single *panda* tree, which died in 1996, and are known from observation of the chimpanzees to have been in use since at least 1975. The excavators recovered 39,600 grams (about 21 pounds) of nutshell and 4500 grams (9.8 pounds) of fractured stone. There was no question that the fractured stone resulted from chimpanzee activity, but the fragments bore no resemblance to early hominid tools, which are much more sophisticated. The stone fragments included some flakes derived from manufacturing hammerstones. The clusters of broken stone were about the same size as that of some early human occurrences.

This unusual excavation shows that chimpanzees leave a material record of nut cracking behind them. They transported stone to their processing place from some distance, gathered nuts, and shaped hammerstones. The patterns of this activity resemble those of early hominids but certainly do not represent formal toolmaking like that of early humans. But the excavation has important implications for palaeoanthropology. Maybe it will be possible to trace such distinctive activities on early nonhuman primate sites occupied as early as the Miocene. And perhaps, too, one day we will be able to show that the stone by-products of nut cracking became the sharp-edged choppers and cutting tools used by the first humans—the Oldowan culture. At the moment, however, the origins of human technology remain a mystery.

Even if the specifics vary in some instances and the natural environments are different, the behavioral pattern of Oldowan hominids was generally similar to that of apes. There are, however, two behavioral differences between apes and early hominids. First, hominids were at an advantage in that they were bipedal, a posture that is far more efficient than walking on four limbs for carrying objects. Second, the Oldowan humans were adapted to savanna living, where they had to organize and cover far larger territories in open country than their primate relatives in the forest. In the long term, this requirement may have resulted in new concepts of space and spatial organization, concepts that were definitely reflected in more complex stone tool forms after a million years ago (Mithen, 1996).

Early hominids, with their larger brains, probably would not have adapted or behaved the same way as modern apes. We can be certain that there were significant differences between nonhuman primates and hominids 2.5 mya, but these differences may not be reflected in stone artifacts. Without question, our ancestors became more and more dependent on technology. The opportunistic nature of primeval stone technology contrasts sharply with the better-designed, much more standardized stone artifacts of later humans.

⚇ The Mind of the Earliest Humans

By 2 million years ago, there were probably several species of early *Homo,* but for convenience' sake, we can group them under a single species, *Homo habilis.* While many stone tools may have been manufactured by *Australopithecus,* who may also have fractured animal bones, we are safe in assuming that most early archaeological sites and their associated artifacts were the work of early *Homo.* What, then, were the specialized cognitive processes involved in the technical intelligence found in these earliest humans, as opposed to much earlier, nontoolmaking hominids (Mithen, 1996)?

Some clues lie in stone tool manufacture. Chimpanzees shape termite twigs with their teeth from convenient wood fragments, removing leaves so they can poke the "artifact" down a small hole. Stone toolmaking requires good hand-eye coordination, the ability to recognize acute angles in stone, and the mental processes necessary to shape one tool by using another. But the Oldowan stoneworkers were carrying out simple tasks: shaping stones so they could hold them in one hand to crack bones, and striking off sharp-edged flakes. Their artifacts defy precise classification in the way that one can subdivide later stone tools into forms such as choppers, scrapers, and knives, for example. Their lumps and flakes display continuous variability, an understanding of basic fracture mechanics, not the ability to impose standardized forms or to choose easily worked raw materials. Could chimpanzees have made such tools, as has been suggested? Nicholas Toth tried to train a bonobo named Kanzi to make Oldowan tools by demonstration. Kanzi learned by trial and error. Ten years later, his learning curve has risen sharply, where his skills are much closer to Oldowan toolmakers. But there are significant differences between Kanzi's artifacts and those of the Oldowan (Schick et al., 1999). Stephen Mithen (1996) argues for two possibilities: Either a more general intelligence had evolved or some specialized cognitive processes for basic stoneworking had appeared—intuitive physics in the mind of *H. habilis.*

Oldowan stone tools were mainly used to process animal carcasses: skinning, cutting joints and meat, and breaking open bones. But how did *H. habilis* interact with the natural world?

One obvious and significant difference between *H. habilis* and chimpanzees appears in the archaeological record of 2 million years ago: a dramatic rise in meat consumption. As we have seen, prolonged controversies have surrounded the issue of hunting as opposed to scavenging by the earliest humans, with a consensus leaning toward a major emphasis on scavenging. In practice, *H. habilis* was probably a behaviorally flexible, nonspecialized forager whose lifeway was marked by diversity: by shifts between hunting and scavenging and between food sharing and feeding on the move. As biological anthropologists Leslie Aiello and Peter Wheeler have pointed out (1995), the larger brain of *H. habilis* would have required the consumption of more energy and a higher-quality diet. The stable basal metabolic rate was maintained by a reduction in the size of the gut, which could become reduced only as a result of a higher meat diet, as a high-fiber diet requires more intestinal action.

Mithen (1996) believes that this need for more meat required another cognitive ability besides that for toolmaking: being able to use one's knowledge of the environment to develop ideas about where to find predator kills and high densities of animals. He argues that the presence of toolmaking stone up to 10 km (6 miles) from its source is a sign that *H. habilis* was moving not only stone but meat to different, sometimes third, ever-changing locations. Such ability suggests a relatively sophisticated interaction with the environment when compared with that of chimpanzees, which transport "tools" only to fixed locations.

Homo habilis appears to have been confined to tropical Africa and to a relatively narrow range of savanna and grassland environments, in contrast with later humans, who adapted to every kind of climate imaginable. Many groups lived close to permanent water, tethered, as it were, to places like the shallow lake at Olduvai, where sites were stacked one above another over considerable periods of time. Many animal species appear in the Olduvai caches, as if our ancestors ranged widely over the surrounding landscape, but they may have transported much of their food to well-defined locations.

Homo habilis shared the ability of its earlier ancestors to "map" resources over wide areas. But it may also have possessed additional cognitive abilities: to develop ideas about where food might be found and to use telltale signs such as animal droppings to find it—within a relatively narrow environmental setting. At the same time, its general intelligence was supplemented by some specialized abilities in artifact manufacture that were to be an important foundation for environmental intelligence in later millennia.

Social intelligence may have evolved significantly. Anthropologist Robin Dunbar (1992) has studied living primates and discovered evidence of larger brain size in individuals living in larger groups, developing an equation for relating brain to group size. He then estimated the brain size of *H. habilis* and applied his figures to the chimpanzee equation. Chimpanzees live in predicted group sizes of about 60 individuals. In contrast, Dunbar hypothesized, australopithecines lived in groups with a mean size of about 67 individuals, whereas *H. habilis* flourished in larger groups of about 81. Group living was an essential for *H. habilis,* which lived in an environment teeming with carnivores, often competing with them for meat with only the simplest of weaponry for protection. Large-group living has dramatic advantages for hominids living in environments where resources come in large "parcels" that are irregularly distributed across the landscape. Members of a group can search for food individually or in pairs, then share it with others, so that the group as a whole can cover a much larger area. Mithen (1996) believes that the larger brain of the first humans allowed for greater social intelligence, that is, for coping with the complexities of living in closer juxtaposition to others, where assuming that others know things is of vital importance.

〰 The Development of Language

Cooperation, the ability to get together to solve problems of both subsistence and potential conflict, is a vital quality in human beings. We are unique in having a spoken, symbolic language that enables us to communicate our most intimate feelings to one another. One fundamental question about early prehistory surrounds this development: At what point did hominids acquire the ability to speak (Lieberman, 1991)?

Our closest living relatives, the chimpanzees, communicate with gestures and many voice sounds in the wild, whereas other apes use sounds only to convey territorial information. However, chimpanzees cannot talk to us because they do not have the vocal apparatus to do so. In the 1960s, Beatrice and Allen Gardner trained a chimpanzee named Washoe to use American Sign Language (Gardner and Gardner, 1969). Within three years, Washoe had acquired at least 85 signs and could conduct a form of conversation with humans. But can chimpanzees construct sentences? Some argue that flawed methodology has exaggerated chimpanzee linguistic abilities and that chimpanzees are incapable of sentence building.

Sue Savage-Rumbaugh and her colleagues have used a bonabo named Kanzi to suggest otherwise (Savage-Rumbaugh and Rumbaugh, 1993). Kanzi was raised in a 22-ha (55-acre) forest (not in a laboratory), where much communication was concerned with normal chimpanzeelike activities. He was taught how to understand spoken words, and he learned the symbols for them on a computer keyboard. By age 6, he could identify 150 different symbols and also understand the meaning of sentences that consisted of several words strung together. By age 8, he had the linguistic abilities of a 2-year-old.

Savage-Rumbaugh's team claims that Kanzi constructs sentences using some grammatical rules, but the sentences are a far cry from those used by a human 6-year-old. Almost all Kanzi's sentences are demands for things, whereas a 6-year-old human has a vocabulary of about 13,000 words and goes far beyond asking for things. In short, the ways in which humans and chimpanzees acquire language are totally different, to the point where linguist Stephen Pinker has called Kanzi and other "talking" chimpanzees "highly trained animal acts" (1994, p. 151)—perhaps a harsh judgment but one that recognizes that humans acquire specialized language modules after age 2 and that they possess linguistic intelligence.

Clearly, articulate speech was an important threshold in human evolution because it opened up whole new vistas of cooperative behavior and unlimited potential for the enrichment of life. When did hominids abandon grunts for speech? We cannot infer language from the simple artifacts made by *H. habilis,* but two potential lines of research are open. One uses **endocasts.** The endocasts of the early australopithecines are apelike. The brain cell of Skull 1470 (see Figure 2.9) is about 300 cc larger, and the frontal lobe of its endocast is more humanlike, especially in Broca's area, where speech control is located.

Endocast research is much more generalized than detailed anatomical studies of the position of the voice box (the larynx), another way to glean clues about the development of speech. Both comparative anatomy and actual fossils can be used to study differences between apes and humans. Jeffrey Laitman and others (Laitman, 1984; Laitman et al., 1991) studied the position of the larynx in a wide variety of mammals, including humans. They found that all mammals except adult humans have a larynx high in the neck, a position that enables the larynx to lock into the air space at the back of the nasal cavity. Although this position allows animals like monkeys and cats to breathe and swallow at the same time, it limits the sounds they can produce. The pharynx (the air cavity part of the food pathway) can produce sounds, but animals use their mouths to modify sounds because they are anatomically incapable of producing the range of sounds needed for articulate speech.

Until they are about 18 months to 2 years old, human children's larynxes are also situated high in the neck. Then the larynx begins to descend, ending up between the fourth and seventh neck vertebrae. How and why are still a mystery, but the change completely alters the way the child breathes, speaks, and swallows. Adult humans cannot separate breathing and swallowing, so they can suffocate when food lodges in an airway. However, an enlarged pharyngeal chamber above the vocal cords enables them to modify the sounds they emit in an infinite variety of ways, which is the key to human speech.

Fortunately, the shape of the base of the skull is highly informative. Most mammals have flat-based skulls and high larynxes, but humans have an arched skull base associated with their low larynx. Using sophisticated statistical analyses, Laitman and his colleagues (1991) ran tests on as many complete fossil skulls as possible. They found that the australopithecines of 4 million to 1 million years ago had flat skull bases and high larynxes, whereas those of *H. erectus,* dating to about 1.5 million years and later, show somewhat more curvature, suggesting that the larynx was beginning to descend to its modern position. It was only about 300,000 years ago that the skull base finally assumed a modern curvature, which allowed fully articulate speech to evolve.

Anthropologist Robin Dunbar (1991) has studied grooming, the process of picking out fleas and lice, in primate groups. This seemingly trivial activity was vital to socialization, because the individual being groomed, the length of time the grooming took, and those allowed to watch it were part of a process of sending social messages. Dunbar believes that as primate group size increased, so the necessity for transferring social information increased. He believes language evolved as a means of exchanging social information within increasingly large and more complex groups, initially as a supplement to grooming and later as a replacement for it. Language, he says, is more efficient than grooming. Using computer simulations, he found that *H. habilis* spent about 28 percent of its time grooming, very close to a projected maximum time allocation for such an activity of 30 percent. But with so much time taken up with grooming, he believes that these hominids began to embed social information into their vocalizations, in ways somewhat akin to the contented purring of cats or the chattering among groups of modern gelada baboons.

Chimpanzees, our closest living relations, seem to have a natural talent for learning symbolic language under controlled conditions. As we have seen, the chimpanzee Washoe was trained to communicate with humans, using language gestures similar to those of American Sign Language (Gardner and Gardner, 1969). After more than a year, Washoe could associate particular signs with specific activities, such as eating and drinking. There is no evidence that chimpanzees can combine visual symbols to create new meanings or use syntax. Sequences of signs produced by trained chimpanzees may have a superficial resemblance to the first multiword sentences produced by children, but beyond the stage of learning isolated symbols, an ape's language learning is severely restricted.

The real value of language, apart from the stimulation it gives brain development, is that with it we can convey feelings and nuances far beyond the power of gestures or grunts to communicate. We may assume that the first humans had more ways to communicate than the gestures and grunts of nonhuman primates, but it appears that modern articulate speech was a more recent stimulus to biological and cultural evolution.

!!!!! Social Organization

The first phase of human evolution involved shifts in the basic patterns of subsistence and locomotion as well as new ingredients: food sharing and toolmaking. These led ultimately to enhanced communication, information exchange, and economic and social insight, as well as cunning and restraint. Hominid, then, later, human, anatomy was augmented with tools. Culture became an inseparable part of humanity, and social life acquired a new, and as yet little-understood, complexity.

What sort of social organization did *Homo habilis* enjoy? However much we look at contemporary nonhuman primates, we cannot be sure. Most primates are intensely social and live in groups in which the mother-infant relationship forms a central bond. The period of infants' dependency on mothers found in, say, chimpanzees was probably lengthened considerably in *H. habilis*. The larger brain size would mean that infants were born with much smaller heads than adults, at an earlier stage of mental maturity. This biological reality would have had a major impact on social organization and daily habits.

Chimpanzees have flexible matriarchal social groups and may even have different cultures. They occupy a relatively small territory, one with sufficient vegetable resources to support a considerable population density; this pattern contrasts sharply with that of the average hunter-gatherer band, typically a closely knit group of about 25 people of several families (Figure 2.17). The kind of systematic hunting such people engage in requires much larger territories and permits much lower densities per square kilometer. The few sites that have been excavated suggest that *H. habilis* tended to live in bands that were somewhat like those of modern hunter-gatherers. But in all probability, their social organization resembled more closely those of chimpanzees and baboons, which are very different from that of humans.

Chimpanzees and baboons live in a world created in their brains by the integration of sight, sound, smell, and touch. The more complex the inputs and their neural processing are, the more complex is the inner world built by the brain. It may well be that this increase in complexity is what underlies the cumulative growth in brain size that is such a distinctive feature of mammalian evolution, from amphibians to reptiles and then through mammals to humans. The world of *H. habilis* was much less predictable

FIGURE 2.17
Chimpanzees foraging in the Gombe region of Tanzania. Like other primates, they occupy fairly small territories, smaller than those occupied by humans.

and more demanding than that of even Australopithecus. What was it that was more complex? Why do we have to be so intelligent? Not for hunting animals or gathering food, but for our interactions with other people. The increased complexity of our social interactions is likely to have been a powerful force in the evolution of the human brain. For *H. habilis,* the adoption of a wider-based diet with a food-sharing social group would have placed much more acute demands on the ability to cope with the complex and the unpredictable. And the brilliant technological, artistic, and expressive skills of humankind may well be a consequence of the fact that our early ancestors had to be more and more socially adept.

The first chapter of human evolution ended about 2 million years ago, with the appearance of the first true humans, classified generically as *Homo erectus,* described in Chapter 3.

Summary 🐾

The story of human evolution begins with the separation of the chimpanzee and human lines from a common, and as yet unknown, ancestor about 5 million to 6 million years ago. The first hominids were tree-living, with long arms and legs and broad chests, who eventually became bipedal, walking on two limbs. They adapted to more open country in Africa, which resulted from global cooling over 4 mya, by broadening their diet to include more meat and by achieving great mobility and behavioral flexibility.

The earliest known possible hominid is *Sahelanthropus tchadensis* from Chad, which may date to between 6 and 7 mya. A small bipedal hominid named *Ardipithecus ramidus* flourished in Ethiopia 4.5 million years ago. A later hominid, *Australopithecus afarensis,* was ancestral to later hominids and flourished 3.5 to 3.0 mya. By 2 million years ago, the hominid line had radiated into many forms, among them robust and more gracile australopithecines and the larger-brained *Homo habilis,* another hominid form. *Homo habilis* was a forager who also scavenged game meat and perhaps hunted. These hominids used a simple stone technology, had some ability to communicate, and had a very rudimentary social organization. New definitions of the genus *Homo* make a major distinction between the more apelike hominids described in this chapter, which flourished before 2 million years ago, and the true humans, beginning with *Homo erectus,* which evolved after 1.9 million years before the present.

Three lines of evidence can be used to test hypotheses about human behavior: artifact scatters, manufactured artifacts, and food remains. The earliest known artifact scatters were not "central places," or camps, as was once thought. They were places to which food was carried, processed, and eaten by hominids, who scavenged much of their meat from predator kills rather than hunting large animals. Plant remains were also important. The earliest human technology, known as the Oldowan, was a simple, effective use of stone cobbles and sharp-edged flakes, which eventually evolved into artifacts flaked on both sides—bifaces.

Homo habilis shared the ability of their earlier ancestors to "map" resources over the landscape, their intelligence amplified by toolmaking. These hominids may have lived in larger groups, something made possible by greater social intelligence resulting from larger brain size. Despite these enhanced skills at communicating with others, the first humans probably had only the most rudimentary forms of speech, in addition to the grunts and gestures of other primates.

Key Terms 🐾

Adaptive radiation A burst of evolution in which a single species diverges to fill a number of ecological niches, the result being a variety of new forms.

Anthropoids A suborder of Primates that includes apes, humans, and monkeys.

Bipedal Walking on two feet, two-footed posture.

Carrying capacity The ability of an environment to sustain a certain density of population per square kilometer.

Central place A location where hominids and, later, hunter-gatherers returned repeatedly to sleep, eat, and for other activities.

Endocasts Natural casts of the interior of the braincase.

Hominid/Hominidae Primates of the family Hominidae, which includes modern humans, earlier human subspecies, and their direct ancestors.

Hominoidia A superfamily that includes apes and humans.

Knuckle walking A four-footed posture, with the forelimb knuckles acting as bearing surfaces.

Microwear studies Microscopic examination of tool-working surfaces to establish their use.

Pleistocene The last geological epoch, which began about 1.6 mya and ended about 15,000 years ago. Commonly called the Ice Age or Great Ice Age.

Pongid Humanity's closest living relatives such as chimpanzees.

Primates A mammalian order that includes prosimians, apes, humans, and monkeys.

Prosimians A suborder of Primates that includes lemurs, tarsiers, and other "premonkeys."

Quadrupedalism Walking on four limbs.

Sexual dimorphism Size difference resulting from one's sex.

Stratigraphy In geology, the study of the earth's layers; also applies to archaeological layers.

Taphonomy The study of how bones decompose after being discarded or after an animal dies.

Ungulate A hoof-footed mammal.

Guide to Further Reading 🐾

Blumenschine, Robert, and John Cavallo. 1992. "Scavenging and Human Evolution." *Scientific American* October: 90–96.
An elegant discussion of a sophisticated scavenging hypothesis. Impressive for its multidisciplinary perspective and detailed field observations.

Foley, Robert. 1995. *Humans Before Humanity.* Oxford: Blackwell.
A provocative book on the ecological background to the evolution of humankind. Thoughtful commentary and imaginative theorizing on the emergence of humanity.

Johanson, Donald C., and Maitland A. Edey. 1981. *Lucy: The Beginnings of Humankind.* New York: Simon & Schuster.
A well-written, racy account of the Hadar hominids that ranges widely over the major controversies of paleoanthropology. Superb descriptions of the research process and dating methods.

Klein, Richard. 1999. *The Human Career,* 2nd ed. Chicago: University of Chicago Press.
Klein provides an authoritative summary of all chapters of human evolution for the more advanced reader.

Lewin, Roger. 1987. *Bones of Contention.* New York: Simon & Schuster.
An entertaining account of the major personalities and controversies surrounding paleoanthropology. Admirable for the general reader.

_____. 1998. *Principles of Human Evolution,* rev. ed. Cambridge, MA: Blackwell.
Engaging and up-to-date, this is about the best textbook on the subject currently on the market.

Mithen, Steven. 1996. *The Prehistory of the Mind.* London and New York: Thames & Hudson.
A brilliant synthesis of the evidence from archaeology and other disciplines for the evolution of the human mind. Engagingly written for a general audience.

Schick, Kathy, and Nicholas Toth. 2001. "Palaeoanthropology at the Millennium." In *Archaeology at the Millennium: A Sourcebook.* Gary M. Feinman and T. Douglas Price, eds. Pp. 39–108. New York: Plenum/Kluwer.
An up-to-date synthesis of research into the archaeological record of early prehistory. Excellent bibliography.

Tattersall, Ian. 1996. *The Fossil Trail: How We Know What We Think We Know About Human Evolution.* New York: Oxford University Press.
Nicely illustrated, well-written account of the fossil record for laypeople.

HOMO ERECTUS AND *HOMO SAPIENS SAPIENS*

1.9 MILLION TO 40,000 YEARS AGO

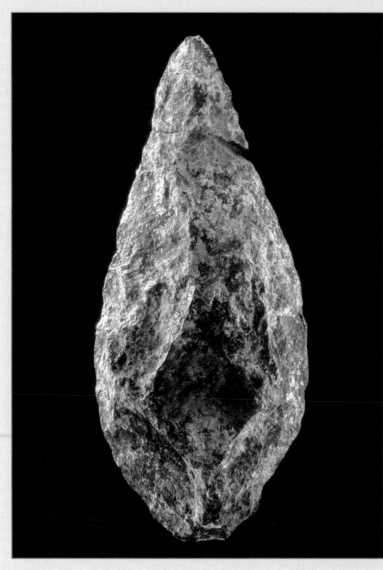

An Acheulian hand ax from Olorgesaillie, Tanzania, East Africa.

Eugene Dubois was a Dutchman obsessed with the "missing link," the mythical human that was the evolutionary connection between apes and modern people. A surgeon by profession, in 1887 young Dubois wangled a posting as an army physician to distant Sumatra in Southeast Asia, where, he was convinced, the missing link would be found. He remembered the words of the great biologist Alfred Russel Wallace, who had developed a theory of evolution parallel to Darwin's. "With what interest must every naturalist look forward to the time when the caves of the tropics be thoroughly examined," Wallace wrote, theorizing that the ancestors of humankind had originated in a "warm forest-clad land." Incredible though it may seem, Dubois actually found what he claimed was such an ancestor on nearby Java in 1891. Digging into fossil-rich ash and river sediments at Trinil on the Solo River in northeastern Java, he found not only the bones of extinct animals but a human tooth, a thick-walled skull, and a human thigh bone.

Dubois was ecstatic and named his fossil *Pithecanthropus erectus*, "ape-human which stood upright." This, he claimed, was the missing link between apes and humans, a very primitive human being. On his return to Europe in 1895, he was greeted with skepticism, then scorn. Dubois's reaction was to withdraw from the scientific arena. He is said to have kept his fossils under his bed, becoming increasingly convinced that they were the bones of an ancestor of the apes rather than of human beings. Modern science has vindicated Eugene Dubois, for he was the first to discover what is now known as *Homo erectus*, a direct ancestor of modern humanity (Lewin, 1987).

We must now describe this long-lived human ancestor and the evolution of modern humanity from these primordial roots. We shall see how the successors of the now-extinct australopithecines and those of early *Homo* were humans capable of a far more complex and varied lifeway. These were hominids, who used fire, made systematically manufactured rather than opportunistic tools, developed seasonal central places, and were the first to settle outside Africa.

Pleistocene Background

The archaic world of *Homo erectus* and the first modern humans was one of constant climatic change, which began about 2.5 million years ago and intensified with the beginning of the Pleistocene (the Great Ice Age) about 1.6 million years ago. These climatic changes were the backdrop for an accelerating pace of human biological and culture change that culminated in the appearance of modern humans and the spread of hunter-gatherer groups to all corners of the world in the late Ice Age (see Chapter 4).

Lower Pleistocene (1.6 Million to c. 780,000 Years Ago)

The Pleistocene began about 1.6 mya, after an intensification of glaciation about 2.5 mya (Figure 3.1a, Table 3.1). This arbitrary boundary for the beginning of the Pleistocene coincides with a major geomagnetic reversal in the earth's magnetic field, which can be recognized on a worldwide basis. By this time, great mountain chains had formed in the Alps, the Himalayas, and elsewhere. Landmasses had been uplifted; there was a reduction in the connection between these latitudes and southern areas, lessening their heat exchange and causing greater temperature differences between them. Three million years ago, northern latitudes were still warmer than today, but they were much cooler by the beginning of the Pleistocene.

The Lower Pleistocene is distinguished by surviving Pliocene animal forms and by the appearance of horses, cattle, elephants, and camels. Deep-sea cores tell us that climatic fluctuations between warmer and colder regimens were still relatively minor during this, the first million years of the Ice Age (Kurtén, 1968). This was a critically important time, when *Homo erectus* evolved in Africa and moved out of the tropics into Asia and Europe.

FIGURE 3.1a Climatic events of the Pleistocene. Stratigraphic record of the Pleistocene from deep-sea core V28-238, from the Solomon Plateau in the Pacific Ocean (Shackleton and Opdyke, 1983). The Matuyama-Brunhes boundary occurs at about 780,000 years ago, at a depth of 1200 cm (39.3 feet). Above it, a sawtoothlike curve records the relative size of the world's oceans and ice caps and identifies eight complete glacial and interglacial cycles, a more complete record of the Middle and Upper Pleistocene than comes from land sediments. The Vostok ice core from Antarctica covers the past 335,000 years and documents a periodicity of about 100,000 years for transitions from cold to warm conditions.

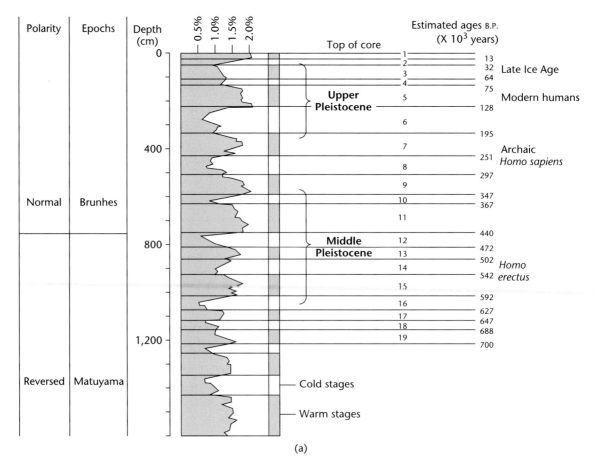

(a)

TABLE 3.1
Homo erectus **and early modern humans**

Years B.P.	Africa	Southwest Asia	Asia	Europe	Americas
50,000					
		Qafzeh			
	Klasies River	Neanderthals and modern humans	Human physical type unknown	Neanderthals	
100,000			?		
	Homo sapiens sapiens			Archaic *Homo sapiens*	
				Atapuerca	
250,000	**Olorgesaillie**	Human physical type unknown		? **Torralba**	
				Tautavel	
	Archaic *Homo sapiens*		**Zhoukoudian**		
500,000				**Boxgrove** **Mauer**	
	Kilombe		**Ban Mae Tha**		
750,000					
				Gran Dolina	
1 Million		*Homo erectus*	*Homo erectus*	*Homo erectus*	
	East Turkana	**Ubeidiya**			
	Olduvai Gorge			**Dmanisi**	
1.8 Million	*Homo erectus**	?	**Sangiran**		

NO SETTLEMENT

*   The term *Homo erectus* is used generically here.

Middle Pleistocene (c. 780,000 to 128,000 Years Ago)

An abrupt reversal of the earth's magnetic field, back from reversed to normal, occurred about 780,000 years ago, an event that has been identified all over the world in both deep-sea cores and terrestrial deposits. This **Matuyama-Brunhes boundary,** named after the geologists who first identified it, marks the arbitrary division between the Lower and Middle Pleistocene (Butzer and Isaac, 1975). The seesaw pattern of deep-sea-core changes tells of constant climatic change from this point on. Consistently, the cores tell us, ice sheets formed gradually, but deglaciation took place with great rapidity, during phases that geologists call **terminations.** These corresponded with major rises in sea level that flooded low-lying coastal areas. Glaciers covered a full third of the earth's surface during glacial maxima. Great ice sheets mantled Scandinavia and the Alps, as well as much of northern North America (Figure 3.1b). The recently drilled Vostok ice core from Antarctica, which reached a depth of 3623 m (11,886 feet) in the Antarctic ice sheet, has produced a record of four transitions from cold to warm periods going back some 335,000 years, with a periodicity of about 100,000 years, the last occurring 18,000 years ago, at the end of the Ice Age (Petit et al., 1999).

During **interglacials,** the glaciers were about as extensive as they are today. Thus, during interglacials, sea levels were within 5.5 to 6.0 m (18 to 20 feet) of present shorelines. Much less is known about changes in tropical regions. It is known that the southern fringes of the Sahara expanded dramatically during cold periods.

The outlines of Middle Pleistocene climatic change are still imperfectly known, but we know that there was a major glacial episode, called by European geologists the Elster glaciation, about 525,000 years ago. At its height, there was ice as far south as present-day Seattle, St. Louis, and New York in North America, and sea levels were about 197 m

FIGURE 3.1b Pleistocene glaciers in the Northern Hemisphere at their maximum extent. Shorelines caused by low sea levels are not known.

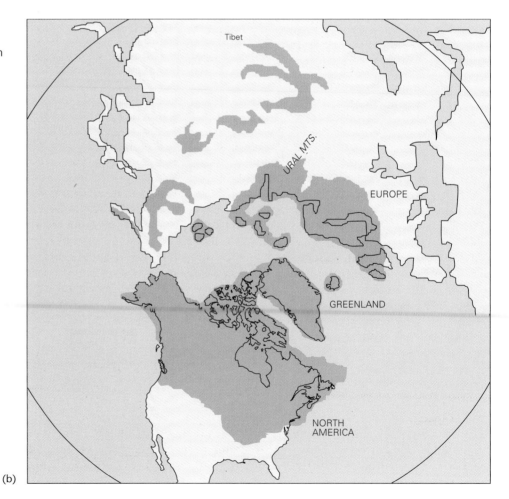

(b)

(650 feet) below modern levels. In contrast, there were periods of more temperate conditions between about 515,000 and 315,000 years ago, with colder incidents breaking up the warmer climate. It was during this interglacial that the human settlement of temperate latitudes really took hold as small bands of hunter-gatherers exploited the rich animal and plant resources of European and Asian river valleys and woodlands.

The Middle Pleistocene ended with another intense glaciation, the Saale (known as the Illinoian in North America), which lasted from about 180,000 to 128,000 years ago. As we shall see, this colder cycle coincided in general terms with the period when anatomically modern humans (*Homo sapiens sapiens*) were evolving in tropical Africa.

Both *H. erectus* and *H. sapiens* evolved during a period of constant climatic transition between warmer and colder regimens in the northern latitudes. Experts believe that the world's climate has been in transition from one extreme to the other for over 75 percent of the past 730,000 years, with a predominance of colder climate over the entire period. These constant climatic changes played an important role in the spread of archaic humans throughout the temperate and tropical latitudes (Gamble, 1999).

The climatic events of the Upper Pleistocene are described at the beginning of Chapter 4.

〽 *Homo erectus*

Early hominid evolution forms a complex pattern of constant diversification, to the point where there were probably about five or six species of living hominids at the beginning of the Ice Age some 1.6 million years ago. By a million years ago, the only known survivor was *Homo erectus,* a larger human with overall skeletal proportions much more like those of modern humans. As we saw in Chapter 2, true humans, in the sense of members of the genus *Homo,* may only have appeared about 1.9 mya, with the evolution of *Homo erectus,* a powerfully built human with massive brow ridges and a large face and with a long, low skull to accommodate a much larger brain. It flourished in Africa, Asia, and probably Europe until about half a million years ago. Over this enormous area, *H. erectus* displayed considerable, and still little understood, variation.

〽 *Homo erectus* in Africa

Current estimates place the emergence of *H. erectus* (the earliest African form is sometimes called *H. ergaster*), probably in Africa, at about 1.9 million years ago. That the new human evolved from a *H. habilis*–like hominid seems unquestionable, but we still await the discovery of larger-brained transitional forms.

Homo erectus
1.9 mya

The earliest East African specimens come from the Lake Turkana region of northern Kenya, where current estimates place the appearance of *H. erectus* at about 2 mya or slightly later (Figure 3.2). The early East African specimens come from the Turkana area of northern Kenya. Skull KNM-ER 3733 from East Turkana dates to between 1.6 and 1.5 mya. This fossil, with its massive brow ridges, enlarged brain size, and high forehead, is morphologically very close to examples of *H. erectus* dating to a million years ago and earlier (Figure 3.3). We also know that *Australopithecus boisei* survived alongside *H. erectus* until at least 1.5 mya (Suwa et al., 1997).

Richard Leakey and anatomist Alan Walker discovered the virtually complete skeleton of an 11-year-old *H. erectus* boy at Nariokotome on the western shores of Lake Turkana dating to about 1.6 million years ago (Walker and Leakey, 1993). The footprints of hippopotamuses and other animals nearby suggest that the decomposing corpse was trampled to pieces. From the neck down, the boy's bones are remarkably modern-looking. The skull and jawbone are more primitive, with brow ridges and a brain capacity perhaps as much as 700 to 800 cc, about half the modern size. The skeleton shows that the boy stood about 1.6 m (5 feet 4 inches) tall, taller than many modern 12-year-olds. This Turkana find tends to confirm many scientists' view that different parts of the body evolved at different rates, the body achieving fully modern form long before the head.

Nariokotome
1.6 mya

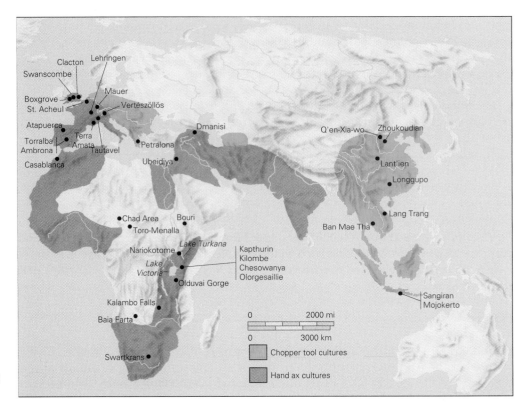

FIGURE 3.2
Archaeological sites mentioned in this chapter. (For Neanderthal sites, see Figure 3.16.)

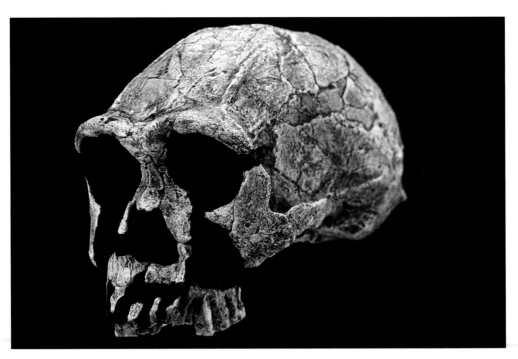

FIGURE 3.3 Skull KNM-ER 3733, East Turkana, Kenya. This important early *Homo* fossil has a rounder skull than that of an australopithecine. The distance between the temples is less pronounced, owing to a large brain size of about 750 cc.

🐾 The Radiation of *Homo erectus*

We know that the earliest hominids could adapt to a variety of climates and habitats. Both the australopithecines and *Homo habilis* adjusted to plunging global temperatures during a glacial episode between about 2.7 and 2.5 million years ago. The colder conditions turned much of Africa's moist woodlands into much drier, open savanna. The hominids thrived in these conditions, as tree-dwelling primates yielded to bipedal forms better able to survive in the open. Around 2 mya, hominids were adjusting to cyclic alterations among savanna, forest, and desert, as the Ice Age began. They did so by migrating with changing vegetational zones, as many mammals did, or by adapting to new environments and changing their dietary emphasis from meat to plant foods. Finally, they could move out of tropical latitudes altogether into habitats that human beings had never occupied before.

Very likely, *H. erectus* adapted to changed circumstances in all these ways, radiating out of Africa by way of the Sahara, when the desert was capable of supporting human life. Neil Roberts (1998) has likened the Sahara to a pump, sucking in population during wetter savanna phases and forcing hunter-gatherers out northward to the margins of the desert during drier cycles. In radiating out of Africa, *H. erectus* behaved just like other mammals in its ecological community. *Homo erectus* was an omnivore and thus was linked ecologically with other predators. There was widespread interchange of mammals between Africa and more temperate latitudes during the Pliocene and the Lower Pleistocene. For example, a major change in the mammalian populations of Europe took place about 700,000 years ago. Hippopotamuses, forest elephants, and other herbivores and carnivores such as the lion, leopard, and spotted hyena seem to have migrated northward from Africa at this time. Migrations by the lion, leopard, and hyena—the animals with which hominids shared many ecological characteristics— were in the same direction as that taken earlier by *H. erectus.* That the first successful human settlement of tropical Asia and of temperate Europe coincided with radiations of mammalian communities out of Africa seems plausible (Figure 3.4).

During the long history of *H. erectus,* humanity adapted to many different environments, from tropical savannas in East Africa to forested Javanese valleys, temperate climates in North Africa and Europe, and the harsh winters of China and northern Europe. *Homo erectus* was certainly capable of a far more complex and varied lifeway than that of previous hominids. With such a wide distribution, it is hardly surprising that some physical variations in populations also appeared (F. C. Howell, 1999). For example, some had more robust skulls than others, although it is said that the Zhoukoudian *H. erectus* skulls from China display a gradual increase in brain capacity from about 900 cc in 600,000-year-old specimens to about 1100 cc in 200,000-year-old individuals (Figure 3.5).

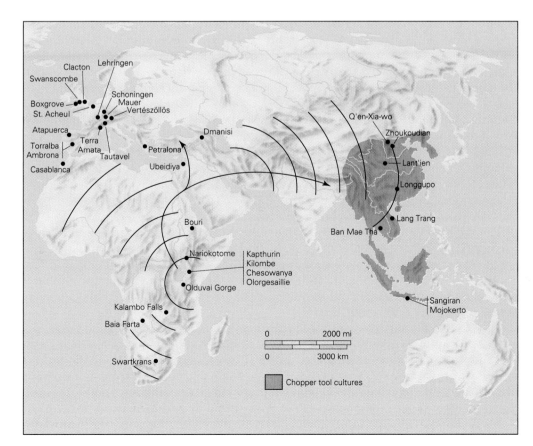

FIGURE 3.4 The radiation of *Homo erectus.* Map shows key sites and the major technological provinces of the world of *H. erectus.* The radiating lines are meant to give an impression of radiation outward from tropical Africa. A recent fossil discovery of *H. erectus* in Ethiopia dating to 1 mya strongly suggests that there was movement both in and out of Africa after the initial radiation.

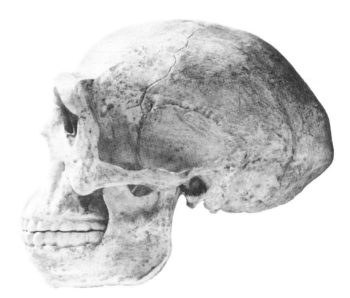

FIGURE 3.5 A plaster cast of *Homo erectus* from Zhoukoudian, China. The skull bones of *H. erectus* show that these hominids had a brain capacity between 775 and 1300 cc, showing much variation. Their vision was probably excellent, and it is probable that they were capable of extensive thought. The *H. erectus* skull is more rounded than that of earlier hominids; it also has conspicuous brow ridges and a sloping forehead. With a massive jaw, much thicker skull bones, and teeth with cusp patterns somewhat similar to those of *Australopithecus africanus* and modern humans, *H. erectus* also had limbs and hips fully adapted to an upright posture. It stood over 1.8 m (5 feet 6 inches) tall and had hands fully capable of precision gripping and many kinds of toolmaking.

In any case, *H. erectus* was far more "human" than *H. habilis* and was a habitual biped that had probably lost the thick hair covering that is characteristic of nonhuman primates. Unfortunately, we are unlikely to know when we lost our dense facial hair because soft parts are never preserved. But it seems possible that this loss occurred when the dramatic enlargement of hominid brains recycled the developmental "clock"— perhaps with *H. habilis* (Rightmire, 1990).

Modjokerto Sangiran 1.8 to 1.6 mya

Until recently, scientists believed that *H. erectus* radiated out of tropical Africa about a million years ago. Now *H. erectus* fossils from Modjokerto and Sangiran, on the Solo River in Indonesia, have been dated (somewhat controversially) to about 1.8 to 1.6 mya, comparable in age to the earliest *H. erectus* finds from East Africa (Swisher et al., 1994). But despite the apparent contemporaneity of the earliest *H. erectus* fossils in both East Africa and Southeast Asia, most scientists still believe *H. erectus* originated in Africa. They point to the continuous record of human evolution in that continent, from *Ardipithecus ramidus* to the australopithecines, then *H. habilis* and *H. erectus*. However bushlike the evolutionary tree—and it was much more complicated than we know today—the best and longest fossil record comes from tropical Africa. And as we shall see later in this chapter, the same continent may also have been the cradle of modern humans, *H. sapiens sapiens*.

If we accept that *H. erectus* evolved in Africa, it may have radiated rapidly out of that continent into Southwest Asia and farther afield, perhaps within a mere 100,000 years. Why did this sudden movement occur, and could it have taken such a short time? The 100,000-year time frame is entirely feasible, given the sparse human populations of 1.9 million years ago and with *H. erectus* occupying large territories of open landscape where food resources were scattered unevenly over the landscape. Under these circumstances, even a rate of expansion of 32 to 48 km (20 to 30 miles) a year soon translates into hundreds, even thousands, of miles within a few generations.

The radiation of *H. erectus* out of Africa remains one of the great mysteries of early prehistory, for we have only a scatter of fossil finds and potassium-argon dates to chronicle this most crucial of human movements. Despite claims to the contrary, *H. erectus* was the first human form flexible and mobile enough to adapt to temperate, even bitterly cold, environments. It did so with the aid of more elaborate toolkits and by domesticating fire (Foley, 1987b).

Bouri 1 mya to 800,000

The plot has thickened recently with the discovery of a *H. erectus* skull and fragments of six other individuals at Bouri, in Ethiopia's Middle Awash, dating to between 1 million and 800,000 years ago (Asfaw et al., 2002). The cranium displays both African and Asian features, as one might expect if there was ebb and flow of populations to and from Africa, perhaps as a result of cooling temperatures in northern latitudes. The new discovery casts doubt on the existence of *H. ergaster* as a separate African form. Most likely, there was constant intermingling and interbreeding between the continents over many hundreds of thousands of years.

Fire

It may be no coincidence that the earliest human settlement of Europe and Asia, of more temperate latitudes, occurred after *Homo erectus* appeared in East Africa and (perhaps) mastered fire nearly 2 million years ago. Desmond Clark and Jack Harris (1985) think it not unlikely that the conservation and taming of fire—as much as food sharing, meat eating, and new forms of sexual behavior—helped to forge close-knit family groups among hominid bands. The distribution of archaeological and hominid sites approximately 1.5 mya may reflect greatly increased home ranges and may have been the time when humans domesticated fire.

Fire caused by natural conflagrations was certainly part of the savanna environment in which our earlier ancestors lived. Great grass and brush fires swept across open and wooded country during the dry months, especially, perhaps, when markedly drier conditions were widespread in East Africa about 1.7 million years ago. This was a time when the faunal communities of East Africa adapted to drier, more open grassland conditions. From this point on, there are signs that human behavior changed. Archaeological sites now appear at higher East African elevations, in less densely vegetated areas more intensively occupied.

We can assume the early hominids had learned to live with natural fires and were not afraid of them (Clark and Harris, 1985). Fire offers protection against predators and an easy way of hunting game—even insects and rodents—fleeing from a line of flames. Many common vegetable foods can be roasted or parched in hot ashes to neutralize toxins and allow people to use a wider range of plants in their diet (Stahl, 1984). The prevalence of such toxins may be the reason chimpanzees eat so many insects—still an important protein source for many African peoples and perhaps for early hominids, too. Perhaps *H. erectus* had the habit of conserving fire, taking advantage of long-smoldering tree stumps, which had been ignited by lightning strikes and other natural causes, to kindle flames to light dry brush or simply scare off predators.

Hominid body size had increased dramatically with the appearance of *H. erectus*. An ecological consequence of enlarged body size is extension of the home range, a fact well documented from animal behavior studies (Foley, 1984b). Larger quantities of food are needed because of higher metabolic rates. This may have been the time when hominids not only relied on smoldering tree stumps but also began to carry simple firebrands as protection against large predators. The new weapon would also allow them to move into more open country, where trees were much rarer, and to extend their home ranges into unfamiliar habitats.

The earliest traces of what may have been tamed fire come from Swartkrans in South Africa, dating to about 1.6 million years ago, and from Chesowanya in the Kenya Rift Valley. Both examples are assumed to be the work of *H. erectus*. Chesowanya yielded evidence of hearthlike arrangements of stone artifacts, fragmentary bones, and baked clay that had been hardened in antiquity. Unfortunately, it has not been possible to demonstrate that the inhabitants controlled the fire that hardened the clay. The date when fire was first domesticated is still a matter of debate, and may be much later than we often assume.

**Swartkrans
1.6 mya
Chesowanya**

𖢔 *Homo erectus* in Asia

The earliest traces of human occupation in Asia date to somewhere around 1.8 million years ago. Despite claims to the contrary, no australopithecine or *Homo habilis* fossils have yet come from any part of Asia. Most scientists believe humans first settled in South, Southeast, and East Asia after the first appearance of *H. erectus* in distant Africa.

Southeast Asia

The Modjokerto and Sangiran fossils in Indonesia's Solo River valley are dated to between 1.8 and 1.6 mya, dates acquired with a still-experimental chronometric method (Swisher et al., 1994). (The dates have been questioned on geological grounds.) The earliest traces of human settlement consist of three artifacts found in gravel deposits

Ban Mae Tha
700,000

at Ban Mae Tha in northern Thailand. These split and flaked cobbles have been dated through paleomagnetic studies (a method using dating clays containing evidence of the earth's magnetic field) and potassium-argon studies to about 700,000 years ago (G. Pope et al., 1986). Given what we know about the earliest prehistory of Southeast Asia, it seems almost certain that these tools were made by *H. erectus*. Dubois's *H. erectus* finds and other more recent discoveries from Indonesia are thought to date to no earlier than about 700,000 years ago (G. Pope, 1984). Offshore, some *H. erectus* fragments from Flores Island date to between 900,000 and 800,000 years ago (Morwood et al., 1999).

Five *H. erectus* specimens dating to about 500,000 years ago come from Lang Trang Caves in Vietnam. They are the earliest securely dated human fossils in Southeast Asia. *Homo erectus* may have reached Southeast Asia in the very late Lower Pleistocene, perhaps via the so-called Sunda shelf, low-lying ground that joined many of the Southeast Asian islands during cooler cycles (see Figure 6.6). This shelf appears to have acted as a faunal filter, preventing many tropical ungulate species from reaching the east. Southeast Asia was a tropical forest environment, with extensive patches of dense forest even during the driest periods of the Pleistocene. Geoffrey Pope (1984) believes that bamboo and other wood resources from these forests were of vital importance for the highly portable toolkit used by *H. erectus* in this environment. He also points out that fire, perhaps tamed by these people, is an important component in forest technology. Thus, the crude stone choppers and flakes that may have formed the simple stone technology of Asia for tens of thousands of years were only a limited part of forest material culture (Schick, 1994). Such implements are all that remain of a Stone Age lifeway that was based not on the pursuit of large savanna animals but on smaller game and forest resources, many concentrated around natural springs, sinkholes, and caves.

China

No one knows when humans first settled in what is now China, but it was probably at about the same time as they arrived in Southeast Asia. Hominid bones and stone tools from Longgupo Cave in south-central China have been paleomagnetically dated to nearly 2 million years ago (Larick and Ciochon, 1996). The middle levels of the cave have yielded a hominid jaw fragment, together with bones from more than 10,000 animals. The hominid fragments are somewhat ambiguous but are claimed to be early *H. erectus*. The only two stone tools from Longgupo are crude choppers. Two other sites, Lant'ien and Q'en-Xia-wo in central China, have yielded *H. erectus* specimens that date to earlier than 600,000 years ago.

Longgupo
?? 2 mya

Lant'ien
600,000

Zhoukoudian
460,000 to 230,000

The most famous, and the largest Middle Pleistocene, site in China is the Zhoukoudian Cave, 46 km (28.5 miles) west of Beijing (Figure 3.6a). Zhoukoudian consists of many caverns and fissures, the most famous of which is Locality I, where both stone implements and human fossils have been found. These caverns were visited by *H. erectus* over an immensely long period of time, from about 460,000 to 230,000 years ago (Chang, 1986). At least 40 *H. erectus* individuals have been found at Zhoukoudian, most of whom died before they were 14 years old. Many of them appear to have perished from injuries.

The Zhoukoudian people visited the caves when the climate was perhaps a trifle warmer and moister than it is today. They hunted deer and other animals; more than 60 species are represented in the deposits.

About 100,000 stone implements come from Zhoukoudian, most of them made on flakes of rough-vein quartz. The people made choppers and scrapers, awls, crude points, and many multipurpose artifacts (Figure 3.6b). The toolkit evolved over the millennia, with the earliest artifacts tending to be larger and made with simple percussion techniques. As time went on, the toolmakers produced smaller implements, many of them made of finer raw materials.

Taken together, the Asian fossils are remarkably homogeneous. They have broad-based skulls, low, receding foreheads, and **prognathous** faces. The upper skull bones are thick and show every sign that these humans had strong chewing muscles. These

(a)   (b)

FIGURE 3.6 (a) Zhoukoudian Cave, China. (b) A crude chopping tool from Zhoukoudian, front and side views (one-half actual size).

people were up to 1.67 m (5 feet 6 inches) tall and had a brain capacity between 775 and 1300 cc. One has the impression of a biologically conservative human population that changed little over enormously long periods of time.

The latest Asian *H. erectus* finds come from Java and from Narmada in India. They date to about 230,000 years ago.

Narmada
230,000

Early Asian Technology

The early Asians took full advantage of the forest resources available to them. Instead of stone, they turned to wood, fiber, and bamboo, all of them organic materials that survive poorly in archaeological sites. In other words, our view of early Asia is biased simply because we lack evidence of the whole range of their forest cultures. Tropical forests are rich in animal and plant foods, but they are widely dispersed. Thus, human groups subsisting off forest foods must move constantly, carrying their artifacts with them. Under these circumstances, it is logical for people to use for their toolkits bamboo, wood, and other fibrous materials—the most convenient and lightweight materials at hand.

Bamboo, one of the most versatile materials known to humankind, was efficient, durable, and portable (G. Pope, 1989). It could be used to manufacture containers, sharp knives, spears, weapon tips, ropes, and dwellings. To this day, it is widely used in Asia as scaffolding for building skyscrapers (Figure 3.7). It is an ideal material for people subsisting not on large game but on smaller forest animals such as monkeys, rats, squirrels, lizards, and snakes, as well as plant foods. Simple stone flakes and jagged-edged choppers would be ideal for working bamboo and may indeed have been used for this purpose over many millennia (Schick, 1994).

Not that the early Chinese were incapable of expert stone toolmaking. About 803,000 years ago, a meteorite struck southern China. The impact caused huge fires, which burnt off dense forest across the Bose basin, exposing large tracts of red earth and deposits of large cobblestones. Local hunter-gatherer groups took advantage of the cleared land with its natural stone outcrops and settled along the banks of the Youjiang River. Hundreds of their stone artifacts lie in the fourth terrace above the modern river, dating to soon after the meteorite event, many of them chipped cobbles

FIGURE 3.7 Bamboo scaffolding in use to build a modern high-rise. This flexible and versatile material has been used by Asians since the earliest times.

turned into simple axes and bifacial tools. The basic technology is very similar to that used by Acheulian peoples in the west, except that the characteristic teardrop-shaped Acheulian hand ax is absent. The Bose find shows that the archaic people of the region were perfectly capable of using stone technologies as sophisticated as those used in the west at the time when they settled in deforested areas (Yamei and others, 2000).

〰 The Settlement of Temperate Latitudes

We must think of the first human settlement of temperate latitudes as part of a broader set of ecological processes, one of them the simultaneous radiation of modern grazing animals and new vegetational communities into Europe and other northern latitudes of the Old World. Humans were part of this vast animal community. Their long-term success resulted from their ability to adapt to the cyclical changes in the Ice Age environment, from temperate to much colder, then to full glacial conditions and an abrupt deglaciation as the climate warmed up again rapidly. These early human populations may have flourished in regions where dense, abundant, and predictable resources were to be found, isolated from other regions where similar conditions existed. The climatic changes of the Ice Age sometimes brought these isolated populations together, then separated them again, ensuring gene flow and continued biological and cultural evolution over the millennia (Butzer, 1982).

The first settlement of temperate latitudes was not simply a case of an opportunistic species seizing a set of favorable environmental circumstances (Gamble, 1993). By 500,000 years ago hominids had mastered the necessary hunting and foraging strategies to survive in much more diverse environments than tropical savanna. Most regions of the temperate world had the energy and resources for hominid settlement even when *H. habilis* flourished. But *H. habilis* had not evolved the long-term solutions such as clothing for coping with cyclic climatic change and all the resource changes that resulted from it.

Most evidence for Middle Pleistocene settlement, between about 500,000 and 130,000 years ago, falls in periods when the climate was colder than today but not fully glacial, as it has been for most of the past 700,000 years—times when grazing animals formed the principal food resource in cooler latitudes. Plant and marine foods were much more costly to exploit and often sparse. The successful colonists of northern latitudes were those hominids who could exploit game animals distributed unevenly, and at times very densely, over the landscape.

That is not to say, of course, that the hominids lived by hunting alone. They had to cope with long, sparse winter months, when their prey dispersed so widely that it was beyond human capacity to hunt them effectively. Perhaps people searched for frozen animal carcasses, a winter strategy that was adaptive for highly mobile predators like humans. This would have been a lower-risk strategy if a large group worked together, searching for the predictable refrigerated carcasses of large animals that died during the winter months (Gamble, 1999). During the spring and summer, the people could concentrate on hunting migratory game, eating their kills quickly and stripping them of meat before other predators moved in. Many known sites are near lakes and streams, perhaps the places where the bands most commonly hunted and also where wood might have been found for toolmaking and for the fires used to thaw frozen meat. The key to this entire adaptation was mobility; the bands could respond quickly to changes in resource distribution by moving into new areas. Gamble believes that this was a primarily opportunistic adaptation based on a knowledge of resource distribution rather than on deliberate planning.

🐾 Earliest Human Settlement in Southwest Asia and Europe

While most experts agree that Asia was settled soon after 2 million years ago, the evidence for first settlement in Southwest Asia and Europe is more uncertain. To judge from the Southeast Asian dates, *Homo erectus* moved rapidly eastward out of Africa, but settling the more northerly latitudes of Europe and Eurasia may have presented a more formidable challenge, especially during glacial cycles. Male and female skulls of *H. erectus* (*ergaster*) have recently been discovered at Dmanisi, southwest of Tbilisi in Georgia, in association with crudely shaped choppers and flakes. The crania came from river deposits dated by argon isotope and paleomagnetic methods to c. 1.7 million years ago, making them the earliest humans to be unearthed in Eurasia and predating the earliest Western Europeans by half a million years. These new finds are evidence that archaic humans foraged widely in search of food, their movements driven perhaps as much by hunger as by superior technology (Gabunia and others, 2000).

Dmanisi
? 1.7 mya

Southwest Asia

The Dmanisi skulls are an isolated find, for all other evidence of archaic human occupation is considerably later. Human artifacts date to at least a million years ago in Morocco, while the Ubeidiya site in Israel has yielded both stone tools and some very fragmentary human remains dating to about 1.4 mya (Bar-Yosef, 1999).

Ubeidiya
1.4 mya

Europe

The earliest settlement of temperate Europe itself took place at least 800,000 years ago, perhaps earlier, presumably as a result of gradual movement northward from warmer regions, or, perhaps, also from the east. The Gran Dolina site at Atapuerca, near Burgos in northern Spain, has yielded human remains from layers immediately below a paleomagnetically dated horizon of 800,000 years ago (Gutin, 1995). The human remains are probably from *H. erectus*, called by Spanish scientists *Homo antecessor*, a form ancestral to later Archaic Europeans.

Gran Dolina
800,000

The first widespread European settlement appears to coincide with the appearance of Acheulian hand ax technology about 600,000 years ago, with several important fossil finds dating to about 500,000 years B.P. (Roebroecks and von Kolfschoten, 1994). Among them are the celebrated *H. erectus* jaw from Mauer, Germany, which was the oldest known European for almost a century. The robust thigh bone of another *H. erectus* has come

500,000

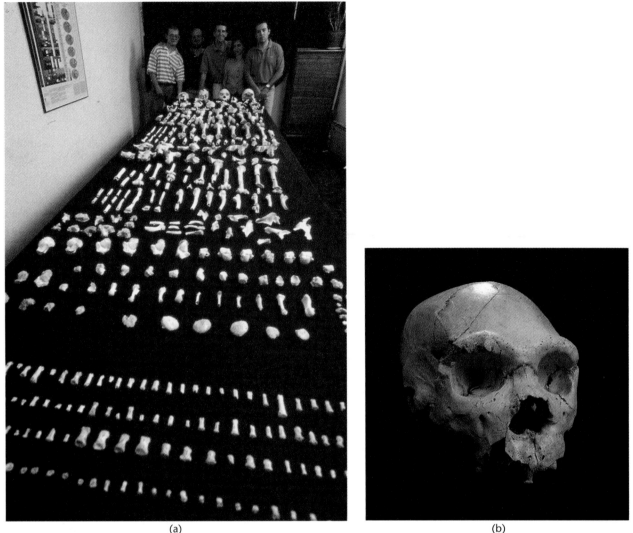

(a)　　　　　　　　　　　　　　　　(b)

FIGURE 3.8 Two-hundred-thousand-year-old Europeans. (a) Some of the 1600 human bones from the Sima de los Huesos (Pit of Bones), Sierra de Atapuerca, Spain. (b) The best preserved of the Archaic *Homo sapiens* skulls from Atapuerca.

Boxgrove

from Boxgrove in southern England, dated by highly diagnostic vole (small rodent) bones to between 524,000 and 475,000 years ago (see Site box, p. 90).

By 400,000 years ago, human settlement was widespread throughout western and central Europe and perhaps farther east (Arsuaga et al., 1993). Fossil remains from sites like Tautavel, France, and Vertésszöllös, Hungary, display larger cranial vaults and more receding faces, foreshadowing some features of the Neanderthal anatomy of later millennia (see p. 94).

Sima de los Huesos

300,000

The Sima de los Huesos (Pit of Bones), in northern Spain's Sierra de Atapuerca, has yielded a mass of fossil human bones dating to about 300,000 years ago, the remains of between 32 and 50 individuals (Figure 3.8). All are archaic *H. sapiens,* a human form intermediate between *H. erectus* and the Neanderthals. The human remains are from young adults and adolescents.

〰 The Technology Used by *Homo erectus*

Both Oldowan technology and the artifacts fashioned by *Homo erectus,* sometimes generically called Lower Paleolithic technology, remained in use in various forms for immensely long periods of time. Oldowan stoneworking lasted for as much as a million

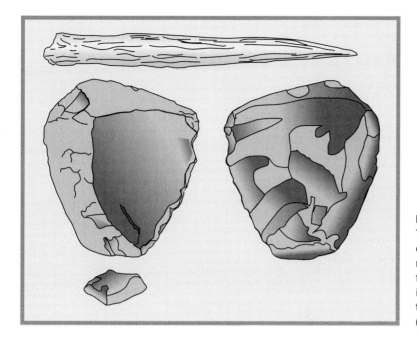

FIGURE 3.9 European wood and stone tools. Top, a wooden spear tip from Clacton, England, dating to about 200,000 years ago (approximately one-eighth full size). Bottom, views of a flake from the same location. The upper surface is shown at the left, the flake (lower) surface on the right. The striking platform is at the base (one-third actual size).

years, its more diverse successor for nearly half as long again. There is a tendency to think of both technologies as monolithic, unchanging chronicles of human prehistory, fixed stages in human cultural evolution, partly because of the time scales involved and also because stone tools appear to have changed so little over hundreds of thousands of years. In fact, however, the technology of *H. erectus*, like that of *H. habilis*, displays considerable variability and development (Ambrose, 2001).

Homo erectus did not rely exclusively on stone, for we can say with confidence that our remote ancestors also made use of wood, one of the most versatile raw materials known to humanity. The earliest known wooden artifacts are three throwing spears and a possible thrusting spear dated to 400,000 years ago, found with broken animal bones and stone tools in an open coal mine at Schoningen, Germany (Thieme, 1997). The spears are between 0.78 and 2.30 m (2 feet 9 inches and 7 feet 6 inches) long, with tapering tails to give them better direction when thrown. These are 200,000 years older than a wooden spear tip from Clacton in eastern England, dating to about 200,000 years ago (Figure 3.9), and a 150,000-year-old wooden spear from Lehringen in Germany. Most insights into the technology of *H. erectus* come from stone tools and the by-products associated with them, because wood and other organic materials are rarely preserved.

Schoningen
400,000

Hand Axes and Other Tools

In Africa, Europe, and some parts of Asia, *H. erectus* is associated with a distinctive toolkit that includes not only a variety of flake tools and sometimes choppers but also bifacially flaked hand axes. These hand ax industries are grouped under the technological label *Acheulian*, after the town of St. Acheul in northern France, where many such artifacts have been found. Hand axes come in many sizes and shapes; they are sometimes artifacts of such great refinement and beauty that people ignore all the other tools *H. erectus* made. In fact, human stone tool technology between 1.5 million and 150,000 years ago shows considerable diversity, probably associated with local adaptations and the availability of suitable raw materials.

Acheulian tradition
1.5 mya to 150,000

The hand ax occurs over a vast area of the Old World in all shapes and sizes, from crude teardrop-shaped forms to ovals and from tongue-shaped to occasional finely pointed specimens. Unlike the crude scrapers and choppers of the Oldowan, the Acheulian hand ax was an artifact with converging edges that met at a point. The maker had to envisage the shape of the artifact, which was to be produced from a mere

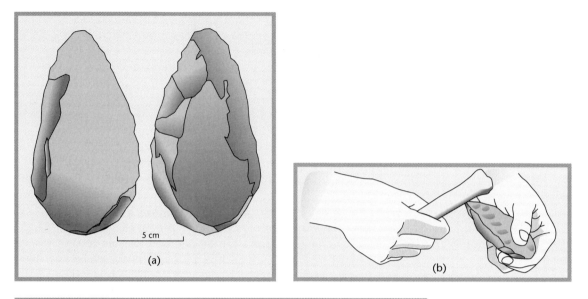

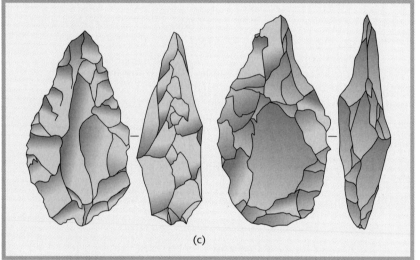

FIGURE 3.10 Acheulian technology. Hand axes were multipurpose artifacts that were shaped symmetrically around a long axis. (a) As the hand ax from Kilombe, Kenya, of 700,000 years ago shows, the stoneworker would sometimes use a minimum of blows with a simple hammerstone to achieve the desired shape. (b) Sometimes a hammer made of animal bone served to strike off the shallower flakes that adorn the margins of these tools.

Later hand axes assume many forms, among them the finely pointed shape in (c), which shows front and side views of two early hand axes from Bed II, Olduvai Gorge, Tanzania (three-quarters actual size). As time went on, the stoneworkers used carefully prepared cores to fashion large flakes that served as blanks for axes and other artifacts. They also produced flakes that were used as opportunistic artifacts, for woodworking and for many other purposes.

lump of stone, and then fashion it, not with opportunistic blows but with carefully directed hammer blows (Figure 3.10). Acheulian hand axes come in every size, from elegant oval types a few inches long to heavy axes more than 0.3 m (1 foot) long and weighing 2.3 kg (5 pounds) or more. They must have been a versatile, thoroughly practical artifact to have continued in use for so long.

What exactly were hand axes used for? Almost certainly they were held in the hand rather than being hafted on the end of a wooden shaft. They were simply too cumbersome, and in any case, hafted tools probably did not come into use until much later. Conventional wisdom has it that they were multipurpose artifacts, used for grubbing up roots, working wood, scraping skins, and especially skinning and butchering large and small game. There is no question that they were highly effective butchery tools. Many archaeologists have tried not only cutting up antelope carcasses with them but also slicing through hippopotamus and elephant hide—with great success. In some ways, the hand ax was ideal for this purpose because it could be sharpened again and again, and when it became a useless lump of stone, it could be recycled into flake tools. But effective butchery can be achieved with simple flakes as well, and a number of researchers have wondered whether the hand ax, which took longer to make, was not used for other purposes, such as for throwing or for digging up edible roots.

In addition to hand axes, the new technology resulted in scrapers and other artifacts for woodworking, skinning, and other purposes. But hand axes remain the most characteristic artifact of many *H. erectus* populations (Figure 3.11). Fine specimens are scattered in the gravels of the Somme and Thames rivers in northern Europe, in North African quarries and ancient Saharan lake beds, and in sub-Saharan Africa from the Nile Valley to the Cape of Good Hope. Acheulian tools are common in some parts of India, in Arabia, and in Southwest Asia as far as the southern shores of the Caspian Sea and perhaps even farther north. They are rare east of the Rhine and in East Asia, where chopping tools were commonly used until comparatively recent times (Butzer and Isaac, 1975; Howell and Clark, 1963). No one has been able to explain why hand axes have this distribution. Were such multipurpose tools used only in big-game hunting camps? Was their use restricted by the availability of flint and other suitable raw materials? Did environmental conditions affect the hunters' choice of toolkits? Or were they used as projectiles in areas where big game abounded? We do not know.

Hand Axes and the Evolution of the Human Mind

While we recognize that *H. erectus* made a wide variety of artifacts, the fact remains that the Acheulian hand ax is the most characteristic and one of the most widely distributed tools made between 1.5 million and 150,000 years ago. It also provides us with an opportunity to consider the relationship between an artifact and the evolution of the mind. Hand axes were the logical result of long-used stone technology, made to a degree of standardization unimaginable in earlier times. For example, the hand axes from Kilombe, Kenya, date to over 700,000 years ago. They display a very high statistical correlation among length, breadth, and thickness, standardization within a length of 8 to 24 cm (3.14 to 9.40 inches). Such a correlation implies a well-defined mental image of the ideal end product shared by more than one person (Figure 3.12).

Homo erectus had a geometrically accurate sense of proportion, which was imposed accurately on stone (Gowlett, 1978). Symmetrical hand axes resulted from careful selection of the stone cobble used as a blank, both for shape and for potential fracture dynamics. Then the stoneworker had to rough out the axe with a stone hammer and finish it off with a more delicate, softer bone or wood striker. Each hand ax required careful planning and the application of toolmaking knowledge acquired over a considerable period of time, not just mindless flaking on either side of the nodule. No mechanical set of rules led to hand axes. The maker had to "feel" the raw material and use visual clues to decide where to strike next, constantly adjusting plans as the artifact emerged from the raw material. A much higher degree of technical intelligence lay behind Acheulian hand-ax manufacture than behind Oldowan technology.

For example, another East African site, Kapthurin, near Kenya's Lake Baringo, contains hundreds of late Acheulian hand axes dating to about 230,000 years ago. The stoneworkers there used elaborately **prepared cores,** fashioned with perhaps 40 or more strokes, as the blanks for a single large flake—a dramatic contrast to the three or four flakes removed in earlier millennia (see Figure 3.12). The large flake that resulted was then bifacially flaked into an elegant, versatile hand ax in a wide variety of useful shapes (see Figure 3.11).

Yet puzzling questions remain: Why did archaic humans ignore antler, bone, and ivory, staples of later Stone Age technology? Why did they make only multipurpose tools, none of which were mounted on handles or spear shafts, as was commonplace in later millennia? And finally, why did they manufacture such a limited range of stone

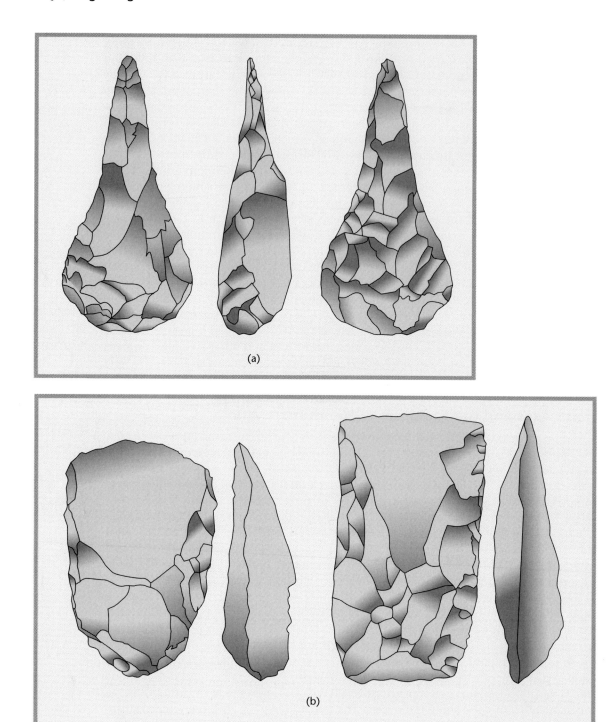

(a)

(b)

FIGURE 3.11 Hand ax technology. (a) Acheulian hand ax from Swanscombe, England (one-third actual size), (b) Two Acheulian cleavers, from Baia Farta, Angola (left), and Kalambo Falls, Zambia (right) (both one-half actual size). Cleavers are thought to have been butchering tools, artifacts with a single unfinished edge that modern experiments have proved effective in skinning and dismembering game.

artifacts, despite their ability to exploit a remarkable range of natural environments? Steven Mithen (1996) believes that the ability of *H. erectus* to exploit markedly seasonal environments reflects a high degree of what he calls "natural history intelligence," the ability to think one's way through a wide variety of often savage landscapes with only a simple technology. He argues that *H. erectus* lacked the ability to integrate toolmaking

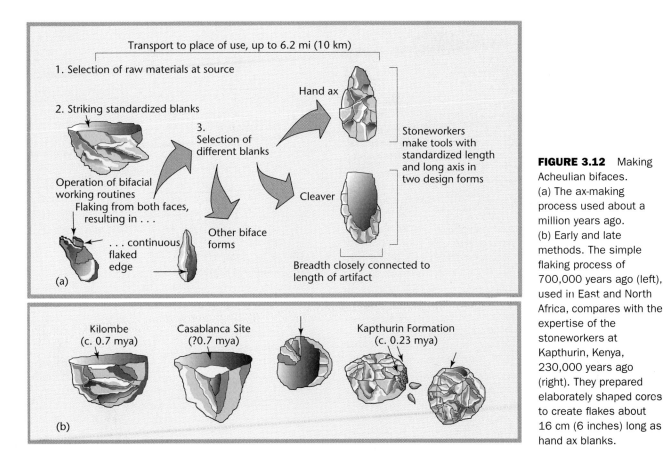

FIGURE 3.12 Making Acheulian bifaces. (a) The ax-making process used about a million years ago. (b) Early and late methods. The simple flaking process of 700,000 years ago (left), used in East and North Africa, compares with the expertise of the stoneworkers at Kapthurin, Kenya, 230,000 years ago (right). They prepared elaborately shaped cores to create flakes about 16 cm (6 inches) long as hand ax blanks.

with its knowledge about the environment and animal behavior. This would account for the lack of specialized tools used for specialized tasks or of composite artifacts made from several parts. The same compartmentalized reasoning would account for the great conservatism of Archaic human technology. The making of stone tools was never integrated with subsistence activities except at the most generalized level.

𑿋 Evidence for Behavior: Boxgrove and Torralba

What do we know of the subsistence activities of *H. erectus?* Without question, these archaic humans hunted and foraged for food, probably in far more effective ways than their ancient predecessors. Time and time again, hand axes and other butchering artifacts have been found in association with the bones of large game animals, which those tools were used to butcher. No one doubts that *H. erectus* butchered such animals. But did the hunters actually kill such formidable herbivores as the elephant and rhinoceros? The Schoningen wooden spears of 400,000 years ago hint at considerable hunting ability. To hunt large animals would require social mechanisms to foster cooperation and communication abilities far beyond those of earlier hominids.

Evidence of these activities comes from the Boxgrove site in southern England (see Site box, page 90).

Boxgrove is not alone. Evidence for butchery and perhaps big-game hunting also comes from two Acheulian sites, at Torralba and Ambrona, northeast of Madrid in Spain (F. C. Howell, 1966). The Acheulians probably lived in this deep, swampy valley either 200,000 or 400,000 years ago (the date is disputed). Torralba yielded most of the left side of a large elephant that had been cut into small pieces, and Ambrona contained the remains of 30 to 35 dismembered elephants. Concentrations of broken food bones were found all over the site, and the skulls of the elephants had been

**Torralba
Ambrona
400,000 to 200,000**

SITE

Boxgrove, England

The Boxgrove site in Sussex, southern England, comprises a series of isolated activity areas used by *Homo erectus* (or *H. heidelbergensis*, depending on your classificatory preference) over tens of thousands of years about 500,000 years ago. During this long period, the setting at this strategic location changed from a coastal and marine environment to open grassland and near-glacial tundra. For much of the occupation, the climate was very similar to that of today. At the northern end of this area is a cliff that stood 75 to 100 m (250 to 330 feet) high at the time of human occupation, with a shallow lake at its foot, fed by a spring. Archaeologist Mark Roberts and his colleagues have investigated the area beneath the cliff, where the people hunted and butchered large mammals, using flint tools made from rock obtained from the crag (Roberts and Parfitt, 1999). Only large stone hand axes used for butchering, as well as flint blocks used as anvils, hammerstones, and bone and antler toolmaking artifacts, have come from the bone-laden deposits below the cliff. The people must have lived elsewhere, for no traces of occupation have been found. They probably lived in the dense forests above the cliffs, where they were relatively safe from the numerous predators in more open country.

Boxgrove provides convincing evidence of successful hunting of large mammals, among them rhinoceroses, bison, deer, horse, and bear in the prime of life. One horse shoulder blade displayed a hole made by a wooden spear about 50 mm (2 inches) across. A forensic pathologist suspects the spear was spinning when it made the wound. Weapons like the Schoningen spears from Germany may have been used by the Boxgrove hunters. Further evidence that they were hunting comes from butchery marks on the skulls, which show the hunters removed the tongues and eyes from their prey. Had the animals been scavenged, birds would have already removed these soft pieces. Much of the prey was butchered near a water hole where the animals gathered, suggesting that *H. erectus* lay in wait for game at the same location over many generations. How many people were involved is unknown, but at least six butchering sites have been excavated near a single horse skeleton. The meat yields from the larger animals were enormous, if the marrow and entrails are included. A rhinoceros would yield 700 kg (1550 lb) of meat alone. Everything points to the butchery having been thorough, with much of the meat and skin removed for later use, as if considerable amounts of flesh were dried in the sun. One hand ax bears the distinctive wear patterns associated with scraping hide.

The Boxgrove people were capable of sophisticated hunting, an activity that requires considerable forethought and planning. But their technology was extremely simple and barely changed over 200,000 years. Mark Roberts argues that they must have required some form of speech more advanced than that of their remote predecessors. Of the people themselves, only two teeth, and part of a lower shin bone (tibia) gnawed by predators have come to light, thought to resemble the fragmentary and little known *Homo heidelbergensis*. The massive tibia comes from a male in his 20s. The two teeth exhibit cuts made by stone tools during life, perhaps while eating and cutting meat.

---

broken open to expose the brains (Figure 3.13). Both kill sites were littered with crude hand axes, cleavers, scrapers, and cutting tools.

The elephant bones at both sites were buried in clays that were once treacherous marsh. The original scenario for the sites had hunters watching the valley floors where the elephants roamed. At a strategic moment, several bands would gather quietly, set brushfires, and drive the unsuspecting beasts into the swamps, where they could be killed and butchered at leisure. Torralba and Ambrona were on important game trails between summer and winter grazing areas (Butzer, 1982). The hunters thus preyed on migrating elephants each spring and fall (Figure 3.14), dispersing into smaller groups during the other seasons. Other archaeologists believe that the hunters were actually scavenging meat from animals that had perished when enmired (Shipman and Rose, 1983).

FIGURE 3.13 From Torralba, Spain, a remarkable linear arrangement of elephant tusks and leg bones that were probably laid out by those who butchered the animals.

FIGURE 3.14 Reconstructed model for seasonal movement by Acheulian hunters at Torralba-Ambrona, Spain. (a) Interception of migrating animals in spring and fall. (b) Use of topography to secure game. (c) Schematic model of how the populations moved. The reconstructions were based on information recovered from excavations (Butzer, 1982).

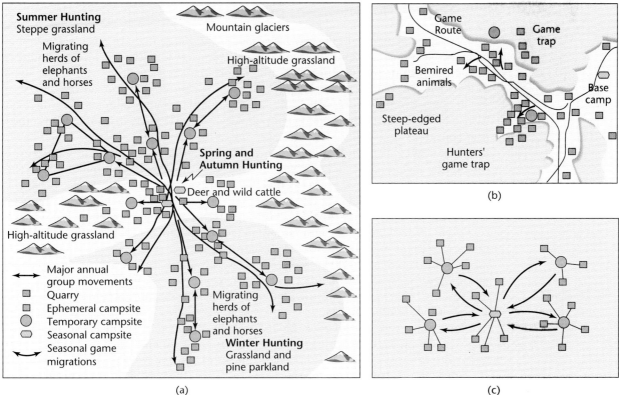

Everything indicates that *Homo erectus* and archaic *Homo sapiens* were eclectic and flexible hunter-gatherers who relied on hunting, scavenging, and plant foods. They may have understood the telltale signs of the passage of seasons, the meanings of cloud formations, the timing of game and bird migrations, and the geography of their territories. But they never exploited small game, birds, fish, or sea mammals on any significant scale, as modern humans did almost at once.

Both archaic *H. sapiens* and *H. erectus* probably lived in relatively large groups at times, both to reduce the danger from carnivores and to improve the chances of finding food, especially from larger animals. At other times, band size may have been much smaller, especially when plant foods were more abundant and easily obtained by individuals. All of this argues for considerable social flexibility and intelligence in *H. erectus*, reflected in their larger brain size. But as was true of their natural history intelligence, they may have been unable to integrate their social intelligence—their ability to share food and cooperate in the hunt—with other aspects of human intelligence.

Language

Homo erectus had a large brain with a well-developed Broca's area, the zone associated with speaking ability. Its vocal tracts were more modern than those of *Homo habilis*, which suggests considerable potential for articulate speech. Anthropologists Leslie Aiello and Robin Dunbar (1993) have argued that the basis for language ability appeared in humans by at least 250,000 years ago. They believe it first evolved as a way to handle increasingly complex social information. As group sizes increased, so did a capacity for language, used primarily to talk about social relations. It was only later that humans developed the kind of general-purpose language we use today, which allows us to communicate freely, whatever the behavioral domain. So like us in many ways, *H. erectus* lacked the cognitive flexibility characteristic of modern humans, yet it was from this archaic human that *H. sapiens sapiens* ultimately evolved. Nor had the larynx shifted into a position where the range of sounds modern humans use were possible.

Archaic *Homo sapiens* in Europe: The Neanderthals

Much of what we know about early *Homo sapiens*, the descendant of *Homo erectus*, comes from the Neanderthals, long-term inhabitants of Europe and Eurasia, whose anatomical features appear in archaic European populations such as those from Atapuerca, Spain, at least 200,000 years ago (see Figure 3.8). The Neanderthals are still the subject of much controversy among physical anthropologists. Some people use the word *Neanderthal* to describe dim-witted, ugly people who are like apes, an insult aimed at those they consider stupid. This stereotype and that of the shambling cave people so beloved by cartoonists come from mistaken studies of Neanderthal skeletons in the early years of the twentieth century. In fact, the Neanderthals were strong, robustly built humans with some archaic features. For example, their skulls display retreating foreheads, projecting faces, and sometimes eyebrow ridges. But there is every reason to believe that they were expert hunters and beings capable of considerable intellectual reasoning.

There are, of course, striking anatomical differences between Neanderthals and modern humans, both in the robust postcranial skeleton of the Neanderthal and in its more bun-shaped skull, sometimes with heavy brow ridges and a forward-projecting face (Figure 3.15). These features are the reason that this extinct hominid form is classified as *Homo neanderthalensis*, a subspecies of *Homo sapiens*, and not as *Homo sapiens sapiens*, a fully modern human.

Homo neanderthalensis
before 100,000
to c. 30,000

In the century and a half since the first Neanderthal skull from the German village of that name was unearthed, substantial numbers of Neanderthal individuals have been found, mostly in western Europe but also in Southwest Asia, Africa, and Asia (Figure 3.16). Neanderthals first appeared during the Eem interglacial, well before 100,000 years ago, but they were apparently few in number (see the Dating the Past box).

DATING THE PAST

Radiocarbon Dating

The later Neanderthals can be dated by the most universal of all archaeological dating methods: radiocarbon (^{14}C) dating. Radiocarbon dating is based on the knowledge that living organisms build up their own organic matter by photosynthesis and by using atmospheric carbon dioxide. The percentage of radiocarbon in the organism is equal to that in the atmosphere. When the organism dies, the carbon-14 (^{14}C) atoms disintegrate at a known rate, with a half-life of 5730 years. It is possible then to calculate the date of an organic object by measuring the amount of ^{14}C left in the sample. The initial quantity in the sample is low, so the limit of detectability is soon reached, making the oldest reliable radiocarbon dates about 40,000 years old.

Radiocarbon dates can be obtained from many types of organic material, including charcoal, shell, wood, and hair. The beta-particle decay rate is conventionally measured with a proportional counter, but the use of accelerator mass spectrometry has refined the procedure dramatically. Every radiocarbon date arrives with a statistical error, a standard deviation. For example, a date of 2200 ± 200 years means that the date has a probable range of 200 years, with a two-out-of-three chance the date lies between the span of one standard deviation (2400 and 2000 years).

Unfortunately, the concentration of radiocarbon in the atmosphere has varied considerably over time as a result of alterations in solar activity and changes in the strength of the earth's magnetic field. It is possible to correct dates by calibrating them against accurate dates from radiocarbon-dated tree rings and developing a master correction curve. Dates as far back as nearly 7000 B.C. can be calibrated with tree rings, and experiments are currently under way with highly accurately dated fossil coral beds to extend the calibration back much farther into the past.

Radiocarbon dating is the most universally applied chronological method in archaeology, but unless calibrated with tree rings or coral, such dates should be recognized for what they are: statistical estimates of radiocarbon age. Accelerator mass spectrometers (AMS) are now used in radiocarbon dating for much greater accuracy (see Chapter 8).

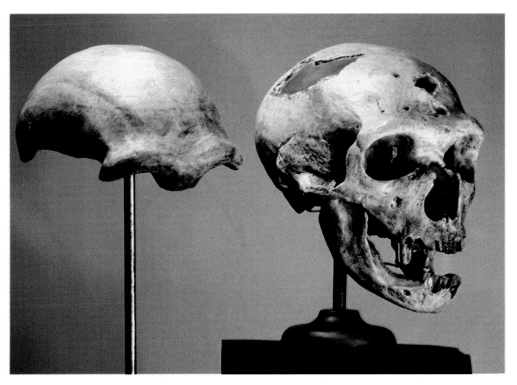

FIGURE 3.15 Two classic Neanderthal crania, showing the prominent brow ridges, prognathous faces, and massive jaw.

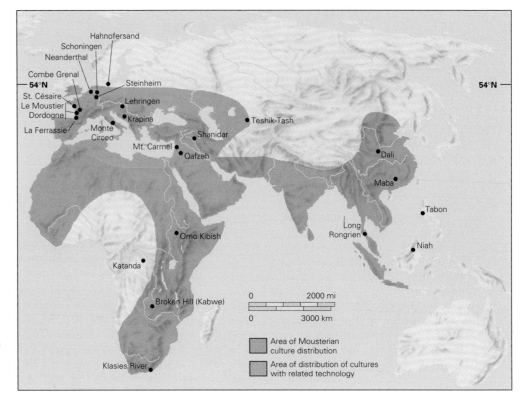

FIGURE 3.16

Distribution of the Neanderthals, their culture, and related technologies. Also shown are sites mentioned in the remainder of Chapter 3.

Large Neanderthal sites occur in the Dordogne area of southwest France, where deep river valleys and vast limestone cliffs offered abundant shelter during the Weichsel glaciation (Stringer and Gamble, 1993; Trinkaus and Shipman, 1992).

The skeletons found in French caves may look like anatomical anachronisms, with massive brow ridges and squat bodies, but they walked upright and as nimbly as modern humans. They stood just over 153 cm (5 feet) tall, and their forearms were relatively short compared with those of modern people. This "classic" variety of Neanderthal is confined to western Europe and is more noticeably different from *H. sapiens* than its contemporary populations found elsewhere, especially around the shores of the Mediterranean and in Asia (Figure 3.17). We find much variability among nonclassic Neanderthals, who most often display less extreme features, particularly brow ridges and other cranial features, than the classic variety of western France. This variability is well demonstrated at the Mount Carmel sites of et-Tabun and es-Skhul in Israel, as well as at Krapina in central Europe (Stringer, 1984).

The morphological differences apparent between many Neanderthals and modern *H. sapiens* are startling. How do these heavily built, beetle-browed people fit into the picture of human evolution? In the 1930s the great French physical anthropologist Marcellin Boule believed that the classic Neanderthals were clumsy, shambling people, so specialized that they became extinct while other populations provided the evolutionary basis for modern humans (Boule and Vallois, 1957). We now know that the Neanderthal anatomical pattern took approximately 50 millennia to evolve, from 150,000 years ago, then stabilized for another 50,000 years before changing rapidly to essentially modern human anatomy within a brief period of 5000 years, approximately 40,000 years ago. We know, too, that Boule was mistaken partly because his definitive studies were made on an elderly individual suffering from arthritis and partly because much more skeletal material is now available.

The Neanderthals had the same posture, manual abilities, and range and characteristics of movement as modern people (Figure 3.18). They differed in having massive limb bones, often somewhat bowed in the thigh and the forearm, features that reflect the Neanderthals' greater muscular power. For their height, the Neanderthals were

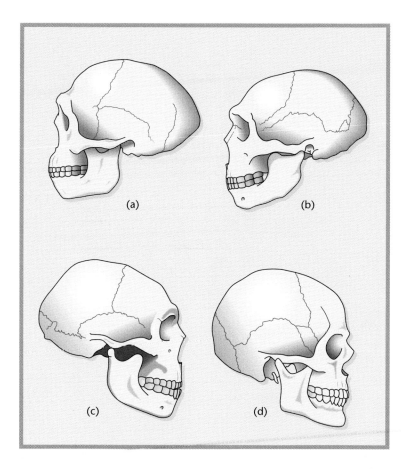

(a)   (b)

(c)   (d)

FIGURE 3.17 Comparisons of four fossil skulls and jaws. (a) The reconstructed skull has prominent brow ridges, a bun-shaped rear to the cranium, and a retreating chin. (b) A "classic" Neanderthal skull found at Monte Circeo, Italy, still has well-marked brow ridges and a bun-shaped cranium but an increased brain capacity. The skull is lower and flatter than those of modern humans, and the jaw is chinless. (c) The Shanidar Neanderthal from Iraq is a less extreme example, with a higher forehead, somewhat reduced brow ridges, and a much more rounded skull. (d) A modern skull, with well-rounded contours, no brow ridges, a high forehead, and a well-marked chin.

bulky and heavily muscled, and their brain capacity was slightly larger than that of modern humans. Their antecedents are chronicled by the archaic individuals from the Sierra de Atapuerca in northern Spain, dating to more than 200,000 years ago. The more complete of these specimens display anatomical features closer to those of archaic *H. sapiens* than to *H. erectus,* as if the evolutionary roots of the Neanderthals lie deep in earlier times (Arsuaga et al., 1993).

Like their predecessors, Neanderthal bands occupied large territories, which they probably exploited on a seasonal round, returning to the same locations year after year when game migrated or vegetables came into season. The Neanderthals were skilled hunters who pursued large game animals like the mammoth as well as reindeer and wild horses. They also caught birds and fish. It appears that many western European bands lived in caves and rock shelters during much of the year as a protection against arctic cold. During the summer months they may have fanned out over the tundra plains, living in temporary tented encampments (for details, see Stringer and Gamble, 1993). But theirs was a precarious existence, dependent on hunting skills and an expert knowledge of animal habits, which required the hunter to come within such close range that he literally had to touch his prey before being able to spear, club, or wrestle them to the ground. As a result, many of these hunters' injuries are reminiscent of those of modern rodeo riders.

Clive Gamble (1993) argues that the Neanderthal adaptation in Europe was significantly different from that of earlier human populations. He points to major changes in human settlement patterns—that is, to a greater use of rock shelters and caves, as well as the repeated use of open sites as temporary stopping places for people away from the larger main group. This may have been a time when technology became more organized, when planning assumed greater importance—to reduce the risk of starvation. People were now developing hunting and foraging strategies based on four main herd species: bison, horse, red deer, and reindeer. Gamble theorizes that storage assumed much greater importance for surviving winter shortages by maximizing the

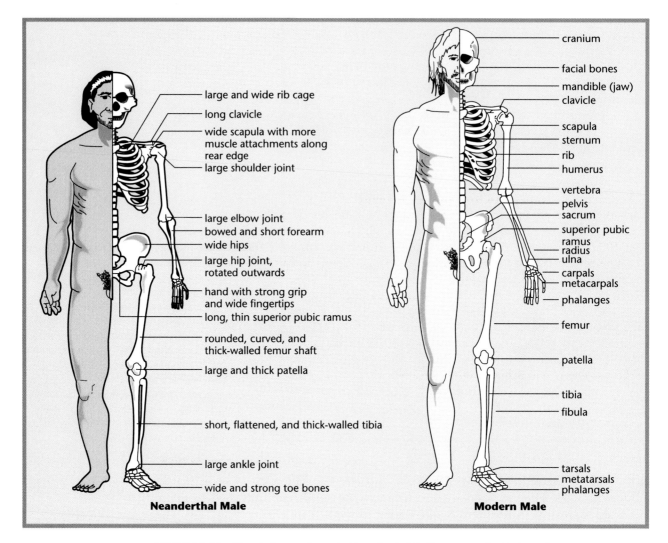

Neanderthal Male labels:
- large and wide rib cage
- long clavicle
- wide scapula with more muscle attachments along rear edge
- large shoulder joint
- large elbow joint
- bowed and short forearm
- wide hips
- large hip joint, rotated outwards
- hand with strong grip and wide fingertips
- long, thin superior pubic ramus
- rounded, curved, and thick-walled femur shaft
- large and thick patella
- short, flattened, and thick-walled tibia
- large ankle joint
- wide and strong toe bones

Neanderthal Male

Modern Male labels:
- cranium
- facial bones
- mandible (jaw)
- clavicle
- scapula
- sternum
- rib
- humerus
- vertebra
- pelvis
- sacrum
- superior pubic ramus
- radius
- ulna
- carpals
- metacarpals
- phalanges
- femur
- patella
- tibia
- fibula
- tarsals
- metatarsals
- phalanges

Modern Male

FIGURE 3.18   The skeleton of a male Neanderthal (left) compared with that of a modern male. The Neanderthal is more robust and stockier than his modern counterpart. (After Stringer and Gamble, 1993.)

meat culled from seasonally migrating animals. There may have been higher population densities, greater population stability, and more adaptive stability, with less risk of local populations' dying out in times of stress.

For the new adaptive strategies in the cold north, environmental knowledge and larger group sizes were keys to effective survival. Factors such as herd size, migration seasons, and predictability of animal movements assumed vital importance. This pattern of adaptation resulted in considerable interregional differences within the Neanderthal world. The southwestern areas of Europe, with their deep river valleys and large rock shelters, were occupied continuously, whereas more open areas to the north and east were more extensively exploited during periods of warmer climate and were largely abandoned during glacial times. No Neanderthal sites have yet come to light north of 54°N (see Figure 3.16).

𖤐 A More Complex Technology

Mousterian

The Neanderthals' Mousterian technology (named after the Le Moustier rock shelter in southwest France) was far more complex and sophisticated than its Acheulian predecessor, with many regional variations (Stringer and Gamble, 1993; Mellars, 1996).

The stone technology used by the Neanderthals and other early *Homo sapiens* forms has often been subsumed under the label *Middle Paleolithic* (Greek: *paleos,* "old," and *lithos,* "stone") on the grounds that the techniques used were distinct from those of *H. erectus.* In fact, the basic differences are much less radical than has often been assumed. There was a basic continuum in stoneworking skills that began in the Lower Paleolithic and continued through the Middle into the Upper Paleolithic and even later in prehistory. Even the more efficient technological changes associated with the spread of *H. sapiens sapiens* after 40,000 years ago had a strong basis in much earlier, simpler technologies (Figure 3.19).

Levallois and Disk-Core-Reduction Strategies

At Kapthurin and other East African sites, Acheulian stoneworkers demonstrated a remarkable skill in preshaping cores to produce large flakes for making axes and other artifacts. With such prepared-core techniques, which were to assume great importance after 100,000 years ago, the core was shaped to predetermine the flake or blade that was to be removed. The **Levallois technique,** named after the Paris suburb where specimens were first found, produces broad, flat flakes, large blades, and triangular points (Figure 3.20). This is a very difficult technique to execute successfully. Probably no more than about a score of modern flint knappers can rival the Neanderthals' skill in conceiving and making Levallois flakes. The **disk core technique** was used to produce as many flakes of varying size as possible and resulted in residual cores with an approximately round shape. The size of the raw material lumps available to the stoneworker probably had a major effect on the flakes produced, for both techniques, as well as simpler flaking, were widely used in Europe, Africa, and Asia.

Tool Forms and Variability

For the most part, Mousterian and other Middle Paleolithic tools were made of flakes, the most characteristic artifacts being points and scrapers (Figure 3.21). Some of these were composite tools, artifacts made of more than one component, for example,

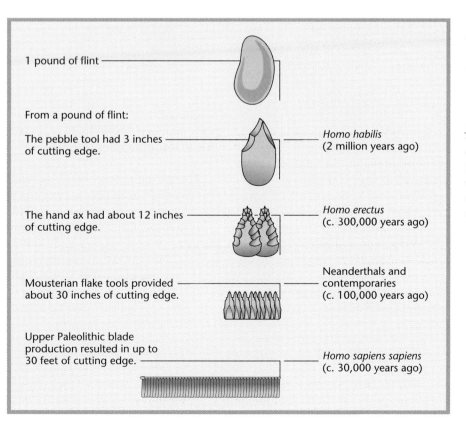

1 pound of flint

From a pound of flint:

The pebble tool had 3 inches of cutting edge. — *Homo habilis* (2 million years ago)

The hand ax had about 12 inches of cutting edge. — *Homo erectus* (c. 300,000 years ago)

Mousterian flake tools provided about 30 inches of cutting edge. — Neanderthals and contemporaries (c. 100,000 years ago)

Upper Paleolithic blade production resulted in up to 30 feet of cutting edge. — *Homo sapiens sapiens* (c. 30,000 years ago)

FIGURE 3.19 The growing efficiency of Stone Age technology is shown by the ability of ancient stoneworkers to produce ever-larger numbers of cutting edges from a pound of flint or other fine-grained rock. The Neanderthals were far more efficient stone artisans than their predecessors. By the same token, *H. sapiens sapiens* used a blade technology (see Figure 4.4), which produced up to 9.1 m (30 feet) of blades per pound of flint.

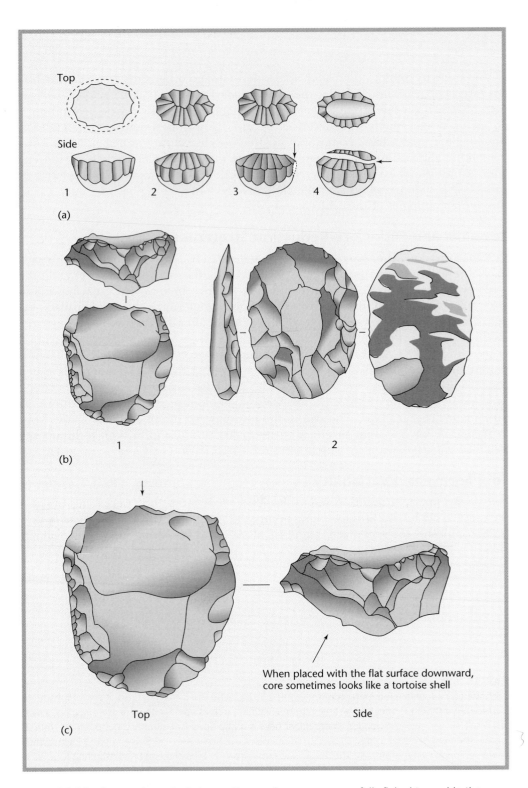

FIGURE 3.20 Prepared-core techniques. Prepared cores were carefully flaked to enable the toolmaker to strike off large flakes of predetermined size. The Levallois technique meant that the stoneworker would shape a lump of flint into an inverted bun-shaped core (often compared to an inverted tortoise shell). The flat upper surface was struck at one end, the resulting flake forming the only product from the core. Another form was the disk core, a prepared core from which several flakes of predetermined size and shape were removed. The core gradually became smaller, until it resembled a flat disk. Disk cores were often used to produce points and scrapers. (a) Making a Levallois core: (1) The edges of a suitable stone are trimmed; (2) the top surface is trimmed; (3) a striking platform, the point where the flake will originate, is made by trimming to form a straight edge on the side; (4) a flake is struck from the core and removed. (b) (1) A Levallois core from the Thames Valley, England, with a view of the top of the core (top left) and the resulting flake (2). (c) When placed with the flat surface downward, the core sometimes looks like a tortoiseshell. One-half actual size.

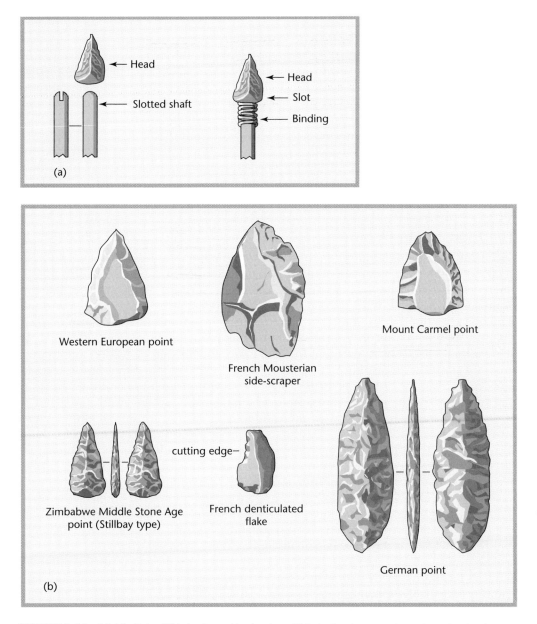

FIGURE 3.21   Middle Paleolithic tools and technology. This technology was based on simple stone techniques that were used for tens of thousands of years before the emergence of early *Homo sapiens*. By 100,000 years ago, artifacts of many types were of composite form, that is, made from several different parts. A wooden spear might have a stone tip, a flint scraper a bone handle. Unfortunately, we know almost nothing about the bone and wood tools used. (a) Stone-tipped Mousterian spear (a hypothetical example). The spear was made from a pointed stone head attached to a wooden handle to form the projectile. The head probably fitted into a slot in the wooden shaft and was fixed to it with resin or beeswax; a binding was added to the end of the shaft. (b) Mousterian artifacts.

a point, a shaft, and the binding that secured the head to the shaft to make a spear. The edges of points and scrapers were sharpened by fine trimming, that is, the removal of small, steplike chips from the edge of the implement. These artifacts, almost universally distributed in Middle Paleolithic sites, were used in the chase, in woodworking, and in preparing skins. However, recent microwear research has revealed that many untrimmed flakes were used for cutting, scraping, and other tasks; they were convenient working edges when needed at a moment's notice (Gamble, 1999). In spite of their technical proficiency, Neanderthals made only a narrow range of artifacts compared with, say, modern Inuit of the Canadian Arctic, who use a wide variety of specialized tools made from a wide variety of raw materials, and all with specific uses.

The French sites have yielded a great diversity of Mousterian artifacts and toolkits (Mellars, 1996). Some levels include hand axes; others, notched flakes, artifacts perhaps used for stripping meat for drying or pressing fibrous plants. Subdivisions of Mousterian technology have been identified by the prevalence of specific tool types. The French archaeologist François Bordes (1968) excavated the Combe Grenal Cave in the Perigord and studied a stratified series of intermittent Mousterian occupations from between 90,000 and 40,000 years ago. Bordes identified no fewer than 60 different Mousterian tool types, made with a variety of toolmaking techniques, including the Levallois method, and with carefully prepared disk cores. He also identified four distinct toolkits in the Combe Grenal levels: one associated with small hand axes, another with thousands of heavy-duty side scrapers, a third with a high proportion of saw-edged flakes, and some that contained an even balance of different tool types.

The Mousterian Debate

Such wide variation in Mousterian toolkits is found not only at Combe Grenal but also at other Neanderthal sites throughout Europe and Southwest Asia and in North Africa, where other archaic *H. sapiens* made similar tools. Bordes (1968) believed that the Combe Grenal toolkits reflected four different Neanderthal groups that all visited the same location but that lived in almost complete isolation and rarely had any contact with one another. Others hypothesize that the variations in toolkits were the result of slow cultural change, with different tools, like the side scraper, in fashion at different times. In contrast, Lewis Binford and Sally Binford (1966) argued that Bordes's traditions reflect various distinct activities carried out within the same cultural system at different times of the year. Nicholas Rolland and Harold Dibble (1990) have studied Mousterian scraper technology on the assumption that the various shapes of these artifacts represent a "reduction continuum," that is, a continuous process of flaking the edge of flake blanks. Thus, collections with more large side scrapers represent less intensive utilization of scrapers than those with greater variability in scraper forms. They argue that neither style nor function was the overriding factor in stone tool variability. Rather, the Neanderthals were using a fundamentally very simple stone technology, with both flaking techniques and reduction processes varying considerably in response to all kinds of external factors—availability and size of raw materials, climate, differing activities, and subsistence needs among them (Mellars, 1996).

The Neanderthals and their contemporaries were developing tools for different activities far more quickly than ever before, perhaps at a time of growing human populations and slightly enhanced social complexity. Fundamentally, Middle Paleolithic technology was simple and highly variable and was a logical development of technologies refined over many millennia.

🐾 The Origins of Burial and Religious Belief

The Neanderthals were hunter-gatherers; and the world's population was still small, but life was gradually becoming more complex. Some experts claim that the Neanderthals regularly buried their dead, showing the first signs of religious ideology and of a preoccupation with the life hereafter. Many Neanderthals were indeed buried by their companions, but all known burials have come from caves or rock shelters in Europe, Southwest Asia, and Eurasia, often found under unscientific circumstances. Christopher Stringer and Clive Gamble (1993) point out that most complete Neanderthal bodies occur in caves where predator bones are rare, as if carnivores were not using such places for their dens. Thus, the abandoned corpses have survived more or less intact, even if they were disposed of underground, for no hibernating bears dug them up and no hyenas scattered the decaying bodies lying in their dens.

Neanderthal burials have been recovered from the deposits of rock shelters and caves as well as from open campsites. Single burials are the most common, normally accompanied by flint tools, food offerings, or even cooked game meat (identified by charred bones); but many such associations are dubious, given unscientific excavation many years ago. One rock shelter, La Ferrassie, near Les Eyzies in France, yielded the remains of two adult Neanderthals and four children buried close together in a camp-site. One band of Siberian mountain-goat hunters lived at Teshik-Tash in the western foothills of the Himalayas. They buried one of their children in a shallow pit, sur-rounding the body with six pairs of wild goat horns.

Another remarkable single burial came from the Shanidar Cave in the Zagros Mountains of Iraq (Trinkaus, 1983). There a 30-year-old man was crushed by a rockfall from the roof of the cave. He was buried in a shallow pit. Other single graves from France and central Europe were covered with red ocher powder.

There is no question that the Neanderthals buried some of their dead, but whether such burial was mere corpse disposal or was associated with beliefs in an afterlife is a matter for debate.

🐾 The Origins of Modern Humans

For hundreds of thousands of years, *Homo erectus* and its close relatives flourished in the tropical and temperate regions of the Old World. Except for an overall increase in brain size, *H. erectus* remained remarkably stable in evolutionary terms for more than a million years, until less than 500,000 years ago. Eventually, *H. erectus* evolved into archaic *H. sapiens*, but we do not even know when the gradual transition began or how it took place. Some researchers believe it began as early as 400,000 years ago; others, much later, sometime around or after 200,000 years ago.

Archaic Homo sapiens
? c. 250,000

For hundreds of thousands of years, both *H. erectus* and archaic *H. sapiens* survived and evolved with the aid of what Steven Mithen calls multiple intelligences, separated by walls analogous to those dividing the chapels of a medieval cathedral. As Mithen says (1996), the thoughts in one chapel could barely be heard in another. Archaic hu-mans lacked one vital component of the modern mind: cognitive flexibility, the ability to bridge the walls between their many intelligences. Such flexibility appears to have been the prerogative of modern humans, *Homo sapiens sapiens*.

Homo sapiens sapiens means "wise person," and the controversies surrounding the origins of modern humanity—of ourselves—rank among the most vigorous in archae-ology. What is it that separates us from earlier humans, scientists wonder? First and foremost must be our ability to speak fluently and articulately. We communicate, we tell stories, we pass on knowledge and ideas—all through the medium of language. Consciousness, cognition, self-awareness, foresight, and the ability to express oneself and one's emotions—these are direct consequences of fluent speech. They can be linked with another attribute of the fully fledged human psyche: the capacity for symbolic and spiritual thought, concerned not only with subsistence and technology but also with defining the boundaries of existence and the relationship among the individual, the group, and the universe. Fluent speech, the full flowering of human creativity expressed in art and religion, expert toolmaking—these are some of the hallmarks of anatomically modern humans. With these abilities, humankind eventu-ally colonized not just temperate and tropical environments but the entire globe. With the appearance of *H. sapiens sapiens* we begin the study of people biologically identical to ourselves, people with the same intellectual abilities and potential. It is hardly surprising that controversy surrounds the appearance of our remote ancestors (Lewin, 1993; Nitecki and Nitecki, 1994; Stringer and McKie, 1996).

Homo sapiens sapiens

Continuity or Replacement?

Over generations of debate, two major, and diametrically opposed, hypotheses have developed to explain the origins of modern humans (Figure 3.22):

- *The multiregional model* (Figure 3.22a) hypothesizes that *H. erectus* populations throughout the Old World evolved independently, first to archaic *H. sapiens*, then to fully modern humans. This continuity model argues for multiple origins of

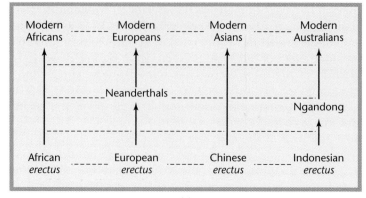

(a)

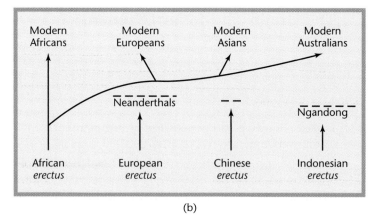

FIGURE 3.22 Theories of the origins of modern humans, each of which interprets the fossil evidence in very different ways. (a) The multiregional model, which argues for the evolution of *H. sapiens sapiens* in many regions of the world. (b) The out-of-Africa model, which has modern humanity evolving in Africa, then spreading to other parts of the world.

(b)

H. sapiens and no migrations later than those of *H. erectus.* Thus, modern geographic populations have been separated from one another for a long time, perhaps for nearly 2 million years (Frayer et al., 1994; Wolpoff et al., 1984). In this scenario, continuous gene flow within the group meant that highly adaptive, novel anatomical features spread rapidly, thereby keeping all human populations on the same fundamental evolutionary path toward anatomically modern people, even if some evolved into fully modern humans before others.

- *The out-of-Africa model* (Figure 3.22b) takes the diametrically opposite view. According to it, *H. sapiens* evolved in one place, then spread to all other parts of the Old World. This model, which assumes population movement from a single point of origin, implies that modern geographic populations have shallow roots and were derived from a single source in relatively recent times (Lewin, 1993).

These two models represent extremes that pit advocates of anatomical continuity against those who favor the rapid replacement of primeval populations. There are intermediate models, too, that allow, for example, for some genetic hybridization between archaic and early modern populations in Africa (discussion in Lewin, 1998). Until fairly recently, most anthropologists strongly favored the multiregional model. The reason was that finds from western Europe and Southwest Asia dominated academic discussion, largely because the largest numbers of fossils came from these areas and seemed to provide evidence for at least two points of origin. Furthermore, many deep, well-excavated caves and rock shelters appeared to document technological change from simple, relatively unsophisticated toolkits to the much more elaborate artifacts characteristic of *H. sapiens.*

A torrent of new discoveries has turned our conception of Europe from one of the cradles of modern humans into somewhat of a backwater, inhabited by a very heterogeneous group of archaic humans whose descendants were the Neanderthals. Apart from the fossil evidence, basic principles of evolutionary biology make it appear unlikely that populations of *H. sapiens* were living in central and western Europe for 200,000 years so isolated from one another that two different lineages could form. Another important group of finds gave support to the candelabra model. These were the highly variable fossil populations found just before World War II in the Mount Carmel caves in what is now Israel (Garrod and Bate, 1937): Neanderthals displaying startling anatomical variation compared with their European contemporaries.

Was Southwest Asia a cradle of *H. sapiens*? Many new discoveries from Southwest Asia and from sites like Qafzeh in Israel have confirmed that Southwest Asian populations were very heterogeneous between 100,000 and 40,000 years ago (see Figure 4.3). However, there is a considerable morphological gap between more Archaic and only slightly older fossils and those displaying more modern features, such as reduced brow ridges, more rounded crania, and larger limbs. Many experts believe that the differences between these individuals make the local evolution of *H. sapiens* from Neanderthals unlikely (Trinkaus and Shipman, 1992).

Such an evolution would require an adequate amount of time for anatomical change to take place. This time frame does not appear to exist in Europe, for finds of Neanderthal-like individuals from Hahnofersand near Hamburg, Germany, and St. Césaire in the Charente region (France) date to as late as 34,000 to 30,000 B.C. Some Neanderthal groups may have survived as late as 28,000 B.C. in southern Spain. Anatomically modern humans were living in western Europe by this time. Very likely, there was a period of coexistence and probably hybridization between the Neanderthals and the modern populations at about this time, when the latter had already replaced Neanderthals in Southwest Asia (Stringer and Gamble, 1993).

Everything points not to anatomical continuity in Europe and Southwest Asia but to replacement of primeval populations by *H. sapiens*. Furthermore, Southwest Asian excavations make it certain that *H. sapiens* populations were living there as early as 92,000 years ago, earlier than they were in Europe. This may indeed have been the area from which modern people spread into the north and replaced the Neanderthals some time later. The out-of-Africa model, then, seems to fit the available fossil evidence better. But the central question remains unanswered: Where did these people come from? We know from distributions of Neanderthal finds that there were contacts and gene flow with North Africa. Might tropical Africa have been the ancestral homeland of modern human beings?

Homo sapiens in Africa

Africa may have been the cradle of humankind, but for years it was regarded as a backwater in later prehistory, a place where modern humans arose very much later than they did in Europe. These ideas were formulated before radiocarbon chronologies and were based on a mere handful of fossil finds, among them the famous robust Broken Hill (Kabwe) skull from Zambia, an archaic-looking cranium that seemed to epitomize a backward continent (Phillipson, 1994).

A new generation of research based on radiocarbon dates and sophisticated cave excavation has painted a radically different picture of African life after 200,000 years ago. We now know that Acheulian hand-ax technology gave way to more sophisticated and versatile toolkits based on flakes, between 200,000 and 130,000 years ago in both eastern and southern Africa. The excavators of the Klasies River Cave, in southeastern Africa, were able to correlate human occupation with deep-sea cores and date it to between 120,000 and 70,000 years ago (Figure 3.23). Numerous fragmentary human remains dating to between 125,000 and 95,000 years ago came from the same levels, remains that displayed astoundingly modern features at a date far earlier than that of anything from Southwest Asia or Europe (Deacon, 1992; Deacon and Geleijinse, 1988).

Klasies River
120,000 to 70,000

In East Africa, Richard Leakey found a large, thick-boned human skull and limb bones at Omo Kibish in Ethiopia, dating to perhaps as early as 130,000 years ago. They came from a tall, well-built male, with a broad forehead and well-defined brow ridges that thinned at the edges (Stringer and Gamble, 1993). There are other sites in both

Omo Kibish
130,000

FIGURE 3.23 Klasies River Cave, South Africa, where some of the earliest modern humans in the world lived about 100,000 years ago.

eastern and southern Africa where skeletal fragments of modern-looking ancient people have been reported—alas, none of them well dated or complete.

At least three "grades" of *H. sapiens* flourished in sub-Saharan Africa (Brauer, 1992). An "early archaic *Homo sapiens*" form was widely distributed from southern to northeast Africa some 200,000 years ago. These archaic populations had evolved from earlier *H. erectus* populations and had larger cranial vaults and many other anatomical features similar to those of anatomically modern humans. The Broken Hill (Kabwe) skull from Zambia belongs in this group. A second group—"late archaic *Homo sapiens*"—includes fossils with mosaics of both archaic and modern features, with the latter tending to predominate. These specimens date to 100,000 years ago and earlier. The last group are anatomically modern individuals, with only a very few archaic features.

Kabwe
100,000

Very early, anatomically modern *H. sapiens* was widely distributed in eastern and southern Africa as far back as the early Upper Pleistocene, some 115,000 years ago, perhaps even earlier (Brauer, 1992). The anatomical developments that led to the emergence of *H. sapiens* in eastern and southern Africa had run their course as early as 100,000 to 70,000 years ago, far earlier than any equivalent developments in Europe or Southwest Asia. At this time, the evolution of the classic and late Neanderthals had run its course in those areas. In evolutionary terms, the transition from *H. erectus* to archaic *H. sapiens* seems to have occurred not quickly but relatively slowly and continuously. It is difficult to draw a line between the two species. In contrast, the "modernization" of the human skull into its present configuration took place considerably faster, sometime at the very end of the Middle Pleistocene or the beginning of the Upper Pleistocene, by 100,000 years ago.

Molecular Biology and *Homo sapiens*

Molecular biology has played a significant role in dating earlier human evolution and is now yielding important clues to the origins of *H. sapiens* (Cann, Rickards, and Lum, 1995; Cavalli-Sforza and Cavalli-Sforza, 1995). Researchers have zeroed in on **mitochondrial DNA (mtDNA),** a useful tool for calibrating mutation rates because it accumulates mutations much faster than nuclear DNA (Figure 3.24). Mitochondrial DNA is inherited only through the maternal line; it does not mix with and become diluted by paternal DNA. Thus, it provides a potentially reliable link with ancestral populations. When genetic researchers analyzed the mtDNA of 182 women from Africa, Asia, Europe, Australia, and New Guinea, they found that the differences among them were

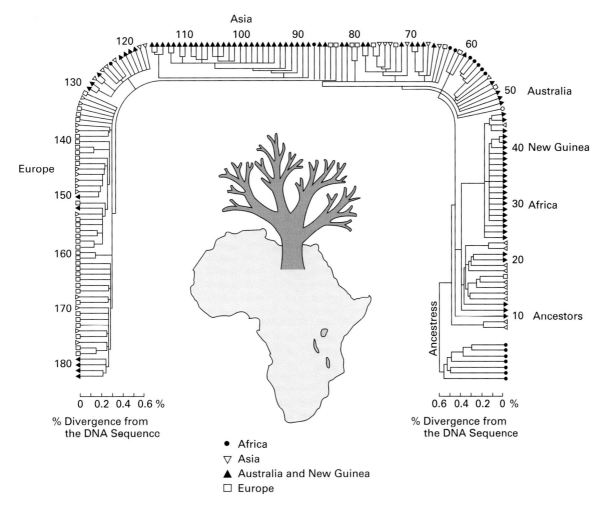

FIGURE 3.24 Allan Wilson and his research team used mitochondrial DNA from 182 women around the world to develop this family tree of modern human origins.

very small. Therefore, they argued, the five populations were all of comparatively recent origin. There were some differences, sufficient to separate two groups within the sample: a set of African individuals and another comprising individuals from all groups. The biologists concluded that all modern humans derive from a 200,000-year-old African population from which populations migrated to the rest of the Old World, with little or no interbreeding with existing, more Archaic human groups. (Research using the Y chromosome, which makes an embryo male, is said to produce somewhat similar results.)

A storm of criticism has descended on the so-called Eve hypothesis, most of it directed against the calculations of the rate of genetic mutation. As Cann and others (1995) have pointed out, the methodology is very new and evolving rapidly. Nevertheless, with mitochondrial data from some 5000 modern individuals, there is evidence that Africans display more diverse types of mitochondrial DNA than other present-day populations elsewhere in the world, a finding that suggests they had more time to develop such mutations. An even larger data base of normal (nuclear) DNA and of its products (blood groups and enzymes) displays a hierarchy of clusters. There was a primary split between Africans and non-Africans, then a later one between Eurasians and Southeast Asians. These findings also imply that modern humans originated in Africa, then dispersed from there to split again in Asia (Cann, 2001). It is thought that the ancestral population lived in Africa about 100,000 years ago. This also means that, assuming a constant rate of genetic diversification, all human variation could have arisen in the past 150,000 years (Powledge and Rose, 1996). The mitochondrial research remains controversial, on statistical grounds and also because the data are still inadequate to reject the multiregional hypothesis completely.

A new generation of research using new models and statistical approaches is showing that the process of origin and spread was more complex than originally thought. One scenario argues for the appearance of an early modern human population in Africa some 100,000 years ago that fragmented into several isolated populations and then spread out to populate the rest of the Old World. There was a severe population bottleneck after the establishment of the modern human population, for reasons that are not understood, that was followed by explosive population growth in different parts of the world. This issue is highly controversial, and research continues (Rogers and Jorde, 1995).

At present, the earliest archaeological evidence for anatomically modern humans in Africa dates to between 130,000 and 100,000 years ago. With so few fossils to work with, all we can be sure of is that there was considerable anatomical variation in Africans between 200,000 and 100,000 years ago. It is also entirely possible that anatomically modern humans evolved in many locations south of the Sahara in highly varied and very isolated African populations.

Ecology and *Homo sapiens*

For generations, anthropologists have tended to treat the origin of *H. sapiens* as a unique event that took place outside the processes of evolutionary biology. As Robert Foley (1984c) argues, one can understand this event only within a comparative ecological framework. Foley points out that modern humans are most likely to have originated within a single location. The savanna woodland of Africa around 100,000 years ago was an ideal environment for promoting the speciation of modern humans, he believes. Foley has studied monkey evolution in Africa and found that the widely dispersed populations had diverged; they did not continue on a single evolutionary course. Africa experienced considerable habitat fragmentation and re-formation during the alternating cold and warmth of the Pleistocene, fluctuations that enhanced the prospects of speciation among the continent's animals and plants. For example, Foley found that one monkey genus alone radiated into 16 species at about the same time that modern humans may have evolved on the continent. The tropical environments of Africa consisted of a constant mosaic of changing environmental patterns, a mosaic that tended to foster local evolution. In contrast, in higher latitudes, environmental changes were more marked, and animal distributions changed significantly and rapidly over short periods of time.

Foley's monkey studies have convinced him that modern humans evolved in such a mosaic of tropical environments, developing distinctive characteristics that separated them from their archaic predecessors. Within tropical Africa's patchy environments were areas where food supplies were both predictable and of high quality. In response to such regions, some humans may have developed wide-ranging behavior, may have lived in larger social groups with a considerable kin-based substructure, and may have been highly selective in their diet. As part of these responses, some groups may have developed exceptional hunting skills, a technology so effective that they could use projectiles to prey on animals from a distance. With more efficient technology, more advance planning, and better organization of both hunting and foraging, our ancestors could have reduced the unpredictability of the environment in dramatic ways.

This ecological approach to modern human origins is still untested against archaeological evidence. Even at this stage in research, there are unexplained anomalies between biology and archaeology. Once modern human beings had evolved, they manufactured a sophisticated tool technology based on antler, bone, wood, and stone blade manufacture. In the long term, similarly improved hunting and foraging technologies took hold throughout Africa, finally turning humans from expert scavengers and occasional hunters into superpredators capable of taking mammals large and small. The link between technology and anatomy is very loose, as if ideas and genes had moved at different rates. A number of lines of evidence strongly suggest that *H. sapiens* originated in Africa and spread from there into other parts of the Old World.

The Spread of *Homo sapiens*

If tropical Africa was the cradle of modern humans, how and why did *H. sapiens* spread into Europe and Asia (Brauer, 1992)? The critical period was between 100,000 and 45,000 years ago, the date by which *H. sapiens* is known to have been living in Southwest Asia. There are two possible routes: the Sahara and Nile Valley and a coastal route across the Red Sea to southern and southwestern Asia. The latter is virtually undocumented except for a recent discovery of an archaeological site on the western shore of the Red Sea with evidence for early shellfish exploitation.

The only major barrier to population movement between tropical Africa and the Mediterranean basin is the Sahara, today some of the driest territory on earth. During the early Weichsel glaciation, the Sahara went through phases of relative aridity and greater rainfall. A cooler and wetter climate prevailed in the desert from before 100,000 until about 40,000 years ago and again between 32,000 and 24,000 years ago. For long periods, the country between East Africa and the Mediterranean was passable, supporting scattered game herds and open grassland. The Nile Valley was always habitable, even during periods of great aridity in the desert. Thus, anatomically modern *H. sapiens* may have hunted and foraged across the Sahara into the Nile Valley and Southwest Asia in the early Weichsel. Then, as Southwest Asia became increasingly dry and less productive, the newcomers may have responded to population pressure and food shortages by moving across the wide land bridge that joined Turkey to southeastern Europe 45,000 years ago and by spreading into the more productive steppe and tundra regions of Europe and western Asia (Fagan, 1990).

〰 The Issue of Cognitive Ability

If we are correct in assuming that anatomically modern humans had settled in southwestern Asia by 100,000 to 90,000 years ago, we then have to explain why 40,000 years or so passed before they spread northward. Furthermore, the first art traditions now appear as well as much more elaborate culture. The answer may lie in a lag between the development of the full cognitive ability of modern humans and other features of their anatomy. Richard Klein (2001) has argued that southwestern Asia was, in a sense, a province of tropical Africa 90,000 years ago, inhabited by both Neanderthals and more modern humans for 40,000 years, a time when new toolkits and vastly enhanced cognitive skills developed. Recent genetic research involving the molecular evolution of gene FOXP2 tends to support Klein's hypothesis (Ervard et al., 2002). Then, after 45,000 years ago, the rapid, and final spread of modern humans began. This is a logical explanation for what the scanty fossil and archaeological record tells us, but we have, as yet, no means of establishing whether he is correct.

〰 *Homo sapiens* in East Asia

For hundreds of thousands of years, from well over a million years ago until perhaps later than 200,000 years ago, *Homo erectus* populations flourished in East and Southeast Asia. These archaic humans adapted to a wide range of environments, but the adaptations were conservative ones, especially in the tropical forests and woodlands of Southeast Asia, where bamboo may have been an important toolmaking material.

Although physical anthropologists argue over the anatomical differences between different Asian *H. erectus* populations, no one doubts that there were gradual changes in human anatomy through time. Unfortunately, there is such a dearth of fossils and accurate dates for them that the experts can do little more than speculate intelligently about human fossils that are often separated in time by as much as 250,000 years. In China, there are scattered finds of what are said to be archaic forms of *H. sapiens*, as opposed to anatomically modern people, dating to about 200,000 years ago from such sites as Dali and Maba. By this time, Chinese biologists believe they can recognize

Dali

Maba

200,000

distinctive "Chinese" anatomical features, and there is general agreement that brain sizes were increasing by that date.

Despite theories that anatomically modern people flourished in China as early as 70,000 years ago, there is a yawning fossil gap until finds in the 35,000-year-old range, much later in prehistory.

In Southeast Asia, where there is a similar chronological gap, physical anthropologists Milford Wolpoff, Xinzhi Wu, and Alan Thorne (1984) compared a *H. erectus* fossil from Sangiran in Java, estimated to be some 700,000 years ago, with a large sample of *H. sapiens sapiens* skeletons from Lake Mungo in southern Australia (see Chapter 6). On the basis of comparisons of selected anatomical features like the jutting forward of the face, they argued that there was strong evidence of anatomical continuity between *H. erectus* and more modern Asian populations. They believe that there was interbreeding of *H. sapiens sapiens* populations from centers of greater morphological variation, like Southwest Asia, with archaic populations farther east. But the farther one got from the "centers," they argue, the later the appearance of modern humans. One of the outer regions was mainland Southeast Asia, where *H. erectus* apparently survived far longer than in Africa and Europe—until as late as 53,000 to 27,000 years ago, according to dates from Ngangdong, Java.

Out-of-Africa critics of this multiregional hypothesis argue that Wolpoff, Wu, and Thorne's research is based on a careful selection of a few anatomical features, some of which may be primitive retentions, and on fossils that are separated by hundreds of thousands of years of prehistoric time. It has to be admitted that if the out-of-Africa hypothesis is correct, the date when anatomically modern humans spread into Asia and the processes by which they did so are a complete mystery.

Niah
40,000
Tabon
23,000

The earliest well-documented *H. sapiens sapiens* fossils in Asia date to long after modern people were living in the western Mediterranean region. A poorly dated *H. sapiens sapiens* skull from the great cave at Niah in Borneo is believed to be about 40,000 years old, and an anatomically modern skull from Tabon Cave in the Philippines may date to about 23,000 years ago. Both of these specimens are said to display features that link them to gene flow from farther north in Asia. The earliest anatomically modern fossils in China date to somewhere between 50,000 and 35,000 years ago. (For a discussion of the earliest human settlement of Australia, see Chapter 6, p. 183.)

Long Rongrien
c. 37,000

The earliest mainland site that might be attributed to *H. sapiens sapiens* is the Long Rongrien Cave on the west end of the Thai-Malay Peninsula in the thick rain forest (D. Anderson, 1990). The lowest occupation levels date to at least 37,000 years ago and are marked by small scrapers, some worked cobbles, and three antler or bone tools. We can only hypothesize about the inhabitants of mainland Southeast Asia between 100,000 and 40,000 years ago. In the forests, as Long Rongrien shows, there was no need for sophisticated stone artifacts when easily split and sharpened bamboo and various woods would suffice for weapons and knives.

In short, we do not know when anatomically modern people settled in Asia, but an intelligent guess would be after 100,000 years ago, by which time *H. sapiens sapiens* was well established in Southwest Asia and Africa.

In Chapter 4, we follow the fortunes of modern humans in northern parts of the world during the late Ice Age.

Summary 〰️〰️

This chapter covers a long period of time, from about 1.9 million to 40,000 years ago. We describe the climatic events of the Great Ice Age (the Pleistocene) between about 1.6 million and 128,000 years ago. These complex fluctuations between glacial maxima and much shorter interglacial periods were the backdrop to the evolution not only of *Homo erectus*, but of modern humans—*H. sapiens sapiens*—as well. *Homo erectus* had evolved from earlier *Homo* in tropical Africa by 1.9 mya, then radiated into Europe and Asia as part of a general radiation of mammalian species soon afterward. The earliest date of this radiation may be as early as 1.8 million years ago, but the chronology is controversial. Sometime after 1.8 million years ago, humans domesticated fire, but the date is much debated. The new humans used a simple technology based on hand axes and basic flake technology in the west, relying heavily on bamboo and other forest products in Southeast Asia. There was a gradual increase in brain size, perhaps beginning as early as about 0.4 million years ago, as archaic forms of *H. sapiens* with enlarged brain capacities evolved in various parts of the Old World.

The best known of these forms are the Neanderthals of Europe and Eurasia, who developed more sophisticated toolmaking technology than *Homo erectus,* were more adept hunters and foragers, and were the first humans to bury some of their dead.

Two competing theories account for the appearance of anatomically modern humans. The multiregional hypothesis for modern human origins has it that modern humans developed independently in Africa, Europe, and Asia, and that the biological diversity of contemporary humankind has very deep roots in prehistory. The out-of-Africa hypothesis argues that modern humans evolved in tropical Africa before 100,000 years ago, then spread into other parts of the world from Southwest Asia after 45,000 years ago (see Chapter 4). The long delay in this later spread is thought by some to be attributable to the later evolution of the full cognitive abilities of modern humans. With the appearance of modern humans, the long prehistory of the archaic world ends.

Key Terms

Disk core technique A stone technology based on disk-shaped cores, shaped so as to produce several relatively similarly sized flakes for manufacture into different tool forms.

Interglacial A warm period between major Ice Age glaciations.

Levallois technique A stone technology based on a core prepared to produce one large flake of predictable shape.

Matuyama-Brunhes boundary A moment when the earth's magnetic field reversed c. 780,000 years ago.

Mitochondrial DNA (mtDNA) DNA inherited through the female line.

Prepared core A stone core preshaped to produce flakes of a predictable shape.

Prognathous Applied to human faces—a prognathous face juts out, whence prognathous jaw characteristic of many Neanderthals.

Termination A period of rapid deglaciation.

Guide to Further Reading

Bordes, François. 1968. *The Old Stone Age.* New York: McGraw-Hill.
A simple manual on the Paleolithic period that is out-of-date except for its simple descriptions of basic Stone Age technologies and European tool types. Ideal for beginners.

Gamble, Clive. 1999. *The Palaeolithic Societies of Europe.* Cambridge: Cambridge University Press.
A full discussion of the fundamental issues surrounding the Middle Paleolithic adaptation in Europe. For advanced readers.

Klein, Richard. 2001. "Fully Modern Humans." In *Archaeology at the Millennium: A Sourcebook.* Gary M. Feinman and T. Douglas Price, eds. Pp. 109–136. New York: Kluwer Academic/Plenum.
Klein discusses current research on modern humans, including the vexing question of cognitive abilities. Comprehensive references.

Lewin, Roger. 1993. *The Origins of Modern Humans.* New York: Scientific American Library.
An excellent introduction to the issues and scientific data.

Lieberman, Philip. 1991. *Uniquely Human: The Evolution of Speech, Thought, and Selfless Behavior.* Cambridge, MA: Harvard University Press.
An authoritative study of the evolution of language in humans.

Mithen, Steven. 1996. *The Prehistory of the Mind.* London and New York: Thames & Hudson.
Controversial and provocative analysis of archaic humans and their intellectual capabilities. Recommended for the general reader.

Roberts, Mark, and Simon Parfitt. 1999. *A Middle Pleistocene Hominid Site at Eartham Quarry, Boxgrove, West Sussex.* London: English Heritage.
An excellent general description of the most important Middle Palaeolithic site found in Europe in recent years.

Schick, Kathy, and Nicholas Toth. 2001. "Paleoanthropology at the Millennium." In *Archaeology at the Millennium: A Sourcebook.* Gary M. Feinman and T. Douglas Price, eds. Pp. 39–108. New York: Kluwer Academic/Plenum.
This up-to-date summary includes a section on *Homo erectus* and its technology. Comprehensive references.

Stringer, Christopher, and Clive Gamble. 1993. *The Search for the Neanderthals.* London: Thames & Hudson.
An eloquent account of what we know about these archaic humans, aimed at the general reader.

Stringer, Christopher, and R. McKie. 1996. *African Exodus.* New York: Holt.
Another popular account of modern human origins.

Trinkaus, Erik, and Pat Shipman. 1992. *The Neanderthals: Changing the Image of Mankind.* New York: Knopf.
Another popular and authoritative account of the Neanderthals.

THE GREAT DIASPORA: THE SPREAD OF MODERN HUMANS

45,000 YEARS AGO TO MODERN TIMES

"I want you to remind yourself," he said, "that you have now spent 1 field season of excavation, 15 years of analyses, and thousands of dollars of taxpayers' money to find out no more than this: what a family of five did during the autumn, on six different occasions, scattered over a 2,000-year period. I earnestly hope that the thought will keep you humble."

"Would you believe 'deeply depressed'?"

Kent Flannery, *Guilá Naquitz* (1986)

The curtain rises on the fourth act of the human past, sometime after 100,000 years ago, with the appearance of anatomically modern humans in Southwest Asia. By 45,000 years ago, only one human actor remained on the world stage: *Homo sapiens sapiens,* modern humans, ourselves. And by that time, too, there was a dramatic cultural florescence—new human behaviors, the use of new artifact materials, the first art—and people ventured over oceans and into hitherto uninhabited continents. Steven Mithen (1996) calls this moment the "Big Bang"—when the human mind ceased to function through multiple intelligences, when all such intelligences functioned smoothly together, harmonizing to create the almost limitless imagination of the modern human mind.

Part II tells the story of the great human diaspora that resulted.

period already covered	period covered in this part	partial coverage

5 mya	2.5 mya	1 mya	100,000 B.P.	10,000 B.C.	A.D. 1	A.D. 1500

c h a p t e r

4

EUROPE AND EURASIA

c. 40,000 TO 8000 B.C.

A Cro-Magnon hand outline on the wall of a French cave.

Spanish landowner Marcellino de Sautuola had a casual interest in archaeology. He had visited an exhibit in Paris of some of the fine stone tools from French caves. In 1875, he decided to dig for some artifacts of his own in the caverns of Altamira on his estate. Sautuola's 5-year-old daughter, Maria, begged for the chance to dig with him, so he good-naturedly agreed. Maria soon tired of the muddy work and wandered off with a flickering lantern into a low side chamber of the cave. Suddenly, he heard cries of "Toros! Toros!" ("Bulls! Bulls!"). Maria pointed excitedly at brightly painted figures of bison and a charging boar on the low ceiling. Daughter and father marveled at the well-preserved paintings, arranged so cleverly around bulges in the rock that they seemed to move in the flickering light.

Sautuola was convinced the paintings had been executed by the same people who had dropped stone tools in the cave. But the experts laughed at him and accused the marquis of smuggling an artist into Altamira to forge the bison. It was not until 1904 that the long-dead Spaniard was vindicated, when some paintings with strong stylistic links to Altamira came to light in a French cave that had been sealed since the prehistoric artists had worked there. Clearly, whoever had painted on the cave walls at Altamira was a far cry from earlier humans like the Neanderthals.

In Chapter 3, we explored current thinking about the emergence of *Homo sapiens sapiens* in tropical Africa and hypothesized that anatomically modern humans spread from the tropics into North Africa and Southwest Asia about 100,000 years ago. From there, *H. sapiens* may have entered Europe at a time of low sea level, crossing the land bridge that connected the Balkans with Turkey across the Bosporus (Nitecki and Nitecki, 1994). This chapter chronicles the culture changes that resulted from this replacement of European Neanderthals by anatomically modern humans and looks at the vigorous hunter-gatherer cultures that flourished in the northern parts of the Old World between 38,000 years ago and postglacial times (Figures 4.1a and 4.1b; Table 4.1).

The Upper Pleistocene (c. 126,000 Years Ago to 8000 B.C.)

The Upper Pleistocene began in about 126,000 B.C. and coincided with the last interglacial and glacial cycles of the Ice Age. The detailed picture we have of this cycle gives us important clues to the general nature of the Ice Age climate: gradual glaciation and rapid deglaciation in cycles of cold, dry weather

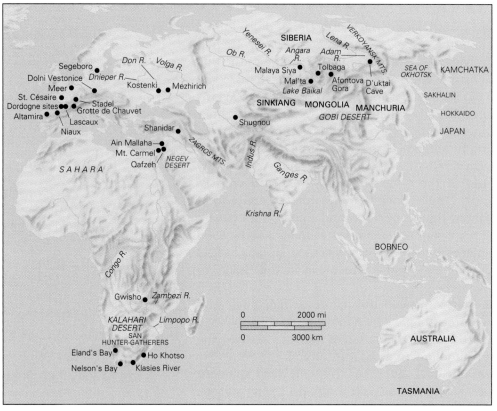

(a)

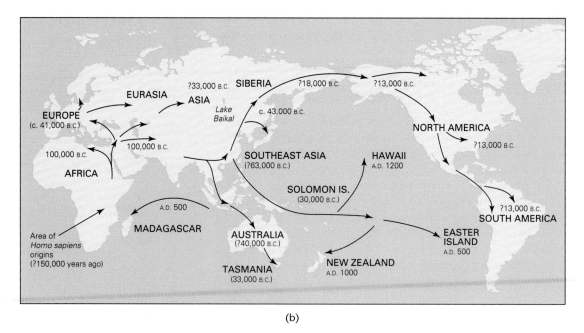

(b)

FIGURE 4.1 (a) Map showing archaeological sites mentioned in this chapter and in Chapters 6 and 7. Some minor and little-known sites are omitted for clarity, but their general locations are clear from the text. (b) The spread of *Homo sapiens sapiens* in the late Ice Age and after.

prevailing over northern latitudes for some 60 percent of the past 730,000 years. Full interglacial conditions, when the climate was warmer than today, brought forest and woodland to Europe (Figure 4.2a). The Upper Pleistocene began with the Eemian interglacial, which lasted only some 10,000 years. About 116,000 B.C., global temperatures started to cool gradually with the onset of the Weichsel glaciation. By 113,000 B.C.,

TABLE 4.1

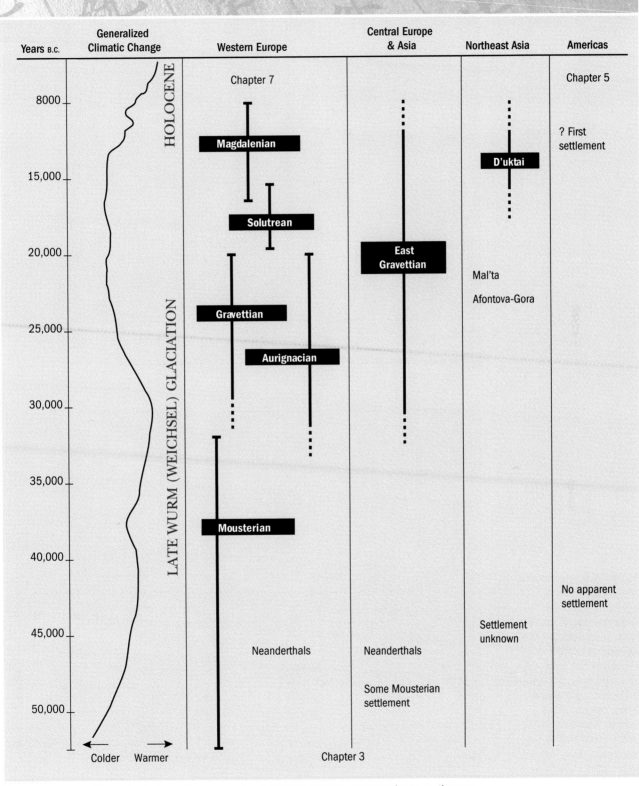

There was considerable overlap between European cultures. Climatic changes are approximate, as they are subject to considerable controversy among experts.

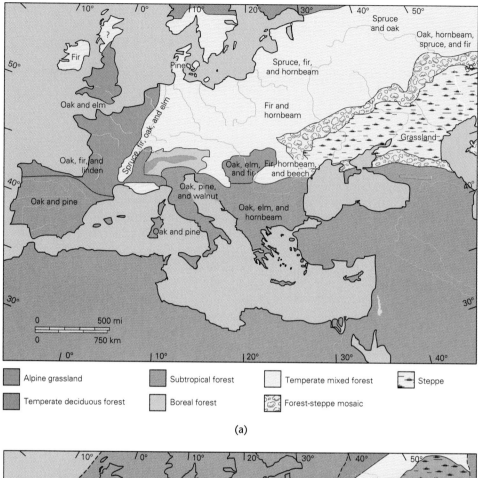

(a)

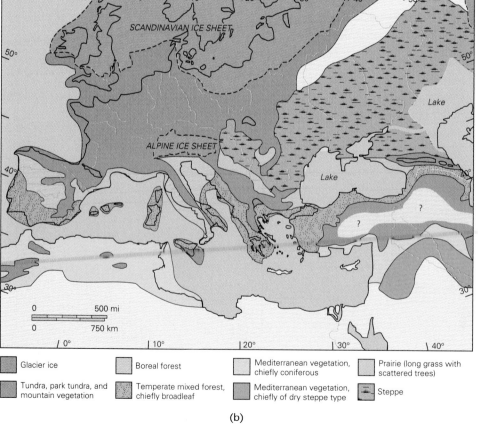

FIGURE 4.2 (a) Generalized distribution of vegetation in Europe during the height of the Holstein interglacial. The succeeding Eemian interglacial was not quite as warm and was of shorter duration, but the same general vegetational patterns prevailed. (After Butzer, 1974.) (b) Generalized vegetation map of Europe at the height of the Weichsel glaciation, showing ice sheets. (After Butzer, 1974.)

(b)

North American and European ice sheets were expanding again and sea levels had already fallen some 70 m (230 feet). Glacial conditions were intense about 73,000 B.C., when the Neanderthals were flourishing in Europe and the Americas were still uninhabited, and again after 27,000 B.C., reaching their height about 16,000 B.C., when sea levels fell to about 130 m (425 feet) below modern levels. This drop led to the exposure of huge continental shelves in Southeast Asia and elsewhere; the Bering Strait was dry land.

At the height of the last glaciation, world temperatures fell by as much as 15.5°C (60°F) near the ice sheets. The world's vegetation was very different at the height of the Weichsel glaciation (Figure 4.2b). Treeless tundra (open scrub) vegetation extended south of the ice sheets, giving way to a wide belt of cold continental steppe (open plain) that extended from the Low Countries into China and from Siberia to the Mediterranean. The steppe was much narrower in North America, soon giving way to coniferous forest farther south. Huge zones of desert occupied more than half the earth's surface between latitudes 30°N and S, but some of today's desert areas—like the American Southwest, the northern Sahara, and the southern African deserts—were more hospitable, supporting scrub, grassland, and shallow lakes. The rain forests of tropical Africa and Asia gave way to open woodland and grassland; coral reefs and mangrove swamps contracted drastically as a result of cooler temperatures. However, despite the harsh world climate, humankind managed to survive and flourish in this very different world.

⸘⸘ Modern Humans in Southwest Asia

In Chapter 3, we theorized that anatomically modern *Homo sapiens* had spread from Africa into Southwest Asia by about 100,000 years ago. The number of people involved must have been very small; indeed, it has been estimated that the original Southwest Asian breeding population may have been no larger than 50 people, and only 500 after 200 years (Jones and Rouhani, 1986). Such small numbers would have created a genetic "bottleneck," reducing the great genetic variability of African-derived populations dramatically—and possibly accounting for the lesser degree of genetic variability among modern non-African populations.

The archaeological evidence for both indigenous Neanderthals and modern humans in Southwest Asia is still very sparse. We know *H. sapiens sapiens* was living at the Qafzeh Cave in Israel by at least 100,000 B.C., almost as early a time as modern humans are known to have flourished in southern Africa (Stringer and Gamble, 1993) (Figure 4.3). The Qafzeh dates imply that Neanderthals and anatomically modern people were living in Southwest Asia at the same time and coexisted there without biological or cultural interaction for thousands of years, perhaps from before 90,000 B.C. until at

Qafzeh
c. 100,000

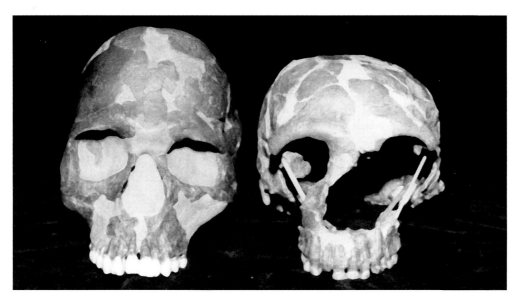

FIGURE 4.3 The early modern human skull from Qafzeh 9 (cast) compared with a Neanderthal from et-Tabun at Mount Carmel, both from Israel.

least 43,000 B.C. Stone tools from Qafzeh, from caves on Mount Carmel, and from the Negev Desert chart a slow evolution of human technology between about 100,000 and 40,000 B.C.

Does this mean that Neanderthals evolved into anatomically modern people in Southwest Asia, as the multiregional hypothesis implies (see Chapter 3)? Alternatively, did Neanderthal groups move south from Europe to escape extreme cold, perhaps as late as 50,000 B.C., settling in a region where anatomically modern humans from Africa were already living? At present, we do not know. What is significant, however, is that after **45,000 years ago** 45,000 years ago, new technologies based on fine stone blades and associated with *H. sapiens sapiens* become dominant in Southwest Asian toolkits. Perhaps it was not until these new technologies developed that fully modern people had the competitive edge that enabled them to move northward into the new, challenging environments of late Ice Age Europe. As we also saw in Chapter 3, this may have been the moment when modern humans finally developed their full cognitive abilities (Ervard et al., 2002; Klein, 2001).

〰 The Upper Paleolithic Transition

The biological transition from Neanderthals to *Homo sapiens sapiens* is still the subject of much debate; however, the replacement theory is most strongly favored. Can we, then, document the transition in technological and cultural terms (Bar-Yosef and Vandermeersch, 1993)?

Considerable technological changes accompanied the final chapter of human biological evolution, but these changes were far less dramatic than has sometimes been claimed. For generations, experts on the Stone Age assumed that the appearance of *H. sapiens sapiens* coincided with the invention of radically new, much more advanced technologies that involved, among other things, the use of punches to produce fine, parallel-sided blades and a proliferation of specialized tools, not only in stone but in antler and bone as well (Figure 4.4). Although there is no doubt that such innovations did appear in the Upper Paleolithic, careful examination of earlier technological traditions shows that they were foreshadowed tens of thousands of years earlier. Rock shelters and caves in eastern and southern Africa have yielded large tools made of blades fabricated by skilled percussion from carefully prepared cores. The same peoples of 100,000 years ago were using composite tools and a wider range of artifacts than many of their predecessors. In Southwest Asia, great caves and rock shelters, like the Mount Carmel sites et-Tabun and Mugharet el-Wad in Israel and Shanidar in Iraq, document thousands of years of Neanderthal toolmaking. These sites were visited again and again by hunter-gatherer bands from more than 70,000 years ago right into modern times.

The Mousterian levels in these caves contain tens of thousands of carefully retouched flakes and side scrapers, as well as the bones of large deer and wild cattle (Marks, 1983). This technology was a very simple and conservative one that displayed considerable variability within fairly restricted limits. This variability included some horizons (occupation levels) in which large, bladelike blanks were made with sophisticated percussion flaking. Later occupation levels containing different toolkits covered the Mousterian horizons. The new tools gradually replaced earlier artifact forms and technologies. In these later levels, the long, parallel-sided blades that were the first stage in making stone tools came from cylindrical flint cores with a punch and a hammer stone (see Figure 4.4). Some blades were up to 15.2 cm (6 inches) long. The tools made from them varied greatly, were designed for specific tasks, and, in later millennia, were mounted in handles.

Anthony Marks (1983) studied hunter-gatherer camps in Israel's Negev Desert and found an interesting change in ancient settlement patterns. The climate was wetter and the hunting population tended to concentrate in more circumscribed areas by 45,000 years ago. As the climate dried up, the people became more mobile. Instead of camping close to convenient sources of toolmaking stone, they moved around constantly, a reality that necessitated new ways of using precious fine-grained rock. Instead of using wasteful Levallois techniques (see Figure 3.20), they experimented with more

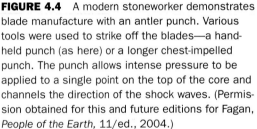

FIGURE 4.4 A modern stoneworker demonstrates blade manufacture with an antler punch. Various tools were used to strike off the blades—a handheld punch (as here) or a longer chest-impelled punch. The punch allows intense pressure to be applied to a single point on the top of the core and channels the direction of the shock waves. (Permission obtained for this and future editions for Fagan, *People of the Earth,* 11/ed., 2004.)

economical flaking methods, which evolved into the long, parallel-sided blades favored by Upper Paleolithic stoneworkers. So Upper Paleolithic **blade technology** was the logical result of millennia of gradual adjustment to more mobile lifeways, in which careful **curation** of toolmaking stone was essential.

A Cultural Explosion?

Early *Homo sapiens sapiens* flourished in Africa before 100,000 years ago, but with the exception of an occasional bone tool, human technology and behavior were very little different from those of millennia before. After 100,000 years ago, early modern humans in Southwest Asia buried their dead with animal jaws, as did some Neanderthals. There was nothing to distinguish their behavior or material culture from that of earlier humans. As much as 60,000 years passed before there were dramatic changes in human life, what has been described as a "cultural explosion" (Mithen, 1996). As Steven Mithen points out, there was no one explosion but, rather, a series of "sparks": There would be rapid culture change in one area but not in others. One such spark was the development of blade technology in Southwest Asia by 50,000 years ago; another, the first appearance of art objects in Europe about 40,000 years ago; a third, the first settlement of Australia by 35,000 years before the present. Only about 30,000 years ago, during the late Ice Age, did rapid culture change take hold in all parts of the world.

Many explanations have been invoked for these sudden developments, among them increased economic specialization, the restructuring of social relations, a major technological revolution, and even the development of fully articulate speech (for references, see Klein, 2001; Mithen, 1996). But Mithen believes that the new types of behavior associated with the cultural explosion resulted from the knocking down of the barriers between different parts of the human mind. With full cognitive fluidity, human beings developed new connections between the previously isolated domains of natural history, technical, and social intelligence.

One of the consequences was much more sophisticated social relations; another was visual symbolism, the development of art as a means of expression and communication. As the great cave paintings of western France (described later in this chapter) show, humankind now had the ability to bring the natural and the social worlds together in a seamless synthesis that is characteristic of many human societies, whether hunter-gatherers or farmers, to this day. The evolution of cognitive fluidity gave *H. sapiens sapiens*, spreading throughout the world after 45,000 years ago and perhaps earlier, a competitive edge over resident earlier human populations. With their superior intellectual capabilities, they pushed earlier populations into extinction, perhaps occasionally interbreeding with them. Once the move toward cognitive fluidity began, there was no stopping the process.

〰️ Modern Humans in Europe

Nowhere did cognitive fluidity play a more vital role than in the first settlement of Europe by modern humans. Environmental conditions may have militated against earlier settlement. From 100,000 to about 45,000 years ago, Europe was locked into extremely cold, fully glacial conditions, with very long, severe winters. It may be no coincidence that *Homo sapiens sapiens* first appears in continental Europe during a brief spell of more temperate climate after 50,000 years ago. Even then, climatic conditions and seasonal contrasts may have been severe enough to require new artifacts and more sophisticated hunting skills to exploit northern environments to the full.

Blade technology, with its portable cores and efficient small blanks, was highly adaptive for late Ice Age hunter-gatherers exploiting large hunting territories close to and around ice sheets. This technology has been likened to the Swiss army knife, with its strong hinge and many blades. The knife is a foundation for many tool forms, as was the blade core (Figure 4.5). The stoneworker knocked off numerous blade blanks, which could be fashioned into a great variety of scrapers, awls, and knives, to say nothing of fine-edged graving tools—or **burins,** as archaeologists call them. This versatile stone technology produced the fine, sharp working edges necessary for grooving bone and antler, raw materials available in abundance in the periglacial north (areas close to ice sheets). The development of blade technology may well have enabled modern humans to move north from Southwest Asia (Mellars, 1993).

A scatter of radiocarbon dates and stone tools chronicles the spread of modern humans into late Ice Age Europe. Characteristic blade technology appeared in Bulgaria as early as 41,000 B.C.; in Hungary, by 38,000 B.C.; and in western Europe, within a few millennia, perhaps as early as 38,000 B.C. There are clear signs that Neanderthals and newcomers lived alongside one another, for Mousterian occupation layers in some central European caves date to much later than 38,000, and there were Neanderthals making blade tools at St. Césaire in France by 34,000 B.C. After 31,000 B.C., *H. sapiens sapiens* was the only human form in Europe, and Upper Paleolithic blade technologies were universal. (These modern people are often called Cro-Magnons, after the rock shelter of that name near the village of Les Eyzies in southwestern France.)

What form this population replacement took remains an enigma in some locales (Stringer and Gamble, 1993). It was a long process of gene flow and small-scale population movement, as well as cultural innovations—new technologies and fresh strategies for the hunt. The flow of ideas may have been accelerated in situations in which hunters exploited large hunting territories and wandered far and wide in search of game and, perhaps, good toolmaking stone. Under such circumstances, technological innovation may have preceded gene flow and population movement, resulting in the

38,000 B.C.

St. Césaire
34,000 B.C.
Cro-Magnons

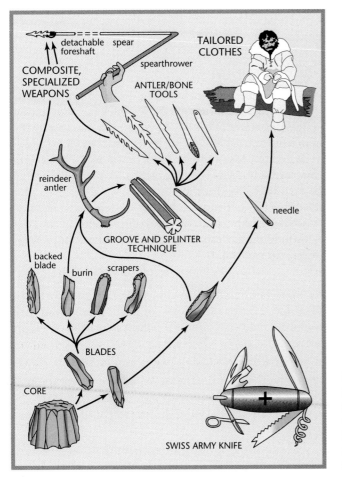

FIGURE 4.5 The Swiss army knife effect. Blade technology acted like the celebrated Swiss army knife, producing blanks for making many specialized artifacts for working bone and antler.

Neanderthals' experimenting with more sophisticated artifacts, as apparently was the case at St. Césaire. Not that the process of replacement was necessarily rapid. There is consensus among experts that Neanderthals survived for between 5000 and 10,000 years after the arrival of modern humans in the different, drier ecological conditions of the Ebro Valley region of southern Spain, where there may even have been some intermarriage between the two populations. A Neanderthal lower jaw from the Zafarraya site in Andalusia has been radiocarbon-dated to as late as about 28,000 B.C. (Mellars, 1998).

The late Ice Age archaeology of Europe has been so well studied that we can discern a series of long-term trends that took hold in hunter-gatherer societies throughout the world after 35,000 years ago. The changes were by no means simultaneous, nor did they occur everywhere, but they were cumulative and led in the long term to major economic, social, and political changes everywhere, especially in southwestern France and parts of Australia, where food resources were abundant and seasonally predictable.

Randall White (1982) cites the significant changes for late Ice Age Europe, many of which were mirrored elsewhere:

- A tendency toward higher population densities after 33,000 B.C.
- More regular social gatherings.
- Much more stylistic variation in stone artifacts, which lay in precise and scientifically recorded contexts in time and space. Perhaps this variation represents different territorial or social boundaries.
- A much greater emphasis on the working of bone and antler. Again, these tools display formal stylistic variation, perhaps with social significance.
- Some shift toward the hunting of herd animals that carried antlers for much of the year, especially in cold latitudes.

- The growing importance of personal ornamentation as a way of communicating communal and personal identity.
- The acquisition of materials from distant sources, probably through structured exchanges involving cooperation with other groups.

White believes there was a total restructuring of social relations during the critical transition period. It was then that corporate and individual identities became important and were enhanced by the skilled working of antler, bone, and stone and by the use of ornaments. The Upper Paleolithic may have seen more structured relationships between the inhabitants of different geographic areas, expressed not only in trade but in better-defined hunting territories and other social relationships. White believes that we should examine this transition on a very broad canvas.

One of the most important questions is establishing whether *H. sapiens sapiens* had to adapt to the close presence of other human groups as a matter of survival. In later prehistoric times, relationships with neighbors were to assume ever-increasing importance in adaptive strategies for long-term survival.

In these pages, we concentrate on the following major developments:

- The hunter-gatherer cultures that flourished in southwest France and northern Spain between 33,000 and 6000 B.C. These cultures are of particular importance because of their adaptation to the last cold snap of the Weichsel glaciation and their remarkable artistic traditions.
- The societies that developed on the western Russian plains and in Siberia.
- The early settlement of the arctic latitudes of northeast Asia, from which the first settlement of the New World may have developed.
- In Chapter 5, the first human settlement of the Americas and the cultural traditions that stemmed from it.
- In Chapter 6, the early history of surviving hunter-gatherers in tropical latitudes, especially the Australians and the San peoples of southern Africa.

〰 European Hunter-Gatherers (45,000 Years Ago to 8000 B.C.)

Central and western Europe were cold and dry during much of Upper Paleolithic times, with great ice sheets covering large expanses of the northern latitudes. South of the ice sheets, thousands of square kilometers of steppe-grassland, with occasional stands of trees, covered much of the unglaciated land. There were many local variations, with extensive tree growth in deep river valleys and other sheltered areas. A rich mammalian community flourished in these diverse environments. It included bison, horses, reindeer, and mountain goats in more rugged areas; large herbivores like the mammoth, the woolly rhinoceros, and the wild ox were common on the open steppe. The human inhabitants could exploit not only a rich animal biomass but also a wide variety of plant foods, including blueberries, raspberries, acorns, and hazelnuts. The climate was changing constantly, so the people had to readapt by altering their diet, their hunting and gathering strategies, and their technology. Much of the great variability in Upper Paleolithic culture resulted from such readaptations.

The Upper Paleolithic of Europe began about 35,000 years ago and witnessed constant changes in human behavior over the next 25,000 years (Mellars, 1993). These millennia have been subdivided into a series of cultural periods, each with its own technology and technological innovations (Figure 4.6; see Table 4.2). At first, French archaeologists, who developed this cultural sequence from excavations in caves and rock shelters, thought of each period as a rigid "epoch," like a geologic layer. Today, the cultural phases are seen as changes stimulated by a variety of complex and little-understood factors (Knecht et al., 1993). Some of them may have been responses to practical needs; others, purely dictates of fashion or small technological innovations (Geneste and Plisson, 1993).

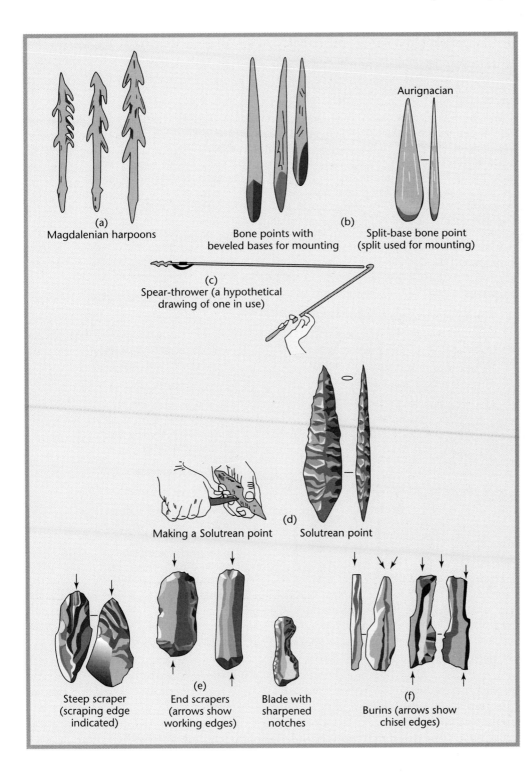

(a)
Magdalenian harpoons

(b)
Bone points with
beveled bases for mounting

Aurignacian

Split-base bone point
(split used for mounting)

(c)
Spear-thrower (a hypothetical
drawing of one in use)

Making a Solutrean point

(d)
Solutrean point

Steep scraper
(scraping edge
indicated)

(e)
End scrapers
(arrows show
working edges)

Blade with
sharpened
notches

(f)
Burins (arrows show
chisel edges)

FIGURE 4.6 Characteristic artifacts used by Upper Paleolithic groups in western Europe. Antler and bone artifacts were of vital importance, especially harpoons (a) and bone points (b) mounted on wooden shafts. The spear-thrower (c) was a hooked shaft, used to propel a spear a longer distance with great accuracy. Upper Paleolithic stone tools were made from blades for the most part, reaching their highest degree of sophistication about 20,000 years ago, with pressure-flaked Solutrean points (d), named after the Solutré site in southwestern France. Every group relied heavily on scrapers (e), used for processing skins, for working bone and antler, and for woodworking. The most important artifact was the chisel-ended burin (f), employed for grooving wood, bone, and especially reindeer antler.

As time went on, major regional differences emerged throughout central and western Europe (Gamble, 1999). These can be identified from stone and antler tool types of contrasting stone technologies. As Randall White (1986) remarks, it is almost as if barriers to communication were arising, as if there were regional dialects in Europe for the first time.

Settlement Strategies and Lifeways

The Upper Paleolithic peoples of southwest France have long been thought of as one of the prehistoric models for the cave people so beloved of modern-day cartoonists.

TABLE 4.2
Much simplified outline of the Upper Paleolithic traditions of western Europe from 40,000 to 10,000 B.C.

The most commonly accepted scheme has two parallel cultural traditions: the Gravettian, characterized by backed knives, and the Aurignacian, favoring scrapers and sharpened blades. The Gravettian, with increasingly finer backed knives, became dominant after 30,000 years ago. Thereafter, there were considerable regional variations, reflected in different tool traditions.

The Solutrean, a culture that relied on sophisticated "cooking" of large pieces of flint so that they became porcelainlike in texture, flourished in France and Spain. The stoneworker could exert pressure on the flake edge to produce magnificent leaf-shaped spear points. Many variations of the Gravettian culture are found in central and eastern Europe. In the west, the Magdalenian tradition, which relied heavily on antler and bone, emerged about 18,000 years ago. (For artifacts, see Figure 4.6.)

Years B.C.	Climate	Cultures	Characteristics
	Temperate	Mesolithic cultures	Forest and coastal adaptations
10,000			
	Warming up after 12,000 B.C.		• Apogee of cave and antler art • Skillful bone and antler work
15,000		Magdalenian	
	Very cold		Magnificent pressure-flaked stone spearheads
20,000		Solutrean	
			Bas-relief sculpture
25,000	Cold	Gravettian Aurignacian	• "Venus" figurines, cave art • Gradual elaboration of stone and bone technology
30,000	Somewhat temperate		• Aurignacian—sharpened and etched woodworking tools • Gravettian—backed stone knife blades
35,000			
	Cold	Arrival of *Homo sapiens sapiens*	Middle Paleolithic technology
40,000		Mousterian ↓	

Although it is true that much of our knowledge of their cultures comes from French caves and rock shelters, these were by no means the only settlements occupied after 38,000 B.C. Southwest France is remarkable for its high density of Upper Paleolithic sites within a restricted area, sites that were sometimes intensively occupied over long periods of time.

33,000 B.C.   Between 33,000 and 10,000 B.C., the climate of this region was strongly oceanic, with cool summers and mild winters by Ice Age standards. Summer temperatures may have been in the 12°C to 15°C (53.6°F to 59°F) range, with winter readings around 0°C (32°F). The plant-growing season was longer than on the open plains to the north and east, and snow cover was considerably less. Thus, the increase in food resources for large and small herbivores may have resulted in a much higher density of game animals as well as more plentiful edible plant foods.

This was a region of diverse food resources, reflected not only in tree pollens in shel-tered archaeological sites but also in the range of animals recovered from them. The people subsisted mainly on reindeer, but they also took wild ox, red deer, bison, ibex, chamois, woolly rhinoceros, and mammoth, as well as numerous smaller animals such as rabbits and birds. The sheer diversity of the environment gave the human inhabitants some economic security. In years when reindeer migrations were unpredictable, there were other sources of animal protein close at hand, to say nothing of plant foods (Straus, 1993).

Many of these resources were relatively predictable. There were seasonal reindeer migrations, from the higher ground of the east in summer to the deep river valleys of the west in winter, where food resources could be found even in the coldest months. The hunters could intercept animals from a broad range of species, many of them migratory, from an ecological range extending perhaps some 100 km (62 miles) on either side of their central places. Michael Jochim (1983) argues that large-scale salmon fishing during seasonal runs was a major factor in the evolution of complex hunter-gatherer societies in this region. The concentration of settlement along riverbanks, at places where the salmon runs were most prevalent, was a logical response to predictable food resources. Unfortunately, Jochim's argument has a serious weakness, for very few salmon bones have been found in the region's Upper Paleolithic sites (Mellars, 1985). Rabbits and other small game, perhaps taken with nets, were also a major food source (Adovasio et al., 1996).

Although fishhooks and harpoons, as well as fine engravings of salmon and seals, are known from many later Upper Paleolithic sites, it appears likely that hunting mammals of all kinds, large and small, was the predominant subsistence activity between 33,000 and about 8000 B.C. Fishing does seem to have assumed much greater importance at the very end of the Ice Age, perhaps as forests encroached on open grazing grounds and rising sea levels brought more fish to French rivers. Whatever the precise makeup of the Upper Paleolithic diet in southwest France, there were direct adaptive responses to these highly favorable ecological conditions. Population densities were locally much higher than in other parts of Europe, and groups lived in the same locations for much of the year, close to seasonal concentrations of food resources. They exploited these resources with high efficiency, and some part of the population lived almost permanently in certain key locations. Smaller groups then exploited more distant resources in summer and according to need.

The people tended to choose many of their settlement sites with reference to plentiful water supplies and good views of the surrounding landscape so that they could observe game and perhaps their neighbors. More than 90 percent of all known sites are close to springs or riverbanks. The bands could live wherever they wanted to, for they had the technology to survive hard winters in the open. Some of the largest cave and rock shelter sites lay close to river fords, places, perhaps, where migrating reindeer would cross each year. One such site is Laugerie Haute, near Les Eyzies in the Dordogne, where the skeletons of several reindeer lay between the great rock shelter and the river ford. When the people occupied a rock shelter or cave, it invariably faced south so they could benefit from the sun's rays on cool days. They appear to have erected tents and hide curtains in the shelters for additional protection. Some shelters lay near places where it was possible to stampede reindeer, horses, and other herd animals over cliffs. In the open, some groups laid out pavements of river cobbles as foundations for wood, skin, or sod structures. Sometimes they heated the pebbles first, perhaps so they could lay them over frozen ground to form a secure platform.

Laugerie Haute

Social Life and Group Size

Many of the largest Upper Paleolithic French sites are close to places where seasonally abundant resources like reindeer or small animals could be exploited by large numbers of people, perhaps, sometimes, with nets as opposed to spears. Other settlements were much smaller, little more than temporary camps occupied by a few families. Perhaps it is significant that the larger sites—like Laugerie Haute and Laugerie Basse, or La Madeleine, the type site of the Magdalenian—contain many more art objects. To cooperate in the food quest, the bands may have come together into larger social units

Magdalenian culture

at locations where abundant resources were available for a few months or weeks. Such aggregations could not have lasted year-round, partly because the environment would not have supported so many people in one place for long. If modern hunter-gatherers are any guide, the bands probably had no mechanisms for resolving disputes, except that practiced by the modern San of southern Africa: walking away. This is what anthropologist Richard Lee (1979) calls "voting with your feet."

The days, weeks, and even months of aggregation are the high point of the year in today's hunter-gatherer societies, as they must have been in the Upper Paleolithic. This was the time of marriage and initiation ceremonies, of highly intense rituals in which the fine art objects of the people may have played important roles. This was when shamans told tales and wove spells, when the forces of the ancestors and the spirit world were invoked to ensure the continuity of life and the success of the hunt. It was also a time when men and women exchanged artifacts, ornaments, and exotic raw materials from near and far. Seashells from the English Channel and the Mediterranean, Baltic amber, and other exotica—items that were sometimes imbued with special magical, social, or prestige value—were apparently exchanged from hand to hand. Many of these may have been given and received as gestures of social obligation between individuals and groups.

The Upper Paleolithic societies of southwest France lived in relatively close juxtaposition, in a diverse environment with rich, predictable food resources. For at least part of the year, these societies may have lived a relatively sedentary existence and come together in much larger aggregations. Under these circumstances, it is reasonable to expect that their social organization would become more complex than was normal among egalitarian band societies.

Magdalenian culture was elaborate and sophisticated, to the point where we can predict that more sedentary living and larger group size may have resulted in social change, in more complex hunter-gatherer societies (Mellars, 1985) (see Chapter 5). Certainly, the sometimes elaborate decoration of seashells, bracelets, and even sewn clothing associated with the dead argues for complex spiritual beliefs, many involving abstract symbolic images of the Ice Age world that we will never be able to recover.

〰️ Upper Paleolithic Art

Sometime between 40,000 and 30,000 B.C., Europeans began making ornaments such as beads, pendants, and perforated animal teeth to adorn their persons. And at about the same time, they painted images of animals, signs, and anthropomorphic figures on cave walls. (Although there are some earlier scratched bones from Neanderthal sites, these hardly constitute art.) But the Europeans were by no means alone. Art was a worldwide phenomenon by 25,000 B.C., perhaps much earlier. Painted slabs dating to

25,500 B.C.   about 25,500 B.C. have come from the Apollo 11 Cave in southern Africa, and wall engravings in Australia are at least as early. We know of only a few paintings and engravings this early, for art does not seem to have become commonplace anywhere until after about 18,000 B.C., the height of the last glaciation. The cave art of western Europe is the best known and most thoroughly studied (Bahn and Vertut, 1988).

As Steven Mithen (1996) has argued, there can be little doubt that the sudden appearance of art was connected with the development of human cognitive fluidity. But this was not art for art's sake; it was art with vital symbolic meaning, with, as it were, a "code" behind it. *Homo sapiens sapiens* created visual images that had complex meanings and great emotional power—and that are beyond our ability to decode. Many of their paintings and engravings hint at anthropomorphic themes, where animals become humans and humans animals. This suggests that late Ice Age artists, like modern hunter-gatherers, linked the social, spiritual, and natural worlds into a single continuum, and that the environment was imbued with great potency.

Nowhere does this close connection between animal and human, the living and the spiritual worlds, appear more vividly than at the recently discovered, and very early, Grotte de Chauvet, deep in southeastern France's Ardèche region (see Site box).

SITE

Grotte de Chauvet, France

Discovered in December 1994, the Grotte de Chauvet is a series of painted and engraved chambers undisturbed since the late Ice Age (Chauvet, Deschamps, and Hillaire, 1996). Hearths on the floor looked as if they had been extinguished the day before. Flaming torches had been rubbed against the wall to remove the charcoal so they would flare anew. More than 300 paintings adorn the walls (Figure 4.7). They include a frieze of black horses, wild oxen with twisted horns, and two rhinoceroses facing one another. The horses have half-open muzzles; the eyes are depicted in detail. There are lions, stags, and engravings of an owl, animals never before seen in painted caves, covering an area of more than 10 m (30 feet). A little farther on in the chamber lies a slab that had fallen from the ceiling. A bear skull had been set atop it. The remains of a small fire lie behind it. More than 30 calcite-covered, and intentionally placed, bear skulls surround the slab. A 10-m (30-foot) frieze of black figures dominated by lions or lionesses (without manes), rhinoceros, bison, and mammoth lies in an end chamber, a human figure with a bison head standing to its right (see illustration). The discoverers wrote that it "seemed to us a sorcerer supervising this immense frieze" (Chauvet et al., 1996, p. 110).

The artists were masters of perspective, overlapping the heads of animals to give the effect of movement and numbers. They even scraped some of the walls before painting them to make the figures stand out better. They would spread the paint with their hands over the rock, obtaining values that showed dimension and color tonality.

Accelerator mass spectrometry (AMS) radiocarbon dates (see Dating the Past box in Chapter 8) from two rhinoceroses and a large bison point to a 1300-year period around 30,000 B.C., making these paintings the earliest securely dated art in the world. Two more dates from torch smears on the walls are around 24,500 B.C., while two charcoal samples on the floor gave readings of about 22,500 B.C., suggesting that humans visited Chauvet on several occasions over at least 6000 or 7000 years. Whether they painted over that long period is still unknown, but AMS dates will ultimately produce some answers.

Grotte de Chauvet was a bear cave, a place where these powerful animals hibernated. Interestingly, many of the animals on the cave walls represent dangerous members of the late Ice Age bestiary: the bear and the lion, the mammoth, rhinoceros, and bison, even, occasionally, the nimble and ferocious aurochs. Perhaps human visitors to the cave, with its claw marks, hollows, prints, and scattered bones, came to the chambers to acquire the potency of the great beast, whose smell probably lingered in the darkness.

FIGURE 4.7 Panel with horses and woolly rhinoceros at Grotte de Chauvet, France. This same wall space was used repeatedly.

FIGURE 4.8 A lion-headed anthropomorphic statuette, carved from a small mammoth tusk, reconstructed from fragments found in the Stadel Cave, southern Germany. One of the earliest known human artworks, it dates to about 30,000 B.C.

Paintings and Engravings

Grotte de Chauvet
30,000 to 24,500 B.C.

Grotte de Chauvet offers dramatic evidence for the very early flowering of late Ice Age art. Until recently, most scholars thought in terms of a steady evolution of Upper Paleolithic art, from simple, unsophisticated beginnings to the magnificent polychrome paintings at Altamira in northern Spain and Lascaux in southwestern France. But both the Chauvet paintings and a lion-headed anthropomorphic figure carved in ivory from the Stadel Cave in southern Germany (Figure 4.8), as well as other animal sculptures from the same site (Hahn, 1993), suggest another scenario: one of brilliant flowerings of art in different areas at different times over a period of more than 20,000 years.

The evidence for these flowerings comes from nearly 200 caves in southwest Europe, mainly France and Spain, bearing wall paintings and engravings. Some 10,000 sculpted and engraved art objects have come from Upper Paleolithic sites across Europe and far into Siberia. Upper Paleolithic people were brilliant artists in stone, antler, bone, clay, ivory, and wood. They used paint on rock walls, sculpted in bas-relief and the round, and made musical instruments like bone flutes (Bahn and Vertut, 1988). The artists created thousands of naturalistic images of animals, sometimes human and humanlike forms, and dozens of enigmatic signs. All this art conveys complex, long-forgotten ideas, a symbolic world of spirit animals and spirit humans, of forces benevolent and evil. Some of the earlier art comprised "Venus" figurines: sculptures and bas-reliefs of

FIGURE 4.9 Paleolithic art: Venus figurines from Willendorf, Austria (left), and Dolní Vestonice, Czech Republic (right). (Right: Neg. No. 39686. Photo, Kirschner. Courtesy Dept. of Library Services, American Museum of Natural History.)

females, sometimes with pendulous breasts, sometimes pregnant, and with exaggerated sexual characteristics (Figure 4.9). They have been found from Russia in the east to the Dordogne region of France in the west, most in deposits dating to about 23,000 B.C. We have no means of knowing what rituals were associated with these figurines, but they seem to have been associated with a relatively short-lived set of beliefs that was prevalent over a wide area of Europe, even, perhaps, with divination ceremonies (Pringle, 1998).

Bas-reliefs in the form of friezes of animals like wild horses came into fashion in about 20,000 B.C. But 80 percent of all known Upper Paleolithic art comes from the Magdalenian, beginning around 16,000 B.C. The earlier Magdalenian saw some remarkable cave painting from places like Lascaux, painted in about 15,000 B.C. (Ruspoli and Coppens, 1987) Lascaux's walls were covered again and again with depictions of wild horses, bulls, reindeer, and many other animals. Many of the animals were painted with long, distorted necks and thick bodies, as if the artists were unaware of perspective (Figure 4.10). The paintings also include squiggles, spaghetti-like patterns, and tentlike symbols. A Great Hall of the Bulls features four immense wild bulls, drawn in thick, black lines, with some of the body details filled in. Horses, deer, a small bear, and a strange unicornlike beast prance with the great bulls in a fantastic display of blacks, browns, reds, and yellows that truly bring the animals to life in a flickering light. It is hard to believe that the paintings are at least 17,000 years old.

Magdalenian artistry reached its height with an explosion of antler and bone work after 16,000 B.C. The people decorated their harpoons, spear points, spear-throwers, and other artifacts with naturalistic engravings, fine carvings of wild animals, and elaborate schematic patterns. Even fine eye details and hair texture were shown by delicate graving strokes (Figure 4.11). But the Magdalenians are most famous for their beautiful

Lascaux
15,000 B.C.

FIGURE 4.10 The wild ox or aurochs, *Bos primigenius*, cavorts over a row of wild horses on the walls of Lascaux, France.

FIGURE 4.11 Mobile art from French Upper Paleolithic caves and the Venus of Willendorf (lower right). The artifacts depicted include a double-barbed harpoon (right), a thong straightener engraved with wild horses (top), a bison licking its flank (upper center), a spear-thrower (right), and a magnificent engraving of reindeer swimming across a river among salmon (bottom).

rock art, paintings and engravings deep in the caves of northern Spain and southwest France. At Altamira, in northern Spain, you walk deep into the hillside to enter a low-ceilinged chamber, where the painters left fine renderings of bison in red and black (Figure 4.12) (Beltran et al., 1999). By painting and engraving the animals around natural bulges in the rock, the artists conveyed a sense of dimension and life.

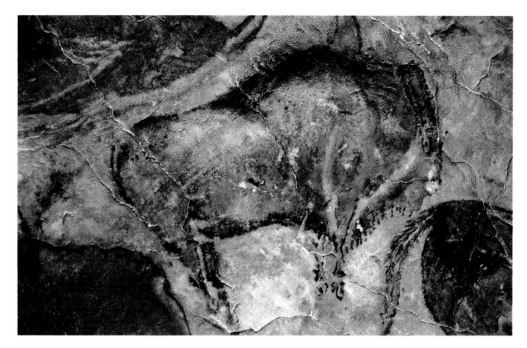

FIGURE 4.12 A bison in a polychrome cave painting from Altamira, Spain.

Explaining Upper Paleolithic Art

An enormous and highly speculative literature concerns the motives behind this remarkable art. Originally, Henri Breuil (1952) and other experts argued that the caves were sacred places where the hunters gathered to perform rituals and sympathetic magic that would ensure the fertility of game and the success of the hunt. Even the signs on the cave walls were interpreted as snares and traps. Today we know a great deal more about symbolic behavior and the art that goes with it and much more about how hunter-gatherer societies function.

French prehistorian André Leroi-Gourhan argued (1965, 1984) that the art was not random but part of a system of meanings, an expression of a worldview that organized Upper Paleolithic life. By counting the associations of subjects and the clusters of motifs, Leroi-Gourhan found that certain themes, among them female figures, appeared in rock shelters and better-lit locales, whereas others were in dark caverns. Leroi-Gourhan and his contemporaries lacked ways of dating individual paintings, so many of their theories were too generalized to stand up to close scrutiny.

The development of AMS radiocarbon dating, which requires only tiny paint samples, has allowed the dating of individual figures in caves like Niaux in southern France. There, Jean Clottes (1995) has combined AMS dating with chemical analysis of the paintings. He has dated Niaux's bison to between about 11,850 and 10,890 B.C. He has also been able to show that the paintings in such accessible chambers as the famous Salon Noir (Figure 4.13) were painted much more carefully than hastily executed figures in deep, inaccessible chambers, painted, perhaps, by individuals on solitary vision quests (searches for spiritual enlightenment).

Niaux
11,850 to 10,890 B.C.

Today, we know that many hunter-gatherer groups use ritual and art, creating and manipulating visual forms to structure and give meaning to their existence (Boyer, 1994). Many ethnographic studies show that symmetry and other artistic principles may underlie the designs of many art traditions and characterize every aspect of daily life, from social relationships to village planning. The people may use relatively few symbols to communicate meanings. Very often, it is the context of the symbols that reveals the meaning. For the Upper Paleolithic artists, there were clearly continuities between animal and human life and with their social world. Thus, their art was a symbolic depiction of these continuities. The artists did not choose just any wall or piece of antler or bone for their drawings, nor just any animal or geometric form to depict. Their selections were deliberate, symbolic acts that provide clues to the significance of

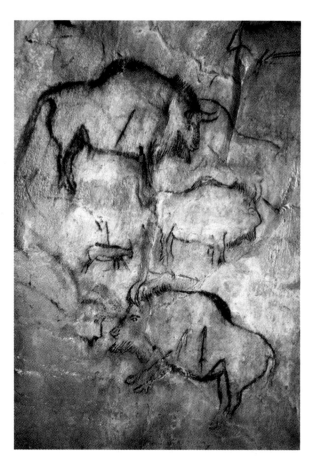

FIGURE 4.13 Bison from the Salon Noir, Niaux, France, AMS radiocarbon-dated to about 11,000 B.C.

the world's earliest artistic tradition (Bahn and Vertut, 1988). Ancient San rock art from southern Africa, some from the Paleolithic, has strong shamanistic associations that have been partially reconstructed from historical records and oral traditions (Clottes et al., 1998; Lewis-Williams, 1981, 1995, 2002) and provide at least some general clues to the kinds of activities that may have been associated with European cave art (see Chapter 6). (This does not, of course, imply that San art can be used to interpret art traditions of 18,000 years ago.)

Engraved portable objects, such as the spear-throwers and harpoons found in Magdalenian caves, may have had a quite different significance, perhaps as a new form of tool for recording information. Alexander Marshack (1972) has carried out detailed microphotographic studies of the portable art and argues that many of the visual forms are ecologically and seasonally related. Rather than concentrating on the naturalistic pictures of animals, he has studied hundreds of nonnaturalistic pieces, with their patterns of lines, notches, dots, and groupings of marks (Figure 4.14). On some pieces, the marks were made with different tools at different times. These pieces, which Marshack named "time-factorial" objects, were used, he believes, as sequential notations of events and phenomena, predecessors of calendars. The Magdalenian and earlier notations were for the engraver alone to read, even if this person explained them to others on occasion. To formulate such a system required thought and theoretical abstractions far more advanced than those hitherto attributed to the hunter-gatherers of this age.

Marshack's ideas are highly controversial. His research has been criticized by Francesco d'Errico, who uses more rigorous methodology, checking his own interpretations against replicas of engraved artifacts produced under controlled conditions. D'Errico believes many engraved notations were an "artificial memory system with a complex code based on the morphology and spatial distribution of the engraved marks" (1995, p. 163).

About 11,000 B.C., the Magdalenians seem to have stopped painting and engraving deep caves. Most art after that appears at cave entrances and in rock shelters, always

FIGURE 4.14 Engraved bone, 21 cm (8.2 inches) long, from La Marche, France, which was intensively studied by Alexander Marshack. The close-up shot shows tiny marks in two groups, each engraved by a different point, with a different type of stroke. Recent research using microscopic and experimental methods has suggested that these marks were a form of early artificial memory system. (© Alexander Marshack, 1972.)

exposed to the light of day. The paintings and engravings were no longer naturalistic, and they vanished altogether about 9000 B.C. By this time, much warmer climatic conditions had brought forest to the open plains, and the large arctic animals depicted in the earlier art were largely extinct. The brilliant efflorescence of Magdalenian culture had been replaced by new adaptations—to forests, rivers, and coasts. By this time, cave and antler art had given way to a complex symbol system, incompletely recorded on flat pebbles (Courand, 1985).

🐾 Human Settlement in Eurasia (35,000 to 15,000 Years Ago)

The vast, undulating plains of western Russia and central Europe as far east as the Ural Mountains were a much less hospitable environment for Stone Age hunter-gatherers than the deep, well-watered valleys to the west (Hoffecker, 2002). There were no convenient caves or rock shelters. For warmth and shelter, the inhabitants of this area had to create artificial dwellings with their own tools and locally available raw materials. It may be no coincidence that few archaeological sites are found on these frigid plains, with their nine-month winters and short summers, until Upper Paleolithic times. The Neanderthals and early Upper Paleolithic populations may have ventured onto the steppe during the warmer summer months. It took some significant technological innovations, providing better cultural adaptations to bitter cold, to allow people to live there year-round. One important invention may have been the perforated bone needle, which enabled people to fabricate tailored layers of clothing, for layered garments provide the best protection against subzero temperatures. Advances in bone and antler technology may also have played a decisive role in arctic adaptation, for they allowed not only more efficient hunting but also the development of such important artifacts as the spear-thrower, a highly effective weapon against large, gregarious animals.

Between about 28,000 and 8000 B.C., a series of Upper Paleolithic hunting-and-gathering societies known to archaeologists as the Eastern Gravettian complex flourished on the plains and the varied terrain of central and eastern Europe (here the Gravettian flourished much later than in western Europe). There were many local groups within this large complex, people adapted to life on frigid, open plains

Eastern Gravettian complex 28,000 to 8000 B.C.

(Hoffecker, 2002; Roebroeks et al., 2000). Many of their campsites contain mammoth bones; in fact, many earlier interpretations of these societies referred to them as "mammoth hunters."

Actually, the Eastern Gravettians exploited a wide range of late Ice Age mammals, ranging in size from bison to rabbits and arctic fox, the latter much prized for its soft fur. They may indeed have killed some mammoth, for such animals provided not only bones for constructing dwellings in treeless environments but also an abundance of meat and hide. But this would have been a memorable occurrence by any standards. Many of the mammoth bones may have come from animals that died of natural causes, or even from mammoth "cemeteries," places where animals perished in large numbers in spring floods, such as are known from Siberia. At the famous Dolní Vestonice and Pavlov sites in the Czech Republic, for example, the nearby landscape is rich in calcite and other minerals that, when licked, provide vital magnesium and calcium for elephants in late spring and summer, at a time when fresh grass is high in potassium. The most common animal bones come from rabbits and other small animals, which were clearly a staple food, as they may have been over much of late Ice Age Europe (Pringle, 1997).

Dolní Vestonice

Dolní Vestonice and Pavlov were occupied again and again between about 25,000 and 23,000 B.C., with campsites overlooking the Dyje River valley and a nearby swamp. Perhaps between 100 and 120 people dwelled at Dolní Vestonice, sometimes in summer, at other times in oval bone-and-timber winter huts with hide roofs, dug partially into the ground (Figure 4.15a). Both sites are remarkable for their numerous burnt clay figures, which were fired in a small, oval-shaped oven inside a winter house, the earliest fired-clay objects in the world by at least 15,000 years. Burnt clay fragments also preserved traces of basketry and twined textiles made from plant fibers that are the earliest known in the world (Figure 4.16) (Adovasio et al., 1996). James Adovasio and his colleagues believe that the inhabitants of both sites used nets to capture large numbers of rabbits and other small game in cooperative hunts that involved men, women, and children. Such hunts yielded so much food that larger, more densely occupied settlements may have been more common than in earlier times (Soffer et al., 1998).

FIGURE 4.15 Late Ice Age houses. (a) An artist's reconstruction of a winter house excavated at Dolní Vestonice, Czech Republic, dating to c. 25,000 B.C. The timber-and-bone structure supported a hide roof. This dwelling contained an oval oven used to bake clay figurines. (b) An artist's impression of two mammoth-bone huts at Mezhirich, Ukraine.

(a)

(b)

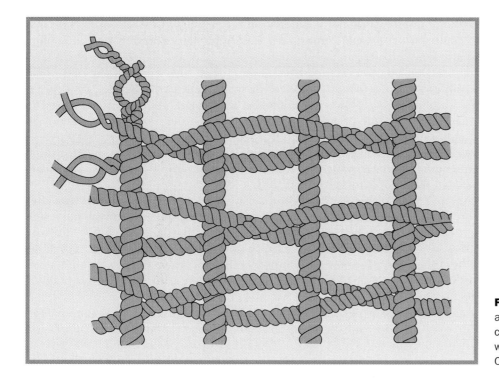

FIGURE 4.16 An impression of a woven fragment preserved on clay: an open diagonal twining with an S twist weft, from Pavlov, Czech Republic.

Groups living in what is now the Czech Republic were highly mobile and habitually visited the Danube region of Austria, southern Poland, and northern Hungary. As the late Ice Age climate grew colder and resources grew scarcer, some of these people moved southward; others followed game herds onto the open steppe of the central Russian plains. This west-to-east population movement took at least 4000 years, with constant abandonment and resettlement of different regions in response to climate and resource changes (Hoffecker, 2002).

Only a few rivers dissect the Russian plains, among them the Don and the Dnieper. It is no coincidence that ancient river terraces were the most common locations for Stone Age hunting settlements. These were often promontories overlooking the river, where the hunters could spy on the movements of the herds of arctic elephant (mammoth), woolly rhinoceros, and wild horse that flourished in the valleys, as well as prey on smaller mammal populations. At the height of the last glaciation, this area was a treeless periglacial landscape, a meadow steppe in warmer periods. It was a very inhospitable environment but one where hunter-gatherer societies flourished for thousands of years.

The earliest Upper Paleolithic sites, probably settlements of anatomically modern people, date to at least 33,000 B.C. (Hoffecker, 2002). The most intensive (Eastern Gravettian) occupation dates to the period between 16,000 and 12,000 B.C., when scattered hunter-gatherer bands lived in what were often spectacular mammoth-bone structures (Soffer, 1985). The Mezhirich site overlooks the Dnieper River southeast of Kiev; it is a 15,000-year-old settlement of five houses, covering an area of some 10,219 sq m (110,000 square feet). Each house was about 4 to 7 m (13 to 22 feet) across and up to 79 m (850 square feet) in area (Figure 4.15b). Foundation walls of massive mammoth bones supported an intricate framework of smaller limb bones, vertebrae, and other parts, sometimes arranged in fine herringbone patterns. Uprights stuck into holes broken through large mammoth bones supported the roof. Elephant hide or sod covered the entire structure. Hearths and work areas were inside the houses, which seem to have been occupied over long periods of time. More hearths, as well as deep storage pits that kept meat refrigerated in the permafrost, were between the houses.

Mezhirich
13,000 B.C.

The Mezhirich dwellings housed about fifty people, each dwelling taking ten men about five or six days to complete, a considerable investment of effort. Since mammoth-bone dwellings found at other locations are less elaborate, it may be that this settlement was of unusual importance. The inhabitants hunted not only mammoth but also many smaller mammals such as rabbits, as well as taking river fish and river birds. Judging by the evidence from several sites, they pursued the occasional mammoth in autumn and winter, reindeer in spring and early summer, fur-bearing animals in winter, and waterfowl in summer. So many mammoth bones were used in house construction that the people must have scavenged them from carcasses on the plains in addition to using their own kills. Russian archaeologists report that seashells from between 640 and 800 km (400 and 500 miles) away were found in the Mezhirich houses, and amber, a stone thought by many prehistoric peoples to have magic qualities, was traded from 160 km (100 miles) away.

Kostenki
22,000 B.C.

The famous Kostenki sites on the Don River were occupied about 2000 years after those to the west, between 22,000 and 21,000 B.C. They contain large hollows filled with bones and other debris. Their plans are so irregular that it is difficult to be sure whether they were dwellings or storage pits. In some cases, several circular structures up to 4.6 m (15 feet) in diameter were built together in a huge depression with a row of hearths down the middle. Bands of considerable size must have congregated in these tented areas.

To the east of the western plains stretches central Asia, a vast area of continental territory that covers not only northern Afghanistan but also the arid Turan Depression and the central Asian highlands. The archaeology of this area is still little known, although research has made rapid strides in recent years (Davis, 1987). There are numerous Mousterian sites dating to the early part of the Weichsel glaciation, as they do in the West, displaying different toolkit variations that probably reflect different seasonal activities. It is not yet known when the transition to the Upper Paleolithic took place, but one hunting camp at Malaia Suja, on the White Iyus River west of Lake Baikal, has been radiocarbon-dated to about 32,500 B.C. (Goebel and Akensenov, 1996). Here people hunted mammoth, horse, reindeer, and other steppe animals, which they also engraved on bone, some of the earliest art in the world. Undoubtedly, however, the human population of this harsh country was very small.

Malaia Suja
32,500 B.C.

Shugnou
18,000 to 13,000 B.C.

The Upper Paleolithic of central Asia is known from a late Ice Age culture that was widespread in caves, rock shelters, and open sites but is still not well known. The Shugnou site, southwest of the city of Samarkand, lies at an altitude of 2000 m (6700 feet), one of the highest Upper Paleolithic sites in the world. Russian archaeologists found five occupation layers in a site above a mountain river, yielding evidence of big-game hunting and of horses, wild oxen, wild sheep, and goats, dating to at least 18,000 to 13,000 B.C. Pollen grains suggest that weather conditions were somewhat cooler and wetter than today. The hunter-gatherer population of central Asia may have been sparse for thousands of years, perhaps because of unfavorable climate conditions, but this is pure conjecture. Population densities rose at the end of the Pleistocene, and human settlement expanded into higher elevations.

Central Asia was subjected to cultural influences from both the flake and the blade traditions of the West and the chopper-chopping-tool traditions of the Far East. Consequently, stone tools here were frequently based on stone cobbles and were simple, highly effective artifacts that rarely achieved the sophistication or artistry of western traditions. The same amalgam of cultural traditions filtered into Siberia in Far East Asia (Larichev et al., 1987).

🐾 Siberia (?33,000 to 13,000 Years Ago)

Remote from Atlantic and Pacific weather patterns, Siberia is dry country with harsh, dry winters and short, hot summers. Treeless plains predominate in the far north and extend to the shores of the Arctic Ocean. Rainfall was so sparse during the Weichsel glaciation that the great ice sheets of the west never formed here. Herds of gregarious mammoths grazed on the tundra and on the edges of the river valleys, where small bands of hunter-gatherers weathered the long winters. The archaeology of this enormous area and of northeast Asia is still little known, despite long-term excavation campaigns in recent years (Dolukhanov et al., 2002; West, 1996). Nonetheless, Siberia and northeast Asia are of vital importance, for they were the staging areas from which the first settlement of the Americas took place, across the Bering Strait.

There is no reliable evidence of human settlement in northeast Siberia before the late Ice Age. Local archaeologists claim that sites contemporary with Malaia Suja lie east of Lake Baikal, including one at Tolbaga said to date to as early as 32,900 B.C., but few details of the site have been published (Larichev et al., 1988). All these settlements contain well-developed blade technology and also artifacts made by using Middle Paleolithic techniques. There is far less variation in tool forms than in later Stone Age cultures in the region.

By 20,000 B.C., two very different cultural traditions were flourishing in Siberia and into northeast Asia. The Mal'ta tradition is known from clusters of sites west of Lake Baikal and the Yenesei River valley, many of them located in places sheltered from the prevailing northerly winds. The Mal'ta site itself, one of semisubterranean houses, covers more than 600 sq m (6458 square feet) and may have been reoccupied many times between 24,000 and 18,000 B.C. Mal'ta was probably a winter base camp of houses framed with large animal bones and covered with a lattice of reindeer antler to support a skin or sod covering. The hunters pursued mammoth, woolly rhinoceros, and reindeer, as well as small animals. The Mal'ta people were expert bone workers who carved female and bird figurines (Figure 4.17).

Mal'ta
24,000 to 18,000 B.C.

The Afontova Gora-Oshurkovo tradition flourished over a much wider area not only in the Yenesei River valley but also over an enormous area of northern Asia, perhaps all the way from the Altai Mountains to the Amur River. The oldest sites, Afontova Gora itself on the Yenesei and Mogochino on the Ob' River, date to between 19,000 and 18,000 B.C. Again, the people hunted periglacial steppe mammals, making large tools fashioned on cobbles, blade artifacts, large cobble scrapers known locally as skreblos, and occasionally small blade artifacts.

Afontova Gora-
Oshurkovo tradition
?19,000 B.C.

There are many general similarities between the Mal'ta and Afontova Gora-Oshurkovo traditions that tend to transcend the local differences between them. Together, they reflect a varied adaptation by *Homo sapiens sapiens* to an enormous area of central Asia and southern Siberia from well west of Lake Baikal to the Pacific Ocean far to the east. Late Ice Age populations in this harsh area were never large and were concentrated for the most part in river valleys and near lakes. In general terms, their lifeway may have resembled that of plains big-game hunters on the steppe-tundra to the west, but it would be a mistake to argue that these Siberian groups originated in western Eurasia. They may have moved north or northeastward onto the open steppe-tundra from more temperate environments, perhaps at about the same time as Cro-Magnons

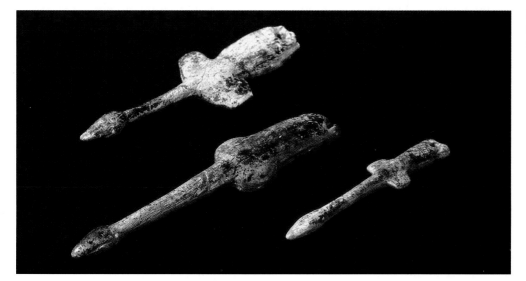

FIGURE 4.17 Ivory figurines from Mal'ta, Siberia.

moved into Europe. Although Neanderthal settlements are known in the mountainous Altai region of central Asia, there are no signs of Middle Paleolithic sites on the steppe-tundra itself. Anatomically modern humans may have been the first to venture north into periglacial regions.

D'uktai and the Settlement of Far Northeast Asia

The first human settlement of periglacial northeast Asia appeared between 38,000 and 28,000 B.C. and was well established just before the late glacial maximum of about 16,000 B.C. The Mal'ta and Afontova Gora-Oshurkovo traditions peter out as one moves north and east into the far frontiers of northeast Asia. The Ver-koy-ansk Mountains are thought to have been a major barrier to late Ice Age human settlement (Hoffecker et al., 1993). The western slopes of the range adjoin the Lena River basin, which we know had been settled by humans by 20,000 to 13,000 B.C. Beyond the Ver-koy-ansk unfolds the vast landscape of extreme northeast Siberia, which ends at the shores of the Bering Strait. During the height of the last glaciation, around 20,000 years ago, this was an extremely cold and windy desert environment, extremely forbidding for any form of human settlement until sporadic warming began after 18,000 B.P. But, at some point, this harsh and unforgiving region of periglacial steppe-tundra, occasional large river valleys, and icebound coasts was the homeland of the first Stone Age people to cross into the Americas. They reached the uninhabited New World by traversing a low-lying land bridge that still connected Siberia and Alaska several thousand years after the end of the Ice Age.

Archaeologist Yuri Mochanov (1978) has identified a late Ice Age culture that once flourished in the Middle Aldan Valley, far north and east of Lake Baikal. He excavated

D'uktai
?16,000 B.C.

D'uktai Cave, close to the river floodplain. There he found mammoth and musk-ox remains associated with large stone choppers, bifacially flaked stone points, burins, and small blade artifacts. The cave deposits had been much disturbed by freezing, thawing, and other natural phenomena, but Mochanov was able to date the occupation levels to between 16,000 and 10,000 B.C. He soon found more D'uktai-like sites on the banks of the Aldan, sites that contained not only points and choppers but also highly distinctive small blades and the characteristic wedge-shaped cores from which they had been formed (see Figure 4.18).

〰 Bifaces, Microblades, and the First Americans

Clearly, the D'uktai tradition owes little to the well-defined big-game-hunting plains traditions of central and western Eurasia. It is marked by small blades, also by bifaces and some stone spear points. Since this is the only known late Ice Age culture from extreme northeast Asia, it may be one of the cultural traditions from which the culture of the first Americans came. Some of the D'uktai stone points recall those made by Clovis people in the New World, but without the distinctive "flute," a longitudinal thinning flake at the base of the head (see Chapter 5). However, there are no signs of small blades in the earliest human cultures of the Americas. These distinctive artifacts do appear, though, later, in Alaska, by about 9000 B.C.

The most important artifacts used by the first Americans were stone-tipped spears and stone knives made from flakes of fine-grained stone struck off large cores, often themselves fashioned into bifaces so they could be carried around from one camp to the next. Such artifacts must also have been important on the steppe-tundra of northeast Asia long before small blades came into use. Unfortunately, we know so little of D'uktai that we can only guess that it may represent more than one cultural tradition, one using bifaces and stone-tipped spears—a technology that spread early into the Americas—and perhaps a later version that relied more heavily on small blades, often called **microblades.**

The origins of microblade technology are somewhat better documented. If there is one significant trend in human stoneworking technology during the late Ice Age, after 23,000 B.C., it is a progressive elaboration and diminution of stone tools. This trend is well documented in Africa, Europe, and southern Asia, and in the Far East as well. Chinese archaeologists Tang Chun and Gai Pei (1986) believe that a primitive microblade tradition emerged in Asia quite soon after *Homo sapiens sapiens* appeared in the region. In time, microblade technologies were to dominate stone technology throughout northern China, Korea, Japan, and far to the northeast in Siberia and possibly extreme northwestern America as well.

Microblades are diminutive blades that were struck in the thousands off carefully prepared conical or wedge-shaped cores (Figure 4.18). By their very size, microblades were designed to be mounted in antler, bone, or wooden handles to serve as spear barbs, arrow points, or small knife or scraper blades. Microblade technology first appeared in northern China about 28,000 B.C. and soon spread over an enormous area, even into tropical environments far to the south (Chun and Pei, 1986). They were widely used in China by 18,000 B.C., in Japan by about the same time (Reynolds and Barnes, 1984), and at the Studenoe-2 site southeast of Lake Baikal in Siberia by 15,800 B.C. (Goebel et al., 2000). However, no human occupation whatsoever is yet known from the Kamchatka Peninsula or extreme northeast Siberia that dates to earlier than about 13,000 B.C. (Goebel, 2000; Kuzmin and Tankersley, 1996).

Studenoe-2
15,800 B.C.

If, in fact, no Stone Age peoples ever settled in the far northeast adjacent to what is now the Bering Strait before about 13,000 B.C., it was clearly impossible for anyone to have crossed into the Americas earlier than that date (Figure 4.18).

?13,000 B.C.

We can propose a scenario for what occurred. Perhaps microblade technology first developed in temperate Asia, in areas like the Gobi Desert and Mongolia, where people hunted over enormous areas. Here, they needed a stone technology that was

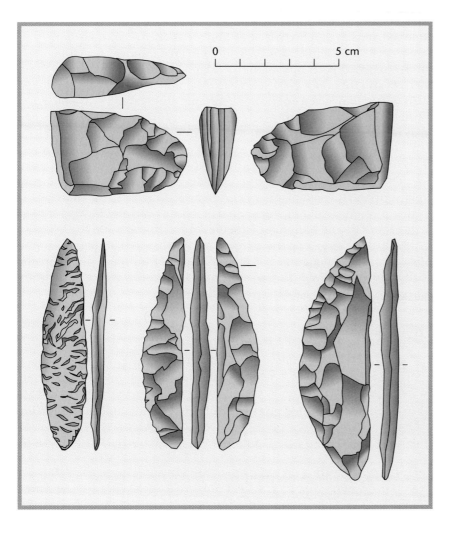

FIGURE 4.18 Artifacts of the D'uktai tradition. Top, four views of a wedge-shaped core, used to make tiny blades. Bottom, two bifacially flaked projectile points. The wedge-shaped core is a characteristic artifact found on both sides of the Bering Strait in contexts of about 8000 B.C. It is, of course, a by-product of the production of fine microblades.

economical, easy to carry and manufacture, and yet capable of arming spears. And perhaps, very late in the Ice Age, they needed bows and arrows with sharp, lethal points for taking game on the run in open country. In time, the same technology spread north and east into the harsh periglacial landscapes of Siberia, where small-scale and highly portable toolkits were highly adaptive, especially when used against such migratory periglacial animals as the reindeer. In time, small groups of microblade-using people may have carried the same technology across the dry land of the Bering Strait into Alaska, perhaps after simpler biface and spear point toolkits had spread into the Americas. But, if the present field evidence is correct, there were no such population movements before about 13,000 B.C., some time after post–Ice Age warming began.

This scenario receives some support from the dental research of Christy Turner (1984). He has shown that the characteristic tooth features of Native Americans include specialized attributes, such as shovel-shaped incisors, that are mirrored in northern Chinese skeletons dating to about 18,000 B.C. He calls this group of features *sinodonty,* features that are never found on European Stone Age teeth. Turner believes that the first Americans originated in northern China, reaching their new homeland through eastern Mongolia and northeast Siberia. With that momentous development, *H. sapiens sapiens* eventually reached the Americas.

Summary

Chapter 4 documents the spread of *Homo sapiens sapiens* into Europe and Eurasia from Africa and Southwest Asia after 43,000 B.C., during the late Ice Age. By this time, there was increasing specialization and flexibility in hunting and foraging, as anatomically modern humans replaced Neanderthal groups by 33,000 B.C. The sheer diversity of the late Ice Age environment gave the Cro-Magnon people of western Europe great flexibility. They developed more complex societies and developed elaborate bone and antler technology, as well as a complex symbolic life reflected in intricate artistic traditions. These cultures reached their apogee in the Magdalenian culture, which flourished after 16,000 B.C. and for about 5000 years. Cro-Magnon art traditions developed before 30,000 years ago and involved engraving, painting, and sculpture, as well as the adornment of portable objects. The motives behind the art are much debated. Some of the cave art may be connected with shamanistic activity and initiation ceremonies.

The Eastern Gravettian cultural complex of eastern Europe and Eurasia was contemporary with Cro-Magnon societies in the west and was based on the exploitation of open plains and steppe. The many groups within this complex spread slowly eastward from the Czech Republic onto the Russian plains, relying heavily on game of all kinds.

Far to the northeast, western Siberia was settled at least as early as 28,000 B.C., but the extreme northeast was devoid of human settlement until the very late Ice Age, perhaps as late as 13,000 B.C. Most experts agree that northeastern Siberia was the stepping-off point for the first settlement of the Americas. From there, humans first crossed the Bering land bridge into Alaska, either during the late Ice Age or when global warming began after 15,000 B.C.

Key Terms

Blade technology A distinctive technology that uses a punch to strike off flakes from a carefully prepared, cylindrical core. The blades are then turned into a wide variety of specialized tools.

Burin A chisel-like blade tool used for grooving antler and bone and for engraving and woodworking.

Curation Careful use of toolmaking stone and other special materials that are in short supply.

Microblade Greek: *micros,* "small." A diminutive version of the blade used for manufacturing small barbs and scraping tools.

Guide to Further Reading 〰〰

Bahn, Paul, and J. Vertut. 1988. *Images of the Ice Age*. New York: Viking.
  A superb general account of Paleolithic art, illustrated with magnificent photographs. Excellent on the motives behind the art.

Chauvet, Jean-Marie, Eliette Brunel Deschamps, and Christian Hillaire. 1996. *Dawn of Art: The Chauvet Cave*. New York: Harry Abrams.
  An account of the discovery of the Grotte de Chauvet by the people who found it, and a preliminary assessment of its date and significance. Superb color illustrations.

Gamble, Clive. 1993. *Timewalkers: The Prehistory of Global Colonization*. Stroud, England: Alan Sutton.
  Covers much of the ground in this chapter in more detail.

_____. 1999. *The Paleolithic Societies of Europe*. Cambridge: Cambridge University Press.
  Provocative essay on the European Stone Age. Essential for all serious students of the subject.

Hoffecker, John F. 2002. *Desolate Landscapes*. New Brunswick, NJ: Rutgers University Press.
  An up-to-date summary of what is known about the late Ice Age societies of Eurasia.

Mithen, Steven. 1996. *The Prehistory of the Mind*. London and New York: Thames & Hudson.
  This groundbreaking synthesis is essential reading for the material in this chapter.

Soffer, Olga. 1985. *The Upper Paleolithic of the Central Russian Plains*. New York: Academic Press.
  An account of Mezhirich and other Upper Paleolithic sites. An exemplary essay on the Stone Age of Ukraine.

White, Randall. 1986. *Dark Caves, Bright Images*. New York: American Museum of Natural History.
  Up-to-date, well-illustrated, and readable account of Cro-Magnons and their culture. Recommended for the general reader.

c h a p t e r

5

THE FIRST AMERICANS

?14,000 B.C. TO MODERN TIMES

An artist's impression of a bison drive at Head-Smashed-In, Alberta, Canada.

One fine spring morning in 1908, a black cowboy named George McJunkin was riding slowly along the edge of a dry gully near Folsom, New Mexico. He was casting over the range in search of stray cattle. Suddenly, he saw some sun-bleached bones protruding from the side of the arroyo. He pried some out with his knife. As he did so, a sharp stone fragment came loose in his hands, a stone spear point like the ones he had seen lying on the surface elsewhere on the ranch. McJunkin took his finds back to the ranch house, where they lay around for 17 years.

Years later, in 1925, someone was curious enough to send the bones to Jesse Figgins, the director of the Colorado Museum of Natural History. Figgins realized they were from an extinct form of plains bison, apparently from the same level as the stone point. The following year, he dug into the arroyo, finding more stone tools and bison bones. He realized he had the proof that humans had lived in North America at the same time as long-extinct animals. Soon, experts came to Folsom and were convinced that Figgins had finally found proof of the considerable antiquity of humankind in the Americas.

The controversies over the first Americans raged long before the Folsom excavations, and they are still among the most vigorous of all debates in archaeology. How long ago did humans set foot in the Americas? What manner of people were they? By what route did they reach the New World? These questions have preoccupied scientists since soon after Columbus landed in the West Indies. This chapter discusses these controversies and describes the diverse later hunter-gatherer societies of the Americas.

The First Settlement of the Americas

Almost all archaeologists agree that the first inhabitants of the Americas set foot in the New World by way of the Bering land bridge, at a time when the strait of that name was dry land (Figure 5.1). However, for all the agreement about the Siberian route, intense controversies surround the beginnings of human settlement in the Americas (Adovasio, 2002; Dillehay, 2000; Dillehay and Meltzer, 1991) (see Table 5.1). These controversies revolve around three fundamental questions:

- How long ago did humans first settle in the Americas?
- What toolkit did they bring with them, and what was their lifeway?
- What was the ultimate ancestry of the first Native Americans?

FIGURE 5.1 Ancient hunter-gatherers in the Americas. Sites mentioned in the text are indicated. (For the Bering land bridge, see Figure 5.2.)

Two competing hypotheses account for first settlement, each with passionate advocates:

- One (minority) school of thought holds that the Americas were colonized by some time during the Wisconsin glaciation, perhaps as early as 40,000 B.C. or even earlier.

- A second hypothesis argues that the first Americans crossed into the New World considerably later, perhaps about 20,000 years ago, during the late Ice Age. Some scholars of this school suspect that settlement took hold even later than this, at the very end of the Wisconsin glaciation, perhaps as recently as about 13,000 B.C. or even later, and penetrated south of the Upper Pleistocene ice sheets as they retreated.

Intense controversy surrounds not only the specific archaeological evidence for the first settlement but also the criteria that can be used to establish it. However, most archaeologists agree that securely radiocarbon-dated, well-stratified cultural remains of undoubted human manufacture are the only acceptable evidence. So far, data whose quality is universally acceptable have eluded even persistent search, leaving one of the major mysteries of world prehistory still unsolved. In recent years, a flood of new genetic and linguistic information has added to the controversy.

TABLE 5.1

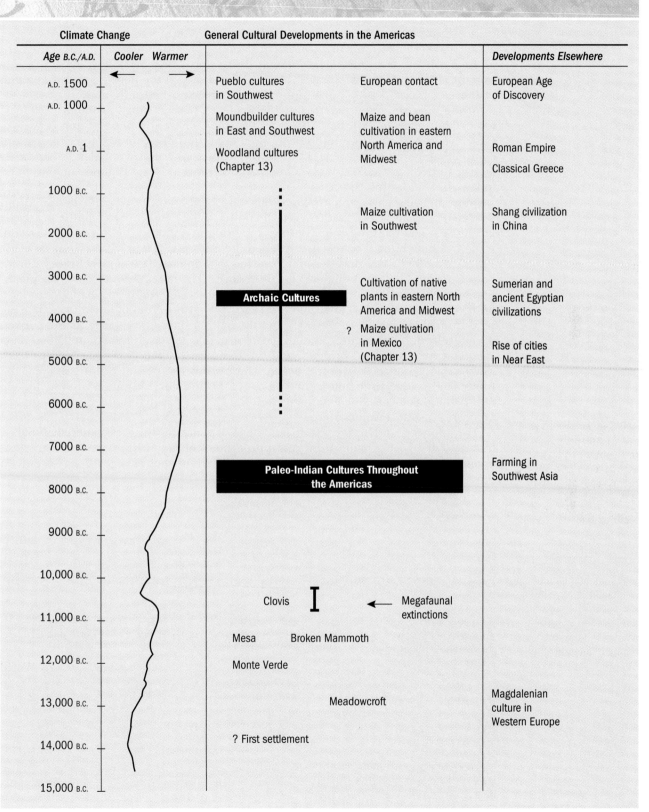

Climate Change			General Cultural Developments in the Americas			Developments Elsewhere
Age B.C./A.D.	Cooler	Warmer				
A.D. 1500	←	→	Pueblo cultures in Southwest	European contact		European Age of Discovery
A.D. 1000			Moundbuilder cultures in East and Southwest	Maize and bean cultivation in eastern North America and Midwest		
A.D. 1			Woodland cultures (Chapter 13)			Roman Empire
						Classical Greece
1000 B.C.						
				Maize cultivation in Southwest		Shang civilization in China
2000 B.C.						
3000 B.C.				Cultivation of native plants in eastern North America and Midwest		Sumerian and ancient Egyptian civilizations
			Archaic Cultures			
4000 B.C.				? Maize cultivation in Mexico (Chapter 13)		
5000 B.C.						Rise of cities in Near East
6000 B.C.						
7000 B.C.						
			Paleo-Indian Cultures Throughout the Americas			Farming in Southwest Asia
8000 B.C.						
9000 B.C.						
10,000 B.C.						
			Clovis	← Megafaunal extinctions		
11,000 B.C.						
			Mesa Broken Mammoth			
12,000 B.C.			Monte Verde			
13,000 B.C.				Meadowcroft		Magdalenian culture in Western Europe
			? First settlement			
14,000 B.C.						
15,000 B.C.						

〽 Ice Sheets and the Bering Land Bridge

As we saw in Chapter 4, human settlement in extreme northeastern Siberia and far northeast Asia is documented as early as 13,000 B.C. Judging from sites in western and central Europe, the human settlement of extreme arctic environments expanded after about 16,000 B.C., with the first consistent warming, so a somewhat later first settlement of the harsh and unforgiving extreme northeast would be logical. If we accept the notion that *Homo sapiens sapiens* was living near the shores of the Bering Strait after about 13,000 B.C., how did people cross into Alaska, only a short distance away?

At the time we are considering, world sea levels were as much as 100 m (330 feet) lower than today—so low that a land bridge stood where the Bering Strait now separates Asia and Alaska. (Sea levels drop when quantities of ocean water are frozen into continental ice sheets.) The strait formed part of a now almost submerged landmass known to geologists as Beringia. Only parts of west and east Beringia are dry land today—in Siberia and Alaska.

Some 18,000 years ago, central Beringia was an exposed coastal plain, denuded and dissected by many rivers, that covered the floors of the Chukchi Sea and the northeast Bering Sea. This was the famous Bering land bridge, commonly believed to be the land route by which human beings first reached the Americas (Figure 5.2) (Hopkins et al., 1982; West, 1996). The Bering land bridge has a complicated geological history, known both from land-based studies and deep-sea cores. The cores show that the last glaciation began about 100,000 years ago, with a gradual cooling trend that exposed the land bridge from about 75,000 to 45,000 years ago. A lengthy period of less cold climate ensued from about 40,000 to 25,000, when the land bridge was no more than a narrow, periodically flooded isthmus. Bitter cold returned as sea levels fell about 25,000 years ago. This time, the land bridge lasted until around 11,000 years ago, perhaps later, when rapid postglacial warming began. During this last period of intense cold, the windy land bridge stretched from Asia to Alaska and covered much of the Chukchi Sea. Its southern coastline extended from the Gulf of Anadyr in Siberia to the Alaska Peninsula in North America.

The low-lying land bridge was no landscape of gently waving grass, where half-naked hunters pursued big game from Asia into a new continent. Beringia was a treeless, arctic land, covered with a patchwork of very different types of vegetation. Recently, a

FIGURE 5.2 The Bering land bridge at the last glacial maximum, as reconstructed by the latest research. The land bridge is thought to have been the major route by which humans first colonized Alaska and the Americas, during or immediately after the late Ice Age.

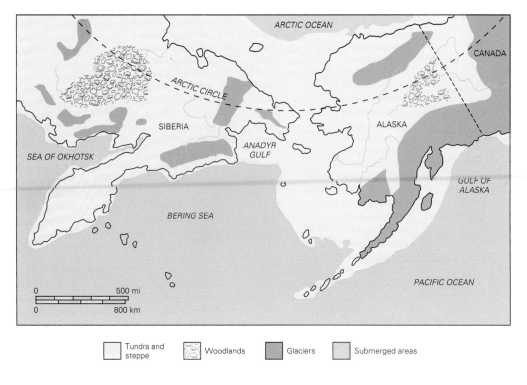

1000-sq-km (400-square-mile) patch of the Beringian landscape of 17,000 years ago has come to light under a thick volcanic ash. The plant samples include grasses, sedges, mosses, and many other varieties in a nearly continuous ground cover. But the root mat was thin, with no soil formation, meaning that the plant cover enjoyed little long-term stability (Geotcheus et al., 1994). The land bridge was a place of violent climatic extremes and strong winter winds, which may have kept animal and human population densities low. John Hoffecker and others (1993) have gone so far as to argue that a shortage of firewood during the late Ice Age would have inhibited human settlement until warmer temperatures enabled trees to be established in Beringia.

The land bridge could have supported a diversity of large and small herbivores, provided it had sufficient variety, and quantity, of plant communities to do so. It never teemed with game animals, for they were probably scattered throughout the landscape, concentrated at dozens of special sites, in lowland meadows and near rivers. They would have succeeded one another, utilizing patches of the bare, treeless environment in an endless succession of grazing patterns that persisted as long as the continental ecosystem of the land bridge remained intact.

Hardly surprisingly, no archaeological remains have yet come from the floor of the Bering Strait, so we can only assume that there was once a sparse human population dwelling on the land bridge, preying on the large and small animals that lived there. There may have been coastal settlements on the southern shores, too, settlements now flooded by rising sea levels, where people might have taken fish and sea mammals. However, without effective canoe technology, they would have been severely limited in their ability to take maritime resources. In all likelihood, the first Beringians were terrestrial and, perhaps, sea mammal hunters, practicing a lifeway that had flourished for thousands of years on the steppe-tundra.

When human beings first set foot on the land bridge remains a complete mystery, but, given the present dates for D'uktai sites in Siberia, it may have been after 18,000 radiocarbon years ago. And at some point afterwards, some of these people foraged their way across to higher ground in the east and ultimately into the Americas. At present, it is not possible to give an even slightly precise date for this crossing. Alternatively, it may have been a response to the rapid flooding of the land bridge after 14,000 years ago, although it was at least partially in existence until around 11,000 years ago.

Could the first Americans have made their way along the shores of the land bridge by boat? We know that people colonized the remote landmass of Australia before 35,000 B.C. and that they could have done so only by crossing over some 88.5 km (55 miles) of open water even at the height of the glaciation, when sea levels were much lower than today (see Chapter 6). These were more benign tropical waters, where such hazards as floating ice, strong arctic winds, and the ever-present danger of hypothermia were unknown. The risks in the far north were much greater. Even in summer, fogs and rough seas make the strait a chancy place, and to cross winter pack ice is to invite disaster.

Unfortunately, we have no means of knowing whether early northeast Asians had skin boats, or even kayaks, for their long-abandoned settlements lie under modern sea levels. We do know that the predominant dietary source for Stone Age hunters over an enormous area of Europe and Asia was land mammals of all sizes, with apparently much less concentration on seasonal vegetable foods, fish, and marine mammals. To venture onto the Bering land bridge required no new skills, merely the same foraging expertise that characterized generations of Ice Age hunters. That the first crossing into Alaska was by land rather than by boat seems likely, simply on deductive grounds. It may have been only later that arctic peoples adapted to postglacial coasts and crossed freely from Asia to Alaska, maintaining social and cultural ties on both sides of the Bering Strait.

ⱳ The First Settlement of Alaska

Finding human occupation in Alaska is, as Richard Morlan (1983) says, rather "like looking for a needle in a haystack (and a frozen one at that)." The first Alaskans are still a very shadowy entity, known only from a few stratified locations, but they appear to date to just after 10,000 B.C. (Bever, 2001).

About 20,000 years ago, glaciers covered the Alaska Range and the Alaska Peninsula, as well as the Brooks Range, but much of the land immediately east of the Bering Strait was dry and ice-free. Some archaeologists believe these ice-free areas of Alaska were uninhabitable during the late Wisconsin glacial period. Others have considered Alaska little more than a passageway, a "natural highway" to more temperate latitudes. In fact, a sparse population spread over this vast arctic landscape, adapted to it in many ways, and evolved distinctive cultures over very long periods of time indeed. Unfortunately, the archaeological potential of Alaska and the Yukon has hardly been tapped. The level of speculation about first settlement vastly exceeds the amount of archaeological data. Only a handful of sites gives us clues (see a summary in Reanier, 1995).

Broken Mammoth
11,700 B.C.

The Tenana Valley, 97 km (60 miles) southeast of Fairbanks, has yielded a series of temporary encampments on well-drained ridges overlooking marshy lowlands where game would have grazed in summer (see the summaries in West, 1996). The Broken Mammoth, Mead, and Swan Point sites contain stratified occupation layers with stone tools and animal bones. AMS dates from the three locations place the earliest occupation to about 11,700 B.C. The Swan Point levels contain unmistakable microblades as well as swan bones, which means that some form of terrestrial flyway between the heart of North America and Alaska existed at this time—an argument for the existence of some form of ice-free corridor with ample water and marshes at the time.

Dry Creek I
11,500 B.C.

To the north, the Nenana River valley in the northern foothills of the Alaska Range contains two radiocarbon-dated levels. The earliest, Dry Creek I, dates to about 11,500 B.C. and contains some cobble and flake tools, as well as broken blades, thin bifacial knives, and points. Roger Powers compares the artifacts to tools from the Kukhtyi III site in eastern Siberia, a site belonging within the D'uktai tradition (Powers and Hamilton, 1978). Dry Creek II dates to about 8700 B.C., and this level contains microblades and other artifacts associated with such technology.

Walker Road
11,400 to 11,100 B.C.

Walker Road, about 16 km (10 miles) north of Dry Creek in the Nenana River Valley, has been AMS-dated to between 11,400 and 11,100 B.C. Walker Road's cultural occupation, stratigraphic position, and age are similar to those of Dry Creek I. Two concentrations of stone tools, including small bifacial points and scrapers but no microblades, cluster around small hearths and represent a single Nenana occupation. Broken Mammoth, Dry Creek, and Walker Road belong within a generalized, and as yet poorly defined, "Northern Paleo-Indian traditions," which is thought of as a northern equivalent of the Paleo-Indian traditions like Clovis to the south, described later in this chapter.

If one were to use a global terminology, the earliest Alaskan archaeological sites would belong within the Upper Palaeolithic, a term used to describe late Ice Age cultures and technology over a broad area of Europe and Eurasia. Under this argument, the Clovis Paleo-Indian tradition of North America, with its links to projectile point–using groups in Alaska of 11,500 B.C., also belongs in the Upper Paleolithic, thereby confirming the Siberian origin of the earliest Native Americans (West, 1996).

Alaskan archaeologists have grappled with the problem of classifying the little-known Northern Paleo-Indian cultures, although they all agree that they may form part of a highly varied cultural tradition that reflects adaptations to a complex mosaic of local environments at the end of the Ice Age. The same hunting and foraging cultures may have been the ancestors of the first human societies to flourish south of the ice sheets that mantled northern North America during the Wisconsin glaciation.

Many experts favor a relatively late settlement of the Americas, one that coincided with the general global warming between 15,000 and 10,000 B.C. that submerged the Bering land bridge. As far as can be established, the predominant lifeway in the northern latitudes of Eurasia and northeast Asia during the last glacial climax was based on large- and small-game hunting (Gamble, 1993). That this lifeway was pursued in Beringia seems unquestionable. Once the ice sheets retreated, however, many Ice Age game species became extinct, and human bands had to adapt to a far more diverse tundra and birch forest environment (Dumond and Bland, 1995). This environmental diversity is reflected in considerable toolkit variation within early Alaskan settlements.

A possible scenario for first settlement, then, has tiny groups of hunter-gatherers crossing into Alaska either during the very late Ice Age or as climatic conditions improved dramatically—if the Siberian evidence is correct after about 13,000 B.C. The crossing was not a single population movement but, rather, dozens of such migrations over many centuries. Some of these people, perhaps numbering only in the dozens, were the first to move southward either by land or sea into the temperate latitudes that lay beyond the great ice sheets covering much of Canada and the Rocky Mountains.

There remains one fundamental question: Why did humans settle in the New World at all? Was it an inner urge that caused the first Americans to endure the harsh climate of the Bering land bridge? Or was there some more prosaic reason?

Two great population dispersals occurred during prehistory, the first when *Homo erectus* radiated from the tropics nearly 2 million years ago. The second took place after the evolution of *H. sapiens sapiens,* when the first human populations crossed from the Old World into the New and when Australia was inhabited for the first time. The exact dates of this later dispersal are still highly uncertain, but it seems to have occurred soon after modern peoples appeared. The explanation for these sudden radiations seems to lie mostly in the fact that humans tended to behave as other animals did. Rather than responding to an inborn restlessness, the first Americans were probably behaving in the same way as other animal predators. They spent their days tracking the game herds, and perhaps sea mammals, that formed an important part of their subsistence. When Siberian game herds moved onto the Bering land bridge toward the end of the last glaciation, their human predators followed. The higher ground to the east—Alaska—formed part of the same hunting grounds.

🐾 Biological and Linguistic Evidence for the First Americans

For more than a century, anthropologists have pointed to biological similarities between Siberians and North American Indians. Christy Turner (1984) of Arizona State University has studied the changing physical characteristics of Native American teeth, especially their crowns and roots, and has compared them with those of Old World populations. These dental features are more stable than most evolutionary traits, with a high genetic component that minimizes the effects of environmental differences, sexual dimorphism, and age variations. After examining more than 4000 individuals, ancient and modern, Turner has developed a series of hypotheses, based on dental morphology, about the first settlement of the Americas (Figure 5.3).

Turner points out that ancient Americans display many fewer variations in their dental morphology than do eastern Asians. He calls these characteristics sinodonty, a pattern of dental features that includes incisor shoveling, single-rooted upper first premolars, triple-rooted lower first molars, and other attributes. Sinodonty occurs only in northern Asia and the Americas. Turner's earliest evidence for sinodonty comes from northern China in about 18,000 B.C., but he believes that it emerged much earlier, perhaps as early as 40,000 years ago. European Upper Paleolithic skeletons do not display sinodonty. Turner believes that the sinodont northern Chinese may have evolved from a primeval Southeast Asian *Homo sapiens* population, whom they resemble more closely than they do northeastern Asians and American Indians.

Using statistics to study evolutionary divergence, Turner has estimated the approximate dates at which sinodont populations split off from ancestral Chinese groups. He hypothesizes that the first settlement of the Americas resulted from a population movement through eastern Siberia and across the now-submerged continental shelf around 12,000 B.C. Two subsequent population movements brought the present-day Athabaskan and Eskimo-Aleut populations into the Americas a few thousand years later. Neither of these groups penetrated deep into the continent.

Turner's dental work gains support from both genetic and linguistic researches (M. Crawford, 2001; Renfrew, 2000). As we saw in Chapter 3, mitochondrial DNA has proved a useful tool for calibrating mutation rates and studying human genealogies, because it is inherited through the female line and accumulates mutation rates much faster than nuclear DNA. Mitochondria trace modern human ancestry back to tropical Africa at least 100,000 years ago, while no less than five mitochondrial DNA

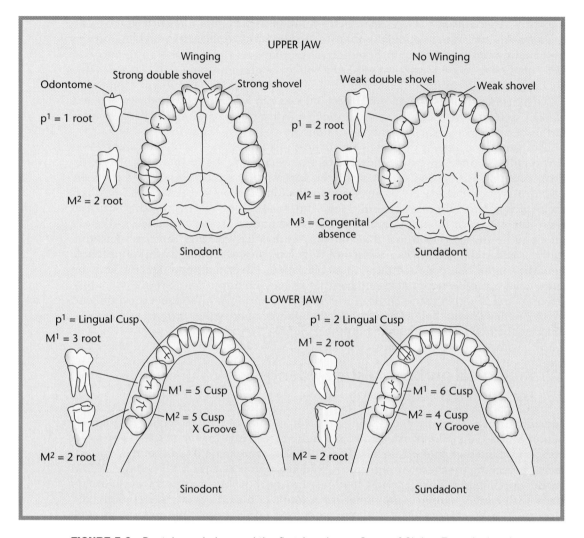

FIGURE 5.3 Dental morphology and the first Americans. Some of Christy Turner's theories about the peopling of the Americas are based on differences between the teeth of the so-called "sinodonts" (northern Asians and all Native Americans) and "sundadonts" (eastern Asians). Sinodonts display, among other features, strong incisor shoveling (scooping out on one or both surfaces of the tooth), single-rooted upper first premolars, and triple-rooted lower first molars.

lineages are shared by ancient and modern Native American populations in North and South America. The molecular biologists believe that all Native Americans are descended ultimately from a single, somewhat diverse group of Asians, from eastern Siberia and Beringia (for a survey, see Torroni, 2000). But the date for this genetic migration is not established accurately, because different researchers have assumed different mutation rates. Estimates range from 40,000 to 20,000 years, with little agreement between the experts.

Back in 1956, the Stanford linguist Joseph Greenberg proposed that most North American and all South American languages were part of a single, large "Amerind" family. Aleut-Eskimo and Na-Dene were quite separate linguistic groups, making a total of three for the whole of the Americas. Greenberg then spent years compiling a vast data base on the vocabulary and grammar of the 140 families of American Indian languages, which confirmed his belief that there were three linguistic groups that corresponded to migrations into the Americas. Greenberg estimated that his Amerind group arrived before 9000 B.C., Na-Denes around 7000 B.C., and that Aleuts and Eskimos diverged about 2000 B.C. (Greenberg, 1987). Greenberg's large grouping of many languages into an Amerind family has been severely criticized by other linguists (see the surveys in Golla, 2000, and Kaufman and Golla, 2000). Despite this drumbeat of criticism, some geneticists claim that the genetic evidence agrees well with Greenberg's tripartite subdivision of Native American languages. The controversy is unresolved.

〰 The Earliest Sites South of the Ice Sheets

Exactly the same problem—lack of sites—arises when we look for archaeological evidence of early settlement south of the great ice sheets. Decades of ardent search have produced only a handful of sites that may date to earlier than 13,000 B.C. (Adovasio, 2002; Dillehay, 2000).

The lack of evidence is striking, to the point where many claims are based on emotionalism and specious argument from minimal data. There are numerous claims for early North American settlement based on poorly dated scatters of projectile heads and flaked tools from deep caves and open sites in many parts of the United States. Many of these claims have been disproved by later investigation, through improved dating methods or more sophisticated artifact analysis techniques. Intense debate surrounds both the dating of first settlement and the routes by which it occurred.

Settlement Routes: Ice-Free Corridors and Seacoasts

If tiny bands of hunter-gatherers penetrated the plains of central Beringia during the late Wisconsin glaciation, how, then, did they reach the heart of the Americas? Again, the first settlement is fraught with controversies about hypothetical routes and the boundaries of ice sheets.

North America was very different during the Wisconsin glaciation. We know from studies of deep-sea cores that the Wisconsin began some 117,000 years ago, with an inexorable cooling of world temperatures. Great ice sheets covered much of northern North America during the early Wisconsin, until about 60,000 years ago. Between about 60,000 and 25,000 years ago, there was a prolonged period of glacial retreat, and sea levels rose. With the possible exception of a much-reduced ice sheet around Hudson Bay, most of North America was freed of glacial barriers. For these 35,000 years, any (hypothetical) human settlers would have encountered environments not very different from modern tundra and boreal forest.

The late Wisconsin glaciation, the earliest time period when human settlement seems possible, began about 23,000 B.C. The Laurentide glaciers, centered on Labrador and in the Keewatin areas of Canada, expanded south, west, and east, eventually fusing into a huge frozen wilderness. At its maximum, in about 16,000 B.C., the Laurentide ice sheet extended from the Atlantic seaboard across the Great Lakes region into southeast Alberta. The mountain ranges of southern Alaska and British Columbia were heavily glaciated at the time, forming the Cordilleran glacier complex in the west. The Cordilleran extended about 48 km (30 miles) south of Seattle as recently as 12,500 B.C., apparently reaching its maximum extent after the Laurentide.

Clearly, these great late Wisconsin ice barriers would have inhibited travel between Beringia and the southern latitudes of the New World. Did they stop human settlement altogether? In the 1950s, Canadian geologists reported that the Cordilleran ice flowed down the eastern flanks of the Rockies but apparently did not join the Laurentide ice sheet. The idea of an ice-free corridor soon took hold of archaeologists' imaginations. "Doubtless it was a formidable place," wrote Thomas Canby of the National Geographic Society, "an ice-walled valley of frigid winds, fierce snows, and clinging fogs . . . yet grazing animals would have entered, and behind them would have come a rivulet of human hunters" (1979, p. 221). The picture is a compelling one—but was it reality?

The ice-free corridor has been mapped more thoroughly in recent years, to the point where we can be sure it was no superhighway for Stone Age hunters. In some places, the ice sheets merged. In others, especially in the far north and the south, there was a corridor, but it twisted and turned through the roughest of terrain, country restricted by chill meltwater lakes, often with biologically sterile shores. At best, the late Wisconsin ice-free corridor was a barren and impoverished landscape. Even if it were passable, there is a good chance that there was no incentive to cross it between about 23,000 and 13,000 B.C., for much better food resources lay in Beringia. In any case, we lack evidence that human settlers had made Beringia their homeland earlier than 13,000 B.C. If an interior route was used, chances are that it was traversed during a time of glacial retreat, sometime after 13,000 B.C., when the Laurentide glaciers shrank rapidly.

If the ice-free corridor was a barrier to human settlement, could people have passed down ice-free coastal areas along the Alaskan and British Columbian coasts into temperate regions (Erlandson, 2001)? Perhaps the late Wisconsin northwest coasts were relatively warmer and more productive than other areas, to the extent that they might have sustained human life. Unfortunately, however, we do not know whether these areas were accessible from mainland Beringia, or indeed whether there were late Wisconsin populations on the land bridge at all. If such people did exist, their sites are buried deep beneath modern sea levels. The earliest documented coastal settlement in south Alaska occurs around 8000 B.C., but is estimated to have begun perhaps 2000 years earlier (Ames and Maschner, 1999). Many archaeologists believe that much earlier coastal settlement is unlikely, on the (perhaps dangerous) assumption that everything we know about the earliest settlers suggests they were terrestrial hunters and gatherers, with a lifeway adapted in part to the pursuit of large Ice Age mammals.

A number of sites throughout the Americas have been claimed as evidence for late Wisconsin settlement, mainly caves and rock shelters (Adovasio, 2002). The most important are worth individual review.

Late Wisconsin Settlement in North America?

Meadowcroft
A.D. 1300 to
?14,000 B.C.

Meadowcroft Rock Shelter lies 48 km (30 miles) southwest of Pittsburgh, Pennsylvania, a sheltered location close to permanent water supplies. James Adovasio excavated and dated the 11 levels of the shelter with more than 70 radiocarbon dates. They show that it was occupied from about A.D. 1300 back to at least 10,000 and perhaps to 14,000 B.C. (Adovasio et al., 1981, 1998).

Controversy swirls around the lowest levels of the rock shelter, which were claimed to date to as early as 17,600 B.C. The earliest date of human occupation at Meadowcroft has now been estimated as being between 2000 and 3000 years before 9500 B.C., that is, perhaps as early as 12,500 B.C. (Adovasio et al., 1998). But by no means does everyone agree with this estimate. Recent discoveries of mammoth kills in Florida and Virginia, dating to about 12,000 B.C., add some indirect credibility to the latest Meadowcroft chronology.

There are a number of other sites from all parts of North America that may date to earlier than 12,000 B.C., but none of them are of any size or completely watertight chronologically.

Central and South America?

The evidence for late Wisconsin human occupation is also sparse south of the Rio Grande (for a review, see Dillehay, 2000). The earliest well-documented site comes from Chile, but there are other possible, but usually discounted, sites (see Meltzer, Adovasio, and Dillehay, 1994).

Monte Verde
11,800 to 12,000 B.C.

The Monte Verde site lies in a small river valley in southern Chile, a streamside settlement covered by a peat bog, so that not only stone and bone but also wooden artifacts survive (Figure 5.4). The site has been thoroughly excavated and has been radiocarbon-dated to between 11,800 to 12,000 B.C. (Dillehay, 1989, 1997). Thus far, only a portion of the site has been excavated, revealing two parallel rows of what are said to be rectangular houses, joined by connecting walls. The skin-covered houses were 3 to 4 m (9 to 13 feet) square, with log and crude-plank foundations and a wooden framework. Clay-lined hearths, wooden mortars, and large quantities of vegetable foods were found in the houses. A short distance away lay a wishbone-shaped structure associated with chewed bolo-plant leaves (used today to make a form of medicinal tea), mastodon bones, and other work debris. This may have been a work area.

FIGURE 5.4
Excavations at Monte Verde, Chile. This site is strong evidence for early settlement of southern South America soon after the Ice Age.

The Monte Verde people exploited a wide range of vegetable foods, including wild potatoes; they also hunted small game and perhaps mammals such as extinct camels and mastodons (it is possible that they scavenged such meat, however). Monte Verde was in a forest, with abundant vegetable foods year-round. The site was almost certainly a long-term campsite. What is fascinating is that 90 percent of the stone artifacts are crude river cobbles. It is clear that wood was the most important raw material. It was certainly used for spears and digging sticks and for hafting stone scrapers, three of which have survived in their wooden handles. Sites yielding simple flaked stone artifacts like those from Monte Verde have been found elsewhere in South America, as far south as Patagonia, but this is the first place that anyone has been able to make more complete discoveries.

The Monte Verde site is currently the most convincing evidence for pre-Clovis human occupation in the Americas. However, archaeologist Stuart Fiedel (2000) has dissected the lengthy monographs on the site and drawn attention to what he considers to be inconsistencies in the excavations. His criticisms do not necessarily undermine the credibility of the site. (It should be noted that there is a 33,000-year-old level at Monte Verde, but it has not been investigated for human occupation.)

A Scenario for First Settlement

Assuming that the earliest evidence for human activity dates to well after 20,000 years ago, as most experts currently believe, we can describe a tentative scenario for first settlement, which goes as follows: Few human beings lived in frigid Beringia during the height of the last glaciation (Fiedel, 1999). So far, there is no evidence that there were many people living in extreme northeast Siberia before 15,000 years ago, if then. Somewhere around 12,700 B.C., temperatures rose rapidly in the far north. The vast Laurentide ice sheet melted rapidly, releasing enormous amounts of freshwater into northern oceans. This may have been when the first human groups crossed the vanishing Bering land bridge and settled in Alaska. By this time, too, the ice-free corridor was already passable, even if it was not an attractive place to live. The rapidly warming climate may have drawn tiny numbers of Paleo-Indians southward into the heart of an uninhabited continent after 12,700 B.C.

These initial forays into new lands must have involved a diversity of paths. Judging from Monte Verde and some other locations, the first settlers ranged widely and far to the south. Computer modeling offers new opportunities to examine possible paths along which first settlement occurred (Anderson and Gillam, 2000). Analyses based on the notion of "least cost" assume that people took the least arduous routes into unknown territory that gave them the best chance of finding food and stone for tool manufacture. Such analyses suggest that the Americas could have been traversed and been filled up by hunter-gatherer populations fairly quickly, perhaps in about 2000 years from the date of first arrival. This process of settlement could have taken place linearly, with bands splitting off from one territory into another as population densities increased, along main lines of spread, with people then branching out into neighboring areas. However, the earliest known sites are scattered thinly over enormous regions, not in lines, which makes a form of "leapfrog" model more plausible, in which hunter-gatherer groups fissioned from one territory into another, often separated from the original one by long distances. This model would explain the wide separation of very early sites with uninhabited areas between them that were filled in by later generations.

The leapfrog model would explain why first settlement took hold in some areas well before that in others. Under this scenario, the well-known Clovis and other fluted point cultures, described later in this chapter, may well have been founder populations in hitherto unoccupied areas, while earlier groups had already leapfrogged their way through resource-rich areas to the southern extremities of the Americas.

11,400 B.C.   After 11,400 B.C., the world entered another near-glacial cold snap called the Younger Dryas (see Chapter 7). In most parts of the Americas, especially North America, the climate was probably relatively cold and arid. But a change in the jet stream path may have brought dry conditions to the Pacific Northwest but wetter, more favorable circumstances to the Great Plains and the Southwest, where the Clovis culture expanded over much of North America. People using fluted point technology may now have occupied many hitherto empty areas and adapted to a wide range of environments over several centuries. This process explains the increasing diversity of artifact forms as a result of what is called *stylistic drift*. Not that human populations were large or densely packed anywhere in the Americas. Most groups were isolated, with relatively few contacts with neighbors.

All this is, of course, still little more than a theoretical scenario. There is only one certainty: About 11,200 B.C., the Clovis culture appears, marked by a veritable explosion in the number of archaeological sites throughout North America, from the California deserts to the Eastern Woodlands.

〰 The Paleo-Indians: Clovis

Clovis
11,200 to 10,900 B.C.   About 11,200 B.C., the highly distinctive Clovis culture appeared all over eastern North America, on the Great Plains, and much farther afield. These Paleo-Indian people are the first well-documented inhabitants of the New World. Many questions still remain about their ancestry and lifeway, but what is certain, however, is that the Clovis culture was relatively short-lived. Judging from dated sites in western North America, most sites were occupied during the three centuries after 11,200 B.C. We now move onto solid ground, for the archaeological record suddenly mushrooms from nothing to a well-documented scatter of locations from coast to coast in North America, with well-established Paleo-Indian occupation in Mesoamerica and Latin America as well (Fiedel, 1999; Haynes, 2002; Hofman and Graham, 1998).

Although Paleo-Indian occupation is known from both eastern and western North America, the Clovis culture is best known from the Great Plains. At the end of the Wisconsin glaciation, the areas in the rain shadow of the western mountains of North America were dominated throughout the year by the dry mid-Pacific air mass. Most rain fell, and still falls, in spring and early summer, supporting short grasses that keep much of their biomass beneath the soil. This structure helps retain moisture in the roots and provided mammoths, bison, and other ruminants with high-quality nutrients in the dry fall and into the winter. These grasslands expanded at the end of the Wisconsin and were colonized by herds of ruminants that were selective feeders. The grasslands were also the home of scattered bands of Clovis people. Within a few centuries, tiny hunter-gatherer bands had spread to both North American coasts and as far south as Guadalajara, Mexico, adapting to the different environments they encountered.

The western plains of North America offer a highly diverse range of environments with a variety of protein-rich grasses and shrubs that once supported a browsing and grazing mammalian fauna, which in turn provided subsistence for a small number of hunter-gatherers (Frison, 1992). However, life was not easy for the bands, as they had to respond to different distributions of animals and plants each year, conditions that depended on rainfall, snowfall, runoff from the mountain peaks, and so on. The realities of the climate meant that the people had to collect dried meat and vegetable foods in the summer months and store them against the bitter winter. Each family group probably moved frequently, tending to visit the same campsites year after year and taking all their belongings with them. Archaeologically, they left very little behind, so the evidence for prehistoric occupation of the plains is usually limited to remains of large bison kills and scatters of broken flakes and projectile points.

The Clovis culture is known mainly from kill sites in western North America. At Murray Springs, Arizona, for example, the people killed mammoth and bison, butchering them at separate locations, with a campsite nearby. Eleven bison died at Murray Springs, yielding enough meat to support up to 50 to 100 people, perhaps many fewer. Distinctive Clovis projectile points and other tools were found among the bones. At Naco, Arizona, no fewer than eight points lay in one mammoth carcass. Perhaps between 4 and 8 hunters, a fifth of a band of 20 to 40 people, killed or scavenged the great beast (Figure 5.5). The hunters partially dismembered their quarry, sometimes making piles of the disarticulated bones. The Clovis people who camped in Blackwater Draw, New Mexico, a natural arroyo trap, could drive large animals into swampy ground. There they took mammoth, bison, horse, camel, and deer. Lehner, also in Arizona, is another well-known waterside site, where Clovis hunters may have killed 13 mammoth in one hunt.

Everyone agrees that the Clovis people hunted both big game and smaller animals, besides foraging for wild vegetable foods during spring, summer, and fall. Big-game hunting was probably an important part of their subsistence, but the prevalence of kill sites in the archaeological record may give us a misleading impression of people who

FIGURE 5.5 Four Clovis points from an unknown location on the Great Plains.

must also have relied heavily on edible plant foods. Large animals like the mammoth and the bison could provide meat for weeks on end, as well as valuable by-products for household possessions, tents, and even clothing. But plant foods collected by women were as significant a part of the diet, even in places where game abounded. George Frison (1992) and others believe that Clovis hunters tended to concentrate on solitary mammoths, for their spear technology could not stop an elephant in its tracks, just wound it severely. They would stalk herds, concentrating on straying animals, sometimes perhaps driving them into swamps (for an extended discussion, see Haynes, 1982). The hunters would wound an animal, then take their time to kill it with thrusting spears.

Clovis people, and other Paleo-Indian groups, used a portable toolkit that included bone, cordage, stone, and wood artifacts. Preservation conditions allow us to know most about their stone technology, often based on precious fine-grained rock from widely separated outcrops. The hunters traveled great distances for their stone, carrying it in core form for hundreds of miles. These cores were like a savings account, carried around so that flakes could be used to make finely pressure-flaked projectile points. The finished heads were mounted in wood or bone foreshafts set on the end of spear shafts. Once the spear penetrated an animal, the foreshaft would break off. The hunter could then rearm the spear with a new foreshaft in a few moments. Damaged points were resharpened and used again; some exceptionally large ones may even have been ceremonial artifacts.

Besides projectile points, the Clovis toolkit included butchering tools, scrapers, and dozens of untrimmed stone blades and flakes used as convenient knives. The people used bone, and presumably wood, for foreshafts, spears, and other artifacts. The origins of this technology are unknown but must lie ultimately in Upper Paleolithic big-game-hunting traditions in the Old World. Are there, then, archaeological links between Clovis artifacts and Stone Age tools made in the far north at the same time, or earlier? Distinctive Clovis points with or without fluted bases are found in all the Canadian provinces and throughout North America. In Alaska, the new discoveries at Broken Mammoth, Dry Creek, and Mesa include bifaces and other artifacts that are reminiscent of early Paleo-Indian points and tools from temperate North America. There are still too few artifacts from any Alaskan site to make detailed, meaningful comparisons, but it seems increasingly likely that Clovis origins, and those of its immediate, and putative, ancestors, are among very early cultural traditions in Alaska. The Clovis point itself may have been an indigenous development, first fabricated south of the ice sheets and not in the Arctic at all (Hoffecker and others, 1993; Tankersley, 1994).

Clovis people lived in small bands, ranged over enormous distances, and relied significantly on hunting large and small animals. They shared the same basic cultural traditions and toolkits over vast areas, giving at least a superficial impression of cultural standardization, even if recent discoveries in the southeastern United States and elsewhere point to far more diverse lifeways than merely big-game hunting (Anderson and Sassaman, 1996). Within a few centuries of their arrival, Clovis people and their relatives were scattered all over the Americas, many of them adapting to more forested environments. In most areas, Paleo-Indian groups made extensive use of plant foods from the earliest times.

Central and South American Paleo-Indian societies may have been more diverse than those to the north. Certainly, many of them relied heavily on plant foods. The **Caverna da Pedra Pintada** lies in the Amazon basin near the town of Monte Alegre in northern Brazil (Figure 5.6). Anna Roosevelt of Chicago's Field Museum found stone projectile points, as well as charred plant and animal remains, in levels radiocarbon-dated to about 9000 B.C. Unlike other early groups, the inhabitants of this site subsisted in a humid and forested tropical environment, where plant foods such as Brazil nuts and palm seeds were all-important. According to Roosevelt (1996), the earliest inhabitants of the cave visited the site irregularly over a period of 1200 years—evidence for a considerable diversity of human culture in the Americas from the time of first settlement onward.

This scenario for first settlement is almost as inadequately documented as those espousing earlier dates. However, the cumulative sum of the limited data tends to support rather than undermine it (Meltzer, 1995).

Caverna da Pedra Pintada
c. 9000 B.C.

FIGURE 5.6
Excavations at Caverna
da Pedra Pintada, Brazil,
an early settlement in
a rain forest environment.
This site shatters
stereotypes of the first
Americans as purely
big-game hunters.

〰 Big-Game Extinctions

The Clovis people flourished for about 300 years and then, about 11,000 B.C., evolved into a multitude of hunting-and-gathering cultures. This sudden change coincides with one of the great mysteries of modern science: the catastrophic extinction of Ice Age big-game animals in the Americas. Many large animals became extinct throughout the world at this time but nowhere as drastically as in the Americas. Three-quarters of the large mammalian genera there vanished abruptly at the end of the Pleistocene (Martin and Klein, 1984). Speculations about this extinction have been long and lively. One long-established theory argues that the large mammals were killed off by the Paleo-Indian bands' intensive hunting, as they preyed on large herds of animals that had formerly had relatively few predators to control their populations. In fact, many Pleistocene animals disappeared before the heyday of the Paleo-Indians. Besides, the Indians existed in very small numbers, and they had other subsistence activities as well. Surely the animals would have adapted to changed conditions and new dangers. Instead, the extinctions accelerated after the hunters had been around for a while; the modern bison, for example, never adapted to mounted hunters.

10,900 B.C.

Another hypothesis argues that changing environments, spreading aridity, and shrinking habitats for big game after the Ice Age may have reduced the mammalian population drastically. This theory faces strong objections, too. The very animals that became extinct had already survived enormous fluctuations in Pleistocene climate without harm. If they had once migrated into more hospitable habitats, they could have done so again. Furthermore, the animals that became extinct were not just the browsers; they were selected from all types of habitat. This hypothesis assumes that desiccation leads to mass starvation in game populations, an idea refuted by ecological research in Africa. What actually occurs is that the smaller species and those with lower growth rates adapt to the less favorable conditions, leaving the population changed but not defunct.

A third hypothesis cites the great variation in mean temperatures at the end of the Pleistocene as a primary cause of extinction. In both the New and Old Worlds, the more pronounced seasonal contrasts in temperature climates would have been harder on the young of species that are born in small litters, after long gestation periods, and at fixed times of the year. These traits are characteristic of larger mammals, precisely those that became extinct. The less equable climate at the end of the Pleistocene, then, would have been a major cause of late Pleistocene extinctions in North America (Grayson, 2001).

All three hypotheses have some validity. Complex variables must have affected the steps that led to extinction, with intricate feedback among the effects of intensive big-game hunting, changing ecology, and the intolerance of some mammalian species to seasonal contrasts in weather. It may be that the hunters, being persistent predators, were one of the final variables, causing more drastic mammalian extinctions than might otherwise have occurred.

〽〽 Later Hunters and Gatherers

As the world climate warmed up rapidly at the end of the last glaciation, American environments changed drastically. The great ice sheets of the north shrank, mountain snow lines and sea levels rose, and forest vegetation established itself in hitherto glaciated regions. If one word can be used to describe these momentous changes, it is diversity, a great diversity of local environments: lush river floodplains, great deserts, grassy plains, miles upon miles of boreal and deciduous woodland. The late Paleo-Indians and their successors adapted to this great diversity with brilliant success and ingenuity (see a summary in Fagan, 2000b).

In general, the western and southwestern United States became drier, but the east coast and much of the Midwest became densely forested. The large Pleistocene mammals became extinct, but the bison remained a major source of food. In the Southeast, the more favorable climate brought drier conditions, which meant less standing water, markedly seasonal rainfalls, and specialization among humans in fishing or intensive gathering. Many areas had much economic diversity, as we see among the desert forager peoples of the Tehuacán Valley in Mexico. They flourished between 10,000 and 7000 B.C., at the same time hunter-gatherers in the Pacific Northwest were probably taking advantage of seasonal salmon runs in the fast-moving rivers.

North American climate and sea levels seem to have coincided with social change in many areas, which was still climaxing as European explorers and colonists arrived in the Americas. The human population of North America was still sparse, scattered in myriad isolated hunter-gatherer bands. Judging from sites in many areas, people spent most of the year living in small family groups and exploiting large hunting territories. They may have come together with their neighbors for a few weeks during the summer months at favored locations near rivers or nut groves. The bands would have held ceremonies, arranged marriages, and traded fine-grained rocks and other commodities. Then they would have gone their separate ways, following migrating game, trapping small animals, and foraging for wild vegetable foods.

At first there was plenty of vacant territory to go around, continues this hypothetical scenario. In time, natural population growth and the low carrying capacity of the land combined to restrict mobility. Several long-term adaptive trends developed.

First, the extinction of the Ice Age megafauna meant that hunters focused even more on smaller mammals, especially the white-tailed deer. Inevitably, people turned to alternative food sources, including wild vegetable foods, birds, mollusks, and fish. Wild vegetable foods were a particularly favored dietary source, especially in areas like river valley bottoms and lakeshores, where they were seasonally abundant and diverse. From the earliest times, Native Americans developed a remarkable expertise with wild plant foods, which preadapted them in later millennia to the cultivation of native grasses and tubers.

Second, there was a long-term trend toward less mobility, toward base camps that were occupied for many months of the year. These served as anchors for larger territories, which were exploited seasonally from outlying settlements. This settlement pattern was by no means universal, but it took hold in areas where there was an unusual diversity of food resources. Examples of base settlements are to be found in the desert West, in midwestern and southeastern river valleys, and in the Northeast.

Third, some areas witnessed a move toward sedentary settlement, occupation of the same settlement year-round or for most of the year. This type of settlement is different from a base camp used on a seasonal basis, even if the latter lasts for many months. It implies a permanent settlement within a highly restricted territory, a settlement lying within easy reach of sufficient game, vegetable, and aquatic resources, that enables the occupants to stay through every season of the year. Sedentary settlement is hard to identify in the archaeological record, except by the presence of substantial dwellings or cemeteries. Such occupation was well established in some midwestern river valley bottoms by 2000 B.C. and perhaps in favored coastal areas, such as southern California and the Pacific Northwest, somewhat later.

These trends coincided with accelerating population growth in more favored areas after 2000 B.C. Such was the diversity of North American environments in Holocene times that only a few relatively limited areas witnessed sedentary settlement and large-scale population growth. Perhaps it is no coincidence that it was in some of these areas, notably midwestern and southeastern river valleys and the Southwest, that people turned to the cultivation of domesticated plants.

🐾 Plains Hunters

In only one region—the arid grasslands from the frontiers of Alaska to the Gulf of Mexico—did big-game hunting survive. This was the "great bison belt," which lay in the rain shadow of the western mountains. The short-grass range of the plains was an ideal environment for the bison, one of the few Ice Age big-game species to adapt to Holocene conditions. The postglacial descendants of the Ice Age steppe bison have increased digestive efficiency to cope with the high-fiber, low-nutrient dead grass of winter. They can feed in deep snow and are less selective eaters than many of the Ice Age species that died out. By 10,500 B.C., bison were the dominant species in all archaeological sites in the bison belt.

At first glance, the Great Plains appear homogeneous, even monotonous. Close examination reveals many subtle differences: stream courses and water holes where game congregated, places where longer grass and seasonal water favored larger bison herds. The late Paleo-Indians and their successors, who preyed on the herds right into historic times, could survive only by a careful, planned utilization of the plains' complex ecosystem (Wood, 1998).

Plains hunting cultures
10,900 B.C. onward

After 10,000 B.C., numerous variations of bison-hunting cultures appeared on the plains, all of them using portable toolkits that bear a strong resemblance to those of their Clovis ancestors. Stone-tipped projectile points with carefully thinned and ground bases made spear-throwers and spears effective weapons for bison hunting. At least seven major forms are known, with names like Eden, Folsom, Plainview, and Scottsbluff—to mention only a few (Figure 5.7). Whether all these forms actually represent distinct cultural entities is a matter of controversy. The entire Paleo-Indian toolkit was highly portable and capable of being used for a wide variety of purposes, everything from woodworking to bison butchery. Many plains sites are kill locations, strategic places where mass game drives could be organized. Such drives were far from daily events, perhaps taking place every couple of years or so. To pursue bison on foot means days of patient stalking and an intimate knowledge of the animals' habits. Perhaps several bands would cooperate in a game drive. They would encircle a few beasts or, more often, stampede a herd into a swamp or a narrow defile. In some cases, they would drive the frightened animals over a cliff or into dune areas. The archaeological evidence for such activities comes from a series of sites, among them the Agate Basin site in eastern Wyoming, where, judging from the age of the animals, the hunters apparently maneuvered 10 to 20 animals into an arroyo bottom in late February or early March (Frison, 1992). The hunters then drove them upstream until they reached a natural trap in the gully, where the confused bison could be killed with stone-tipped spears.

The Olsen-Chubbock site in Colorado is an example of a kill site, where approximately 200 bison of all ages were stampeded into a deep, narrow arroyo, probably during the summer or fall (Wheat, 1972). Because the skeletons of the ancient bison faced north, the excavators concluded that the wind was blowing from the south on the day

Olsen-Chubbock
c. 6000 B.C.

FIGURE 5.7 A Paleo-Indian Folsom point from Folsom, New Mexico, lying next to two ribs of an extinct bison. This find (c. 10,500 B.C.) proved that humans were contemporary with extinct animals in North America.

of the hunt (Figure 5.8). The stampeding herd was driven into a gully and could not catch the scent of the people waiting for them at the arroyo. The hunters' artifacts were scattered around the carcasses of their quarry: scraping tools, stone knives, and flakes used to dismember the bison.

Garnsey
A.D. 1540

Smaller communal hunts were probably much more commonplace. John Speth's (1983) excavations at Garnsey, New Mexico, chronicle such a kill. About 400 years ago, a group of hunters visited a small gully where they knew bison would congregate in late March or early April. Instead of killing every animal on sight, they tended to concentrate on the males because, Speth believes, male bison are in better condition in the spring, when their bone marrow has a higher fat content. Fatty meat is an important source of energy and essential fatty acids, and is difficult to come by after the lean winter months. So if Garnsey hunters killed a cow, they consumed only the choice, fatty parts.

Bison hunting was practiced on the plains right up to the advent of the horse and the repeating rifle, but Paleo-Indian peoples flourished throughout North America. Clovis-like projectile points are known from many locations in the East. Herds of caribou may have provided sustenance in northern sites around the Great Lakes and in the Northeast at locations such as present-day Robert, Nova Scotia, where caribou hunters flourished (Meltzer, 1988). Paleo-Indian hunting-and-gathering economies may have varied a great deal from region to region, some bands specializing more heavily in big game, others in fishing or gathering, depending on the resources available in each territory. This diversity is reflected in Paleo-Indian archaeological sites, which vary from kill locations to shell middens. That hunting was important in places where large game was abundant seems unquestionable, but this activity diminished rapidly in importance as the big game became extinct.

〰️ The Desert West

Economic emphasis shifted in the arid West and Southwest. As big game became scarce, many hunting bands relied more heavily on wild vegetable foods that required much more energy to collect and process than game meat. In the Great Basin, smaller

FIGURE 5.8   The bison bone bed at Olsen-Chubbock, Colorado.

animals such as rabbits, squirrels, and deer became more common prey. At the same time, gathering of vegetable foods grew to dominate economic life, combined with some fishing and, in maritime areas, exploitation of shellfish. We are fortunate that arid climates in Utah, Nevada, and elsewhere have preserved many plant and vegetable foods eaten by these early hunter-gatherers. By 9000 B.C., a distinctive, desertlike form of Archaic culture had been developed over much of the western United States by small bands camping in caves, rock shelters, and temporary sites (Grayson, 1993).

Excavations at later sites like Danger Cave in Utah and the Gypsum and Lovelock sites in Nevada reveal that the hunters were making nets, mats, and baskets, as well as rope (Figures 5.9 and 5.10) (D'Acevedo, 1986; Jennings, 1957). Hogup Cave in Utah has yielded one of the world's most complete and longest archaeological culture sequences (Aikens, 1970). The site displays gradual adaptations at one settlement, changing it from a base camp to a short-stay camp that was associated with other base camps or with horticultural villages after people learned how to produce food. At all these sites, the inhabitants used digging sticks to uproot edible tubers, and much of their toolkit consisted of grinding stones used in preparing vegetable foods. Most Great

Hogup Cave

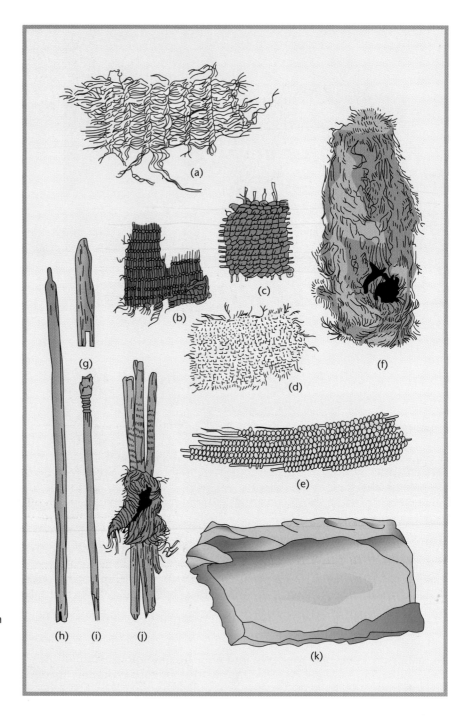

FIGURE 5.9 Artifacts from Danger Cave, Utah, preserved by the dry climate: (a and b) twined matting; (c) twined basketry; (d) coarse cloth; (e) coiled basketry; (f) hide moccasin; (g) wooden knife handle, 7.4 cm (4.5 inches) long; (h) dart shaft, 41 cm (16 inches) long; (i) arrow shaft with broken projectile point in place, 84 cm (33 inches) long; (j) bundle of gaming sticks, 29 cm (11.5 inches) long; (k) milling stone.

Gatecliff
6000 B.C. onward

Basin peoples were obliged to be constantly on the move, searching for different vegetable foods as they came into season and camping near scanty water supplies. For example, the deposits at Gatecliff Rock Shelter near Austin, Nevada, are 12.1 m (40 feet) deep and span more than 8000 years of human occupation. The inhabitants lived by valleyside streams in the winter, then moved up to the shelter in the summer, gathering piñon nuts on the mountain slopes and hunting game, just as Shoshone Indians did in recent times (D. Thomas and Bettinger, 1983).

Most western North American societies continued to live by hunting and foraging right up to European contact. It was only in the most favored areas that people could stay in one place for months on end. One such location was Lovelock Cave in Nevada, where the base camp overlooked a lake rich in fish and waterfowl. The people hunted

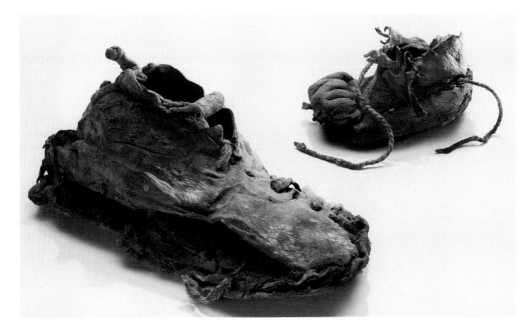

FIGURE 5.10 A fiber moccasin from Hogup Cave, Utah.

their prey with bows and arrows, using extremely lifelike reed duck decoys. Human feces show that over 90 percent of the Lovelock inhabitants' diet came from the lake area, including wetland grasses, fish such as chub, and ducks and mud hens (Grayson, 1993).

The southern California coast was another challenging area, first exploited by small bands combining fishing with marine mammal hunting as early as 11,000 B.C. The coastal population remained sparse except in favored areas, where much more elaborate societies evolved (Erlandson, 1994, 2001). For example, the historic Chumash people of the Santa Barbara Channel area congregated in large, more or less permanent villages ruled by local chiefs, who maintained trading contacts between offshore islands and the mainland (Arnold, 2001). Such sedentism was possible because of exceptional resource diversity, but unpredictable rainfall made large communities a high-risk proposition and required conservative adaptations to the semi-arid environment.

From November to March, the Chumash subsisted on dried meat and stored vegetable foods. They also collected shellfish and caught fish in the dense kelp beds close inshore. Come spring, they ranged far afield, collecting plants and tubers. Summer brought tuna and other warm-water fish to local waters. The people caught enormous quantities of fish from their canoes. Pine nuts and acorns were gathered in the fall and stored for the leaner months ahead. The Chumash hunted marine mammals and scavenged stranded whales whenever the opportunity arose. This maritime bounty resulted from an upwelling that replenishes the surface layers of the Santa Barbara Channel with nutrients and zooplankton. At least 125 fish species flourished in local waters, part of an incredibly diverse range of food resources that enabled not only relatively sedentary settlement but also higher population densities—as many as 15,000 people living near the shores of the channel and on the offshore islands at the time of European contact. However, periodic strong El Niños and severe droughts made life precarious, even in good years, and there is evidence of fighting between different groups, perhaps over territory and resources.

♨ Eastern North America

Whereas the Great Plains are dominated by grasslands, eastern North America, the region from the Mississippi Valley eastward, is covered by deciduous woodlands and the Southeast by evergreen forest. Superficially, this could be considered a homogeneous natural environment with no sharp geographic barriers to interaction between different human groups, but in fact, the area includes an almost bewildering array of microenvironments. As a result, it is almost impossible to generalize about cultural developments after first settlement before 11,500 B.C.

Paleo-Indian bands settled widely over the Eastern Woodlands from as far north as Nova Scotia to southern Florida (Meltzer, 1988). They combined hunting with foraging, turning to the pursuit of the white-tailed deer and other small mammals as the Ice Age megafauna vanished. By 11,000 B.C., a widespread shift to more generalized hunting and gathering was under way, as the peoples of the Eastern Woodlands exploited a broad variety of foods: forest resources, like gray squirrels and annual nut harvests, and pioneer seed-bearing grasses. It seems certain that small game, fish, mollusks, and vegetable foods assumed greater importance in the eastern diet after about 10,500 B.C. Inhabitants were part of the broad-spectrum hunting-and-gathering tradition known as the Archaic, which lasted until about 1000 B.C. in many areas (Sassaman and Anderson, 1996).

During the many millennia of the Archaic, there was a long-term trend toward increased efficiency and success in exploiting forest and river valley resources. The Archaic has been subdivided into early, middle, and late stages on the basis of stylistic changes in projectile points and the introduction of slate tools, copper artifacts, and other technological innovations (see Griffin, 1967, for details), but the basic patterns of Archaic life were established early on and are known to us from excavations and surveys in northeast Arkansas and the Little Tennessee River valley (Chapman, 1994).

Dalton
9950 to 7900 B.C.

The Dalton Archaic tradition flourished over a wide area of the Southeast and the Midwest from about 9950 to 7900 B.C. Dan Morse and Phyllis Morse (1983) argue that in northeast Arkansas, Dalton band organization allowed a network of stable local family bands of 20 to 30 people who regularly used base camps centered on watershed territories (Figure 5.11). There they exploited easily accessible shallow-water fish, vegetable foods, seasonal nut harvests, and deer; the women married into neighboring bands in nearby river valleys, thereby maintaining trading links between each area drained by a river system, contacts that ensured ample supplies of fine-grained chert over large areas (see also D. G. Anderson and Sassaman, 1996).

6000 to 4000 B.C.

By about 6000 B.C., warmer and drier climates were developing in the East, culminating between 4500 to 4000 B.C. The major rivers of the Midwest and the Southeast

11,000 B.C.

FIGURE 5.11 Artist's reconstruction of an Archaic camp on the Little Tennessee River (c. 6300 B.C.), which gives a general impression of foraging lifeways in a woodland environment after the Ice Age.

stabilized their courses, while the population densities were still low. The highest concentrations of population were in major river valley bottoms and lakeshores, which offered the greatest diversity of aquatic, game, and vegetable foods. In some favored areas, there was a slow trend toward living within more circumscribed territories and toward more sedentary settlement, made possible by an abundant constellation of seasonal foods. The famous Koster site in the Midwest's Illinois Valley chronicles this trend (see Site box).

A similar trend is documented at other midwestern sites, among them the Modoc Rock Shelter near the Mississippi River (Brown and Phillips, 1983; Fowler, 1958). Modoc was occupied between about 8000 and 2000 B.C. As time went on, it became more and more of a base camp, where people lived for much of the year while they caught fish and exploited nut harvests. Both Koster and Modoc show that the middle Archaic adaptation was a conservative one, requiring at least a degree of careful scheduling to maximize the potential of nut harvests and to capitalize on the game that fed on the rich forest mast (undergrowth) each fall.

By about 2500 B.C., there had been a dramatic increase in the use of riverine resources over much of the Southeast and the Midwest, when stabilized river bottoms provided an abundance of oxbow lakes and swamps where fish abounded and native grasses, shellfish, and other foods were to be found. Some of the river valleys lay on seasonal waterfowl migration routes, too, providing a bounty of food in spring and fall. This enhancement of aquatic habitats increased potential food supplies over long sections of river floodplains. In response, many groups adopted more sedentary lifeways, perhaps best described as a shift toward centrally based wandering, which involved a seasonally mobile lifeway and a regular return to the same base location for much of each year, especially during the summers.

Archaic populations in the East increased sharply after 4000 B.C., especially in favored areas. Rising sea levels and warming ocean temperatures allowed a steady northward expansion of fish and shellfish habitats. Flooded estuaries allowed more upriver fish runs in spring and fall. Nut-bearing forests spread farther north, into parts of the Great Lakes region, and river valley bottoms were exceptionally diverse and rich environments for Archaic hunter-gatherers (Yerkes, 1988).

In all probability, Archaic population growth was a response not only to environmental change but also to technological and subsistence advances, as well as new settlement patterns that took advantage of new riverine environments. The more sedentary living that accompanied the growth in many areas allowed people to store nuts and other winter foods on a much larger scale than if they were always on the move. This storage, in turn, created larger food surpluses, the ability to support higher population densities year-round, and opportunities for kin groups and individuals to play important roles in controlling labor and the redistribution of food and luxury goods. By the same token, people lived within more restricted territories, and there was far more local cultural variation.

There were also long-term changes in the ways people interacted with one another and their neighbors. The smaller territories inhabited by more people contained a diversity of food resources and raw materials, but there was always something lacking. Such items as obsidian for toolmaking had to be sought elsewhere, by a special journey or regular economic and social contacts with groups living nearer to the sources of what was needed. Over time, these trading connections assumed ever greater importance in the yearly round. They became a source not only of valued possessions and raw materials but also of social connections and prestige—a way of maintaining "diplomatic" relations with the outside world. These interactions also affected population densities, especially when the demand for prestige items, such as copper objects or seashells, soared. More and more hands would be needed to increase the output of food and trade goods. The intensification of hunting and foraging to meet these demands would lead to population increases—and to the emergence of social ranks based on prestige and social and economic power within previously egalitarian societies.

The late Archaic witnessed much greater regional variety in hunter-gatherer culture in the East (B. Smith, 1986; Snow, 1980). The so-called Central Riverine Archaic was the most developed of all eastern late Archaic traditions, for it was centered on midwestern and southeastern river valleys with a superabundance of aquatic, game, and

Koster
7580 B.C. to A.D. 1200

Modoc
8000 to 2000 B.C.

SITE

Koster, Illinois

The famous Koster site in the Illinois River valley, with its 14 stratified occupation levels separated by sterile layers, provides an extraordinary chronicle of human exploitation of a midwestern river valley from about 7500 B.C. until A.D. 1200 (Struever and Holton, 1979). The first visitors to camp at Koster were Paleo-Indians, who visited the locality occasionally. By about 6500 B.C., an early Archaic camp at Koster covered about 0.3 ha (0.75 acre). This was a seasonal camp with temporary buildings, visited by an extended family group of about 25 people who came to the same site every few years over many centuries, perhaps to exploit rich fall nut harvests. Between 5600 and 5000 B.C., a large permanent camp with longhouses covered in hides or mats came into use; the inhabitants focused on a narrow spectrum of abundant foods throughout much of the year. The substantial dwellings were occupied for most if not all the year, the settlement covering about 0.7 ha (1.75 acres). During spring and summer, the inhabitants took thousands of fish, gathering freshwater mussels and hickory nuts in fall and migratory birds in spring. Perhaps the people moved to the nearby uplands to hunt deer. As long as this middle Archaic population remained stable, they could find most of their food resources within 5 km (3 miles) of their settlement.

Horizon 6 at Koster dates to between 3900 and 2800 B.C., a time when people lived there year-round. The village covered about 2 ha (5 acres), perhaps housing 100 to 150 people. Stuart Struever and his colleagues found six houses, built on sunken earthen floors that were cut like shallow terraces about 45 cm (18 inches) into a hill slope. The builders erected rows of stout posts along the long walls, then filled in the gaps between them with woven brush and clay. Apparently they covered the ends with skins, mats, or more brush. Each dwelling covered between 12 and 15 sq m (96 and 140 square feet), sufficient space for a nuclear family.

The food remains from this settlement reveal striking contrasts with earlier Archaic diet in the Illinois Valley. Earlier fisherfolk had concentrated mainly on fish species that preferred faster-moving river water. Their Horizon 6 successors exploited the shallow backwater lakes and swamps that now abounded near Koster. They speared and netted vast numbers of sluggish, shallow-water fish like bass, buffalo fish, and catfish, species that can be eaten fresh or be dried or smoked for consumption during the winter. Dozens of fish could also be taken by poisoning the water with the chemicals in powdered hickory nut husks, or by driving fish into oxygen-starved pools where they could be scooped up with baskets. One Illinois fisheries biologist has estimated that Koster's inhabitants could have taken between 136 and 272 kg (300 and 600 pounds) of fish flesh per acre every year from backwater lakes that covered hundreds of acres. The same shallow lakes also contained rich mollusk beds that could be used as a supplementary food source.

Like their predecessors, the people relied on the fall hickory and acorn harvests, as well as black walnuts, pecans, and hazelnuts. But they now exploited many more seed plants, including marsh elder (sumpweed), a swampside grass, grinding the seeds with stone pestles and mortars. The hunters took deer and other small mammals, but they also harvested another seasonal food—waterfowl that paused to feed and rest on the shallow lakes of the Illinois Valley during spring and fall migrations. The Illinois River is on the Mississippi flyway, the narrow migration route used by millions of waterfowl flying north and south to and from their Canadian breeding grounds each year. The Koster people could take hundreds of ducks, geese, and other migrants with bows, or by trapping them with light, weighted nets cast over sleeping birds, or by using silently paddled canoes to drive them into waiting cages during stealthy dawn raids.

Everything in Koster Horizon 6 points to the exploitation of a much broader spectrum of animal, aquatic, and vegetable foods. This implies larger food surpluses used to feed more people. Enhanced food procurement abilities coincide with more commonplace sedentary occupation, perhaps resulting in part from even more restricted territorial mobility than in the middle Archaic.

The Koster excavations yielded a treasure trove of chronological information that provided a framework for studying major changes in Native American society over many thousands of years.

Moseley, Michael. 2000. *The Incas and Their Ancestors*, 2nd ed. London and New York: Thames & Hudson.
  The definitive popular account of Andean archaeology for the general reader.

Sassaman, Kenneth E., and David G. Anderson, eds. 1996. *Archaeology of the Mid-Holocene Southeast*.
  Pp. 259–287. Gainesville: University Presses of Florida.
  A set of technical reports that summarize a great deal of CRM-acquired data.

Struever, Stuart, and Felicia Antonelli Holton. 1979. *Koster: Americans in Search of Their Past*. New York:
  Anchor Press/Doubleday.
  A vivid account of the Koster site for laypeople. Tells a lively story of archaeology, people, and science.

West, Richard H., ed. 1996. *American Beginnings*. Chicago: University of Chicago Press.
  A series of reports on what is now known of the archaeology of Siberia and Beringia. A specialist work
  but a useful reference source.

chapter

AFRICANS
AND AUSTRALIANS

45,000 YEARS AGO TO MODERN TIMES

San hunter-gatherers dance around a dying eland. Rock painting from Natal, South Africa.

he wind blows strongly toward the open sea on a stormy day 40,000 years ago, swishing through the dense mangrove swamps. A man and a woman pole their wooden raft across the shallow lagoon, making their way to a shallow bank close offshore. They reach the shoal, driving wooden poles into the seabed to hold the heavy raft against the wind. Oblivious to the wind, they set fishing lines where the bottom fish lie. A sudden squall descends on the raft, tearing it loose from the restraining poles. Frantically, the crew try to stop their craft over the shallows, but the wind carries them out into deep water. Ashore, their relatives watch helplessly as the raft vanishes over the horizon far downwind. They know that they will never see the man and woman again.

Perhaps it was by some such accident that a crude raft was blown far offshore, to drift helpless on the open ocean and to ground days, even weeks, later on an unknown, uninhabited land over the horizon. Or perhaps it was by deliberate water-borne voyage that human beings first came to offshore Southeast Asia, to New Guinea, Australia, and the Pacific islands during the late Ice Age.

Having followed the complex population movements that took anatomically modern humans throughout Europe and Eurasia and then into the Americas, we now examine cultural developments in southern latitudes (Table 6.1). Instead of attempting a detailed chronicle of dozens of local cultures in Africa and Asia, we focus on two adaptations of particular interest: those of the San peoples of southern Africa and of the first settlement of New Guinea, the southwestern Pacific, and Australia, involving population movements made possible by the first open-water voyages in human history.

African Hunter-Gatherers, Past and Present

As we saw in Chapter 4, *Homo sapiens sapiens,* anatomically modern humans, probably evolved in Africa, perhaps as early as 150,000 years ago. The long millennia of the Weichsel glaciation saw the peoples of Africa developing ever more efficient ways of hunting and foraging (Phillipson, 1994). Some fascinating indications come from coastal caves in South Africa, among them Klasies River Mouth and Nelson's Bay (Deacon and Deacon, 1999; Klein, 1979). Richard Klein found that the people who inhabited these caves lived not only off vegetable foods but off game and marine resources as well. Klasies River was occupied between about 120,000 and 70,000 years ago, then abandoned until about 3000 B.C. The early inhabitants collected limpets and also pursued seals and penguins. They took few fish; they preferred game on the hoof, especially such docile animals as the eland and the

TABLE 6.1

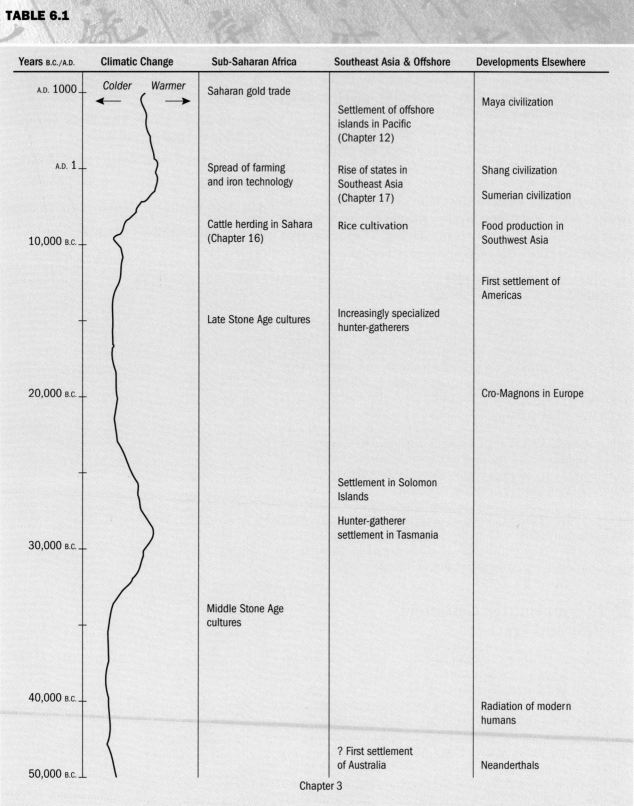

Years B.C./A.D.	Climatic Change	Sub-Saharan Africa	Southeast Asia & Offshore	Developments Elsewhere
A.D. 1000	Colder ← → Warmer	Saharan gold trade		Maya civilization
			Settlement of offshore islands in Pacific (Chapter 12)	
A.D. 1		Spread of farming and iron technology	Rise of states in Southeast Asia (Chapter 17)	Shang civilization
				Sumerian civilization
		Cattle herding in Sahara (Chapter 16)	Rice cultivation	Food production in Southwest Asia
10,000 B.C.				
				First settlement of Americas
		Late Stone Age cultures	Increasingly specialized hunter-gatherers	
20,000 B.C.				Cro-Magnons in Europe
			Settlement in Solomon Islands	
			Hunter-gatherer settlement in Tasmania	
30,000 B.C.				
		Middle Stone Age cultures		
40,000 B.C.				Radiation of modern humans
			? First settlement of Australia	Neanderthals
50,000 B.C.				

Chapter 3

hartebeest. They did kill some more formidable beasts like the buffalo, the black wilde-beest, and the roan antelope, but in much smaller numbers, and some of the meat was perhaps scavenged. Interestingly, the bones of these individual species came from either very old or young individuals, which is the sort of age pattern found in predator kills. Only the eland and hartebeest were taken at all ages. Klein concluded that they may have been driven into traps or over cliffs.

Nelson's Bay Cave was occupied by modern *H. sapiens* populations after 13,000 B.C. Again, eland and hartebeest were common and taken at all ages, perhaps by game drives. The Nelson's Bay folk took bush pigs and warthogs, much fiercer and more formidable prey. Not only that, they used nets and fishhooks to catch a wide range of ocean fish. They also lived off flying sea birds such as cormorants. One could argue, of course, that the Klasies River people simply preferred game on the hoof, but the rela-tive abundance of wild pigs strongly suggests that the Nelson's Bay hunters were much more expert and capable of exploiting a far wider range of game. They may have used the bow and arrow. Although the eland lives in widely dispersed herds, other antelope do not and would have been much more vulnerable to efficient hunting. Klein (1979) notes that several large mammal species became extinct between 10,000 and 8000 B.C.

By about 7000 B.C., the world's southern oceans were warmer than today. It was not until 3000 years later, during the so-called postglacial climatic optimum, that the northern seas achieved higher temperatures. This delay was due to different land and water distributions in the two hemispheres, Antarctica being much colder than the Arctic Ocean. Warmer, drier conditions in southern Africa led to more succulent veg-etation at the expense of grassland and heath, with major changes in human subsis-tence. These changes are hard to document. John Parkington (1987) has chronicled one changing scenario at Eland's Bay Cave in the far south. In 11,000 B.C., the inhabi-tants hunted large and medium-sized antelope. But between 9000 and 7000 B.C., they turned their attention to smaller browsing animals, with estuarine and marine animals as well as limpets becoming ever more common. By 6000 B.C., the entire coastal plain was flooded, with only small browsing animals, mussels, and fish being taken. Then, Eland's Bay Cave was abandoned suddenly, never to be reoccupied.

After 9000 B.C., the quantity of food bones increases dramatically, as does the variety of ostrich-eggshell beads, water containers, bone tools, decorated bone work, and other artifacts (Figure 6.1). Parkington believes that this intensification in domestic ac-tivity was due to environmental change, that is, to the dramatic encroachments of the postglacial ocean. Eland's Bay Cave was first visited, then lived in for long periods of time as the coastal plain shrank. Finally, the people moved into the interior or else-where along the shore when this stretch of coastline was no longer productive. It would be a mistake to describe the major changes in artifact inventories or subsistence as evolving culture change. Rather, they may reflect continual adaptation to rapidly altering climatic conditions, changes that were reflected by other adaptive shifts elsewhere on the coast, as at Nelson's Bay, and also in the warm interior.

The long-term trend over the past 15,000 years may have been toward hunting smaller game and increased specialization in plant collecting (Parkington, 1987). Many late Stone Age caves and rock shelters in southern Africa were used much more regularly in postglacial times, as if mountain and near-coastal locations were extremely favorable places to settle, places where smaller browsing animal herds would be concentrated. The warming trend in the earlier millennia of postglacial times may have led to increased aridity in many parts of the interior, with the densest human pop-ulations concentrated in areas of abundant water and diverse animal and plant resources. A great diversity of hunter-gatherer societies now developed throughout much of Africa.

Hilary Deacon (1979) has excavated several late Stone Age rock shelters and caves with exceptional care. He believes that there was a trend toward hunting smaller game and especially toward the exploitation of plant foods. Rabbits, tortoises, and both grasses and root plants became vital components in the hunter-gatherers' diet. Just when plant foods came to be of overwhelming importance is much debated, but they were especially significant after about A.D. 1, when herding peoples were settled in extreme southern Africa (see Chapter 11), perhaps when the newcomers squeezed hunter-gatherers into more limited territories, away from cattle-grazing grounds.

Klasies River
120,000 to 70,000

Nelson's Bay
13,000 B.C.

7000 B.C.

Eland's Bay
11,000 to 6000 B.C.

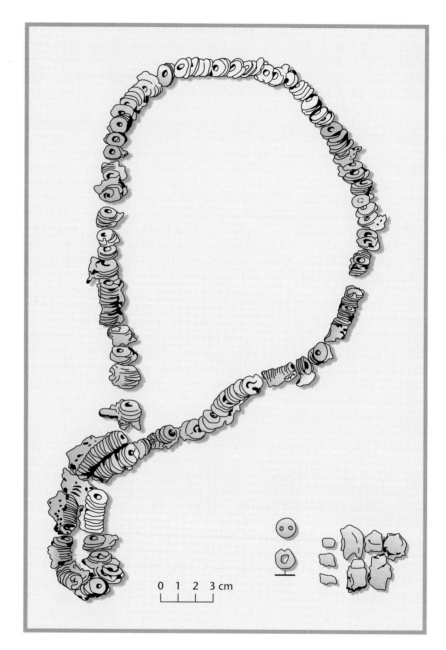

FIGURE 6.1 An ostrich-eggshell-bead necklace from a burial at Gwisho, Zambia, Central Africa (c. 1500 B.C.). The bead maker cut the beads to a roughly circular shape, then ground them against a fine, rocky surface to produce beads of even size.

The same general trend toward increasingly specialized subsistence strategies may also have developed in other parts of sub-Saharan Africa, just as in other parts of the world. The peoples of the open savanna lived off the abundant game populations and supplemented their diet with seasonal gathering of the rich vegetable resources of the woodland. Other bands settled on the shores of lakes and on riverbanks and lived by fishing. This valuable and reliable source of protein encouraged more lasting settlement and increased specialization. The rain forest peoples of the Congo River basin in Central Africa were unable to hunt as wide a range of game as their savanna counterparts, so they relied heavily on vegetable foods and wild roots.

The later Stone Age hunter-gatherers of the eastern and southern African savanna are comparatively well documented, not only from archaeological sites but also from their own rock paintings and engravings. Unfortunately, preservation conditions are usually such that only stone implements and sometimes animal bones are preserved, making study of cultural diversity a challenging task. Only a handful of sites, among them the Gwisho hot springs in Central Africa, offer a more complete picture (see Site box).

Gwisho

1000 B.C.

We should not, of course, assume that the 3000-year-old Gwisho site was a prototype for historic San lifeways, but the general similarities are striking, at least at a superficial

SITE

Gwisho Hot Springs, Zambia, Central Africa

The Gwisho hot springs in central Zambia lie on the edge of the seasonally inundated floodplain of the Kafue River and provide an unusually complete picture of hunter-gatherer life along the river over 3000 years ago (Fagan and van Noten, 1971). At least four forager camps once nestled among the bubbling hot springs, all locations that were occupied repeatedly over many centuries. The reed-surrounded springs offered both abundant water, protection from predators, and a fine view of the floodplain, which teemed with game animals, especially during the spring flood, when the river was high. Abundant plant foods were within easy reach, too.

The Gwisho sites remained waterlogged after their abandonment, so not only bone fragments but also wooden tools and all kinds of plant remains survived in excellent condition, giving an unrivaled picture of late Stone Age life in this region. The Gwisho people hunted many species of small and medium-sized antelope and caught fish in shallow pools of the nearby Kafue River. Despite the abundance of game, plant foods were an important part of the Gwisho diet. The waterlogged levels contained more than 10,000 plant remains, most from only eight species, especially the edible fruit of the *Bauhinia*. The emphasis on only a few edible species suggests that food supplies were relatively abundant, to the point that the people could focus on a few plants to the exclusion of others. The deposits also yielded the remains of plants that yield vegetable poisons, known to have been used by modern-day San for arrow poison. Nearby lay some fine arrowheads and some of the wooden artifacts made by the inhabitants, including some simple digging sticks used for uprooting tubers. These tools are identical to those used by Kalahari San today. There were traces of a grass-and-stick shelter, of hearths, and of layers of grass that may have served as bedding. Thirty-five

burials were deposited in the soil of the campsites. The deposits were littered with hundreds of stone arrow barbs and tiny scraping tools that lay alongside pestles and grinding stones used to process the vegetable foods that were an important part of the Gwisho diet (see Figure 7.7). So little have gathering habits changed in the past 3000 years that a San from the Kalahari was able to identify seeds from the excavations and tell archaeologists what they were used for. The economy and the material culture of the Gwisho people show a striking resemblance to those of modern San peoples in the Kalahari, although, of course, there are environmental differences (Lee, 1979).

The Gwisho hot springs are informative, for they confirm ethnographic observations made about the present-day San. Like that of their modern successors, the toolkit of the Gwisho people was highly portable, and much of it was disposable. Except for bows and arrows, modern-day Kalahari San improvise many of their tools from the bush as they need them, making snares from vegetable fibers and clubs from convenient branches. The women use digging sticks like the Gwisho artifacts for digging tubers and a softened antelope hide, or kaross, as a garment and carrying bag. Their only other artifacts are a pair of pounding stones for breaking up nuts. The Gwisho site contained both digging sticks and pounders. We know from cave paintings that the San used karosses for thousands of years, and we can assume they were employed at Gwisho and elsewhere.

Like those of the San, the Gwisho home bases were little more than small clusters of brush shelters, part of a complex annual round, of which we know only part from these remarkable sites. It may be that the Gwisho camps were occupied somewhat longer than modern-day San settlements, because of the abundant water and diverse local food supplies, but we lack the means of establishing this.

level. The comprehensive studies of Kalarai San provide us with a useful data base for looking at earlier societies known only from archaeology. For example, the average present-day San camp holds approximately 10 to 30 people, just as the Gwisho camps probably did. The small population of a San territory leads to a continual turnover of the composition of camp populations. This constant change is a reality reflected in the San's highly flexible kinship system. Every member of a band has not only close family ties but also kin connections with a much wider number of people living all over San territory. The San kinship system is based on an elaborate network of commonly

FIGURE 6.2 San hunter-gatherers depicted in a rock painting from Natal, South Africa. This scene has deep symbolic meaning that defies modern interpretation, but the human figures are elongated to depict an altered state of consciousness (see also Figure 6.3).

possessed personal names, which are transmitted from grandparent to grandchild. People with similar names share kin ties even if they live some distance from one another. This network is such that individuals can move to a new camp and find a family with which they have kin ties to accept them. The resulting flexibility of movement prevents total social chaos and also provides a network for mutual assistance in times of food scarcity. Presumably, the ancient San had similar political and social systems to aid in survival.

Ancient San paintings and engravings depict the game hunted, the chase, and life in camp (Lewis-Williams, 1995, 2002; Vinnecombe, 1976). The San drew running hunters, people fishing from boats, and scenes of gathering honey and vegetable foods (Figure 6.2). The hunters can be seen stalking game in disguise, hotly pursuing wounded quarry, and even raiding the cattle herds of their agricultural neighbors of later centuries. David Lewis-Williams, who has studied ethnographic records of San bands, has shown convincingly (1981, 1995) that many of the paintings depict complex metaphors that represent symbolic values in the San world. Each superimposition of paintings and each relationship between human figures and animals had profound meaning to the artists and the people. For instance, many of the paintings depict eland

FIGURE 6.3 San dancers performing on loose sand.

with dancers cavorting around them (see chapter opener). Lewis-Williams believes that the dancers were acquiring the potency released by the death of the eland. The dancers go into trances so powerful (Figure 6.3) that they become eland themselves. This symbolism survived into the nineteenth century. When Victorian anthropologist George Stow showed some rock-painting pictures to an elderly San couple, the woman began to sing and dance. The man begged her to desist because the old songs made him sad. Eventually, he joined in, and Stow watched the couple reliving the symbolism of past days. Only now, more than a century later, are archaeologists trying to probe this forgotten world. (For a contrary view, see Solomon, 1997.)

Stone Age hunter-gatherers enjoyed the savanna woodlands of eastern and southern Africa undisturbed until approximately A.D. 1, when the first farming peoples (other African folk) settled by the banks of the Zambezi and Limpopo rivers. The San placed second in the resulting competition for land: The farmers wanted grazing grass and prime land for cultivating, so they drove off the bands of San hunter-gatherers, who had to retreat into less favored areas. Some took up the new economies and married into farming communities. White settlement in South Africa increased the isolation of the San. As the pressure on their hunting grounds grew, the San moved into mountainous areas and desert regions. Even there, they were harassed and hunted. Some of the white settlers made a sport of shooting them on Sunday afternoons. The doomed San of South Africa calmly continued to paint scenes of cattle raids and of European ships and wagons. They even depicted red-coated English soldiers on expeditions into the mountains. By the end of the nineteenth century, there was no San painting in South Africa, and the art of stone toolmaking had all but died out. The last stoneworkers used glass bottle fragments to make their sharp arrowheads. They found this unusually pure "stone" vastly preferable to their usual quartz pebbles (Barnard, 1992).

⁂ Sunda and Sahul: The First Settlement of Island Southeast Asia

On the other side of the world, island Southeast Asia, New Guinea, and Australia underwent far more profound change than tropical Africa after the Ice Age. The Australian Aborigines encountered by British navigator Captain James Cook and other early European explorers in the eighteenth century A.D. were still living as hunter-gatherers (Figure 6.4). For two centuries, anthropologists and historians have puzzled

FIGURE 6.4 An Australian Aborigine hunting in a marsh.

over the ancestry of these remarkable people. Where did the Australians come from, and how long ago did people first settle on this remote continent (J. Allen, 1994; Mulvaney and Kamminga, 1999)?

At the height of the last glaciation in about 18,000 B.C., sea levels were over 100 m (300 feet) below modern levels. Dry land joined Sumatra to Borneo, and great plains were exposed between many of the islands, which were connected to the Southeast Asian mainland. Great rivers dissected the now-sunken plains, known to geologists as Sunda (Figure 6.5). Farther offshore, nearly 30 km (19 miles) of open water separated Sunda from the island of Wallacea (modern Sulawesi and Timor); 100 km (62 miles) farther offshore lay a vast landmass, Sahul, consisting of what are now Australia (including Tasmania), New Guinea, and a low-lying shelf between them that is now the Arafura Sea. These are, of course, the coastlines of the glacial maximum, and sea levels were considerably higher for most of the last glaciation. For most of the period between about 100,000 and 13,000 B.C., people would have had to cross much wider stretches of ocean than those at the glacial maximum. Even at the height of the last glaciation, the colonization of Wallacea and Sahul would have required some form of watercraft and the technology to build them. This necessity raises a fundamental and deeply interesting question: How long ago did people go offshore and cross wide tracts of ocean, perhaps paddling out of sight of land?

The earliest known occupation of Sunda comes from the island of Flores, where *Homo erectus* fragments have been fission-track-dated to between 900,000 and 800,000 years ago (Morwood et al., 1999). But the few Archaic humans who ventured out from the mainland were long gone when the first modern humans settled on Sunda. If *H. sapiens sapiens* had settled in mainland Southeast Asia by about 75,000 years ago, as we hypothesized in Chapter 4, we can reasonably expect colonization of offshore landmasses to have occurred some time after that date. At the time, the plains of Sunda were relatively dry. Human settlement was probably concentrated in areas, such as coasts, lakeshores, and rivers, that had more diverse and predictable food resources. As in the rain forests, easily split bamboo and other woods sufficed for many tasks. Relatively benign waters lapped the coastlines that faced Wallacea and Sahul. Here people could take plenty of shallow-water fish and shellfish to supplement game and plant foods. Perhaps the people living along these shores fashioned simple rafts of bamboo and mangrove logs lashed together with forest vines (R. Jones, 1989). Such rafts were stable platforms for fishing in sheltered, shallow water and for reaching

FIGURE 6.5 Late Ice Age Southeast Asia. Low sea levels exposed dry land off mainland Asia and between Australia and New Guinea during the last glaciation, creating Sahul and Sunda.

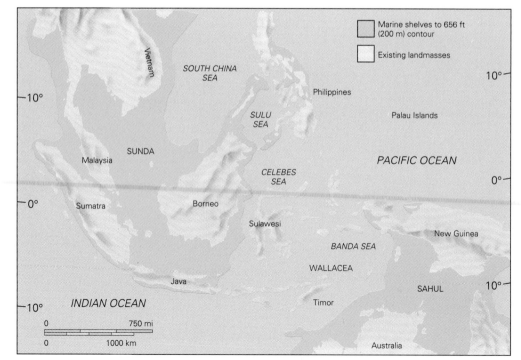

offshore shell beds. Perhaps it was in such craft that some people crossed to Wallacea and Sahul well before the glacial maximum of 18,000 B.C. In support of this hypothesis, the Lene Hara Cave on East Timor contains traces of occupation dating to before 30,000 years ago (O'Connor, Spriggs, and Veth, 2002; O'Connor and Veth, 2000).

**Lene Hara
29,000 B.C.**

Two main routes led offshore to Sahul. One went from southern Sunda to Wallacea, then across to the Australian shore. The other was from southern China, across the Philippines and Borneo, and into New Guinea via Sulawesi (see Figure 6.5). Whichever route was used, the process of colonization involved both island hopping and open-water travel, the earliest instance of seafaring by human beings. As is always the case with ocean crossings, scholars debate endlessly about whether the first settlement was accidental or deliberate. In the case of Southeast Asia, with its strong northerly monsoon winds of summer, colonization was probably the result of dozens of accidental driftings offshore over thousands of years. Computer simulations have shown that there are moderate chances of a raft drifting from Timor to Australia in about seven days in front of strong monsoon winds. Undoubtedly, many of these strandings resulted in the group dying out. Computer simulations show that the chances of survival, even with both men and women in the party, were very small. Eventually, however, a viable population (or populations) was established along the more than 3000-km (1850-mile) coastline of Sahul.

🐾 New Guinea and Adjacent Islands

Much of Sahul was rolling, semi-arid lowlands—what is now Australia, with New Guinea in the far north offering a quite different landscape of rugged mountains and highland valleys (Figure 6.6). The earliest evidence for human settlement in New Guinea comes from Bobongara on the Huon Peninsula, where archaeologist Les Groube found ground axes, with indented waists for mounting them, and a single stone flake sealed under volcanic ash. The ash dates to at least 38,000 B.C. (Figure 6.7). Groube believes that these waisted axes were used to ring trees and clear forests, perhaps to encourage the growth of plants on the forest fringes—a form of deliberate manipulation of wild plants to enhance the growth of wild plant foods such as yams, sugarcane, and perhaps taro and fruit trees (Groube et al., 1986; Hope and Golson, 1995).

**Bobongara
?38,000 B.C.**

The Huon Peninsula faces the Bismarck Strait, with the island of New Britain only a 50-km (30-mile) or so passage offshore. From there, it is only a short voyage to New Ireland. These two islands are visible from one another but are separated by deep water and were never joined during the last glaciation. Open-water voyages were needed to colonize them and may have been commonplace by 33,000 B.C. (Pavlides and Gosden, 1994). Excavations in four limestone caves on New Ireland have yielded traces of human occupation by at least 30,000 B.C. (J. Allen, Gosden, and White, 1989).

30,000 B.C.

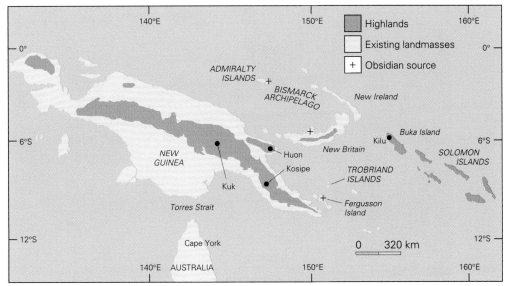

FIGURE 6.6 Map showing New Guinea and adjacent islands mentioned in Chapters 7 and 12.

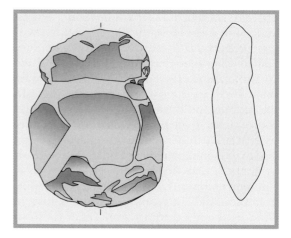

FIGURE 6.7 Waisted stone axe from the Huon Peninsula, New Guinea, perhaps early evidence for forest clearance in island Southeast Asia.

These were fisherfolk who took shellfish and fish and hunted bats, reptiles, and birds. By 18,000 B.C., their successors were regularly trading obsidian for toolmaking across 30 km (19 miles) of open water to west New Britain, from a volcanic source 350 km (217 miles) in a straight line from their home.

Kilu
26,000 to 18,000 B.C.

Even farther offshore to the south, the Kilu Rock Shelter on Buka Island in the northern Solomons contains human occupation dating to between 26,000 and 18,000 B.C. (Figure 6.8) (Wickler and Spriggs, 1988). Open-water crossings of at least

FIGURE 6.8 Excavations at Kilu Rock Shelter, northern Solomon Islands, where evidence of human occupation dates to as early as 26,000 B.C.

130 to 180 km (81 to 112 miles) would have been required to settle on Buka, depending on the route selected. Voyaging over this distance would certainly have required some form of open-water craft, as well as foods that could be preserved for use during long voyages of days on end. Substantial water containers would also have been essential. From Buka, it would have been an easy matter to colonize the rest of the Solomon chain, for the islands are separated only by short distances (J. Allen et al., 1989).

Farther offshore lay the limits of the late Ice Age world, for sea distances become much larger. More than 300 km (186 miles) lie between the Solomons and the environmentally impoverished Santa Cruz Islands, which were a much smaller target area even for expert navigators. The islands to the south and east of the Solomons lie within a region with no indigenous terrestrial mammals except bats and a progressively impoverished flora and fauna. Such remote oceanic environments were insufficient to support hunter-gatherers. It was not until much later that the development of larger offshore canoes, much more sophisticated navigational skills, and easily storable food crops enabled humans to colonize islands far offshore (see Chapter 12).

Everything points to a relatively rapid spread of hunter-gatherer peoples with expert seagoing abilities throughout northern Sahul and contiguous islands at least as early as 33,000 B.C. Favorable climatic conditions helped. Generally good weather and predictable winds and currents carried people in small crafts from island to island without the necessity of elaborate technology. The Sunda-Sahul area was a superb "nursery" for seafaring expertise. It is no coincidence that islanders in the western Pacific were venturing far offshore long before Westerners undertook ambitious voyages in the Mediterranean, after 12,000 B.C. (Irwin, 1992; Irwin, Brickler, and Quirke, 1990).

〰 Australia

Intense controversy surrounds the first settlement of Australia, just as it does that of the Americas (J. Allen, 1994; Frankel, 1991; Murray, 1998). The earliest human occupation is said to date to between 55,000 and 60,000 years ago, on the basis of thermoluminescence dates from northern Australia and early dates for the Lake Mungo skeletons (Roberts, Jones, and Smith, 1994; Thorne et al., 1999). Human settlement is well documented after 36,000 to 38,000 B.C., but traces of earlier occupation are very thin (J. Allen and Holloway, 1995). It is, of course, possible that there was a long period of what archaeologist Jim Allen calls "invisible colonization" for thousands of years by peoples who are not represented in the archaeological record.

First settlement
?60,000

33,000 B.C.

Whatever the date of initial colonization, recent geomorphological researches have shown that humans could have walked over dry land all the way from New Guinea into Tasmania far to the south throughout the late Ice Age (Kershaw, 1995).

Traces of human occupation immediately before and around 28,000 B.C. have accumulated rapidly in recent years (Figure 6.9). Some hunter-gatherers visited Devil's Lair Cave, near Perth in the southwest part of Western Australia, as early as 30,500 B.C. and used the site more regularly from 21,000 B.C. to the end of the Ice Age (Dortch and Merrilees, 1973). The Purritjarra Rock Shelter in the arid center of Australia, near the Northern Territory's Cleland Hills, was occupied from at least 25,000 to about 4000 B.C.

Devil's Lair
30,500 B.C.

Purritjarra
25,000 to 4000 B.C.

Far to the east, in the Willandra Lakes region of western New South Wales, early sites cluster around long-dried-up lakes. One group of sites includes shell middens located in dune systems dating to around 30,000 B.C., perhaps earlier. The Lake Mungo site of 24,000 B.C. comes from the same general area—a thin scatter of stone artifacts, hearths, and fish bones and other food remains (Bowler et al., 1970). Humans were living in the arid zones of Australia, at places like Koonalda Cave on South Australia's Nullabor Plain, by 22,000 B.C. People lived there until 13,000 B.C., visiting the site to quarry stone and making patterned lines or "flutings" on the cave walls during their stays. Arnhem Land in the north was certainly occupied well before 18,000 B.C., with radiocarbon-dated occupations of about 20,900 B.C. from Malangangerr Rock Shelter. Ocher pencils with traces of wear date to at least 17,000 and perhaps 28,000 B.C. There are even claims of 60,000-year-old ocher. It is possible that some of the earliest Arnhem Land paintings depict extinct animals, but the interpretation is much debated. Dates from coatings of "desert varnish" from engravings on rocky outcrops at Mannahill in

Koonalda
22,000 B.C.

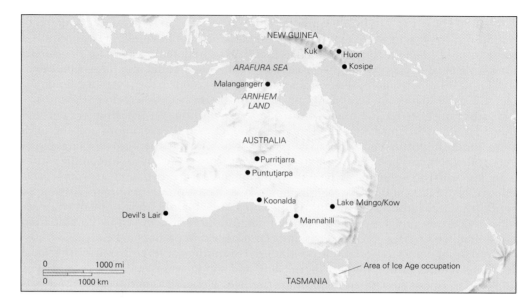

FIGURE 6.9
Archaeological sites in Australia and Tasmania.

South Australia are said to span a period from 29,000 to 14,000 B.C., but the dating method is still experimental (Dorn, Nobbs, and Cahill, 1988). There seems little reason to doubt, however, that Aboriginal Australians were painting as early as were artists in Europe and Africa (Figures 6.10 and 6.11). Hunter-gatherers were living around the coast and on the fringes of the central Australian desert by 18,000 B.C. By 8000 B.C., they were exploiting every major environmental zone.

As for the first settlement itself, scientists are deeply divided. Some believe that initial colonization was a slow and gradual process along coasts and then into the interior by people forced to adapt not only to a new maritime environment but also to unfamiliar animal and plant foods (White and O'Connell, 1982). Others argue for a rapid colonization, with small groups expanding rapidly over the continent as a result of their highly mobile lifeway (J. Allen, 1994). Anthropologist Joseph Birdsell (1977) hypothesized that a mere doubling of the Australian population every 20 years after the first settlement would have resulted in a natural population growth to eighteenth-century levels within only 2000 years. Recent discoveries of evidence of late Ice Age wallaby hunters in Tasmania tend to support his hypothesis.

FIGURE 6.10   An extinct Tasmanian wolf (thylacine) depicted in a rock painting from Arnhem Land, Australia. The thylacine has been extinct for more than 3000 years.

FIGURE 6.11 Australian Aboriginal painting of a figure carrying two spears and a shieldlike object, from Arnhem Land, northern Australia, dated to the past 3000 years. The dashes near the head may depict sounds, one of the earliest such records in Australia. Like San art, Australian paintings had deep symbolic meaning, forming part of the "Dreamtime," the spiritual world.

༔ Ice Age Wallaby Hunters in Tasmania

Tasmania is now an island, but it was connected to mainland Australia by a land bridge for at least 55,000 years of the late Ice Age, so that first settlement was a matter of hunting and foraging across dry land. During much of the last glaciation, climatic conditions throughout Tasmania were quite severe, with ice sheets on higher ground in the interior and temperatures at the glacial maximum as much as 6°C (10.8°F) lower than today. Human settlement dates to about 32,000 B.C. at the Parmerpar Meethaner Rock Shelter in the Forth Valley in the central southwest of the island, occupied until about 780 years ago (Cosgrove, 1995). Another site, Warreen Cave, was first visited in about 33,000 B.C. (Porch and Allen, 1995). Richard Cosgrove has excavated the Bluff and ORS 7 Rock Shelters in south-central Tasmania. The Bluff site (Figure 6.12) was first occupied about 28,500 B.C., whereas ORS 7 was in use by 28,800 B.C. Both of these occupation levels contain emu eggs, which can be collected only during late winter and early spring, a bitterly cold time of year (Cosgrove, Allen, and Marshall, 1990).

These sites were occupied before the glacial maximum, but people continued to live in the rugged landscape of southwestern and central Tasmania through the coldest millennia of the last glaciation. The Kutikina Cave was occupied between 18,000 and 12,000 B.C., when what is now dense forestland was open tundra and grassland. The inhabitants hunted red wallabies, as did the people who lived in at least 20 other occupied caves nearby. Slightly to the east, in another rugged area that is now rain forest, is Bone Cave, occupied between 15,000 and 11,000 B.C. The groups in these areas appear to have been part of a common social system that flourished over a large area for many thousands of years. Some groups used Darwin glass, a natural glass from a meteorite crater a minimum distance of 45 km (28 miles) from Kutikina and over 100 straight-line km (62 miles) from the Bluff Rock Shelter area. Some of these people were painting hand stencils and other designs long before the end of the Ice Age.

Parmerpar Meethaner
32,000 B.C.
Warreen
33,000 B.C.
Bluff
28,500 B.C.

Kutikina
18,000 to 12,000 B.C.

FIGURE 6.12 Excavations at the Bluff Rock Shelter, Tasmania, visited by late Ice Age wallaby hunters as early as 28,500 B.C.

These were the southernmost people living on earth during the last glaciation. With the severing of the land bridge, their successors remained isolated from the outside world for thousands of years until French explorer Marion du Fresne met some Aboriginal Tasmanians face to face in A.D. 1772. The occupation levels of the Parmerpar Meethaner Rock Shelter document how the Tasmanians adapted to warmer, more forested conditions over many millennia.

〽️ Later Australian Cultures

Between 23,000 and 8000 B.C., the population of Australia may have reached approximately modern levels, perhaps as many as a million people. Cultural change was gradual right into modern times, reflecting much regional diversity and the basic efficiency of ancient Australian technology. (For a summary of later archaeology, see Mulvaney and Kamminga, 1999.) The same traditions of stoneworking and bone technology found in early sites survived almost unchanged for thousands of years. For instance, flakes showing wear patterns characteristic of adze blades made by modern Aborigines date back as far as 18,000 B.C., and the same bone points used to fasten skin clothes in historic times have been found deep in the prehistoric levels of Devil's Lair. The Australian Aborigines were famous for their artistic traditions and elaborate ceremonial life. Abundant traces of ritual belief have been found in Australian sites. The Devil's Lair site yielded stone plaques, a deep pit, and human incisor teeth that had been knocked out with a sharp blow: Such evulsion of teeth was an ancient Australian tradition.

18,000 B.C.

Despite the essential conservatism of Australian stoneworking practices, some regional variations did appear over the millennia. Steep-edged scrapers, which were probably used as woodworking tools, were made over a wide area of Australia during much of the Upper Pleistocene. These and plainly crafted flake tools remained in use until recent times; in some areas, they were joined after 4000 B.C. by stone points, set

FIGURE 6.13
Australian Aborigines making stone tools. Late Australian stone technology depended on composite tools such as scrapers and spear points mounted on wooden handles, as well as stone axes like those depicted in the photograph.

on shafts, and other microliths. There is good reason to believe that Aboriginal technology developed within Australia over a long period in response to local needs and without the benefit of cultural innovation from outside (Hiscock, 1994) (Figure 6.13).

Some idea of the dynamics of early Australian life can be obtained from the saga of the Tasmanians (Plomley, 1969). When the first European voyagers visited Tasmania in 1642, they found bands of hunter-gatherers living on the island. The Tasmanians lasted precisely 80 years after European settlement in 1802. They had no shafted tools (that is, tools made of stone heads or points with wooden shafts or handles) and relied instead on scrapers and choppers somewhat like those used by early hunter-gatherers on the mainland; they lacked the boomerangs, spear-throwers, shields, axes, adzes, and lightweight stone tools the Australians of the mainland had when they first entered written history. Tasmania's isolated population, although forming part of the Australian cultural group, never received the later cultural innovations that spread throughout Australia because of rising sea levels. Henry Lourandos (1987) and others have suggested that Tasmanian adaptations preserved a rather specialized lifeway that was typical of much of Australia from the late Ice Age into modern times.

Fortunately for archaeology, at least some investigations of Aboriginal culture have been made that have an important bearing on the interpretation of the archaeological record. Richard Gould (1977) spent many months among the Ngatatjara people of the Western Desert, carrying out ethnographic investigations that had objectives somewhat similar to those of Richard Lee among the San in Africa: He was interested in their cultural ecology and in the ways ethnographic observations could be used to interpret the archaeological record. His Aboriginal informants took him to Puntutjarpa Rock Shelter, a site that they still visited regularly. Gould excavated the occupation levels in the shelter and found that people had lived there for more than 6800 years. The later stone implements were almost indistinguishable from modern Ngatatjara tools, to the extent that Gould was able to compare the wear patterns on both ancient and modern artifacts and decide which 5000-year-old tools had been mounted on shafts and which had not. He also compared modern living surfaces with equivalent features found in the rock shelter (Figure 6.14).

The study of living Aborigine bands shows just how conservative Australian lifeways have been. There were few major technological innovations during Australia's

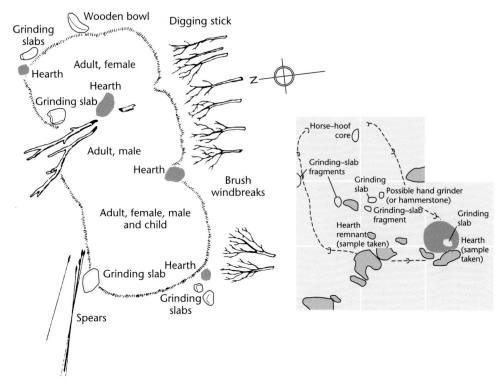

FIGURE 6.14 Comparison of a prehistoric campsite at Puntutjarpa Rock Shelter, Australia (right), with a modern Aboriginal camp in the same area (left). Note that the modern encampment can be subdivided into living areas by use of the informants' data and anthropological observation (left), whereas the archaeological site is devoid of such information, consisting merely of artifact patterns (right).

pre-European past. Indeed, it was possible for the Aboriginal Australians to maintain a thoroughly viable lifeway with minimal technology and only the simplest of artifacts. The Tasmanians, for instance, used only two dozen or so tools to hunt and forage (R. Jones, 1995). The great elaboration of Australian and Tasmanian culture was in social and ritual life, neither of which can be readily recovered by archaeological investigation. That much of this activity was designed to maintain the delicate balance between the Aborigines and the available resources in their environment was no coincidence. A belief in such balance lay at the core of Australian life.

Summary ᘆ᙮᙮᙮᙮᙮᙮᙮᙮

As the Ice Age ended, hunter-gatherer groups living in Africa and Asia adopted increasingly diverse adaptations to local environments. In sub-Saharan Africa, people turned their attention to smaller browsing animals, continually adapting to changing environmental conditions, a change well documented at Eland's Bay in South Africa. They focused heavily on edible plant foods. The densest populations concentrated in areas of abundant water and diverse animal and plant resources. It was from these diverse societies that modern-day African hunter-gatherer groups are descended.

The later hunter-gatherers of southern Africa are well documented from rock paintings and archaeology. Controversy surrounds the interpretation of San art from this region, which may be connected with shamanistic rituals and altered states of consciousness.

During much of the last glaciation, New Guinea and Australia formed a single landmass, called Sahul. Sahul was settled perhaps as early as 50,000 to 70,000 years ago, but the earliest documented settlement is about 38,000 B.C. People using open-water craft had settled in the Solomon Islands of the southwestern Pacific by 26,000 B.C. First settlement of Australia dates to at least 33,000 B.C., but may be as early as 60,000 years before present. The controversy over first settlement continues. Securely dated sites proliferate after 35,000 years ago. Late Ice Age hunters flourished in Tasmania by 29,000 B.C. The later archaeological record shows that the Australian lifeway changed little over the millennia, except for some significant innovations in tool technology.

Guide to Further Reading

Deacon, Hilary, and Jeanette Deacon. 1999. *Human Beginnings in South Africa: Uncovering the Secrets of the Stone Age*. Walnut Creek, CA: Altamira Press.
> A general account of the archaeology of southern Africa for laypeople and students. Strongly recommended for its clear exposition and multidisciplinary emphasis.

Frankel, David. 1991. *Remains to Be Seen: Archaeological Insights into Australian Prehistory*. Melbourne: Longman Cheshire.
> An attractive general account of methods and approaches to Australian prehistory for the beginning student. Especially strong on the links between archaeology and anthropology. Well illustrated.

Lee, Richard B. 1979. *The !Kung San*. Cambridge: Cambridge University Press.
> If there is one classic ethnographic study of hunter-gatherers, this account of the Kalahari San and their complex ecology is it. Strongly recommended to give the reader a clear understanding of hunter-gatherer lifeways.

Lewis-Williams, David. 1981. *Believing and Seeing: Symbolic Meanings in Southern San Rock Art*. New York: Academic Press.
> A superb, well-argued study of the meaning of prehistoric rock art in southern Africa that should be read by anyone interested in this subject.

Mulvaney, John, and Johan Kamminga. 1999. *The Prehistory of Australia*. Washington, DC: Smithsonian Institution Press.
> A useful overview of Australian research for students and interested general readers.

Phillipson, David. 1994. *African Prehistory*, 2nd ed. Cambridge: Cambridge University Press.
> A somewhat technical synthesis of the African Stone Age and Iron Age; summarizes recent research.

White, J. Peter, and James O'Connell. 1982. *A Prehistory of Australia, New Guinea, and Sahul*. New York: Academic Press.
> The definitive analytic synthesis of the prehistory of Australia. A superb, even masterly, account, but somewhat outdated.

INTENSIFICATION AND COMPLEXITY

BEFORE 10,000 B.C. TO MODERN TIMES

A replica of a Chumash Indian planked canoe, a *tomol,* navigates Southern California waters.

n about 7000 B.C., a small group of hunters and foragers camped in a sandy clearing near Meer in northern Belgium. They built a hearth and presumably erected brush or skin shelters, but no signs of these survive. After a while a right-handed artisan walked a short distance away from the settlement, sat down on a small boulder, and made some stone tools with prepared blanks he had brought along with him. Among them were three borers for working wood or hide. Minute abrasions on the tips reveal that he turned them clockwise, showing that he was right-handed. Later, a left-handed stoneworker came and sat down next to him, bringing a core. He proceeded to knock off some flakes, the scars from which showed clearly that he was a southpaw.

This remarkable, fine-grained research was the work of two Belgian archaeologists, David Cahen and Francis van Noten (1981). It demonstrates a high level of detail, using refitting, edge-wear analysis, and other analytical techniques that are needed to understand the new hunter-gatherer societies that developed after the Ice Age.

Despite the harshness of late Ice Age climates, especially in northern latitudes, *Homo sapiens sapiens* adapted successfully to a remarkable range of global environments. The last 50,000 years of the Ice Age saw human settlement of the globe reach its premodern limits, with two major exceptions. The subarctic lands and eastern arctic regions of North America were mantled by ice and were uninhabitable until long after the Ice Age (see Chapter 5). The far offshore islands of the Pacific were not to be settled until much later, after the development of the twin-hulled offshore canoe and new navigational techniques that allowed seafarers to voyage far out of sight of land during the last 5000 years of ancient times (see Chapter 12) (see Figure 4.1b).

All later cultural developments, including a new focus on both agriculture and animal domestication and the establishment of much more complex human societies, which included the first civilizations, stemmed ultimately from the progressive settlement of the globe by *Homo sapiens sapiens* during the last glaciation (Fagan, 1990). The immediate consequences of the end of the Ice Age affected many hunter-gatherer societies scattered across the world when the great ice sheets finally retreated.

The Holocene (After 10,000 B.C.)

When the last cold episode of the Ice Age ended in about 13,700 B.C., widespread global warming ensued, followed by an abrupt cold snap. Paleoclimatologists divide the earliest part of the **Holocene** into two phases:

Bølling-Allerød Interstadial (c. 14,700 to c. 12,950 years ago).   This 2000-year period saw dramatic global warming, massive ice sheet retreats, sea level rises, and much higher temperatures. It conventionally marks the end of the Würm glaciation.

Younger Dryas Interval (c. 12,950 to 11,650 years ago).   The Younger Dryas witnessed a dramatic fall in temperatures, back to near glacial conditions in a mere decade or so. This 1100-year-long cold snap ended as abruptly as it began, with the renewed onset of warmer conditions. But, as we shall see, it had a lasting effect on human life (see Chapter 9).

Changes in ice distribution and sea levels were very irregular. Using core borings from coral beds off Barbados in the Caribbean, Richard Fairbanks (1989) has shown that sea levels at the glacial maximum were 121 m (396 feet) below modern levels. They rose by 20 m (66 feet) between about 15,000 and 10,500 B.C. Then there was an abrupt rise of 24 m (79 feet) in a mere 1000 years, a slight rise at about 9000 B.C. and another 28-m (92-foot) rise after 8500 B.C. that culminated in 7500 B.C. These new levels led to major changes in world geography. The Bering Strait was dry land as late as 13,000 B.C. and ocean again by 7000 B.C. By this time, sea levels were rising rapidly, especially in areas such as Scandinavia, where the earth's crust was depressed by the massive weight of retreating ice sheets. The North Sea was flooded, and Britain was separated from the continent by approximately 6000 B.C. Enormous areas of North America and northern Europe were exposed by retreating ice sheets and were available for human settlement for the first time in nearly 100,000 years.

We have hardly begun to understand the dramatic changes in temperature, rainfall, and vegetation that occurred during the early millennia of the Holocene, between about 13,000 and 5000 B.C. (Björk et al., 1996; N. Roberts, 1998) (Table 7.1). Recent ice core research shows that the Holocene's atmosphere is about a third richer in carbon dioxide than at any time during the preceding 120,000 years of the late Ice Age. This enrichment increased photosynthesis, biomass, and seed yield, so that Holocene plants were more productive and more cold- and drought-tolerant than Pleistocene plants (Sage, 1995). This greater productivity may have been an important watershed for hunter-gatherers, who were now adapting to a very different world, one that was more productive and more climatically stable than its constantly changing Pleistocene predecessor.

The most striking environmental transformations took place in northern latitudes, in areas like western and central Europe and in regions of North America contiguous to the great ice sheets. During the height of the Weichsel glaciation, for example, central Europe had been treeless periglacial tundra and the Baltic Sea did not exist. Only 5000 years after the Scandinavian ice sheet began retreating, forests covered most of Europe and sparse human populations had settled on the shores of a newly exposed northern sea.

Throughout the world, game populations changed radically in the millennia after the Ice Age. By 10,000 B.C., the familiar mammoth and woolly rhinoceros hunted by the Cro-Magnons were extinct in central and western Europe, as were steppe bison and reindeer—all replaced by forest animals like the red and roe deer. In North America, mammoths, mastodons, camellike species, and many other large animal species vanished abruptly about 9000 B.C. (Martin and Klein, 1984). Even in tropical Africa, the rich and diverse savanna faunas suffered losses at the end of the Ice Age. The extent to which humans were responsible for the rapid extinction of late Ice Age animals is a matter of great, and unresolved, controversy (see Chapter 5).

There were major and highly significant vegetational changes in warmer latitudes, too. For much of the last glacial maximum, for example, the Sahara had been as arid as it is today, but rainfall patterns changed at the end of the Ice Age, bringing large, shallow lakes and short grasslands to the desert. As late as 6000 B.C., hunter-gatherer populations flourished in the heart of the Sahara, in areas that are now arid wilderness. In Southwest Asia, the late Ice Age climate of the Tauros and Zagros mountains was so cold and dry that no trees grew in the uplands. After about 9000 B.C., new plant assemblages immigrated into the now warmer highlands, among them wild cereal grasses that were to become the ancestors of domesticated crops. These cereals had long been native to the region, having survived the late Ice Age in sheltered locales.

TABLE 7.1
Climatic and generalized archaeological sequence in Europe and Southeast Asia after the Ice Age

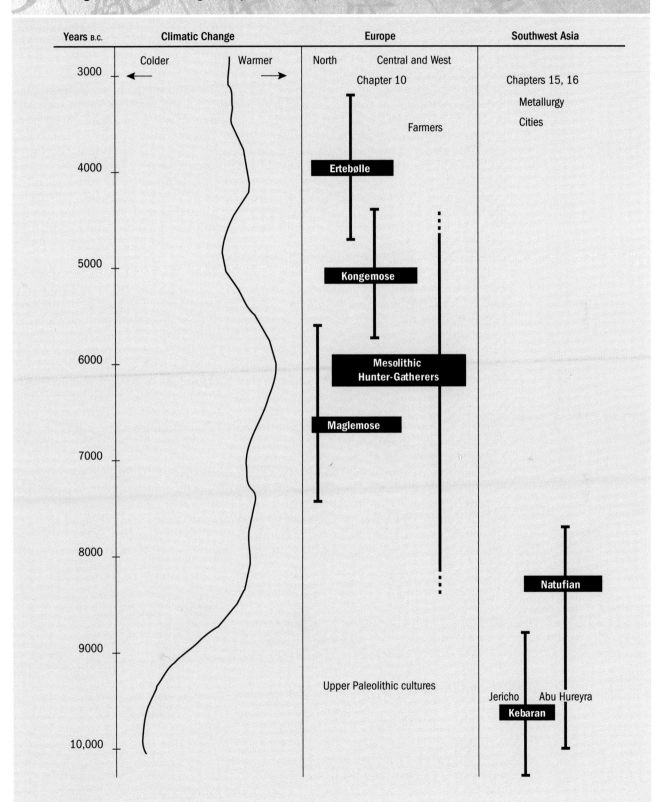

With the onset of warmer conditions, their distribution expanded greatly, so that they were accessible to many more hunter-gatherer bands distributed over a vast area.

In Mexico, the climate of 18,000 B.C. was drier and colder than today. At the end of the Ice Age, temperatures rose, bringing a rich forest of cacti and legume trees to the mountain valleys of Puebla and Oaxaca. This thorn-scrub-cactus forest included many wild ancestors of domesticated plants, including the maguey, squash, bean, and teosinte, the wild grass that was the ancestor of domesticated maize.

These and other Holocene climatic changes had profound effects on hunter-gatherer societies throughout the world, especially on the intensity of the food quest and the complexity of their societies. Why had such changes not occurred earlier in prehistory? There had been climatic changes of similar, if not even greater, magnitude in early millennia, say, during the early part of the last interglacial, some 128,000 years ago. One reason may have been population density. Then, human populations were much smaller, and a great deal of the world was uninhabited. It was possible for human populations living in large hunting territories to move around freely and to adapt to rapid climatic shifts by traveling to new areas, even over large distances. This ability enabled them to develop highly flexible survival strategies that took account of the constant fluctuations in food availability. If, for example, an African band experienced two dry years in a row, it could move away or fall back on less nutritious edible foods, perhaps species that required more energy to harvest.

By 10,000 B.C., circumstances were very different. The world's hunter-gatherer population was probably approaching about 8.5 million people (Hassan, 1981). The **carrying capacity** of the earth still exceeded that required by the human population, largely because humans were becoming more efficient in their exploitation of a broad spectrum of food resources. After 10,000 B.C., the population curve approached that of carrying capacity in many areas (Figure 7.1). This development may have set off behavioral changes resulting from restricted mobility and greater competition. Notable among these changes would have been a necessity to solve problems locally rather than just moving away from them. People would have tended to exploit a wider range of local resources, both to avert starvation and to protect themselves from food shortages caused by short-term droughts and other unpredictable changes. The increased plant productivity of the Holocene meant that people became much more dependent on vegetable foods of all kinds.

In a sense, the world was full, or at least occupied sparsely, by people who lived off its game, plant, and other food resources. *Homo sapiens sapiens* had settled in **periglacial** regions, in tropical rain forests, on offshore islands, and in the Americas. There were scattered hunter-gatherer populations throughout the world, many of them living in areas such as central Australia, for example, where the carrying capacities of the land were very low indeed (Figure 7.2). Human populations had risen considerably, too,

FIGURE 7.1 Increases in world population during the Ice Age matched against the carrying capacity of the globe for humans.

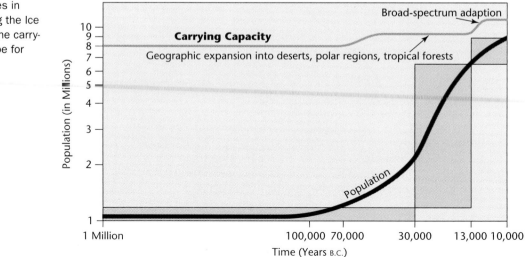

FIGURE 7.2 San hunter with weapons from Ho Khotso rock shelter, Lesotho, southern Africa, from a late Stone Age painting colored purple-red. The figure is approximately 21 cm (8 inches) high. Such paintings provide invaluable generalized information on ancient lifeways, as well as insights into ancient rituals.

especially in areas with diverse and seasonally predictable food resources. Even in sparsely inhabited environments, hunting territories were more confined. There was less room to move around; there were often more mouths to feed; and new adaptive strategies were needed, strategies aimed at more efficient and productive exploitation of the environment. As a result of these new strategies, hunter-gatherer societies underwent profound changes and, in some areas, acquired much greater complexity (for a series of area surveys, see Straus et al., 1996).

The technology used by Holocene hunter-gatherer societies for the most part comprised adaptations of much earlier toolkits for new, more specialized roles. Some of these artifacts, such as microblades, baked clay objects, ground stone tools, and woodworking implements, clearly come from earlier prototypes. Between 10,700 B.C. and 8800 B.C., the climate was more stable and becoming warmer, a period when many societies turned to fish, smaller game, and, above all, newly productive plant foods. The result—more specialized toolkits and a narrower focus on food resources that could be procured in large quantities. Among the innovations were more elaborate traps, hunting nets, fishhooks, harpoons, and fishing weirs. But the big breakthrough was the bow and arrow, which was in widespread use throughout much of the Old World by 8000 B.C. But this new weapon only spread into the heart of North America after the time of Christ, when it came rapidly into use. (It was in use in the Arctic by 2000 B.C.) Bows allowed individual hunters to pursue quite large game alone, without the cooperation of others, a major change with obvious social implications (for a discussion, see Bettinger, 2001).

⚬ Coping with Environmental Variation

Increasingly during the late Ice Age and more frequently in Holocene times, hunter-gatherer populations were confronted with new challenges, challenges created both by major climatic changes at the end of the Pleistocene and by local population growth. Everywhere, much more circumscribed hunter-gatherers were forced to improve their strategies for coping with local environmental variations, both in predictable seasonal resources and in unpredictable shifts in such phenomena as rainfall patterns or game migration routes (see the extended discussion in Bettinger, 2001).

This shift can be seen clearly in the Americas. As we saw in Chapter 5, the Americans of 11,500 B.C. were small in numbers, highly mobile, and sparsely distributed on the ground. They subsisted in some part off Ice Age big game, which became extinct very rapidly after 11,000 B.C. The archaeological record now shows a much greater diversity of local adaptations over the millennia, as thousands of isolated hunter-gatherer

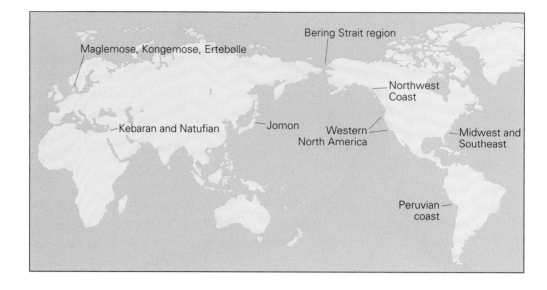

FIGURE 7.3 Map showing general areas where affluent hunter-gatherers mentioned in this book flourished.

groups became more and more restricted in their movements. The change was especially marked in areas of exceptional resource diversity like the Pacific Northwest coast, the southern California coast, and the fertile river valleys of the southern Midwest and the southeastern United States (Figure 7.3). In all these areas, hunter-gatherer populations became more sedentary and developed often highly specialized technologies for hunting, foraging, or fishing (Figure 7.4).

The **intensification** of hunting and gathering was marked by two long-term technological trends that went hand in hand. The first was the gradual downsizing of stone artifacts and the perishable antler, bone, and wood toolkit that went with them. The second was the development of highly efficient, often very specialized, sets of hunting weapons or food-processing implements designed for the intensive exploitation of specific food resources such as reindeer, sea mammals, birds, or acorns. The trend toward diminution in stone technology began during the late Ice Age and coincided in general terms with the last glacial maximum of about 18,000 B.C. Spear barbs and knife blades became smaller and lighter in weight, as if the hunters were relying more heavily on spear-throwers for propulsion velocity. It was sometime during the late Ice Age, too, that the bow and arrow came into use; it is a weapon with many advantages, among them greater accuracy, enhanced portability, and the ability to fire off several missiles within a very short space of time. The bow was also far more versatile than the spear,

FIGURE 7.4 Salmon fishing in the Pacific Northwest; nineteenth-century painting by Paul Kane. Harvesting salmon runs required a carefully organized "production line" to process, dry, and store the fish as they were speared and netted by the thousands.

FIGURE 7.5 An Inuit hunter casting a harpoon at the edge of an ice floe in northern Canada.

for the hunters could carry many more lightweight lethal points with them in a small quiver, arrows that could be brought into use in a few moments. Under these circumstances, the chances of a kill were greatly enhanced (Figure 7.5).

We do not know exactly when the bow and arrow first came into use, but there is a good reason to believe that this versatile hunting weapon was in Europe by 9000 B.C. and perhaps in Africa and Southwest Asia at about the same time. In contrast, it reached the Americas very much later, in some areas as late as 200 B.C. As early as 28,000 B.C., and even more intensively after 13,000 B.C., stone tool technologies became more and more standardized and more and more oriented toward the production of parts of composite tools, especially small arrow and knife barbs, scrapers, and awls. In Europe and Southwest Asia, this technology involved the production of thousands of small **microliths,** geometrically shaped barbs used on all manner of weapons (Figure 7.6). These standardized artifacts were made by striking small bladelets off a conical core, then notching and snapping off the thicker end to form a small microlith. Microlith-tipped and barbed wooden arrows have been found intact in Danish swamps, environments where they were used to hunt forest game, rodents, and birds for many centuries.

The diminution of stone technology reflected a much greater emphasis on specialized but versatile toolkits that were modified to reflect local needs. The early Holocene saw a much greater localization of artifacts of all kinds, a development reflected in a proliferation of new archaeological "cultures"; these, in fact, reflected a world in which movement was more circumscribed, in which thousands of small bands and occasionally larger population groups adapted to constant local environmental variation. This localization is well documented in areas like Europe, Australia, Southwest Asia, and the North American Great Basin, as well as by Kent Flannery's important work on a small forager band that visited Guilá Naquitz Cave, Mexico, between about 8750 and 6670 B.C. As Flannery has eloquently pointed out, the new local toolkits were part of a process whereby humans coped not only with long-term climatic change but also with the constant uncertainties of local climates. "Humans are well suited to the working out of resilient strategies for environmental variability," Flannery writes, "since they possess multigenerational memory and have unique methods for exchanging information and establishing cooperative relationships over long periods" (1986, p. 76).

The new subsistence strategies often involved highly intensive exploitation of locally abundant and predictable resources such as salmon or nuts. Such intensive exploitation

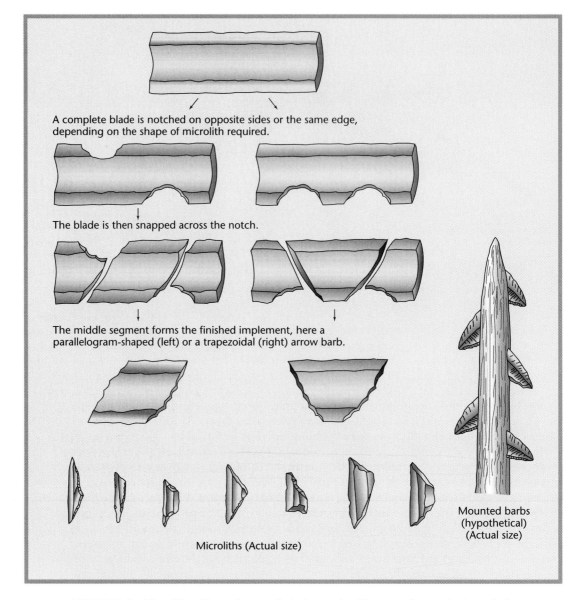

A complete blade is notched on opposite sides or the same edge, depending on the shape of microlith required.

The blade is then snapped across the notch.

The middle segment forms the finished implement, here a parallelogram-shaped (left) or a trapezoidal (right) arrow barb.

Microliths (Actual size)

Mounted barbs (hypothetical) (Actual size)

FIGURE 7.6 Microliths. Stages in manufacturing a microlith, a small arrow barb or similar implement made by notching a blade and snapping off its base after the implement is formed.

was adaptive in environments where seasonal phenomena such as salmon runs, caribou migrations, or hickory harvests required not only the harvesting of enormous quantities of food in a short time but also their processing and storage for later use. Storage technology now assumed a new and pressing importance; thousands of fish were dried on racks in the sun or in front of fires, and the nut and wild cereal harvest was placed in basket- or clay-lined pits for later consumption. There was nothing new in the notion of storage; much earlier, big-game hunters, for example, dried meat and pounded it up to eat on the march. What was new, however, was the notion of large-scale storage in more sedentary settlements, where mobility was no longer a viable strategy. By the use of storage and by the careful seasonal "mapping" of game, plant, and aquatic resources, early Holocene hunter-gatherers compensated for periodic food shortages caused by short-term climatic change and seasonal fluctuations. At the same time, they broadened their diet to include foods that were less nourishing, another way of ensuring fallback in the diet in the event of staple shortages.

As early as 18,000 B.C., and more markedly after 10,000 B.C., toolkits displayed much greater specialization and elaboration. We have already mentioned the development of the needle as a catalyst for layered, tailored clothing in periglacial environments,

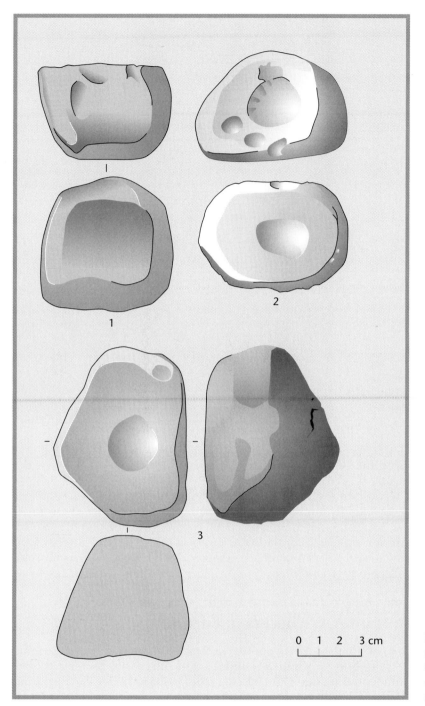

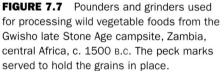

FIGURE 7.7 Pounders and grinders used for processing wild vegetable foods from the Gwisho late Stone Age campsite, Zambia, central Africa, c. 1500 B.C. The peck marks served to hold the grains in place.

and both the Magdalenians and the Eastern Gravettian hunters used a wide variety of specialized, and sometimes elaborate, antler and bone tools in the chase and in domestic life, as well as nets and cordage (see Chapter 4). Holocene hunter-gatherer societies worldwide developed even more specialized toolkits for many purposes. Many African and North American societies relied heavily on seeds and nuts. They developed many forms of grinders and pestles to process such harvests (Figure 7.7), and the rich organic deposits of such sites as the Hoko River and Ozette on the Olympic Peninsula in the Pacific Northwest document a highly effective halibut-fishing and whale-hunting technology based on wood, bone, slate, and fiber (Figure 7.8) (Croes and Hackenberger, 1988). Canoes, bone-tipped fish spears, and wooden birding arrows were part of the specialized fishing and **fowling** toolkit of Holocene groups in northern Europe. Perhaps the ultimate in specialized hunting technology for sea

FIGURE 7.8 Replica of an ancient halibut fishhook used for fishing, from the Hoko River site, Olympic Peninsula, Washington, USA.

mammals comes from the Bering Sea coasts of Alaska and the Thule culture of the Canadian Arctic (see Chapter 5).

More restricted territories, less mobility, rising local population, and new strategies for dealing with seasonal and unpredictable environmental variations—these problems were common to postglacial hunter-gatherer societies throughout the world. A few of these societies, especially those living in areas with rich and diverse food resources that included fish or sea mammals, achieved a high degree of social complexity, with signs of some social ranking.

〽️ Mesolithic Hunter-Gatherers in Europe

An excellent example of how late Ice Age hunter-gatherers adapted to global warming comes from northwestern Europe, where **Mesolithic** forest and coastal hunter-gatherers replaced tundra reindeer hunters after 11,000 B.C. (J. G. D. Clark, 1975). The European Mesolithic spanned about 4500 years, from about 8000 B.C. to the beginnings of farming in northwestern Europe about 3500 B.C.

11,000 B.C.

The environmental changes in Europe after 13,000 B.C. were so dramatic that the Magdalenian and other late Ice Age cultures vanished relatively quickly. The traditional view held that Europe was now populated by impoverished Mesolithic hunters and gatherers who had lost much of their capacity for economic and social relations. This notion of a cultural hiatus has crumbled in the face of recent sophisticated ecological researches. Instead of impoverished environments, each change in postglacial forest composition probably brought greater ecological productivity. A range of forest **ungulates** such as red and roe deer replaced the migratory reindeer that were so important in the Ice Age. Plant foods such as nuts assumed much greater importance in Mesolithic life (Zvelebil, 1994).

These food sources may have contributed to an increase in Mesolithic populations. Coasts, estuaries, and lakes were highly productive, especially with such seasonal resources as salmon, water birds, and sea mammals, many of them relying on seasonal plankton production in the oceans. Many of these aquatic foods could be taken and stored, especially by people who occupied relatively permanent encampments nearby. Thus, larger populations were possible in some areas among people who relied on seasonal resources and used such nonseasonal foods as shellfish to plug the gaps (Rowley-Conwy, 1986). Some of these more sedentary groups enjoyed a bounty of food sources and a complexity of life that has been called *affluent foraging.*

Were all European Mesolithic groups affluent foragers? The interplay of different resources varied dramatically throughout Europe, with its seasonal climates and productive environments. This was not a hostile environment peopled by only minimally complex hunter-gatherer bands but one where a great variety of adaptations was possible. At least two general models have been proposed for Mesolithic Europe:

- Lower latitudes supported somewhat generalized environments where highly mobile bands exploited evenly dispersed animal and plant resources, shifting camp regularly as local resources were exhausted.

- Higher-latitude environments were more uneven in productivity and resource reliability, having few species in large numbers. These were specialized environments, where human groups moved less often and frequently directed their moves toward the exploitation of a single seasonal resource such as caribou. Larger numbers of people sometimes congregated for seasonal hunts.

These are, of course, by no means the only models for Mesolithic life that could be put forward, but they serve to remind us that this was a period when European populations enjoyed a wide range of adaptations—from peoples with highly mobile lifeways to permanently settled, "affluent" groups that dwelled in large villages or base camps, such as those found in northwestern Europe and by the Iron Gates area of the Danube River. Without question, the Mesolithic was a period of broad variation in economic and social life, with some intensification of the food quest where uncertain environmental conditions dictated it (see Site box).

Clive Gamble (1986) points out that the adaptive trends seen in the European Mesolithic are not particularly innovative; indeed, most of them had their roots in a much earlier restructuring of the organization and use of resources with the arrival of modern humans in temperate latitudes some 35,000 years ago. The Upper Paleolithic saw much greater exploitation of regional resources and an enhanced ability to adapt to extremes of both glacial and fully interglacial climates. This restructuring gave Europeans the ability to solve the problems of exploiting not just a few resources but many different ones at once. This ability became vital at the end of the Ice Age, when food management strategies could cope with extremely varied combinations of food resources. These strategies included some elements that were of critical importance when people began to grow crops and tame animals: adaptations that were attuned to the scheduling of seasonal activities connected with growing and harvesting seasons and systems of information sharing. The Mesolithic hunters' schedule was comprehensive and flexible enough to cope with anything and could easily accommodate strategies that relied on deliberate cultivation of the soil or careful animal husbandry.

Efficient food management strategies involved more effective technology, too—more diverse toolkits for hunting forest animals and exploiting coastal resources such as sea mammals and shallow-water fish. The Mesolithic peoples who lived along the shores of the newly emerging Baltic Sea developed an astonishing range of fish spears, nets, harpoons, and traps, many of them preserved in waterlogged sites. Spears and arrows were tipped with tiny stone, bone, or antler barbs. Ground-edged tools were used for woodworking and processing forest plants. Large canoes, some of them dugouts hollowed from tree trunks, were in evidence. We know that Stone Age people were crossing open water as early as 10,000 B.C., for miners were visiting the island of Melos in the Mediterranean to collect obsidian that was traded far and wide (Torrance, 1986).

In a trend toward increasing **sedentism,** many Mesolithic groups lived in larger, more permanent settlements, a number of them located on strategic bays or near lakes or rivers. Some locations were probably used year-round or certainly for many months, anchored by abundant aquatic resources nearby. There were smaller camps and specialist activity areas, too. Everything points to greater internal differentiation in society

Star Carr
8700 to 8400 B.C.

Star Carr, England

Star Carr, probably the most famous Mesolithic site in the world, lies in northeastern England. One of the first Stone Age locations dug with environmental experts on site, Star Carr has become a classic example of ecological archaeology for generations of students. The site came to light in 1947, when amateur archaeologist John Moore unearthed some flint tools and broken bones at the edge of a long dried-up glacial lake in northeastern England, only a few miles from the North Sea coast. Cambridge University archaeologist Grahame Clark recruited the services of pollen experts Harry Goodwin and Donald Walker, and spent three seasons (1949–51) excavating a tiny birchwood platform crammed with stone tool fragments, bone and wooden artifacts, and a wealth of food remains. Using archaeology, animal bones, pollen analysis, and all manner of esoteric identifications, as well as a liberal dose of traditional European folklore, Clark reconstructed Star Carr as a small hunting camp set in a patch of reeds by a lake. Pollen samples placed Star Carr to a time when birch forests first spread into northern Britain and much of the southern North Sea was still dry land. Radiocarbon pioneer Willard Libby of the University of Chicago dated Star Carr to 7538 ± 350 B.C. Clark and his experts argued from the red deer antlers that the site was occupied in winter. He analyzed the methods used to make bone spear points, linked the technology of the stone tools to those made in Scandinavia at the time, and described a remarkable series of bone and wooden tools, including elk antler mattock heads, one with the tip of its wooden handle still in place; a single wooden canoe paddle; awls; even bark rolls and lumps of *pragmites*, moss used for fire-lighting (Figure 7.9).

Grahame Clark published his classic monograph, *Excavations at Star Carr*, in 1954. Since then, Star Carr has become an important testing ground for new ideas on ancient hunter-gatherer societies. Just recently, archaeologists Paul Mellars and Petra Dark (1998) published a new report on Star Carr that highlights the staggering advances in archaeological science since Clark's excavations. They report on 12 years of highly selective paleoecological and archaeological investigations, from 1985 to 1997. An entirely new vision of the site is coming from archaeological science unimaginable in Clark's day.

When Clark first excavated Star Carr, he concentrated on a small waterlogged area in a gully. After three seasons, he interpreted the site as a small settlement, perhaps used irregularly by four or five families. The new excavations extended onto drier areas and showed that the site was of a far greater extent than Clark suspected. By fieldwalking and careful test pitting, the excavators plotted flint artifact scatters over more than 122 m (400 feet) of the ancient lake shore. Thus, Star Carr saw much more widespread activity than Clark originally suspected. By carefully surveying the original topography of the site, Mellars and his colleagues located a clay-filled channel that once flowed through the center of the site, separating Clark's wetland area from the drier locations.

The new excavators were able to bring a far wider range of dating methods to bear on Star Carr. Grahame Clark believed the site was occupied on and off for a considerably longer period of time than his single radiocarbon date suggested, basing his argument on differences between barbed antler point forms. A new trench 66 feet east of Clark's original excavation produced 12 closely spaced accelerator mass spectrometry (AMS) radiocarbon dates on charcoal and minute plant remains taken from a stratigraphic column excavated for paleoecological analysis (for AMS dating, see Chapter 8). By correlating these dates with tree-ring readings from central European pines, Mellars and Dark dated the occupation to between 8700 and 8400 B.C., a good 1000 years earlier than Clark's original date. But two AMS dates from organic artifacts recovered in the Clark excavations dated to between 7400 and 7100 B.C., as if the site was occupied later as well. Instead of simplifying the picture, the new, finer-grained chronology complicates it and gives the site a life of at least 300 years, confirming Clark's suspicions of a lengthy occupation.

Grahame Clark originally hypothesized that the inhabitants of Star Carr had little impact on their surroundings. Petra Dark was able to use much higher resolution microscopes to examine the distribution of charcoal particles associated with the AMS dates. She showed that there was an initial period of intense charcoal deposition that lasted for about 80 years, then a century with little activity, followed by fairly continuous distribution for a further 130 years. Botanist Jon Hather identified the charcoals as those of reeds, burnt off when they were dry between autumn and spring, when new growth begins. Mellars and Dark believe the reeds were fired repeatedly by humans, largely because the samples of high charcoal frequency are localized at the site, as if burning was tightly controlled. Such conflagrations, commonplace among historic foragers, could have provided people with a better view of the lake and surrounding terrain, as well as a convenient landing place for canoes. They also fostered new plant growth, which would attract feeding animals.

Clark claimed that Star Carr was based on a crude birchwood platform. Excavations in 1985 revealed another, quite different wooden structure 18 meters (60 feet) east of the original trenches, this time a concentration of large timbers, some split like planks, all laid in the same direction. The timbers are willow and aspen, species that grew by the lake at the time of occupation. Only a small portion of the structure was uncovered, for the excavators lacked the large-scale conservation facilities to uncover more of it. But they theorize it may have been some form of trackway leading down to water's edge. Clearly, Star Carr was more elaborate than Clark suspected.

The original report described Star Carr as a winter settlement, but later investigators like Anthony Legge and Peter Rowley-Conwy restudied the bones and argued for late spring and early summer occupation. Now x-ray analysis of unerupted teeth deep in deer jaw bones and comparisons with modern samples have identified many 10- to 11-month-old animals, which would have been killed in March or April. This new seasonality data agree with minute finds of tightly rolled leaf stems of reeds burnt in early growth between March and April, as well as with aspen bud scalers that date to the same time of year. No winter settlement, Star Carr may have been occupied from March until at least June or early July.

Forty years of new interpretations at Star Carr, which look further afield than the confines of the site, confirm that this lakeside location was very attractive to local foragers over several centuries. The comparatively well-sheltered and sunny site lies near a large lake promontory, ideal for spotting and driving animals. Above all, the inhabitants were not passive users of their landscape, but modified it repeatedly with burning. The site was occupied at a time when dense birch forests pressed on the lake, confining human activity to lakeshore areas. This is why the appearance of stone axes at Star Carr is so important, for they may represent the first efforts of Europeans to cope with dense forest and to develop basic woodworking skills for laying trackways and other large-scale projects.

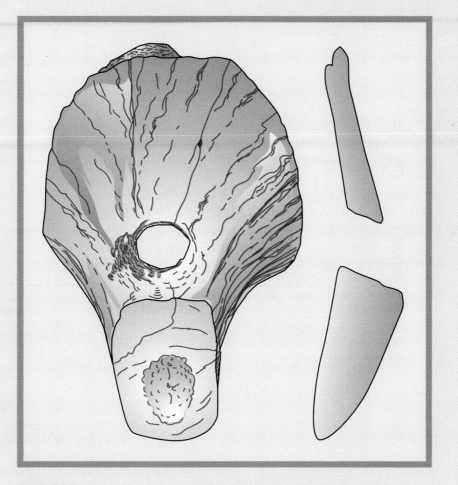

FIGURE 7.9 Elk antler mattock from Star Carr, England (two-thirds actual size).

and to more intensive subsistence activities. Nuts and shellfish became far more important, and hunters took a far wider range of game than their Ice Age predecessors. It was not the dietary staples but merely the diversity of exploited food resources that changed.

Perhaps the most profound changes were those in population densities and social organization, both notoriously difficult phenomena to identify in the archaeological record. J. G. D. Clark (1977) has identified three major "social territories" at the end of the Upper Paleolithic, between the Netherlands, Poland, and southern Sweden. Three distinct cultures (Ahrensburgian, Swiderian, and Bromme) each covered territories of about 100,000 sq km (38,610 square miles). As the Holocene wore on, these territories were rapidly reduced in size. By 6000 B.C., at least 15 territories were in this same area, identified by different artifact styles or distributions of raw materials. Each of these zones was 15,000 to 20,000 sq km (5791 to 7722 square miles) in extent. This pattern may reflect major changes in the regional distribution, density, and social organization of Mesolithic populations.

6000 B.C.

Douglas Price (1983) points out that as these changes were taking place, new artifact forms and presumably other innovations were spreading across wide areas of Europe. Among them was a characteristic trapeze-shaped microlith, widely used as an arrow barb by later Mesolithic peoples, that appeared all over the continent about 6000 B.C., perhaps somewhat earlier in southeast Europe (J. G. D. Clark, 1958). The Mesolithic ended with the rapid spread of agricultural economies into southeastern Europe about 6000 B.C. From there, they spread sporadically into central Europe by 4500 B.C. and to the northwest after 3500 B.C.

The European Mesolithic testifies to a continuity in human culture from Ice Age times, but this continuity was based on continuous adjustment to changing postglacial environments. In time, the same Mesolithic societies readapted to the warmest millennia of postglacial times, not only by shifting their hunting and foraging methods but also by taking up new subsistence practices, often within the context of their existing society.

〰 Mesolithic Complexity in Scandinavia

This continuity is well documented from waterlogged Mesolithic sites in Britain and Scandinavia, where three broad subdivisions of the northern Mesolithic are known (Price, 1985).

The Maglemose Period (7500 to 5700 B.C.)

Maglemose
7500 to 5700 B.C.

The Maglemose was a time of seasonal exploitation of rivers and lakes, combined with terrestrial hunting and foraging. Inland, late spring and early summer settlements are represented by the Ulkestrup site in Denmark, where the people lived in large huts with bark and wood floors, on a peat island in a swamp by a lake. One hut lay close to poles where canoes were once moored. A large wooden paddle lay nearby. The Maglemose people fished with bone- and antler-barbed points, trapped birds, and hunted red deer, wild ox, and pig. In fall, the bands foraged for hazelnuts and other edible plant foods, killing elk and other game in winter, when fishing was apparently less important.

The Kongemose Period (5700 to 4600 B.C.)

Kongemose
5700 to 4600 B.C.

Kongemose sites are mainly on Baltic Sea coasts, along bays and near lagoons, where the people exploited both marine and terrestrial resources. Many Kongemose sites are somewhat larger than Maglemose ones; among the better known is the Segebro settlement, now submerged in brackish water near the southwestern Swedish coast. This settlement covered 50 m by 25 m (164 feet by 82 feet) and was occupied year-round, but mainly in spring and summer. Carbon isotope analyses of human bones from Segebro show that fish and sea mammals constituted most of the diet, with no fewer than 66 species of animals found in the site. Not only freshwater and saltwater fish but also red deer, elk, boars, and seals were commonplace.

The Ertebølle Period (4600 to 3200 B.C.)

Ertebølle was the culmination of Mesolithic culture in southern Scandinavia (Price, 1987). By this time, the Scandinavians were occupying many coastal settlements year-round, subsisting off a very wide range of food resources indeed. These included forest game and waterfowl, shellfish, sea mammals, and both shallow- and deep-water fish. There were smaller seasonal coastal sites, too, many for specific activities such as deep-water fishing, sealing, or hunting of migratory birds. The Aggersund site in Denmark was occupied for a short period in the autumn, when the inhabitants collected oysters and hunted some game, especially migratory swans. Ertebølle technology was far more elaborate than that of its Mesolithic predecessors; a wide variety of antler, bone, and wood tools for specialized purposes such as fowling and sea mammal hunting were developed, including dugout canoes up to 10 m (32.8 feet) long.

Ertebølle
4600 to 3200 B.C.

With sedentary settlement comes evidence of greater social complexity. Some Ertebølle communities buried their dead in cemeteries, placing the bodies in various positions, with dog interments alongside the human. The Vedbaek Bogebakken cemetery in Denmark dates to about 5000 B.C. and contains the graves of at least 22 people of different ages. Everyone was buried in an extended position (Figure 7.10); at least three people were buried after injury or a violent death. Men and women were deposited with different grave goods, and older people with red deer antlers. Other Ertebølle cemeteries from Denmark contain evidence of violent death; some people have projectile points in their ribs. There are also traces of cannibalism (Price, 1985).

5000 B.C.

FIGURE 7.10 Burial of a man, a woman, and, between them, a small child, from Vedbaek, Denmark, c. 5000 B.C. A bone point is embedded in the man's throat; the woman wears a ring of animal teeth, which lies on her chest. (Burial from Vedbaek, Denmark. National Museum of Denmark, Danish Collections.)

FIGURE 7.11 A 35-year-old man from Porsmose, Denmark, who died of bone arrow wounds c. 3000 B.C. One went through his nose and into his brain.

3000 B.C.

The trend toward more sedentary settlement, the cemeteries, and the occasional social differentiation revealed by elaborate burials are all reflections of an intensification among these relatively affluent hunter-gatherers of 3000 B.C. Mesolithic societies intensified the food quest by exploiting many more marine species, making productive use of migratory waterfowl and their breeding grounds, and collecting shellfish in enormous numbers. This intensification is also reflected in a much more elaborate and diverse technology, more exchange of goods and materials between neighbors, greater variety in settlement types, and a slowly rising population throughout southern Scandinavia (Figure 7.11). These phenomena may, in part, be a reflection of rising sea levels throughout the Mesolithic, inundations that flooded many cherished territories. There are signs, too, of regional variations in artifact forms and styles, of cultural differences between people living in carefully delineated territories and competing for resources.

Mesolithic cultures are much less well defined elsewhere in Europe, partly because the climatic changes were less extreme than in southern Scandinavia and because there were fewer opportunities for coastal adaptation. In many areas, settlement was confined to lakeside and riverside locations, widely separated from one another by dense forests. Many Mesolithic sites were located on ecotones, so that the inhabitants could return to a central base location, where for much of the year they lived close to predictable resources such as lake fish. However, they would exploit both forest game and other seasonal resources from satellite camps. For example, Michael Jochim (1976) believes that in central Europe, some groups wintered in camps along the Danube, moving to summer encampments on the shores of neighboring lakes. In many areas, like Spain, there appears to have been intensified exploitation of marine and forest resources. There was a trend nearly everywhere toward greater variety in the diet, with more attention being paid to less obvious foods and to those, like shellfish, that require more complex processing methods than do game and other such resources.

Thus, in parts of Europe, there was a long-term trend among hunter-gatherer societies toward a more extensive exploitation of food resources, often within the context of a strategy that sought ways to minimize the impact of environmental uncertainty. In more favored areas, such as southern Scandinavia, some such societies achieved a level of nascent social complexity that was to become commonplace among later farming peoples. When farming did come to Europe, this preadaptation was an important catalyst for rapid economic and social change (Chapter 10).

⠿ Hunter-Gatherer Complexity

"Hunter-gatherers move around a lot and live in small groups." This statement has been a universal label for hunter-gatherer societies, ancient and modern, for a generation (Lee and DeVore, 1976). It paints a picture of hunter-gatherers in prefarming times who lived in small, temporary camps; were constantly on the move; and possessed a highly portable technology and a flexible social system. However, these models were based in large part on anthropological research among living societies like the !Kung San of the Kalahari Desert in southern Africa or the Inuit of the Canadian Arctic (Binford, 2001a). Most of them are populations living and dwindling in areas of the world, like tropical rain forests, Arctic regions, or semideserts, where agriculture is an impossibility. Almost invariably, they have been in touch with farmers, and the wider world, for many centuries, which suggests they may have little to tell us about ancient foraging societies. Only a handful of hunter-gatherer societies, peoples like the Ainu of Japan or the Northwest coast Indians of North America, enjoyed complex adaptations at the time of European contact around the eighteenth century A.D. Generalizations about highly mobile, small-scale hunter-gatherer societies took little account of the great diversity among the many hunting and foraging societies that once existed on earth. This diversity, known almost entirely from archaeological research, developed during the late Ice Age and the Holocene. Above all, the archaeological record of the world of 13,000 to 4000 B.C. reveals a global trend toward great complexity in hunter-gatherer societies in well-defined regions as widely separated as northern Europe, southern Africa, Japan, the North American Midwest, and coastal Peru.

Conditions for Greater Complexity

Complex hunter-gatherer societies did not appear everywhere, but they occurred in a remarkable variety of environments, from fertile river valleys to coastal deserts. Whatever the environment, however, certain general conditions were necessary. First, population movements had to be limited by either geography or the presence of neighbors. Thus, one could not move away from resource shortages; solutions had to be found on the spot. Second, resources had to be abundant and predictable in their seasonal appearance. Small, numerous organisms with high reproductive rates played an especially important role in intensifying hunting and gathering. Such organisms included fish, shellfish, nuts, and seeds (Hayden, 1981, 1990), species that were available in abundance and seldom exhausted. Third, population growth might reach a point at which food shortages occurred and there was an imbalance between people and their food supply. Again, a solution was to intensify the food quest, an intensification that might result in a more complex society.

Attributes of Greater Complexity

What features distinguish a more complex hunter-gatherer society from its less elaborate neighbors? The following appear to be of fundamental importance:

- Higher than normal population, concentrated in relatively small and restricted territories, such as individual river valleys, where movement is circumscribed by either geography or neighbors.
- A more intensive, more diversified, and more specialized food quest. Selected species such as nuts and seeds become more important, and foods that were not exploited previously because they required more effort are adopted into the diet. In some cases, people deliberately sow wild plants to ensure an adequate harvest.
- A system of food storage and preservation.
- Permanent and nearly permanent settlements, often base camps of much greater size than in earlier times. Settlements are often linear, distributed along, say, riverbanks; contain different forms of structures; and are often associated with burial grounds, which may serve as territorial boundaries.
- Highly developed hunting, fishing, or plant-processing equipment.
- Division of labor not only by sex and age but also by activity, such as whale hunting, or a craft specialty like canoe building.

- Some form of simple social ranking, probably based on differences between lineages or other kin groupings, such as wealth, diet, and burial customs.
- Often, intensive exchange in exotic objects and raw materials with neighboring groups.
- More elaborate ritual beliefs and ceremonial life.

Debates About Social Complexity

We do not know when the first more complex hunter-gatherer societies appeared, but at least some late Ice Age societies may have enjoyed some level of complexity. Possible candidates include the Magdalenians of southwestern France and northern Spain as well as the Eastern Gravettian plains hunters, with their mammoth-bone houses, who lived in the river valleys of Ukraine in 16,000 B.C. (see Chapter 4).

Complexity among hunter-gatherer societies became widespread after the Ice Age, especially in areas where freshwater or marine fish, shellfish, or sea mammals were available in abundance. Aquatic resources have the advantage of being both relatively plentiful and predictable, so that there are strong incentives for people to adopt sedentary lifeways along rivers and at lake and ocean shores. However, the full potential of marine and freshwater resources was realized in only a relatively few areas of the world, and then within the past 10,000 years.

The debates about social complexity among hunter-gatherers revolve around two opposing viewpoints. One viewpoint sees the oceans as a kind of Garden of Eden (Binford, 2001b). Proponents of this theory point to the enormous abundance of shellfish in many areas of the world and to the great productivity of many estuaries and coastal waters easily exploited by shore-dwelling fisherfolk. This abundance allowed societies to become sedentary and to maintain population densities (Moseley, 1975).

In contrast, another group of archaeologists, many of them studying post–Ice Age hunter-gatherers in Europe, argue that aquatic resources were a strategy of last resort, a response to population pressure and shortages of terrestrial resources such as game and plant foods (Gamble, 1986). These authorities assume that marine and freshwater resources, no matter how productive, were more labor-intensive to harvest and were less nutritionally valuable than food sources on land.

David Yesner (1987) takes a somewhat different perspective. He argues that the shift to the exploitation of aquatic resources was the result of decisions made in periods of rapid environmental change, when population pressure was causing food shortages. The "optimal" strategy for people under these circumstances would have been to turn to a resource that did involve more work and was, perhaps, as productive as big game.

All of these viewpoints assume, however, that maritime resources played a key role in the emergence of social complexity among Stone Age hunter-gatherers. The debate is unresolved, for we do not know exactly how decisive marine or riverine resources were in allowing dense populations and sedentary living, both essential prerequisites for social complexity. Nor do we know whether we can make comparisons between the elaborate and socially complex Northwest coast Indian cultures that flourished a few centuries ago in North America and early Holocene hunter-gatherer groups living thousands of years earlier, in the past (for a discussion, see Bettinger, 2001).

〰 Hunter-Gatherer Societies in Southwest Asia

13,000 B.C.

Southwest Asia has provided a fascinating picture of emerging social and cultural complexity among hunter-gatherers at the end of the Ice Age. Between 13,000 and 8000 B.C., the simple hunter-gatherer societies of the eastern Mediterranean, the coastal zone of present-day Israel and Syria, gave way to more complex hunting and gathering societies and eventually to farmers (for a site map, see Figure 9.1). For years, scientists have discussed the origins of agriculture in Southwest Asia, believing it to be a more radical transformation in human life than almost any other development in prehistory (see Chapter 8). In fact, recent research has suggested that the earlier transition to more complex hunter-gatherer societies may have been much more profound.

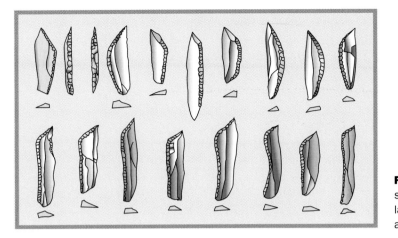

FIGURE 7.12 Geometric Kebaran microliths, full size. Such small artifacts were manufactured in large numbers and mounted on wooden shafts as arrowheads or barbs.

In 13,000 B.C., small and highly mobile hunter-gatherer bands inhabited the **Levant,** subsumed under the general cultural name of Kebaran. Kebaran sites, marked by thousands of small geometric microliths, occur not only in wooded country but also in the steppe and desert of the Negev and the Sinai (Henry, 1989). The Kebarans are found in a wide variety of environments, which may account for the great variation in their toolkits (Figure 7.12). Everything points to the Kebarans' having enjoyed a simple hunter-gatherer strategy, which placed a high premium on mobility (Bar-Yosef, 1987). In some areas, the people may have dispersed to the uplands in summer, moving into caves and rock shelters near lowland lakes in the winter. Apparently, plant foods were not overwhelmingly important, and the Kebaran toolkit lacks the specialized grinders and pounders found in later cultures, except at lower elevations, where some wild cereal grasses grew.

Kebaran
13,000 to 11,000 B.C.

By about 11,000 B.C., warming temperatures throughout Southwest Asia brought significant environmental and vegetational changes. During the late Ice Age, warmth-loving plants like wild emmer wheat and barley, oaks, almonds, and pistachio trees were restricted to refuge areas lying below modern sea level. These sandy-soil areas would have given only poor yields of wild cereals. As early Holocene temperatures rose, these plant and tree species colonized higher country, where clayey soils produced much higher yields (Henry, 1989). New, denser cereal stands were now much more resistant to short-term climatic change and were also harvestable over a longer period of time each year. Many hunter-gatherer sites on higher ground, from after 11,000 B.C., contain ground stone tools: pestles and mortars, implements used to process seed harvests for storage, an essential in much more seasonal, and increasingly arid, climates.

These abundant cereal and nut resources within the Mediterranean hill zone stimulated the development of more intensive foraging strategies, more sedentary settlement, and rapid territorial expansion until the most favored territories were filled. The emergence of these more plentiful plant resources coincided with the emergence of the Natufian culture from the earlier Kebaran, a culture that expanded rapidly to the edges of the Mediterranean zone within about 1500 years.

The Natufians used a more complex hunting and foraging strategy than the Kebarans. They exploited wild emmer and barley intensively, as well as acorn, almond, and pistachio, all highly productive resources that were easily stored (Byrd, 1989). The new subsistence strategies encouraged more sedentary lifeways and the development of much larger settlements, averaging about 700 sq m (7500 square feet) in area. These villages, which contained semisubterranean houses, storage pits, and pavements, were associated with nearby small, transitory camps, where food was collected and processed (Figure 7.13). The Natufian toolkit contained all manner of specialized plant-processing tools, including querns, grinding slabs, pestles, mortars, and bone sickles with flint blades (Figure 7.14). These bear a characteristic "sickle gloss" caused by the silica in cereal grass stalks.

Natufian
11,000 to 8500 B.C.

Natufian hamlets were confined to the Mediterranean hill zone, where wild cereals and nut-bearing trees had their natural habitat. The larger sites are close to the

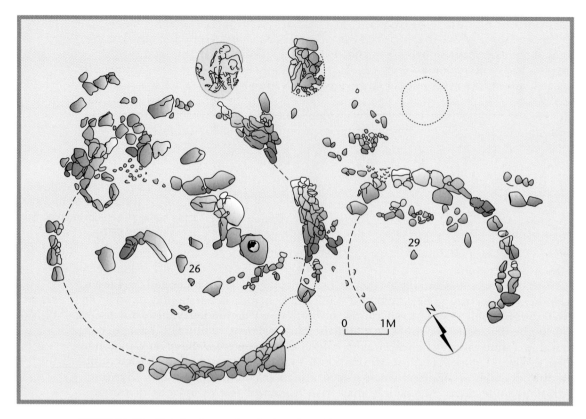

FIGURE 7.13 Natufian house foundations from Ain Mallaha, Jordan. There are mortars, pestles, and storage areas in Structure 26 (left) and a burial in a shallow pit immediately outside the north wall. The smaller hut (right) may have served as a storage area.

FIGURE 7.14 Natufian bone-handled sickle and flint blades.

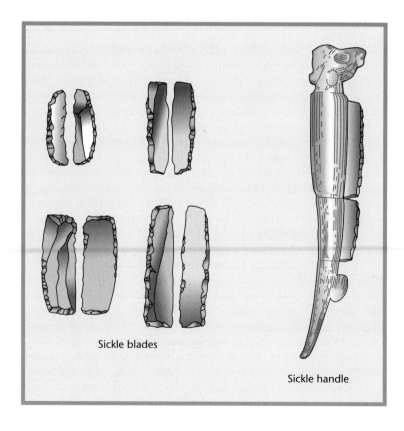

Sickle blades

Sickle handle

boundaries between the coastal plains or grassland valleys and the hill zone. Some were placed strategically to take advantage of good toolmaking stone. Such settlements enabled the Natufians to exploit spring cereal crops, fall nut harvests, and the game that flourished on the lowlands and on the rich nut **mast** on the forest floor in the hills above. Unlike their more mobile ancestors, the Natufians enjoyed many months of plentiful food by exploiting spring cereals and then following nut harvests up the slopes as the nuts ripened at progressively higher elevations. Gazelle hunting assumed great importance at certain seasons of the year, with neighboring communities cooperating in game drives, ambushes, and other mass-hunting enterprises.

By the end of Natufian times, about 8500 B.C., local populations were considerably higher than in earlier times. Natufian society offers intriguing glimpses at a new, more complex social order. The Natufians buried their dead in cemeteries, which have yielded a wealth of information on their society. There are clear signs of social ranking. One common and constantly recurring symbolic artifact, the *dentalium* seashell, is confined to a few burials, whereas the elaborate grave furniture such as stone bowls found with some individuals, including children, hints strongly at some form of social differences. Perhaps this social ranking was the result of a need for the redistribution of food surpluses and to maintain order within much larger sedentary communities. Also, the stone slab grave covers and mortar markers associated with the cemeteries may have served as ritual markers of territorial boundaries, perhaps of lands vested in revered ancestors.

After 9000 B.C., the Natufians faced much drier climatic conditions at a time when their populations were expanding. The effect of increased aridity was to shrink the cereal habitats in the Mediterranean zone, causing the most productive stands to be found at higher altitudes. At the same time, the Natufians were forced to remain in sedentary settlements close to permanent water supplies, a fact of life that made the cost of harvesting cereals and nuts at remote locations much higher. How, then, could people living in a complex hunter-gatherer system solve the problem of declining staples? After nearly 2000 years of close involvement with cereal plants, they would have been well aware of what was needed to plant and grow cereal grasses deliberately. By deliberately planting cereals on a modest scale, the people tried to cope with uncertainty, to augment declining stands of wild wheat and barley with their own supplemental crops. As we shall see in Chapter 9, it was only a short time before full-time farming societies were flourishing widely in Southwest Asia. In a real sense, the development of a more complex hunter-gatherer society in this area preadapted the Natufians to plant crops.

The Natufian scenario from the eastern Mediterranean was mirrored under different circumstances in many parts of the world, where trajectories of culture change followed many paths. In some areas, the new shape of hunter-gatherer societies preadapted people for the deliberate planting of cereal and root crops and for the domestication of animals. In other regions, such as southern California, that were marginal for subsistence farming, complex hunter-gatherer societies flourished until modern times.

Part III describes the origins of food production and early agricultural societies in all parts of the world.

Summary 〰〰〰

The Ice Age ended after 13,000 B.C., ushering in the beginning of the Holocene period. Dramatic climatic changes marked the Holocene, including retreating ice sheets, major shifts in vegetational zones, and rises in sea level. Many large mammal species became extinct. Hunter-gatherer societies throughout the world developed highly localized adaptations to new, less predictable conditions, with a more intensive exploitation of food resources and, in many areas, a trend toward more permanent settlement, the use of storage technologies, and more complex societies.

Complexity among hunter-gatherers became widespread after the Ice Age, especially in areas of exceptional resource diversity. Controversy surrounds the issue of complexity, with one school of thought arguing for a connection between resource diversity and abundant, diverse food supplies, and the other considering fishing a strategy of last resort resulting from population pressure and shortage of other foods. Alternatively, it may be due to rapid environmental change. This increased social complexity is well documented in the Mesolithic cultures of Scandinavia, where groups exploited maritime resources and birds extensively. Such increases in social complexity were marked by higher population densities, more intensive food exploitation, more long-distance exchange, and greater social ranking, detected in burial ornaments. These shifts also appear in the eastern Mediterranean region of Southwest Asia, especially among the Natufian people, who were intensive foragers of wild cereals and nuts, as well as expert gazelle hunters. Such intensification of the food quest and greater sedentism preadapted many groups for adopting agriculture and animal domestication.

Key Terms 🐾

Bølling-Allerod Interstadial A 2000-year period of global warming after the Ice Age, which began c. 12,400 B.C.

Carrying capacity The ability of the world's many environments to support animals and people.

Ecotone A transitional zone between different environments.

Fowling Bird hunting.

Holocene After the Greek *holos*, meaning "recent." Defines the geological period after the end of the Ice Age until today; c. 12,000 B.C. to present.

Intensification In archaeology, a more focused exploitation of food resources, or agriculture that uses methods such as irrigation to improve crop yields.

Levant A somewhat old-fashioned but useful label that describes the region of the eastern Mediterranean coastline and immediate hinterland.

Mast (Ma-aast) The rich fruit droppings of oaks and other forest trees.

Mesolithic From the Greek *mesos*, "middle," and *lithos*, "stone": the period of post–Ice Age times in Europe that preceded the introduction of farming.

Microlith From the Greek *micros*, "small," and *lithos*, "stone": a stone artifact of diminutive size, usually employed for arrow and spear barbs.

Periglacial Around or near glaciers.

Sedentism Permanent settlement at one location for all, or sometimes most, of the year, and over more than one year.

Ungulate A hoofed mammal.

Younger Dryas Interval A millennium-long period of sharply colder conditions around the world, which began c. 10,950 B.C.

Guide to Further Reading 🐾

Bettinger, Robert L. 2001. "Holocene Hunter-Gatherers." In *Archaeology at the Millennium*. Gary M. Feinman and T. Douglas Price, eds. Pp. 137–198. New York: Kluwer Academic.
Bettinger summarizes the current state of Holocene hunter-gatherer research and especially theory. This is a superb, highly technical essay that covers the major points with comparative examples.

Clark, J. G. D. 1975. *The Earlier Stone Age Settlement of Scandinavia*. Cambridge: Cambridge University Press.
A fundamental synthesis on Mesolithic northwestern Europe.

Henry, Donald O. 1989. *From Foraging to Agriculture*. Philadelphia: University of Pennsylvania Press.
This essay on Southwest Asia is excellent on the Natufian.

Price, T. D. 1985. "The Mesolithic of Western Europe." *Journal of World Prehistory* 1 (3):225–305.
A well-reasoned synthesis; discusses complexity among hunter-gatherers.

Price, T. D., and James A. Brown, eds. 1985. *Prehistoric Hunter-Gatherers: The Emergence of Cultural Complexity*. Orlando, FL: Academic Press.
Essays on emerging cultural complexity among hunter-gatherers in many parts of the world. A specialist volume.

Roberts, Neil. 1998. *The Holocene: An Environmental History*, 2nd ed. Oxford: Blackwell.
A useful survey of Holocene climate change that is already somewhat outdated by fast-moving climatic research.

Straus, Lawrence G., et al., eds. 1996. *Humans at the End of the Ice Age*. New York: Plenum Press.
This volume of essays explores, from a global perspective, a variety of cultural responses to Holocene climate change. A specialist's book, but an excellent discussion of major themes and controversies.

FIRST FARMERS

c. 10,000 B.C. TO MODERN TIMES

Agriculture is not to be looked on as a difficult or out-of-the-way invention, for the rudest savage, skilled as he is in the habits of the food-plants he gathers, must know well that if seeds or roots are put in a proper place in the ground they will grow.

Sir Edward Tylor, *Anthropology* (1871)

Part III tells the story of how food production began, beginning with a discussion of some of the theories about the origins of agriculture and animal domestication. We then describe the archaeological evidence for the origins of food production in different parts of the world, starting in Southwest Asia.

period already covered	period covered in this part	partial coverage

5 mya	2.5 mya	1 mya	100,000 B.P.	10,000 B.C.	A.D. 1	A.D. 1500

c h a p t e r

8

A PLENTEOUS HARVEST: THE ORIGINS

A boy herding cattle in East Africa.

The men climb high above the ground, lopping off small branches with their stone-bladed axes. The women and children gather up the foliage and pile it around the bare tree trunks. It is hard, backbreaking work that goes on for days on end, as the farmers watch the brazen sky for thunderclouds and signs of rain. A few spits of rain and building clouds bring hope of imminent showers. The people fire the tinder-dry brush, which burns fiercely. The sky fills with dense brown smoke as far as the eye can see, as the women turn over the fresh ash into the cleared soil and plant their precious seed. Then everyone waits for the life-giving rains to conjure bright green shoots from the soil (Figure 8.1).

It is sometimes hard for us to imagine, buying our food from supermarkets, that for more than 99 percent of our existence as humans we were hunters and gatherers, tied to the seasons of plant foods, the movements of game, and the ebb and flow of aquatic resources. Food production, the deliberate cultivation of cereal grasses and edible root plants, is a phenomenon of the last 12,000 years of human existence. This relatively new human subsistence strategy is in large part responsible for the rapidly accelerating rates of population growth and culture change in the past ten millennia. One of the major controversies in world prehistory surrounds the origins of food production: Why, when, and where did people first grow crops and domesticate wild animals? This chapter describes some of the major theories developed over more than a century of research.

 Theories About the Origins of Food Production

As we saw in Chapter 7, changing environmental and demographic conditions at the end of the Ice Age, after 13,000 B.C., caused major long-term changes in hunter-gatherer societies. There was more localization, considerable technological innovation, and a trend toward sedentary settlement in areas with abundant and seasonally predictable food resources. And as we saw with the Natufian culture of the eastern Mediterranean, many of these societies were, in many respects, preadapted to food production. When and why did they choose to grow their own crops?

Early Hypotheses

Late Victorian archaeologists were the first to speculate about agricultural origins. They envisaged a solitary genius who suddenly had the brilliant idea of planting seed. Today, no one looks for a single genius or for the earliest maize cob. Rather, modern theory concentrates on the complex processes that caused gradual changes in human subsistence patterns (B. Smith, 1998).

FIGURE 8.1 Modern-day hoe cultivation in an irrigated field in Kerala state, southern India.

The best-known and longest-lived of the early theories was Vere Gordon Childe's "Neolithic Revolution" **(Neolithic).** He proposed a major economic revolution in prehistory that took place in Southwest Asia during a period of severe drought, a climatic crisis that caused a symbiotic relationship between humans and animals in fertile oases. The new economies ensured a richer and more reliable food source for people on the edge of starvation after the Ice Age (Childe, 1936, 1952). Childe's simple theory was widely accepted, but it was based on inadequate archaeological and environmental data. It has long been surpassed by much more sophisticated formulations (H. Wright, 1993).

Systematic fieldwork on the origins of food production began only in the late 1940s, when Robert J. Braidwood of the University of Chicago mounted an expedition to the Kurdish foothills of Iran to test Childe's theory. He soon rejected any notion of catastrophic climatic change, arguing that economic change came from "ever increasing cultural differentiation and specialization of human communities" (Braidwood and Braidwood, 1983, p. 23). Thus, people were culturally receptive to innovation and experimentation with the cultivation of wild grasses. Braidwood believed that Stone Age hunters had domesticated animals and plants in "nuclear zones," areas such as the hilly flanks of the Zagros Mountains in Iraq and upland areas overlooking the Mesopotamian lowlands. He was convinced that the human capacity and enthusiasm for experimentation made it possible for people to domesticate animals. Most modern theories of food production have their beginnings in Braidwood's work, which focused on the notion that people were culturally receptive to new subsistence practices.

Multivariate Theories

Since the 1960s, theorizing about the origins of food production revolves around complex multivariate models, which combine many factors (Flannery, 1965, 1968). All multivariate models take into account the reality that many early Holocene hunter-gatherer societies were more complex and well preadapted to food production before anyone started planting wild cereal grasses or penning animals. For example, as recently as the eighteenth century A.D., the Kumeyaay Indians of southern California reduced the risk of starvation by "domesticating" their landscape. They lived in semi-arid valleys, encouraging the growth of wild grasses by burning harvested stands, then broadcasting some of the seed over the burned ground. They created groves of oaks and pines by planting edible nuts at high elevations, and they planted agave and other

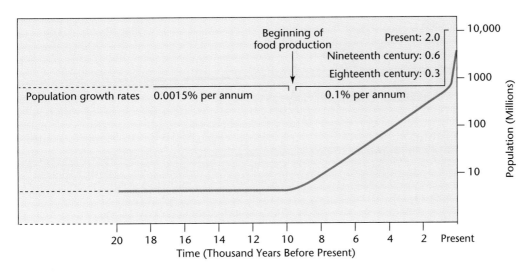

FIGURE 8.2 World population changes since the beginnings of food production. There has been an explosion in human population densities in the past 10,000 years.

desert plants in suitable habitats. In this way, they flourished by means of a complex mosaic of manipulated wild plants (B. Smith, 1998).

Population Pressure.   Now that we can look at world prehistory on a far wider canvas than the pioneers in this field, we know that agriculture appeared at approximately the same time in Southwest Asia and China and somewhat later in the Americas, in **Mesoamerica** and the **Andean** region. This development has led some scholars to think in terms of worldwide population pressure that caused many hunter-gatherer societies to abandon gathering because their growing populations had reached the limit that their food resources could support (Cohen, 1977). No one denies that food production led to higher population densities and indeed ignited a population explosion (see Figure 8.2). But there is no evidence for very high population densities in Southwest Asia or Mesoamerica during the millennia when agriculture was taking hold, certainly not for the sorts of density that cause chronic food shortages (Flannery, 1983).

Social Theories.   Barbara Bender (1985) argues for social factors. She theorizes that some hunter-gatherer societies were becoming more socially complex, with far more elaborate hierarchical social organization. She points to the increasing abundance of trade objects and the appearance of richly decorated burials in preagricultural societies in Southwest Asia, Europe, and elsewhere. Perhaps, she hypothesizes, an expansion of trade and of political alliances between neighboring groups created new social and economic pressures to produce more and more surplus goods, not only foodstuffs but other objects as well. This development, in turn, led to more sedentary lifeways. Bender's social hypothesis tends to ignore the compelling factors of now well-documented environmental changes that were apparently one of the key elements in a move toward cultivation in areas like Southwest Asia.

Population and Resources Theories.   Another category of theories is based on relationships between populations and resources. This category is an extension of a famous argument by economist Ester Boserup (1965) which points out that food production systems of any type are highly flexible. Thus, hunter-gatherers responded to favorable relationships between population densities and available resources by intensifying their hunting and gathering. However, population growth in restricted areas with diverse resources can cause food shortages because there is less mobility and everyone has less territory to move around in, a situation that may have arisen in parts of Southwest Asia (Chapter 9), northwestern Europe (Chapter 10), and the Americas (Chapter 13). So population and resource theories tend to concentrate on interdependent factors: risk and population-resource imbalances. Apart from environmental change, all environments involve some form of risk for hunter-gatherer societies: drought cycles; long, cold winters; or unpredictable floods, to mention only a few possibilities. People respond to these risks by moving, by developing new food storage technologies, and by drying foods like powdered bison meat or salmon. A straightforward solution to rising

SITE

Guilá Naquitz, Mexico

Kent Flannery's investigations in the Valley of Oaxaca, Mexico, offer a classic example of ecological approaches to early food production. As part of a long-term archaeological project, Flannery and his research team excavated Guilá Naquitz Cave, a small shelter used about six times over a 2000-year period between 8750 and 6670 B.C. (Flannery, 1986; Marcus and Flannery, 1996). These sporadic occupations extended from the early Archaic, soon after the extinction of big game in the region, to a period when the occupants were using domesticated plants. The early Archaic occupants spent some of the year in large bands, splitting up to exploit larger areas of territory in much smaller groups, one of which used Guilá Naquitz on occasion.

The multidisciplinary research project revealed a wealth of information about the visitors to this shelter, identifying not only subsistence strategies but also the division of labor between the women, who processed plant foods, and the men, who did the hunting, through the distribution of artifacts and features in the cave's occupation levels. The excavations also produced evidence for the domestication of the gourd *Cucurbita pepo* by 8000 B.C. (B. Smith, 1997). Most important of all, Flannery and his colleagues tried to answer two questions: What was the strategy that led to the choice of the wild plants eaten by the inhabitants, and how did this strategy change when they began planting?

Robert Reynolds (1986) developed a comprehensive and ingenious "adaptive computer simulation model" to approach these questions. He started with a hypothetical, and totally ignorant, band of five people who settle in the area. Over a long period of trial and error, they "learn" how to schedule 11 major food plants over the year, in an environment where the sequence of dry, wet, and "average" years is totally unpredictable. The collective memories of successive generations prove to be vital, for experience is the basis on which they modify their strategies in future years that prove to be the same as experienced ones. For example, a cycle of drought years may yield survival strategies that are remembered through the succeeding wet years, despite the passage of a generation or more, and are then used again during drought years. The strategies rank plants and vegetational zones in order of the size of the harvest, yielding collective decisions followed by the band. By the time the last preagricultural occupation occurs at Guilá Naquitz, the band is so efficient in all conditions that very few modifications improve the adaptation. Basically, there is a stable performance level.

The computer simulation produced a mix of plant species that matched the mix found in the occupation deposits very well. It also showed that one set of strategies was used for wet years, when plant foods were available in abundance and a wide range of them was used, and another in dry

• •

populations, resulting food shortages, or risk factors may be to go one step farther: to cultivate familiar plants and to domesticate common prey so that people can draw on familiar "stored" resources in scarce months (B. Smith, 1998).

Climatic Change.   Climatic changes, such as sudden cold snaps or droughts lasting decades, even centuries, have been invoked as causes of food production. While climatic change was never a prime mover, a harsh drought or some other short-term climatic shift could have a profound effect on peoples' choices of food and their ways of feeding themselves—witness the complex interplay between drought and early farming at Abu Hureyra, Syria (described in Chapter 9).

Ecological Theories.   Another group of theorists focuses on ecological factors such as local variability in food resources and the interactive effects of human exploitation. Proponents of these ecological models talk of "opportunities" for the introduction of agriculture, of people turning to superior local resources when the moment arrived. That is, some resources—say, wild wheat or barley or wild goats—were seen as attractive. People used them more and more, to the point where they were eventually domesticated. Kent Flannery (1968) used this approach to examine the mechanisms by which Mesoamericans took up agriculture. The preagricultural peoples of the region

wet & dry stages

years, when the people took fewer species and those with higher yields. Reynolds's simulation is based on the assumption that the first stages of agriculture were attempts to alter the distributions of the natural densities of specific plants. The wet-year strategies were the ones that were the most flexible and the most capable of incorporating experimentation without risk. At first, deliberate planting may have been a rarity, a strategy that was successful but was employed only in wet years. It was a specialized strategy whose yields were seen eventually to have advantages, to the point where planting became more frequent, occurring not only in wet years but in dry ones as well, once the experiment had been shown to work. If the simulation is correct, the pace of experimentation was very slow, confined at first to wet years; at the same time, centuries-old foraging strategies continued.

This scenario suggests that bean cultivation near the cave itself allowed the people to collect more food and travel less, with, ultimately, a greater emphasis on foraging in the thorn forest near the site rather than farther afield. At the same time, traveling time decreased and collecting time increased; for example, acorns from the thorn forest became much more common. Less time was spent on lower-yielding, more marginal wild plants, as greater emphasis was placed on beans, squash, and maize. As the group gained experience with planting, yields rose, and the people placed ever more emphasis on cultivation as opposed to foraging.

Reynolds's simulation corresponds well with the shifts in plant species found in the six occupation levels at Guilá Naquitz. When he added climatic change and population growth to the equation, he found that two sources of uncertainty—unpredictable climate fluctuations and population shifts—were the factors that led to the most rapid increase in the density of high-yielding domesticated plants near the site. Reynolds believes that a high level of annual climatic variation—with its frequent wet years, for experimentation, and dry years, which put pressure on people to be efficient—was a major factor in the shift to food production in Oaxaca. So were short-term as opposed to long-term fluctuations in population densities, which also led to an accelerating reliance on cultivation not only on hill slopes but also on river plains in Oaxaca, the environments in which the first larger villages have been found.

This sophisticated hypothetical model is remarkable in that it corresponds well with the excavated data. Reynolds demonstrates that these Oaxaca people were well preadapted to food production. There was no "trigger" that started cultivation. The people simply added, first, gourds, then beans, and a simple form of maize to a much earlier foraging adaptation, at first as a wet-year innovation, which came into use in average and dry years once it proved reliable. As Flannery says, "Human hunting and gathering is, after all, economic behavior" (1986, p. 75).

adapted to a few animal genera and plants whose range cut across several environments, such as deer, rabbits, cactus fruit, and wild grasses, including the wild ancestor of maize. They scheduled their annual round so as to be in the right place at the right time to harvest, say, cactus fruit. Over the centuries, genetic changes in the ancestor of maize made it more productive and progressively more important in the diet. As time went on, people spent more and more time cultivating it and rescheduled their annual round accordingly, neglecting foods they had once exploited in favor of cultivated crops.

The crux of ecological models is trying to identify the processes that caused people to make the shift to deliberate cultivation, again a very difficult task. For example, did cultivation enable people to widen their adaptive niches? Were these new cost-benefit realities that favored farming? What about such factors as the nutritive value and the seasonal availability of foods? Did genetic changes in animals and plants play a role?

Most theories about the origins of food production are far from easy to test. It is difficult to link complex models with actual field data, largely because the models do not lend themselves to easy documentation. Such documentation will come from very meticulous excavations at single sites that will be combined, eventually, into larger regional models (H. Wright, 1993). Such research has been conducted successfully at Abu Hureyra, Syria; in the southern part of the eastern Mediterranean (Chapter 9);

and at Guilá Naquitz, Mexico (see Site box). In the final analysis, however, no one theory of the origins of food production embraces all regions of the world (Gebauer and Price, 1992). As Bruce Smith has pointed out (1999), the shift from plant gathering to food production was much more complicated, as people adapted to very localized cultural and environmental challenges. These changes may have taken many centuries, even millennia, in some places. But everywhere the key element was human decision making in the face of various selective pressures.

The Guilá Naquitz excavation shows us that foragers make decisions about the distances to travel and the plants and territory to exploit. When they shift to agriculture, they are changing the pattern of their decision making, not in an irreversible way but probably as one of several alternatives open to them. This change "has to be understood in terms of their previous decision-making pattern, the options open to them, and that new situation" (Flannery, 1986, p. 76). At the same time, this culturally based explanation also emerges from circumstances arising from larger processes, among them a worldwide climatic change at the end of the Ice Age and long-term evolutionary processes. In time, for example, early farmers anywhere acquired a selective advantage by virtue of their ability to disperse seeds from "a group of plants whose genetic program they had altered, in defiance of natural selection" (p. 77).

The Guilá Naquitz research, with its sophisticated computer simulations, is an example of what some future research into agricultural origins holds. In the final analysis, Flannery seems to prefer what he calls a "probabilistic ecosystem model." This model allows people to respond to changes in the ecosystem in several ways. The Guilá Naquitz people reduced their search area for wild plants, which may have led to protein deficiencies. Their solution was to grow beans, a protein-rich crop that allowed them to reduce their search area still more. In other parts of the world, like southern California and the Pacific Northwest, people intensified fishing and sea-mammal hunting, and agriculture was never adopted on any scale, even if the people were well aware of it. Agriculture was not the only option. It was one of many, and one that achieved remarkable success in the regions where it did develop.

ſ꜅꜅꜆ Differing Dates for Food Production

As we shall see in Chapters 9 to 13, food production began at very different times in various parts of the world, being well established in Southwest Asia by 10,000 B.C., in Mesoamerica by 5000 B.C., but in tropical Africa by about 1000 B.C., and then only in some locations (Harlan, 1992). What were the local variations that accounted for this time lag? David Harris (1980) argues that hunter-gatherers in subtropical zones such as Southwest Asia and highland Mesoamerica were beginning to manipulate potential domesticates among wild grasses and root species at the end of the Ice Age. Dependence on such foods probably came earlier in these regions, where there were only a few forageable species. Such dependence was essential to long-term survival. In contrast, populations in more humid tropical regions, like the African and Amazonian rain forests, probably did little more than manipulate a few wild species to minimize risk in lean years; as a corollary, many African agricultural peoples turn to hunting and gathering in lean years to this day. The archaeological record shows that agriculture was established considerably earlier in subtropical Southwest Asia, Middle and South America, Southeast Asia, and India than it was in humid, tropical zones, undoubtedly because these regions were rich in game and wild vegetable foods. Furthermore, domesticated crops and animals were more susceptible to irregular rainfall, locusts and other insect attacks, and endemic stock diseases. A strong and sustained incentive to obtain food must have been a prerequisite for a lasting shift from foraging to agriculture.

Harris points out that many variables must be understood before we can reconstruct the conditions under which agriculture was first regarded as a profitable activity. We are searching for sets of conditions in which population pressure, the distribution of plants, the rate at which the environment was changing, and even the techniques of harvesting wild grasses all played their part in making agriculture work. Then there are variations among the potentially domesticable plants and animals, some of which resisted domestication because of their long life span or because parts of their lives took place outside human control. The seasonal distribution of wild vegetable foods or game may also have prevented experiments in domestication, when the seasons during which these wild foods were exploited coincided with the times of year when it was important that experimenting farmers stay near their growing crops. Under these circumstances, people would tend to pursue their traditional food-getting strategies rather than risk their lives for an uncertain outcome.

〰 Studying Early Food Production

The study of early plant domestication has been revolutionized by the use of **flotation** methods, which pass soil samples through water and recover substantial samples of even the tiniest seeds. The development of accelerator mass spectrometry (AMS) radiocarbon dating now allows the dating of individual seeds, not just the levels they come from (see Dating the Past box). This has allowed investigators to pin down with great precision the dates for domesticated wheat and barley at sites like Abu Hureyra, Syria. Maize domestication is now AMS-dated to earlier than 2500 B.C. in Central America, a far later date than the crudely based 5000 B.C. chronology of only a few years ago (B. Smith, 1998).

Scanning electron microscopy (SEM) is providing vital information on the micromorphology of tiny wild and domesticated seeds. SEM has allowed scientists to identify domesticated native quinoa seeds in the Peruvian Andes dating to between 3000 and 2000 B.C. (B. Smith, 1998). And by using genetic fingerprinting, botanists have been able to identify the present location of populations of wild einkorn wheat that led to domesticated einkorn in southeastern Turkey, less than 250 km (155 miles) from Abu Hureyra in Syria, one of the earliest farming villages in the world (see Chapter 9) (Heun et al., 1997).

The invention of agriculture was not, in and of itself, that important an event. What was of all-embracing significance was the transition from hunting and gathering to cultivation, which was the catalyst for all the elaborate cultural developments of later millennia, of which urban civilization was but one (B. Smith, 2001). In strictly archaeological terms, we will never document the moment of invention, but over many years we have chronicled the rapid spread of the new economies, which soon reached all parts of the world where farming or animal herding were possible. Thanks to new and cutting edge research we now know that the process of spread was a very complex one, involving both long periods when people subsisted off wild foods as well as domestic crops, then moments when the new economies spread rapidly.

Twenty-first-century science is documenting new information not only about seeds but also phytoliths, or vegetable tissues. For the first time, root crops are coming to the fore, a hitherto neglected aspect of early agriculture (Hather, 1994). Staggering advances in knowledge will shortly come from pioneering work on the genetic fingerprinting of modern wild grain populations, on their similarities to domesticated relatives, and on their original homelands (Bellwood, 2001; Blumer, 1991; Jones and Brown, 2000). For example, we now know that the heartland of einkorn was in eastern Turkey (Heun et al., 1997), and that of maize in the Rio Balsas region of Mexico (Doebley et al., 1999). Parallel studies on the genetic makeup of modern animal domesticates show that there were multiple origin centers for cattle, horses, sheep, goats, and pigs (Zeder et al., 2002).

DNA and other multidisciplinary research into the transition from hunting and gathering to agriculture has only just begun, but is likely to revolutionize our knowledge of this all-important chapter in human history. Chapter 8 in future editions of *People* is likely to be very different from this one!

〰 Why Did Food Production Take Hold So Late?

Once successful, food production spread rapidly, partly because the resulting population growth prevented people from reverting to hunting and gathering. An interesting question remains: Why did food production not take hold much earlier in prehistory? Surely, there were many previous occasions during the Ice Age when conditions were favorable for people to start cultivating plants. Here, population models for prehistory offer some clues. We know there was gradual population growth during the Stone Age. The constant, cyclic changes of the past 700,000 years must have led to conditions in

DATING THE PAST:

Accelerator Mass Spectrometry (AMS) Radiocarbon Dating

Until about ten years ago, dating the rate of decay (beta counts) from different radiocarbon samples had a calculated ratio that gave only approximations. Using carbon-14 (^{14}C) and carbon-12 (^{12}C), scientists could detect and count individual decay events with radiocarbon. They would observe the emission of beta particles to determine the rate of radioactive breakdown and so estimate the number of ^{14}C atoms remaining in the sample. Since only a small number of ^{14}C atoms break down over the many hours of the sample count, the samples had to be large enough to provide an adequate number of beta counts.

Back in the 1960s, archaeologists collected handfuls of charcoal from hearths in plastic bags, the rule being, the larger the sample, the better. Scientists could not date small objects like maize cobs or tiny wood fragments embedded in the sockets of prehistoric bronze spearheads. Since they make up too-small samples, such objects are especially hard to date—and very difficult to pin down chronologically when the ratio can be only approximate. Minute samples such as seeds can easily move upward or downward into older or younger occupation layers, either through human agencies such as trampling or through natural phenomena such as burrowing animals. The development of a new radiocarbon method based on accelerator mass spectrometry (AMS) in 1983 revolutionized radiocarbon chronologies and the study of early food production (Figure 8.3).

An accelerator mass spectrometer can date the age of sample material by counting the number of ^{14}C atoms present. Rather than counting decay events (beta counts), researchers estimate the remaining ^{14}C by directly counting ^{14}C atoms. By doing this, they can date samples 1000 times smaller than the handful of charcoal used a generation ago. The development of small, high-energy mass spectrometers solved a major problem, that of background noise from ions or molecules of a similar mass to the ^{14}C masking their presence. The new instruments filter out background, as a proportion of the sample's atoms are propelled through an accelerator toward a detector (see Figure 8.3). Ionized carbon atoms from the sample are pulled in beam form toward the accelerator. A magnet bends the beam, so lighter atoms turn more sharply than heavier ones and move to the inside of the diverging beam. A filter blocks the passage of all charged particles except those of atomic mass 14. The accelerator pushes the stripped beam through a second beam-bending magnet filtering out any last non-^{14}C particles. A magnetic lens focuses the beam as a ^{14}C detector counts the number of remaining ions, allowing the calculation of the age of the sample.

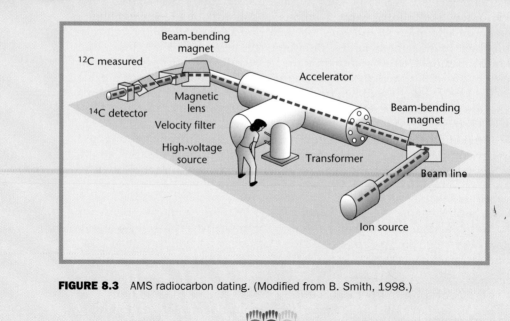

FIGURE 8.3 AMS radiocarbon dating. (Modified from B. Smith, 1998.)

some areas that presented human societies with the challenge of constant environmental change and population shifts. However, as we saw in Chapter 7, it was not until the end of the Ice Age that global populations rose sufficiently to limit mobility, and the easiest strategy for people faced with food shortages is to move. There was initially a slow and then a rapidly accelerating intensification of hunter-gatherer lifeways during and after the last glacial maximum, especially during Holocene times. This intensification preadapted many societies to food production for the first time (McCorriston and Hole, 1991). And, as we saw in Chapter 7, increased plant productivity resulted from higher carbon dioxide levels in the atmosphere after the Ice Age.

﷽ Consequences of Food Production

The new food-producing economies proved dramatically successful. In 10,000 B.C., virtually everybody in the world lived by hunting and gathering. By A.D. 1, most people were farmers or herders, and only a minority were still hunter-gatherers. The spread of food production throughout the world took only about 8000 years. The problem for anthropologists is to explain not only why people took up agriculture but also why so many populations adopted this new, and initially risky, economic transition in such a short time. Food production spread to all corners of the world except where an environment with extreme aridity, heat, or cold rendered agriculture or herding impossible, or where people chose to remain hunters and gatherers.

Food production resulted, ultimately, in much higher population densities in many locations, for the domestication of plants and animals can lead to an economic strategy that increases and stabilizes the available food supplies, although more energy is used to produce them (see Figure 8.2). Farmers use concentrated tracts of territory for agriculture, and for grazing cattle and small stock if they practice mixed farming. Their territory is much smaller than that of hunter-gatherers (although pastoralists [animal herders] need huge areas of grazing land for seasonal pasture). Within a smaller area of farming land, property lines are carefully delineated as individual ownership and problems of inheritance arise. Shortages of land can lead to disputes and to the founding of new village settlements on previously uncultivated soil.

More enduring settlements brought other changes. Heavier toolkits and more lasting houses replaced the portable and lightweight material possessions of many hunter-gatherers (Figure 8.4a). Grindstones and ground-edged axes were even more essential to farming culture than they were to gathering societies. Hoes and other implements of tillage were vital for the planting and harvesting of crops. New social units came into being as more lasting home bases were developed; these social links reflected the ownership and inheritance of land and led to much larger settlements that brought hitherto scattered populations into closer and more regular contact.

Food production led to changed attitudes toward the environment. Cereal crops were such that people could store their food for winter (Figure 8.4b). The hunter-gatherers exploited game, fish, and vegetable foods, but the farmers did more: They altered the environment by the very nature of their exploitation. Expansion of agriculture meant felling trees and burning vegetation to clear the ground for planting. The same fields were then abandoned after a few years to lie fallow, and more woodland was cleared. The original vegetation began to regenerate, but it may have been cleared again before reaching its original state. This shifting pattern of farming is called slash-and-burn, or **swidden, agriculture.** Voracious domesticated animals stripped pastures of their grass cover; then heavy rainfalls denuded the hills of valuable soil, and the pastures were never the same again. However elementary the agricultural technology, the farmer changed the environment, if only with fires lit to clear scrub from gardens and to fertilize the soil with wood ash. Hunter-gatherers had deliberately set fires to encourage the growth of new grass for their grazing prey. In a sense, shifting to slash-and-burn agriculture was merely an extension of the age-old use of fire to encourage the regeneration of vegetation.

Food production resulted in high population densities, but disease, the available food supplies, the water supplies, and particularly famine, controlled population increases. Also, early agricultural methods depended heavily on a careful selection of the soil. The technology of the first farmers was hardly potent enough for the extensive

(a)

(b)

FIGURE 8.4 (a) A farming village in Ivory Coast, West Africa. (b) A grain bin from an African village, used for cereal crops. Storing food is a critical activity of many hunter-gatherers and farmers.

clearing of the dense woodland under which many good soils lay, so only accessible land was cultivated. Gardens were probably scattered over a much wider territory than is necessary today. One authority estimates that only 40 percent of the moderately fertile soil in Africa is available for cultivation (Allan, 1965). This figure must have been lower in the early days of agriculture, with their simpler stone tools and fewer crops. In regions of seasonal rainfall, such as Southwest Asia, other parts of Asia, and sub-Saharan Africa, periods of prolonged drought are common. Famine was a real possibility as population densities rose. Many early agriculturalists must have worriedly watched the sky and had frequent crop failures in times of drought. Their small stores of grain from the previous season would not have carried them through another year, especially if they had been careless with their surplus. Farmers were forced to shift their economic strategy in such times.

We know that the earliest farmers availed themselves of game and wild vegetable foods to supplement their agriculture, just as today some farmers are obliged to rely heavily on wild vegetable foods and hunting to survive in bad years (Scudder, 1962, 1971). Many hunter-gatherer bands collect intensively just a few species of edible plants in their large territories. Aware of many other edible vegetables, they fall back on these only in times of stress; the less favored foods can carry a comparatively small population through to the next rains. A larger agricultural population is not so flexible and quickly exhausts wild vegetables and game in the much smaller territory used for farming and grazing. If the drought lasts for years, famine, death, and reduced population can follow.

🐾 Nutrition and Early Food Production

Was food production a real improvement in human lifeways? For generations, archaeologists have argued that human health improved dramatically as a result of agriculture, because people worked less and lived on more reliable food supplies (Butzer, 1982). But some have argued that, in fact, agriculture brought diminishing returns in relation to the labor expended in the new systems that were adopted to feed many more people. Richard Lee's (1979) studies of the !Kung San of the Kalahari Desert tend to support these views. They show that, at the time of the studies, these hunter-gatherers, and presumably others, had abundant leisure and worked less than farmers. Some nutritionists point out that foragers may have had better-balanced diets than many farmers, who relied heavily on root or cereal crops. Further, farmers, with their sedentary settlements and higher population densities, were much more vulnerable to famine than their hunter-gatherer predecessors. They would also have been more vulnerable to gastrointestinal infections and epidemics because of crowded village populations (Cohen, 1988).

Nutrition studies based on the skeletons of early farmers suggest some incidence of anemia and slow growth resulting from malnutrition. Regional studies of prehistoric populations have suggested a decline in mean age life expectancy in agricultural populations, a suggestion that contradicts the commonly held perception. Taken as a whole, **paleopathological** studies suggest a general decline in the quality, and perhaps the length, of human life with the advent of food production. However, many unknowns are involved, among them changes in fertility and population growth rates, which caused the world's population to rise even if general health standards and life expectancy fell (C. Larsen, 1995). What impact these studies will have on population pressure theories about the origins of agriculture is still uncertain. Certainly, any shift to food production caused by increasing population pressure could be reflected in a decline in the overall health and nutrition displayed by prehistoric skeletons.

In the final analysis, some people probably turned to food production only when other alternatives were no longer practicable. The classic example is the Aborigines of extreme northern Australia, who were well aware that their neighbors in New Guinea were engaged in intensive agriculture. They, too, knew how to plant the top of the wild yam so that it resprouted, but they never adopted food production, simply because they had no need to become dependent on a lifeway that would reduce their leisure time and produce more food than they required.

🐾 Herding: Domestication of Animals

Potentially tamable species like the wild ox, goat, sheep, and dog were widely distributed in the Old World during the Upper Pleistocene. New World farmers domesticated only such animals as the llama, the guinea pig, and the turkey, and then only under special conditions and within narrow geographic limits. It is possible that the domesticated dog crossed into the New World with the first Americans before 12,000 B.C. or that it was domesticated elsewhere in the Americas. But the evidence is uncertain.

Having one's own herds of domesticated mammals ensured a regular meat supply. The advantages to having a major source of meat under one's control are obvious. Later, domesticated animals provided by-products such as milk, cheese, and butter, as well as skins for clothes and tent coverings and materials for leather shields and armor. In later millennia, people learned how to breed animals for specialized tasks such as plowing, transportation, and traction (Clutton-Brock, 1989).

Domestication implies a genetic selection emphasizing special features of continuing use to the domesticator. Wild sheep have no wool, wild cows produce milk only for their offspring, and undomesticated chickens do not lay surplus eggs. Changes in wool bearing, lactation, or egg production could be achieved by isolating wild populations for selective breeding under human care. Isolating species from a larger gene pool produced domestic sheep with thick, woolly coats and domestic goats providing regular supplies of milk, which formed a staple in the diet of many human populations.

No one knows exactly how the domestication of animals began. Three elements are vital to domestication: constraint on the movement of the target populations, regulation of their breeding, and control of their feeding to shape future generations (Meadows, 1989). During the Upper Pleistocene, people were already beginning to concentrate heavily on some species of large mammals for their diet. The Magdalenians of southwest France directed much of their lives toward pursuing reindeer. At the end of the Pleistocene, hunters in Southwest Asia were concentrating on gazelles and other steppe animals. Wild sheep and goats were intensively hunted on the southern shores of the Caspian Sea. Gregarious, highly social animals like goats and sheep are the most easily domesticated beasts; they follow the lead of a dominant herd member or all move together. They also tolerate feeding and breeding in a confined environment.

Hunters often fed off the same herd for a long time, sometimes deliberately sparing young females and immature beasts to keep the source of food alive. Young animals captured alive in the chase might be taken back to the camp and might grow dependent on those who caged them, thus becoming partially tamed. A hunter could grasp the possibility of gaining control of the movements of a few key members of a herd, which would be followed by the others. Once the experience of keeping pets or of restricting game movements had suggested a new way of life, people might have experimented with different species. As part of domestication, animals and humans increased their mutual dependence.

The archaeological evidence for early domestication is so fragile that nothing survives except the bones of the animals kept by the early farmers, and the differences between wild and domestic animal bones are often so small initially that it is difficult to distinguish them unless very large collections are found. In the earliest centuries of domestication, corralled animals were nearly indistinguishable from wild species. The process of animal domestication was undoubtedly prolonged, developing in several areas of Southwest Asia at approximately the same time. Although animal bones are scarce and often unsatisfactory as evidence of early domestication, most authorities now agree that the first species to be domesticated in Southwest Asia were goats and sheep, about 8000 B.C. Goats and sheep are small herd animals whose carcasses yield much meat for their size. They can readily be penned and isolated to develop a symbiotic relationship with people. By 8000 B.C., goat bones at sites like Ganj Dareh in the Iranian highlands display the characteristic mortality profile of managed herds: Surplus males were slaughtered before adulthood, with females being kept for breeding and milk purposes. Earlier hunting mortality profiles show a focus on adult males (Zeder and Hesse, 2000).

Cattle are much more formidable to domesticate, for their prototype was *Bos primigenius*, the wild ox much hunted by Stone Age people (Figure 8.5). Andrew Smith

FIGURE 8.5 *Bos primigenius*, the aurochs or wild ox, as depicted by S. Von Herbenstain in 1549. It became extinct in Europe in 1627, although modern breeding experiments have reconstructed this formidable beast.

(1992) believes that the first domesticated animals came from better-disciplined wild herds in arid environments, where it was easier to control the movements of animals. Such conditions may have pertained over much of Southwest Asia and the Sahara as the climate became drier after 7000 B.C.

Some animals, such as sea mammals, resist domestication because much of their lives is spent out of the range of human influence. Most early successes with domestication took place with gregarious animals. They can be thought of as a food reserve, as "grain on the hoof."

〰 Plant Cultivation

Many fewer wild vegetable foods were domesticated than foraged over the millennia. In the Old World, wheat, barley, and other cereals that grow wild over much of Asia and Europe became cultivated. In the New World, a different set of crops was tamed (D. Harris and Hillman, 1989; Zohary and Hopf, 1988). These included Indian corn (*Zea mays*), the only important wild grass to be domesticated. Root crops such as manioc and sweet potatoes, chili peppers, tobacco, and several types of bean were grown. As Christine Hastorf (1999) remarks, very often the plants first domesticated were "flavorful, spicy, sweet, industrial, hallucinatory, or medicinal." (Common to both Old and New Worlds are gourds, cotton, and two or three other, minor crops; see B. Smith, 1998).

In the Old World, tropical regions had many potential domesticates such as the yam and gourds. In Southeast Asia and sub-Saharan Africa, a long period of intensive gathering and experimenting with the deliberate planting of wild root crops probably preceded the beginnings of formal agriculture. Perhaps, however, the transition from the gathering to the cultivation of root crops was almost unconscious, for many tubers are easy to grow deliberately. The African yam, for example, will sprout if its top is cut off and buried in the ground. The hunter-gatherer bands that were familiar with this easy means of conserving their food supplies may simply have intensified their planting efforts to supplement shortages caused by changed circumstances. As with animals, however, certain heavily exploited species tended to resist domestication; among them were long-lived trees like the oak and plants whose life spans were so long that they inhibited human selection. They also tended to cross-pollinate, a process that undoubtedly discouraged human efforts to trigger or control their genetic variation.

In the Old World, the qualities of wild wheat, barley, and similar grains are quite different from those of their domestic equivalents (D. Harris and Hillman, 1989). In the wild, these grains occur in dense stands. One can harvest them by tapping the stem with the hands and gathering the seeds in a basket as they fall off, or by uprooting the plant. The tapping technique is effective because the wild grain is attached to the stem by a brittle joint, or **rachis**. When the grass is tapped, the weak rachis breaks and the seed falls into the basket.

The first cultivated wheat and barley crops were of the wild, brittle-rachised type, and the resulting crops would probably have been large enough to generate domestic-type mutants in the first two to five years (Figure 8.6). Selection for the semitough rachised forms was an unconscious process during the earliest stages of domestication, perhaps accelerated by the use of sickles or the uprooting of individual plants to harvest ripe seeds rather than merely tapping them into waiting baskets. Computer simulations have shown that semitough rachised domestic forms may have been rare at first, but they would have been fully domesticated within 20 to 30 generations—for these cereals, between 20 and 30 years. Even with less intense selective pressures than those assumed in the experiment, domestication could have been achieved within one or two centuries (Figure 8.7) (Hillman and Davis, 1990). This conclusion is confirmed by DNA fingerprinting studies on einkorn in southeastern Turkey, where alterations in just one or two genes transformed wild wheat into a useful crop with a tough rachis.

Archaeobotanist Gordon Hillman believes that the farmers would have started conscious selection as soon as the domesticates became sufficiently common to be recognized, perhaps 1 to 5 percent of the crop. From then on, domestication would have been completed in three or four years.

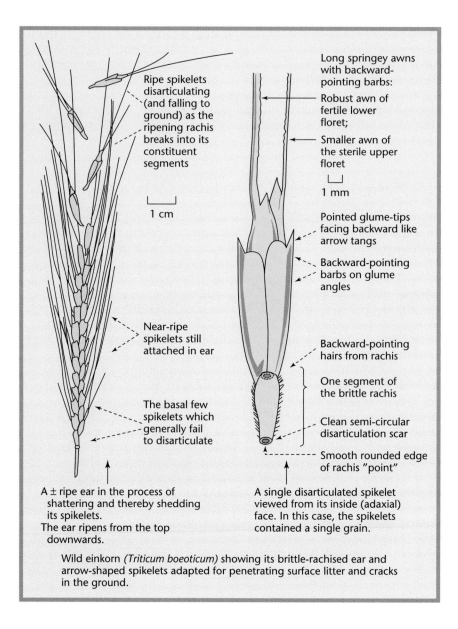

Ripe spikelets disarticulating (and falling to ground) as the ripening rachis breaks into its constituent segments

1 cm

Near-ripe spikelets still attached in ear

The basal few spikelets which generally fail to disarticulate

A ± ripe ear in the process of shattering and thereby shedding its spikelets.
The ear ripens from the top downwards.

Long springey awns with backward-pointing barbs:
Robust awn of fertile lower floret;
Smaller awn of the sterile upper floret

1 mm

Pointed glume-tips facing backward like arrow tangs

Backward-pointing barbs on glume angles

Backward-pointing hairs from rachis

One segment of the brittle rachis

Clean semi-circular disarticulation scar

Smooth rounded edge of rachis "point"

A single disarticulated spikelet viewed from its inside (adaxial) face. In this case, the spikelets contained a single grain.

Wild einkorn (*Triticum boeoticum*) showing its brittle-rachised ear and arrow-shaped spikelets adapted for penetrating surface litter and cracks in the ground.

FIGURE 8.6 The features affecting seed dispersal and spikelet implantation in wild and domesticated einkorn wheat.

Although the broad outlines of the process of domestication can be reconstructed through controlled experimentation and computer simulation, it is most unlikely that anyone will ever find "transitional" grains in Southwest Asian sites that will document the actual process under way. Botanists have, however, located in southeastern Turkey the wild populations of einkorn that were the source of the first domesticated wheat crops. The changeover from wild to domesticated strains was so rapid that we are more likely to find wild seeds in one level and domesticated ones in the next. This is precisely what has been found at Southwest Asian sites such as Abu Hureyra, Syria, where farming appeared abruptly about 10,000 B.C. (see Chapter 9).

🐾 Technology and Domestication

The technological consequences of food production were, in their way, as important as the new economies. A more settled way of life and some decline in hunting and gathering slowly led to long-term residences, lasting agricultural styles, and more substantial housing. As they had done for millennia, people built their permanent homes with the raw materials most abundant in their environment. The early farmers of Southwest Asia worked dried mud into small houses with flat roofs; these were cool in summer and warm in winter. At night during the hot season, people may have slept on

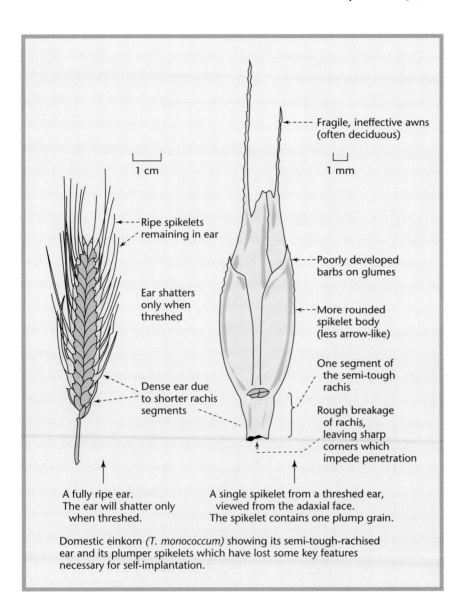

Fragile, ineffective awns
(often deciduous)

1 cm

1 mm

Ripe spikelets
remaining in ear

Poorly developed
barbs on glumes

Ear shatters
only when
threshed

More rounded
spikelet body
(less arrow-like)

One segment of
the semi-tough
rachis

Dense ear due
to shorter rachis
segments

Rough breakage
of rachis,
leaving sharp
corners which
impede penetration

A fully ripe ear.
The ear will shatter only
when threshed.

A single spikelet from a threshed ear,
viewed from the adaxial face.
The spikelet contains one plump grain.

Domestic einkorn (T. monococcum) showing its semi-tough-rachised
ear and its plumper spikelets which have lost some key features
necessary for self-implantation.

FIGURE 8.6   (Continued)

the flat roofs. Some less substantial houses had reed roofs. In the more temperate zones of Europe, with wetter climates, timber was used to build thatched-roof houses of various shapes and sizes. Early African farmers often built huts of grass, sticks, and anthill clay. Nomadic pastoralists of the northern steppes had no concern with a permanent and durable home, yet they, too, took advantage of the related benefits of having a domestic food supply: They used animal skins to make clothing, as well as tents to shelter themselves during the icy winters.

Agriculture is a seasonal activity, with long periods of the year in which the fields are lying fallow or are supporting growing crops. Any farmer is confronted with the problem of keeping food in ways the hunter-gatherer never has to ponder. Thus, a new technology of storage came into being. Grain bins, jars, or clay-lined pits became an essential part of the agricultural economy for stockpiling food for the lean months and against periods of famine. The bins may have been made of wattle and daub, clay, or timber (see Figure 8.4b). Basket and clay-lined silos protected valuable grain against rodents.

Hunter-gatherers use skins, wood containers, gut pouches, and sometimes baskets to carry vegetable foods back to base. Farmers face far more formidable transport problems: They must carry their harvest back to the village, keep ready-for-use supplies of foods in the house as opposed to storage bins, and store water. Early farmers began to use gourds as water carriers and to make clay vessels that were both waterproof and capable of carrying and cooking food (Figure 8.8). They made pots by coiling rolls of

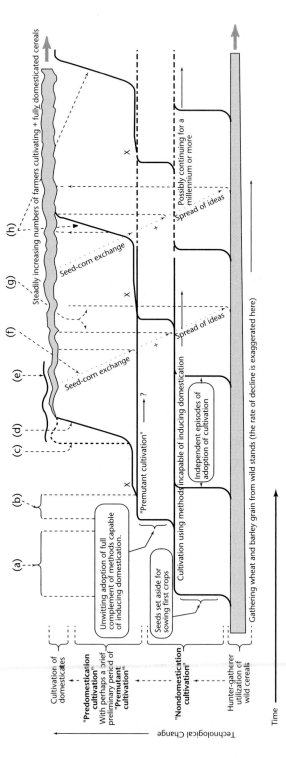

FIGURE 8.7 A summary of the principal events associated with the domestication of wheat and barley. For the sake of argument, this diagram assumes that the domestication of both the wheats and the barleys occurred at several settlements independently. Key to the table: (a) Nonhusbandry domestication. Husbandry (cultivation) methods are incapable of causing domestication. This process may have continued for a long time at some sites but was not universal. (b) A possible temporary period (at some settlements) of premutant cultivation of crops in which domestication-inducing methods were now applied but domestic-type mutants were still absent, so that the start of domestication was delayed even further. (c) Effect of imposing conscious selection midway through the selection process. (d) The primary domestication curve—without conscious selection. (e) Fluctuations in the completeness of domestication due to the incomplete fixation of modifier genes. (f) Transmission of seeded stocks of domesticates to farmers practicing sporadic cultivation and even to hunter-gatherers. Also, transmission of the knowledge of domestication-inducing methods of husbandry to farmers lacking the technology. (g) Abrupt appearance of domesticates in settlements that had just acquired domesticated seed stocks through exchange. (h) Later (independent) domestication of crops at other settlements.

FIGURE 8.8 Pottery manufacture. A common method of pot making was to build up the walls from clay coils (top). The pot was then smoothed and decorated (left) and fired, either on an open hearth (right) or in a kiln. These pictures illustrate modern-day Pueblo Indian pottery-manufacturing techniques from the southwestern United States and are, of course, not necessarily typical of all potters, especially ancient ones.

clay or building up the walls of vessels from a lump and firing them in simple hearths. Clay vessels were much more durable than skin or leather receptacles. Some pots were used for several decades before being broken and abandoned.

Pottery did not appear simultaneously with agriculture. It came into use at different times in many widely separated places. For example, the Jomon hunter-gatherers of Japan were making simple clay pots by at least 9000 B.C. They lived a more or less sedentary life by their shell middens, using clay vessels long before agriculture became part of their way of life (Barnes, 1993). In Southwest Asia, however, farmers first used pottery by approximately 6000 B.C. (Mellaart, 1975).

For tens of thousands of years, people dug up wild edible roots with simple wooden sticks, sometimes made more effective with the aid of a stone weight. The first farmers continued to use the digging stick to plant crops a few inches below the surface, probably in readily cultivable soils. They also used wooden or stone-bladed hoes (and much later, iron hoes) to break up the soft soil. These they fitted with short or long handles, depending on cultural preferences. European and Southwest Asian farmers made use of the ox-drawn plow in later millennia, at first with a blade tipped with wood, then with bronze, and later with iron (Chapter 15). The plow was an important innovation, for it enabled people to turn the soil over to a much greater depth than ever before. Every farmer has to clear wild vegetation and weeds from the fields, and it is hardly surprising to find a new emphasis on the ax and the adze. In Southwest Asia, the simple axes of pioneer farmers were replaced by more elaborate forms in metal by 2500 B.C.

FIGURE 8.9 Using a stone ax to fell a tree. A Tefalmin farmer at work in New Guinea in 1966. (Copyright The British Museum.)

Present-day experiments in Denmark and New Guinea have shown that the ground and polished edges of stone axes are remarkably effective in clearing woodland and felling trees (Figure 8.9). In later millennia, the alloying of copper and bronze and, later, the development of iron cutting edges made forest clearance even easier.

New tools meant new technologies to produce tougher working edges. At first, the farmers used ground and polished stone, placing a high premium on suitable rocks, which were traded from quarry sites over enormous distances. Perhaps the most famous ax quarries are in western Europe, where ax blanks were traded the length of the British Isles. Grand Pressigny flint from France was prized over thousands of square miles. In Southwest Asia and Mexico, one valuable toolmaking material, not for axes but for knives and sickles, was obsidian, a volcanic rock prized for its easy working properties, sharp edges, and ornamental appearance. Early obsidian trade routes carried tools and ornaments hundreds of miles from their places of origin. By using spectrographic techniques, scientists have been able to trace obsidian over long distances to such places of origin as Lipari Island off Italy and Lake Van in Turkey (Torrance, 1986).

All these developments in technology made people more and more dependent on exotic raw materials, many of which were unobtainable in their own territory. We see the beginnings of widespread long-distance trading networks, which were to burgeon even more rapidly with the emergence of the first urban civilizations.

We still know tantalizingly little about the ways humankind began to exercise control over food resources. We know that in Southwest Asia there was a dramatic shift in human subsistence patterns by 9500 B.C., in northern China by 5000 B.C., and in Mesoamerica about 3500 B.C. Some fascinating clues, such as the example of southern California's Kumeyaay Indians, suggest that people were exercising some sort of control over their food supplies very much earlier. Perhaps Upper Paleolithic people who specialized in hunting reindeer or mountain goats made some attempts to manage their prey herds. Conceivably, too, hunter-gatherers living on the fringes of tropical rain forests may have engaged in deliberate opportunistic horticulture, planting yams and other food plants that could be regenerated for future use. The beginnings of the agricultural revolution took hold many thousands of years before the explosion came. After all, we should never forget that humans have always been opportunistic, and the planting of food crops and the first taming of animals may have been one simple result.

Summary 🐾

Many late Ice Age and early Holocene hunter-gatherer societies were preadapted to food production, as they were already exploiting some food resources intensively and living more sedentary lifeways. Most of these societies were in regions where food resources were diverse and seasonally predictable. Higher levels of carbon dioxide in the atmosphere after the Ice Age resulted in much higher plant productivity and increased the importance of such foods in human diet. In contrast to early theories that food production was a revolutionary development, modern hypotheses invoke social relations, population growth, and ecological factors as multivariate causes of food production. Its development was a gradual process, one that saw increasing reliance on food crops, especially in areas with constant and unpredictable environmental change.

Food production resulted in more sedentary human settlement, more substantial housing, elaborate storage technologies, and special implements for agricultural tasks. All these technological developments led to greater interdependence and to more long-distance exchange of raw materials, as well as increasing human social complexity.

Key Terms 🐾

Andean That part of South America where state-organized societies arose.

Archaeobotanist A specialist in the study of ancient plants.

Flotation A method of recovering seeds from archaeological excavations by passing them through water and fine screens.

Mesoamerica That part of Central America where state-organized societies developed.

Neolithic A widely used general label in the Old World that refers to early, Stone Age, farmers who hadn't the use of metal tools.

Paleopathology The study of ancient disease.

Rachis The joint that attaches a seed to its stem.

Scanning electron microscopy (SEM) A method using electron microscopes for studying the micromorphology of seeds.

Swidden agriculture Sometimes called slash-and-burn agriculture, swidden farming involves burning off of natural vegetation, planting of crops, and then allowing the land to regenerate before reuse.

Guide to Further Reading 🐾

Childe, V. Gordon. 1936. *Man Makes Himself.* London: Watts.
     Classic Childe argues for a "Neolithic Revolution" in a book that summarizes all the evidence in favor of a revolutionary change in prehistory when food production began.

Cohen, Mark. 1977. *The Food Crisis in Prehistory.* New Haven, CT: Yale University Press.
     An original and thought-provoking essay on the beginnings of agriculture that advocates population as a major factor.

_____. 1988. *Health and the Rise of Civilization.* New Haven, CT: Yale University Press.
     An essay on paleopathology and the origins of more complex societies that contains much original thinking.

Flannery, Kent V. 1986. *Guilá Naquitz.* Orlando, FL: Academic Press.
     A case study of a site occupied during the transition from hunting and gathering to food production, with an excellent theoretical discussion.

Gebauer, A., and T. D. Price, eds. 1992. *Transitions to Agriculture in Prehistory.* Madison, WI: Prehistory Press.
     A useful series of essays on origins, addressed to more advanced readers.

Harris, David, and Gordon Hillman, eds. 1989. *Farming and Foraging.* Oxford: Clarendon Press.
     Articles on the basics of agriculture and plant foraging crammed with useful background information. Somewhat specialized, but fascinating reading.

Smith, Bruce D. 1998. *The Emergence of Agriculture,* 2nd ed. New York: W. H. Freeman.
     A clear account of the origins of food production for the general reader. Smith uses AMS radiocarbon dating and other scientific advances to date major crops in the archaeological record.

THE ORIGINS OF FOOD PRODUCTION IN SOUTHWEST ASIA

Figures from 'Ain Ghazal, Jordan.

It was the final day of the 1953 excavation season at Jericho. For weeks, the top of a human skull had projected from the side of the trench dug deep into one of the earliest farming communities in the world. Excavator Kathleen Kenyon (1981) had given strict instructions that it was not to be disturbed until the stratigraphic layers in the trench wall had been drawn and photographed. Drawing completed, she somewhat unwillingly gave the site supervisor permission to remove the skull from the wall. That evening, he carried back to camp a complete cranium, carefully covered in clay, the human features modeled in, the eyes inset with shells.

The next morning, Kenyon looked closely at the small hole in the wall. She could see two more plastered skulls within. They were removed. Three more now appeared behind them, then a seventh, and final head. It took five days to extract the nest of skulls from the wall, for the crushed bones were packed tightly with stones and hard earth. They formed the earliest portrait gallery in the world, each head modeled with individual features—nose, mouth, ears, and eyebrows molded with delicacy. Kenyon believed she had found the heads of revered ancestors who were critical intermediaries between the living and the spiritual world. They were symbols to their makers of a new spiritual order that linked people closely to the land that brought forth their crops.

Much of the theorizing about early food production has stemmed from archaeological research in Southwest Asia, where many early farming settlements have been found (Figure 9.1 and Table 9.1) (B. Smith, 1998). The time when food production began is called the **Neolithic,** the "period in which a pattern of village settlement based on subsistence farming and stockbreeding became the basis of existence for communities throughout southwest Asia" (Moore, 1985, p. 223). The Neolithic of Southwest Asia began about 9500 B.C. nearly everywhere and lasted until the sixth millennium B.C. in Mesopotamia and until as late as 4000 B.C. along parts of the eastern Mediterranean coast (Henry, 1989).

A Scenario for Early Agriculture

Deep-sea cores and pollen studies tell us that the Southwest Asian climate was cool and dry from about 21,000 to 16,000 B.C., during the late Weichsel glaciation (Moore and Hillman, 1992). Sea levels dropped more than 100 m (300 feet); much of the interior was covered by dry steppe, with forest restricted to the eastern Mediterranean and Turkish coasts. After 16,000 B.C., the climate warmed up considerably. Forests expanded rapidly at the end of the Ice Age, for the climate was still cooler than

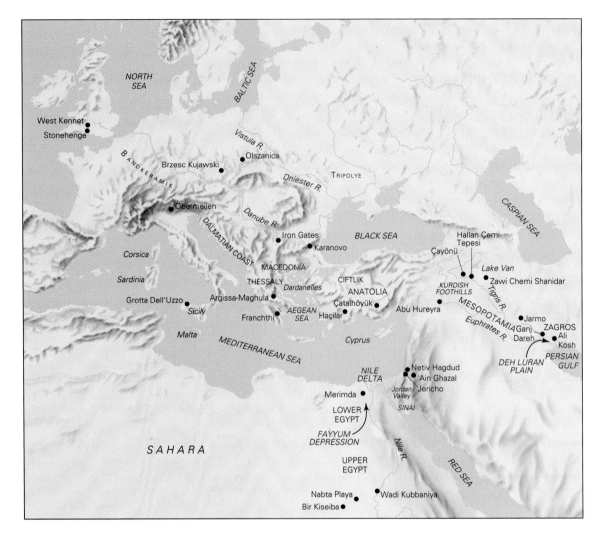

FIGURE 9.1 Early farming sites in Southwest Asia, Europe, and the Nile.

16,000 B.C.   today and considerably wetter. Many areas of Southwest Asia were richer in animal and plant species than they are now, so that they were highly favorable for human occupation.

A widely accepted scenario for the first farming goes as follows: The extreme eastern Mediterranean coast lay at the junction of mediterranean, continental, and monsoon-influenced climates and nurtured a unique and ever-changing set of **ecotones**. In the early Holocene, the climate shifted from continental to mediterranean, with warmer temperatures, more forest cover, and increasing summer aridity. The vegetation became far more diverse, with a dramatic increase in annual cereal grasses that flowered and produced seed in spring and became dormant through the long, dry summer months. These cereals appeared first in the west and spread eastward. At the same time, hunter-gatherer groups may have disturbed and unconsciously diversified the vegetation by firing it in the dry season to encourage new grass growth, for the deer and other animals that fed on it.

The millennia after the Ice Age were ones of constant climatic change, with an abrupt change to cooler, very dry conditions with the onset of the Younger Dryas in

10,500 B.C.   about 10,500 B.C. The colder, much less hospitable climate may have triggered experimentation with the deliberate cultivation of cereal grasses like rye and wheat at many locations, among them the village of Abu Hureyra on the Euphrates River, where rye cultivation began as early as 10,000 B.C.

Only those hunter-gatherer groups with an ability to cope with such constant climatic change and marked seasonality could flourish. They responded by developing storage

TABLE 9.1

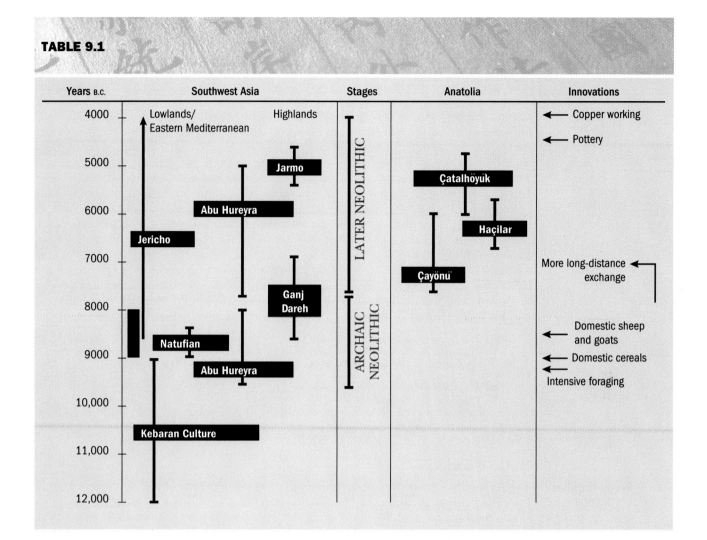

Years B.C.	Southwest Asia	Stages	Anatolia	Innovations

technology, intensively exploiting cereals and grinding their seeds, and adopting much more sedentary lifeways. All this was not so much a shift toward broad-spectrum hunting and foraging as an adjustment to climatic fluctuations. With scarcer surface water and months on end when plant foods and game were in short supply, people depleted their environments. Some groups converged around lakes, where they domesticated cereals and legumes as a way of amplifying the available wild food supplies. They also congregated in villages, for permanent settlement preceded agriculture in some places.

In Chapter 7, we recounted the dramatic changes in hunter-gatherer life throughout this region during the early Holocene. We described the simple Kebaran culture, which flourished over a wide area of the coastal zone and inland at a time of more severe climate than today. The Kebaran evolved into the much more sedentary and more complex Natufian culture. These people exploited the Mediterranean zone intensively, foraging on the slopes for cereal grasses and nuts while exploiting gazelle and other game on the grassy lowlands. This same pattern of specialized hunting and gathering is documented elsewhere in Southwest Asia in about 11,000 B.C. The inhabitants of the Abu Hureyra site in Syria, for example, were hunting gazelle virtually to the exclusion of all other species. More than 80 percent of the mammal bones in this small settlement were from gazelle; at the same time, the people exploited half a dozen staple wild plants as well as more than 200 other species for a wide variety of purposes, among them hallucinogens and dyes. To this extent, they were managing and tending their environment to a significant degree (Moore et al., 2000). At the same time, they, and the Natufians, were coping with increasingly dry seasonal climates. If the scenario outlined is correct, these were the conditions that caused people living on drier steppes, and soon afterward other groups, to switch over to food production. In a sense, this climatic change and the peoples' adjustments to it represented a point of no return that led to agriculture.

Everything points to initial plant domestication having taken hold during the 1000-year-long Younger Dryas, between about 10,500 and 10,000 B.C., when people began to harvest wild cereal grasses such as rye with sickles or by uprooting entire plants. As we saw in Chapter 8, those spikelets that remained attached to the plants during harvesting were most likely to be part of next year's fields of cultivated plants. Within a short time, domesticated plants with semitough rachises dominated in cultivated fields; they were humanly created forms unable to compete on their own against the wild grasses. The harvesters imposed entirely new selective pressures on cultivated stands of wild grasses. This new set of selective pressures seems to have developed first in a small region of Southwest Asia called the Levantine Corridor, an area up to 40 km (25 miles) wide running from the Damascus basin in the north into the lower Jericho Valley (Bar-Yosef and Belfer-Cohen, 1989; McCorriston and Hole, 1991; H. Wright, 1993), and extending into the Euphrates Valley. This corridor had reliable water supplies and a relatively high water table, enabling foragers to shift wild grains from their natural habitats into well-watered areas near streams and lakes. The earliest farming sites in the world lie within the Levantine Corridor, among them Netiv Hagdud, Abu Hureyra, and Jericho (B. Smith, 1998).

〰️ The First Farmers: Netiv Hagdud, Abu Hureyra, and Jericho

Three important archaeological sites document this all-important transition in human life, giving us at least a general impression of the changeover.

Netiv Hagdud

Netiv Hagdud
10,000 B.C.

The tiny settlement of Netiv Hagdud, 80 km (50 miles) north of Jericho in present-day Israel, flourished for about 300 years after 10,000 B.C. and documents an early state in agricultural economies (Bar-Yosef et al., 1991). Perhaps 100 to 200 people, as many as 30 families, lived on a tributary of the Jordan River, hunting gazelle, taking fish and waterfowl, and collecting more than 50 species of wild plants, especially wild cereal grasses harvested with flint-bladed sickles. This small village of oval and circular mud-brick houses collected so much plant food that the grain was stored in small storage bins. The seeds included semitough rachised two-row barley, a domesticated grain raised in small fields on nearby, easily tilled soils close to the alluvial plain and a small freshwater lake. Netiv Hagdud is vitally important because it documents early efforts at farming only one cereal crop, probably as an important supplementary food. In contrast, farmers at Abu Hureyra, Jericho, and other sites cultivated several domestic crops together.

Abu Hureyra

Andrew Moore's long-term research on his excavations at the Abu Hureyra site near the Euphrates in Syria has led him to believe that agriculture and stock herding developed in this region remarkably quickly, perhaps in no more than a few hundred years, around 10,500 to 10,000 B.C.

Abu Hureyra
10,500 to 6000 B.C.

Abu Hureyra began life as a small village settlement of a few families that lived in pit dwellings with simple reed roofs supported by wooden uprights (Moore et al., 2000) (Figure 9.2). Using fine screens and flotation equipment, the excavators recovered thousands of seeds of wild vegetable foods, including wild einkorn and rye. Abu Hureyra lies outside the present-day range of these wild cereals. However, between 10,500 and 10,000 B.C., when the site was first occupied, the climate was somewhat warmer and damper than it is today. As a result, the village lay in a well-wooded steppe area where animals and wild cereals were abundant. At any rate, some hunter-gatherer groups, such as the Abu Hureyra people, came together in more permanent settlements and harvested wild cereals as a deliberate subsistence strategy.

FIGURE 9.2 Abu Hureyra, Syria. *Top,* the mound of Abu Hureyra from the southwest. The site, which overlooks the Euphrates floodplain, consists of two superimposed settlements. *Bottom,* the earlier settlement, comprising a series of interconnecting pits dug into the natural subsoil. These were roofed with poles, branches, and reeds to form huts. Part of a later rectilinear house can be seen near the top of the picture.

The inhabitants also had access to a reliable meat source: Persian gazelles that arrived from the south each spring. The arrivals were apparently killed en masse each year, and the meat was stored. With such a favorable location, Abu Hureyra slowly increased in size to 300 to 400 people, until much more arid conditions, and perhaps deforestation due to heavy firewood consumption, caused them to leave (Moore and Hillman, 1992). In its heyday, its people may have enjoyed a higher degree of social organization than that found in nomadic hunter-gatherer societies.

Deliberate farming began in about 10,000 B.C. in Abu Hureyra's earlier village (AH 1). It was based on rye, einkorn, and lentils. The agricultural economy developed continuously, leading to the formation of the much larger second settlement (AH 2). Just about half a millennium separated the first, gazelle-hunting settlement at Abu Hureyra and the subsequent, much larger farming settlement. About 9000 B.C., a new village, which grew to cover nearly 12 ha (30 acres), rose on the low mound. At first, the inhabitants still hunted gazelle intensively. Then, about 9000 B.C., within the space of a generation or two, they switched to herding domesticated sheep and goats. Visitors to the village would have found themselves wandering through a closely knit community of rectangular one-story mud-brick houses joined by narrow lanes and courtyards. The multiroom dwellings had polished black plaster floors, sometimes decorated with red designs. A single family occupied each one. We know the women did most of the food preparation because their knee joints bear the telltale signs of arthritis from kneeling (Molleson, 1994). Abu Hureyra was finally abandoned in about 6500 B.C. (see Site box).

Jericho

Jericho
10,000 B.C. and later

Most early Neolithic villages covered, at most, a couple of acres. In dramatic contrast, the settlement at Jericho extended over at least 4 ha (9.8 acres). A temporary Natufian camp had flourished at the bubbling Jericho spring by at least 10,000 B.C. (Kenyon, 1981), but a more lasting farming settlement quickly followed. Soon these people, whose technology did not include clay vessels, were building massive walls around their settlement. A finely built stone wall complete with a tower bordered a rock-cut ditch nearly 3 m (9 feet) deep and 3.2 m (10 feet) wide (Figure 9.3). The beehive-shaped huts of Jericho were clustered within the defenses. The communal labor of wall building required both political and economic resources on a scale unheard of a few thousand years earlier. Why walls were needed remains a mystery, but they may have been for defense from group competition for scarce resources. Some geomorphological research hints that the walls may have been flood-control works, but the theory is controversial (Bar-Yosef, 1986).

Types of houses similar to those at Abu Hureyra occur at Jericho and other contemporary settlements, where the dead were buried within the settlement, sometimes under house floors. At Jericho, 'Ain Ghazal in Jordan, and elsewhere, the people would sever the head and deposit it alone or with a cache of skulls. At both sites, they sometimes modeled the features of the deceased in painted plaster, perhaps in some form of ancestor cult (Figures 9.4 and 9.5). There are no signs of differences in individual status in this society.

FIGURE 9.3 Excavated remains of the great tower in early Jericho. Part of a massive stone wall, a passageway inside the tower contained many human skeletons deposited at a later date.

FIGURE 9.4 Plastered skull from Jericho, perhaps evidence of an early ancestor cult.

FIGURE 9.5 Plaster figurines from 'Ain Ghazal, Jordan. Found on a small platform, these may be domestic house figures.

SITE

n's and Women's Work at Abu Hureyra, Syria

ier times, many people spent most of their
working at specific tasks, labor that left tell-
tai gns on their bones. For instance, people who
squat habitually develop specific anatomical conditions of their hips, knees, and ankles.

Biological anthropologist Theya Molleson of
London's Natural History Museum examined the
fragmentary skeletons of about 162 people from
the early farming village at Abu Hureyra in Syria
(Molleson, 1994). She found ample evidence of
repetitive tasks. Some people's neck bones displayed enlarged upper vertebrae, the result of
carrying heavy loads on their heads. Others
showed the characteristic facets at the forward side
of the ankles that are found in people who squat
habitually from an early age. This condition
occurred in men, women, and children.

Many Abu Hureyra skeletons from people in otherwise good health displayed collapsed lower vertebrae, grossly arthritic big toes, and muscular arms
and legs (as revealed by prominent muscle attachments). The toe bones were very revealing: Older
individuals displayed a degenerative condition of
the metatarsals, and even younger people showed
changes in the big toe and second toe joints that had
resulted from kneeling with the toes tucked under
the foot. This position was used by people who
spent long periods of time laboring at household
tasks such as grinding grain. When Molleson examined pictures from ancient Egyptian and Assyrian
tombs, she found just such a position being used by
grain grinders, metalworkers, and other artisans.

At Abu Hureyra, a metal-less community, the
inhabitants must have been grinding grain on shallow querns. The weight of the body was used to
grind the grain, the toes being used as a base for
applying force to the grinding motion. This was a
very painful and tiring activity indeed, hard on the
arms as well as the toes (Figure 9.6). The Abu
Hureyra skeletons displayed well-marked attachments for the deltoid muscles on the upper arms,
which probably resulted from the movement at
the end of the pushing stroke during grinding.

Theya Molleson measured the first metatarsal
bone of the feet bones in her sample. She found
the larger ones belonged to males, the smaller to
females. On the latter, the arthritic condition associated with grinding was found. The constant,
daily use of saddle querns (saddle-shaped grinding
stones) caused this condition to develop in the
knees and the lower back of many Abu Hureyra
individuals. Grinding with such a quern is very
laborious; it involves pushing a rubbing stone over
a slightly tilted quern set as close to the knees as
possible. Many passes are needed to produce flour
for baking. This grinding method places severe
stress on knees, wrists, and lower back, reflected in
the bones of those who carried out this constant
daily work—the women of the community.

The Abu Hureyra people had heavily abraded
teeth, resulting from eating coarse grain. But they
may have sifted grain through fiber baskets, as
some of the teeth display the characteristic grooving resulting from chewing basket fiber to soften it.

FIGURE 9.6 Deformed toe bones of an Abu
Hureyra woman.

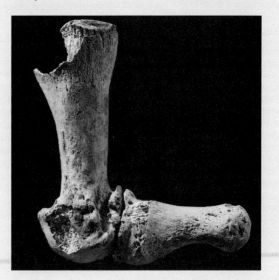

Diverse Farming Economies and Trade

9000 B.C.   The farmers of 10,000 to 9000 B.C. hunted gazelles, wild cattle, pigs, goats, and other
species. None of the bones shows the characteristic morphological features of domesticated animals. Judging from the proportions of immature gazelles at some sites, the

people were very efficient, selective hunters. This pattern of animal exploitation had begun millennia earlier, during the Upper Paleolithic. Sheep and goats very rapidly replaced gazelles as the principal meat supply at Abu Hureyra and elsewhere after about 8000 B.C. At the same time, there are signs that cattle and pigs were subject to increasing human control. By this time, the domestication of sheep and goats had proceeded to the point where surplus males were slaughtered for meat before adulthood, a characteristic mortality profile for managed herds. By about 7500 B.C., it appears that the local gazelle herds were depleted. Sheep and goats now composed 60 percent of all meat consumed (Legge and Rowley-Conwy, 1987).

Emmer wheat, barley, lentils, and peas were grown in the early Neolithic from about 9000 B.C. Even quite early, agricultural methods were relatively sophisticated, cereals being rotated with pulses to ensure high crop yields and to sustain soil fertility. An effective system of allowing fields to lie fallow also made larger sites possible. Abu Hureyra and Jericho were occupied continuously over many centuries as a result. Many settlements became trading centers, for the numbers of imported materials and exotic objects rose dramatically after 8000 B.C. The farmers were using obsidian from Anatolia, turquoise from Sinai, and seashells from the Mediterranean and the Red Sea. The volume of trade was such that many villagers used small clay spheres, cones, and disks to keep track of the commodities traded. These tokens are thought by some archaeologists to have been a simple recording system that later evolved into written script (Schmandt-Besserat, 1992).

8000 B.C.

By 7000 B.C., there was considerable variation in farming culture throughout Southwest Asia, caused by local cultural developments. But the farmers maintained fleeting contacts with communities many hundreds of miles away, even with peoples living in quite different culture areas in the Zagros and Anatolia (Kozlowski, 1999).

ꙮ The Zagros and Mesopotamia

As along the coast, the sequence of Neolithic cultures in the Zagros foothills and Mesopotamia can be divided into an earlier stage, from about 10,000 to 6000 B.C., and later Neolithic, lasting until about 5000 B.C. There were sporadic contacts between these areas and the Mediterranean coast, but cultural developments in this region were parallel to and independent of those at Abu Hureyra, Jericho, and other western locations.

Thanks to the pioneering work of Robert Braidwood, who looked for agricultural origins on the hilly flanks of Mesopotamia, we know more about the highlands, where agricultural conditions were less favorable, than we do about early food production in the lowlands, the undulating northern Mesopotamian steppe, where the Assyrian civilization flourished millennia later (Kozlowski, 1999). To the south, the sandy Mesopotamian plain accumulated deep layers of silt throughout the Holocene. Early farming settlement there is probably buried under several feet of alluvium. Some small farming villages are preserved under great city mounds like those of Ur and Eridu, and they date to not much earlier than about 5800 B.C.

During the late Ice Age, human groups probably lived in the warmer lowlands. In the very early Holocene, the mountains were cool and dry, so agriculture probably began in the lowlands first, a natural habitat for wild cereals and pulses. As the climate warmed up, people moved into the mountain valleys of Zagros, open steppe country with seasonal resources spaced vertically up hill slopes. This was ideal country for herding sheep and goats, to the extent that herding may have developed earlier here than in other parts of Southwest Asia (Moore, 1985).

Zawi Chemi Shanidar

About 10,500 B.C., wild goats were a primary quarry for the hunters and gatherers exploiting the resources of the foothills. The people of a small encampment named Zawi Chemi Shanidar in the mountains of Kurdistan were hunting and gathering at this time, living in small circular huts. The inhabitants were killing large numbers of immature sheep, as if they had fenced in their grazing grounds for efficient, intensive

Zawi Chemi Shanidar
10,500 B.C.

hunting. Zawi Chemi may have been a summer encampment on the steppe. Pollen studies show an increase in cereal grasses during the occupation, perhaps evidence of cultivation.

Ganj Dareh

High in a mountain valley nearby lies another early farming village, named Ganj Dareh, first occupied about 10,000 B.C. (P. E. L. Smith, 1978). The earliest settlement was probably a seasonal camp used by hunters and gatherers, but a later occupation, around 8000 B.C., consisted of a small village of rectangular mud-brick houses, some two stories high. The lower stories may have been used for storage because clay bins have been found there. Ganj Dareh represents the beginnings of permanent settlement in the Zagros, based on goat and cattle herding and possibly agriculture. The goat bones reveal a high proportion of sub-adult males and mostly older females, the characteristic mortality profile of domesticated and managed herds (Zeder and Hesse, 2000).

Jarmo

One of the best-known Zagros farming villages is Jarmo, a permanent hill village southeast of Zawi Chemi occupied in about 7000 B.C. (Braidwood and Braidwood, 1983). Jarmo was little more than a cluster of 25 houses built of mud bricks and forming an irregular huddle separated by small alleyways and courtyards. Storage bins and clay ovens were an integral part of the structures. The Jarmo deposits yielded abundant traces of agriculture: Seeds of barley, emmer wheat, and minor crops were found with the bones of sheep and goats. Hunting had declined in importance—only a few wild animal bones testify to such activity—but the toolkit still included Stone Age–type tools with sickle blades, grinding stones, and other implements of tillage. Jarmo contains exotic materials such as obsidian, seashells, and turquoise traded into the Zagros from afar. There are also numerous clay tokens, perhaps again evidence of a recording system connected with long-distance trade. Jarmo was a fully permanent, well-established village engaged in far more intensive agriculture than its predecessors. More than 80 percent of the villagers' food came from herds or crops.

Ali Kosh and the Lowlands

Below, in the lowlands, farming began along the eastern edge of the flat Mesopotamian plain at least as early as along the eastern Mediterranean coast. The Ali Kosh site on the Deh Luran plain of Khuzistan, north of where the Tigris and Euphrates join waters, chronicles human occupation from about 7500 B.C. Ali Kosh began life as a small village of mud-brick rectangular houses with several rooms (Hole et al., 1969). As time went on, the houses became larger, separated from one another by lanes or courtyards. The people herded goats and sheep, which may have been driven to highland pastures in the mountains during the hot summer months. This *transhumance pattern*—the seasonal movement of herding peoples to new pastures—continues in the area to this day. Emmer, einkorn, barley, and lentils were cultivated from the earliest days of Ali Kosh. Hunting and gathering were important, as were the fish and waterfowl from a nearby marsh. This well-excavated site documents the maturing of farming and herding on the lowlands, with the development of improved cereal strains and the first appearance of irrigation as a way of intensifying agricultural production.

Agriculture and herding were well established in the lowlands when Ali Kosh was founded in about 7500 B.C. As along the coast, cereal cultivation and animal husbandry were probably developed first by hunter-gatherer groups in the very early Holocene.

🐾 Anatolia

Anatolia (Turkey) was a diverse, favorable highland and lowland environment for human settlement from early in the Holocene. Sites like Hallan Çemi Tepesi in eastern Anatolia, occupied during the Younger Dryas, document sedentary settlement before agriculture, pig domestication, and extensive obsidian trade as early as 9500 B.C. (Özdogan and Basgelen, 1999; Rosenberg et al., 1998). Food production probably began in this region at about the same time as it did in the Levant, but archaeological research is still in its early stages (for a useful survey, see Özdogan and Basgelen, 1999).

Çayönü

Çayönü, about 100 km (62 miles) west of Hallan Çemi Tepesi, was occupied from about 8600 to 7000 B.C. (R. J. Braidwood and Cambel, 1980; Özdogan and Basgelen, 1999). The first phase of occupation lasted about 650 years, when the inhabitants lived in separate rectangular houses of various designs. The people cultivated cereals and pulses, collected wild vegetable foods, and relied increasingly on domesticated sheep for meat after 7700 B.C. Çayönü represents a relatively developed form of farming life, remarkable only for the sudden adoption of sheepherding, a phenomenon also found at Abu Hureyra in Syria. Perhaps the inhabitants of both sites started herding sheep as a result of contact with shepherd peoples from the highlands to the east, who had been herding small stock for a long time.

Çayönü
8600 to 7000 B.C.

Other sites in the same general region document similar occupation at the same time as the first settlement at Çayönü. Settlements like Nevali Çori on a tributary of the Euphrates and Göbekli Tepe contain rectangular buildings and elaborate carvings of humans and animals, evidence for a sudden explosion of rituals that may be connected with fertility.

Haçilar

The Anatolian Plateau was also an early center for food production, as well as a major source of obsidian for toolmaking since the end of the Ice Age. As early as 8300 B.C., villages flourished near major outcrops. (For a summary of work on obsidian sources and local sites, see Özdogan and Basgelen, 1999.)

Most Neolithic sites in central and eastern Anatolia were within easy reach of the rich obsidian sources near Lake Van and elsewhere. Villages close to the volcanic flows where the fine stone came from used it almost exclusively for artifacts, trading a great deal of obsidian to communities near and far in the form of prepared blade cores. Small quantities of Anatolian obsidian traveled hundreds of miles along the eastern Mediterranean coast and as far as the Persian Gulf. Trace element analyses of artifacts from many sites show that the patterns of exchange were exceedingly complex, as different sources came into and went out of fashion.

In western Anatolia, James Mellaart (1975) excavated a remarkable early farming village at Haçilar, which was founded in approximately 8000 B.C. Seven phases of occupation took place at Haçilar before its inhabitants moved. They lived in small rectangular houses with courtyards, hearths, ovens, and plastered walls. No pottery was used at Haçilar, but basketry and leather containers probably were. Barley and emmer wheat were cultivated, and some wild grass seeds were also eaten. The bones of sheep or goats and cattle and deer are present, but there is no evidence of the domestication of any animal except the dog. Haçilar was a simple and unsophisticated settlement, probably typical of many communities in Southwest Asia in the early millennia of farming.

Haçilar
8000 B.C.

Çatalhöyük

The simplicity of many Anatolian farming villages contrasts dramatically with a more complex settlement engaged in widespread trading activity. The great mound of Çatalhöyük covers 13 ha (32 acres); it was a large village or town of numerous small houses built of sun-dried brick, which were designed to back onto one another, occasionally separated by small courtyards. Roofs were flat, and the outside walls of the houses provided a convenient defense wall (Figure 9.7). The town was rebuilt at least 12 times after approximately 7000 B.C., presumably when the houses began to crumble or the population swelled (Mellaart, 1967). The site is currently being excavated on a large scale by an international team of researchers (Hodder, 1996; Özdogan and

Çatalhöyük
7000 B.C.

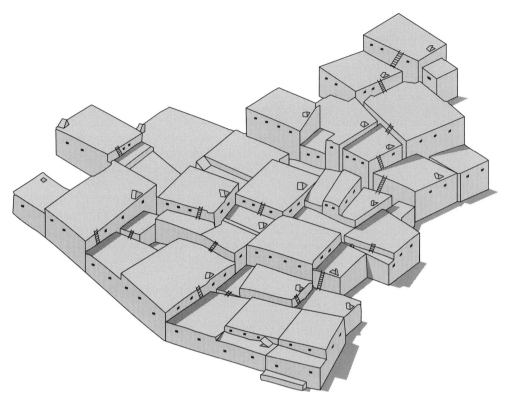

FIGURE 9.7 Schematic reconstruction of houses and shrines from Level VI at Çatalhöyük, Turkey, showing the flat roof architecture and the roof entrance.

Basgelen, 1999). More than likely their work will change the interpretation of the site offered here (Figure 9.8).

Çatalhöyük preserves a flourishing artistic tradition that clearly has roots in earlier paintings and carvings, preserved on carefully plastered walls and in sculptures adorning what appear to be household shrines (Figure 9.9). Most depict women or bulls, scenes of birth, shamanistic dances, and ancestors. We can never hope to reconstruct the symbolic world of the Çatalhöyük people except in the most general terms. We know there was a duality between male and female, some form of divine family personified, perhaps, by

FIGURE 9.8
Excavation of a house at Çatalhöyük.

FIGURE 9.9 Reconstruction of the east and south walls of Shrine VI.14 at Çatalhöyük, Turkey, with sculpted ox heads, horns, benches, and relief models of bulls and rams. A ladder at right entered the shrine.

two deities: mother/daughter (a great goddess) and a lesser father/son (her paramour) (Mellaart, 1967).

Much of Çatalhöyük's prosperity resulted from its monopoly on the obsidian volcanic glass trade from quarries in nearby mountains. Obsidian, however, was only one of many materials traded by Southwest Asian farmers after 9000 B.C. Marine shells, jadeite, serpentine, turquoise, and many other exotic commodities moved from village to village through myriad barter transactions. Perhaps these regular exchanges were used not only to obtain exotic materials but also to cement social relationships. Andrew Moore (1985) believes that this widespread exchange of raw materials accelerated the diffusion of all manner of innovations far and wide, among them sheepherding, the introduction of pottery, and eventually copper and bronze metallurgy.

Just how important the obsidian trade was in the area has been shown by spectrographic analyses of fragments of the volcanic glass in hundreds of sites between Turkey and Mesopotamia. The trace elements in obsidian are so distinctive that it is possible to identify the natural source of the glass by this analysis and to reconstruct the distribution of obsidian from dozens of localities. Thousands of obsidian samples document widespread exchange of this most desirable of toolmaking stones throughout Anatolia and deep into the Levant. The percentages of obsidian fall away rapidly the farther one gets from the source, which suggests that much early farming trade was probably a form of "down-the-line" bartering that passed various commodities from one village to the next.

〰 Two Stages of Farming Development

Until about 6000 B.C., cultural development proceeded independently in each of these three regions: the eastern Mediterranean coast, the highlands, and Anatolia. In each area, herding and agriculture emerged separately. Not that they were isolated one from another; far from it. There were regular trading contacts between each area, contacts that may have led to the spread of cereal crops, herding, pottery, religious beliefs and ideologies, and other innovations. In time, well-established barter networks helped spread both economic and technological innovations throughout ancient Southwest Asia, and that is why similar developments and intensifications of agricultural production occur at about the same time in several places. By 6000 B.C., the new economies had become the foundations of human diet throughout Southwest Asia. Major changes in settlement patterns ensued. Sustained population growth took hold a while after farming became commonplace and agriculture sufficiently productive to feed many more people.

6000 B.C.

The development of the new food-producing economies took place in two stages. The first saw some agriculture and control of animals, but much of the diet still came from game and wild vegetable foods. Then, about 6000 B.C., more productive cereal grains and the domestication of cattle, sheep, goats, and pigs created the fully agricultural and stock-raising economy that was to persist into historic times and in much more elaborated forms.

This was a time of profound social change, when human societies developed new mechanisms for social control, the settlement of disputes, and the regulation of the cultivation and inheritance of land. Evidence of ranked societies appears in the form of richly adorned burials at Çatalhöyük and, perhaps, the plastered skulls from Jericho; both were large, important settlements that were the focus of long-distance exchange and important religious rituals. Some scholars even refer to these large centers as towns, or "protocities," locations where new forms of ranked society first developed in Southwest Asia. For the most part, however, the new societies were still egalitarian, their economies based on the productive abilities of the household and the nuclear family. The plastered skulls from 'Ain Ghazal, Jericho, and other Neolithic sites (see Figures 9.4 and 9.5) and complex rituals and ancestor cults show farmers already defining the relationship between living people and the spiritual world, the world of soil fertility, bountiful crops, and revered ancestors.

Summary 〰〰

Southwest Asia was cool and dry immediately after the Ice Age, with dry steppe over much of the interior. Human populations were sparse and highly mobile as forests spread more widely throughout the region. The development and spread of food production took place under conditions of climatic change that favored wild annual cereal grasses. There was a general trend toward more sedentary lifeways and a greater emphasis on storage technology and seed grinding after 10,000 B.C., epitomized by the Natufian culture and related societies in the Levant and Anatolia, groups who foraged intensively for wild cereals.

Farming began at Abu Hureyra on the Euphrates River in about 10,000 B.C. Sheep and goats replaced gazelle hunting abruptly at the same site and at other settlements after 8000 B.C. Abu Hureyra was not unique. Food production began in several regions more or less simultaneously, the Levant being one area, southeastern Anatolia another.

Herding was well established somewhat earlier in the Zagros highlands, while Anatolia was inhabited by farming communities linked by long-distance exchange routes handling obsidian and other exotica by at least 8500 B.C.

Cultural development then proceeded separately in each area of Southwest Asia, but there were increasingly frequent trading connections between each region, which accelerated even more after 3000 B.C.

Key Terms 〰〰

Ecotone A location where several ecological zones meet.

Neolithic After the Greek *neos*, "new," *lithos*, "stone." A generic term used to refer to Stone Age farmers, mainly employed in Europe and Southwest Asia.

Guide to Further Reading 〰〰

Aurenche, O., and S. Kozlowski. 1999. *La naissance au néolithique au Proche Orient, ou le paradis perdu.* Paris: Editions Errance.
A useful synthesis of the origins of food production in Southwest Asia with excellent illustrations.

Bar-Yosef, O. 1987. "Late Pleistocene Adaptations in the Levant." In *The Pleistocene Old World: Regional Perspectives.* Olga Soffer, ed. Pp. 219–236. New York: Plenum Press.
An authoritative synthesis of late Upper Paleolithic cultures in Southwest Asia. Designed for the serious reader.

Cauvin, J. 2000. *The Birth of the Gods and the Origins of Agriculture.* T. Watkins, trans. Cambridge: Cambridge University Press.

Provocative and controversial, this book by a French scholar offers a thought-provoking analysis of early food production in Southwest Asia.

Kenyon, Kathleen. 1981. *Excavations at Jericho,* vol. 3. Jerusalem: British School of Archaeology.
A monograph on the early levels at Jericho; a fascinating specialist publication.

Moore, Andrew T. 2000. *Village on the Euphrates.* New York: Oxford University Press.
Arguably the finest and most comprehensive monograph on an ancient farming settlement ever written.

Özdogan, M., and N. Basgelen, eds. 1999. *Neolithic in Turkey: New Discoveries.* Istanbul: Arkeoloji ve Sanat Yayinlari.
This edited volume, compiled by two Turkish scholars, contains articles summarizing recent work in Anatolia. A seminal work, but, alas, somewhat inaccessible.

Smith, Bruce D. 1998. *The Emergence of Agriculture,* 2nd ed. New York: W. H. Freeman.
An up-to-date account of high-technology science and the origins of agriculture, written for a popular audience. A wonderful introduction to the subject, with much on Southwest Asia.

10

THE FIRST
EUROPEAN FARMERS

The interior of a Neolithic house at Skara Brae, Orkney Islands, United Kingdom.

For many years, fishermen on the Swiss lakes had spread rumors of submerged forests that snagged their nets. Then a drought in the 1850s shrank the lakes dramatically and exposed veritable "forests" of wooden pilings set in the mud. Zurich archaeologist Ferdinand Keller dug around the piles at Obermeilen on Lake Zurich. The mud had preserved all manner of objects, large and small, not only prehistoric ax handles and weapons but fruit and ripe hazelnuts, thousands of animal bones, and all the perishable debris of a long-abandoned farming settlement of "high antiquity," as Keller (1866, p. 53) put it.

Keller's methods were rough and ready, for he merely dug into the mud around the pilings to recover as much as he could. He theorized that "lake dwellings" had been built on piles over the water, and that the inhabitants had dropped their artifacts, food remains, and garbage into the lake. It was not until the 1920s that more meticulous excavators showed that the villages had flourished on dry land before being flooded by rising lake levels. But Obermeilen and other Swiss sites were the first evidence for early farming in Europe, sites that are now known to be relatively late in the history of European farming (Coles and Coles, 1989). In this chapter, we examine the evidence for the spread of food production throughout temperate Europe.

Mesolithic Prelude

In Chapter 7, we described the Mesolithic hunter-gatherers of central and western Europe, the indigenous peoples of those densely forested regions concentrated by seashores, lakes, and rivers and in forest clearings (Table 10.1). The Mesolithic lasted for about 4000 years, from about 8000 B.C. until the introduction of farming in northwestern Europe about 4000 B.C. This temperate and boreal forest adaptation displayed considerable location variation. Except in areas of abundant aquatic resources and predictable food supplies, population densities were very low. In some areas, however, such as the Danube's Iron Gates region and the Baltic shores of Scandinavia, population densities were unusually high, and there are some signs of social ranking and great complexity in some late Mesolithic groups (Price, 1987).

These trends toward greater complexity, more sedentary lifeways, and more intensive hunting, foraging, and fishing took hold in Mesolithic societies throughout Europe when Southwest Asian societies were already experimenting with the deliberate cultivation and domestication of crops and animals. After about 6000 B.C., farming was well established in parts of the Aegean and in southeastern Europe. During the 2000 years that followed, European Mesolithic societies apparently embraced these new subsistence practices quite readily

TABLE 10.1

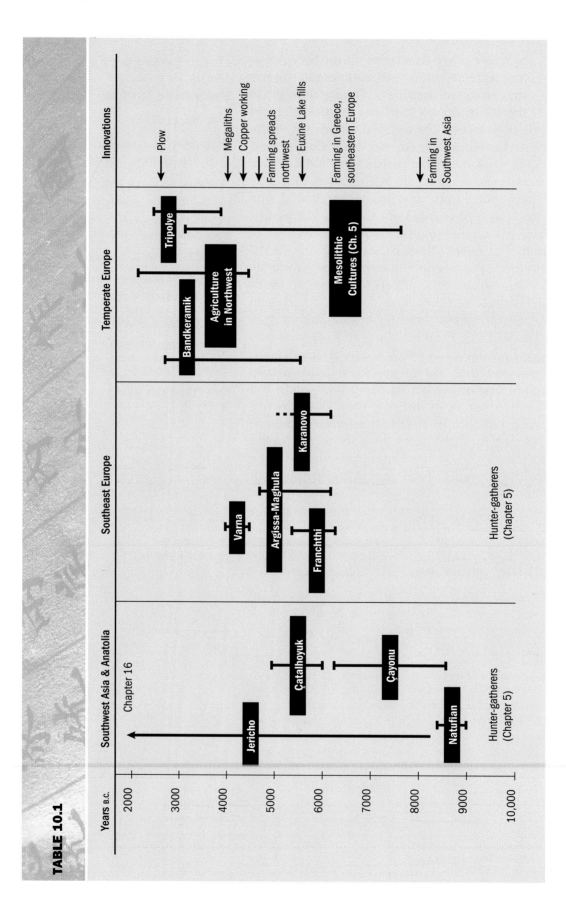

(Barker, 1985; Bogucki, 1993), abandoning the hunter-gatherer lifeways that had sustained their immediate and more remote ancestors for hundreds of thousands of years (Bonsall, 1989). The details of this transition are still little understood, but it can be argued that the Mesolithic population was preadapted to cultivation and animal domestication, especially in areas where short-term population shifts and local environmental change may have required conservative subsistence strategies.

🐾 The Transition to Farming in Europe

Did farming spread into Europe as a result of diffusion from Southwest Asia, or did food production develop independently in the temperate zone? There are almost as many theories about this controversial subject as there are archaeologists; the theories pit diffusionists against those who argue that Europeans developed their own farming culture in southeastern Europe before 6000 B.C. (Van Andel, Tjeerd, and Runnels, 1995).

One reason why many scholars have assumed that agriculture spread into Europe from Southwest Asia is that they have thought of Europe as one geographic entity, and of Turkey and the rest of Southwest Asia just across the Dardanelles as another (Thorpe, 1996). They also assumed that rising population densities caused surplus farmers to spill over into Europe, bringing goats, sheep, and Southwest Asian cereal crops with them. There is no evidence of uncomfortably high population densities anywhere in Anatolia at this time (although our knowledge is incomplete). Furthermore, the earliest farming sites in southeastern Europe are situated in very favorable places, which could have been familiar only to people who had lived in the region for many generations. However, it is undeniable that food production began in Southwest Asia about 10,000 B.C. and some 2000 years later in southeastern Europe. Thus, it is most likely that the new economies spread into temperate lands from Southwest Asia (Figure 10.1). But how are we to account for the chronological gradient?

We begin our discussion with some hypothetical scenarios. The assumption that the natural distributions of wild cereals and of potential animal domesticates have

FIGURE 10.1 Map showing early farming areas in Southwest Asia and southeastern Europe. Arrows show possible routes by which the new economies spread. (1) Jordan Valley and the eastern Mediterranean; (2) Çayönü region; (3, 4) Anatolian region, including Çatalhöyük and Haçilar; (5) Cyprus; (6) Crete; (7) Franchthi Cave; (8) Macedonia; (9) Balkans region.

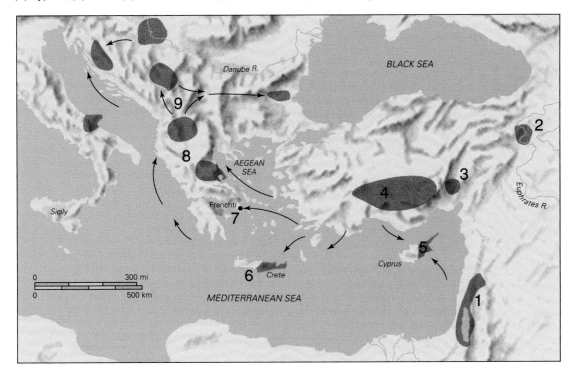

remained unchanged since the early Holocene is at best questionable (Thorpe, 1996). As many authors have pointed out, human activity alone may have drastically reduced present-day ranges to the point where all we record are residual distributions. Late glacial and early Holocene pollen diagrams from northern Greece demonstrate that barley and perhaps other cereals were present in southeastern Europe long before farmers appeared, about 6000 B.C. Cereal grasses may have moved into temperate Europe ahead of woodlands in early Holocene times. Pulses may also have grown in Europe—the evidence is uncertain. As for potential animal domesticates, wild sheep are known to have flourished, although in scattered groups, in Upper Paleolithic Europe.

Robin Dennell (1983) argues that the development of food production in southeastern Europe went through three phases. First, climatic conditions in the early Holocene favored more plant growth. Grasses like einkorn and barley became more abundant, growing in dense stands that could be harvested in sufficient quantities to support a family for a year. However, most groups probably relied on shorter-term supplies, as wild plant harvests were unpredictable. So they moved on and obtained much of their diet from hunting and other foraged foods.

A second stage began when trees colonized the areas previously occupied by grasses. This change would have scattered grass stands, decreasing the amount of the grasses worth harvesting by human groups. The grasses were worth maintaining as a seasonally important food, so the people may have ring-barked tree trunks or burned the forest to clear space for wild grasses to grow. The harvested plots would gradually revert to woodland, where young shoots would attract deer, wild sheep, and other animals. Dennell (1983) believes that a simple interdependence between plant harvesting and animal exploitation developed in areas where woodlands were expanding at the expense of cereals. In such areas, human beings lived in small transitory settlements, many of them seasonal camps—just the kinds of sites found in the southern European Mesolithic (Zvelebil, 1986).

A third phase saw the establishment of permanent agricultural settlements. Through either local bartering or natural means, large-grained tough-rachis cereals were introduced into southeastern Europe (Thorpe, 1996). These were Southwest Asian cereals like emmer and bread wheat that were more predictable and productive than wild cereals. They required much more work to cultivate and careful sowing in specially prepared and selected fields. The farmers had to weed and protect their growing crops. All this extra effort involved creating special fields and gardens for crops, a mosaic of cultivated land based on carefully chosen soils and a rotation system that allowed exhausted soils to rest. Both domestic emmer and bread wheat take large quantities of nutrients from the soil, which could be replaced by the underplanting of nitrogen-fixing legumes and the use of animal manure. This new farming habitat involved the integration of cultivation and animal husbandry into a closely knit subsistence strategy based on individual households' supplying their own food needs.

This model envisages food production in southeastern Europe as a largely indigenous development, stimulated in part by the immigration of some domestic plants and animals from across the Dardanelles, perhaps as a result of trading activity (B. Smith, 1998). It also accounts for the chronological gradient, a time lag that resulted from the gradual "drift" of new crops and domesticated animals from Southwest Asia.

🐾 Farming in Greece and Southern Europe

The earliest known evidence of food production in southern Europe comes from the Argissa-Maghula village mound on the plains of Greek Thessaly (Demoule and Perlès, 1993; Perlès, 2001) (Figure 10.2). These once-empty plains with their many rivers and lakes provided a favorable environment for natural irrigation of easily cultivatable floodplain lands. As early as 7000 B.C., farmers settled in this region, cultivating emmer wheat and barley and herding cattle, sheep, and pigs. Van Andel et al. (1995) have argued convincingly for a spread of farming from Anatolia into this fertile area and into southeastern Europe (see Figure 10.1).

7000 B.C.

Within a few centuries, farmers were well established elsewhere in Greece's mountainous terrain. The Franchthi Cave in southern Greece was occupied in Mesolithic

Franchthi

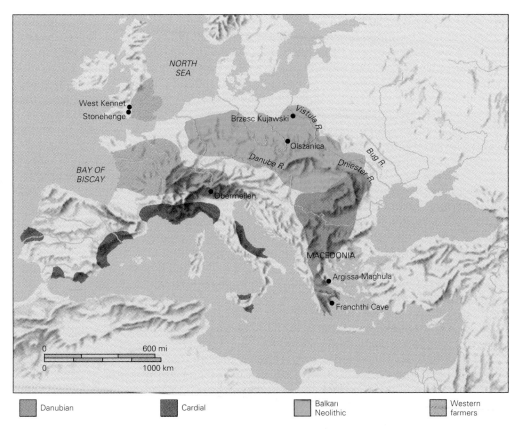

FIGURE 10.2
Archaeological sites in temperate Europe and the distribution of Bandkeramik (Danubian) pottery, Cardial ware, and western Neolithic cultures.

| Danubian | Cardial | Balkan Neolithic | Western farmers |

times and continued in use for many thousands of years. Farming appeared there about 6000 B.C., when the people began herding goats and sheep and extended their settlement outside the cave itself. These people had trading contacts with the Aegean islands (Jacobsen and Farrand, 1987). Since domesticated crops appeared abruptly at Franchthi, it is reasonable to suppose that cereal agriculture had been developed somewhat earlier or elsewhere. By 5500 B.C., established farming settlements were commonplace in Greece, also along the Adriatic Sea's Dalmatian coast.

6000 B.C.

Like Franchthi Cave in Greece, the Grotta dell'Uzzo on the northwest coast of Sicily was occupied for many millennia by hunter-gatherers. Between 6000 and 5800 B.C., the cave's inhabitants abruptly began raising einkorn, wheat, barley, and lentils. They also kept cattle and small stock, continuing, however, to hunt and to gather wild plant foods on a considerable scale. This was selective agriculture, in which indigenous hunter-gatherers adopted some Southwest Asian domesticates as supplemental foods. Sheep, for example, represent only about 2 to 20 percent of the animal bones at dell'Uzzo. But by 5000 B.C., sheepherding and sedentary agriculture were well established along the Mediterranean coast and inland.

Grotta dell'Uzzo
6000 B.C.

🐾 The Spread of Agriculture into Temperate Europe

The beginnings of farming in Europe have traditionally been explained as a process of colonization from Southwest Asia (Barker, 1985; Price, 2001). According to this theory, the newcomers spread across Europe from about 6000 B.C., ending with the introduction of farming to northwestern Europe in about 3500 B.C. The new economies effectively terminated hunter-gatherer societies in Europe. In fact, the process was much more complicated, a combination of both local and intrusive developments (Milisauskas and Kruk, 1989).

6000 B.C.

The adaptive processes and population movements involved are still little understood. These temperate zones have year-round rainfall and marked contrasts between winter and summer seasons. Timber and thatch replaced the mud-brick architecture used so effectively for houses in Southwest Asian villages. Agricultural techniques had to reflect the heavier soils and perennial rainfall of European latitudes, but the first introduction of farming coincided with a warm, moist phase, when midsummer temperatures were at least 2°C (3°F) higher than today. The forest cover was mainly mixed oak, shadier tree cover that reduced the grazing resources of large game animals such as deer and wild cattle. Many of the indigenous Mesolithic populations lived by coasts, lakes, and rivers on ecotones, where they could exploit several ecological zones from summer and winter camps. The first European farmers settled on the mostly **loess** soils of central Europe, which were lightly wooded, fertile, and easily tilled with simple digging sticks and hoes (Starling, 1985).

No one questions that there was a directional movement of farming from the southeast to the northwest (Dennell, 1983), but whether this was a matter of population replacement, as claimed by some geneticists, or of the adoption of the new economies by indigenous Europeans is a matter of continuing debate (Cavalli-Sforza and Cavalli-Sforza, 1995; Powledge and Rose, 1996). This is a far cry, however, from thinking in terms of a wave of Southwest Asian colonists, eager for new land, pouring into Europe. In fact, the first European farming societies were sparse in numbers, and the land had the potential to support far larger numbers of cultivators. Furthermore, indigenous Mesolithic peoples were probably important players in the adoption of the new economies. Indeed, European farmers have been remarkable for the ways in which they have adapted to the challenging and varied environments of temperate Europe. Here, as in Southwest Asia, China, and the Americas, early farming was a matter of trial and error, of success and sometimes failure.

Recent excavations have also raised the possibility that some animals and plants were actually domesticated in southeastern Europe and not introduced from Southwest Asia. The natural ranges of sheep and such plants as barley, einkorn, and some legumes may have once extended into southeastern Europe (Dennell, 1983). Only emmer and bread wheat were certainly domesticated in Southwest Asia. There is a real possibility, then, that hunter-gatherer societies in southeastern Europe developed food production on their own, in response to such stresses as population pressure or environmental change. The exact stresses are still a mystery.

One potentially major stress has emerged from remarkable deep-sea core research in the Mediterranean and Black seas. In about 6200 B.C., four centuries of much cooler, drier conditions may have caused widespread drought across southeastern Europe. Under these circumstances, farming settlements would have tended to concentrate near lakes, seacoasts, and rivers. At the time, the Black Sea was an enormous freshwater lake, for the brackish Mediterranean had not risen sufficiently from its late Ice Age low to breach an earthen barrier that lay at the mouth of the Bosphorus Valley. Better rainfall and wetter conditions returned in about 5800 B.C.; the Mediterranean continued to rise, lapping at the crest of the barrier that separated it from the Black Sea, 150 m (492 feet) below. Suddenly, around 5500 B.C., seawater cascaded over the rim in a violent waterfall that cut deep into the underlying bedrock. The Euxine Lake rose rapidly and became part of the ocean, inundating thousands of square kilometers of low-lying coastal terrain. Although we have no archaeological evidence to document the now-submerged settlements, there must have been massive population disruptions in the face of this natural catastrophe, which may have brought farmers to the fertile Danube Valley, well away from the rising Black Sea (Ryan and Pitman, 1999).

Graeme Barker (1985) proposes a general scenario: In Greece, farming villages were well established by 6000 B.C. and were based on sheep husbandry and the cultivation of crops sown each fall. North of Greece, about 5500 B.C., the expansion of farming activity appears to have coincided with a cycle of higher rainfall, warmer winters, and the rise of the Black Sea, which brought Mediterranean styles of farming viable in the southern Balkans and somewhat different forms of agriculture possible to the Danube basin.

About 5500 B.C., farming based on cattle herding combined with spring-sown crops developed during a period of wetter conditions over enormous areas of continental Europe, especially on optimum loess soils. This agricultural system was perfectly adapted to such conditions, whereas stock herding assumed much greater importance in nearby, more low-lying regions. At the same time, hunter-gatherer societies continued to flourish for at least another millennium in areas that were marginal for cultivation or herding. Eventually, distinctive local farming adaptations replaced hunting and gathering in

6200 B.C.

5800 B.C.

5500 B.C.

southern Scandinavia and lowland Britain, as well as along the Atlantic Coast and at higher altitudes. Hunting, foraging, and fishing remained dominant subsistence strategies only in the farthest north, in areas that were vulnerable to minor climatic change.

The Balkans

In the Balkans, the earliest farmers settled on fertile agricultural soils on floodplains and elsewhere (Tringham, 1971; Whittle, 1996). Many of them lived in compact villages of one-room dwellings built of baked mud plastered on poles and wicker (Tringham et al., 1980). These Karanovo culture settlements, named after the first site dug, were occupied over long periods. The economy was based on cultivated wheat and barley and domesticated sheep and goats. A number of culture traits, including *Spondylus* shells (a characteristic Mediterranean mussel much used for ornamentation), clay seals and figurines, and reaping knives, show continuing connections with the Mediterranean world. This is an area with great environmental variability and ranges in temperature. For example, there are fertile plains and spring areas where the soils are permanently moist. It was here that many farming communities settled in the same locations for centuries, just as Southwest Asian and Anatolian farmers had done. The largest mounds are found where good arable soils are most widespread. It was in this area that metallurgy developed in approximately 3000 B.C. (see Chapter 20).

Karanovo culture
5500 B.C.

Bandkeramik Cultures

Very complete radiocarbon chronologies characterize the spread of farming in Europe as a stop-and-start process. There were major expansions and then long pauses, not gradual waves of advance. Barker (1985) believes that the expansions coincided with climatic changes that affected local landscapes and made farming viable in new areas. In short, the spread of farming was a complex process that involved major cultural change over many centuries.

The best-known early European farming culture is called the Bandkeramik (or the Danubian) complex, named after its distinctive linear-decorated pottery (Figure 10.3). Its first colonization of the Middle Danube was on a small scale about 5300 B.C. It appears that small groups of people migrated along river valleys, avoiding areas where Mesolithic folk lived. Their farming territories were widely spaced and apparently very small, perhaps on the order of about 200 ha (500 acres), of which about a tenth to a third was in cultivation at one time (J. M. Howell, 1987). The people lived in hamlets made up of individual farmsteads, separated by about 90-m (100-yard) intervals. Individual houses were rectangular, from 5.5 to 14 m (18 to 46 feet) long, made of timber and thatch, and presumably sheltering families, their grain, and their animals (Champion et al., 1984).

Bandkeramik complex
5300 B.C.

The Bandkeramik people cultivated barley, einkorn, emmer wheat, and minor crops including flax. These they grew by using systems of crop rotation and fallowing, which enabled the farmers to remain in the same place for long periods of time, sometimes

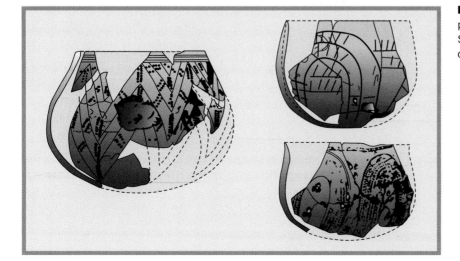

FIGURE 10.3 Linear Bandkeramik pottery (linear-decorated pottery) from Sittard, Holland, with characteristic line decoration (one-fourth actual size).

even growing hedges to delineate their fields and to fence in their animals. Cattle were the most important animal in Bandkeramik life; indeed, they may have been domesticated from wild strains locally. The people also kept sheep, goats, and dogs. Population estimates of between 40 and 60 people per village seem reasonable, with a new settlement being founded as the population expanded. Population growth after first settlement was slow. The founding of companion villages gradually filled in the gaps between widely spaced neighboring communities. Within four or five centuries, population densities in parts of Germany rose from 1 per 1000 sq. km (386 square miles) to 1 per 120 sq km (46 square miles) (Milisauskas and Kruk, 1989).

4000 B.C. By 4000 B.C., cereal crops and domesticated animals were widespread in southeastern and central Europe and perhaps also in southern France. These farming communities were surrounded by scattered hunter-gatherer societies.

The Bandkeramik people had spread far west to southern Holland, where they had settled by 4800 B.C., and east to the Vistula River and the upper Dniester. In the prime agricultural areas, the people relied heavily on their cattle, sheep, and pigs. They may have moved their herds onto the northern European plain for part of the year. The Brzesc Kujawski site in southern Poland was inhabited by summer cattle herders, who also gathered wild vegetable foods and caught perch in northern streams (Bogucki, 1993; Bogucki and Grygiel, 1986). Eventually, farmers settled on heavier soils. We find regional variations of Danubian culture in many parts of central Europe. Some farmers had to rely more on hunting and gathering because the soils of their gardens did not yield enough food to support their families. Defensive earthworks appeared later, as if vigorous competition for land had caused intertribal stress.

🐾 Frontiers and Transitions

The Bandkeramik expansion created a "frontier" in many parts of Europe between farming communities and Mesolithic groups. It would be a mistake to think of this as a rigid boundary between different peoples, although both hunter-gatherer and farming societies have a tendency to stay within their own territories and to continue the way of life with which they are familiar (Dennell, 1983). By the same token, however, the peoples who lived on either side of the frontier inhabited a far from closed world. They knew of one another's presence, traded with one another, and interacted through an intricate web of contacts that were beneficial to both sides. Mesolithic people were well aware of cereal crops and domesticated animals. In many cases, they saw no advantage in adopting a new way of life that involved a great deal more work for few significant changes in the diet.

More likely, as Robin Dennell (1983) has argued, they incorporated some aspects of Neolithic culture into their lives, those that gave them an immediate advantage. These may have included clay vessels for storage and cooking, perhaps status items acquired by trade that were soon copied by local artisans. Cereal crops and sheep may have been valuable simply because they solved problems of winter food supplies. Sheep have lower feeding requirements than deer, have higher reproductive and growing rates, and can be used to keep woodland open for cereal growth. Stored nuts, wild cereal grains, and dried deer meat or fish may have been Mesolithic winter staples. It would have been easy for Mesolithic people to graft sheep and domestic cereals onto their existing hunting and gathering practices. Dennell believes that these processes of assimilation caused farming to spread over much of temperate Europe from after 6000 B.C. to as late as 3500 B.C., when many Scandinavian groups finally adopted food production.

Marek Zvelebil and Peter Rowley-Conwy (1984) take the argument a stage farther, distinguishing three transition phases from hunting and gathering to farming:

- An availability phase, when farming was known to Mesolithic peoples and there was some exchange of materials and information. Both farmers and hunter-gatherers were still independent units.
- A substitution phase that had two forms: (1) Farmers moved into and settled hunter-gatherer territory in competition with the indigenous residents, and (2) hunter-gatherers added cultivation or animal husbandry to their range of subsistence

activities. During this phase, there was competition for land, food, and raw materials, and perhaps social competition as well.

- A consolidation phase, when food production became extensive and widespread, with hunting and gathering becoming subsistence strategies in emergencies. Farmers had now occupied the best soils and were using secondary areas with more intensive farming methods. By this time, the frontier had vanished.

The Zvelebil–Rowley-Conwy model serves as a descriptive device for analyzing the spread of food production into western and central Europe, but more data are needed to bolster it.

☙ Social Changes, Lineages, and the Individual

Bandkeramik communities settled on very specific parts of the landscape: gravel river terraces overlooking medium-sized streams in areas of loess soils (J. M. Howell, 1987). These forest farmers deliberately selected places where damp lowland pasture coincided with tracts of light, friable upland soils. They cultivated fertile soils, land where hoe-using farmers could grow emmer wheat and other crops year after year, fertilizing their fields with cattle dung and domestic waste. Cattle were an important element in the Bandkeramik economy, pointing to a "pioneer" economy introduced from southeastern Europe rather than an indigenous farming culture that made full use of local plants and game animals.

After 4550 B.C.

The Bandkeramik people built large, permanent timber houses, investments in time and labor that would have been totally uneconomical if they had been engaged in slash-and-burn agriculture and had shifted their villages regularly (Figure 10.4). Bandkeramik sites formed clusters of settlements, separated from one another by distances of 20 to 30 km (12 to 19 miles). The houses were apparently rebuilt again and again in much the same place. Bandkeramik settlements were occupied over long periods of time, so that a basic site, and the social structure within it, were maintained over many generations. There was continuity of residence location and inheritance from one generation to the next. In some areas, settlements were closely packed within small areas, each hamlet owning a territory of 15 ha (37 acres) or so—not because land was in short supply but because factors such as trade and local outcrops of flint and other materials may have played a role (Figure 10.5).

All of these characteristics point to farming societies that were producing food at the household level but with cooperation between different lineages at the settlement level—to build houses, erect enclosures, and herd cattle (J. Thomas, 1987). The first settlement in an area was, perhaps, the senior one, the place where the elders of the senior lineage lived. In burials, there were two general distinctions among grave goods: between graves of males and females and between those of young and old. Many graves of Bandkeramik women, members of families who lived in longhouses, are richly decorated. Such dwellings are commonly associated in modern societies with *matrilineage,*

FIGURE 10.4 Plan of a Bandkeramik house from Olszanica, Poland, with wall trenches, postholes, pits, and other features. Such structures housed extended families, perhaps each with its own hearth, and also domestic animals.

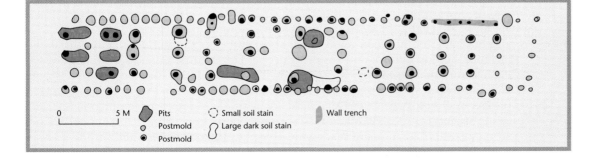

| 0 | 5 M | Pits | | Small soil stain | | Wall trench |
| Postmold |
| Postmold |
| Large dark soil stain |

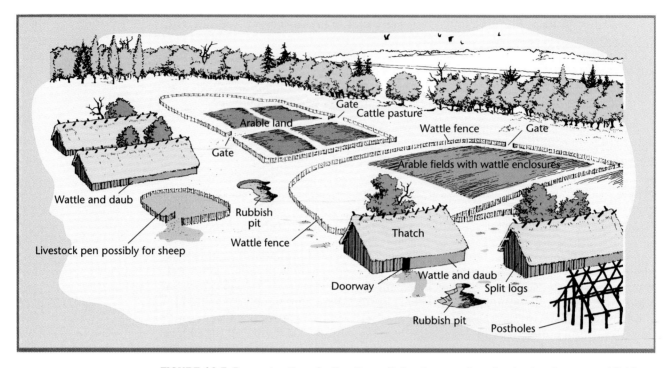

FIGURE 10.5 Reconstruction of a Bandkeramik farming complex, showing longhouses and field boundaries.

a kin group that traces its lineage through the maternal line. In such circumstances, women have high status, and this may have been so in Bandkeramik society. Political power and social authority, however, may have been in the hands of a group of older men, who controlled cattle ownership and the exchange of cattle and other exotic commodities with other settlements. In Bandkeramik society, then, a complex network of social relations controlled productivity. Lineages within the society formed the links between people and the lands of their ancestors.

About 4500 B.C., Bandkeramik settlements became more clustered and turned into villages. Many were protected by earthen enclosures. Divergent pottery styles hint that different settlement clusters had well-defined territories (J. Thomas, 1987). This was a time when more elaborate burial customs developed throughout Europe as ancestor cults became more complex.

In western Europe, communal tombs came into fashion, among them the celebrated megaliths, sepulchers fashioned from rough-hewn boulders and buried under earthen mounds (see "The Megaliths," pp. 264–266). Such corporate burial places may have been where revered kin leaders were buried, along with people who had genealogical ties to the ancestors and thus were of paramount, collective importance to a group of farming communities, where ancestors were guardians of the land. In time, communal tombs may have become important power symbols among local groups that were linked with their neighbors and others by both lasting kin ties and the burgeoning exchange networks that were expanding throughout Europe at this time (J. Thomas, 1987). It has been suggested, for example, that the communal burial mounds of northern Europe embody in earth and stone the notion of linearity, perhaps an ideology that came from Bandkeramik longhouses (Hodder, 1990).

2800 B.C.   Somewhat later, between about 2800 and 2400 B.C., another change in burial customs took hold in central and eastern Europe. For the first time, individual graves as well as communal sepulchers appeared. S. J. Shennan (1993) has argued that group-based ideologies were replaced by new beliefs that reinforced individual power and prestige. It would have been very hard for a single elder to preempt political and economic authority in Bandkeramik society. There were simply too many kin ties and reciprocal obligations to overcome, as well as the collective bond with the ancestors. By being buried separately, however, in a burial adorned with elaborate grave furniture, a prominent elder could take on the role of sole male ancestor, the fountain of authority over land ownership, a role now assumed by his successor. Inheritance of land and wealth was now legitimized.

This is, of course, a speculative scenario, but one supported by telling clues. There are many cases in which men and women were buried together in a single grave. This practice, argue some archaeologists, indicates monogamous marriages rather than the polygamous ones of lineage-based Bandkeramik society. The dominance of male burials from this period suggests that men were of great importance in establishing descent and rights of inheritance. Many individual graves were dug into older communal monuments, perhaps to reinforce the idea that individual ancestors were more important than collective ones. The rich grave goods found in such burials reveal new emphases in society: Many weapons such as daggers and swords appear, as well as battle axes, fine copper ornaments, and drinking cups. Everything points to the emergence of individuals who thought of themselves as warriors. Personal achievement and prestige were associated with males, who were involved in expanding exchange networks that handled luxury goods such as amber, gold ornaments, and weapons. The beginnings of metallurgy in Europe may have been tied to a rising demand for shiny, prestigious ornaments. Luxury artifacts were the symbols of prestige, the means of cementing individual relationships, political links, and reciprocal obligations. There are striking differences in the people buried, too. Bandkeramik farmers lavished their finest goods on older individuals. The later individual burials are those of men in their prime, indicating that personal achievement was the avenue to power and prestige.

🐾 The Introduction of the Plow

Andrew Sherratt (1994a) believes that the introduction of plow agriculture was a seminal development in Europe. Plows are known to have been used as early as 3600 B.C., but Sherratt says they came into far more widespread and intensive use about 2600 B.C., when a number of other innovations reached Europe from Southwest Asia. These included sheep shearing, milking, horse riding, and the use of oxen for traction. He goes so far as to argue for a "secondary products revolution," which transformed both settlement patterns and social organization throughout Europe.

2600 B.C.

Plow agriculture allows fewer people to work an acre of land; thus, more land would be cleared and an individual's fields would be more widely scattered, sometimes close to the outer limits of daily walking. The result was a much more dispersed settlement pattern, with a rapid expansion onto heavier soils and hitherto uncultivated areas around 2600 B.C. With much more acreage to clear and the technology to do it, the farmers of 2600 B.C. were less tied to ancestral lands and the realities of household production and to the kin ties these imply. Fewer people worked in the field, so that there were "unproductive" individuals in greater numbers and therefore compelling needs for social change. Thus, in place of the kin-based society, a new social order arose in which individual success, prestige, and inheritance of land were the norm—with momentous consequences for the Europeans.

🐾 Plains Farmers: Tripolye

While the Bandkeramik complex was developing in central Europe, a mosaic of different subsistence patterns emerged on the Russian plains to the east between 6000 and 4500 B.C. (Telegin, 1987; Zvelebil and Dolukhanov, 1991). Agricultural peoples settled the areas best suited to farming, such as intermountain basins, while hunter-gatherers continued to exploit the river basins, such as that of the Dniester River. The farmers and foragers interacted with one another, living in complementary environments where one did not threaten the other. By 4500 B.C., Bandkeramik peoples had moved as far east as Ukraine, bringing a mixed farming economy with them. They settled on the higher terraces of major rivers, still interacting with Mesolithic folk in the valley bottoms. Both Mesolithic and Neolithic peoples maintained their own identities.

6000 B.C.

Farming reached its greatest extent in the forest-steppe regions of western Russia with the Tripolye culture in about 4000 B.C. (Zbenovich, 1996). Soon after, the farmers finally submerged the Mesolithic foragers of the valleys, perhaps because the cultivators relied extensively on cattle, whose grazing demands may have competed with hunter-gatherers'

Tripolye culture
4000 B.C.

2800 b.c.   foraging needs. In about 2800 b.c., the climate deteriorated, making cultivation less viable. At this point, balanced economies emerged, relying on stock breeding on the steppe and farming in the forest-steppe, a balanced dynamic that survived into recent times, with important historical consequences.

〰 Mediterranean and Western Europe

New artifacts, such as pottery, and food sources, such as sheep, were added to hunter-gatherer adaptations as farming took hold in central Europe and farther afield. This transitional phase lasted for centuries throughout Europe. In many areas, the new items added to existing practices, but they did little to change the fundamental structure of Mesolithic society or lifeways. The full-scale adoption of farming economies in areas such as western Russia took a long time to achieve, whereas in other areas, such as Britain, a full changeover occurred within five centuries or so.

In the Iron Gates region of the Danube Valley, coastal Yugoslavia, central Italy, and southern France, pottery, cereal crops, and sheep appeared, but there was little immediate change in daily life. Many sites where such artifacts occur are in the same type of setting as Mesolithic settlements, where hunting continued for centuries, even millennia. The shift to farming was only partial in many areas, for game and wild plant foods continued to be important; witness the well-preserved berries and nuts in waterlogged lakeside villages in Switzerland (Coles and Coles, 1989). In the Mediterranean basin, the long-term changes were an expansion in the use of obsidian and much wider ranging trade in this material after 5000 b.c. Obsidian was found on three Mediterranean islands, including Sardinia, and was now regularly traded to neighboring islands and the mainland. This trade was part of a widespread network of contacts, linked partly by sea, that carried seashells, exotic rocks, and, later, copper ore the length and breadth of the Mediterranean.

5000 b.c.

This trade also coincided in general terms with the manufacture of distinctive pottery styles decorated with impressions of seashells, among them the shell of the cockle *Cardium* (Figure 10.6). This motif has given rise to the term *Cardial ware* to describe a range of indigenously developed pottery styles that mark the first use of clay vessels by western peoples. Like sheep and goats and perhaps cereal crops, pottery was selectively adopted, as were other elements of farming culture, by different groups, long before full-time farming took hold.

Cardial ware

FIGURE 10.6 *Cardium*-shell-impressed pottery from southern France (one-fourth actual size). The *Cardium* shell was widely traded and used for ornamentation.

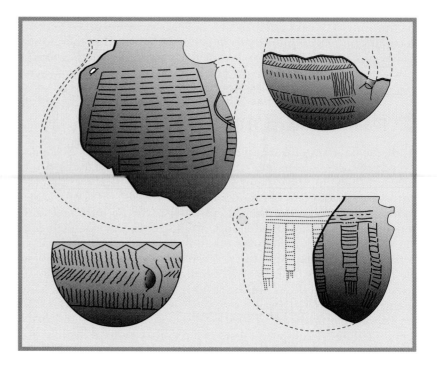

The decisive shift from hunting and gathering in the west took place in the sixth millennium before Christ, with sheep and goats being acquired by trade, exchange, or theft considerably earlier, and cereal crops arriving somewhat later. By 4000 B.C., a series of fishing villages was thriving on the shores of the Swiss lakes (Coles and Coles, 1989). These were peopled by cattle and sheep farmers, who cultivated barley and wheat as well as many minor crops, including cider apples and flax (to make linen cloth) (Figure 10.7). Their houses stood on the damp ground between the lake reed beds and the scrub brush of the valley behind. The first dwellings were small rectangular huts, but they eventually gave way to larger two-room houses. Some villages grew to include between 24 and 75 houses clustered on the lakeshore, a density of population much the same as that of modern Swiss villages, which have approximately 30 households.

In the extreme northwest, food production was adopted comparatively late. From 6000 through 4000 B.C., the newly isolated Mesolithic peoples of Britain developed with little or no significant contact with the continent. The earliest traces of pottery and forest clearance appeared soon after 4000 B.C., with well-documented cereal agriculture by 4300 B.C. The same processes may have operated here as in western Europe. Robin Dennell (1983) theorizes that European farmers did not cross the channel and settle in Britain. Rather, Mesolithic peoples in Britain experienced population pressure about 4000 B.C., perhaps as a result of forest expansion due to warmer climate and also because of population growth. Hunting became more difficult, so the people began clearing woodland to provide more animal forage and plant foods and to make hunting more predictable. The people also increased their exploitation of marine resources, and seafaring techniques developed, leading to contacts with other coastal communities in Britain and on the continent. Eventually, Mesolithic populations in Britain became aware of new food resources, like domestic cereals and sheep, and acquired them. Ample open grassland was available for herding and cultivation in southern Britain. Within five centuries or so, Mesolithic populations had transformed themselves into farmers with their own distinctive cultural traditions. Somewhat similar processes probably led to the adoption of agriculture and stock rearing among Mesolithic Scandinavians.

4000 B.C.

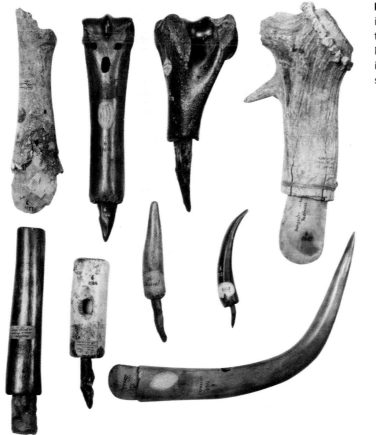

FIGURE 10.7 Simple prehistoric stone axes mounted in deer antler handles from the Swiss lake dwellings, typical of those used by early farmers in Europe. Modern experiments have shown that such implements were surprisingly effective in clearing small trees and woodland.

𝕄 The Megaliths

Early European farming societies were basically egalitarian, the family being the basic productive unit at the center of a web of intricate kin ties and reciprocal social relationships that linked communities near and far and tied people to the land of their ancestors (for the British Neolithic, see J. Thomas, 1999). There was probably equal access to resources, with sufficient food being produced to feed individual families. In a real sense, the subsistence farming economy was society (Champion et al., 1984). In general, early Neolithic burials in Europe do not reflect any social differentiation between individuals.

There are signs of variation, notably in the intensity of trading activities through barter networks and in burial customs. A slow process of social change can be documented throughout Europe after 4000 B.C., moving toward a greater emphasis on craft specialization and burial ritual and the emergence of regional trading centers that controlled exchange networks, and perhaps ritual as well. The famous megalithic tombs of the Mediterranean and western Europe are one symbol of this trend toward social change.

Megaliths
4500 B.C. and later

As early as 4500 B.C., some French farmers were building large communal stone tombs, known to archaeologists as **megaliths** (Figure 10.8). Megaliths are found as far north as Scandinavia, in Britain, Ireland, France, Spain, the western Mediterranean, Corsica, and Malta. For years, scholars thought that megaliths had originated in the eastern Mediterranean in approximately 2500 B.C. and had spread westward into Spain with colonists from the Aegean who had carried a custom of collective burial and their religion with them (Daniel, 1973; Renfrew, 1983). Megalithic tombs were believed to have been built in western Europe, witnesses to a lost faith perhaps spread by pilgrims, missionaries, or merchants.

This popular and widely accepted hypothesis was badly weakened by carbon-14 dates from France that turned out to be earlier than others from western Europe (Renfrew, 1972). Furthermore, new calibrated dates have placed Spanish megalithic sites and their associated culture as early as approximately 4500 B.C., much earlier than their alleged prototypes in the Aegean. Thus, megaliths were being built in western Europe at least a millennium before massive funerary architecture became fashionable in the eastern Mediterranean. This remarkable freestanding architecture is a unique local European creation.

What, exactly, were megaliths? Were they the surviving remains of a powerful religious cult that swept western Europe, or did they symbolize the emergence of new, more sophisticated political and social structures in the West? Colin Renfrew (1983) has argued that the tradition of communal burial developed in very early western European farming societies. He believes that it is manifested by the famous long

FIGURE 10.8 The megalithic tomb at New Grange, Ireland, c. 3200 B.C. The structure measures up to 85 m (280 feet) across. The rising sun shines directly into the burial chamber at the winter solstice (December 21) every year.

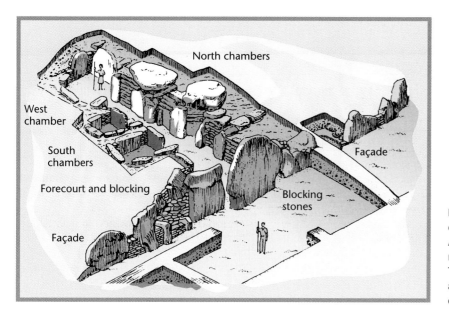

FIGURE 10.9 Interior of a megalithic chamber tomb in West Kennet, near Avebury, England, ^{14}C-dated to approximately 3500 B.C. (After Piggott, 1965.) The West Kennet sepulcher was probably a communal grave, used by a kin group over many generations.

barrows of southern Britain (Figure 10.9), many of which had stone-boulder megalithic interiors. The long barrows were fairly small structures, requiring not more than about 5000 to 10,000 worker-hours to build (a figure equivalent to 20 workers taking 50 days). Ian Hodder (1990) believes they may be a reflection of long-held ideologies surrounding longhouses that were perpetuated in tomb design, on the grounds that ideology was a vital component in early European farming societies. Between 4000 and 3500 B.C., these barrows were associated with more elaborate monuments, among them enclosed earthworks (often called causewayed camps), which are known to have been protected by timber palisades. Recent excavations have shown that these camps were littered with human bones, many of them skeletons from which the flesh had weathered in the open. Perhaps these camps were places where the dead were exposed for months before their bones were deposited in nearby communal burials.

Easton Down
3200 B.C.

As time went on, the argument goes, burial ceremonies revolved around even larger monuments, the so-called **henges,** stone- and wood-built circles of which Stonehenge in southern Britain is the most famous (see Figure 20.8). In this sense, megaliths of all types formed a kind of settlement hierarchy on the prehistoric landscape, a hierarchy that may have reflected profound changes in European society.

Another ingenious theory argues that megalithic monuments appeared in western Europe at just the time when farming took hold all across Europe. This final colonization must have had a major impact on the stable Mesolithic societies that were exploiting coastal resources along the Atlantic Ocean and North Sea shores from the Bay of Biscay in France to the Baltic. Ian Kinnes (1982) believes that megaliths first appeared in the margins of Neolithic society, along the Atlantic Coast, where the competition with Mesolithic groups may have been most acute. Perhaps, he believes, the megaliths served as territorial markers, signs of ancestral ownership of the surrounding land. (For a closely argued assessment, see J. Thomas, 1999.) (See Site box.)

Avebury
2550 B.C.

Colin Renfrew and others have called megaliths the "tombs of the living," lasting, human-made symbols of the continuity of human life as well as symbols of the continuity of ownership of land from one generation to the next. The annual round of religious rituals at places like Stonehenge reinforced this continuity; and at a time when population densities were rising sharply, the megaliths associated with the rituals became important symbols of political and social continuity. They also reinforced the political, economic, and spiritual power of those who supervised the building and worship at places such as Stonehenge. That such supervision was necessary is certain, for it has been estimated that Stonehenge required at least 30,000 worker-hours to complete. So the appearance of megaliths and the hierarchy of more elaborate stone and wooden monuments associated with them may have foreshadowed profound social changes in prehistoric Europe that came with the increasing use of bronze and other metals (Chippindale, 1994).

SITE

Easton Down and the Avebury Landscape

The great earthworks and megalithic monuments of western Europe did not stand alone. For example, Avebury in southern England (Figure 10.10) lies at the center of a vast, long-vanished sacred landscape that was marked by burial mounds, enclosures, charnel houses, and other sites for commemorating the ancestors (Malone, 1989; Whittle, 1993). Avebury itself was built in about 2550 B.C., in a natural amphitheater ideal for a large stone circle. In its final form, its earthwork and ditch dug into the underlying white chalk encompassed 11.5 ha (28.5 acres) and measured about 350 m (1150 feet) across. Four causewayed entrances divide the monument into four unequal arcs. Ninety-eight standing stones set up inside the ditch once adorned the interior, some of them up to 14 m (46 feet) high. Two inner circles stood within the outer circle. This staggering construction was built by farming communities with no wheeled carts and only the simplest levers, rollers, and stone, antler, and wooden tools. When new, the white earthworks with their exposed subsurface chalk must have stood out for kilometers.

Generations of archaeologists have excavated Avebury, but only recently have they paid close attention to its now-invisible landscape, very different from the rolling farmland of today. Obtaining evidence of ancient landscapes requires careful excavation and sample collection, most often of the original land surfaces under burial mounds and earthworks. When archaeologist Alisdair Whittle excavated some test trenches into a long burial mound at Easton Down in southern England, he exposed the original land surface, as well as the core of stacked turves, chalk, and topsoil under the mound. These discoveries gave him an unusual opportunity to obtain a portrait of the local vegetation in about 3200 B.C. (Whittle and others, 1993).

First, he turned to pollen analysis. Small amounts of pollen grains from the land surface were predominantly from grasses, showing that no woodland grew close to the tumulus when it was built. A well-sealed section of the pre-mound soil yielded 11 mollusk samples, which chronicled a dramatic change from woodland to open grassland forms over a short period of time. Whittle located an ancient tree hollow under the mound, which, hardly surprisingly, contained woodland mollusks. A sudden increase in open-country mollusks followed, a change so rapid that human clearance of the land seemed the only logical explanation. Interestingly, soil scientists found signs of lateral movement of the soil below the mound, which can have resulted only from cultivation before the mound was built.

Excavations such as Easton Down can give us only snapshots of the complex mosaic of cleared and uncleared land that characterizes any agricultural landscape. For example, mollusks and soil samples under nearby Avebury itself tell us that the great temple of 2550 B.C. rose on long-established but little-grazed natural grassland close to a forest that had regenerated after being cleared for farming.

This kind of environmental archaeology is now so precise that we can fix the exact seasons when monuments were built or buildings erected. For example, soil samples from carefully cut sod laid under the original ground surface of the 40-m (130-foot) Silbury Hill, built in about 2200 B.C. and close to Easton Down, show that the builders started work in the late summer, most likely after the harvest when people had time for construction work. We know this because the well-preserved sods contain ants and anthills. The ants were beginning to grow wings and fly away from their anthills, as they do in late summer.

As environmental and landscape studies continue, we will learn a surprising amount about the setting, and perhaps the meaning, of major religious sites like Avebury and Stonehenge.

FIGURE 10.10 Aerial view of Avebury stone circles in southern England. (See also Chapter 1 opener.)

A complex set of processes governed the emergence of food production in temperate Europe, processes only rarely involving the movement of entire populations from one region to the next. Here, as in other parts of the world, one should think of agriculture not as a miracle invention or in terms of conquest but as yet another instance of how readily hunter-gatherers adapted to new opportunities and conditions. As is so often the case in prehistory, continuity was as important as change, but this continuity was born of inherent flexibility, an ability to adapt to new circumstances.

Summary

The European Mesolithic lasted from about 8000 to the introduction of farming in northwestern Europe in about 4000 B.C. There were considerable local variations, with a trend toward more permanent settlement in more favored areas. By about 6000 B.C., farming was well established in parts of the Aegean area and in southeastern Europe. Agriculture and animal husbandry developed in southeastern Europe because of a local shift to the more intensive exploitation of cereals and wild sheep, and also because of a "drift" of domestic animals and cereals from Southwest Asia. This was a largely indigenous development.

The widely distributed Bandkeramik complex documents the first settlement of southeastern European farmers in the middle Danube Valley and on the light loess soils of central Europe around 5000 B.C. This may be connected, at least in part, with fallout from the flooding of the Euxine Lake, which became the Black Sea. The flooding may have caused people to move into forested lands, away from the lake. During the next millennium, food production spread widely throughout Europe, largely among indigenous Mesolithic peoples, who adopted sheep, pottery, and cereals, which they considered of immediate advantage to them.

From about 4500 B.C., new religious ideologies spread widely in central and western Europe, as indicated by the building of communal burial mounds and megalithic monuments. Some of these new beliefs reflected centuries-old ideologies connected with the longhouses and the communal ethics of the Bandkeramik farmers. Others, derived from central and eastern Europe, were beliefs growing out of the appearance of individual power and prestige as a potent factor in local life, power reflected in the growing numbers of exotic artifacts and materials.

Key Terms

Henge A British term for a wooden or stone circle—whence Stonehenge.

Loess Glacial windblown dust from Ice Age glaciers that formed light soils for early European farmers.

Megalith Greek for "large stone" (*megos lithos*), a term applied to communal stone tombs built widely throughout western Europe after 4500 B.C.

Guide to Further Reading

Barker, Graeme. 1985. *Prehistoric Farming in Europe*. Cambridge: Cambridge University Press.
    An analysis, aimed at specialists, of the spread of farming into temperate Europe.

Cunliffe, Barry, ed. 1994. *The Oxford Illustrated Prehistory of Europe*. Oxford: Oxford University Press.
    This edited volume offers a definitive and up-to-date summary of what we know about ancient Europe.

Hodder, Ian. 1990. *The Domestication of Europe*. Oxford: Blackwell.
    A provocative survey of later European prehistory that places heavy reliance on ideology and changing religious beliefs. An excellent counterpoint to much more traditional writing about Europe's prehistoric past.

Thorpe, I. J. 1996. *The Origins of Agriculture in Europe*. London: Routledge.
    Surveys the archaeological evidence for agriculture.

Whittle, Alastair. 1996. *Europe in the Neolithic: The Creation of New Worlds*. Cambridge: Cambridge University Press.
    A summary of the European Neolithic for the more advanced reader.

Zvelebil, Marek, ed. 1986. *Hunters in Transition*. Cambridge: Cambridge University Press.
    A collection of articles that describe basic Mesolithic theory and analyze the Neolithic transition in various parts of Europe.

11

FIRST FARMERS IN EGYPT AND TROPICAL AFRICA

The Nile River at Aswan, Egypt

"O ur finds caused quite a stir," 80-year-old Gertrude Caton-Thompson told me. "People didn't believe us when we showed them carbonized emmer and barley seeds from the baskets. They told us they were modern seeds that were mixed into the pits by accident." Caton-Thompson's memories of her late-1920s excavations in early farming settlements in Egypt's Fayyum Depression were as vivid as if they had been from yesterday. She told me how she had worked almost alone, camping in the wilderness at the edge of a dried-up lake. It was there that she had uncovered the remains of small oval-shaped pole-and-reed dwellings and small storage pits lined with baskets still containing domestic grains.

Caton-Thompson's finds were revolutionary in the late 1920s, for they pushed the origins of agriculture back to earlier than 4000 B.C. Though she worked with almost no money and facilities, her research started a quest for the first farmers on the Nile that continues to this day (Caton-Thompson and Gardner, 1934).

The Nile slashes like a green arrow through the arid wastes of the eastern Sahara, rising high in the Ethiopian highlands and flowing northward more than 4800 km (3000 miles) to the Mediterranean. For most of its last 1100 km (700 miles), the Nile has cut a deep gorge through the desert, which it has filled with layer after layer of fertile river silt. This was a land of bounty but also an uncertain one, dependent on rainfall far upstream. If there were good winter rains in the highlands, then the annual flood would inundate the fertile floodplain and replenish plant life. Poor rains would trigger only a meager flood, leaving the Nile Valley baking under the summer sun. Occasionally, too, record rainfall in Ethiopia would bring catastrophic floods downstream that swept everything before them. For all these uncertainties, the Nile Valley was always an isolated oasis, a strip of green, fertile land between desert bastions. The valley floor itself consisted for the most part of seasonally flooded natural basins that supported grass and brushland. People lived on higher levees along the river, where trees grew and settlements escaped the annual inundation. For tens of thousands of years, the region was a paradise for hunters and foragers (Table 11.1; for map, see Figure 9.1).

Hunter-Gatherers on the Nile

During the last millennia of the Ice Age, the Nile Valley was a rich, diverse habitat, abounding in game of all sizes and in wild vegetable foods. Fish and waterfowl added to the bounty of resources. But those who lived there had to employ both flexible and conservative ways of life to adjust to constant fluctuations in the flood levels.

TABLE 11.1

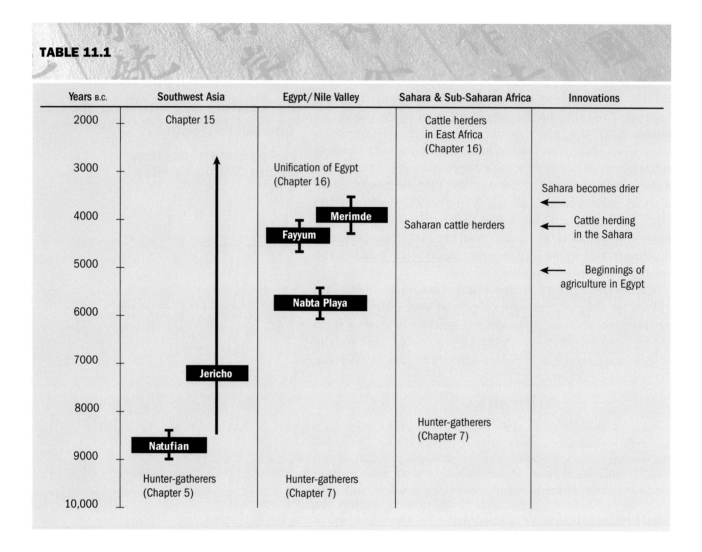

Years B.C.	Southwest Asia	Egypt/ Nile Valley	Sahara & Sub-Saharan Africa	Innovations
2000	Chapter 15		Cattle herders in East Africa (Chapter 16)	
3000		Unification of Egypt (Chapter 16)		
4000		**Merimde** **Fayyum**	Saharan cattle herders	Sahara becomes drier ← ← Cattle herding in the Sahara
5000				← Beginnings of agriculture in Egypt
6000		**Nabta Playa**		
7000				
8000	**Jericho**		Hunter-gatherers (Chapter 7)	
9000	**Natufian**			
10,000	Hunter-gatherers (Chapter 5)	Hunter-gatherers (Chapter 7)		

Wadi Kubbaniya
17,000 to 15,000 B.C.

We know something of their lifeways from excavations at ancient camps in Wadi Kubbaniya dating to between 17,000 and 15,000 B.C., northwest of Aswan in Upper Egypt (Wendorf et al., 1980). The tiny settlements, little more than scatters of stone tools, bones, and charcoal, lay atop sandy dunes about 3 km (1.9 miles) from the narrow Nile floodplain. Rising floodwaters inundated the dunes for some weeks each summer, but for the rest of the year the inhabitants looked out over a marshy floodplain. The annual cycle at Wadi Kubbaniya began with rising floodwaters in July, when vast numbers of catfish congregated in the shallows to spawn. After mating, they lay sluggish in the water for several hours. It was then that the inhabitants would flock to the water's edge, catching fish with their hands, impaling them with spears, or even trapping them with upturned containers. Hundreds of fish were gutted and laid out to dry in the sun during the precious few days of spawning.

When the floodwaters reached their height, flooding root plants in the wetlands, the people fished and foraged at water's edge, harvesting ripe dates and acacia seeds from trees at the edge of the desert. As the inundation receded, men and boys would comb the shallow pools left by the retreating water for trapped catfish. Meanwhile, the women, armed with wooden digging sticks, turned their attention to the ripe swards of nut grass and club-rush tubers in the newly exposed wetlands. Even today, nut grass is abundant along the Nile, yielding small, bitter-tasting tubers high in carbohydrates and fiber. But they are toxic, especially during later stages of growth, so the women would rub and grind them, then leach them before consumption. A family armed with digging sticks could have gathered enough carbohydrates for several days within a matter of hours.

As fall and winter came, the foragers would turn to water lilies, sedges, wild millets, and other wetland plants, while the hunters would take migratory coots, ducks, and geese. Come spring, the people would eat acacia seeds and dates and cattail and other wetland plants, relying on a broad spectrum of edible plant foods that were vital when staples were in short supply.

Not that the Wadi people enjoyed a comfortable life, for the annual floods varied so much that they lived in a constant state of uncertainty. A high flood could delay plant harvests, and low waters caused the marshlands to dry up for months on end. For this reason, the people exploited a very broad range of food resources, seeking in any way possible to adapt to their demanding environment.

The same broad-based hunter-gatherer economies persisted for the remainder of the Ice Age and well into Holocene times, with, however, a trend toward more sedentary settlement and a more intensified exploitation of plants and fish. In all probability, numerous local groups lived in the valley, all the way from the Nile Delta in the north into the Sudan (Nubia) in the far south, distinguishable in the archaeological record by minor differences in their toolkits.

One such group was the so-called Qadan culture from central Egypt, best known from microlithic tools found at riverside campsites near the Nile (J. D. Clark, 1971). In the earlier stages of the Qadan, fishing and big-game hunting were important, but large numbers of grindstones and grinding equipment came from a few localities, which seem to show that gathering wild grains was significant in at least part of the economy. Some Qadan settlements were probably large and occupied for long periods. The dead were buried in cemeteries, in shallow pits covered with stone slabs. Some pits held two bodies. In six instances, small stone tools were embedded in the bones of these Qadan people, who must have met a violent end.

Qadan culture
10,000 B.C.

These war casualties are a sign that life was not easy along the bountiful Nile, probably because of the sheer unpredictability of the annual flood and because of constant drought, especially after 6000 B.C. Most groups settled close to permanent water supplies, relying on predictable seasonal foods to tide them over during the lean months of the inundation.

The end of the Ice Age brought increased rainfall to northern Africa. Raging floods cut through the Nile floodplain, sweeping away rich marshlands and fertile soils, until rising Holocene sea levels reduced the river gradient and the inundation again deposited rich silt on the valley floor. At the same time, more rainfall brought semi-arid grassland and shallow lakes to much of the Sahara, making it possible for hunters and foragers to live in hitherto uninhabited lands. There was also regular movement between the desert and the Nile Valley.

Perhaps about 1000 people lived in tiny family groups in this unpredictable, harsh environment between 8000 and 3000 B.C. As much as 80 percent of their diet may have come from edible plants, as well as from gazelles, hares, and other small animals that flourished on the stony terrain. Life became much harder in the Sahara after 6000 B.C., when the drought cycles became longer and the lakes shrank rapidly. By this time, desert populations may have risen to the point where there were well-defined territorial boundaries and no unexploited lands. The Saharans responded to drier conditions by settling closer to permanent water, where they faced the same problem as the people of the Nile: seasonal food shortages and the constant threat of starvation.

⁂ Agricultural Origins Along the Nile

For years, people assumed that cereal crops and domesticated animals had been introduced into the Nile Valley from Southwest Asia sometime after 8000 B.C. (Childe, 1952). In recent years, this view has been challenged by those who believe that food production arose independently in Egypt, the Sudan, and even the Sahara (Hassan, 1986). The evidence for such a development, however, is both fragmentary and controversial, for the deep alluvium of the Nile Valley has long buried the relevant settlements near the valley. Prevailing expert opinion seems to favor an outside introduction. This scenario goes as follows.

In about 6000 B.C., severe drought conditions prevailed over much of Southwest Asia, decimating game populations and causing widespread crop failures among the tiny farming populations that flourished in what are now Israel and Syria. The farmers

6000 B.C.

responded by moving from drier zones into the Mediterranean forest zone near the coast, one day to be the source of the famed "cedars of Lebanon" mentioned in the Scriptures. During these years of dislocation and resettlement, some nomadic groups with goats and sheep may have crossed the Sinai into Lower Egypt, bringing domesticated barley, emmer wheat, and other crops with them.

The Nile Valley was also gripped by drought. Human populations moved closer to the shrinking river, where animals still grazed and plant foods were still plentiful. Inevitably, group territories shrank, too, so people responded by turning to domesticated plants and animals as part of a complex safety net that protected them against a very unpredictable environment. Not that there was any drastic change in daily life, for initially the new economies were practiced on a very small scale. Early Nile agriculture may have been a form of insurance, practiced sporadically and on the smallest of scales when circumstances merited, by people who were preadapted to the new lifeway (Hassan, 1986).

Agricultural methods were probably of the simplest. Some villagers would plant wheat on damp ground at the receding floodwaters' edge, a crop timed to ripen when food was short. The plots were small and left to fend for themselves. Thus, farming began along the Nile when people living in an unpredictable riverine environment wanted to amplify their food supplies. Within a remarkably short time, probably only a few centuries, domesticated forms of these same cereals became important staples. These new strains were much more demanding than their wild ancestors, needing constant attention, weeding, and watering. Each village was now tied to its herds and gardens.

Nabta Playa
6000 B.C.

Archaeological evidence for early farming is virtually nonexistent. Domesticated barley is known from the Nabta Playa site in the Western Desert and dates to about 6000 B.C. These cultivators and their neighbors at Bir Kiseiba, to the west, were living in large settlements with houses set in rows or in an arc. Perhaps as many as 14 families lived in these villages, dwelling in low pit houses sunk into the ground (Wendorf et al., 1984).

Farther north, in the Fayyum Depression west of the Nile, small fishing camps flourished along the water's edge at the time of Bir Kiseiba and Nabta Playa (Wenke et al., 1988). Unlike their relatives far to the south, they did not use cereals. For reasons still not understood, the Fayyum was abandoned after about 6000 B.C. Then, about 4350 B.C., the lakeshores were home to people living in short-term seasonal camps that were moved as the lake level rose or fell. These people cultivated wheat and barley, locating their gardens on patches of fertile soil whose distribution changed as the lake did. They also herded cattle, sheep, and goats, but fish were overwhelmingly important in their diet. Unlike their contemporaries in Southwest Asia, the Fayyum people never built permanent villages, for their environment was too unpredictable to allow complete dependence on agriculture.

Fayyum
4350 B.C.

Considerable debate surrounds the Fayyum discoveries, which have long been hailed as evidence for the earliest farming in the Nile area (Caton-Thompson and Gardner, 1934). In fact, this lake-filled depression may have supported groups that only partially adopted the new lifeways because of the unpredictable environment. Dozens of farming villages may have flourished in the fertile Nile Valley as early as 5000 B.C., if not earlier, settlements that are now inaccessible beneath deep alluvial deposits laid down by thousands of years of river floods.

4300 to 3300 B.C.

The earliest dated farming settlements from the Nile Valley, both from Egypt and the Sudan, date to between 4300 and 3300 B.C. Hassan (1986) believes that the nomadic peoples of the desert now included the fertile river valley in their wanderings, moving in and out of the desert as conditions warranted, as they do in the Sahel region at the southern fringes of the Sahara today. These movements, he believes, were especially significant after 2500 B.C., when conditions became very arid indeed. This was also a time of exceptionally low Nile floods, so the sparse agricultural sites dating from early farming times are probably buried under many feet of later river alluvium. Hassan argues that irregular population movements into the valley, involving small numbers of people from many desert regions, continued for thousands of years. The result was considerable cultural diversity within the Nile Valley, caused by both immigration and fusion with existing populations.

Merimde
3900 B.C.

Many of the new floodplain settlements may have been like the village of Merimde Beni Salama near the Nile Delta. There, a cluster of oval houses and shelters was built half underground and roofed with mud and sticks (Hoffman, 1979). An occupation mound 2 m (7 feet) high accumulated over 600 years, from approximately 3900 B.C. Farming at a subsistence level was characteristic of large areas of the Nile floodplain for thousands of years (Hassan, 1988).

Cemetery burials are our main source of information on the other farmers who flourished along the Upper Nile. Like their northern neighbors, they used bows and arrows in the chase, many tipped with finely flaked arrowheads. Emmer wheat and barley were cultivated, and cattle and small stock provided much of the meat. Settlements here were typified by mud-brick and transient architecture. The dead, however, were buried with some ceremony—in linen shrouds and covered with skins. The women wore ivory combs and plaited their hair. This culture, named the Badarian after a village where the first settlements were found, is thought to have been broadly contemporary with that of Merimde (Hassan, 1988). The early farming communities of the Nile continued to use the forested riverbanks for settlement (Butzer, 1976). Animals grazed on the flat grasslands of the plain for most of the year, and crops were planted on wet basin soils as the waters receded. Game was still abundant in the Nile Valley in 4000 B.C.; even so, the people ventured to the edge of the desert in search of gazelles and other small animals. They buried their dead in cemeteries overlooking the Nile, where the graves would not take up valuable agricultural land.

By 3500 B.C., the inhabitants of the Nile Valley were living almost entirely off agriculture, with hunting playing a negligible role in daily life. The density of population was probably low enough so that the people had no need of either centralized government or government-regulated irrigation canals. They farmed without any form of large-scale irrigation. The modern Egyptian landscape bears no resemblance to the riverine environment of 3000 B.C. We know little of the narrow floodplain's original appearance. We can only draw analogies from other large rivers like the North American Mississippi or the African Zambezi, which flood each year.

3500 B.C.

The Nile must have had a well-defined channel that meandered between natural banks. Shallow basins and swamps retained receding floodwater, capturing fertile silt. Small farming villages flourished on higher ground or on the riverbanks, in strategic locations near good soils. As the floodwaters receded, the farmers planted their crops in the fresh silt, grazing their cattle in nearby meadows and scrublands. By the time the waters rose again, the harvest was over. The villagers' herds grazed on dry lands at the margins of the flood. The Egyptian farmer of 5500 years ago had no need of elaborate irrigation technology, just the ability to exploit flood basins and a varied environment teeming with edible plants, fish, and game animals. The first appearance of irrigation seems to have coincided with the unification of Egypt and is described in Chapter 16.

Saharan Pastoralists

Many people think of the Sahara as a vast sand sea, one of the most desolate places on earth. In fact, the Sahara is a highly diverse, albeit dry, region that has undergone major climatic changes since 10,000 B.C. (McIntosh and McIntosh, 1988). As recently as 6000 B.C., the southern frontier of the desert was far to the north, and semi-arid grassland and shallow freshwater lakes covered much of what are now arid plains. This was a landscape where antelope of all kinds abounded, as well as *Bos primigenius,* the wild ox. The areas that are now desert were, like all arid regions, very susceptible to cycles of higher and lower rainfall, resulting in major, sudden changes in distributions of plants and animals. The people who preyed on the sparse desert fauna responded to drought by managing the wild resources they hunted and gathered, especially wild oxen, which had to have regular water supplies to survive.

6000 B.C.

Even before the drought, the Sahara was never well watered. Both humans and animals were constantly on the move, in search of food and reliable water supplies. Under these circumstances, archaeologist Andrew Smith believes (1992), the small herds of *Bos primigenius* in the desert became closer-knit, smaller breeding units. The beasts were more disciplined, so that it was easier for hunters to move among them, predict their habits, and cull animals at will. At the same time, both cattle and humans were more confined in their movements, staying much closer to permanent water supplies for long periods of time. As a result, cattle and humans came into close association.

Smith believes that the hunters were well aware of the more disciplined ways in which their prey behaved. Instead of following the cattle on their annual migrations, the hunters prevented the herd from moving from one spot to another. They did this in such a way that they were no threat to the beasts, moving around and through the herd on its home range. At first, they controlled the movement of the herd while still maintaining their all-important ritual relationships with their prey and ensuring continuance of their meat diet. But soon they also gained genetic control of the animals, which led to rapid physical changes in the herd. South African farmers who maintain herds of wild eland report that the offspring soon diminish in size, unless wild bulls are introduced constantly from outside. The same effects of inbreeding may have occurred in controlled cattle populations, with some additional, and perhaps unrecognized, advantages. The newly domesticated animals behaved better, were easier to control, and may have enjoyed a higher calving rate, which in turn yielded greater milk supplies. We know from rock paintings from deep in the Sahara that the herders were soon selecting for different horn shapes and hide colors (Figure 11.1).

It is still unclear whether domesticated cattle were tamed independently in northern Africa or introduced to the continent from Southwest Asia. Whatever the source of the original tamed herds, it seems entirely likely that much the same process of control and juxtaposition occurred in both Southwest Asia and northern Africa, and even in Europe, among peoples who had an intimate knowledge of wild cattle's behavior. The experiments with domestication probably occurred in many places, as people living in ever-drier environments cast around for more predictable food supplies.

The cattle herders had only a few possessions: unsophisticated round-based pots and flaked and polished adzes. They also hunted with bow and arrow. The Saharan people left a remarkable record of their lives on the walls of caves deep in the desert. Wild animals, cattle, goats, humans, and scenes of daily life are preserved in a complicated jumble of artistic endeavor extending back perhaps to 5000 B.C. (Muzzolini, 1995). The widespread distribution of pastoral sites of this period suggests that the Saharans ranged their herds over widely separated summer and winter grazing grounds.

3500 B.C.

About 3500 B.C., climatic conditions again deteriorated. The Sahara slowly became drier and lakes vanished. Rainfall rose in the interior of western Africa, and the northern limit of the **tsetse fly** belt moved south. So the herders shifted south, following the major river systems into savanna regions. By this time, the Saharan people were probably using domestic crops, experimenting with such summer rainfall crops as sorghum and millet as they moved out of areas where they could grow wheat, barley, and other Mediterranean crops (J. D. Clark, 1984; McIntosh and McIntosh, 1988).

FIGURE 11.1 Cattle in a Saharan rock painting from Tassili n'Ajjer. Saharan rock paintings had symbolic meaning to those who painted them. For archaeologists, they are a source of vital information on early cattle herders and trade in the desert.

🐾 Early Food Production in Sub-Saharan Africa

At the end of the Pleistocene, the indigenous inhabitants of sub-Saharan Africa were already adapted to many kinds of specialized environments (Phillipson, 1994). Some lived by intensive fishing and others by gathering or hunting, depending on their environment. In a simple way, the techniques of food production may already have been employed on the fringes of the rain forests of western and central Africa, where the common use of such root plants as the African yam led people to recognize the advantages of growing their own food (J. D. Clark, 1984). The yam can easily be resprouted if its top is planted. This primitive form of **vegeculture** may have been the economic tradition onto which the cultivation of summer rainfall cereal crops was grafted as it came into use south of the grassland areas on the Sahara's southern borders (Harlan, 1998; Harlan et al., 1976).

As the Sahara dried up after 5000 B.C., pastoral peoples moved southward along major watercourses into the savanna belt of West Africa and the Sudan. By 3000 B.C., just as ancient Egyptian civilization was coming into being along the Nile, they had settled in the heart of the East African highlands far to the south. The East African highlands are ideal cattle country and the home of such famous cattle-herding peoples as the Masai today. Hunter-gatherers living around mountains near the plains inhabited the highlands until about 3300 B.C., when the first cattle herders appeared. These cattle people may have moved between fixed settlements during the wet and dry seasons, living off hunting in the dry months and their own livestock and agriculture during the rains (Ambrose, 1984; Bower, 1984).

As was the case elsewhere, cattle were demanding animals in Africa. They required water at least every 24 hours and large tracts of grazing grass if herds of any size were to be maintained. The secret was the careful selection of grazing land, especially in environments where seasonal rainfall led to marked differences in graze quality throughout the year. Even modest cattle herds required plenty of land and considerable mobility. To acquire such land often meant moving herds considerable distances, even from summer to winter pastures. At the same time, the cattle owners had to graze their stock in tsetse fly–free areas. The only protection against human and animal **trypanosomiasis** was to avoid settling or farming such areas—a constraint severely limiting the movements of cattle-owning farmers in eastern and central Africa. As a result, small cattle herds spread south rapidly in areas where they could be grazed. Long before cereal agriculture took hold far south of the Sahara, some hunter-gatherer groups in the savanna woodlands of eastern and southern Africa may have acquired cattle, and perhaps other domesticated animals, by gift exchange or through raids on herding neighbors.

Contrary to popular belief, there is no such phenomenon as "pure" **pastoralists,** a society that subsists on its herds alone. Almost certainly, the Saharan herders who moved southward to escape drought were also cultivating sorghum, millet, and other tropical rainfall crops. By 1500 B.C., cereal agriculture was widespread throughout the savanna belt south of the Sahara. Small farming communities dotted the grasslands and forest margins of eastern West Africa, all of them depending on what is called *shifting agriculture.* This form of agriculture involves clearing woodland, burning the felled brush over the cleared plot, mixing the ash into the soil, and then cultivating the prepared fields. After a few years, the soil is exhausted, so the farmer moves on, exploiting new woodland and leaving the abandoned fields to lie fallow. Shifting agriculture, also called *slash-and-burn,* is highly adaptive for savanna farmers without plows, for it allows cereal farming with the minimal expenditure of energy. It is also wasteful of land.

The process of clearance and burning may have seemed haphazard to the uninformed eye, but it was not. Except in favored areas such as regularly inundated river floodplains, tropical Africa's soils are of only moderate to low fertility. One expert has estimated that only about 40 percent of such soils are cultivable, even with plows (Allan, 1965). Farmers using simple axes, digging sticks, and hoes would have been at an even greater disadvantage, especially on the heavily wooded, clayey soils so common on the African savanna (see Figure 8.1). The art of farming was careful soil selection, that is, knowing which soils were light and easily cultivable, could be readily turned

3000 B.C.

1500 B.C.

FIGURE 11.2
Traditional iron smelting in central Africa. The furnace, made of sticks and anthill clay, is in the form of a woman giving birth. The goatskin bellows operate from the back. The man in the foreground with a stick is raking out the smelted iron.

with small hoes, and would maintain their fertility over several years' planting (cereal crops rapidly remove nitrogen and other nutrients from the soil).

Iron technology, which appeared south of the Sahara about 700 B.C., was one catalyst for the spread of farming throughout sub-Saharan Africa (Schmidt, 1996) (Figure 11.2). Once it had taken hold, slash-and-burn agriculture expanded its frontiers rapidly, as village after village took up new lands, moving forward so rapidly that one expert has estimated it took a mere two centuries to cover 2000 km (1250 miles) from eastern to southern Africa. By A.D. 1, farming villages flourished on the banks of the Zambezi River. Other farmers and cattle herders had crossed into what is now South Africa within a few centuries (see Chapter 16).

Summary 〰

Food production was probably introduced into the Nile Valley at a time of drought, by 6000 B.C. The hunter-gatherers of the Nile and of the then-inhabitable Sahara were preadapted to the new economies, which they may have taken up as a means of staving off food shortages in drought years. By 4000 B.C., agriculture was well established along the Nile, and cattle were being domesticated and herded in the depths of the Sahara. Nile Valley communities soon became dependent on agriculture; they relied on natural flooding to water their gardens until about 3000 B.C. As the Sahara dried up after 5000 B.C., pastoralists with cereal crops moved south of the desert, introducing cattle herding as far south as the East African highlands. Cereal cultivation, based on shifting agriculture, did not take hold in much of sub-Saharan Africa until the introduction of ironworking south of the desert in the first millennium B.C.

Key Terms 〰

Pastoralist A cattle herder, someone who subsists predominantly off domesticated animals.

Trypanosomiasis Sleeping sickness, a disease carried by the tsetse fly in Africa, which is fatal to cattle.

Tsetse fly An African insect that carries trypanosomiasis. Tsetse is endemic to much of Africa, which affects the distribution of cattle throughout the continent.

Vegeculture A simple method of growing wild root crops like yams by cutting off the tops and planting them.

Guide to Further Reading

Butzer, Karl. 1976. *Early Hydraulic Civilization in Egypt.* Chicago: University of Chicago Press.
A fundamental source on ancient Egyptian agriculture that has great relevance to this chapter.

Clark, J. Desmond, and Steven A. Brandt, eds. 1984. *From Hunters to Farmers.* Berkeley: University of California Press.
A set of scholarly essays summarizing evidence for early agriculture in Africa. Excellent for specialists; definitive but slightly outdated.

Hassan, Fekri. 1988. "The Pre-Dynastic of Egypt." *Journal of World Prehistory* 2 (2):135–186.
A definitive critical summary of early agricultural and later societies on the Nile. For the advanced reader.

Hoffman, Michael A. 1979. *Egypt Before the Pharaohs.* New York: Knopf.
A fascinating study of prehistoric Egypt that not only recounts key discoveries but also recalls the archaeologists who made them. The first detailed account of this subject for many years, written for the general reader.

Phillipson, David. 1994. *African Archaeology,* 2nd ed. Cambridge: Cambridge University Press.
Comprehensive summary of sub-Saharan African archaeology from the earliest times to the arrival of Europeans. For the more advanced reader.

Schmidt, Peter, ed. 1996. *The Culture and Technology of African Iron Production.* Gainesville: University of Florida Presses.
An important work on indigenous African ironworking that has much to tell us about early metallurgy.

Smith, Andrew B. 1992. *Pastoralism in Africa.* Johannesburg: Witwatersrand University Press.
A specialized monograph on pastoralism that has a far wider application than merely to African archaeology. A must for the serious student of the past.

chapter

12

ASIA AND THE PACIFIC: RICE, ROOTS, AND OCEAN VOYAGES

Huang Ho Valley, China.

"I n these Proes or Pahee's as they call them from all accounts we can learn, these people sail in these seas from Island to Island for several hundred leagues, the Sun serving them for a compass by day and the Moon and Stars by night. When this comes to be prov'd we Shall no longer be at a loss to know how the Islands lying in these Seas came to be people'd" (Beaglehole, 1974, p. 178). Captain James Cook landed on Tahiti in the heart of the South Pacific in A.D. 1769. He befriended a Polynesian navigator named Tupaia, who accompanied him southwest to New Zealand. "We may trace them from Island to Island quite to the East Indias," wrote Cook prophetically. Ever since then, scientists have been fascinated by the origin of these remarkable Polynesian seamen. This chapter explores the beginnings of food production in Asia and the developments that led up to the settlement of the remotest landmasses of the Pacific Ocean (Table 12.1).

The Origins of Rice Cultivation

Rice was the staple of ancient agriculture over an enormous area of southern and southeastern Asia and of southern China. Today, rice accounts for half the food eaten by 1.7 billion people and 21 percent of the total calories consumed by all of humankind (B. Smith, 1998). Unfortunately, we still know almost nothing about the origins of this most important of domesticated crops.

Rice was one of the earliest plants to be domesticated in the northern parts of Southeast Asia and southern China. Botanists believe that the rices and Asian millets ancestral to the present domesticated species radiated from perennial ancestors around the eastern borders of the Himalaya Mountains at the end of the Ice Age. The initial cultivation of rice is thought to have taken place in an alluvial swamp area, where there was plenty of water to stimulate cereal growth. The first form to be domesticated may have flourished in shallow water, where seasonal flooding dispersed the seed on the border zone between permanently dry and permanently inundated lands (B. Smith, 1998). Perhaps this cultivation occurred under conditions in which seasonal flooding made field preparation a far from burdensome task.

It may be that the first attempts to cultivate rice resulted from deliberate efforts to expand seasonally inundated habitats by constructing dams to trap runoff. The dams could then be breached, so that the flooded land could be used for rice planting, creating additional stands of wild rice. From there, it was a short step to deliberate sowing and harvesting in wet fields (paddies). Most likely, a sedentary lifeway based on the gathering of rice developed at the beginning of the Holocene in low-lying, seasonally flooded areas. Systematic cultivation resulted from a response to population growth, climatic change, or some other stress (Higham and Glover, 1996).

TABLE 12.1

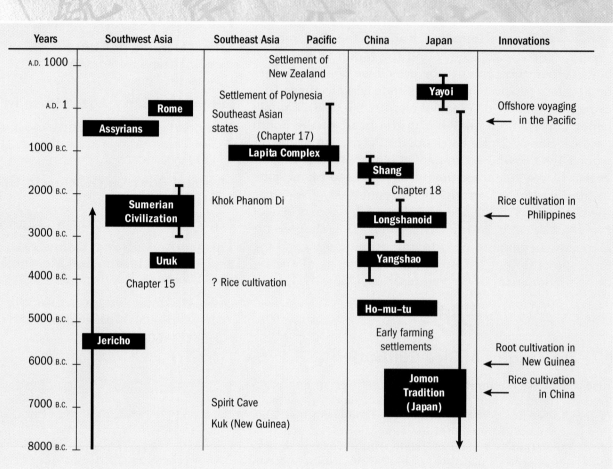

At the time of this writing, the earliest known rice-farming sites were believed to have come from the Yangzi River region of southern China, a contradiction of earlier theories which held that the first domestication took place farther south. Although the Yangzi Valley now lies outside the modern range of uncultivated rice, warmer, more humid conditions before 6000 B.C. supported extensive wetlands where the cereal once flourished. Many Chinese scholars believe that the middle and lower Yangzi was the most likely heartland of rice domestication before 6500 B.C. (Underhill, 1997).

🐾 Early Farming In China

At about the same time as farming began in southern Europe, two quite distinct agricultural lifeways developed along two great Chinese river systems: the Huang Ho, or Yellow River, in the north and the Yangzi in the south (Murowchick, 1994; B. Smith, 1998) (Figure 12.1).

Southern and Eastern China

Southern China is a strong candidate as the region where rice cultivation first began (Higham and Lu, 1998). During the early Holocene, warmer conditions may have allowed wild rice to colonize the lakes and marshes of the middle and lower Yangzi Valley, when hunter-gatherer societies throughout China were exploiting a broad spectrum of animal and plant resources. An international team of researchers led by

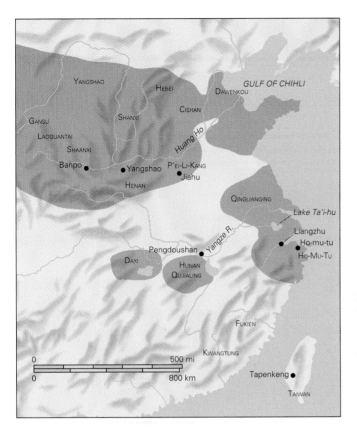

FIGURE 12.1 Early Chinese farming cultures, with names of some major local variants. Yangshao sites occur both within the northern shaded area and outside it. Southern sites of corded pottery are found in the Kwangtung, Fukien, and Taiwan areas.

Richard MacNeish and Yan Wenming has excavated the important Xianrendong and Wangdong Cave sites, where they have identified four phases of occupation going back deep into the late Ice Age, when the inhabitants ate wild rice. Between 9200 and 7550 B.C., the inhabitants may have begun cultivating rice, for a wider range of artifacts possibly used for cultivation appears, as well as phytoliths of domesticated rice (MacNeish and Libby, 1995). Climatic data reveal a long period of warming conditions, followed by a cooler interval, during which rice cultivation may have begun, just as food production took hold in northern China during the same cooler interval.

Xianrendong
9200 B.C.

The Pengtoushan site, in the middle Yangzi Valley, dates to between 6500 and 5800 B.C. and provides definite evidence for rice farming. It was part of an agricultural culture that may have begun as early as 7000 B.C. and flourished for as long as 1500 years. This large settlement with substantial dwellings and 19 graves was a rice-farming village, occupied for seven centuries at a time when agriculture was spreading rapidly in southern China (Underhill, 1997). From southern China, rice farming appears to have spread into India and Southeast Asia.

Pengtoushan
6500 to 5800 B.C.

Other farming cultures flourished in other parts of southern China, where rice cultivation was well established by at least 7000 B.C. The best known is the Hemudu culture, south of Shanghai, dating to about the same period as Majiabang. The Hemudu site itself lies in a marshy area and was once surrounded by forests and ponds and a great diversity of natural resources. Four cultural layers have been radiocarbon-dated to between about 5000 and 4500 B.C. The lowest level of this remarkable site has yielded beautifully mortise-and-tenon-joined building planks, bone hoes, and coarse black pots decorated with cord impressions. This is ideal rice-growing country, and it was hardly surprising to find abundant rice in the site as well as the remains of bone shovels, bottle gourds, and numerous wild vegetable foods (Figure 12.2). The Hemudu people were skilled hunters who kept water buffalo, pigs, and dogs.

Hemudu culture
c. 7000 B.C.

Much of the earliest agricultural development may be associated with the widely distributed cord-decorated pottery traditions found in Ho-mu-tu and other mainland sites. Offshore, the Dapenkeng culture of Taiwan is one of the better known of early farming traditions, a culture of people who lived close to lakes and rivers. As early as

Dapenkeng culture
c. 5000 B.C.

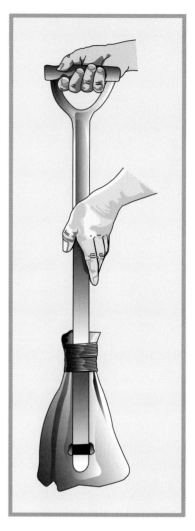

FIGURE 12.2 Artist's reconstruction of a Hemudu culture shovellike agricultural implement, based on well-preserved examples of such artifacts at the site. The blade was formed from a shoulder blade of a water buffalo.

5000 B.C., perhaps a millennium earlier, the Dapenkeng people were engaged in intensive fishing and shellfish collecting, as well as hunting and foraging. There is no archaeological evidence for agriculture, but it seems certain that rice and root crops were farmed. It is likely that this is only one of many cord-decorated pottery traditions that flourished throughout southern China and its offshore islands in the millennia after the first development of agriculture.

By 3000 B.C., much more sophisticated agricultural societies were flourishing on the Yangzi River and farther afield (Barnes, 1993). The archaeology of these traditions is known primarily from cemetery excavations that show slow changes in grave goods. The earliest graves indicate few social differentiations, but later sepulchers show not only a much wider variety of artifacts—pottery, bone and stone tools, jade objects, and other ornaments—but also an increase in the number of elaborately adorned burials. Richard Pearson, who has analyzed several cemeteries, argues that they demonstrate an increase in the concentration of wealth, a trend toward ranked societies, and a shift in the relative importance of males at the expense of females (Pearson et al., 1986). This last trend may be associated with the development of more intensive agriculture, an activity in which males were valued for their major roles in the cultivation and production of food.

Northern China

The second great center of early Chinese agriculture lies nearly 650 km (400 miles) north of the Yangzi, where the Huang Ho flows out of mountainous terrain into the low-lying plains of northern China. Northern Chinese agriculture was based on millet, whereas the southern staple was rice. However, rice was cultivated as early as 6500 to 5500 B.C. at the Jiahu site in the Huai River valley, 800 km (500 miles) south of Beijing. The southern staple arrived in the north many centuries after millet was domesticated.

Jiahu
6500 to 5500 B.C.

The earliest farming site in northern China may be Nanzhuangtou, in Hubei province, which flourished during a period of warm and moist climate, around 12,000 B.C., and may be a site where some cultivation took place, although the evidence is uncertain (Underhill, 1997). Certainly, wild plant foods were of great importance. If there was cultivation of cereal grasses this early, then there is a gap of 3000 to 4000 years before firm archaeological evidence of millet agriculture appears. The first well-attested northern agricultural communities were sited in the central regions of the Huang Ho valley (Figure 12.1). The area is a small basin, forming a border between the wooded western highlands and the swampy lowlands to the east. As in the south, the early Holocene saw a warming trend, followed by a cooler interval, then a more prolonged period of climatic amelioration. It was during the colder period, dating to about 6500 B.C., that the first sedentary farming villages are documented in the Huang Ho valley.

During Pleistocene glaciations, loess soils formed over a wide area of the north. The fine, soft-textured earth was both homogeneous and porous and could be tilled with simple digging sticks. Because of the concentrated summer rainfall, cereal crops, the key to agriculture in this region, could be grown successfully. The indigenous plants available for domestication included the wild ancestors of foxtail millet, broom-corn millet, sorghum, hemp, and the mulberry. Many villages lay near small streams on lower-level river terraces, along foothills and plains. Ancient Chinese farmers developed their own cultivation techniques, which persisted for thousands of years. Although irrigation gradually became the basis of the agricultural economies of Egypt, the Indus Valley, and Mesopotamia, it was not important in northern China until much later (Ho, 1984).

How, then, did northern Chinese agriculture begin? There are two possible scenarios. We can assume that the inhabitants of the Huang Ho region passed through a long phase of experimental cultivation and intensive exploitation of the indigenous flora before developing their own distinctive agricultural techniques, or we can assume that food production was developed farther south in China and adopted later in the north. Neither hypothesis can be tested with the available evidence. It is known that early farming villages were associated with the coarse, cord-marked pottery found on the banks of the Huang Ho in western Henan province. Perhaps these vessels are related to the cord-decorated pottery traditions of southern China.

The earliest farming villages in central and northern China date to as early as 6300 to 5100 B.C. Four groups of sites belong within a loosely defined Peiligang culture (Barnes, 1993; B. Smith, 1998). Many settlements consisted of semisubterranean houses with large storage pits. Their owners grew foxtail millet and kept dogs and pigs. Other regional cultures are slowly being identified from new research (for a discussion, see Underhill, 1997).

Peiligang culture
6300 to 5100 B.C.

By far the best known of China's early farming cultures is the Yangshao, which flourished over much of the Huang Ho basin, an area as large as the early centers of agriculture in Egypt or Mesopotamia, from before 4800 B.C. to about 3200 B.C. Each Yangshao village was a self-contained community, usually built on a terrace overlooking fertile river valleys and situated to avoid flooding and to allow maximal use of floodplain soils (Figure 12.3). Using hoes and digging sticks, the farmers cultivated foxtail millet as a staple, mainly in riverside gardens that were flooded every spring. Hunting, foraging, and fishing were still important, and the people moved their villages when local soils became exhausted. Yangshao culture evolved over many centuries. By 3200 B.C., it boasted of a characteristic, and thoroughly Chinese, culture, with its own naturalistic art style (Figure 12.4) and expert potters who made cooking pots for steaming food, the technique that forms the basis of much Chinese cuisine to this day. The Chinese language may have its roots in Yangshao culture as well.

Yangshao culture
4800 to 3200 B.C.

Over the centuries, Yangshao culture expanded as new villages split off from older communities and brought new land under cultivation. Yangshao villages and other settlements tended to follow a pattern of river valleys as many regional variations of peasant farming culture developed throughout China (Figure 12.5). Agriculture

FIGURE 12.3
Reconstruction of
Yangshao houses from
Banpo, China.

developed over wide areas at about the same time, with people adapting their crops
and farming techniques to local conditions. In time, the success of the new economies
led to local population increases, more complex cultures, and the concentration of
wealth in privileged hands.

Longshanoid cultures
3000 B.C.
     By 3000 B.C., Longshanoid farming cultures (named after the Longshan site) flour-
ished throughout much of northern China, based on larger, more permanent, and
often earthen-walled settlements. Longshanoid cultures were based in part on irrigation and rice cultivation, for the new tropical crop had been introduced from the lush
water meadows of the south and had reduced dependence on dry agriculture. These
much more elaborate, and wealthier, farming cultures were among the foundations of
Chinese civilization (Figure 12.6). (For Korea, see Nelson, 1993.)

FIGURE 12.4
(a) Yangshao pottery from
Banpo, China (approxi-
mately one-fourth actual
size). (b) The fish motifs
often used to decorate
Yangshao vessels can be
clearly seen (other motifs
are drawn separately).

(a)

(b)

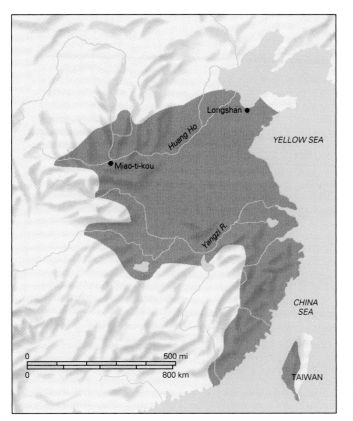

FIGURE 12.5 Approximate distribution of later farming cultures in China (dark shaded area).

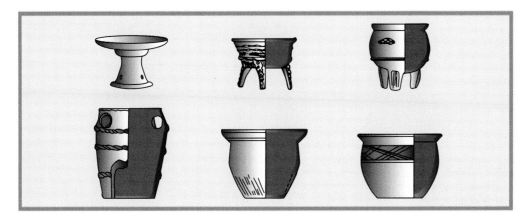

FIGURE 12.6 Some typical Longshanoid vessels used for cooking and other purposes from Miao-ti-Rai, China (scale not recorded). From the earliest times, Chinese ceramics reflected the distinctive Chinese cuisine based on steaming and stir-frying.

In both northern and southern China, village farming life was well established by 6500 B.C. The agricultural economies of the two regions were very different, but both supported large, stable settlements; increasingly complex ranked societies; and more advanced agricultural technologies than the simpler earlier methods. This parallel development of large, kin-based communities was to endure throughout rural China until modern times.

🐾 Jomon and Early Agriculture in Japan

By 10,000 B.C., sea levels around Japan were rising, and the area of landmass available to hunter-gatherers had shrunk considerably. In postglacial times, many Asian groups settled along coastlines and lakeshores, just as they did in Europe. They began exploiting a wide range of land and maritime resources in many different climatic zones. In

FIGURE 12.7 Three Jomon gray-colored vessels from the Yamanashi region of Japan. Jomon pottery, the earliest in the world, achieved great elaboration and evolved over many centuries.

Jomon culture
10,500 to 300 B.C.

some areas where resources were concentrated, people began to adopt more sedentary settlement patterns and live in well-defined territories. In Japan, for example, shellfish collecting provided a relatively stable subsistence base for the Jomon people. As early as 10,500 B.C., they made clay vessels, which they used for steaming mollusks and making vegetable foods palatable (Figure 12.7) (Pearson et al., 1986). These are some of the earliest clay pots ever made, but the same cultural development may have taken hold elsewhere as Stone Age people adapted to radically new environmental conditions and exploited an even wider resource base. As postglacial times continued, the people turned to another logical adaptive strategy: the deliberate growing of crops and taming of animals to ensure more reliable food supplies (Reynolds and Barnes, 1984).

More than 30,000 Jomon sites are known, most of them from Honshu in central Japan. All are linked by a common cultural tradition that lasted for thousands of years, but there were probably different ethnic groups that perhaps spoke different languages and adapted to diverse environments. The Jomon people hunted deer and other game with bows and arrows, collected shellfish, mainly in the spring, and fished much of the year. At first, they caught all types of fish, but as time went on, they concentrated on a few carefully selected species, inshore and lake fish as well as deepwater forms such as the bonito and the tuna. Above all, their diet depended heavily on wild vegetable foods, such as acorns, nuts, and edible seeds. They lived in relatively sedentary settlements, perhaps because of carefully scheduled seasonal hunting, gathering, and fishing activities. Some believe that they supplemented these activities with the cultivation of root crops and cereals or simply by the careful management of nut trees. The evidence for agriculture is still sketchy, but it seems possible that the Jomon people flourished by developing an elaborate technology for processing and storing huge stocks of nuts, an activity they may have combined with the cultivation of milletlike plants (Crawford, 1992).

The Jomon tradition lasted from as early as 10,500 B.C. until as late as 300 B.C. During this period, the focus of settlement shifted from the coasts to central Honshu and to the northern shores of Japan. By 5000 B.C., the inhabitants of Honshu were enjoying an elaborate material culture, including finely made ritual clay pots adorned with intricate decorations. The people often lived not in the caves and simple pit houses of earlier times but in large clusters of wooden houses with elaborate hearths. After 3000 B.C., the climate became cooler, overpopulation may have strained the carrying capacity of arable land, and the clearance of natural vegetation affected hunting activities. Hence, the population declined and the major centers of Jomon occupation moved toward the coasts. In the south, the inhabitants of Kyushu took up rice and barley cultivation after 1000 B.C.

Yayoi period
after 300 B.C.

The basis for what was to become traditional Japanese society was formed during the Yayoi period, which began after 300 B.C., when new crops and technologies spread throughout the islands. Japan was unified into a single state in approximately A.D. 600, by which time complex, stratified societies were commonplace throughout the archipelago.

🐾 Early Agriculture in Southeast Asia

The development of agriculture in Southeast Asia was an important element in the eventual colonization of the offshore islands of the Pacific, some of the last landmasses on earth to be settled by modern humans.

In 13,000 B.C., hunter-gatherer groups inhabited much of Southeast Asia. Their stone toolkits reveal remarkable uniformity over large areas of the mainland and islands (Higham, 2000). These stone assemblages do not necessarily reflect a stagnation of cultural innovation or a simple lifeway. Rather, it seems certain that the people were exploiting a broad range of game and vegetable foods. For example, Spirit Cave, in northeast Thailand, overlooks a small stream (Figure 12.8) and was first occupied before 9000 B.C. (Bellwood, 1997). The inhabitants exploited all manner of wild plants, including almonds, betel nuts, broad beans, gourds, water chestnuts, peppers, and cucumbers. The seeds found in Spirit Cave were from plants that can still be collected in the wild and have a variety of dietary, medicinal, and other uses. The large range of animal species found in the sites indicates a broadly based hunting economy that focused on deer, pigs, and arboreal creatures such as monkeys.

Spirit Cave
before 9000 B.C.

Hunter-gatherer groups exploited a wide variety of yams and other potential domesticates in Thailand and elsewhere in Southeast Asia at the end of the Pleistocene. As we have pointed out, yam planting is very simple, and hunter-gatherers are well aware that deliberate cultivation is possible. The problem is to identify the factors that led people to deliberate experimentation with various plants. In the absence of firm archaeological evidence, we can speculate that primitive shifting agriculture, with a combination of diverse crops and some animal herding, may have had its origins in a broad spectrum of hunting and gathering, as it did in other regions of the world. In the final analysis, all that is needed for a culture to make the transition

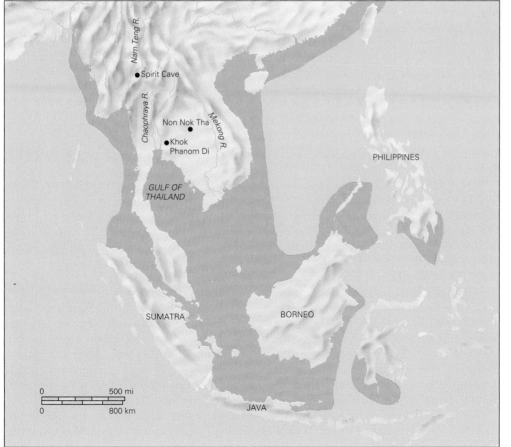

FIGURE 12.8
Southeast Asian sites mentioned in this chapter. Shaded areas show the extent of low sea levels during the last glaciation.

SITE

The Princess of Khok Phanom Di, Thailand

Charles Higham of the University of Otago in New Zealand is one of the world's experts on the archaeology of Southeast Asia. Working closely with Thai archaeologist Rachanie Thosarat, he has made spectacular discoveries of coastal hunter-gatherer communities and in well-established Bronze and Iron Age settlements (Higham and Thosarat, 1998). In 1984, he began excavations at the large Khok Phanom Di mound on the floodplain of the Bang Pakong River. From a previous test excavation carried out by a Thai colleague, he knew the occupation deposits were nearly 9 m (30 feet) deep, the mound resting on layers of shell midden debris. In the trial pit Higham spotted "the hollow eye sockets of some prehistoric person," so he knew he would probably find burials (Figure 12.9).

After digging through the uppermost levels, he found lighter, more sandy soil about 1 m (3 feet) below the surface. He cleaned the surface of the deposit carefully and spotted the telltale outline of the dark filling of a grave. Soon the excavators uncovered a row of graves close to the foundation of a raised platform with a building on it. Their trowels traced the walls of beautifully polished black vessels, many of them decorated with curvilinear designs. Higham's excitement mounted as he uncovered 14 burials. From the platform, "I could look down the row of skeletons and see the remains of men, women, and children, and even a tiny grave with the intertwined bones of two newly born infants, probably twins. It looked like a family group running through a couple or more generations" (Higham, 1994).

The excavation penetrated downward into a large burial chamber, uncovering a pyramid of circular clay cylinders once destined to become pots. When the pyramid was removed, the skeleton of a woman in her mid-thirties appeared, her wrist muscles well formed, probably from kneading clay. She had borne one or two children. Her chest was covered with a carpet of tiny shell beads and a necklace of large, white I-shaped beads. Higham lifted the top half of the body in a single block of soil and dissected it in the laboratory, where he recovered no less than 120,787 shell beads, once sewn onto two ornate upper garments. The princess must have shimmered in the sunlight, her wealth and social position coming from her expertise at potmaking, witness the burnished polishing pebbles found by her feet and the broken vessels covering her legs. Just 2 m (6 feet) away, Higham found another

are some clearings at the edge of the forest and a simple digging stick, already used for gathering, to plant the crop.

When rice cultivation actually spread into Southeast Asia from China remains a mystery. Did farming immigrants from the north import the new crop, or did indigenous hunter-gatherers adopt new economies? We know that rice farming was well established south of the Yangzi Valley by 2800 B.C. and in Vietnam's lower Red River valley by 2500 to 2000 B.C. A date for the first arrival of rice farming in Southeast and South Asia of about 2500 B.C. is not unreasonable, with well-documented agricultural communities on Thailand's Khorat Plateau by 2200 B.C. (Higham, 2000).

2800 to 2500 B.C.

Not that rice cultivation was universal, especially near low lying coasts with saline soils. Charles Higham (1994) has excavated a large and wealthy hunter-gatherer community at Khok Phanom Di, a settlement that was close to coastal mangrove swamps between 2000 and 1400 B.C. but is now more than 19.3 km (12 miles) from the sea (see Site box). The site covers 5 ha (12.3 acres) and is 12 m (39 feet) deep. It contains rice grains, but Higham and Thosarat (1998) believe that most of the domestic grains were imported from elsewhere since the local soils are unsuitable for growing the crop, despite a brief interlude when lowered sea levels allowed rice farming.

**Khok Phanom Di
2000 to 1400 B.C.**

During the late third millennium B.C., new dry-rice-farming villages appeared far inland, but few of them are known archaeologically. There was a slow expansion in farming activity, which was to affect societies living far from the coast in coming centuries.

identical grave covered by another heap of clay cylinders, this time of an infant only 15 months old. The child was adorned with identical decoration to that of her mother and lay with a tiny potmaking anvil, a smaller version of those used by adults, by her side. Higham is convinced this is the princess's daughter.

By the time the excavation finished six months later, Higham and his colleagues had recovered another 139 burials, representing 17 to 20 generations of expert potters who traded pots to obtain exotic shell ornaments. But none of them rivaled the splendor of the Princess of Khok Phanom Di.

FIGURE 12.9   Excavation at Khok Phanom Di. Thailand. This site has yielded important evidence of early rice cultivation.

Southeast Asia did not suffer from the drastic climatic changes of the northern latitudes, but its long dry season makes food storage essential, an important characteristic of domesticated rice. Only dramatic rises in low sea levels altered the geography and environment of Southeast Asia, creating islands from dry land and reducing the amount of coastal floodplain available to hunters and gatherers. Conceivably, these major changes in the coastline and the available land surface were among many factors that moved the inhabitants of Southeast Asia to experiment with plants and domestic animals.

⁊⁊⁊⁊ Rice and Root Cultivation in Island Southeast Asia

Offshore from mainland Asia one enters what archaeologist Peter Bellwood has called "a totally different Neolithic world" (1997, p. 121). He believes that the swamp cultivation of rice was introduced from the north, where it had taken hold considerably earlier. Rice agriculture dates to around 3500 B.C. on Taiwan, perhaps earlier. It dates back to only about 1200 B.C. in the Philippines, although agriculture may have occurred as early as 3000 B.C. there and on Sulawesi (Spriggs, 1989). Farmers were living on East Timor before 2100 B.C. and offshore in the Bismarck Archipelago by 1900 to 1500 B.C.

A relatively homogeneous Neolithic culture of farmers who settled mainly by coasts and rivers marks this first settlement. Canoes played a major role in intervillage

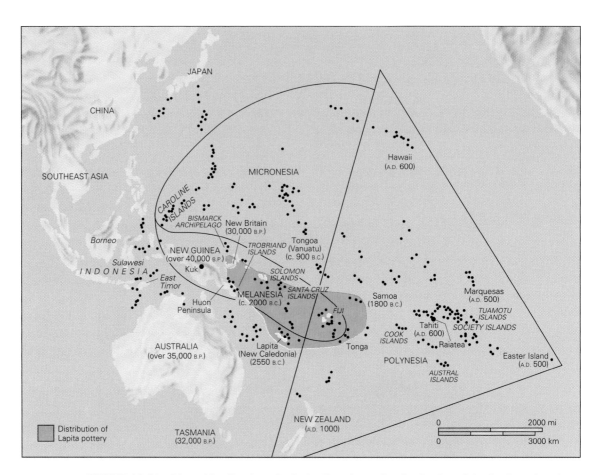

FIGURE 12.10 Map of Pacific sites. Dark shading shows the distribution of the Lapita cultural complex. Lines delineate Melanesia, Micronesia, and Polynesia. Dates are for first settlement.

exchange, which persisted for 2000 years. These constant exchanges meant that such items as clay vessels, adzes, and axes were fairly standardized over large areas, and communities as far separated as Taiwan and Manus enjoyed the same general economy, material culture, and social organization (see Figure 12.10). The same exchange networks carried New Britain obsidian and occasional metal objects over hundreds of miles.

This culture does not appear to have penetrated highland New Guinea, where agriculture developed quite independently. Here hunter-gatherers lived in damp, often densely forested environments, where the cultivation of root crops like taro and yams and fruit trees such as bananas required less forest clearance. Agricultural systems of this type became widespread in parts of Indonesia and in island Melanesia after 2500 B.C.

Archaeologists Jack Golson, Peter White, and others have researched early horticulture in the New Guinea highlands, using both pollen analysis and the study of old irrigation channels to amplify the archaeological record (Golson, 1977; Golson and Gardiner, 1990). There are traces, at approximately 7000 B.C., of a deliberate diversion of river water in the Kuk basin; these traces have been interpreted to mean that the people were cultivating taro or yams at a very early date. The evidence is still uncertain, although signs of increased erosion in the area may be the result of forest clearance for taro or yam gardens or possibly for the deliberate growing of indigenous New Guinea plants (B. Smith, 1998).

By 4000 to 3500 B.C., much more organized horticultural works were found in the Kuk basin. There is pollen evidence for quite extensive forest clearance in the general area. These works may have been created for yam and taro crops, while indigenous plants were grown on the better-drained soils between the channel banks. After 2000 B.C., the

Kuk
7000 B.C.

2000 B.C.

first highly developed drainage systems appeared in the area, a sign that people were farming much more intensively.

After 500 B.C., the people depended more and more on dry and wet agriculture, for an environment altered permanently by human activity had replaced the forest resources of earlier times. A slow population growth resulted eventually in the taking up of uncleared land. After that was exhausted, the only option was to shorten the fallow periods in cleared gardens—a choice that, if taro was the crop, would have resulted in lower crop yields.

The archaeological investigations and pollen analysis of Golson (1977) and others have produced firm evidence for sedentism, forest clearance, stone agricultural tools, and water-control techniques in the New Guinea highlands by 4000 to 3000 B.C. What is uncertain, however, is the means by which food production began in New Guinea. Was it developed locally with introduced plants after the local hunter-gatherers had manipulated indigenous plants for centuries? Or did the people manipulate local plants as a result of adopting a few introduced crops first? Whatever the answer, it appears that the New Guinea highlands were an area where people created an artificial garden environment as a result of a long period of experimentation in which they raised plants native to their natural environment. By exploiting a wide range of tropical animals and plants, the people became more sedentary and later started to plant small plots of root crops; ultimately, they would have intensified their food production until they had modified their environment beyond recognition. This hypothetical model of early agriculture in New Guinea may serve as a possible model for other tropical areas in Asia as well.

🐾 Agriculture in the Pacific Islands

The origins of the peoples of the Pacific islands have fascinated scientists since the seventeenth century. Today, most authorities look to Southeast Asia for the origins of the Melanesians, Micronesians, and Polynesians (Blust, 1995). They point out that the settlement of the offshore islands depended on the successful cultivation of root crops such as taro and yam, as well as breadfruit, coconuts, and sugarcane. Chickens, dogs, and pigs were also valued as food and were domesticated in Asia before being introduced to the Pacific. Oceanic islands lack much in the way of wild food resources, so domesticated plants and animals were essential for successful colonization. Small animals such as pigs and chickens could have been carried readily from island to island in canoes, as could easily germinating root plants such as the yam. Both food sources allowed a sizable population to spread to many hundreds of small islands separated by miles of open water.

The settlement of the remoter Pacific islands is closely connected to the early cultivation of yams, and especially of taro. As we pointed out earlier in this chapter, taro and yams were probably domesticated in Southeast Asia before the development of rice cultivation, but exactly when and where they were first grown is unknown (Yen, 1995). Late Ice Age seafarers settled not only on New Guinea but also on close island chains like the Solomons and perhaps the Bismarck Archipelago as early as 35,000 B.C. (Gosden, 1995) (see Chapter 6). Beyond the Solomons and farther offshore was a biologically more impoverished world that awaited domesticated crops and animals and more sophisticated seafaring and navigational techniques for human colonization.

🐾 The Lapita Cultural Complex and the Settlement of Melanesia and Western Polynesia

The settlement of remoter Melanesia covered a distance of 5000 km (3100 miles) of island chains and open ocean during a period of six centuries from about 1600 to 1000 B.C. (Bellwood, 1987). This was human settlement that followed on the domestication of plants and animals and the development of new maritime technologies, presumably including oceangoing double-hulled sailing canoes. In archaeological terms,

FIGURE 12.11 Lapita pottery from Melanesia. The distinctive shell-impressed motifs used by Lapita potters can be employed to trace the extent of human settlement.

Lapita cultural complex 1600 to 1000 B.C. and later

this development is associated with the highly distinctive Lapita cultural complex, named after a site on New Caledonia island. Most experts agree that the Lapita people were Austronesian-speakers who traded widely through the southwestern Pacific. Their settlements are marked by characteristic stamp-decorated pottery, often adorned with elaborate designs (Figure 12.11).

The original homeland of the Lapita people is a matter of considerable debate. One school of thought believes that they originated in western Melanesia, whereas others believe that they arrived in the islands from the Southeast Asian mainland (Kirch, 1988; White et al., 1988). Lapita people moved obsidian from New Britain Island 3700 km (2300 miles) eastward to Fiji and 3800 km (2400 miles) northwestward to northern Borneo through exchange networks that carried the same toolmaking stone as far west as farming settlements on the eastern coast of Borneo (Bellwood and Koon, 1989). That is not to say, of course, that Lapita canoes traveled all the way to Borneo. Rather, by 1000 B.C., there was what Peter Bellwood (1997) calls a "linked chain" of exchange networks over more than 8100 km (5000 miles) throughout the Southeast Asian islands deep into the central Pacific.

People living on small islands usually depend on their neighbors for many important commodities, an interdependency that was reflected in these complex exchange networks spanning many miles of open ocean. The commodities carried in canoes ranged from foodstuffs to manufactured items and may have included ceremonial objects as well. The social and economic complexities of Melanesian trading systems have long excited anthropologists, starting with Bronislaw Malinowski (1922) in his famous fieldwork on the celebrated *kula* ring of the Trobriand Islanders that circulated shell necklaces and bracelets from island to island in complex circles. The *kula* ring, with its elaborate ceremonial, was just one of many related exchange trading systems that linked all parts of coastal New Guinea and much of Melanesia. These networks were reciprocal and self-perpetuating; they had their ancestry in much earlier exchange patterns that began, although in a simpler form, among the Lapita people (Allen and White, 1989; Terrell, 1988).

The Lapita homeland was probably the Bismarck Archipelago area, which was inhabited during the late Ice Age (see Chapter 6) as far back as about 35,000 B.C. (Gosden et al., 1989). There is clear evidence for open-water voyaging by 2900 B.C. as far as Manus Island, where obsidian is to be found, some 200 km (124 miles) straight-line open-water away. An Australian research team has identified widespread human occupation throughout the Bismarck Archipelago before Lapita pottery appeared about 1500 B.C., and it may be that some, if not most, elements of the Lapita cultural complex came from local roots. By identifying the sources of island obsidians and pottery clays, the Australians have been able to show that local trading patterns changed constantly during pre-Lapita times and throughout the Lapita occupation of the archipelago. Clearly, Lapita cultures were dynamic, ever-changing systems.

These excavations show that there is a very long history of human occupation indeed in the Bismarck Archipelago, one that stretches far back into the Ice Age. Throughout most of this long period, obsidian was moved through the islands and far beyond them toward Southeast Asia. The region was never isolated from the outside world. Its inhabitants were part of a vast network of interconnections that linked the entire western Pacific and island Southeast Asia over a period of at least 1500 years. It was not until sometime after 2000 years ago that these broad links vanished, to be replaced by more local cultural developments.

The Lapita cultural complex was either a migration of new peoples from Southeast Asia into the islands, as was once thought, or a vast exchange system that linked island after island through reciprocal trading between kinspeople (Clark, Andrews, and Vunidilo, 2001). Archaeologically, we know that Lapita pottery from the Santa Cruz Islands, decorated with stamped designs and made of clay tempered with shell, is found as far east as Vanuatu (Tongoa), Fiji, Tonga, and Samoa. We know it dates generally to the last thousand years before Christ but seems to have gone out of fashion by A.D. 200 (Kirch, 1982). To associate this pottery distribution with a migrating ethnic group is to oversimplify a very complex picture of long-distance exchange, ocean voyaging, and island settlement.

Clearly, one catalyst for this expansion was the development of the oceangoing double-hulled canoe (Finney, 1994). This canoe was the means by which efficient exchange networks were maintained from island to island over distances up to 600 km (372 miles) from Melanesia far out into the Pacific, into western Polynesia. The rapid expansion from island to island that carried Lapita pottery far to the east developed among societies living in an island environment that extended from the Southeast Asian mainland far southeastward. The inhabitants of this vast archipelago lived on relatively benign coasts and maintained contacts with one another that extended over hundreds of miles. That there was some standardization of artifacts and culture among them after 2000 B.C. is hardly surprising. It is only when one reaches off-lying islands such as Fiji and Tonga that one can legitimately think in terms of Lapita "colonists" who were the first settlers of the Pacific. Here, open-water distances are much longer, involving, for example, voyages of nearly 592 open-water km (600 miles). In Fiji, Samoa, and Tonga, the first settlers carried Lapita artifacts with them, but subsequent cultural development proceeded along local lines.

Long-Distance Voyaging in the Pacific

From Melanesia, canoes voyaged through western Polynesia, taking the plants and domesticated animals of their home islands with them. As distances grew longer, so did the navigational challenges, challenges so formidable that many early scholars argued that the Polynesian islands were settled by accidental voyages (Finney, 1994). Some compelling studies of Polynesian navigation and voyaging by both anthropologists and small-boat sailors have dispelled any lingering doubts about the navigational abilities of the early Polynesians. Geoffrey Irwin (1992), himself an expert sailor, has used computer modeling and his own voyages to suggest that the exploration was rapid and deliberate, a systematic process that led to ever more improved navigational techniques. At the same time, he believes that rather than sailing randomly downwind, the early voyagers made their explorations upwind, against the prevailing winds, knowing that they could always turn downwind and return home with ease.

Nearly all the long trips attributed to the Polynesians were from north to south and therefore involved simple dead-reckoning calculations and an elementary way of measuring latitude from the stars. Several modern studies have collected navigators' lore from surviving practitioners of the art (Finney, 1994) (see Science box). The pilots were a respected and close-knit group. Young apprentices learned their skills over many years of making passages and from orally transmitted knowledge about the stars

SCIENCE

Indigenous Pacific Navigation

When British navigator Captain James Cook visited Tahiti in 1769, he puzzled over a question that has always fascinated scholars: How had the Tahitians colonized their remote homeland? How had humans, with only simple canoes and no metals, sailed across vast tracts of open ocean and settled on the remotest islands of the Pacific? Cook met the great Tahitian navigator Tupaia and asked him how canoe skippers made their way from island to island out of sight of land. Tupaia explained how they used the sun as a compass by day and the moon and stars by night. When Cook marveled at the Polynesians' ability to sail against the prevailing trade winds for hundreds of miles, Tupaia pointed out that westerlies blew from November to January, and so these were the months when canoes could make good progress to windward.

Tupaia carried a mental file of Polynesia with him. He listed islands, the number of days required to sail to them, and their direction, which Cook made up into a rough sketch map. Modern scholars believe Tupaia could define an area bounded by the Marquesas in the northeast, the Tuamotus to the east, the Australs to the south, and the Cook Islands to the southwest. Even Fiji and Samoa to the west lay within his consciousness, a mental map of an area as large as Australia or the United States.

No later explorers interviewed Tahitian navigators. Many scholars assumed the Pacific islands had been colonized by canoes blown accidently offshore. But in 1965, English cruising sailor David Lewis encountered aged canoe navigators in the Caroline Islands of Micronesia. He learned how the navigators used the zenith passages of key stars to navigate far from land, as well as swell direction, waves reflected off distant land, and even the flights of sea and land birds to make landfall on island archipelagos far from the departure point. These navigators were also able to return to their homes safely, using the same signs of sea and sky. Determined to preserve a rapidly vanishing art, Lewis sailed his European-designed, oceangoing catamaran from Rarotonga in the Cook Islands to New Zealand, using only a star map and a Polynesian navigator to help him. In the 1970s, Lewis apprenticed himself to the pilots of the Caroline Islands, learning how they made passages with the aid of sun, moon, stars, and cloud and swell formations, even by passing birds.

In the late 1960s, anthropologist Ben Finney (1994) began long-term experiments with replicas of ancient Polynesian canoes. Finney's first replica was *Nalehia*, a 12-m (40-foot) copy of a Hawaiian royal canoe. Tests in Hawaii's windy waters showed that the vessel could sail across the wind, so Finney planned a voyage from Hawaii to Tahiti and back, using a replica built from a composite of known canoe designs from throughout the Pacific Islands. *Hokule'a*, designed by Hawaiian Herb Kawainui Kane, is 19 m (62 feet) long, with double hulls and two crab-claw-shaped sails. Finney, Micronesian navigator Mau Piailug, and a mainly Hawaiian crew sailed *Hokule'a* from Hawaii to Tahiti and back in 1976. This journey was followed by a two-year voyage around the Pacific using only indigenous pilotage. Thanks to the successful *Hokule'a* experiments, ancient Polynesian navigational skills have been preserved for posterity.

---

and the oceans accumulated by generations of navigators. The navigational techniques used the angles of rising and setting stars, the trend of ocean swells, and the myriad inconspicuous phenomena that indicate the general direction and distance of small islands. The navigators were perfectly capable of voyaging over long stretches of open water; their geographic knowledge was astonishing. They had no need for the compass or other modern aids, and their landfalls were accurate.

The Settlement of Micronesia and Eastern Polynesia

The colonization of Micronesia and eastern Polynesia took place within the last 2000 years, some 1300 to 1600 years after the first settlement of western Polynesia. The sudden, and apparently rapid, expansion may have resulted from population growth in already settled islands that sent voyagers farther eastward looking for pristine new

FIGURE 12.12 Bone fishhooks from Polynesia. Fishhook forms vary greatly from island to island and through time, allowing chronological comparisons between different island culture sequences. (The Field Museum, Neg. #100629, Chicago.)

lands (Kirch, 2000; Spriggs and Anderson, 1993). It is thought that the Polynesians originated in the Fiji area before the great elaboration of Melanesian culture after A.D. 1. After a lengthy period of adaptation in western Polynesia, small groups began to settle the more remote islands. The Marquesas were settled by A.D. 500 and the Society Islands and Tahiti by A.D. 800. The first canoes arrived in Hawaii in about A.D. 600 and on Easter Island by A.D. 500 (Kirch, 1985; Kirch and Sahlins, 1992).

Offshore Pacific settlement
Before A.D. 1 to 800

The settlement of Polynesia seems to have taken approximately 2500 years from its beginnings by people who were still, technologically speaking, in the Stone Age. They relied heavily on stone axes and adzes and an elaborate array of bone and shell fishhooks (M. Allen, 1995) (Figure 12.12). The crops planted varied from island to island, but breadfruit, taro, coconut, yams, and bananas were the staples. Sweet potato, a South American plant, was a staple when Europeans first arrived. No one knows how this crop reached eastern Polynesia—perhaps by (as yet unidentified) Polynesian voyaging to the South American mainland (Hather and Kirch, 1991). The food surpluses generated on the larger islands were used as a form of wealth (for surveys of island perspectives on culture change, see Kirch, 1996, and Kirch and Hunt, 1996).

When the French and British visited Tahiti in the eighteenth century, they chanced upon the center of a vigorous eastern Polynesian society (Oliver, 1977). Tahiti and the surrounding islands were ruled by a powerful hierarchy of chiefs and nobles, many of them descendants of the canoe crews that had settled the archipelago. The chiefs had acquired prestige by controlling and redistributing wealth and food supplies. Their formidable religious and social powers had led them to warfare and to the undertaking of elaborate agricultural projects and the erection of monumental shrines and temples of stone: The famous *maraes* (temples) of Tahiti are typical examples (Figure 12.13). On remote Easter Island, the people erected *moaes*, vast statues up to 9.8 m (32 feet) high (Figure 12.14). They are thought to be images of deified ancestors associated with different kin groups (Bahn and Flenley, 1992; van Tilburg, 1994). The full diversity of Polynesian culture is still imperfectly understood, for archaeological research has hardly begun in the South Seas, but it is certain that the Polynesians were making ocean voyages on a large scale when the Greeks and Romans were little more than coastal navigators.

FIGURE 12.13 Tahitian *marae* at Tuputaputia on Raiatea Island, where many ancient long-distance voyages began. This *marae* has been restored and is shown decorated to commemorate its restoration.

FIGURE 12.14 *Moae* statues at Ahu Nau Nau on the north coast of Easter Island. The ancestral figures bear topknots of red volcanic rock.

The Settlement of New Zealand

New Zealand is the largest and among the most remote of all of the Pacific islands; it is actually two large islands. It has a temperate climate, not the tropical warmth enjoyed by most Polynesians. Despite this ecological difference, Polynesians voyaged southward in comparatively recent times and settled on the North Island. Maori legends tell of a migration from Polynesia in the mid-fourteenth century A.D. The first settlers—including a chief named Toi Ete'hutai, who came to New Zealand in search of two grandsons blown away from Tahiti during a canoe race—may have arrived about 400 years before. The earliest carbon-14 dates for New Zealand archaeological sites are a matter of controversy, but a careful study places first settlement between A.D. 1000 and 1200 (A. Anderson, 1991).

A.D. 1000 to 1200

The temperate climate of North Island formed a southern frontier for most of the basic food plants of Polynesia. Taro, yams, and gourd can be grown only there, but the sweet potato can be cultivated in the northern part of South Island if adequate winter storage pits are used. The Polynesian coconut never grew in New Zealand. The earliest settlers relied heavily on hunting, fishing, and gathering. Even later, though some peoples specialized in food production, others did not, especially on South Island, where many settlements were close to abundant ocean resources (Davidson, 1987).

The first settlers found great flocks of moa birds, flightless creatures that were helpless in the face of systematic hunting. The settlers hunted the moa into extinction within a few centuries (A. Anderson, 1992; A. Anderson and McGlone, 1991). Fish, fern roots, and shellfish were important throughout New Zealand's short prehistory (Shawcross, 1967). The introduction of the sweet potato made a dramatic difference to the New Zealanders, for the tubers, if carefully protected from cold, could be eaten in the winter months, and some could be kept for the next year's planting. Sweet potatoes have a large crop yield and are thought to have contributed to a rapid population buildup, especially on North Island. This buildup, in turn, led to competition among groups for suitable agricultural land on which to grow the new staple (Davidson, 1987).

When the moa became extinct, the Maori had few meat supplies except birds, dogs, and rats. Their only other meat source was human flesh. The archaeological record of Maori culture from approximately A.D. 1400 onward shows not only population growth but also an increasing emphasis on warfare, marked by the appearance of numerous fortified encampments, or *pa*, protected with earthen banks (Figure 12.15). The distribution of *pa* coincides to a large extent with the best sweet-potato lands (Bellwood, 1970). In the course of a few centuries, warfare became a key element in Maori culture, to the extent that it was institutionalized and was an important factor in maintaining cohesion and leadership in Maori society. The booty of war was not only *kumara* (sweet potato) but also the flesh of captives, which became a limited part of the Maori diet.

Maori warfare, mainly confined to North Island, where more than 5000 *pa* have been found, was seasonal and closely connected with the planting and harvest of sweet potatoes, when everyone was busy in the gardens. Military campaigns were short and

FIGURE 12.15 Maori *pa* painted by early nineteenth-century artist Augustus Earle.

FIGURE 12.16 Maori war canoe, drawn in 1769 by Captain James Cook's artist, Sidney Parkington.

intense, very often launched from the sea in war canoes up to 24 m (78.7 feet) or more in length (Figure 12.16). These elaborately carved vessels could hold as many as 150 men on a short expedition. So formidable was the reputation of the Maori that European ships avoided New Zealand ports for years before permanent white settlement was achieved. The last Maori war ended in 1872, by which time the indigenous population had been decimated by disease, warfare, and European contact.

Summary 🐾🐾

As in Southwest Asia, food production began in Asia during the early Holocene, perhaps as early as 10,000 B.C., but became fully established in a cold interval that followed initial warming, around 6500 B.C. In southern China, some rice was cultivated perhaps as early as 9000 B.C. Widespread rice agriculture was well established by 6500 B.C. The staple in the Huang Ho Valley of northern China was millet, cultivated at least as early as 6500 B.C., perhaps much earlier. The Yangshao culture flourished over much of the Huang Ho basin, a society of self-contained villages, replaced by the more elaborate Longshanoid cultures by 3000 B.C.

In Southeast Asia, the staple crop was rice, probably first cultivated along low-lying, swampy coasts. The new economies soon spread inland during the third millennium B.C., bringing village life to much of the region. Island Southeast Asia was settled by hunters and foragers at least as early as 35,000 B.C., and simple root horticulture had been established in highland New Guinea by 6000 B.C. The people of the Lapita cultural complex traded widely through the southwestern Pacific after 1600 B.C., but it was not until the past 2000 years that offshore canoes settled Micronesia and Polynesia, and New Zealand was colonized between A.D. 1000 and 1200.

Guide to Further Reading 🐾🐾

Barnes, Gina L. 1993. *China, Korea, and Japan.* London and New York: Thames & Hudson.
 An up-to-date synthesis of recent research in East Asia by a scholar who commands the local literature. Strongly recommended as a starting point.

Bellwood, Peter. 1997. *The Prehistory of the Indo-Malaysian Archipelago,* 2nd ed. Sydney: Academic Press.
 A valuable summary of Southeast Asian mainland prehistory.

Davidson, Janet. 1985. "New Zealand Prehistory." *Advances in World Archaeology* 4: 239–292.
 An exemplary article on general trends in New Zealand prehistory with a very complete bibliography.

Finney, Ben. 1994. *Voyage of Rediscovery*. Berkeley: University of California Press.
   A popular account of recent research into Pacific voyaging, including modern reenactments. Readable and authoritative.

Irwin, Geoffrey. 1992. *The Prehistoric Exploration and Colonization of the Pacific*. Cambridge: Cambridge University Press.
   Irwin is an archaeologist and practical sailor, so his sophisticated analysis of the offshore settlement of the Pacific is doubly convincing. A truly fascinating work.

Kirch, Patrick V. 2000. *On the Road of the Winds: An Archaeological History of the Pacific Islands Before European Contact*. Berkeley: University of California Press.
   A general account of Pacific archaeology. Strongly recommended.

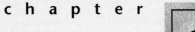

chapter

13

THE STORY OF MAIZE: EARLY FARMERS IN THE AMERICAS

Cliff Palace at Mesa Verde, Colorado.

hen Harvard archaeologist Alfred Kidder dug into the complex layers of Pecos Pueblo, New Mexico, in 1915, he was searching for the ancient roots of Pueblo Indian culture deep in the middens of this long-occupied site. Kidder had visited archaeological sites in Egypt and Greece and had seen at first hand that careful stratigraphic observation had yielded rich chronological dividends. Over many field seasons, he sunk enormous trenches into the depths of the Pecos deposits, uncovering dozens of small occupation layers and dense concentrations of potsherds. Back in the laboratory, he pored over thousands of painted potsherds and turned them into a long cultural sequence that has been the foundation of all subsequent research in the North American Southwest. "It is safe enough to postulate the former presence in the Southwest of a more or less nomadic people, thinly scattered over the country, ignorant of agriculture and pottery making," he wrote (1927, p. 56) of the earliest occupants. Ever since, American archaeologists have searched for the first Native American farmers not only in the North American Southwest but also throughout the Americas.

The Native Americans domesticated an impressive range of native New World plants, some of which—like maize, potatoes, and tobacco—were rapidly adopted by farmers on other continents after European contact (Table 13.1). The most important staple crop was Indian corn, properly called *maize,* the only significant wild grass in the New World to be fully domesticated (B. Smith, 1998). It remains the most important food crop in the Americas, being used in more than 150 varieties as both food and cattle fodder. Root crops were another substantial food source, especially in South America, and included manioc, sweet potatoes, and white potatoes. Chili peppers were grown as hot seasoning; amaranth, sunflowers, cacao, peanuts, and several types of bean were also significant crops. Some crops, such as cotton and gourds, are common to both the Old and New Worlds but were probably domesticated separately.

In contrast to Old World farmers, the Native Americans had few domesticated animals, but they included the alpaca and the llama of the Andes, which provided wool. Dogs appeared in the Americas, and the raucous and unruly turkey and the Muscovy duck were domesticated. Most archaeologists now agree that there were at least two, perhaps three, major centers of plant domestication in the Americas: Mesoamerica for maize, beans, squash, and sweet potatoes, and the highlands of the central Andes for root crops. The lowland tropics in Panama, Colombia, Ecuador, and Peru may have been a center for taming squashes and other tropical plants. There were also four major areas of later cultivation activity: tropical (northern) South America, the Andean area, Mesoamerica, and eastern North America (B. Smith, 1998).

TABLE 13.1

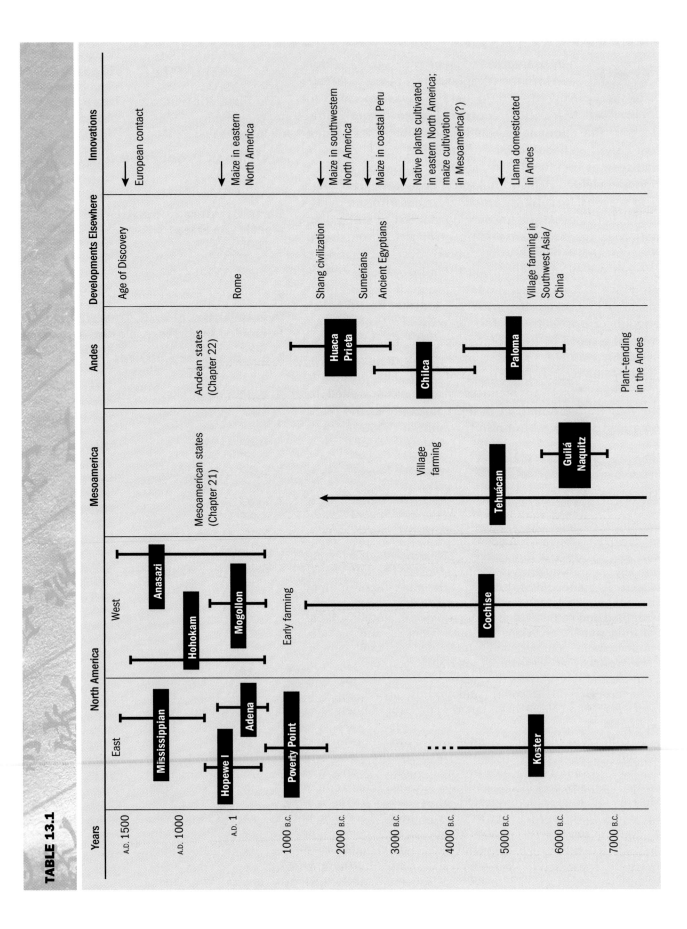

Years	North America				Mesoamerica	Andes	Developments Elsewhere	Innovations
	East		West					
A.D. 1500							Age of Discovery	European contact
A.D. 1000	Mississippian		Anasazi		Mesoamerican states (Chapter 21)	Andean states (Chapter 22)		
A.D. 1	Hopewe I	Adena	Hohokam	Mogollon			Rome	Maize in eastern North America
1000 B.C.	Poverty Point				Village farming	Huaca Prieta	Shang civilization	Maize in southwestern North America
2000 B.C.			Early farming			Chilca	Sumerians	Maize in coastal Peru
3000 B.C.					Tehuácan		Ancient Egyptians	Native plants cultivated in eastern North America; maize cultivation in Mesoamerica(?)
4000 B.C.					Guilá Naquitz	Paloma		
5000 B.C.			Cochise					Llama domesticated in Andes
6000 B.C.	Koster						Village farming in Southwest Asia/China	
7000 B.C.						Plant-tending in the Andes		

🌾 The First Plant Domestication

As long ago as 1952, cultural geographer Carl Sauer expressed the belief that agriculture first began in the Americas in humid tropical forest environments. His ideas have been largely forgotten in recent years, as researchers focused on the origins of maize, then thought to have been domesticated in more open environments. Recent investigations using pollen analysis, **phytoliths,** and plant remains have, however, supported Sauer's belief, with researchers now theorizing that tropical food production first began in small-scale house gardens in forest villages in Panama as early as the ninth millennium B.C. (Piperno and Pearsall, 1998). This "dooryard" horticulture of wild plants developed eventually into slash-and-burn (swidden) farming and, ultimately, into fully settled village life, a process that took as long as 5000 years in the lowland tropics.

By 5000 to 4000 B.C., extensive forest clearance for fields appears to have been under way. In Panama, surveys show that population growth accompanied the new farming methods, which may have come into use as maize, manioc, and sweet potato became available over wider areas. Slash-and-burn agriculture may also have spread because of drier conditions at the time. Piperno and Pearsall believe the humid tropical lowlands were an important setting for the development of early American agriculture and that the more arid highland areas of Mesoamerica, long claimed as the cradle of maize domestication, acquired domesticated crops later. New support for their theory comes from recent excavations at the San Andrés site on the Gulf Coast of Tabasco in Mexico, where evidence of forest clearance and maize pollen date to about 5100 B.C. (K. Pope et al., 2001).

Squashes and a plant called *leren* were probably the first domesticates. Bottle gourds were invaluable containers for holding liquids both before and after domestication. Domesticated gourd remains come from Guilá Naquitz in the Valley of Oaxaca as early as 8000 B.C. This gourd may have originated in Africa, where it is widely used as a fishing-net float. Perhaps, argue some experts, it floated across the Atlantic and washed up on New World shores before European settlement. At any rate, the seeds would have provided tropical hunter-gatherers with an easy source of water containers, a preadaptation that might have led to the cultivation of wild squashes and other cucurbits. Domesticated squash was also in use in Mesoamerica as early as 8000 B.C.

As is well known, maize, beans, and squash, which can be grown in the same garden, are a classic triumvirate of food crops in the Americas. Initially, this association probably occurred in the wild, for runner beans and squashes grow naturally around the stalks and bases of teosinte, a wild grass thought to be the ancestor of maize. In the end, humans disturbed the land by clearing it, observed the association of teosinte, beans, and squash, and domesticated the three in combination. Of these three crops, by far the most complex and most debated is *Zea mays,* maize.

The Origins of Maize Agriculture

Maize was the staff of life for many Native Americans when Christopher Columbus landed in the New World. It was cultivated over an enormous area of the Americas, from Argentina and Chile northward to Canada, from sea level to high in the Andes, in low-lying swampy environments and in arid lands. Hundreds of races of domesticated maize evolved over the millennia, each a special adaptation to local environmental conditions.

The origins of domesticated maize are still the subject of controversy, which centers on the relationship between a wild grass named teosinte (*Zea mexicana*), which grows over much of Mesoamerica, and early strains of domesticated maize (Galinat, 1985; MacNeish and Eubanks, 2000). Botanist George Beadle (1981) theorized that a teosinte of about 13,000 to 6000 B.C. was the direct ancestor of modern corn and was transformed into a primitive corn through human selection. According to Beadle, there was a mutation in a gene in an ancestral form of teosinte that converted the hard fruit cases of the grass into shallow, softer cupules (cups) that carried elongated glumes (husks) enclosing and protecting the kernels. This change made wild teosinte much easier to thresh. The transformation into a domesticated form of early maize may have taken place more or less simultaneously in many areas.

Impressive grounds exist for considering teosinte the wild ancestor of domesticated maize. There are major differences between this grass and corn. Teosinte has long branches tipped with tassels, while maize has short branches tipped with ears. Botanist John Doebley and his colleagues (1999) have identified the gene that controls this difference and think that changes in the regulatory regions of this gene (named tb1 [teosinte branched 1]) were involved in the switch from teosinte to maize. The tb1 protein suppresses production of lateral branches, and the greater the accumulation of tb1, the shorter the branches. Thus, it is a mutation that increases the amount of tb1 that controls the teosinte shape to a maize-like plant. Doebley believes this changeover took many centuries, that it occurred in southwestern Mexico, and that it came about specifically as a result of the modification of teosinte in the deciduous forests of the Balsas Valley region. The process of domestication involved selecting seeds of the preferred form and rejecting those from other, less desirable types. A perennial teosinte found in Mexico in recent years has been crossbred with maize.

Piperno and Pearsall (1998) argue for an origin in the tropical lowlands, which did not have the richness of wild plant foods found in more open areas. From its earliest introduction, maize would have been a more efficient source of calories than many wild forest plants, and thus a source of experimentation (see also MacNeish and Eubanks, 2000). The recent San Andrés find from Tabasco on the Gulf Coast of Mexico adds support to this theory, with maize appearing there by 5100 B.C. (K. Pope et al., 2001).

San Andrés
c. 5100 B.C.

The hypothetical scenario for maize domestication goes as follows (Figure 13.1). The process may have started as an unintentional by-product of gathering wild teosinte, for gathering would lead to selective pressure for harvestable types of the grass, with spikes shrunken into fascicles (bunches). The fascicles would have made it harder for the seeds to scatter. In time, this form of teosinte would become established

FIGURE 13.1 The stages through which teosinte passed on its way to becoming domesticated maize, with (a) showing the earliest teosinte form. (b to d) The harvesting process increased the shrinking of the teosinte branches and led to the husks becoming the enclosures for corn ears. (e) Shows the stabilized maize phenotype. (After Galinat, 1985.)

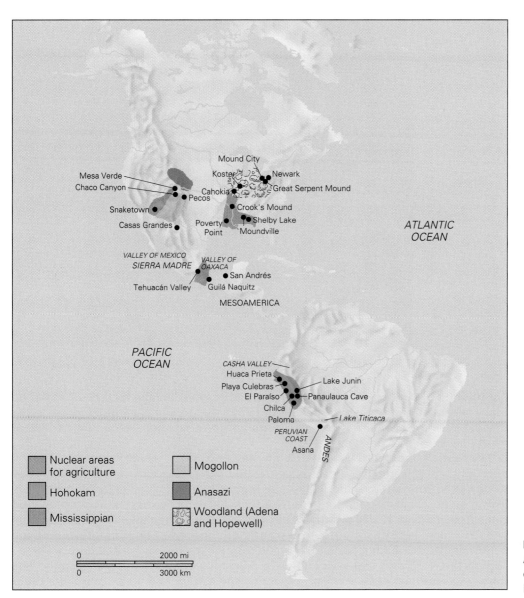

FIGURE 13.2
Archaeological sites and culture areas mentioned in this chapter.

by campsites and in abandoned middens. These colonies would automatically diverge toward greater domestic kinds of variation, from which human beings could select the most useful types. In time, too, humans would remove weeds from these teosinte stands, then start deliberately planting the more useful types. Thus, the female teosinte spike evolved down a pathway leading toward maize. The cultivation and fertilization of semiwild grass populations were followed by attempts to sow selected seed from the most desirable types. At first, the planted teosinte was no more productive than the wild forms, but it was easier to harvest, a critical stage in the process of domestication. When people began the selective harvesting and planting of transitional forms of teosinte, the grass's reproductive strategy changed to dependency on human intervention. A genetic revolution followed, in which attributes that made harvesting easier and favored teosinte's use as a human food had a selective advantage.

The best archaeological evidence for early maize cultivation still comes not from the lowlands but from the dry caves and open sites of the dry highland Tehuacán Valley in southern Mexico (Figure 13.2). This was the valley that Richard MacNeish (1970, 1978) chose as a promising area in which to seek the origins of domesticated maize. In fact, the inhabitants may have received the new crop centuries after its first domestication. MacNeish found domestic maize cobs dating back to approximately 1000 B.C., but

Tehuacán Valley

FIGURE 13.3 Excavations at Coxcatlán Rock Shelter, Tehuacán, Mexico, where evidence for maize agriculture dating to about 2500 B.C. was found.

Coxcatlán
10,000 B.C. and later

not until he began digging in the small Coxcatlán Rock Shelter (Figure 13.3) did he find maize that even vaguely resembled what at that time was considered the hypothetical ancestor of maize. Coxcatlán contains 28 occupation levels, the earliest of which dates to approximately 10,000 B.C.

MacNeish found that the earliest Tehuacán people lived mainly by hunting horses, deer, and other mammals and by collecting wild vegetable foods. These hunters used stone-tipped lances in the chase. They also hunted large numbers of jackrabbits, probably in organized drives. MacNeish estimates that 50 to 60 percent of the people's food

8000 B.C.

came from game in 10,000 B.C. After 8000 B.C., the game population declined, and the people turned more and more to wild plant foods. Instead of hunting year-round, the Tehuacán bands scheduled their food gathering on a seasonal basis and were able to exploit the vegetable and other foods in their environment very intensively. The dietary scenario has been reconstructed from the carbon and nitrogen isotope ratios in the bone collagen of people who lived in the Tehuacán Valley after 6000 B.C.

4500 B.C.

(Farnsworth et al., 1985). By at least 4500 B.C., about 90 percent of the Tehuacano diet consisted of tropical grasses such as *Setaria*, and such plants as cacti and maguey. So much grain was necessary that some form of cultivation or domestication of native plants may have been essential by this time.

2500 B.C.

Crop yields increased after 2500 B.C. People grew foods that, when stored, would tide them over lean months: beans, amaranth, gourds, and maize. They lived in larger and more permanent settlements, grinding their maize on well-made grindstones (*metates*). The maize itself was smaller than modern strains and probably much like teosinte (see Figure 13.1). By this time, more sedentary villages had replaced the scheduled gathering and nomadic settlement patterns of earlier times. Their ample storage facilities helped the people live through the lean months.

The sequence of events at Tehuacán is by no means unique, for other peoples were also experimenting with cultivation (Killion, 1992; MacNeish and Eubanks, 2000). Different hybrid forms of maize are found in Tehuacán sites; these were not developed locally and can have been introduced only from outside. Dry caves elsewhere in northern Mesoamerica show that other cultures paralleled the cultural events in Tehuacán. On the other hand, the highland lakes of the Valley of Mexico and elsewhere may well have supported sedentary communities subsisting on fish and wild vegetable foods as well as experimenting with amaranth and other crops as early as the fourth millennium B.C.

More than 24,000 maize specimens have come from the caves of the Tehuacán Valley. They document a long sequence of maize evolution, beginning with 71 small cobs from the lowest levels of the San Marcos Cave and from deep in the Coxcatlán Rock Shelter. The cobs are less than 20 mm (2 inches) long and lack the ability to disperse their kernels naturally, a clear sign of full domestication. We do not know how much earlier teosinte was transformed into maize, but Bruce Smith believes the process took place more than 250 km (155 miles) west of Tehuacán, in river valleys that flow from the highlands into the Pacific—areas where the wild teosinte most biochemically similar to maize still grows today. His theory has been supported by genetic research (Doebley et al., 1999).

Originally, Richard MacNeish (1970, 1978) used conventional radiocarbon dating to date the layers where the earliest maize cobs were found to between 5000 and 3500 B.C. New accelerator mass spectrometry (AMS) dates on actual early maize cobs from San Marcos date to about 3600 B.C., as much as 1500 years later than originally thought. Future discoveries may, of course, push the date much farther back into the past. Only a millennium later, the precursors of state-organized societies appeared in the Mexican lowlands (see Chapter 21).

San Marcos Cave
Maize
c. 3600 B.C.
and ? earlier

Bruce Smith (1998) estimates that maize was fully domesticated in southwestern Mexico in about 3600 B.C., maybe earlier, reaching Tehuacán some 300 to 400 years later and appearing on the Pacific and Gulf coasts by about 1450 B.C. But the date of its very first domestication remains a mystery (MacNeish and Eubanks, 2000).

Beans and Squash

The domestication of beans and squash may have occurred at much the same time as that of maize, but there is, at present, no archaeological evidence of the first stages of cultivation of these all-important staples. If Kent Flannery's hypothesis is correct, plant domestication in Mesoamerica was not so much an invention in one small area as a shift in ecological adaptation deliberately chosen by peoples living where economic strategies necessitated the intensive exploitation of plant foods. It appears that the evidence from both Tehuacán and Guilá Naquitz bears out this hypothesis.

Earlier theories of the origins of maize assumed that it was domesticated in many areas of the Americas from six or more presumed wild races. Modern pollen studies have shown convincingly that there was never a wild *Zea* with a wide range that extended outside southern Mexico and Guatemala. Apparently, a primitive form of domesticated eight-rowed maize (*maíz de ocho*) with soft glumes, represented at Tehuacán, was the common ancestral corn that spread thousands of miles from its original homeland after 3000 B.C.

🐾 Early Food Production in the Andes

Farming began in two areas of the Andean region: in the mountain highlands and along the low-lying, arid Pacific Coast.

The Highlands

The great eighteenth-century German naturalist Alexander von Humboldt was the first European scientist to explore the high Andes. He marveled at the great variety of wild plants and animals that thrived in the harsh and varied landscape of high peaks and mountain valleys. Only a handful of these many species had been tamed by the farmers living in the foothills of the great mountains. The cultivators lived in terraced environmental zones stacked one above the other on the sides of deep valleys.

Humboldt observed how the ever-growing human populations moved upward and outward into much harsher and more marginal environments. As they did so, they tried to encourage animals and plants living in one zone to adapt to another, to extend their range into unoccupied land. By seeding beans and cereal and transplanting roots and fruit trees, they struggled constantly to maintain a foothold outside natural faunal and floral ranges. The same upward assault continues to this day in the Andes, a quiet battle waged with robust root crops and hardy cereal strains (Moseley, 2000).

Five important Andean species were of vital importance to highland economies: the llama, the alpaca, and the guinea pig, as well as the potato and a grain crop, quinoa (*Chenopodium quinoa*). Llamas were perhaps domesticated alongside quinoa.

FIGURE 13.4
Panaulauca Cave, near Lake Junin, Peru. Excavations here yielded evidence of early quinoa cultivation and llama domestication by 2500 B.C.

Panaulauca Cave
2500 B.C.

Asana
2000 B.C.

Camelid bones from Panaulauca Cave, overlooking the Junin basin 150 km (93 miles) northwest of Lima, display a dramatic increase in younger animals by about 2500 B.C. (Figure 13.4). Eight hundred kilometers (500 miles) to the south, Mark Aldenderfer (1995) found a corral with animal dung dating to about 2000 B.C. at the Asana site southwest of Lake Titicaca. Llama (and perhaps alpaca) herding was widespread throughout the highlands and along the north coast of Peru by 900 B.C. Guinea pigs, an important wild food for many thousands of years, may have been domesticated in high mountain valleys at about the same time.

According to plant biologist Hugh Wilson (1988), quinoa was first domesticated in the south-central Andes. The new crop spread rapidly in the highlands and to the coast. The earliest archaeological occurrence is at Panaulauca Cave, where quinoa seeds with a thickness identical to that of modern domesticated forms comes from levels dating to about 3000 B.C. Direct AMS dates are still awaited, but there is good reason to believe this important highland staple was already widely cultivated by 2500 B.C.

At the time of European contact in the fifteenth century A.D., Andean farmers used literally hundreds of potato varieties. Four major strains were domesticated in the highlands, of which one, *Solanum tuberosum*, is now grown all over the world. Wild potatoes were an important food for highland Andean foragers from the time of earliest settlement. Well-documented potato tubers come from midden sites dating to about 2000 B.C. at the mouth of the Casma Valley on the Peruvian coast, but earlier specimens will, undoubtedly, come to light in the south-central highlands, where other animal and plant species, including lima beans, were domesticated between 3000 and 2000 B.C.

Some form of early plant tending may have persisted in the Andes for many centuries. In the same area, gourds, potatoes, and ulluco (a root crop) were probably grown by 8000 to 7000 B.C. but, like beans, served as a supplementary food and as a means of expanding into hitherto marginal areas. It was many thousands of years before these plants became economic staples.

In both highlands and lowlands, the beginnings of agriculture were a gradual adjustment, food production gradually supplanting gathering as the major subsistence activity.

The Peruvian Coast

On the Peruvian coast, fishing and the gathering of vegetable foods were supplemented by irrigation farming as early as 3000 B.C., and highland peoples were cultivating a

FIGURE 13.5 The Peruvian coast, one of the driest environments on earth.

variety of crops by the same time, crops that amplified the horizontally stacked natural resources of their mountain homeland.

The Peruvian coast forms a narrow shelf at the foot of the Andes, crossed by small river valleys descending from the mountains to the sea (Figure 13.5). These valleys are oases on the desert plain, with deep, rich soils, blooming vegetation, and plentiful water. For thousands of years, Peruvians have cultivated these valley floors, building their settlements, pyramids, and palaces at the edges of their agricultural land. Because conditions for preservation in this arid country are exceptional, the archaeological record is often quite complete. The coast itself forms a series of related microenvironments, such as rocky bars where shellfish are abundant and places where seasonal vegetable foods nourished by damp fogs are common.

One would assume that a combination of these microenvironments would provide a rich and uniform constellation of food resources that could normally be exploited with ease from relatively sedentary base camps (Moseley, 1975). However, the bountiful maritime environment is occasionally disrupted by a warm countercurrent known as El Niño, which can flow for as long as 12 months. El Niño occurs at highly irregular intervals, perhaps every six years, with really major events every quarter century or so. It reduces marine upwelling of cold water so much that in big El Niños, the fish migrate elsewhere, and thus one of the coastal people's staple diet sources is greatly reduced, although replaced to some extent by warm-water fish species. The greatest economic disruption occurred during major El Niños, but even lesser events could cause catastrophic rains that damaged crops. The El Niño phenomenon is so unpredictable that the people could not store food against its arrival; they also could not move from the coast, and they did not have the offshore vessels needed for deepwater fishing. Their only strategy, other than moving or starving, was to limit their population densities to the lowest levels of available natural resources until such time as they developed alternative food sources, such as maize grown by intensive irrigation agriculture.

The archaeological evidence along the Peruvian coast is incomplete for the period immediately preceding early food production. During the dry winter months, the inhabitants collected shellfish and other marine resources, and game and vegetable foods were more plentiful in the summer. After 5000 B.C., however, more efficient collecting strategies came into use, with greater attention to the maximal exploitation of natural food sources. Fishing, in particular, became more important. Between approximately 4200 and 2500 B.C., Peruvian coastal peoples depended on marine resources—fish, sea birds, and mollusks—for much of their diet. During the warmest and driest period after the Pleistocene, the coastal peoples moved closer to the shore, living in larger and more stable settlements. Along with the shift to more lasting coastal dwelling came the development of sophisticated equipment for deep-sea fishing.

Paloma
Before 5500 B.C.

As early as 5500 B.C., the coastal peoples were manipulating plants for their own purposes. The Paloma site on the central coast was occupied earlier than 5500 B.C.; it was a settled community with numerous simple huts and grass-lined pits where the inhabitants stored food for the occasional lean year. The people relied heavily on fishing and gathering but also manipulated some plant species, including tuberous begonias, gourds, squashes, and peppers. They also may have kept llamas, the same species used much later by the Incas for carrying loads in the Andes (Benfer, 1982).

Chilca
3800 to 2650 B.C.

A later coastal settlement that perpetuated the same subsistence pattern flourished at Chilca, 72 km (45 miles) south of present-day Lima. Frédéric Engel excavated refuse heaps there and radiocarbon-dated the earlier Chilca occupation to between 3800 and 2650 B.C. (Engel, 1963). When the site was in use, it probably lay near a reedy marsh, which provided both matting and building materials, as well as sites for small gardens (Figure 13.6). The Chilca people lived on sea mollusks, fish, and sea lions, and apparently hunted few land mammals. They cultivated jack beans and lima beans, gourds, and squashes, probably relying on river floods as well as rainfall for their simple agriculture.

The new emphasis on fish, an increased use of flour ground from wild grass seed, and the availability of cultivated squashes became new sources of nutrition for some coastal groups. This supply may ultimately have set off a sustained period of population growth. Certainly, the succeeding millennia saw many permanent settlements

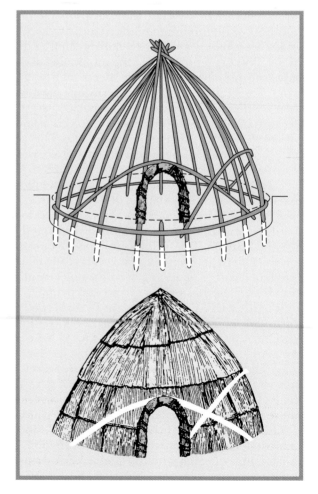

FIGURE 13.6 Reconstruction of a Chilca house. A circular structure, it had a domelike frame of canes bound with rope and covered with bundles of grass; the interior was braced with bones from stranded whales. Seven burials had been deposited in the house before it was intentionally collapsed on top of them. The skeletons were wrapped in mats and all buried at the same time, perhaps because of an epidemic. (After Willey, 1971.)

FIGURE 13.7 A double-headed snakelike figure with rock crabs appended to it, as it appears in a preceramic twined cloth fabric from Huaca Prieta, Peru. The rock crabs are revealed by plotting the warp measurements. The original length was approximately 40 cm (16 inches). The shaded area indicates the surviving textile. Double-headed motifs persisted through more than 3000 years of Andean art.

established near the ocean; the people combined agriculture with fishing and mollusk gathering. Domesticated cotton first appeared around 2500 B.C.

Squashes, peppers, lima beans, and other crops remained staple foods until recent times. Maize and other basic foods were either unknown or of lesser importance, if carbon isotopic analyses are any guide (Burger and van der Merwe, 1990). Agriculture remained a secondary activity much later than it did in Mesoamerica.

One later site is Huaca Prieta, a sedentary village that housed several hundred people on the north coast of Peru between 2500 and 1800 B.C. (Hyslop et al., 1987). The vast refuse mound there contains small one- or two-room houses built partially into the ground and roofed with timber or whalebone beams. The inhabitants were remarkably skillful cotton weavers who devised a sophisticated art style with animal, human, and geometric designs (Figure 13.7). (See also Chapter 22 for more discussion.)

Huaca Prieta
2500 to 1800 B.C.

Maize made its first appearance on the coast at Playa Culebras, another important and contemporary settlement south of Huaca Prieta (Moseley, 2000). The new crop was soon grown on a considerable scale in large irrigation systems in coastal river valleys. Irrigation required the efficient organization and deployment of people to dig and maintain canals, communal work on a scale that could be organized only by a system of taxation by labor, such as was commonplace in the Andes in later millennia. Much higher crop yields resulted as the focus of coastal population moved inland and local kin leaders and priests assumed much more prominent roles in society.

These social changes were reflected in more permanent housing and in large ceremonial pyramids and other public buildings. A complex of stone and mud mortar platforms lies at El Paraíso on the floodplain of the Chillón Valley, some distance from the sea (see Chapter 22). At least one mound had complexes of connected rooms built in successive stages. Settlements such as El Paraíso obviously depended more on agriculture than had earlier sites. By the time the temple complexes were built there, after 1800 B.C., loom-woven textiles and pottery had come into widespread use. All the major food plants that formed the basis of later Peruvian civilization were used.

🐾 Early Farmers in Southwestern North America

In 10,000 B.C., the Southwest of the United States was populated by hunter-gatherers whose culture was adapted to desert living (Cordell, 1997; Lekson, 1999; Plog, 1997). A distinctive foraging culture, the Cochise, flourished in southeastern Arizona and southwestern New Mexico from about this time. The Cochise people gathered many plant foods, including yucca seeds, cacti, and sunflower seeds. They used small milling stones, basketry, cordage, nets, and spear-throwers. Many features of their material

Cochise culture
10,000 B.C. and later

culture remained in use in later times, when cultivated plants were introduced into the Southwest (Matson, 1991).

The earliest Mesoamerican crops to cross the Rio Grande were maize, beans, and squash, which were probably cultivated for some time in northern Mexico before they reached the Southwest. The maize farmers of northern Mexico must have had sporadic contact with Archaic hunter-gatherers living in the deserts to the north, so it would have been easy for knowledge of plants, even gifts of seeds or seedlings, to pass from south to north. Probably, the opportunity for adopting crops was there long before anyone thought it worthwhile.

2500 B.C.   Between about 2500 and 100 B.C., the southwestern climate was relatively stable, perhaps somewhat wetter than it is today. However, it was an environment where hunting and gathering were high-risk occupations, mainly because rainfall patterns were always unpredictable. Despite generally low population densities, local populations may have occasionally risen to the point where there were food shortages. Domesticated plants like maize and beans had one major advantage: They might have low yields, but they were predictable. Cultivators of the new crops could control their location and their availability at different seasons by storing them carefully (Roth and Wellman, 2001).

Perhaps people living in the southern deserts of the Southwest began growing maize because it gave them food supplies to tide them over the lean months until spring. Farther north, in the uplands, growing crops would have enabled hunter-gatherer peoples to exercise more effective control over their environment. In the final analysis, it was probably a combination of rising populations and food shortages that caused the adoption of low-yielding forms of maize. Indeed, one could argue that the people accepted the new crops not because they wanted to become farmers but so they could be more effective foragers (Matson, 1991; Wills, 1989). Linda Cordell (1997) believes that southwestern groups adopted agriculture when what she calls a "situation of regional imbalance" developed between local populations and local resources. Such situations could result from either environmental degradation or population increases. She believes that climatic changes during the Archaic were not sufficient to cause local degradation. Thus, rising population densities may have been a factor.

Maize   The hardy, low-yielding maize that first entered the Southwest was the so-called
2000 to 1500 B.C.   Chapalote form, a small popcorn of great genetic diversity. It may have arrived during a period of higher rainfall between 2000 and 1500 B.C. It was soon crossbred with the indigenous wild teosinte, the result being a highly varied, more productive hybrid maize with larger cobs and more kernel rows.

Maize is a demanding crop, not a cereal that one can rely on to provide all one's food if one plants it casually and simply returns to harvest the resulting stand later, as is possible with many native plants like goosefoot. Maize also lacks two of the vital amino acids needed to make protein, lysine and tryptophan (high in squash), and it is only an effective staple when grown in combination with other crops like beans (lysine-rich) or squash (tryptophan-rich) that provide the necessary protein ingredients for a maize-based diet. Since most southwestern groups continued to enjoy a highly mobile lifeway for at least a millennium after maize first appeared north of the Rio Grande, there is good reason to believe that it first served as a casual supplement to wild plant resources. This was especially so in favorable areas where corn could be planted and then left largely untended, the process of cultivating it not being allowed to interfere with other subsistence activities.

However, a radically different maize, *maíz de ocho*, was the key to new cultural developments in the Southwest. *Maíz de ocho*, with its large, more productive, floury kernels, may have evolved from earlier, highly variable Chapalote maize. It may have resulted from a selection for a large-kerneled corn that was easier to grind and that flowered earlier, both important attributes in the hot and arid Southwest. Here, the irregular timing and distribution of rainfall restrict growing seasons, leaving little time for kernels to fill out. These characteristics of *maíz de ocho* were highly adaptive in North America, with its short growing seasons and very diverse, temperate environments.

Once again, precise AMS dating of actual maize cobs and other domesticated seeds provides the only unimpeachable evidence of cultivation. Broad application of the new dating method has narrowed the window for the arrival of maize and squash in the Southwest to a five-century span between 2000 and 1500 B.C. Both crops spread widely through the Southwest in later centuries, as did other maize forms. Southwestern farmers experimented with the new crop at many elevations. Across the border in northwestern Mexico, Robert Hard and John Roney (Hard and Roney, 1998) have excavated the Cerro Juanaqueña farming village with 7 km (5 miles) of stone house terraces, where maize cobs have been dated to about 1150 B.C. This was also a substantial farming settlement, equivalent to about a 135-room pithouse village, where native grasses may also have been processed.

Cerro Juanaqueña
c. 1150 B.C.

After 500 B.C., southwestern farmers combined maize with beans, for these legumes when underplanted with corn return vital nitrogen to the soil, nitrogen that is depleted by maize. (The earliest known beans date to about 520 B.C.) By planting the two crops together, the southwestern farmer could maintain the fertility of the soil for longer periods of time. The late arrival of beans was probably one reason why some time elapsed between the first appearance of maize and significant dependence on agriculture.

500 B.C.

In the Southwest, as in the Andes, the farmers were working close to the limits of corn's range. Maize is intolerant of too short a growing season, weak soil conditions, and such hazards as crop disease and strong winds. Most important were adequate soil moisture and water supplies. By careful seed selection, the farmers developed higher-elevation varieties with elongated cobs, distinctive root structures, and seeds that could be planted at considerable depths and thus nourished by the retained ground moisture. The farmers became experts at soil selection, favoring soils with good moisture-retaining properties on north- and east-facing slopes that received little direct sunlight. They also favored floodplains and canyon mouths, where the soil was naturally irrigated. They would divert water from seasonal streams, springs, or rainfall runoff to irrigate their lands. As in hunting and foraging, risk management was vital, so the cultivators widely dispersed their gardens to minimize the danger of local drought or flood. Over the centuries, a great diversity of highly effective dry-climate agricultural techniques developed throughout the Southwest.

Between A.D. 300 and 500, another complex of domestic tropical plants, including pigweed, cotton, and several varieties of beans, arrived in the region. (Cotton may have arrived earlier.) These tended to require more irrigation and were confined to the hot regions of the south, where the irrigation-experienced Hohokam adopted them (see next section).

The appearance of maize did not trigger a dramatic revolution in southwestern life. The earlier corns were not very productive and could be planted fairly casually. Under these circumstances, their yields were probably less than those of good piñon nut harvests. Eventually, however, they became of staple importance to many southwestern peoples who were now living in more permanent villages and in more restricted territories. As life became more sedentary, the people invested more time and energy in their crops, which provided protection from shortages of wild plant foods in their smaller territories (Rocek, 1995). The cultural changes of the period culminated in the great southwestern archaeological traditions: Hohokam, Mogollon, and Ancestral Pueblo (Cordell, 1997).

Hohokam

The Hohokam tradition has long been thought to have originated in the Cochise culture. The tradition probably emerged from indigenous roots in the first five centuries of the Christian era, acquiring much greater social complexity through time (Bayman, 2000; Crown, 1990; Crown and Judge, 1991; Gumerman, 1990). One major Hohokam settlement was the Snaketown site (so called after the O'odham name *Skoaquik*, "place of snakes") in the Gila River valley (Figure 13.8) (Haury, 1976).

Hohokam
A.D. 500 to 1450

Snaketown

The Hohokam enjoyed complex trading and ceremonial relationships with peoples living all over the Southwest and in northern Mexico. As time went on, this trade expanded, perhaps within the context of a common ceremonial system centered on the ball courts and other ceremonial structures at Snaketown and other focal points (Whalen and Minnis, 1996).

Hohokam subsistence was based on maize, beans, cucurbits, cotton, and other crops, as well as on gathering. The people planted their crops to coincide with the semiannual rainfall and flooding patterns. Where they could, they practiced irrigation from flowing rivers; otherwise, they cultivated floodplains and caught runoff from local storms with

FIGURE 13.8 The Hohokam settlement at Snaketown, Arizona, during 1965 excavations, showing kivas and dwellings.

dams, terraces, and other devices. Hohokam people occupied much of what is now southern Arizona. Their cultural heirs are the O'odham people of today.

Hohokam culture evolved slowly over as long as 2000 years. In about A.D. 650 to 700, a wave of Mesoamerican influence brought new varieties of maize, the appearance of platform mounds and ball or dance courts at Snaketown and elsewhere, and imports such as copper bells (Ericson and Baugh, 1993). There were at least five stages of the Hohokam culture, culminating in a classical period from approximately A.D. 1100 to 1450, when adobe compounds were built and canal irrigation was especially important.

Casas Grandes
A.D. 1400

Originally, anthropologists believed the Mexican influence was transitory and weak, but this belief changed after excavations at a prehistoric town named Casas Grandes in northern Chihuahua, Mexico (Schaafsma and Riley, 2000; Whalen and Minnis, 2001). (This site should not be confused with Casa Grande, Arizona.) At the height of its prosperity, around A.D. 1400, Casas Grandes boasted approximately 1600 rooms and housed more than 2400 people (Ravensloot, 1988). The dig showed that its inhabitants exchanged turquoise and painted pottery from the Southwest for marine shells, copper bells, and exotic birds (tropical macaws) from Mexico.

Mogollon

Mogollon
c. 300 B.C. to
A.D. 1000

The Mogollon tradition emerged from Archaic roots between 300 B.C. and A.D. 200 and disappeared as a separate entity between A.D. 850 and 1000 to 1150, when it became part of various local traditions (Haury, 1985). The Mogollon is well known from dry caves in New Mexico as an agricultural tradition in which hunting and gathering in the highlands were always important. Mogollon agriculture depended on direct rainfall, with only very limited use of irrigation. The people lived in small villages of pit dwellings with timber frames and mat or brush roofs. Their material culture was utilitarian and included milling stones, digging sticks, bows and arrows, fine baskets, and characteristic red on brown pottery.

At least six regional variants of the Mogollon culture are known, and there were five chronological stages, the fifth ending approximately 500 years ago. Early Mogollon villages were often located on high promontories close to fertile lands. The settlement pattern varied from area to area but had a tendency toward larger sites and increased populations throughout the life of the tradition. By A.D. 1350, pueblos of several hundred rooms had developed in some areas, but by this time the Mogollon tradition had become part of the Ancestral Pueblo tradition. Much of the Mogollon area was completely abandoned by A.D. 1500.

Ancestral Pueblo

The Ancestral Pueblo (formerly called *Anasazi*) tradition is, in general terms, ancestral to the cultures of the modern Pueblo Indians: the Hopi, the Zuni, and others (Cordell, 1997; Plog, 1997). Its emergence is conventionally dated to A.D. 1, but this is a purely arbitrary date, for the Ancestral Pueblo tradition's roots lie in Archaic cultures that flourished for a long time before. The Ancestral Pueblo tradition is centered in the Four Corners area, where Utah, Arizona, Colorado, and New Mexico meet. The Ancestral Pueblo people made heavy use of wild vegetable foods, even after they took up maize agriculture seriously, after A.D. 400. Most of their farming depended on dry agriculture and seasonal rainfall, although they, like the Hohokam, used irrigation techniques when practicable. They made use of flood areas, where the soil would remain damp for weeks after sudden storms. Moisture in the flooded soil could be used to germinate seeds in the spring and to bring ripening crops to fruition after later rains. However, this is a very high-risk type of agriculture, and the Ancestral Pueblo relied on wild resources to carry them through lean years.

Ancestral Pueblo chronology is well established, thanks to the use of tree-ring dating on beams from abandoned pueblos. There are at least six Basketmaker and Pueblo subdivisions of the Ancestral Pueblo; each marked a gradual increase in the importance of agriculture and the emergence of some larger sites. By approximately A.D. 800, the basic Ancestral Pueblo settlement pattern had evolved and above-ground houses were being substituted for the pit dwellings of earlier centuries. The pit dwellings themselves developed into *kivas*, subterranean ceremonial structures that existed in every large village. Pueblos, large settlements of contiguous dwellings, became the rule after A.D. 900 to 1000, with clusters of "rooms" serving as homes for separate families or lineages. Such small towns became more common after A.D. 900.

One major center of Ancestral Pueblo culture developed in Chaco Canyon, New Mexico (Lekson, 1999; Sebastian, 1992) (see Site box). The first sedentary villages appeared there in about A.D. 490. Between the ninth and tenth centuries, summer rainfall was highly variable. Instead of dispersing in response to drought, the Chaco Ancestral Pueblo built a series of "great houses" at the junctions of major drainages. The largest of them, Pueblo Bonito was a huge D-shaped complex of at least 600 rooms rising several stories around the rim of an arc, housing at least 1000 people (Figure 13.9). The

Ancestral Pueblo
A.D. 1 to 1300

Chaco Canyon
A.D. 490 to 1130

Pueblo Bonito

FIGURE 13.9 Pueblo Bonito in Chaco Canyon. The round structures are kivas.

SITE

The Chaco Phenomenon

By 1050, an estimated 5500 people lived in Chaco Canyon, New Mexico, maintaining contacts over an enormous area of the Southwest, as the so-called Chaco Phenomenon reached its apogee. By A.D. 1115, at least 70 communities were dispersed over more than 64,750 sq km (25,000 square miles) of northwest New Mexico, and parts of southern Colorado were linked through the socioeconomic and ritual networks centered on Chaco Canyon.

The Chaco Phenomenon was the center of a vast regional system that extended far beyond the San Juan basin and is famous for its "road system." Over 650 km (400 miles) of unpaved ancient trackways link Chaco in an intricate web with over 30 outlying settlements. The "roads" are up to 12 m (40 feet) wide and were cut a few inches into the soil or marked by low banks or stone walls. Sometimes, the road makers simply cleared the vegetation and loose soil or stones from the pathway, lining some segments with boulders. The roads run straight for long distances, in one instance as long as 95 km (60 miles). They do not follow contours, but change direction in abrupt turns, with stairways and ramps to surmount steep obstacles. These may be little more than toeholds or elaborate stairways with wide steps cut out of bedrock or formed from masonry blocks (Figure 13.10). Each approaches the canyon, then descends via stonecut steps down the cliffs to the valley floor. There they merge in the narrow defiles and split, each leading to a different great house.

By using aerial photographs, fieldworkers have been able to trace roads extending from Chaco almost to the Colorado–New Mexico border and Aztec Ruins, some 80 km (50 miles) away. Other roads connect Chaco to natural resource source areas in modern-day Zuni country and elsewhere. The system may have extended as far north as the San Juan Range in the Rocky Mountains to the north, the Mogollon Mountains to the south, and from the turquoise mines near Santa Fe in the east to the Little Colorado River in the west.

Chaco road construction must have involved the deployment of large numbers of people and considerable group organization. Were they highways for transporting valuable natural resources to major pueblos? Or were they pilgrim roads? Did they have some much more profound spiritual importance? One prevalent hypothesis argues that without draft animals or wheeled carts, the Chaco people had no use for formal roads for their everyday business. Originally, perhaps, people traveled from outlying communities to Chaco to acquire turquoise objects manufactured there, to trade food for ritual paraphernalia. In time, this trade became institutionalized in regular ceremonies and festivals, where people gathered from many miles around for seasonal rituals and where leaders from widely dispersed communities gathered to cement political and economic alliances. Each member of the network would have complex obligations to fulfill, among them, presumably, the supplying of people to construct and maintain the road system, to transport wooden beams for building the great houses in Chaco (more than 200,000 were needed to build them), and for many communal tasks. In other words, the Chaco system was a mechanism for integrating a large number of communities scattered widely in a harsh and unpredictable environment.

This ingenious theory stumbles on two points. First, the focus of Ancestral Pueblo life was the household and ties of kin, which were the means by which people fed themselves and passed on accumulated expertise about making a living from one generation to the next. Second, many of the Chaco roads go nowhere, although they are linked to a great house or kiva. We Westerners tend to think of roads as traveling from A to B, which means that we have tended to join incomplete segments of Chacoan roads with straight dotted lines. The roads may not have actually been joined. While major north and south tracks radiated from Chaco, only about 250 km (155 miles) of the roads have been verified on the ground.

A more likely explanation lies in Pueblo cosmology. The so-called "Great North Road" travels 63 km (40 miles) north from Chaco before it disappears abruptly in Kutz Canyon. North is the primary direction among modern-day Keresan-speaking Pueblo peoples, who may have ancestry among the Chaco people. North led to the origin, the place where the spirits of the dead traveled. Perhaps the Great North Road was an umbilical cord to the underworld and a conduit of spiritual power. The Keresan also believe in a Middle Place, a point where the four cardinal directions converged. Pueblo Bonito is laid out according to these directions and may have served as Chaco's Middle Place. Thus, Chaco and its trackways may have formed a sacred landscape that gave order to the world and linked outlying communities with a powerful Middle Place through spiritual ties that remained even as many households moved away from the canyon.

Think of a giant ideological spider's web with a lattice of obligations among its component parts, and you probably have a credible model for Chaco's role in the eleventh-century Ancestral Pueblo world. Archaeologist Gwinn Vivian calls the landscape a powerful statement, what he calls "We the Chaco."

FIGURE 13.10 Jackson Stairway, Chaco Canyon. Rock-cut steps into the walls of the canyon formed part of the Chacoan road system.

room complexes surrounded courts, with the highest stories at the back. They formed a blank wall; a line of one-story rooms cut off the fourth side. Within the court lay the kivas, usually one great kiva and often several smaller ones. The great kivas were up to 18.2 m (60 feet) in diameter, with wide masonry benches encircling the interior. The roof was supported by four large masonry pillars or upright logs placed around a central hearth. A staircase leading from the floor of the kiva to the large room above it gave access to the sacred precinct.

The Ancestral Pueblo enjoyed a relatively elaborate material culture at the height of their prosperity; at this time, they were making distinctive black-on-white pottery, well-formed baskets, and fine sandals. However, their architecture was neither very sophisticated nor particularly innovative. Rocks and mud were formed into boxlike rooms; a roof of mud rested on horizontal timbers. Room after room was added as the need arose, built from local materials and in a simple architectural style entirely appropriate to its environment.

Tree rings tell us that a great drought in A.D. 1130 endured for a half century. The Chaco population dispersed into smaller settlements as the political gravity of Ancestral Pueblo culture shifted to the Four Corners region. During the twelfth century, large pueblos developed in the Montezuma Valley and outlying regions like Mesa Verde. Some communities moved from the open to under cliff overhangs, the so-called cliff dwellings (Figure 13.11). Some of the features of these sites, such as turrets and loopholed walls, appear to have been defensive (Crown and Judge, 1991). All these larger pueblos were probably communities run for the collective good, with at least some ranking of society under a chieftain. In modern Hopi society, clan superiority and kinship lineages play an important role in the election of leaders. Thrust into close intimacy by the nature of pueblo architecture, the people developed well-integrated religious and ceremonial structures to counteract the tensions of close living. Another serious drought cycle between A.D. 1276 and 1299 saw dozens of Ancestral Pueblo settlements large and small disperse into less affected regions, where they joined groups ancestral to modern Pueblo Indian communities (Adler, 1996) (Figure 13.12).

The southwestern farmer won success by skillfully using scarce water resources and bringing together soil and water by means of dams, floodwater irrigation, and other systems for distributing runoff. Planting techniques were carefully adapted to desert conditions, and myriad tiny gardens supplied food for each family or lineage. This successful adaptation is also reflected in the architecture.

Mesa Verde
A.D. 1130

FIGURE 13.11 The Cliff Palace at Mesa Verde, with three subterranean, and one roofed, kivas in the foreground.

FIGURE 13.12   A painted Mimbres bowl from the North American Southwest.

⁔⁔⁔ Preagricultural and Agricultural Societies in Eastern North America

The Archaic hunter-gatherer traditions of eastern North America enjoyed many regional variations in material culture; these occurred because the people concentrated on different locally abundant food sources (see Sassaman and Anderson, 1996; Yerkes, 1988). In general, however, the lifeway was similar among them: a seasonal one, based on a very broad spectrum of game and vegetable foods. As long as the population density was low, every band could react relatively easily to changes in local conditions. Since many of their favorite vegetable foods were subject to cycles of lean and abundant years, a flexibility in choice and movement was essential. However, as populations grew slowly throughout the Archaic, this flexibility was increasingly restricted and the people tended to specialize in local resources that were available most of the year. They developed better storage techniques and fostered closer contacts with their neighbors through exchange networks that handled foodstuffs and other commodities. The development of these types of response may have required more complex social organization than the simple band structure of earlier times, and it is no coincidence that burial patterns during the late Archaic, in about 1700 B.C., reflect greater differentiation in social status. Cemeteries may also have served as territorial markers.

Late Archaic
1700 B.C.

Under these circumstances, perhaps it was inevitable that late Archaic peoples in the Eastern Woodlands turned to the deliberate cultivation of food plants to supplement wild plant yields. They did so quite independently of other centers of plant domestication (B. Smith, 1998). The four seeds eventually taken under domestication were collected from rich wild stands along river floodplains for many centuries before they were cultivated deliberately. Bruce Smith notes that goosefoot, marsh elder, and the gourd flourished on naturally disturbed flood soils, where they produced abundant seeds in the wild. Sunflowers had numerous small seed heads, which propagated rapidly, and were valued for their oil. Smith hypothesizes that the inhabitants of large riverside settlements gathered seeds from stands of floodplain weeds. Some of the harvested seeds dropped onto disturbed soil, where they established new colonies. Within 50 to 100 years, Smith believes, the foragers would have domesticated the native plants, first by weeding their stands and then by deliberate planting.

AMS dates suggest that such planting began as early as 2500 B.C., all four seeds coming under cultivation within five centuries. This development took hold not at one location but within a number of more or less isolated hunter-gatherer societies living in small river valleys. At first, cultivated plants seem to have filled a small niche in a diverse diet, which comprised game, fish, waterfowl, and plant foods of all kinds. Several plant species were grown outside their natural ranges, but it seems likely that the domestication of these native plants first took hold in locations like the lower Mississippi River Delta, where wild ancestors of these species still grow in abundance. None of the domesticates required the kind of wholesale adaptive shift in year-round routine that maize cultivation demanded of its practitioners.

This form of supplementary cultivation of native plants continued for more than 1500 years. But by 200 B.C., people throughout the region had shifted to a greater reliance on local seed plants, centuries before maize was introduced into the Eastern Woodlands.

🐾 Moundbuilder Cultures

After 2000 B.C., when eastern North American societies still relied heavily on hunting and foraging, we find increasing signs of preoccupation with burial and with life after death, a new ideological foundation for local society in eastern North America. These burial cults shared many practices, among them cremation, the deposition of exotic objects with the dead, and the custom of building burial mounds.

More intensive exploitation of food resources, greater sedentism, regular social interaction and exchange, a degree of social ranking, and increased ceremonialism—these were the culminating elements in late Archaic life in eastern North America. While most groups still lived in temporary encampments or even sizable base camps used for most, if not all, of the year, the Poverty Point culture of the lower Mississippi Valley and the adjacent Gulf Coast offers a dramatic contrast.

Poverty Point culture
2200 to 600 B.C.

The earliest Poverty Point region sites date to about 2200 B.C., forming the oldest component in a cultural sequence that lasted for over 1500 years. Poverty Point itself is the nexus of the culture and stands on Macon Ridge overlooking the Mississippi floodplain, near the confluence of six rivers (Figure 13.13). This was a strategic point from which to trade upstream and downstream, to receive and exchange raw materials and finished products. Some of the exotic materials at Poverty Point came from as far away as 997 km (620 miles).

FIGURE 13.13 Poverty Point, Louisiana. An aerial view taken about a half century ago, showing the concentric earth ridges. The ridges and intervening swales (hollows) show up as light and dark stripes in the fields.

Poverty Point, with its great earthworks, is a remarkable contrast to the humble base camps elsewhere in eastern North America, although it was foreshadowed by other large Archaic earthworks. Six concentric semicircular earthen ridges are divided into segments. They average about 25 m (82 feet) wide and 3 m (10 feet) high and are set about 40 m (131 feet) apart. Their significance is a complete mystery, beyond a suspicion that they were connected with astronomical observations. To the west lies an artificial mound more than 20 m (66 feet) high and more than 200 m (660 feet) long. A person standing on this mound can sight the vernal and autumnal equinoxes directly across the center of the earthworks to the east. These are the points where the sun rises on the first days of spring and fall. Built between 1000 and 600 B.C., Poverty Point itself took more than 35,000 cu m (1,236,007 cubic feet) of basket-loaded soil, a task that would have taken 1350 adults laboring 70 days a year for three years to complete. Estimates of Poverty Point's population are hard to come by, but even a population of 1000 people makes the site unique for the period. The significance of this extraordinary site and the associated culture is still little understood (Gibson, 2001). The Poverty Point culture went into decline in about 600 B.C., just as moundbuilding reached new heights in the Ohio Valley, to the northeast.

Adena

By 700 B.C., the people of eastern North America enjoyed a tradition of long-distance trading that had flourished for centuries. The trade carried not only prosaic commodities such as stone ax blades but also large quantities of prestigious imports such as conch shells and copper artifacts, most of which were deposited in the graves of their owners. These exotic objects may have been status symbols, indicating some social differentiation within groups. As far as is known, these artifacts were buried with their owners at death, and the special status associated with them was not passed on from one generation to the next (Yerkes, 1988).

Between 500 B.C. and about A.D. 400, the Adena culture flourished in the Ohio Valley. The people lived in seasonal camps, relying not only on hunting and gathering but also on the cultivation of squash and local starchy and oily plants. Major camps lay close to ceremonial burial mounds. The construction of even the largest mounds involved relatively few people. This moundbuilding and other earthwork construction may have reflected a strengthening of group identity and the establishment of social and territorial boundaries, which were often marked by cemeteries.

Adena
500 B.C. to A.D. 400

At the same time, the Adena groups developed large exchange networks that extended over enormous distances, the prototypes of even more elaborate trade routes in later centuries. Powerful loyalties to local lineages caused the people to commemorate their dead not only with imposing burial mounds but with extensive earthworks as well.

Adena earthworks follow the contours of flat-topped hills and form circles, squares, and other shapes, enclosing areas perhaps as much as 105 m (350 feet) in diameter. The earth used to make the enclosures came from just inside the walls, giving a false impression of an interior moat. These were probably ceremonial compounds rather than defensive earthworks. The Adena people built large burial mounds, some placed inside enclosures, others standing independently outside. Most are communal rather than individual graves. The most important people lie in log-lined tombs. Their corpses are smeared with red ocher or graphite. Nearby lie ceremonial soapstone pipes and tablets engraved with curving designs or birds of prey. Some prestigious individuals were buried inside enclosures or mortuary structures, which were burned down as part of the funeral rites. Occasionally, the burial chamber was left open so that bodies could be added later. Dozens of people from miles around piled basketfuls of earth to form an imposing burial mound for a single individual (Clay, 1998). More often, the mounds were piled up gradually over the years, as layers of bodies were added. However, the vast majority of less important Adena people were cremated; only their ashes were placed inside the burial mound.

Adena was not so much a culture as a ceremonial complex that flourished over an enormous area of eastern North America. "Adena" is a convenient archaeological term that covers dozens of local early Woodland cultures in the Eastern Woodlands, cultures that were contemporary, often close neighbors, and interacting with one another continuously.

Hopewell

Hopewell
A.D. 1 to 400

For nearly 1000 years, the Midwest experienced a dramatic flowering of artistic traditions and of long-distance trade that brought copper from the upper Great Lakes region, obsidian from Yellowstone, and mica from the southern Appalachians (Baugh and Ericson, 1994). Nowhere is this flowering better documented than in the so-called Hopewell tradition, a later elaboration of eastern North American ceremonial traditions that first appeared in Illinois in about A.D. 1. The Hopewell people themselves lived in relatively small settlements and used only stone artifacts to plant, hunt game, and fish. They wore leather and woven clothes of pliable fibers. Much wealth and creative skill were lavished on a few individuals and on their life after death. At first glance, the exotic artifacts and ritual traditions of the Hopewell culture seem completely alien to the indigenous cultures, but a closer look reveals the links between the underlying traditions and the magnificent art created by Hopewell artisans. Their manufactures were traded in a vast exchange network of prestige goods, which moved between local elites and were used in status-enhancing ceremonies and in burial rituals. Such exchanges also linked kin leaders with lasting obligations to one another.

The cult objects associated with this trade are found in dozens of Hopewell burial mounds and tell us something of the rank and social roles of the people with whom they are buried. Some of the exotic grave goods, such as pipe bowls or axes, were buried as gifts from living clan members to a dead leader. Others were personal possessions, cherished weapons, or sometimes symbols of status or wealth. Hopewell graves contain soapstone pipe bowls in the form of beavers, frogs, birds, bears, and even humans. Skilled smiths fashioned thin copper sheets into head and breast ornaments that bear elaborate animal motifs hammered in relief (Figure 13.14). There were copper axes and arrowheads, trinkets, and beads. Specialists cut mica sheets into striking and lustrous silhouettes of human figures, bird talons, and abstract designs. A few artisans produced most of these artifacts, perhaps in workshops within large earthwork complexes, themselves close to major sources of important raw materials. Some elaborate artifacts may also have been manufactured at special "mortuary camps" for use in the graves of high-status individuals. The same prestigious objects may have been distributed via the trade networks that carried foodstuffs and tools throughout Hopewell territory. Many of them show surprisingly little wear, as if they were soon buried with their owners.

By this time, burial mounds were much more elaborate than those of the Adena predecessors (Greber and Ruhl, 1989). A Hopewell burial mound complex in Ohio, appropriately named Mound City, contains no fewer than 24 mounds inside an enclosure covering 15.2 ha (32 acres) (Figure 13.15). The Newark, Ohio, Hopewell earthworks cover 1040 ha (4 square miles). Farther afield, the Crook's Mound in Louisiana rises 12 m (40 feet) and is more than 30 m (100 feet) across. Its builders followed the established custom when they buried 168 bodies within an extensive earthen platform. Then they placed another 214 corpses on the platform before covering the entire sepulcher with a large mound.

We still know little of Hopewell society, despite the excavation of large mound and earthwork complexes like Marksville in the lower Mississippi Valley. William Dancey and Paul Pacheco (1997) believe that Hopewell communities were made up of single- or multiple-family households scattered across the landscape but were concentrated around centrally located burial mounds and ceremonial precincts. These households were stable, long-term settlements, occupied by people who not only foraged but cultivated indigenous domesticated plants (Wymer, 1996). A dispersed settlement pattern was necessary to accommodate the often conflicting demands of cultivation and intensive foraging activity. Many local communities lie in areas defined by local drainage systems, with household sites, specialized camps, and ritual precincts, normally close to the center of the community and the focus of local life. While individual households were stable units, the constant hiving off of new generations made for a dynamic settlement pattern, where different settlements were occupied for shorter or

(a)

(b)   (c)

FIGURE 13.14   Hopewell ceremonial artifacts found in burial mounds. (a) Raven or crow in beaten copper; (b) bird claw in mica; (c) soapstone frog, Such objects were high-status possessions, often symbols of rank, perhaps acquired in ceremonial gift exchanges. ([b] The Field Museum, Neg. #A90925, Chicago.)

high-status possessions

longer periods of time, with the number of settlement clusters increasing through time. Ceremonial precincts also changed continually through time, with the building of new burial mounds, fresh earthworks, and other features.

On a larger scale, neighboring communities may have formed what one might call "peer polities," anchored by centrally located earthworks and burial mounds.

FIGURE 13.15   Circular Hopewell mounds at Mound City National Monument, Ohio. Each covers a charnel house where cremated dead were deposited.

Hopewell, Newark, and other earthwork groups may represent examples of such larger polities, each strategically located at the intersections of different physiographic provinces. This may reflect a basic self-sufficiency in foodstuffs during good years, but also the need for intercommunity exchange to balance out shortages during cycles of drought and other scarce times caused by short-term climatic shifts. These exchange links also extended to outlying areas where contemporary societies still retained strong Adena ties and did not adopt Hopewell beliefs.

The intricate Hopewell exchange systems endured in the Midwest until about A.D. 400. Then the networks collapsed, interregional art styles broke down, and moundbuilding by entire communities was interrupted. Three theories seek to explain the collapse. The first argues that horticulture became so successful that the ecological incentives for long-distance exchange, for reciprocal gift-giving, were removed. There was much less variation in resource availability between local areas, so ample food was available closer to hand. By the same token, local leadership by talented individuals became less important (Braun, 1989).

The second hypothesis argues that any form of agriculture may increase the carrying capacity of the land, but it carries serious risks with it owing to variations in rainfall and other natural phenomena from one year to the next. The best strategies for minimizing such risks are those of developing food storage systems, diversifying the crops planted and growing them in different, considerably separated fields, and by developing reciprocal ties with kin living outside the immediate local area. Much of Hopewell exchange may have been based initially on competition of individuals vying for prestige and success, rather than on the need to provide for mutual assistance in scarce times. Thus, goes the argument, long-distance exchange networks and personal prestige became less important as maize cultivation became more important, more intensive, and more successful.

William Dancey (1996) argues that specialized food production became common among dispersed, stable groups, of which Hopewell was one, during the first millennium B.C. More fixed territories resulted, which contained such permanent features as earthworks. Population growth resulting from the higher production rates of more specialized production sparked competition for good arable land. This, Dancey argues, may have been the period when Hopewell ceremonialism flowered, with enormous expenditure of energy, perhaps even meant as a device to control growing population. Now larger settlements dominated the landscape. By this time, Hopewell ceremonialism had vanished, since the densely settled communities no longer needed to come together for religious observances at central places, as their more dispersed Hopewell predecessors had done.

None of these theories is fully supported by the scanty archaeological data, but only a few centuries later, between A.D. 800 and 1200, maize cultivation spread throughout eastern North America. Maize may have spread from the Southwest, in forms preadapted to high altitudes and lower temperatures, along riverine areas toward the Northeast. Midwestern twelve-row, or Chapalote, maize was known to southeastern populations by the late first millennium A.D., but it was some time before its dietary staple potential was realized in the late Woodland and Mississippian cultures of the Midwest (B. Smith, 1998). The lush floodplain of the lower Mississippi was ideal for cultivating high-yielding maize strains and, in later centuries, supported considerably denser populations.

Mississippian

Between A.D. 1 and about 450, two important cultural developments emerged in the Southeast. First, mortuary customs became far more elaborate. Second, there are signs that some individuals achieved greater social and political importance in what had been relatively egalitarian societies. These four and one-half centuries saw the construction of hundreds of low, oval, or circular burial mounds throughout much of the Southeast. The burials within them varied considerably in their elaborations, a reflection of the increased social complexity that accompanied accelerating population growth, intercommunity exchange, and more intensive cultivation of native plants and later, maize, between A.D. 450 and 800. Beans arrived after the full potential of maize agriculture was realized. They had not only the advantage of a high protein value but also the asset of compensating for the amino acid deficiencies of corn. These developments were to culminate in a series of remarkable riverine cultures after A.D. 900, in the great Mississippian tradition of the South, the Southeast, and the southern Midwest (D. Anderson, 1994).

The underlying catalysts for the brilliant flowering of Mississippian culture after A.D. 1000 were, first, widespread political and religious changes that saw the appearance of important chieftains; second, the widespread adoption of maize cultivation throughout the Eastern Woodlands after A.D. 800; and last, the efflorescence of sacred ceremonial complexes that led to the emergence of numerous powerful chiefdoms throughout the Southeast.

Mississippian
A.D. 900 to European contact

Major political changes began before widespread maize cultivation, with important thresholds that saw the abrupt appearance of complex chiefdoms at Cahokia and, later, at Moundville and elsewhere. Lesser chiefs must have emulated their more powerful peers in the regions between the major centers, but the sheer size and power of Cahokia and later large centers may have stunted the full historical potential of neighboring areas (D. Anderson, 1997). But what were the remarkable political and religious institutions that distinguished the Mississippian from its predecessors?

The term *Mississippian* defies precise definition. Bruce Smith (1992) used the term to define ancient populations living in the Eastern Woodlands from A.D. 1000 to 1500/1600 that "had a ranked form of social organization, and had developed a specific complex adaptation to linear, environmentally circumscribed floodplain habitat zones." Smith's definition is flexible and allows for great differences in social organization. Another archaeologist, James Knight (1986), believes that distinctive social and religious institutions set the Mississippian apart from other cultural traditions. He argues convincingly that the religious institutions of Mississippian societies were highly distinctive, "a prevalent variety of socio-religious organization crosscutting other cultural and ecological boundaries, recognizable by virtue of shared classes of sacra [sacred artifacts]."

Chiefly Warfare Cult (The So-Called "Southern Cult").

Knight envisages a pluralistic Mississippian institutionalized religion, with a chiefly cult of elite nobles based on warfare, which can be identified by exotic motifs and symbols and by costly raw materials such as seashell or imported copper. Such objects occur in elite burials, together with war axes, maces, and other weapons. These warrior symbols occur alongside other artifacts that bear exotic cosmic imagery, depicting animals, humans, and mythic beasts. This symbolic imagery bound together warfare, cosmology, and nobility into a coherent whole. Some of these categories of artifacts were used as markers of chiefly office, which varied from one location to another.

Dozens of Mississippian cemeteries and mound centers contain finely made pottery and other artifacts associated with this chiefly cult, bearing elaborate decoration and distinctive artistic motifs. They include axes with head and shaft carved from a single piece of stone, copper pendants adorned with circles or weeping eyes, shell disks or gorgets showing woodpeckers, rattlesnakes, elaborately decorated clay pots and effigy vessels, copper plates, and engraved shell cups adorned with male figures in ceremonial dress (Figure 13.16) (Brain and Phillips, 1995).

The themes and motifs have many features in common over a vast area. Generations of archaeologists have grouped these artifact styles and art themes into a distinctive "Southern Cult," which appeared to link sites hundreds of kilometers apart and which originated in earlier centuries. The oldest art objects of any complexity found in the Eastern Woodlands are found in early and middle Woodland sites. These can be shown to have general connections with the basic themes of Southern Cult art. Such themes include widespread use of bird symbolism, "weeping eyes," and circles and crosses. They appear to have been common to all eastern societies, themes that were used, refined, and developed as new traditions and beliefs arose.

The term *Southern Cult* is probably somewhat outdated, for it reflects a complex, highly variable set of religious mechanisms that defy precise definition that supported the authority of local chieftains (for a discussion of the cult, see Muller, 1989).

FIGURE 13.16   Southern Cult. A human effigy vessel with weeping eyes. Themes such as this link Mississippian art traditions to a wide area of the South and the Southeast.

Earth/Fertility.   A second Mississippian cult, a communal earth/fertility cult, was associated with the earthen platform mounds, which may seem like unlikely religious artifacts. However, the act of rebuilding them, of adding additional layers of earth over burials, served as a symbol of renewal, which renewed the earthwork as much as it did human life. The earthen platform served as the earth, a symbolism that endured into historic times. There are historically documented connections between additions to platform mounds and the communal "green corn" ceremony, which celebrated the new harvest and the fertility of the earth. The quadrilateral, flat-topped design of many platform mounds may represent the southeastern Indian belief that the earth was a flat surface oriented toward four quarters of the world.

Ancestor Worship.   Still a third cult may have mediated between the two dominant ones, this one represented by well-preserved temple statuary representing both men and women kneeling in deathlike poses. Such figures occur in many Mississippian centers, among them Moundville and Spiro, as well as dozens of smaller sites. Knight believes that ethnohistorical data link such statues to ancestor cults, which were organized by temple priests, but archaeological finds add little to the ethnohistorical sources.

This triad of Mississippian cult institutions had distinctive features. The warfare cult was exclusive, confined to certain kin groups, and gave privileged rights to chiefly posts within these groups, and in its cosmological aspects serving to underpin and sanctify political power by means of chiefly rituals. In contrast, the platform mound cults were based on communal rituals that involved entire kin groups and communities who labored in their mound construction as part of ceremonies that drew on deeply felt religious beliefs common to all society, such as survived among southeastern Indians until historic times. Priests supervised ancestor cults. They were also responsible for maintaining temples, burial houses, sacred fires, and mortuary rituals. These ancestor rituals, supervised by individuals with special supernatural powers, must have intermeshed with both chiefly and communal cults, to the point that they may have mediated between different interests within society.

James Knight theorizes that the sudden expansion of the Mississippian tradition unfolded within the context of developing political and religious institutions. Newly emerging cults, which themselves developed from much earlier and simpler institutions, provided a framework of changing social forms, where coexisting cult institutions struggled constantly to assimilate ever-expanding spheres of influence by manipulating supernatural beliefs.

If Knight is correct, then the development of the Mississippian tradition was a complex process driven more by political and social changes than by economic considerations. The powerful Mississippian cults, which defined both chiefly and communal society, cut across the South and Southeast and all their different local cultural and ecological boundaries. They created a dynamic, constantly changing, and highly factionalized society. The archaeological record documents the tremendous variation in social complexity in the Mississippian culture area, with major centers like Cahokia in the so-called American Bottom near the modern city of St. Louis at one end of the spectrum and hundreds of small, local centers and minor chiefdoms at the other.

The Mississippian tradition's ultimate roots lay in much earlier Archaic and Woodland cultures that had flourished long before maize agriculture became widespread in the great river valleys of eastern North America (Cobb and Garrow, 1996). But it was the widespread cultivation of maize and beans that helped foster higher population densities and the more complex social and political organization of the centuries immediately before European contact in the sixteenth century. Most likely, the shift to maize agriculture was the result of stress largely precipitated by population pressure or the demands of elites. Such stress could easily have occurred even if plenty of land was available because the start-up labor needed to create maize gardens was much larger than that required for native plants. Begun initially to create more supplemental foods, the new agriculture transformed valley landscapes in such ways that hunting and foraging soon provided less food for the energy expended than maize cultivation. Within a short time, an entirely new economic pattern came into being.

Between A.D. 800 and 1000, there were significant changes in subsistence, material culture, trade, and settlement patterns over much of the South and the Southeast. The Mississippian people not only grew maize, squashes, and beans but also relied heavily on seasonal crops of nuts, fruits, berries, and seed-bearing plants. They hunted deer, raccoon, and turkey and took thousands of migratory waterfowl in spring and fall. Fish and waterfowl may have constituted up to 50 percent of the diet of the villagers living within the floodplain. Maize and bean agriculture now transformed many valley landscapes. Many of the culture changes of these centuries, including new pottery forms, platform mounds, and substantial rectangular houses, may have reflected the adoption of maize not only as a crop to be eaten at once but also as one to be stored for use throughout the year.

Settlements became more complex. Some were palisaded, perhaps for defense. More formal layouts included grouping houses around open plazas and mounds. Regional Mississippian societies developed in river valleys, large and small, over a large area at about the same time and interacted with one another for several centuries (Cobb and Garrow, 1996). Many Mississippian societies flourished on river valley soils fertilized by waterborne nutrients. It has always been assumed that this distribution occurred because of the availability of easily tilled soils. In fact, we know now that this restricted distribution was the result of the complex adaptation that the people developed in an area with well-defined bands of arable soils fertilized by spring floods just before planting season. They lived in valleys with many lakes and swamps, where fish trapped by receding floods were plentiful and migrating waterfowl paused to rest in spring and fall.

The process of volatile political change is best known from the great center at Cahokia, Illinois, one of North America's most spectacular sites. Sedentary villages existed at or near the Cahokia site after A.D. 600, but the huge mound-and-plaza complex we see today was built between the eleventh and thirteenth centuries (Figure 13.17). For these three centuries, a hitherto dispersed rural population was

Cahokia
A.D. 1000 to 1250

(a)

FIGURE 13.17
Mississippian centers.
(a) Central portion of
Cahokia, Illinois, as it
may have appeared
around A.D. 1150, at its
peak. The reconstruction
shows Monk's Mound
and the central precincts,
which were surrounded
by a palisade.
(b) Moundville, Alabama,
another great Mississip-
pian center, showing the
central area.

(b)

suddenly transformed into a much more tightly integrated society (Pauketat, 1994, 1998). Yet, Cahokia only held close sway over a small area of the American Bottom, an area in Illinois and Missouri that encompassed some 100 to 150 km (60 to 90 miles) from its core in the Bottom, although Cahokia-like artifacts and ideas spread much further afield, far north in the Midwest.

The great center emerged as a regional capital with dramatic suddenness, not as a result of external trade or gradual cultural evolution, but through a complicated and still little understood process of political and social negotiation that melded new polit- ical realities with the everyday lives of communities and households (Pauketat, 1998). Instead of early Mississippian villages, hamlets, and farmsteads, a new three-tiered settlement hierarchy suddenly appears—a great capital at Cahokia, several smaller political and administrative centers, and rural homesteads in the northern part of the floodplain, a diverse and highly organized settlement pattern (Emerson, 1997).

Cahokia's population suddenly rose fivefold a few decades after A.D. 1050. Hundreds of people were resettled in small and large villages, even at some distance from Cahokia. This complex process, which involved political negotiations, the use of force, and carefully orchestrated integrative strategies, fostered a common interest between the center and the periphery, between chief and villager. Imposing public structures and shrines, sweat houses, common art traditions, and the promotion of carefully chosen community traditions—all may have been symbols that linked elite and commoner in displays of common cultural meanings and values that helped create a regional chiefdom that combined Cahokia's authority with ancient community interests. The result was a short-lived, imposing polity lasting a century and a half, where competing factions and periodic inabilities to mobilize community labor fashioned an inherently unstable chiefdom that appeared and dissipated with bewildering speed. After A.D. 1100, Cahokia's population gradually tapered off over the next century and a half, as people migrated outward from the American Bottom, and a more dispersed settlement pattern again prevailed.

Cahokia was briefly a magnificent capital. At the height of its power, between A.D. 1050 and 1250, Cahokia extended over an area of more than 13 sq km (5 square miles) (Milner, 1998; Pauketat, 1998; Pauketat and Emerson, 1997). Some 800 ha (2000 acres) of this vast area were covered with dwellings, housing perhaps as many as 16,000 people, although others argue for much smaller numbers. The inhabitants lived in pole-and-thatch houses clustered along a central east-west ridge. Several residences per hectare was the rule, the same building site being used again and again over the generations. The dwellings varied greatly in size, perhaps a reflection of different social status. They may have been grouped in clusters, each associated with mound and plaza complexes, subdivisions of the community.

The Cahokia people erected more than 100 earthen mounds over the centuries, mounds of various sizes, shapes, and functions in an apparently carefully planned layout. Most of them cluster along the central ridge of the site, the driest higher ground in the vicinity. They are grouped around a series of what must have been open plazas. The most extensive grouping is around Monk's Mound, the largest earthwork built by the ancient North Americans.

Monk's Mound was built on four level stages starting before A.D. 1000 and ending some three centuries later. The mound is 30.4 m (100 feet) high, measures 316 by 240 m (1037 by 790 feet), and covers 6.4 ha (16 acres). The builders, probably teams of villagers supervised by expert moundbuilders, heaped up more than 614,478 cu m (21,700,000 cubic feet) of earth in baskets to erect this vast tumulus. The entire earthwork would have taken a theoretical 370,000 workdays to complete, with additional days for contouring and finishing the mound. The mound was built in several stages, with a large thatched structure on the summit.

Some of the largest Cahokia mounds lie in two rows on either side of Monk's Mound with a central 19-ha (47-acre) plaza area immediately to the south. Most of these were platform mounds, flat-topped earthworks where important public buildings or elite residences of pole and thatch lay. Excavators believe that charnel houses once stood on some of the Cahokia mounds, where the dead were exposed while their flesh decayed and before their bones were interred. A large log palisade with watchtowers and gates surrounded the entire 80.9 ha (200 acres) of the central area, perhaps to isolate Monk's Mound and other ceremonial structures and high-status individuals from commoners. The defensive wall was rebuilt at least four times in a similar style to those found at other centers—the result of serious factional conflict in the region.

During Cahokia's heyday, some individuals enjoyed high social status, living in large houses and being buried in great splendor. There is striking evidence for elaborate burial customs in Mound 72 at Cahokia. Melvin Fowler (1997) records a male burial laid out on a platform of 20,000 shell beads. This was an important man, for he was accompanied by three high-status men and women buried nearby. About 800 arrowheads, copper and mica sheets, and 15 polished stone disks used in a spear-throwing game lay with these skeletons, perhaps those of close relatives sacrificed at the funeral. Nearby were the bodies of four men with their heads and hands cut off. More than 50 young women aged between 18 and 23 were buried in a pit close by. Fowler suspects they were strangled to death.

Much of Cahokia's power came not only from compelling ideologies but also from a highly centralized economy, where foodstuffs and communal labor were appropriated by the elite. Most of the prestigious objects manufactured at the site were made from local materials for domestic use. Few of them were exported to distant locations. Cahokia's leaders achieved dominance by appropriating everything to themselves, including ideology, in what can be described as a "centrifugal process" (Pauketat, 1998). During the thirteenth century, this centrally controlled chiefdom fell apart. Cahokia's demise is still little understood, but it was probably as much political as economic, since other major and competing centers arose elsewhere.

Moundville
A.D. 1100

At the height of their powers, Cahokia, Moundville, Etowah, Georgia, and other Mississippian centers formed large, complex chiefdoms, ruled by high-status individuals of great political, social, and religious influence. Increasing control of long-distance exchange, especially in exotic, prestigious goods, and the use of this wealth to control local labor may have been important catalysts for political change. There is every indication that Mississippian chiefs used the exotic, and highly valuable, objects they received from outside as symbols of their legitimacy, of their special relationship to supernatural powers that were theirs alone to control. This form of ideological governance is vulnerable to the uncontrollable forces of long-distance exchange, so stability was achieved by linking the exotic objects used in major ceremonies with ceremonial architecture and with land ownership. Thus, the great earthworks of Cahokia, Moundville, and other centers were a way, albeit an inherently unstable way, of fostering bonds between the people and the elite, between one community and another.

Under these circumstances, Mississippian chiefdoms were fragile institutions, the end products of a constant process of balancing economic interdependence, ideology, and force. These chiefdoms were in a constant state of change, as centers of power changed, some chiefdoms collapsed, and others nearby rose in their place. Local and regional conditions changed frequently, fueled by the competitive political dynamics that are so characteristic of chiefdoms everywhere—societies with few high-status positions. The Mississippian was no political and social monolith, with important rulers maintaining absolute authority over vast areas of the Midwest and South. Rather, hundreds of local societies, large and small, fall under the general category "Mississippian." They enjoyed an infinite variety of local subsistence patterns, which exploited a very diverse resource base, and varied greatly in their dependence on maize and bean agriculture. Long-distance exchange networks brought a degree of cultural continuity to the entire vast area, and there was some common religious tradition among many of them, reflected in widely used art styles and abiding ritual symbolism. The people lived under dozens of chiefdoms, large and small, many of them virtually egalitarian, others, like Cahokia, highly complex, powerful political and social units. But these complex chiefdoms still depended heavily on kin ties and notions of reciprocity to function properly. With their regular feasts and elaborate ceremonies, Mississippian chiefs validated their authority in vivid, symbolic ways, well aware that their power depended on a fine line between coercion and reciprocity and on the balance of the powerful cults that underpinned human existence over wide areas.

Most great Mississippian centers were past the height of their powers by the time European traders and explorers reached the Mississippi Valley. Cahokia declined, then was abandoned by A.D. 1500, even though Moundville may still have been an important center (Knight and Steponaitis, 1998). Numerous chiefdoms still flourished in the mid-South and the Southeast right up to European contact and beyond, some of which, like the Coosa, were visited by conquistador Hernando de Soto during his journey across the Southeast in 1540 to 1542 (M. Smith, 1987). There are grounds to suspect, however, that smallpox and other diseases had spread among the peoples of the interior before the arrival of the Spaniards, weakening and decimating Mississippian society (Ramenofsky, 1987).

In 1720, French explorer Le Page du Pratz spent some time among the Natchez people of the Mississippi Valley. He found himself in a rigidly stratified society—divided into nobles and commoners and headed by a chieftain known as the Great Sun—whose members lived in a village of nine houses and a temple built on the summit of an earthen mound. Pratz witnessed the funeral of the Great Sun. His wives, relatives, and servants were drugged, then clubbed to accompany him in death (Swanton, 1911). Pratz was the first and only European to witness a Mississippian funeral, for epidemics of smallpox and other exotic diseases had already caused the fabric of this most complex of North American societies to fall apart. The Natchez were not the only Mississippian survivors, but within two centuries of the arrival of de Soto, the last vestiges of Mississippian society had been submerged.

Summary

Native American agriculture was based on quite different crops from those in the Old World: root crops like potatoes and sweet potatoes. Maize was the most important cereal. Since there were many fewer potential domesticates than in the Old World, domesticated animals were limited to, for example, the llama, the turkey, and the guinea fowl. The earliest cultivation may have begun in the humid tropical lowlands, for traces of cultivation are said to date to as early as 7000 B.C. in Panama. In drier, more open country, agriculture developed in hunter-gatherer societies that were coping with constant environmental change and unpredictable population shifts. At locations like Guilá Naquitz, Mexico, wet-year subsistence strategies involving deliberate planting eventually became permanent shifts in subsistence activities. Among the staples of Native American agriculture were beans and maize, probably domesticated from a Central American native grass named teosinte as early as 4000 B.C. Maize agriculture spread from southern Mexico and Guatemala thousands of miles to the north and south. There were farmers in the highland Andes and in coastal Peru by 3000 B.C., but maize and cotton did not become vital cultivated staples until about a thousand years later.

Maize agriculture reached the North American Southwest by about 1500 to 2000 B.C. By 300 B.C., sedentary villages and a much greater dependence on farming were characteristic of the Southwest, leading to the emergence of the Hohokam, Mogollon, and Ancestral Pueblo cultural traditions, among which the ultimate ancestry of modern southwestern peoples lie.

Many groups in eastern North America turned to the deliberate cultivation of native plants as food supplements after 2000 B.C., but maize and bean agriculture did not arrive from the Southwest until the first millennium B.C. After 1000 B.C., a series of powerful chiefdoms arose in the Southeast and the Midwest, peoples among whom elaborate burial customs and the building of burial mounds and earthworks were commonplace. The Adena tradition appeared in about 700 B.C. and was overlapped by the Hopewell in approximately A.D. 100. About A.D. 800, the focus of economic, religious, and political power shifted to the Mississippi Valley and the Southeast with the rise of the Mississippian tradition. This tradition, with its powerful religious and secular leaders, survived in a modified form until European contact in the sixteenth century A.D.

Key Term

Phytolith   Minute particles of silica from plant cells produced throughout the life of a plant and used to identify plant species in archaeological sites.

Guide to Further Reading

Cordell, Linda S. 1997. *Prehistory of the Southwest*, 2nd ed. Orlando, FL: Academic Press.
    A definitive, closely argued synthesis of southwestern archaeology.

Emerson, T. E. 1997. *Cahokia and the Ideology of Power*. Tuscaloosa: University of Alabama Press.
    A synthesis of current thinking on Mississippian ideology and Cahokia.

Fagan, Brian M. 2000. *Ancient North America*, 3rd ed. New York: Thames & Hudson.
    A general account of North American archaeology with a long summary of southwestern and Eastern Woodland prehistory. Heavily referenced and aimed at the beginning reader.

Fiedel, Stuart J. 1992. *Prehistory of the Americas*, 2nd ed. Cambridge: Cambridge University Press.
    Discusses the major issues in New World prehistory for beginners. Well-written, continentwide account.

Lekson, Stephen H. 1999. *The Chaco Meridian: Centers of Political Power in the Ancient Southwest*. Walnut Creek, CA: AltaMira Press.
    A controversial but stimulating essay on ancient southwestern societies.

Moseley, Michael E. 2000. *The Incas and Their Ancestors*, 2nd ed. London and New York: Thames & Hudson.
    Comprehensive critical synthesis that is fundamental to understanding Andean archaeology and early food production.

Pauketat, T. R. 1994. *The Ascent of Chiefs: Cahokia and Mississippian Politics in Native North America.*
   Tuscaloosa: University of Alabama Press.
   A useful source on Mississippian culture and development.

Pauketat, Timothy R., and Thomas E. Emerson. 1997. *Cahokia: Domination and Ideology in the Mississippian
   World.* Lincoln: University of Nebraska Press.
   An authoritative and up-to-date synthesis of Cahokia and the Mississippian. It represents a new genera-
   tion of research.

Plog, Fred. 1997. *Ancient Peoples of the American Southwest.* London and New York: Thames & Hudson.
   An excellent popular account of southwestern archaeology.

OLD WORLD CIVILIZATIONS

c. 3000 B.C. TO MODERN TIMES

Rock-tomb, pyramid, and temple succeed in the endlessly similar, endlessly changing landscape. . . . For many centuries they were removed from human lives and emotions. No one living understood their significance or the civilization which built them. Even today, measured, restored, visited, they are difficult to comprehend. How should the 20th century know the heart of Sekhmet the lion-goddess, or fear, like Herodotus, even to pen the name of Osiris?

Robin Feddon, *Egypt: Land of the Valley* (1975)

Part IV deals with the beginnings of complex states and urban civilization, not only in Southwest Asia but also in lesser known parts of the world, such as Africa and Southeast Asia. Research in Africa and Asia has hardly begun; future excavations in these regions are likely to throw significant new light on such much-debated issues as the importance of ceremonial centers and long-distance trade in the emergence of complex societies. The reader is urged to start with the theoretical background in Chapter 14 before embarking on the narrative cultural history in later chapters.

period already covered	period covered in this part	partial coverage

5 mya	2.5 mya	1 mya	100,000 B.P.	10,000 B.C.	1 A.D.	A.D. 1500

THE DEVELOPMENT OF CIVILIZATION

Giant seated figures of the pharaoh Rameses II dominate the facade of the Abu Simbel Temple in Nubia.

Paul Émile Botta was appointed the French consul in Mosul in northern Iraq in 1840, with one official objective: to dig the nearby mounds of biblical Nineveh. Botta had no archaeological qualifications whatsoever, except that he was an experienced traveler who spoke several western Asian languages. At first he dug fruitlessly into Nineveh, finding nothing but inscribed bricks. Then one of his workers told him of similar bricks that formed the chimney of his house at a village named Khorsabad, 23 km (14 miles) away. To get rid of the man, he sent two of his laborers to investigate. A week later, they returned with stories of richly carved walls adorned with strange animals. Botta leaped on his horse and rode to Khorsabad, where he gasped at the curious bas-reliefs in the walls of the small pit—of bearded men in long gowns, winged animals, and wild beasts. He moved his excavations to Khorsabad. Within a few weeks, he had uncovered room after room of sculpted limestone slabs, the wall decorations of a magnificent, exotic royal palace. "I believe myself to be the first who had discovered sculptures which with some reason can be referred to the period when Nineveh was flourishing," he wrote excitedly of the palace (Fagan, 1979, p. 127).

We know now that Botta had uncovered not Nineveh but Assyrian King Sargon's palace, constructed at great expense in the eighth century B.C. Even so, Botta's remarkable discoveries ushered in a classical era of nineteenth-century archaeology. They revealed to an astonished world not only the Assyrians but, in addition, the Sumerians, the Maya, the Minoans, the Mycenaeans, and other hitherto-unknown civilizations (Figure 14.1). Today, there are no more unknown civilizations to be unearthed, but archaeologists are still striving to understand the origins and workings of the world's earliest states. In this chapter, we review some of the attempts to explain their beginnings.

Civilization

Everyone who has studied the prehistory of human society agrees that the emergence of civilization in different parts of the world was a major event in human adaptation. The word *civilization* has a familiar meaning for us. It implies "civility," a measure of decency in the behavior of the individual. Such definitions inevitably reflect ethnocentrism or value judgments because what is "civilized" behavior in one civilization may be antisocial or baffling in another. This simplistic meaning is of no use to students of prehistoric civilizations seeking basic definitions and cultural processes (Scarre and Fagan, 2003).

Today, archaeologists use the term *civilization* as shorthand for urbanized, state-level societies. Those described in these

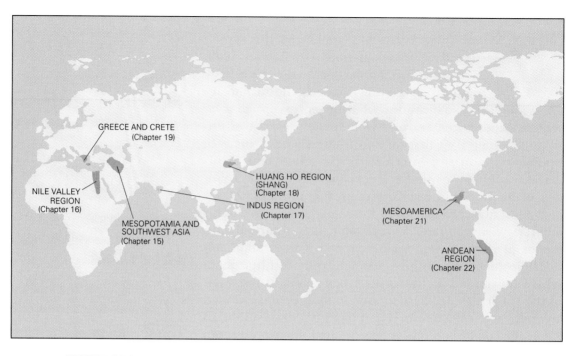

FIGURE 14.1 Locations of major preindustrial states described in this book.

pages are sometimes called preindustrial civilizations, because they relied on manual labor rather than fossil fuels such as coal. There are many variations among the preindustrial civilizations, but the following features are characteristic of them all:

- Societies based on cities, with large, very complex social organizations. The preindustrial civilization was invariably based on a larger territory, such as the Nile Valley, as opposed to smaller areas owned by individual kin groups (Schwartz and Falconer, 1994; Stein and Rothman, 1994).

- Economies based on the centralized accumulation of capital and social status through tribute and taxation. For instance, the Sumerian kings in Mesopotamia monopolized trading activity in the name of the state. This type of economy allows the support of hundreds, often thousands, of nonfood producers, such as smiths and priests. Long-distance trade and a division of labor, as well as craft specialization, are often characteristic of early civilizations.

- Advances toward formal record keeping, science, and mathematics, as well as some form of written script. Such advances took many forms, from Egyptian hieroglyphs to the knotted strings used by the Inca of the Andes.

- Impressive public buildings and monumental architecture, like Khmer or Maya ceremonial centers and Roman temples.

- Some form of all-embracing state religion in which the ruler played a leading role. The Khmer of Cambodia considered their leaders living gods. Such kings lived in great palaces built as depictions of the symbolic Hindu world (Higham, 2002).

〽 Cities

Archaeological research into early civilization concentrates on the origin and development of both state-organized societies (civilizations) and the city. Today, the city is the primary type of human settlement throughout the world, and it has become so since the industrial revolution altered the economic face of the globe. The earliest cities assumed many forms, from the compact walled settlement of Mesopotamia to the Mesoamerican ceremonial center, with a core population in its precincts and a scattered rural population in villages arranged over the surrounding landscape (Figure 14.2) (Nichols and Charlton, 1995). The cities of the Harappan civilization of the Indus River region were carefully planned communities with regular streets and

FIGURE 14.2 The mud-brick ruins of the Sumerian city of Nippur, southern Iraq.

assigned quarters for different living groups. The palaces of the Minoans and the Mycenaeans functioned as secular economic and trading centers for the scattered village populations nearby.

A **city** can be defined by its population, which is generally larger and denser than that of a town or village. A generally used rule of thumb is a lower population limit of 5000 people for a large city. However, numbers are not a sufficient determinant: Many people can congregate in a limited area and still not possess the compact diversity of population that enables the economic and organizational complexity of a city to develop. This complexity, as well as population size and density, distinguishes the city from other settlement types:

- A city is a large and relatively dense settlement, with a population numbered in at least the thousands. Small cities of the ancient world had 2000 or 3000 inhabitants; the largest, such as Rome or Changan in China, may have had over a million.

- Cities are also characterized by specialization and interdependence, between the city and its rural hinterland, and between specialist craftspeople and other groups within the city. The city is a central place in its region, providing services for the villages of the surrounding area, at the same time depending on those villages for food. Most ancient cities, for example, had a marketplace where agricultural produce could be exchanged.

- Cities also have a degree of organizational complexity well beyond that of small farming communities. There are centralized institutions to regulate internal affairs and to ensure security. These usually find expression in monumental architecture such as temples or palaces, or sometimes a city wall. Here we must recognize an overlap between the concept of the city and the concept of the state. States, too, are characterized by centralized institutions. It may be possible to have states without cities, but it is hard to envisage a city that is not embedded within a state.

An ancient city site is usually obvious to archaeologists, both from its size and from the scale of its remains. The state is more difficult to define. It is a political unit governed by a central authority whose power crosscuts bonds of kinship. Kin groups do not disappear, of course, but their power is reduced, and a new axis of control emerges based on allegiance to a ruling elite.

A great deal of new research using aerial photography, remote sensing, and ethnoarchaeology, as well as archaeological survey and excavation, is producing new data on population densities and early urban settlement. Recent fieldwork has also concentrated on agriculture and herding systems that fed early cities, as well as craft production and exchange (see a summary in Stein, 2001).

〰️ Six Classic Theories of the Emergence of States

As we saw in Chapter 1, explanations of human culture change have moved far beyond the ladderlike evolutionary schemes of a century ago. Today's scholars tend to stress social and political organization, to speak of "states" and "complex societies" in contrast to simpler human societies. With its emphasis on the study of culture change and with its long time perspective, archaeology lies at the very core of the study of early civilization.

Few developments in world prehistory have generated as much theoretical debate as the origins of states. These controversies rage in the context of six early and well-established theoretical models for the rise of state-organized societies. They form the starting point for any discussion of the issue.

1. V. Gordon Childe and the "Urban Revolution"

The Victorians, like the Greeks and the Romans before them, assumed that civilization had originated along the Nile, in the "Land of the Pharaohs"—this in spite of the discovery of the Sumerian civilization in Mesopotamia in the 1870s. Eventually, early theorizing took in a broader canvas, embracing all of Southwest Asia. In the 1920s, American archaeologist James Breasted coined the enduring phrase *the Fertile Crescent,* a curve of territory encompassing the Nile and Jordan valleys and the uplands of Iran and lower Mesopotamia. The Fertile Crescent was the cradle of early civilization, of the first complex societies in the world (Scarre and Fagan, 2003).

Australian-born archaeologist V. Gordon Childe formulated the first relatively sophisticated theories about the origins of civilization. Childe (1936, 1952) claimed that an "**Urban Revolution**" followed on the "Neolithic Revolution," which witnessed the beginnings of farming. He theorized that this second revolution saw the development of metallurgy and the appearance of a new social class of full-time artisans and specialists who lived in much larger settlements: cities. Among the Sumerians of Mesopotamia, for example, Childe believed that the new specialists were fed by surpluses raised by peasant farmers. But the artisans' products had to be distributed, and raw materials obtained, often from long distances. Both needs reduced the self-sufficiency of peasant communities, Childe argued. Agricultural techniques became more sophisticated as a higher yield of food per capita was needed to support a growing nonagricultural population. Irrigation increased productivity, leading to the centralization of food supplies and of production and distribution. Taxation and tribute led to the accumulation of capital. Ultimately, said Childe, a new class-stratified society came into being, based on economic classes rather than traditional ties of kin. Writing was essential for keeping records and for developing exact and predictive sciences. Transportation by land and water was part of the new order. A unifying religious force dominated urban life as priest-kings and despots rose to power. Monumental architecture testified to their activities.

Childe considered technology and the development of craft specialization in the hands of full-time artisans a cornerstone of "Urban Revolution." A half century later, most archaeologists associate craft specialization with cultural complexity, to the point where they equate the appearance of specialist artisans with the formation of states. Thus, goes the argument, evidence of increased levels of craft specialization thereafter indicates even further cultural complexity. Many scholars challenge this perspective. They point out that craft specialization is a feature of many more egalitarian societies. Many chiefs, ruling over chiefdoms large and small, patronized specialists with unusual expertise, who produced prestige goods and artifacts, such as canoes. Another theory considers craft specialization the fate of peasant farmers disfranchised from their lands as states expanded and cities grew.

John Clark and William Parry (1990) tested these theories against a sample of data from societies living in widely contrasting environments and with very different cultural institutions. Craft specialization is common in both chiefdoms and states, but these researchers doubt from their studies that it was a major factor in the development of civilization, although there was a strong correlation between full-time craft specialization and civilization. They are intrigued by the possibility that craft specialization supported by the elite was crucial to the emergence of states, for it is associated with rank and may have been a major factor in the acquisition of economic power outside the confines of the kin system. They believe patronizing artisans was one way to acquire social prestige and rank, as well as wealth through production and exchange with other communities, as may have happened along the Nile. Craft specialization was not, in itself, a major cause of civilization, but it may have laid a foundation for more permanent investments in what eventually became inheritable wealth, a major feature of civilizations.

Childe's "Urban Revolution" enjoyed widespread popularity between the 1930s and 1950s. It was a logical synthesis of complex events when relatively little was known about early Southwest Asian civilizations, and even less about complex states in China, South Asia, and the Americas. But the revolution hypothesis has serious flaws. For example, craft specialization is more a sign than a cause of state formation, and it is not unique to civilizations. Furthermore, predicating state and city formation on surplus production does not explain why surpluses came about in the first place.

Robert Adams and other Mesopotamian archaeologists argued in the 1960s that the term *Urban Revolution* implies undue emphasis on the city at the expense of social change, that is, the development of social classes and political institutions. Adams (1966) pointed out that both early Mesopotamian and early American civilizations followed a basically similar course of development in which the communal control of land by kin groups gave way to the growth of private estates owned by noble families. The eventual result was a stratified form of social organization rigidly divided along class lines.

2. Ecology and Irrigation

Most scholars now agree that three elements of Childe's "Urban Revolution" were of great importance in the development of all the world's early civilizations: large food surpluses, diversified farming economies, and irrigation agriculture. Early ecological theories revolved around three broad themes:

a. The Ecological Potential of River Floodplains.   Floodplains have rich, fertile soils. James Breasted's Fertile Crescent hypothesis assumed that the exceptional fertility of the Mesopotamian floodplain and the Nile Valley was the primary cause for the appearance of cities and states in these regions. Larger grain surpluses, as well as social and culture changes, resulted from increased agricultural efficiency and abundant fish (Figure 14.3). The extra food supported non-food-producers such as artisans, priests, and traders, new classes of society that were the backbone of state-organized societies.

FIGURE 14.3 Fishing at Guilin on the Yangtze River, China. Fish were an important food source for many preindustrial civilizations.

Some scholars, among them the economist Ester Boserup (1965), took the opposite tack. They believed that population growth, not food surplus, was the incentive for intensified agriculture and eventually more complex societies. Following Boserup, others have argued that more lasting field agriculture, like that in early Mesopotamia or along the banks of the Nile River, where annual floods inundated the fields, tended to be more intensive and to exploit the environment in a more ordered and systematic way (Spooner, 1972). It created conditions in which more settlements per square mile could exist on foods whose annual yields were at least roughly predictable. The more specialized ecosystems created by these efforts supported more concentrated, rapidly growing populations, and thus civilization. But though important, dense populations did not characterize all state-organized societies, as the Mycenaean and Inca civilizations show.

b. The Ecological Diversity of Local Environments.   Differences in altitude, access to food and other resources, and soil fertility varied greatly from one area to another. Diversified agricultural economies tended to focus on fewer, more productive crops, but the ultimate subsistence base remained wide. The Egyptians farmed wheat and barley on a large scale, but also raised large herds of cattle and goats, for example. The earliest civilizations in the Old World and the New were certainly based on complex subsistence patterns that integrated several ecological zones. For instance, the highland Andean states relied heavily on their lowland neighbors for fish meal, cotton, and other resources. The Harappans of the Indus Valley may have exchanged cotton for semi-precious stones, while highland and lowland Mesoamerican civilizations depended on one another for all manner of commodities, foodstuffs, and artifacts. The resulting diversity of food resources protected the people against famine and stimulated trade and exchange for food and other products, as well as the growth of distributive organizations that encouraged centralized authority. Under these circumstances, a local center might control products from several nearby ecological zones, giving it a vital hedge for managing and controlling food surpluses against crop failure and famine.

c. The Adoption of Irrigation Agriculture.   Irrigation agriculture was a major factor in the rise of civilizations because it supported far higher population densities. Early ecological theories were closely tied to the apparently widespread use of irrigation agriculture by early states to enhance agricultural output. The intensification of agriculture implies a major modification of the environment, which usually means irrigation: the development of canals and other works for storing water and watering fields during dry months. Irrigation theories were popular half a century ago, when anthropologist Julian Steward and historian Karl Wittfogel argued during the 1950s that irrigation lay behind the development of socially stratified societies in Egypt, Mesopotamia, and elsewhere, which Wittfogel famously called "hydraulic civilizations" (Figure 14.4) (Steward et al., 1955; Wittfogel, 1957). In areas where irrigation was practiced, both scholars argued, the relationship between the environment, food production, and social institutions was identical.

Wittfogel, a Chinese specialist, argued that early Asian civilizations became mighty "hydraulic bureaucracies," which owed their despotic control over densely populated areas like China, Egypt, and India to the technological and environmental demands required by large-scale water-control projects in areas of scant rainfall. The state bureaucracy controlled the labor forces that built hydraulic works and maintained them. Thus, the social requirements of irrigation led to the development of states and urban societies in several parts of the Old World. And the same requirements led to remarkable similarities in their economic and social structure.

Wittfogel's arguments were originally formulated in the 1920s and were refined over more than 30 years, during which a mass of new data, including large-scale landscape surveys, sharpened our perceptions of early irrigation. For example, archaeologist Robert Adams carried out major field surveys of ancient irrigation works in Mesopotamia in the 1960s. Adams found that early Mesopotamian irrigation consisted of cleaning natural river channels and building only a few smaller feeder canals (Adams, 1981; Adams and Nissen, 1972). Most settlements lay near major rivers and made the most of the natural hydrology of the waterways. Each community controlled

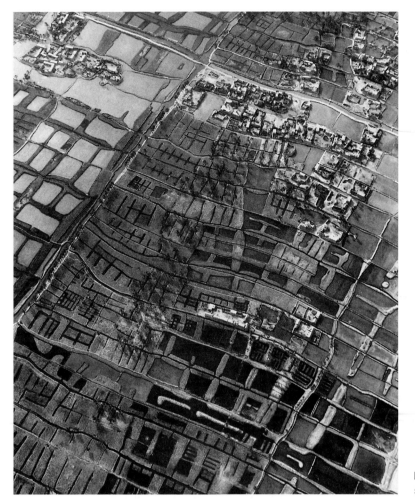

FIGURE 14.4 Irrigated fields in modern-day southern Iraq.

its own small-scale irrigation works. Only centuries later did a highly centralized state government organize irrigation schemes on a massive scale. The same was true in Egypt, where the greatest irrigation works were undertaken during the New Kingdom, using thousands of laborers fulfilling tax obligations to the state (Butzer, 1976). In contrast, early Egyptian agriculture had relied on natural basins to hold back the Nile water—a village-level, small-scale operation requiring no official supervision. Large-scale irrigation requires constant maintenance and supervision, to say nothing of political stability and the control of water sources. For example, the Chimor state on the Peruvian coast was overthrown by the expanding Inca Empire, partly through the latter's acquiring control of the watersheds that fed coastal irrigation schemes (Moseley, 2000) (see Chapter 22).

While some form of irrigation was a necessary precondition for the settlement of the southern Mesopotamian plains, where the world's first cities arose, large-scale irrigation does not everywhere appear to have been a factor in the rise of early civilization. By the same token, modern research has shown that ecology was only one component in a mosaic of many changes that led to state-organized societies. But climate may have been of particular significance in some areas, in view of the major environmental changes, especially shifts in rainfall patterns and rising sea levels, which affected the world during post–Ice Age global warming.

3. Technology and Trade

The origins and evolution of complex societies have long been linked to technological innovation and to growing trade in raw materials like obsidian (volcanic glass used for stone tools, mirrors, and ornaments) and copper and in luxuries of all kinds. Gordon Childe considered metallurgy an important component in his "Urban Revolution," but in fact, copper and other exotic materials were at first used in Southwest Asia for the small-scale production of cult objects and jewelry. In many cases, the technological innovations that did appear, like the wheel in Mesopotamia and the sailing ship in Egypt, were of more benefit in transportation than in production. Not until several centuries after civilization started were copper and bronze more abundant, as demands for transportation and military needs burgeoned. Technology did evolve, but only in response to developing markets, new demands, and the expanded needs of a tiny segment of the population: the elite. Trade developed as local communities exchanged basic commodities on an increasingly large scale. The exchange of luxury goods also played an important part. It is important to note that the nature of trade changed constantly, for elites often used prestigious trade goods as a means to maintain their status and power. In other words, they redefined prestige goods for their own ends (see a summary and references in Stein, 2001).

Any form of trade involves two elements: the goods and commodities being exchanged and the people doing the exchanging. People make trade connections when they need to acquire goods and services that are not available to them within their local area. This trade (more conventionally called an **exchange system**) may be gift-giving, the exchange of gifts that reinforces a social relationship between both individuals and groups as a whole. The gifts serve as gestures that place obligations on both parties and are often a preliminary to bartering for all manner of commodities. This kind of preliminary gift exchange is still commonplace in New Guinea and the Pacific and was widespread in Africa during the past 2000 years.

Bartering, the exchange of commodities or goods, was another basic trading mechanism for many thousands of years, often sporadic, and usually based on notions of **reciprocity,** the mutual exchange of commodities or objects between individuals or groups. The **redistribution** of these goods through society lay in the hands of chiefs, religious leaders, or kin groups. As we have seen, such redistribution was a basic element in chiefdoms. The change from redistribution to an impersonal market economy trade, often based on regulated commerce and involving, perhaps, fixed prices and even currency, was a change closely tied to growing political and social complexity and, hence, to the development of the state (Figure 14.5).

In the 1970s, a number of archaeologists gave trade a primary role in the rise of states. In the Aegean area, British archaeologist Colin Renfrew (1972) attributed the dramatic flowering of the Minoan civilization on Crete and throughout the Aegean to

FIGURE 14.5 A medieval market in Europe epitomizes the market economy of many early states.

intensified trading contacts and to the impact of olive and vine cultivation on local communities. As agricultural economies became more diversified and local food supplies could be purchased both locally and over longer distances, a far-reaching economic interdependence resulted. Eventually, this led to redistribution systems for luxuries and basic commodities, systems that were organized and controlled by Minoan palaces and elsewhere in the Aegean where there were major centers of olive production. As time went on, the self-sufficiency of communities was replaced by mutual dependence. Interest in long-distance trade brought about some cultural homogeneity from trade, gift exchange, and, perhaps, piracy. Thus, intensified trade and interaction, and the flowering of specialist crafts, in a complex process of positive feedback, led to much more complex societies based on palaces, which were the economic hubs of a new Minoan civilization.

Renfrew's model made some assumptions that are now discounted (see Chapter 19). For example, he argued that the introduction of domesticated vines and olives allowed a substantial expansion in the amounts of land under cultivation and helped to power the emergence of complex society. Many archaeologists and paleobotanists now question this view, pointing out that the available evidence for cultivated vines and olives suggests that they were present only in the later Bronze Age. Trade, nevertheless, was probably one of many variables that led to the emergence of palace economies in Minoan Crete.

American archaeologist William Rathje (1971) developed a hypothesis that considered an explosion in long-distance exchange a fundamental cause of Maya civilization. He suggested that the lowland Maya environment was deficient in many vital resources, among them obsidian, salt, stone for grinding maize, and many luxury materials. All these could be obtained from the nearby highlands, from the Valley of Mexico, and from other regions, if the necessary trading networks came into being. Such connections, and the trading expeditions to maintain them, could not be organized by individual villages alone. The Maya lived in a relatively uniform environment, where every community suffered from the same resource deficiencies. Thus, argued Rathje, long-distance trade networks were organized through local ceremonial centers and their leaders. In time, this organization became a state, and knowledge of its functioning was exportable, as were pottery, tropical bird feathers, specialized stone materials, and other local commodities.

Rathje's hypothesis probably explains part of the complex process of Maya state formation, but it suffers from the objection that suitable alternative raw materials can be found in the lowlands. It could be, too, that warfare became a competitive response to population growth and to the increasing scarcity of prime agricultural land, and that it played an important role in the emergence of the Maya states.

Now that we know much more about ancient exchange and commerce, we know that trade can never be looked upon as a unifying factor or as a primary cause of ancient civilization, simply because no one aspect of it was an overriding cause of cultural change or evolution in trading practices (Kohl, 1978). Many ever-changing variables affected ancient trade, among them the demand for goods. This demand prompted a search for supplies, themselves a product of production above local needs. Then there were the logistics of transportation, the extent of the trading network, and also the social and political environment. Intricate market networks channeled supplies along well-defined routes. Authorities at both ends might regulate the profits fed back to the source, providing the incentive for further transactions. There may or may not have been a market organization. Extensive long-distance trade, like large-scale irrigation, was a consequence rather than a cause of civilization.

4. Warfare

Robert Carneiro (1970) used the archaeology of coastal valleys in Peru to argue that warfare played a key role in state formation. His "coercive theory" of state origins argued that the amount of agricultural land in these valleys was limited and surrounded by desert. So a series of predictable events led to the development of states. At first, autonomous farming villages flourished in the valley landscape. But as the population grew and more land was taken up, the communities started fighting over land and raided each others' fields as they competed for limited acreage. Some of the village leaders emerged as successful warlords, became chieftains, and presided over large tribal polities. The valley population continued to grow, and warfare intensified until the entire region fell under the sway of a single, successful warrior, who presided over a single state centered on the valley. Then, this ambitious ruler and his successors started raiding neighboring valleys. Eventually a multivalley state developed, creating a much larger civilization.

Carneiro's theory is hard to test in the field, but an attempt to do so in Peru's Santa Valley showed no sign of autonomous villages. Rather, it depicted a much more complex, evolving settlement pattern over many centuries. Archaeologist David Wilson (1983) points out that the only "coercive" processes came about in about A.D. 400, when the Moche people carved out a multivalley state by their military conquest of neighboring valleys (see Chapter 22). The conquest took place long after complex irrigation-based societies flourished in the Santa Valley. As with irrigation hypotheses, reality is more complex than the straightforward Carneiro scenario. Some of Carneiro's ideas on state formation have formed a basis for more sophisticated theories of the 1990s (see next section).

5. Cultural Systems and Civilization

Most archaeologists agree that urban life and preindustrial civilization came into existence gradually, during a period of major social and economic change. Everyone also agrees that linear explanations rooted in irrigation, trade, or warfare are inadequate. Recent theories of the rise of states invoke multiple, and often intricate, causes and are frequently based on systems models.

In the 1960s, Robert Adams, an expert on ancient Mesopotamia, introduced a new generation of complex theories when he argued (1966) that irrigation agriculture, increased warfare, and "local resource variability" were three factors vital in the newly appearing urban civilizations. Each affected society and the other factors with positive feedback, helping to reinforce each other. The creation of food surpluses and the emergence of a stratified society were critical developments. Irrigation agriculture could feed a bigger population. Larger populations, an increase in permanent settlement, and trade with regular centers for redistributing goods were all pressures for greater production and increased surpluses, actively fostered by the dominant groups in society. The greatly enlarged surpluses enabled those who controlled them to employ larger numbers of artisans and other specialists, who did not themselves grow crops.

Adams argued that some societies were better able to transform themselves into states because of the variety of resources on which they could draw. Higher populations led to monopolies over strategic resources. These communities eventually became more powerful than their neighbors, expanding their territories by military campaigns and efficiently exploiting their advantages over other peoples. Such cities also became early centers of major religious activities, of technological and artistic innovations, and of writing. Literacy, a skill confined to a few people, became an important source of power (Robinson, 1995).

Archaeologists like Kent Flannery (1972), who was working in Mesoamerica, now saw the state as a very complicated "living" system, the complexity of which could be measured by the internal differentiation and intricacy of its subsystems, such as those for agriculture, technology, or religious beliefs (Figure 14.6). The way these subsystems were linked and the controls that society imposed on the system were vital. This model seemed to work well with Mesoamerican states, where pervasive religious beliefs formed close links between public architecture, the economy, and other subsystems of civilization.

The management of a state is far more elaborate and central an undertaking than that of a small chiefdom (Adams, 2001). Indeed, the most striking difference between states and less complicated societies is the degree of complexity in civilizations' ways of reaching decisions and their hierarchical organization, not necessarily in their subsistence activities. Systems models of early states are bound to be complex, for they have to distinguish between the mechanisms and processes of culture change and the socioenvironmental pressures by which we have sought to explain the origins of civilization (Redman, 1978). Religion and control of information now appear to be key elements in

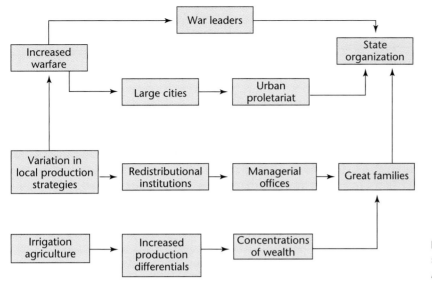

FIGURE 14.6 Hypothetical model of the state's beginnings. (Compiled from R. M. Adams, 1966.)

the regulation of environmental and economic variables in early civilizations and, indeed, in any human society.

6. Environmental Change

Ecologically based theories, which also rely heavily on systems approaches, have enjoyed a relatively long life compared with many other hypotheses. For example, in a classic study of the Valley of Mexico, William Sanders and a group of archaeologists showed how the Aztec state created and organized huge agricultural systems that spread over the shallow waters of the lakes that once filled the valley (Sanders et al., 1979). The variability of the local environment meant that the Aztecs had to exploit every environmental opportunity afforded them. Thus, Sanders argues, the state organized large-scale agriculture to support a population of up to 250,000 just in and close around the Aztec capital, Tenochtitlán. Environmental factors were decisive in each area where civilization began, he believes. Another important factor was centralized leadership.

Some support for this perspective comes from Mesopotamia, where recent studies of rising sea levels have thrown new light on the changing geography of the low-lying Mesopotamian Delta between the Tigris and Euphrates rivers. During the late Ice Age, world sea levels were about 91 m (300 feet) below modern shorelines. The Persian Gulf was dry land 20,000 years ago, with rising seawaters entering the basin in only about 10,000 B.C. At the time, the Tigris and Euphrates river system flowed through the deepest part of the gulf, down a deep canyon caused by the rivers' cutting down to the low sea level of the Indian Ocean. Today's Mesopotamian Delta did not exist, and the entire region was very arid. Between 10,000 and 4000 B.C., shorelines rose rapidly in the Persian Gulf, sometimes at a rate of 11 m (36 feet) a year, at a time when rainfall increased slightly throughout Southwest Asia. By 6500 B.C., the sea had flooded the old river system and had reached the northern shore of the gulf. Sea-level rise slowed in about 5000 B.C., as river estuaries reached their northern limits, extending as far inland as the ancient city of Ur. The vast estuaries filled with windblown sand from the Arabian desert. But the water table remained high, creating large swampy areas in the silt-choked river mouths.

Unfortunately, the archaeological record of these millennia lies buried under deep layers of silt and today's high sea levels. After 7000 B.C., and for about 1500 years, southern Mesopotamia enjoyed an unusually favorable climate, with greater and more reliable rainfall. This may have been a period when people hunted and gathered along the rapidly changing seacoast, using temporary settlements now buried under gulf waters. Some of these communities may have begun cereal farming.

As the climate became drier and the floodplain expanded, some groups may have turned to simple irrigation farming, which provided higher crop yields. Population densities rose proportionately with the yields, increasing competition for agricultural land and other food resources, just when the rising gulf was moving inland at as much as 1 km (0.6 mile) a decade. Under such circumstances, communities living near the water's edge may have moved at regular intervals, eventually coalescing into larger villages. At first, small communities dug their own watercourses, diverting river meanders and side streams. Kin leaders, men and women believed to possess unusual supernatural powers, may have been those who organized canal digging, perhaps even allocating land, as they still do in many village communities. In time, these individuals became the spiritual and political leaders of a farming village in transition, on its way to becoming a settlement and society of far greater complexity. Small villages became towns, then bustling cities, central places with political and economic tentacles extending into settlements near and far. Thus was born the city and, ultimately, Mesopotamian civilization.

This scenario is based on new and highly sophisticated climatic data, but it remains entirely hypothetical in archaeological terms. It contrasts with the traditional view that farming spread into southern Mesopotamia from the north and east. But it does highlight the great importance of local environmental change to the origins of all preindustrial civilizations. Declining Nile floods may have been a factor in the formation of the Egyptian state, for example. The scenario also suggests that centralized organization was of significant importance. A powerful leader has at his or her disposal the information about state-held resources necessary to make decisions, along with the ability to command people's labor and to collect and redistribute the results of that labor. Thus, goes the argument, states arise in social and environmental contexts in which centralized management solves problems effectively.

The ecological approach has serious problems. How, for example, does one tell which environments would foster state formation? Fertile floodplains like those in Mesopotamia and Egypt? Coastal river valleys like those in Peru? Highland plateaus like those of Mesoamerica? Or areas where land is in short supply (also coastal Peru)? States arose in regions where there were few geographic constraints, like the Maya lowlands of Mesoamerica. Further, preindustrial civilizations developed, without any sign of rapid population growth, in Iran and other parts of Southwest Asia. But there can be no doubt that environmental factors were major players in a very complex process of cultural change and response (Feinman and Manzanilla, 2002).

🐾 Social Theories

In recent years, archaeology has shifted away from systems-ecological approaches toward a greater concern with individuals and groups, also with what one might call "state dynamics"—how early states functioned (Stein, 2001). The former theories have often been somewhat impersonal, treating states as rather complex, even mechanical, entities that operated according to complex processes of culture change. A new generation of researchers is carrying social approaches in new directions, arguing that all human societies consist, ultimately, of individuals and groups interacting with one another, and all pursuing their own agendas. The new hypotheses revolve around such phenomena as power, ideology, factionalism, and the role of the individual.

Power in Three Domains

Archaeologically, one can look at power in three domains: economic power, social and ideological power, and political power. The combination of economic control over the sources and distribution of food and wealth, the development and maintenance of the stratified social system and its ideology, and the ability to maintain control by force was vital in early states. Each of these domains was closely linked to the others, but they can be studied separately in the archaeological record (Bowman and Wolf, 1994; Yoffee, 1990).

Economic power depends on the ability to organize more specialized production and the diverse tasks of food storage and food distribution. In time, stored wealth in food and goods develops into relationships of dependency between those who

FIGURE 14.7 A Minoan city ringed by mountains and rivers. People watch departing ships, and a lion hunts deer. A wall painting from Akrotiri, Santorini Island, Aegean Sea. Sixteenth century B.C.

produce or acquire the wealth and those who control and distribute it. A state comprises elites (the noble class), officials (the managers), and dependents (the commoners). In ancient civilizations, the landowning class and the privately owned estate—whether owned by a temple, the ruler, or a private individual—provided security for the estate's dependents. All early states developed where agricultural production became more intensified and diverse. At the same time, early states moved away from purely kin-based organization into centralized structures that crosscut or overrode kinship ties (Figure 14.7).

Economic power also rested in trade and long-distance exchange networks, which provided access to commodities not available locally. Sumer obtained its metal from Anatolia, Iran, and the Persian Gulf. Egypt acquired gold and ivory from Nubia, and highland Andean civilizations imported fish meal from the Pacific Coast. The acquisition of exotic commodities or goods on any scale required organization, record keeping, and supervision. The archaeological record shows that the extent of state supervision of trade and traders varied considerably from civilization to civilization.

Social power means ideological power, and it comes from the creation or modification of certain symbols of cultural and political commonality (Brumfiel, 1983, 1992). This common ideology, expressed in public and private ceremonials, in art and architecture, and in literature, served to link individuals and communities with common ties that transcend those of kin. Those who create and perpetuate ideologies are held in high honor and enjoy considerable prestige, for they are often perceived as interceding with the spiritual world and the deities and sometimes even seen as flesh-and-blood divines themselves. The guardians of ideology are privileged individuals, for their spiritual powers give them special social status and allow them to perpetuate social inequality. So important was ideology in the ancient world that one can speak of the Mesopotamian or Maya areas not in a political sense, for they were made up of patchworks of city-states, but in an ideological sense. Many great cities of the past, like Teotihuacán in the Valley of Mexico or Angkor Thom in Cambodia, were a combination of the spiritual and the secular. They all boasted powerful priesthoods and religious institutions, which owed their wealth to their ability to manage the spiritual affairs of the state and to legitimize rulers as upholders of the cosmic order (see Site box). The temples and public buildings they erected formed imposing settings for elaborate public ceremonies, which ensured the continuity of human life and the universe.

Political power rested in the ruler's ability to impose authority throughout society by both administrative and military means. Those who held positions of authority in either the bureaucracy or the army did not come from within the kin system but were recruited

SITE

The Lord of Sicán at Huaca Loro, Peru

In 1990–1992, archaeologist Izumu Shimada and a team of researchers excavated the Huaco Loro pyramid in the Lambayeque Valley area of Peru's north coast, to investigate the little known Sicán culture, successor to the flamboyant Moche state in the region. The archaeologists unearthed a tomb at the north base of the pyramid that comprised a 3-m (10-foot) square burial chamber at the base of a 10-m (33-foot) vertical shaft sunk into the clay of the river floodplain.

A man of 40 to 50 years of age lay in an inverted position in the chamber, surrounded by his full ceremonial regalia. This included a large textile shawl with almost 2000 small gold foils sewn to the now-vanished cloth. The owner would have glittered and shimmered in the sun when he wore the mantle. A pair of ceremonial gloves were fashioned of gold, silver, and copper, one holding a golden cup, the other a wooden staff ornamented with gold and gold-silver-copper alloy. The man owned several golden headdresses, a semicircular bladed ceremonial knife with silver working edge, and a formal standard. He wore a gold mask with dripping nostrils, symbolic of his role as a shaman and a living personification of the Sicán deity, who is depicted in similar regalia (Figure 14.8).

The burial chamber included the skeletons of two young women and two juveniles, who were sacrificial victims, a disassembled litter, which had once carried the lord to his grave, imported seashells, clusters of beads, and bundles of copper, metal scrap, and thousands of copper sheet fragments, thought to have been a simple form of currency.

The Sicán lord's grave shows the extraordinary skills of Peruvian metalsmiths centuries before the Spanish Conquest. They were well aware of alloying, developed ways of joining metal sheets without solder, and made ornaments by cutting out metal and by hammering decoration into sheets for a repoussé effect. Like other Andean metalworkers, they used depletion gilding, a technique that used acids to deplete baser metals from the surface of alloyed metal objects, leaving them high in gold concentration and with a golden appearance.

FIGURE 14.8 The gold funerary mask of the Lord of Sicán, Huaca Loro, Peru.

---

from outside it (Figure 14.9). This political power lay in foreign relations and in defense and making war. It also operated on a statewide level, dealing with the resolution of major disputes between different factions. But a great deal of power lay outside the political estate, in the hands of community and kin leaders, who handled many legal matters revolving around such issues as landownership and family law.

Norman Yoffee (1990) believes that the interplay between these three sources of power led to the development of new, societywide institutions: supreme rulers and the state. There was, he says, no one moment when civilization came into being, for social evolution did not end with the rise of the state. Preindustrial states functioned in an atmosphere of continual change and constant disputation. Some collapsed; others survived for many centuries.

This theory argues not for neoevolutionary ladders but, rather, for many trajectories for the development of social complexity. Many societies operated under

FIGURE 14.9 An eagle knight, a class of elite warriors that formed an important part of the Aztec power structure in prehispanic Mexico.

significant constraints; they may have lacked, say, dependable crops or domesticated animals or the ability to store large amounts of food. Constraints like these took human societies along very different evolutionary paths from those of the state. That some societies did not become civilizations does not mean that they were stuck in a backward "stage" but simply that constraints on growth prevented the interplay of the major factors that led to state formation elsewhere. Thus, the chiefdom is an alternative trajectory to the state. In the chiefdom, social inequality came from within the kin system; in the state, inequality was based on access to resources and the power this access provided. It is no coincidence that the latest theories on state formation begin with the chiefdom.

Chiefly Cycling: Processes and Agents

The world's first states, politically centralized and socially stratified societies, developed in only a few locations—in Egypt and Mesopotamia by 3000 B.C., and in Mexico and the Andean region by 200 B.C. Invariably, they were formed in a distinctive political environment, in what Kent Flannery calls "the dynamic crucible of cycling chiefdoms" (1999, p. 5). He, and others, believe that states arise in situations where a group of chiefdoms are competing with one another, as they did along the Nile River in the fourth millennium B.C., for example. Eventually, one of the competitors succeeded in achieving political dominance over its neighbors, so that they become provinces of a larger political unit. This competition can arise from many causes: rivalry between chiefly families, factionalism, endemic warfare and raiding, dramatic differences in population densities from one area to the next, crop failure, or just plain weak leadership or outright conquest.

Henry Wright (1984) has described this process among chiefdoms as "cycling," a constant fluctuation between simple and more complex chiefdoms. Each chief presides over a single village and some lesser hamlets nearby. Then one leader usurps the power of his once egalitarian neighbors and forms a much larger political unit, where the former village chiefs become subchiefs. The newly powerful kingdom expands, then breaks down into smaller chiefdoms again, or simply collapses in a recurrent process of emergence, expansion, and fragmentation.

Ancient chiefdoms had the hereditary inequality and hierarchical social structure from which a state could arise, but this rarely happened. Robert Carneiro (1994), an expert on chiefdoms, has suggested no less than six processes for creating one. You defeat neighboring communities in war, then incorporate them into a larger political unit. At the same time, you take prisoners and force them to work for you as slaves. Once you have established control, you appoint close supporters to administer the conquered areas, unless the defeated chiefs are cooperative. Your subjects pay you tribute at regular intervals and are expected to provide fighting men in times of war. States were much larger and more centralized than chiefdoms, as well as being much more stratified socially and politically. Invariably, however, they shared the processes that Carneiro lays out.

Under this argument, then, state formation began with Carneiro's six processes, with the addition of chiefly cycling. Centuries might pass with the usual cycles of simplicity and complexity without any quantum jump in social and political complexity. Then, suddenly, three processes come together (Wright, 1984):

- A standoff of some kind between neighboring and constantly warring chiefdoms develops, reflected in the dispersal of population of the development of "buffer zones" between neighbors.
- One center rapidly acquires additional population, perhaps at the expense of its neighbors. Sometimes highly organized warfare comes into play, as campaigns of conquest replace the constant raiding of earlier times. Conquered areas are incorporated into the new, much larger kingdom.
- A large capital settlement, usually a city, develops as the ultimate level in a four-level settlement hierarchy: city, regional centers, subcenters, and villages.

Carneiro and Wright believe that the formation of states required some form of territorial expansion. But there are limits to the amount of resources that chiefs and their elites can extract from their followers. When that moment comes, they have several options: increase their demands on their subjects, which raises the specter of rebellion; intensify agricultural production with technological innovation; or expand their territory by subjugating their neighbors. If the third alternative is chosen, the kingdom rapidly comes to a point where it becomes larger than the chief himself can administer, so he has to restructure the way he administers his domains and probably make ideological changes to reflect the new political system—a state. This process is reasonably well documented in Mesopotamia and Egypt, also in Mesoamerica and the Andes.

These are, however, generalized, anonymous processes, like those criticized by post-processualists. As scholars of the latter school have often pointed out, it is people, individuals and groups, who are responsible for political and other cultural change. They are the "agents," as opposed to the "processes" (Flannery, 1999). To study ancient agents requires very rich historical records, which enable us to identify individuals and describe their deeds. In some cases, like Egypt, we know the names of seminal rulers like the early Egyptian pharaoh Narmer, but they are little more than shadowy personages on the stage of history. There is no question, however, that people of great ability and charisma were responsible for the rise of many powerful states known from historical times. Flannery (1999) describes the remarkable King Shaka, who set up the Zulu state in South Africa in the early nineteenth century (Figure 14.10), King Kamehameha of Hawaii, and others. All were individuals who were products of their times, whose personal abilities made the most of unusual circumstances, accidental situations, and other moments where they could further their political and military goals. The result was, invariably, a process of historical change.

Flannery goes on to list several qualities that marked Shaka and other agents and argues that they were shared by the chiefs of unusual ability who created the first civilizations. They were members of an elite, people with aggressive and authoritarian personalities, with outstanding military abilities that gave them upward social mobility. They usurped the position of chief by fair means or foul, then conquered their immediate neighbors while seeking a competitive advantage over more distant rivals (this could be technological, a matter of military strategy, and so on). They used this advantage to expand into more distant lands while using forced labor to intensify agricultural production as a means of keeping one's subjects content and of provisioning

FIGURE 14.10   One of the Zulu ruler Shaka's warriors.

armies. If they could not intensify their food production, they acquired additional resources by raiding. Finally, they solidified their position by power-sharing, even if it was nothing more than a nominal gesture. This was definitely not democracy. Strong, able rulers headed the earliest states. They governed autocratically, even if they had nominal councils of advisers.

Much depends on ideology, too, for invariably the preindustrial states were held together by a powerful and distinctive ideology. The famous Epic of Gilgamesh gives us a flavor of Mesopotamian ideology. The pharaohs ruled as the living personification of the sun god. Maya lords were shamans and intermediaries between the people and the ancestors. These ideologies were reflected in sacred places, where lavish ceremonies and public appearances by the ruler were important symbols of continuity and stability, where the ruler's subjects directed their loyalty to the central figure at the pinnacle of the state. Ideology never caused states to come into being, but was an invariable and important part of their fabric once they had come into being.

Both processes and individual agents played vital roles in the formation of states. Aggressive individuals of great ambition have been members of human societies since the beginning, but, until about 6000 years ago, they never lived at a time when conditions of social inequality and chiefly competition were endemic in areas like Mesopotamia and the Nile Valley, or later in Mesoamerica and the Andes. Then these circumstances, competitive advantage, military prowess, and other factors turned a very few of them from powerful chiefs into authoritarian kings, soon supported by compelling new ideologies developed from earlier and less complex worldviews.

⸙ The Collapse of Civilizations

Many historians, among them Paul Kennedy (1987), have written about cycles of history, the rise of civilizations, their brilliant apogees, and their sudden declines. Eventually one civilization falls and another rises to take its place; this replacement in turn goes through the same cycle of rise and fall. The record of early civilizations could easily be written in cyclical terms, for states have risen and then collapsed with bewildering rapidity in all parts of the world within the past 5000 years. In the Mexican highlands, for example, the great city of Teotihuacán flourished between about 200 B.C. and A.D. 700. In A.D. 600, it had a population of more than 125,000 people. For 600 of these years, more than 85 percent of the population of the Valley of Mexico lived in or close to Teotihuacán. Then the city collapsed in the eighth century A.D. Within half a century, the population shrank to a quarter of its former size. A series of lesser states competed to fill the political vacuum left by the great city's fall, until the Toltecs, and later the Aztecs, rose to supremacy (see Chapter 21).

When a complex society collapses, it suddenly becomes smaller, simpler, and much more egalitarian. Population densities fall; trade and economic activity dry up; information flow declines; and the known world shrinks for the survivors. Joseph Tainter (1988), one of the few archaeologists to have made a comparative study of collapse, points out that an initial investment by a society in growing complexity is a rational way of trying to solve the needs of the moment. At first, the strategy works. Agricultural production increases through more intensive farming methods; an emerging bureaucracy works well; and expanding trade networks bring wealth to a new elite who use their authority and economic clout to undertake great public works, such as pyramids and temples, that validate their spiritual authority and divine associations. Maya civilization is an excellent example of these processes in action. It prospered greatly for centuries in the Mesoamerican lowlands until a point of diminishing returns was reached.

As the most costly solutions to a society's needs are exhausted, it becomes imperative to find new organizational and economic answers, which may have much lower yields and may cost a great deal more. As these stresses develop, argues Tainter, a complex society such as that of the Maya is increasingly vulnerable to collapse. There are few reserves to carry the society through droughts, famines, floods, and other natural disasters. Eventually, collapse ensues, especially when important segments of society perceive that centralization and social complexity simply do not work any more and that they are better off on their own. The trend toward decentralization, toward collapse, becomes compelling. Tainter calls collapse not a catastrophe but a rational process that occurs when increasing stress requires some organizational change. The population decline and other catastrophic effects that just preceded, accompanied, or followed collapse may have been traumatic at the time, but they can be looked at as part of what one might call an economizing process.

There is, of course, more to collapse than merely an economizing process. Complete collapse can occur only where there is a power vacuum. In many cases, a powerful neighbor may be waiting in the wings. In early times, numerous city-states traded and competed with one another within a small area. Sumerian cities, Minoan and Mycenaean palace kingdoms in Greece and the Aegean, the Maya centers in Mesoamerica—all existed in close interdependence within their cultural areas, in a state of constant "**peer-polity interaction.**" They traded, fought, and engaged in constant diplomacy. Under these circumstances, to collapse is an invitation to be dominated by one's competitors. There is loss of complexity only when every polity in the interacting cluster collapses at the same time (Yoffee and Cowgill, 1988).

The collapse of early civilizations, then, may be closely connected to declining returns from social complexity and to the normal political processes of factionalism, social unrest, succession disputes, and even civil war (Brumfiel and Fox, 1994).

Summary 〰〰〰

This chapter contrasts the historical and anthropological approaches to the origins of states and summarizes the six main theories developed by archaeologists. Gordon Childe's "Urban Revolution" theory centered on the development of the city. Another group of theories involved the intensification of agriculture and irrigation. Exchange networks and warfare have also been espoused as potential causes of civilization.

Many modern theories revolve around systems-evolutionary hypotheses and explanations involving environmental change. A new generation of social approaches, on the other hand, argues that religious and informational factors, epitomized by centralized authority, have been key elements in the regulation of environmental and economic variables in early civilization. Such theories also stress that the social structure of a society ultimately determines its transformation, so the search for the causes of civilization focuses on ecological variables and the opportunities they present to individuals pursuing political goals in different societies. In other words, how is ecological opportunity or necessity translated into political change? Recent research is now focusing on the dynamics of how ancient civilizations functioned—on factionalism, ideology, and gender as promising areas of inquiry.

The record of early civilizations can be written in cyclical terms. Their collapse may be closely connected to diminishing returns from social complexity, as well as normal political processes such as succession disputes.

Key Terms 🐾

Bartering The exchange, from hand-to-hand, of goods or services for equivalent value.

City Complex, relatively dense settlements with a degree of organizational complexity well beyond that of a village or town. Cities had several thousand inhabitants, the lower limit being between 2000 and 5000 people.

Exchange system A system for exchanging goods and services between individuals and communities.

Fertile Crescent A broad semicircle of land in southwestern Asia that encompasses the areas of the earliest civilizations—a term coined by Egyptologist Henry Breasted in the 1920s.

Peer-polity interaction A state of interdependence between neighboring political units such as city-states, which are equals.

Reciprocity The exchange of commodities or objects between two parties, where each side is obliged to respond, ultimately, in kind.

Redistribution The dispersing of trade goods from a central place throughout a society, a complex process that was a critical part of the development of civilization.

Urban Revolution V. Gordon Childe's term for the time when cities and civilization emerged in southwestern Asia.

Guide to Further Reading 🐾

Adams, Robert M. 1966. *The Evolution of Urban Society*. Chicago: Aldine.
An essay on the origins of civilization that stresses social and economic change; based on the author's fieldwork in Mesopotamia and comparative data from the New World.

Feinman, Gary M., and T. Douglas Price, eds. 2001. *Archaeology at the Millennium*. New York: Kluwer Academic/Plenum.
Chapters 10 to 13 of this useful source book survey many of the issues in this chapter at a more technical level.

Flannery, Kent V. 1972. "The Cultural Evolution of Civilizations." In *Annual Review of Ecology and Systematics*, pp. 399–426. Palo Alto, CA: Annual Reviews.
A masterly summary of the systems approach to early civilization that demonstrates the complexities of explaining the past.

Redman, Charles L. 1978. *The Rise of Civilization: From Early Farmers to Urban Society in the Ancient Near East*. San Francisco: W. H. Freeman.
A book that covers all the theories of the 1960s and 1970s about the origins of civilization and the key sites and concepts. For the advanced student. Strongly recommended as a follow-up to this text.

Robinson, Andrew. 1995. *The Story of Writing*. London and New York: Thames & Hudson.
A delightful and lavishly illustrated introduction to ancient writing. Ideal for enthusiastic beginners.

Sanders, William T., Jeffrey R. Parsons, and Robert S. Santley. 1979. *The Basin of Mexico: Ecological Processes in the Evolution of a Civilization*. New York: Academic Press.
An exemplary area study of highland Mesoamerican civilization that is crammed with wisdom about the study of complex societies. Also an unusually thorough archaeological study. Technical, but strongly recommended.

Yoffee, Norman. 1990. "Too Many Chiefs? Or Safe Texts for the 90s." In *Archaeological Theory—Who Sets the Agenda?* Andrew Sherratt and Norman Yoffee, eds. Pp. 60–78. Cambridge: Cambridge University Press.
A closely argued essay on power and early states that is remarkable for its clarity and compelling arguments.

EARLY CIVILIZATIONS IN SOUTHWEST ASIA

Head of Gudea from Lagash, Iraq.

I n 1872, an earnest banknote-engraver-turned-clay-tablet-expert named George Smith was sorting through the dusty fragments of Assyrian king Assurbanipal's royal library in the British Museum. Suddenly, he came across a tablet bearing a reference to a large ship grounded on a mountain. Immediately, he realized he had found an account of a flood that bore a remarkable resemblance to the biblical story of the Flood in Genesis. A prophet named Hasisadra is warned of the gods' intention to destroy all of sinful humankind. He builds a large ship, loads it with his family, "the beast of the field, the animal of the field." The flood destroys "all [other] life from the face of the earth." The ship goes aground on a mountain. Hasisadra sends out a dove, which returns. Eventually, a raven is dispatched and never returns. Hasisadra releases the animals, becomes a god, and lives happily ever after.

George Smith's discovery caused a public sensation at a time when people believed in the literal historical truth of the Scriptures. Seventeen lines of the story were missing, so the London *Daily Telegraph* paid Smith's way to Nineveh to find the missing fragments. Incredible though it may seem, Smith found them within five days. The tablets can be seen on display in the British Museum, duly labeled "DT," for *Daily Telegraph*.

The Victorians thought of Mesopotamia (Greek for "land between the rivers") as the location of the biblical Garden of Eden. Today, it is a far from paradisal place, for the delta regions and floodplain (Figure 15.1) between the Tigris and Euphrates rivers form a hot, low-lying environment, much of it inhospitable sand, swamp, and dry mudflats. Yet this now-inhospitable region was the cradle of the world's earliest urban civilizations (Table 15.1) (Lloyd, 1983; Pollock, 1999; Postgate, 1993). From north to south, Mesopotamia is approximately 965 km (600 miles) long and 400 km (250 miles) wide, extending from the uplands of Iran to the east to the Arabian and Syrian deserts in the west. The plains are subject to long, intensely hot summers and harsh, cold winters and would be desert but for the Euphrates and Tigris. There are few permanent water supplies other than these great rivers and their tributaries. Rainfall is slight, undependable, and insufficient for the growing of crops. But with irrigation, the alluvial soils of the lower plain can be farmed and their natural fertility unlocked. Farmers can obtain high crop yields from relatively limited areas of land, sufficient to feed relatively dense populations. By 6000 B.C., and perhaps earlier, village farmers were diverting the waters of the rivers. Within 2000 years, the urban civilization of the Sumerians was flourishing in Mesopotamia (Maisels, 1993, 2001).

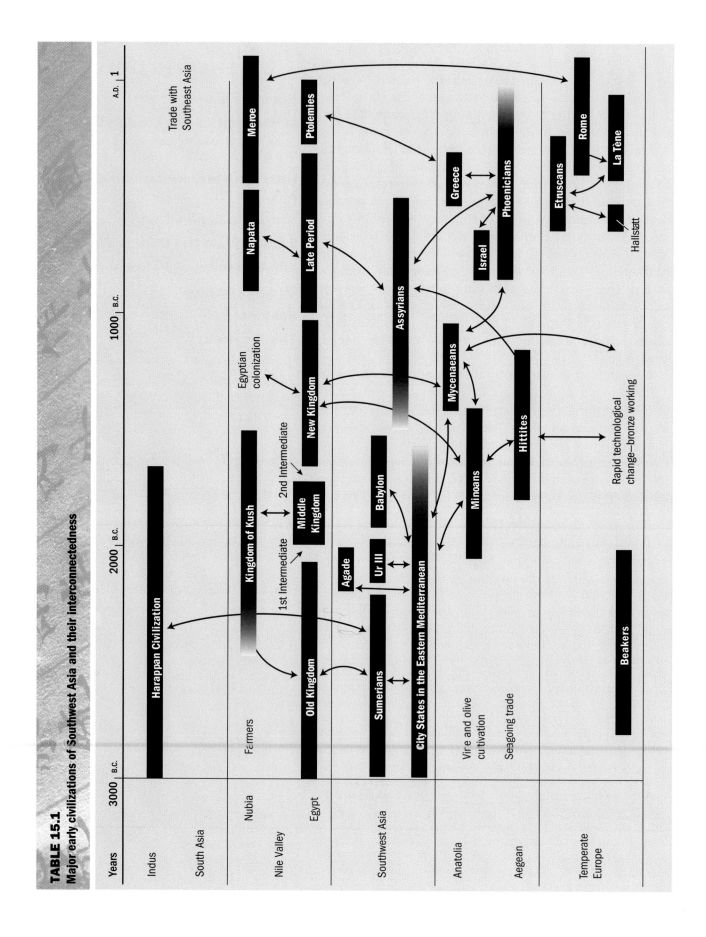

TABLE 15.1
Major early civilizations of Southwest Asia and their interconnectedness

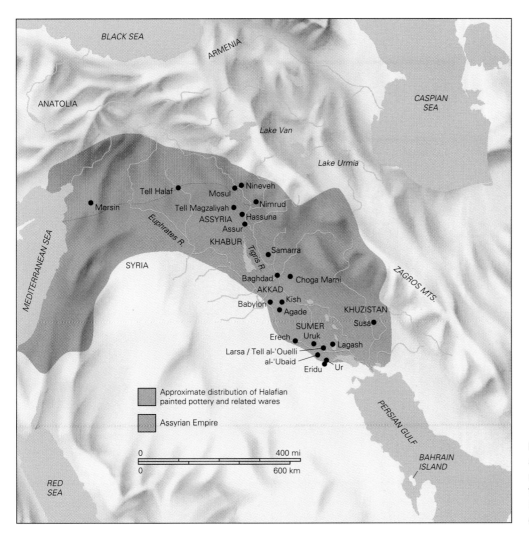

FIGURE 15.1 Sites and cultural distributions mentioned in this chapter. (Tepe Yahya and Shari-i-Shokhta lie to the east of the map.)

〰 Upland Villages

With continued improvement in agricultural methods and the development of such technological innovations as pottery, the village communities of the Zagros foothills, east of Mesopotamia, achieved a more efficient subsistence base that fed a gradually increasing farming population. These technological and economic changes were far from spectacular: By at least 7000 B.C., farmers were living on the Assyrian plains, at first in areas where they could rely on seasonal rainfall to water their crops; later, they settled by the rivers, with animals and crops that could tolerate the climate of the lowlands. There, they developed simple irrigation methods to bring water to their fields (Zeder, 1994).

The first farmers to settle in Assyria were scattered over the undulating plains in compact village settlements like Tell Magzaliyah. The successive occupation layers of these sites are filled with handmade pottery of coarse clay painted or incised with dots, circles, and other designs (Figure 15.2a). Such wares—named Hassunan pottery, after Hassuna, the first excavated village of this type—are found over a wide area of the north, from the upper Tigris Valley to the plains west of the modern city of Mosul.

Hassuna
6000 B.C.

The regions between Mosul in the north and Baghdad in the south were inhabited by irrigation farmers by at least 6000 B.C., and probably many centuries earlier. We know this from discoveries of villages in the region of Samarra, on the fringes of the Mesopotamian Delta. Samarran painted pottery (Figure 15.2b), which comes from such sites as Choga Mami, reveals early farming villages in areas where irrigation agriculture was the only viable means of food production (Oates, 1973). The Samarran sites near Choga Mami are situated along low ridges parallel to nearby hills, where

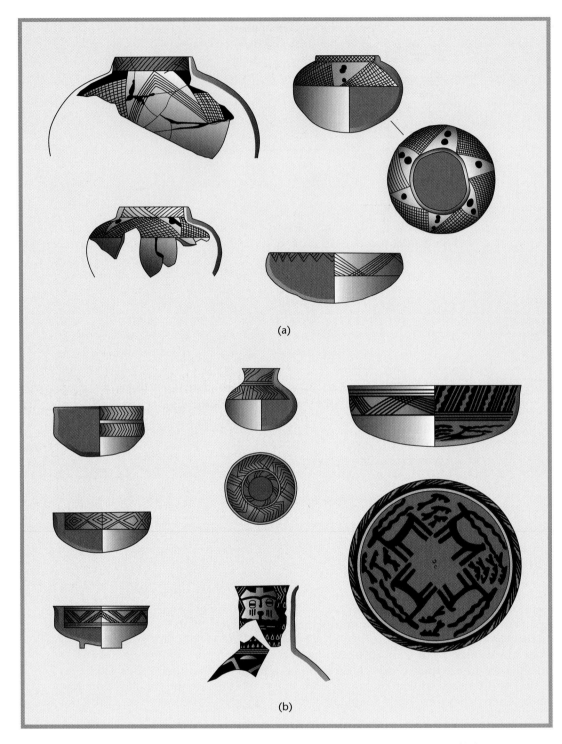

FIGURE 15.2 Early Mesopotamian painted pottery: (a) vessels from Hassuna; (b) Samarra-type vessels from Hassuna. (All one-eighth full size.)

Choga Mami   irrigation could be practiced with the least effort. Traces of canals are found at Choga Mami, as are traces of wheat, barley, and linseed, a crop that can be grown in this area only when irrigation is used. Choga Mami itself lies between two rivers, where floodwaters could be diverted across the fields and then drained away to prevent salt buildup. This is a relatively easy form of irrigation. Presumably, later refinements in technology enabled other farming settlements to move away from naturally flooded areas into regions where more extensive irrigation was necessary. There is every indication that the Samarrans were advanced farmers who lived in substantial villages, which in the case of Choga Mami may have covered up to 6 ha (14.8 acres) and housed more than 1000 souls.

The Samarrans occupied relatively low-lying territory between the arid delta of the south and the dry agriculture areas of the Hassunans to the north. Their newly developed irrigation techniques and heat-tolerant strains of wheat and barley enabled them to settle in areas that previously had been inaccessible. Their sedentary and permanent settlements and great reliance on agriculture allowed them to forge community and external social and economic bonds that provided a catalyst for more complex societies to develop in future millennia.

In about 6000 B.C., many village farmers in Southwest Asia began to make a characteristic style of painted pottery, abandoning the monochrome wares they had made before. The new fashion spread from southwest Turkey around the shores of Lake Van, famous for its obsidian, and as far east as the Zagros Mountains. The most brilliantly painted pottery was made in northern Iraq by the inhabitants of Tell Halaf, whose enormous kilns produced bowls, dishes, and flasks adorned with elaborate, stylized patterns and representations of people and animals (Figure 15.3). The Halafian cultural tradition flourished in what had once been Hassunan territory, and the people maintained regular contact with the Samarrans to the south.

Halafian
6000 B.C.

The Halafians still lived in much the same ways as did their predecessors, and they made no startling agricultural or technological innovations. They developed new contacts between villages hundreds of miles apart, trading such commodities as obsidian, semiprecious stone, and other luxury items, including painted pots with motifs that were standardized over large distances. Neutron activation and other chemical studies of pottery clays have shown that Halafian painted pots, made at a so-far-unidentified location, were traded to settlements like Mersin and Choga Mami, about 960 km (600 miles) apart. In some areas, the main settlement produced most of the fine pottery found in the villages of the surrounding area. It is as if the production and distribution of some items favored by elite members of society were concentrated at key trade centers along water routes. In the Khabur area, the same clay studies hint that both major and minor Halafian settlements produced the goods consumed in their own hinterlands, while restricting the access of nearby subordinate villages to this higher-level trade. This may be a sign that chiefdoms had evolved among Halafian communities in the region. As with the Hopewell in North America, these new elite groups required greater communication and the sharing of status goods, such as painted pottery, to reinforce their authority (Redman, 1978).

FIGURE 15.3 Halafian painted pot from northern Iraq.

〰️ Settlement of the Lowlands

Human settlement along the Persian Gulf shifted as sea levels rose at the end of the Ice Age. The complicated climatic changes in this region since 15,000 years ago form the environmental backdrop to the rise of civilization in Mesopotamia.

Environmental Change

In about 15,000 B.C., during the late Ice Age, the Persian Gulf was dry land, so the Tigris and Euphrates rivers flowed into the Gulf of Oman 800 km (500 miles) south of their present mouths. After 12,000 B.C., sea levels rose rapidly, as they did in other parts of the world, rising from about –20 m (–66 feet) in 6000 B.C. to 2 m (7 feet) above modern levels between 4000 and 3000 B.C. As sea levels rose, riverborne alluvium filled the Persian Gulf, building a vast delta that advanced gradually to the south, leaving freshwater lakes and marshes in its wake (Sanlaville, 1989). These thick layers of alluvium mask the archaeological record of any late Ice Age or early Holocene occupation of the lowlands. Almost certainly, however, both hunter-gatherers and farmers lived off fish and other resources in these low-lying areas for many thousands of years.

The dramatic environmental changes at the end of the Ice Age were significant factors in the development of city-states in southern Mesopotamia. Frank Hole (1994) has developed a hypothetical scenario. Two environmental factors played a vital role: drastic changes in sea level at the end of the Ice Age and intense climatic variability, especially during the fifth millennium B.C., when the so-called climatic optimum after the Ice Age finally ended (Chapter 7). Summer temperatures were considerably higher, with more rainfall, which lasted for a long period, allowing longer growing seasons for crops planted during the winter. The water table may have been higher, so that dry agriculture was possible in areas that a few centuries later could be cultivated only with irrigation.

6000 B.C.　Before 6000 B.C., villages—each of them self-sufficient and egalitarian—supported populations of between 50 and 200 people. In about 6000 B.C., a population decline began; people now lived in much larger towns, and much of the landscape was devoid of settlement. In other words, the gradual expansion of farming communities that had begun 2000 years earlier now ceased. At the same time, contacts between neighboring communities intensified, perhaps in part to make up for shortages of grain and other commodities in different areas during a time of climatic change. By the beginning of the Uruk period, in about 4600 B.C., settlements were linked by canals, once-handmade pottery was now wheel-produced, and the building of temples became more prevalent.

Within a millennium, there were large cities in Mesopotamia. These changes took place as the Mesopotamian landscape changed dramatically. Rising sea levels caused settlements to change locations frequently, rainfall became more irregular, the environment became drier, and agricultural populations were dislocated. Some areas were abandoned altogether, as many groups dispersed into nomadic lifeways and others gathered in favored locations on the Mesopotamian floodplain.

By the mid-fourth millennium B.C., the climate and land had stabilized, so that the development of more extensive irrigation systems and the support of much larger communities were possible. The people who had abandoned dispersed villages and moved to favored areas provided the labor forces that could be organized to develop large-scale irrigation systems and a new economic infrastructure. Within a short time, a new demographic and social order developed that culminated in the appearance of the world's first literate urban civilization. Hole believes it was no coincidence that the first cities in southern Mesopotamia formed between 3500 and 3000 B.C., soon after local sea levels stabilized. Hole's scenario is somewhat hypothetical. What, then, do we know from archaeology?

Archaeological Evidence

The first known lowland farming communities date to around 5800 B.C., small communities located in clusters along the Euphrates channels. The largest of these clusters consisted of small rural communities located around a larger town that covered about 10 ha (28 acres) and housed perhaps between 2500 and 4000 people. Small canals up to 5 km (3 miles) long watered the fields around these settlements. The farmers grew barley and dates and herded cattle, sheep, and goats. These clusters of settlements are subsumed under the term *'Ubaid,* after a small site (al-'Ubaid) near Ur (Huot, 1989).

We do not know anything about how the first inhabitants of the Mesopotamian floodplain acquired or developed the skills needed to survive in their harsh environment. Communal effort was essential because raw materials suitable for building houses had to be improvised from the plentiful sand, clay, palm trees, and reeds between the rivers. Digging even the smallest canal required at least a little political and social leadership. The backbreaking annual task of clearing silt from clogged river courses and canals can have been achieved only by communal effort. As both Robert Adams (1966) and Kent Flannery (1972) point out, the relationship between developing a stratified society and creating food surpluses is close. Distinctive social changes came from the more efficient systems for producing food that were essential in the delta. As food surpluses grew and the specialized agricultural economies of these 'Ubaid villages became successful, the trend toward sedentary settlement and higher population densities increased. Expanded trade networks and the redistribution of surpluses and trade goods also affected society, with dominant groups of 'Ubaid people becoming more active in producing surpluses, which eventually supported more and more people who were not farmers.

'Ubaid sites display considerable variation. The earliest known community is Tell al 'Ouelli, near Larsa, which dates to as early as 5800 B.C. (Forest, 1986). Within a few centuries, some of the larger settlements had substantial buildings, alleyways, and courtyards, but rural settlements like al-'Ubaid itself consisted of mud-brick and reed huts with roofs formed of bent sticks (Adams and Nissen, 1972). Al-'Ubaid and similar small clusters of hamlets shared ceremonial centers and were linked by kin and clan ties, one clan authority overseeing the villagers' affairs and, probably, the irrigation schemes that connected them. In time, the small village ceremonial centers grew, as did the one at Eridu (first settled around 4750 B.C., when the Tell Halaf peoples were still making their painted pottery in the north). Except at the very end of 'Ubaid times, there are no signs of social ranking in cemeteries or of any great differences in wealth between different individuals.

Eridu, a rapidly growing town, consisted of a mud-brick temple with fairly substantial mud-brick houses around it, often with a rectangular floor plan (see Site box, page 362). The craftsworkers lived a short distance from the elite, who were clustered around the temple, and still farther away were the dwellings of the farmers, who grew the crops that supported everyone. By 4500 B.C., the Eridu temple had grown large, containing altars and offering places and a central room bounded by rows of smaller compartments. The population of Eridu was as high as 5000 at this time, but exact computations are impossible.

🐾 Uruk: The Mesopotamian City

As Mesopotamian society grew in complexity, so did the need for social, political, and religious institutions that would provide an integrative function for everyone (Nissen, 1988; Pollock, 1992). The ancient city of Uruk epitomizes cultural developments just before and during the early stages of Sumerian civilization (H. Crawford, 1991; Yoffee, 1995). Archaeologically, we know most, of course, about the later stages of the city. At about 2800 B.C., the city core covered an estimated 250 ha (617 acres), with more people living in the hinterland. Built with an enormous expenditure of work as a community project, the ziggurat complex and its satellite temples were the center of Uruk life. The temples were not only storehouses and places of worship but also redistribution centers for surplus food. Hundreds of craftsworkers labored for the temple as stonemasons, copper workers, and weavers and in dozens of other specialized tasks. None of these people tilled the ground or worked on irrigation; they formed a distinctive class in a well-stratified society. In its earliest manifestations, between 4600 and 3800 B.C., Uruk was a nascent city on a much smaller scale but a settlement that was growing rapidly, many surrounding villages becoming part of the dense urban landscape. An earlier and smaller ziggurat towered over the city, which, just like Eridu, formed the core for the later monumental structure of Sumerian civilization.

'Ubaid
5800 B.C.

Tell al 'Ouelli
5800 B.C.

Eridu
4750 B.C.

Uruk
Before 4600 B.C.

SITE

The Temple at Eridu, Iraq

Sumerian legends called Eridu the earliest city of all, the dwelling place of Enki, God of the Abyss, the fountain of human wisdom. "All lands were the sea, then Eridu was made," proclaims a much later Mesopotamian creation legend. Sumerians considered Enki's word to have created order from the chaos of the primordial waters. Eridu itself once lay in the heart of a fertile riverside landscape. Today, harsh desert surrounds the ancient city. Its ruined temple platform stands at one end of the great city mounds, a low, flat mass of clay and sand with a dune forming downwind of the crumbling mound. For generations, the desolate site defied some of the best archaeologists in the world, who lacked the expertise to distinguish sun-dried mud brick from the surrounding soil. British archaeologist Richard Campbell-Thompson dug into Eridu in 1918 and complained that he found nothing but loose sand.

Thirty years later, Iraqi archaeologist Fuad Safar and his British colleague Seton Lloyd returned to the city with a large labor force and a small mining railroad, which enabled them to move enormous amounts of sand. They also had an expertise with mud-brick structures, using methods developed by German archaeologists at the great city of Babylon just before World War I, which used picks to "feel"

different soil textures. To this simple technique, they added brushes and compressed air, which proved an excellent way to clear mud brick. The two excavators removed enough sand to expose a small complex of mud-brick public buildings, still standing, about 2.4 m (8 feet) high. Then they embarked on a long-term project to decipher the history of the great shrine that had once stood at the heart of the city.

Safar and Lloyd soon found a solid brickwork platform extending from the base of the much later ruined ziggurat (temple). They spent two weeks piecing together scattered brick and reconstructed the foundations of a small, rectangular building surrounded by concentric brickwork triangles. After days of puzzlement, they realized they were looking at a temple platform that had been extended again and again by the simple expedient of adding another layer of brickwork around the shrine to build ever-larger, brilliantly decorated shrines, culminating in the great ziggurat that adorned the city before it was abandoned. At least five temples had stood atop the one exposed by Safar and Lloyd (Figure 15.4). They dismantled the rectangular structure and penetrated deep toward bedrock, uncovering no less than ten earlier shrines, each built atop its predecessor. Temple

● ●

Even as early as 3500 B.C., the entire life of Uruk and its connections with cities, towns, merchants, and mines hundreds of miles away revolved around the temple. The ruler of Uruk and the keeper of the temple was the *en*, both the secular and the religious leader. In its heyday, Uruk was far more than a city. Satellite villages extended out at least 10 km (6 miles), each with its own irrigation system, but population densities around the city were lower than they had been in earlier times. All provided food for those in the city, whether grain, fish, or meat. Each settlement depended on the others for survival, at first because each provided things essential for a well-balanced existence; later, the settlements needed protection from outsiders, who would have plundered their goods (Schwartz and Falconer, 1994). The Mesopotamian city had developed an elaborate system of management with a well-defined hierarchy of rulers and priests, landowners and bureaucrats, traders and peasants. This system organized and regulated society, meted out reward and punishment, and made policy decisions for the thousands of people who lived under it. The countryside became the hinterland of the city and, later, the city-state.

The city was a hallmark of early Mesopotamian civilization, but each urban center had different settlement characteristics and histories. Archaeological surveys record the remarkable fact that over 80 percent of the Sumerian population lived in settlements covering at least 10 ha (25 acres), in a form of "hyperurbanism" in the third

XVI, dated to c. 4500 B.C., lay on clean sand, a small mud-brick shrine 14 m (45 feet) square, with one entrance, an altar, and an offering table. Hundreds of fish bones, including the complete skeleton of a sea perch, still lay on the offering temple. Sea perch live in brackish water, like the shallow estuaries that were once close to Eridu.

Five hundred years later, Eridu's temple platform lay inside a sacred enclosure at least 180-m (200-yard) square enclosure at least 180 m (200 yards) square. A magnificent stepped ziggurat now rose in the center of the city, its facade adorned with brightly colored fired bricks. Crowded residential quarters and markets crowded on the sacred enclosure while the ziggurat was visible for kilometers around. Thanks to months of sophisticated and painstaking mud-brick excavation, we know that this imposing shrine was the descendant of much humbler temples that had commemorated the same sacred place.

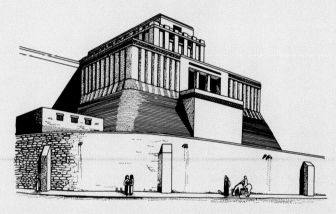

FIGURE 15.4 Artist's reconstruction of an Uruk culture temple at Eridu. Notice the great platform supporting the temple and the drainage pipes in the walls.

millennium B.C., a figure that had declined steadily by just under 50 percent by 2000 B.C. (Adams, 1981; Postgate, 1994).

By 3400 B.C., the first signs of writing appear. One theory has it that the Sumerians' commercial transactions were so complex that the opportunities for thievery and accounting mistakes were endless (Robinson, 1995). It was impossible to keep all the details in one's head. Many people used marked clay tokens, which they carried around on strings. Eventually, some clever officials made small clay tablets and scratched them with incised signs that depicted familiar objects such as pots or animals (Schmandt-Besserat, 1992) (Figure 15.5). Some scholars believe that from there it was a short step to more simplified, conventionalized, wedge-shaped (cuneiform) signs that were modeled so as to be closer and closer to phonetic syllables and spoken language (Figure 15.6). Other authorities disagree, arguing that tokens were supplements to written scripts (Yoffee, 1995). The controversy is still unresolved, but in fact, the earliest economic texts deal with internal administrative matters, usually small numbers and inventories, not with external trade. The new script was also commonly used for compiling lists of all kinds—occupations, places, things in the world, and so on—a common application of writing systems all over the globe, for example, that of the Mycenaeans of Greece (see Chapter 19).

At first, specially trained scribes used cuneiform to record inventories and administrative and commercial transactions (Nissen et al., 1993). Over more than 1000 years,

FIGURE 15.5 A clay tablet from Uruk used to record a transaction in barley, supervised by an official named Kushim. The transaction involved a large quantity of grain, some 135,000 liters (35,663 gallons) and may represent a summary of dealings over a long period of time.

the scribes gradually began to explore the limitless opportunities afforded by the ability to express oneself in writing. Kings used tablets to trumpet their victories and political triumphs. Fathers chided errant sons, and lawyers recorded complicated land transactions. Sumerian poetry includes love stories, great epics, hymns to the gods, and tragic laments bemoaning the destruction of city after city (Kramer, 1963). Temple records and accounts tell us much not only of economic and social organization but also of Mesopotamian folklore and religion.

On the plateau to the north, copper tools and ornaments had been in use for centuries, first appearing as early as the fifth or sixth millennium B.C. (Moorey, 1994). Although many peasant societies were aware of the properties of native copper, and both early Egyptians and Native Americans made hammered ornaments from it, the softness of the metal limits its uses. Eventually, though, people familiar with the kiln firing of pottery developed techniques for smelting copper ore. Copper is fine and lustrous and makes admirable ornaments. At first, it was a high-status metal, valued for its prestige. Copper was in widespread use for ornamentation in Iran during the fourth millennium and was imported into southern Mesopotamia as early as 3500 B.C., perhaps earlier. It enjoyed high status, for utilitarian implements like stone-bladed sickles remained in use throughout the third millennium B.C. Eventually, during the early second millennium, alloying with lead or tin came into widespread use, as metalsmiths learned how to produce bronze and other forms of tougher metal. Once alloying was understood, copper assumed a more central place in agriculture and warfare.

The later development of bronze weapons can be linked to the rise of warfare as a method of attaining political ends, for cities like Eridu and Uruk were not isolated from other centers. Indeed, they were only too aware of their neighbors. The city states of Lagash and Umma were uneasy neighbors and engaged in a tendentious border dispute that dragged on for three or four centuries. Cities soon had walls, a sure sign that they needed protection against marauders. Earlier cylinder seals (inscribed clay cylinders used as seals) bear scenes with prisoners of war.

By this time, too, there were southern Mesopotamian "colonies" in what is now northern Iraq, at Susa across the Tigris, in the Zagros, and elsewhere on the northern and northeastern peripheries of the lowlands. Some of these colonies were entire transplanted communities; others were small enclaves of traders in foreign towns, identified by their characteristic Uruk-style artifacts. Artifacts and artistic styles typical of Uruk and also Susa have come from the Nile Delta during the centuries when long-distance caravan trade was expanding rapidly in Egypt and across the Sinai.

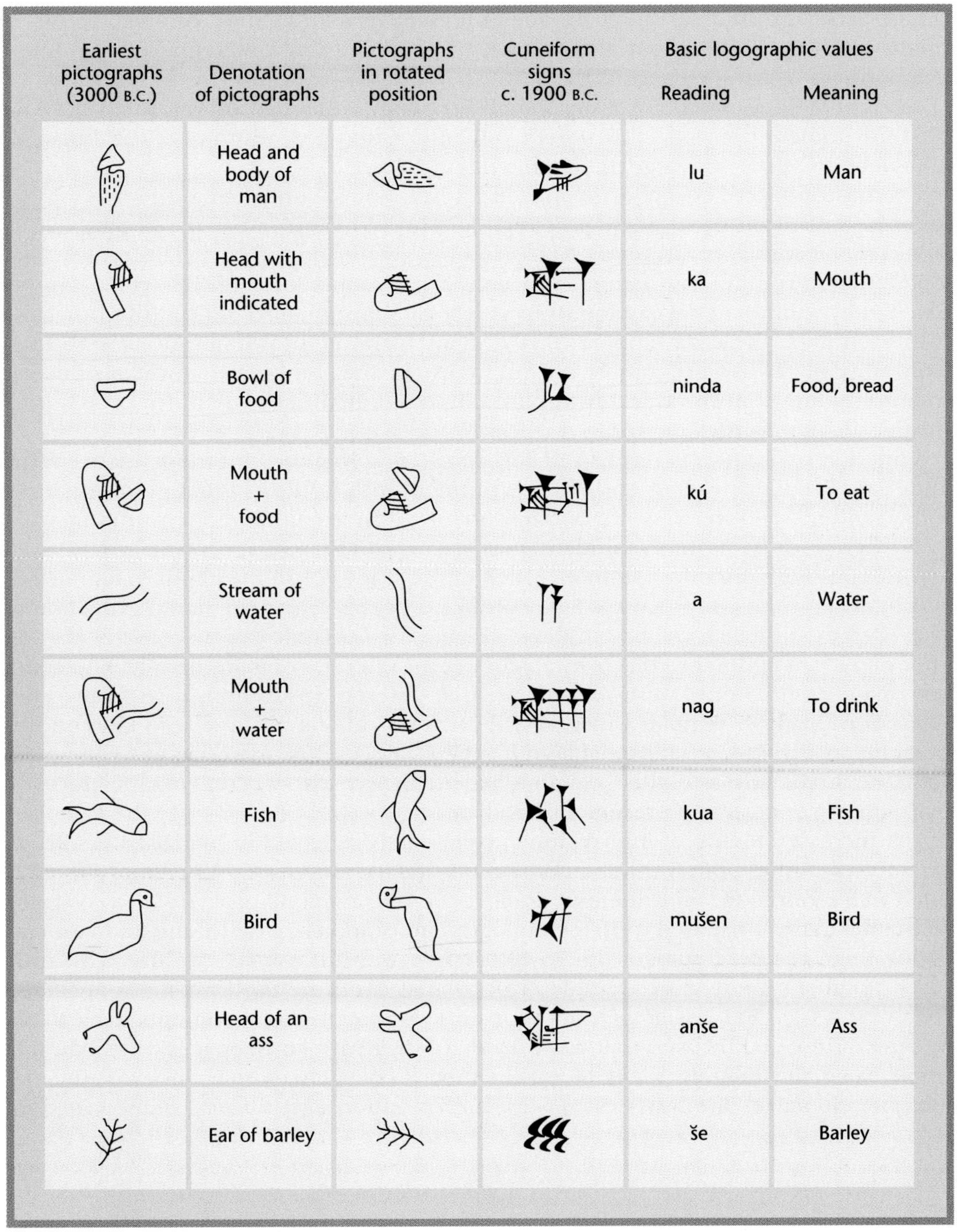

Earliest pictographs (3000 B.C.)	Denotation of pictographs	Pictographs in rotated position	Cuneiform signs c. 1900 B.C.	Basic logographic values	
				Reading	Meaning
	Head and body of man			lu	Man
	Head with mouth indicated			ka	Mouth
	Bowl of food			ninda	Food, bread
	Mouth + food			kú	To eat
	Stream of water			a	Water
	Mouth + water			nag	To drink
	Fish			kua	Fish
	Bird			mušen	Bird
	Head of an ass			anše	Ass
	Ear of barley			še	Barley

FIGURE 15.6
Development of Sumerian writing, from a pictographic script to a cuneiform script and then to a phonetic system. The word *cuneiform* is derived from the Latin *cuneus*, meaning "a wedge," after the characteristic impression of the script.

༄ Sumerian Civilization

With the appearance of the Sumerian civilization in about 3000 B.C., we have entered a new era in human experience, one in which the economic, political, and social mechanisms created by humans began to affect the lives of cities, towns, and villages located hundreds, if not thousands, of miles apart. No human society created by *Homo sapiens sapiens* has ever flourished in complete isolation, and, as we saw in Chapter 7, regular interaction and exchange between neighboring hunter-gatherer groups assumed ever-greater importance in the late Ice Age and the early Holocene. In Southwest Asia, after 9000 B.C., long-distance exchanges in such vital commodities as obsidian, to say nothing of luxury goods like seashells, reached considerable proportions and extended over much of Anatolia, the coastal eastern Mediterranean, and even farther afield (Algaze, 1993). The real launching point in long-distance exchange and organized trade took place during the fourth millennium B.C., the first millennium in prehistory when the history of an individual society can be understood only

Sumerian civilization
c. 3000 to 2334 B.C.

against a background of much broader regional developments. In a real sense, a rapidly evolving "world system" linked, with ever-changing cultural tentacles, hundreds of Southwest Asian societies all the way from eastern Iran and the Indus Valley in Pakistan to Mesopotamia, the eastern Mediterranean, Anatolia, and the Nile Valley. In the third millennium B.C., this system not only embraced Southwest Asia but also extended to Cyprus, the Aegean, and mainland Greece.

This nascent world system developed as a result of insatiable demands for nonlocal raw materials in different ecological regions where societies were developing along very similar general evolutionary tracks toward greater complexity. The broad, and apparently linear, cultural sequence in southern Mesopotamia just described can be matched by equivalent developments in northern Mesopotamia and east of the Tigris.

In each area, these developments and many technological innovations were triggered not only by basic economic needs but also by the competitive instincts of newly urbanized elites, who used lavish display and exotic luxuries to reaffirm their social prestige and authority.

Sumerian civilization is a mirror of this developing regional interdependence. The Sumerians lived in a treeless lowland environment with fertile soils but no metal, little timber, and no semiprecious stones. They obtained these commodities by trading with areas where such items were abundant, perhaps initially on a village-by-village basis and later in a far more organized fashion. Much of this trade was in the hands of temple organizations, for the temples served as centralized storehouses, and many luxury goods were used to embellish public buildings (Figure 15.7). Trade was an integral part of Sumerian life, a multifaceted activity absorbing the energies of many people. Food and many basic commodities were redistributed by different institutions for specific purposes. For example, temples would distribute food rations to those who labored for them. Petty officials were allocated land for their services. Raw materials were obtained from the highlands and the Iranian Plateau to the east for the manufacture of weapons, ornaments, and prestigious luxuries.

The increased tempo of interregional exchange is reflected in increased wealth in archaeological sites both within Sumer and outside its boundaries. Metal tools became much more common, and domestic tools as well as weapons proliferated (Postgate, 1993). Metallurgy benefited from technological innovations carried along trade routes, among them the development of alloying copper with tin to make bronze. This produced tougher-edged, more durable artifacts that could be used for more arduous, day-to-day tasks. One resulting innovation was the metal- and wood-tipped plow, an implement dragged by oxen that was capable of digging a far deeper furrow than the simple hoes and digging sticks of earlier times. The plow, which, incidentally, was never developed in the Americas, evolved as irrigation agriculture assumed greater

FIGURE 15.7 A partial reconstruction of the great ziggurat (temple mound) of Ur, built in approximately 2300 B.C.

importance in Sumer, and the combined innovations increased agricultural yields dramatically. These yields not only supported larger urban and rural populations but also provided a means for the rulers of city-states both in Sumer and farther afield to exercise more control over food surpluses and over the wealth obtained by long-distance exchange. Eventually, Sumerian rulers became more despotic, controlling their subjects by military strength, religious power, and economic incentive (Yoffee, 1995).

Lowland Mesopotamia lacked the mineral and stone resources that were plentiful in distant, more highland environments in Anatolia to the northwest and on the Iranian Plateau to the east. At the same time, the Sumerians controlled not only large surpluses of grain that could be moved in ships but also a flourishing industry in textiles and other luxuries. Demand rose steadily for raw materials, which arrived in Sumerian cities along southern Mesopotamian waterways, especially up the placid Euphrates, easily navigable for long distances. This great river transmitted raw materials from the north and trade goods from the Persian Gulf to the Mediterranean. From the rivers and cities, intricate, centuries-old exchange networks and sometimes formal caravan routes carried metals, timber, skins, ivory, and precious stones over enormous distances and often rugged terrain. Even as early as Sumerian times, caravans of pack animals (in later times, often black asses) joined Anatolia to the Euphrates, the eastern Mediterranean coastal region to Mesopotamia, and Mesopotamia to isolated towns on the Iranian Plateau.

An intricate and ever-changing system of political alliances and individual obligations of friendship linked community with community and city-state with city-state. In time, financial and logistical checks and balances were maintained by an administrative system based in the temples to bring order to what had begun as informal bartering. Specialized merchants began to handle such commodities as copper and lapis lazuli. There was wholesaling and contracting, loans were floated, and individual profit was a prime motivation. Increasingly, every city-state, and indeed entire civilizations, came to depend on what we have called a nascent world system, not so much for political stability but for survival. Reliable, long-term interdependence had become a vital factor in the history of Southwest Asian states by 3000 B.C. (Algaze, 1993; Edens, 1992).

🐾 Exchange on the Iranian Plateau

The rise of urbanization in Sumer was by no means a unique phenomenon, for by 3500 B.C., cities had come into being upstream of the lowlands in areas where only dry farming was possible (Weiss, 1986). Cultural developments remarkably parallel to those in Sumer unfolded in the area between the Zagros foothills and the Tigris and Euphrates (Lamberg-Karlovsky, 1978). These developments did not occur in isolation, for even as early as 3000 B.C., there was regular interaction between the two regions (Curtis, 1993).

During the sixth and early fifth millennia B.C., small farming villages flourished in the heart of Khuzistan. The people were irrigation farmers who herded goats, sheep, and cattle as well. So many of their sites are known that it seems certain that areas such as the Deh Luran plain had been intensively settled by this time. During the next thousand years or so, Khuzistan was still densely populated, and village settlements grew larger and larger. About this time, the famous archaeological site of Susa began to achieve special prominence.

The earliest occupation levels at Susa are broadly contemporary with the late 'Ubaid occupation of Mesopotamia. The first village on the site was 25 to 30 ha (62 to 74 acres) in area and was inhabited by metal-using farmers. Strong Mesopotamian influence can be detected in slightly later levels at Susa, as if there was at least some colonization of Khuzistan by Uruk people from the delta toward the end of the fourth millennium B.C.

Susa
Before 3200 B.C.

By 3200 B.C., a distinctive cultural tradition known as the Proto-Elamite (Elamite is a language) appeared at Susa and elsewhere in Khuzistan (Potts, 1999). The Proto-Elamite state seems to have evolved in what is now southwestern Iran, but within a short time its distinctive tablets, seals, and ceramic types came to be found in widely scattered sites in the Iranian highlands (Carter and Stolper, 1984). Proto-Elamite clay tablets have turned up in settlements in every corner of the Iranian Plateau, in central

Elamite state
3000 to 2000 B.C.

Iran, and on the borders of Afghanistan. Susa, where the trade routes between Mesopotamia and the east converged, itself grew into a great city. The Elamite state emerged in all its complexity after 3000 B.C. and came under the rule of Akkadian kings from central Mesopotamia for a while, but by 2000 B.C., the Elamites were strong enough to attack and destroy Ur in Sumer. The Elamites' power and importance depended on their geographic position at the center of a network of trade routes that led to the Iranian Plateau, to the Persian Gulf, and to most city-states in the lowlands.

From as early as 6000 B.C., raw materials from the Iranian Plateau were traded to the lowlands. As the volume of the plateau trade increased, Susa was in an increasingly strategic position to control access routes. Proto-Elamite developments at Susa followed on the Uruk episode at the site and can be seen as a local reaction to the Uruk domination of lowland Khuzistan, even if the same administrative devices, such as writing and cylinder seals, were retained in local forms.

On the resource-rich Iranian Plateau, long-distance exchange joined widely separated communities in what has been called an interaction sphere, which linked most of the southern part of the region for many centuries. These long-lived networks may have connected major centers near key sources of such commodities as lapis lazuli, turquoise, chlorite, and other materials. Each center became a locus for the manufacture and exchange of prestigious objects made of these commodities, and each center maintained contacts with remote areas such as Sumer and Elam, east of the Tigris River.

Tepe Yahya
3400 B.C. and later

One such center was Tepe Yahya, which was a prosperous rural community between 3400 and 3200 B.C. (Lamberg-Karlovsky, 1973, 1978; Lamberg-Karlovsky and Beale, 1986) (Figure 15.8). The inhabitants exploited local sources of chlorite (steatite). After 3200 B.C., Tepe Yahya grew and was engaged in much more intensive trading activities. Eventually, it became a political and administrative center that manufactured and traded carved chlorite bowls. The bowls produced at Tepe Yahya and elsewhere were definitely luxury items, so highly prized in Mesopotamia that they may have caused keen competition among those rich enough to afford them (Kohl, 1978). Chlorite tools and ornaments were so popular that they have been found over a very wide area of the Iranian Plateau as well as on islands in the Persian Gulf and at Mohenjodaro, one of the major cities of the Harappan civilization of the Indus Valley (see Chapter 17).

Shari-i-Shokhta
2800 B.C.

The plateau trading networks also extended to the settlement of Shari-i-Shokhta, which stood by the shores of Lake Helmand, south of the Hindu Kush in east Iran. An extensive trade in turquoise and lapis lazuli flourished there after 2800 B.C. The lapis was embedded in limestone in the distant Hindu Kush. Shari-i-Shokhta's artisans chipped away the limestone and turned the semiprecious stone into beads. The beads and lumps of raw lapis were then traded across the desert to Mesopotamia and also north into central Asia, probably in exchange for textiles (Tosi, 1983).

The plateau trade handled the work of local artisans but was ultimately founded on the movement of a number of vital, staple commodities, among them textiles and timber (Possehl, 1986). This trade is the subject of some controversy. Some scholars believe

FIGURE 15.8
Excavations at Tepe Yahya, Iran. This settlement was a major center of an international trade with Mesopotamia in steatite vessels.

that the commerce was based on markets in, and was in the hands of traders controlled by, Sumer and Elam, who could affect the trade by a simple application of the laws of supply and demand (Kohl, 1978). Another viewpoint suggests that the trade itself may have been in the hands of entrepreneurs, but that the areas of high demand for its products were both local and at a distance in Sumer and Elam. Although some of the commodities found on the Iranian Plateau may have been transported in large quantities, much exchange proceeded in more informal ways, through occasional purchases, gift exchanges, tribute, booty taking, and individual initiative. It was not until the third millennium B.C. that much larger-scale, highly organized trade became the rule rather than the exception. The Iranian Plateau trade may have developed as an indigenous exchange system, which later spilled over to the west in response to demands from the lowlands. However, this latter trade was a question of people's getting what they could get rather than of a high degree of organization. In other words, supplies were irregular, in sharp contrast to the much more highly organized regional trade organizations that evolved after 2000 B.C. (Possehl, 1986).

Whatever the mechanisms of the Iranian trade, it is clear that an extensive network of interdependence was linking widely separated city-states and polities all over Southwest Asia by 2500 B.C. This network of interaction was highly flexible and continued to develop over many centuries, as different city-states and larger states vied with one another to control and administer ever-larger kingdoms.

ᛘᛘ The Widening of Political Authority

By 2800 B.C., Mesopotamia held several city-states, each headed by a ruler who vied with the others for status and prestige. The Sumerians were in contact with other states and urban centers in northern Mesopotamia and across the rivers in Elam and farther afield to the east. They maintained regular contacts with Anatolia, with the eastern Mediterranean coast, and sporadically with the Nile Valley. Political authority was still most effective at the city level, with temple priests as the primary controllers of trade, economic life, and political matters. Inevitably, as the societies became more complex, so the city rulers became more secular. At the same time, the volume of long-distance trade rose dramatically, to the point, some experts believe, where Sumerian rulers made a conscious decision to develop a formal maritime trade, through the Persian Gulf, with areas to the east such as the Indus Valley (see Chapter 17).

The population shifts of the third millennium B.C. may also reflect a much greater concern with defense, for both Sumerian tablets and the archaeological record tell of warfare and constant bickering between neighbors. Competition over natural resources intensified as each city-state raised an army to defend its water rights, trade routes, and city walls. As the wealth and power of the two dozen or so Sumerian cities increased, so did internecine strife. Such city-states as Erech, Kish, and Ur had periods of political strength and prosperity when they dominated their neighbors. Then, just as swiftly, the tide of their fortunes would change and they would sink into obscurity. There was a constant threat from nomadic peoples of the surrounding mountains and deserts, who encroached constantly on settled Sumerian lands. At times they disrupted city life so completely that any form of travel became an impossibility. In a real sense, the city-states were the settings for economic and social strife in early Mesopotamia (Yoffee, 1995).

Some Sumerian cities nurtured powerful leaders. When Sir Leonard Woolley (1934) excavated the Royal Cemetery in Ur (Figure 15.9), he found a series of wealthy individuals who had been buried in huge graves with their entire retinue of followers. One tomb contained the remains of 59 people who had been poisoned to accompany the deceased—courtiers and soldiers as well as serving women. Each wore his or her official dress and insignia and, having taken the poison, lay down to die in the correct order of precedence. Unfortunately, Woolley's records are too incomplete for present-day archaeologists to check his funerary scenario.

Inevitably, the ambitions of some of these powerful and proud Sumerian rulers led them to entertain bolder visions than merely the control of a few city-states in the lowlands (Postgate, 1993). They were well aware that they lived in a wider world of prosperous and not-so-prosperous neighbors, in a world in which the control of lucrative

FIGURE 15.9 A famous ornament from the Royal Cemetery at Ur, titled Ram in the Thicket. The wood figure of a goat was covered with gold leaf and lapis lazuli, the belly in silver leaf, and the fleece in shell. ("Ram in the Thicket." Ascension #30-12-702. University of Pennsylvania Museum Neg. #T4-1000.)

sources of raw materials and trade routes was the secret of vast political power. The first recorded success in such an endeavor was that of Lugalzagesi (c. 2360 to 2335 B.C.). Not content with the control of Uruk, Ur, Lagash, and several other cities, he boasted of overseeing the entire area from the Persian Gulf to the Mediterranean. The god Enlil, king of the lands, "made the people lie down in peaceful pastures like cattle and supplied Sumer with water bringing joyful abundance" (Kramer, 1963, p. 212). Lugalzagesi's boasts must be taken with a large pinch of historical salt and must be judged not in terms of conquering armies but in the context of a nascent world system of interaction and trading, which carried Sumerian political and religious ideas as far as the shores of the Mediterranean.

The tenuous and sometimes more regular contacts maintained by Mesopotamia with dozens of city-states in Anatolia and along the eastern Mediterranean coast foreshadow the constant political and economic rivalry that was to dominate Southwest Asian history during the second millennium B.C.—rivalry over the control of Mediterranean coastal ports. Here two oceans and three continents meet. The eastern Mediterranean coast had no natural harbors, so the control of its overland routes was the key to dominating a vast area of the known world, including resource-rich Anatolia and grain-rich Egypt. There were also important copper deposits in the region.

Khirbat Hamra Ifdan
2700 to 2200 B.C.

Copper production exploded, especially in the copper-rich Jordan region. Recent excavations at Khirbat Hamra Ifdan, in the Faynan district of southern Jordan, have uncovered the largest early Bronze Age metal workshop in southwestern Asia, dating to between 2700 and 2200 B.C. (Levy et al., 2002). This was a time of major political upheaval and social change throughout the region, yet the Khirbat workshops produced copper implements on a large scale, larger than that of major copper sources in Cyprus to the northeast. Using GIS (Geographic Information Systems) maps, Thomas Levy and his colleagues have been able to reconstruct all the stages of metal processing at the site, which operated like a production line, from mining to finished artifacts. The smelting and casting of metal took place on the south side of the site. Then the metal objects were moved north into rooms on the north side of the site, where grinding and other specialized processes took place.

Khirbat Hamra Ifdan documents a quantum leap in metal production at a time when urban centers in the Levant were growing and Old Kingdom Egypt was achieving much greater complexity. The copper from the site passed along ancient trade routes to the north and even to the southwest, to the Nile Valley.

As we shall see in Chapter 19, the history of this region was bound inextricably to the fortunes of the larger powers that surrounded it.

🐾 The Akkadians

While Sumerian civilization prospered, urban centers waxed and waned in neighboring areas. In these regions, too, lived rulers with wider ambitions, who had a vision of a larger role (Sinapoli, 2001). By 2500 B.C., Akkadian cities to the north of Sumer were competing with lowland cities for trade and prestige. In approximately 2334 B.C., a Semitic-speaking leader, Sargon, founded a ruling dynasty at the town of Agade, south of Babylon. By skillful commercial ventures and judicious military campaigns, his northern dynasty soon established its rule over a much larger kingdom that included both Sumer and northern Mesopotamia (Liverani, 1993).

Akkadian state
c. 2334 to 2112 B.C.

After a short period of economic prosperity, northern Mesopotamia went through a catastrophic drought that lasted some 300 years (Weiss, 2000). Starving farmers thronged to the rich southern cities. Violent clashes ensued, and the Akkadian kingdom collapsed. Fifty years of political instability followed before King Ur-Nammu of Ur took control of Sumer and Akkad in 2112 B.C. and created an empire that extended far to the north. Sargon had forged an empire by military conquest but had never followed up his victories with proper administrative governance. Ur-Nammu and his successors of III Dynasty of Ur were a new breed of ruler who placed great emphasis on consolidating their new empire into a powerful and well-organized bureaucracy. We know much of this kingdom from thousands of administrative tablets from III Dynasty levels at Ur (Steinkeller, 1989). With the Akkadian and Ur empires was forged a persistent tradition of Mesopotamian civilization: the combination of trade, conquest, ruthless administration, and tribute to forge large, poorly integrated, and highly volatile empires that sought to rule an enormous territory between the Mediterranean and the Persian Gulf.

III Dynasty of Ur
2112 to 1990 B.C.

🐾 Babylon

Ur in turn gave way to Babylon and its Semitic rulers by 1990 B.C. Babylon's early greatness culminated in the reign of the great king Hammurabi in 1792 B.C. He integrated the smaller kingdoms of Mesopotamia for a short period, but his empire declined after his death, as Babylonian trade to the Persian Gulf collapsed and trade ties to Assur in the north and for Mediterranean copper in the west were strengthened.

🐾 The Assyrians

By this time, the various masters of Mesopotamia had became major players in a much wider eastern Mediterranean world (see Chapter 19). They vied with the Hittites of Anatolia, with the city of Mitanni on the Euphrates, and with the Egyptians for control of the eastern Mediterranean coast. Perhaps the most successful of these Mesopotamian masters were the Assyrians, who rose to prominence in the mid-fourteenth century B.C. as Babylon declined.

Assur on the Tigris had been a major force in Southwest Asian trade since Sumerian times (Postgate, 1993; M. Larsen, 1995). The merchants of Assur traded far to the east and west and controlled the trade down the Tigris to Babylon and beyond. The city came into great prominence during the reign of King Assuruballit (1365 to 1330 B.C.). He created a great state through ruthless and efficient conquest and political maneuvering that maintained diplomatic relations with the pharaohs of Egypt, with the Hittite

FIGURE 15.10
Assyrian King Sennacherib reviews prisoners and booty paraded before him after a successful siege.

and Mitanni kingdoms of Anatolia (see Chapter 19), and with Babylon. His power was based on control of trade routes and of the rich cereal-growing lands of northern Iraq, as well as on military prowess. His armies swept everything before them and occupied Babylon for a while. The empire collapsed soon after the king's death.

Assyrian Empire
c. 1000 to 612 B.C.

A second imperial expansion occurred in the ninth century B.C. under Assyrian monarchs based in northern Iraq, who expanded their domains with annual campaigns of military conquest. These were absolute despots, vain and grandiloquent men, who boasted of their conquests on their palace walls (Figure 15.10) (Russell, 1991). When King Assurnasirpal completed his palace at Nimrud, he threw a party for the 16,000 inhabitants of the city, 1500 royal officials, "47,074 men and women from the length of my country," and 5000 foreign envoys (Postgate, 1993). The king fed this throng of more than 69,000 people for ten days, during which time his guests ate 14,000 sheep and consumed more than 10,000 skins of wine. Following a succession crisis, the Assyrian Empire collapsed but was revived in a more bureaucratically efficient form by King Tiglath-pileser III.

Babylonian Empire
612 to 556 B.C.

The last of the great Assyrian kings was Assurbanipal, who died in approximately 630 B.C. When he died, the Assyrian Empire entered a period of political chaos. The Babylonians achieved independence, and Assyrian power was finally broken in 612 B.C., when their capital at Nineveh was sacked by the Persians and Babylonians. For 43 years, the mighty King Nebuchadnezzar of Babylon ruled over Mesopotamia and turned his capital into one of the showpieces of the ancient world (Wiseman, 1985). His double-walled city was adorned by magnificent mud-brick palaces with elaborate hanging gardens, a great processional way, and a huge ziggurat. It was to Babylon that a large contingent of Jews were taken as captives after Nebuchadnezzar's armies sacked Jerusalem, an exile immortalized by the lament "By the waters of Babylon we sat down and wept" (Psalms 137:1).

539 B.C.

The Babylonian Empire did not long survive the death of Nebuchadnezzar in 556 B.C. His successors were weak men who were unable to resist the external forces that now pressed on Mesopotamia. The armies of Cyrus the Great of Persia took Babylon virtually without resistance in 539 B.C., and Mesopotamia became part of an empire even larger than that of the Assyrians. By this time, the effects of constant political instability and bad agricultural management were beginning to make themselves felt. The Mesopotamian Delta was a totally artificial environment by 2000 B.C., and poor drainage and badly maintained irrigation works in later centuries led to inexorable rises in the salt content of the soil and to drastic falls in crop yields in some areas. Nothing could be done to reverse this trend until modern soil science and irrigation techniques could be imported to the delta at vast expense.

Summary 🐾

By 7000 B.C., highland peoples had settled in northern Mesopotamia in areas where agriculture was possible through the use of seasonal rainfall. These Hassuna people lived in close contact with other societies downstream that developed irrigation agriculture. In about 6500 B.C., Halafian painted wares appeared over a wide area of upland northern Mesopotamia and Anatolia; they are thought to have coincided with the emergence of chiefdoms in this area.

The delta lowlands may have supported farmers before 6500 B.C., but the first traces of them appear in the 'Ubaid culture of the sixth millennium. They practiced small-scale irrigation and lived in groups of communities linked by trade networks. In time, some villages, like Eridu, became ceremonial centers and towns. A rapid evolution to urban life ensued, marked by fast population growth, the congregation of people in small cities, and the development of long-distance trade. This new urban society was organized in distinctive stratified social classes. Copper metallurgy developed at about the same time in the highlands and soon came into widespread use.

By 2900 B.C., Sumerian civilization was in full swing and was part of what we call a nascent world system, which linked polities as far afield as the Iranian Plateau and the Indus in the east and the Mediterranean and the Nile Valley in the west. Mesopotamia never achieved political unification under the Sumerians. Rather, dozens of city-states vied for political and economic supremacy and competed with other societies in northern Mesopotamia and close to the Zagros Mountains. Sumerian civilization flourished until about 2000 B.C., when it was eclipsed by Akkadian and then Babylonian power.

In the late second millennium B.C., the city of Assur in the north nurtured the Assyrian Empire, which was extended by vigorous and despotic kings during the first half of the succeeding millennium. At one time, the Assyrian Empire stretched from the Mediterranean to the Persian Gulf. The Assyrian Empire fell in 612 B.C., and the power vacuum was filled by the Babylonians under the rule of Nebuchadnezzar. Babylon fell to Cyrus the Great of Persia in 539 B.C., and Mesopotamia became part of the Persian Empire.

Guide to Further Reading 🐾

Crawford, Harriet. 1991. *Sumer and the Sumerians.* Cambridge: Cambridge University Press.
An up-to-date summary of Sumerian civilization from a multidisciplinary perspective.

Kramer, Samuel. 1963. *The Sumerians.* Chicago: University of Chicago Press.
The classic account of Sumerian civilization, written by one of the foremost experts on Sumerian cuneiform tablets and literature. A model of what such books should be, although now somewhat outdated.

Larsen, Mogens. 1995. *The Conquest of Assyria.* London: Routledge.
A stirring account of the discovery of Assyrian civilization for general readers.

Lloyd, Seton. 1983. *The Archaeology of Mesopotamia,* 2nd ed. London: Thames & Hudson.
A synthesis of Iraqi archaeology that concentrates mainly on the early civilizations. Strong on archaeological data, well illustrated, and informative on architecture.

Nissen, Hans J. 1988. *The Early History of the Ancient Near East, 9000 to 2000 B.C.* Chicago: University of Chicago Press.
A useful, up-to-date introduction to Mesopotamian history and archaeology for beginning students.

Postgate, Nicholas. 1993. *Early Mesopotamia: Economy and Society at the Dawn of History.* London: Kegan Paul.
An authoritative, articulate summary of early Mesopotamian civilization. Amplifies the issues discussed in this chapter.

c h a p t e r

EGYPT, NUBIA, AND AFRICA

Bas-relief of the goddess Ma'at.

Painted stone relief. Egypt, 19th dynasty. Museo Archeologico, Florence, Italy. Copyright Scala/Art Resource, NY.

N early overcome, I...contrived to sit; but when my weight bore on the body of an Egyptian, it crushed it like a band-box.... I sank altogether among the broken mummies, with a crash of bones, rags, and wooden cases, which raised such a dust as kept me motionless for a quarter of an hour, waiting till it subsided again." Thus did the notorious Giovanni Belzoni, circus performer turned tomb robber, explore ancient Egypt in 1817.

Belzoni and his ilk thought nothing of using gunpowder, even of going after rivals with a gun, for everyone was out for spectacular finds and all the loot they could gather. Yet the modern science of Egyptology sprang from these adventurous roots. A gentler breed of patient scientists and hieroglyph experts followed Belzoni. They have spent more than a century piecing together the portrait of ancient Egyptian civilization we enjoy today (Fagan, 2004).

〽 The Origins of the Egyptian State

Archaeological evidence tells us that by 5000 B.C. simple farming based on cattle herding and cereal agriculture had replaced a combination of foraging and cultivation along the Nile as far south as what is now the Sudan, ushering in the pre-Dynastic period of Egyptian history (Bard, 1994; see relevant articles in Shaw, 2000; Wenke, 1991b). Two thousand years later, a patchwork of small kingdoms and villages had become a unified state with a distinctive, common ideology (Figure 16.1; Table 16.1).

From the earliest centuries of farming, Egypt formed two broad regions. Lower Egypt encompassed the Nile Delta and Mediterranean coast and the Nile River as far upstream as modern Cairo. Upper Egypt extended upstream as far south as the First Cataract, just above the modern town of Aswân. The process of unification brought these two regions under a single government.

Ancient Monopoly?

Most explanations of the origin of the state focus on population growth and competition for land and natural resources. In Egypt's case, state formation took place where population densities were still relatively low and there was plenty of vacant land, so neither of these factors played a significant role. Egyptologist Barry Kemp (1989) believes that the village farmers of 4000 B.C. had strong ties to their ancestral lands, expressed in deeply symbolic terms. At first, dozens of small communities, each with its own patchwork of farming land, competed and traded with their neighbors.

Kemp likens the behavior and long-term effects to those in a game of Monopoly. In Monopoly, each player maximizes the opportunities presented by a throw of the dice. In Egypt, both

TABLE 16.1
The web of relationships between Asia, Africa, and other regions after 500 B.C.

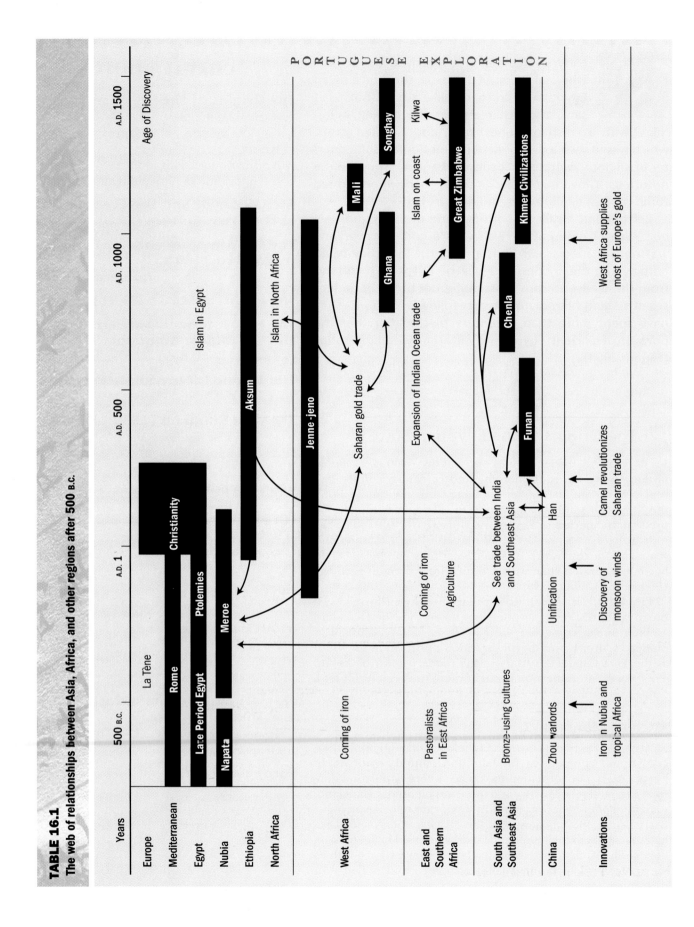

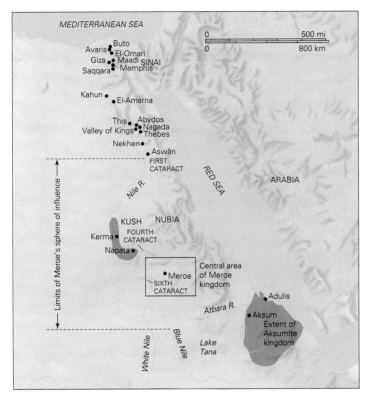

FIGURE 16.1 Ancient Egypt, Ethiopia, and Nubia.

individuals and entire villages took full advantage of favorable locations; of their access to desirable resources, like potting clay; and of chance breaks that came their way. At first the communities, like Monopoly players, were basically equal, but inevitably someone, or some hamlet, gained an unforeseen advantage, perhaps from trading expertise or unusually high crop yields. Equilibrium gave way to a seemingly inevitable momentum in which some communities acquired more wealth and more power than their neighbors—the prehistoric equivalent of building Monopoly hotels on Park Avenue. Their victory was inevitable, as they established a monopoly over local trade, food surpluses, and so on, which overrode any threat posed by other political or economic players (Figure 16.2).

In pre-Dynastic times, there were probably hundreds of such "games" in progress. As time went on, the number of players decreased, but the stakes were higher as increasingly large chiefdoms vied for economic power and political dominance. Just as in Monopoly, the players changed over time, some acquiring great power, then losing it as charismatic individuals died or trading opportunities changed. Kemp points out that Egypt had more than enough fertile land and resources to enable such games to play out over many generations. Surplus resources like grain or toolmaking stone were the foundation of power. But he believes that the Egyptians also had a genius for weaving a distinctive ideology that connected leadership and authority with elaborate symbols and rituals. These ideologies became a powerful factor in promoting unification.

The elaborate processes of state formation leave few signals in the archaeological record. In Egypt, such changes triggered the formation of larger settlements, small towns with all their potential for intensive interaction among individuals. Their leaders were buried with elaborate grave goods and with symbols denoting an emerging ideology of power.

Naqada, Nekhen, and Maadi

At least three pre-Dynastic chiefdoms flourished in Upper Egypt in about 3500 B.C.: Naqada, Nekhen, and This near Abydos (little known and not discussed here), the ancestors of a larger "proto-kingdom" that eventually formed the nucleus of a unified Egypt (Figure 16.3). Another chiefdom, centered on Maadi, ruled part of the delta.

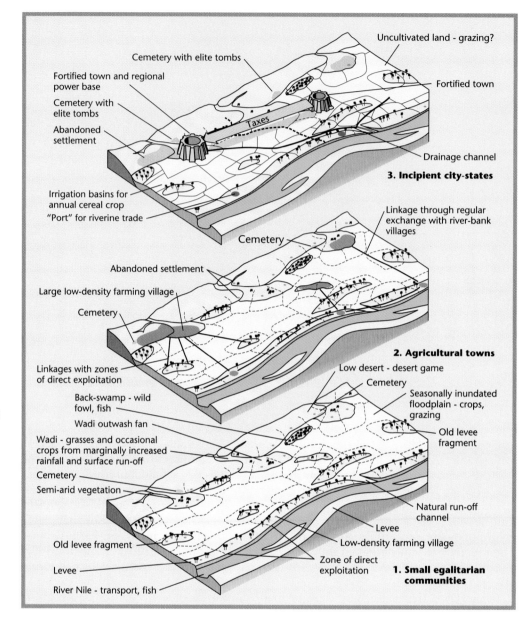

FIGURE 16.2 Early Egyptian "Monopoly." (1) Small egalitarian agricultural communities exploited the diverse floodplain environments of the Nile. (2) The small villages became agricultural towns, often at the edge of the valley, maintaining links with one another and with trade routes along the river. (3) Incipient city-states formed with a strong tax base of subordinate communities. Major towns were fortified, and the elite were buried in cemeteries.

Naqada
c. 4000 B.C.

Naqada. Major changes in human settlement can be seen at Naqada in Upper Egypt, 25 km (15.5 miles) south of Thebes, where small hamlets were spaced about 1 km (0.6 mile) apart in 4000 B.C. (Midant-Reynes, 2000). Demographic archaeologist Fekri Hassan (1988) has calculated that these small settlements grew enough grain on land at the edge of the floodplain to support 76 to 114 persons per square kilometer (0.36 square mile). By clearing trees and removing dense grass growth, and by building dikes and digging drainage canals to clear still-inundated acreage, the farmers opened up much larger tracts of agricultural land. By the time the farmers had taken four, or even eight, times more ground under cultivation, they could support as many as 760 to 1520 people per square kilometer, many of them nonfarmers: officials, traders, and artisans living in permanent towns. A walled town with cemeteries stood in the heart of the Naqada area by 3600 B.C. The housing form was new: rectangular mud-brick dwellings that were typical of later Egyptian villages. In some settlements, larger, more palatial residences housed a prosperous elite who enjoyed contacts with other communities up- and downstream. Naqada may have been the capital of a major chiefdom.

Nekhen. Nekhen (the Greek name is Hierankopolis) flourished upstream, the "City of the Falcon" in Upper Egypt (Hoffman et al., 1982). In 3800 B.C., Nekhen was still a

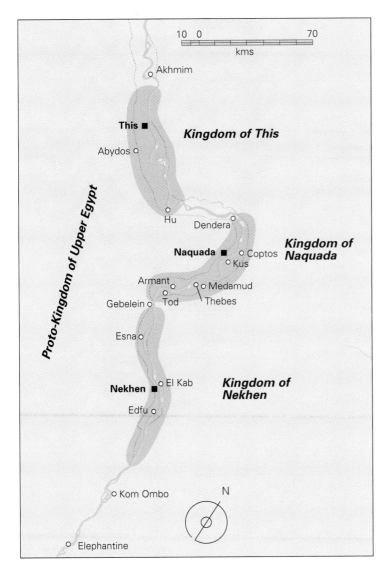

Proto-Kingdom of Upper Egypt

Kingdom of This

Kingdom of Naquada

Kingdom of Nekhen

10 0   70
kms

Akhmim

This ■

Abydos ○

Hu ○   Dendera ○

Naquada ■   ○ Coptos
○ Kus

Armant ○   ○ ○ Medamud
Gebelein ○   ○ Tod   ○ Thebes

Esna ○

Nekhen ■ ○ El Kab

Edfu ○

○ Kom Ombo   N

○ Elephantine

FIGURE 16.3 The spread of the Upper Egyptian proto-kingdom through the Nile Valley, c. 3300 B.C. This is a gross simplification of a very complex, and ever-changing, political situation.

small, insignificant community inhabited by a few hundred people. During the next three centuries, the population mushroomed to as many as 10,500 townsfolk. People lived in closely clustered mud-brick and plaster dwellings, the wealthier artisans and traders in larger houses with separate compounds. For the first time, there were signs of social differentiation in Egyptian society. The Abu Suffian cemetery near Nekhen housed prominent citizens, many of them prosperous traders who had profited from locally made, fine-quality Plum Red pottery, which was used to adorn tombs up and down the river. These people became powerful members of the community, having widespread contacts with settlements near and far. One "royal" tomb was adorned with wall paintings depicting a ruler smiting his enemies and sitting under an awning. Both motifs survived into later pharaonic times.

Nekhen
3800 B.C. to 3000 B.C.

About 3500 B.C., the fragile ecological balance of desert and grassland collapsed, perhaps as a result of overgrazing by goats and sheep and of intensive pottery firing by local artisans, both of which stripped local tree cover. Hoffman believes that some of the local leaders profited from the disaster by using their wealth to foster irrigation agriculture and settlement closer to the Nile. Their venture was successful and yielded large grain surpluses under the control of the new elite. They used their wealth to increase trade, erect public buildings like temples, and invest in imposing sepulchers. The ambitious leaders of Nekhen were buried in the same Abu Suffian cemetery, which straddled a dry gulch, their graves laid out on either side of the wadi (gully) in what Hoffman believes is a symbolic map of a unified Upper and Lower Egypt.

FIGURE 16.4 The Narmer palette, a slab of slate carved on both sides with scenes commemorating King Narmer of Nekhen. Narmer lived just before the First Dynasty. On this side, he wears the white crown of Upper Egypt. He carries a pear-shaped macehead in his right hand and is about to smite a captive, perhaps from the delta in Lower Egypt. Above the victim, a falcon head (the southern Horus) emerges from papyrus reeds carrying a human head. A sandal bearer follows the king, who stands on two dead enemies. The other side shows the ruler wearing the red crown of Lower Egypt as he inspects decapitated enemies from the town of Buto in the delta. Below, a central design of two mythical beasts with intertwined necks symbolizes harmony. The palette symbolizes not only Narmer's military victories but the complex process of unification, which took several centuries, much fighting, and complex diplomatic maneuvering. Palette height: 63 cm (29 inches).

Nekhen yielded the celebrated Narmer palette (Figure 16.4), which commemorates King Narmer's victory over a northern ruler in about 3000 B.C. Narmer wears the crowns of Upper and Lower Egypt. He is faced on one side by the god Horus. The palette displays the full artistic canon of pharaonic Egypt and is a powerful symbol of unification.

Maadi. There were certainly other polities downstream in Lower Egypt, but their capitals lie under thousands of years of accumulated silt. A poorly defined Maadi culture flourished over much of the delta, made up of small towns and farming villages. The Maadi site itself, on the outskirts of modern Cairo, was a major trading center in about 3650 B.C., a place with large, roofed oval or rectangular cellars up to 4 m (13 feet) long and 1 to 2 m (3 to 7 feet) deep. They contained jars, grains, animal and fish bones, stone vases, beads, and lumps of imported asphalt. Rows of large clay storage pots held grain, cooked meat, dried fish, flint tools, spindle whorls, and other objects. Maadi was a key link in a major trade network that brought commodities from the eastern Mediterranean coastal region and perhaps even from Mesopotamia to the Nile, probably by donkey caravan (Caneva et al., 1987; Wenke, 1991b).

Maadi
3650 B.C.

The delta's archaeological record also reflects major political and social change in other places. At the El-Omari sites, one location contains more than 100 dwellings, as well as the burial of a chief or ruler holding a well-made wooden staff or scepter. This remarkable object, pointed at one end and flat at the other, foreshadows the ceremonial staffs carried by later Egyptian pharaohs and gods. Many imports have been found in the El-Omari settlements, among them seashells, ostrich eggshells, mother of pearl, and necklaces and pendants fabricated from Red Sea gastropods.

In contrast to the simpler burials of earlier centuries, the El-Omari dead were buried in cemeteries outside the settlement, the body wrapped in a mat or coarse fabric and placed on its left side, facing south. One cemetery associated with a small village contained the burials of higher-status individuals, graves covered with stone mounds. Interestingly, the village contained many cellarlike storage areas that held large numbers of stone tools and roughed-out blanks for such implements as knife blades and arrowheads. The settlement may have belonged to traders, who apparently maintained contacts with the eastern Mediterranean coast (Rizkana and Seeher, 1984).

Expanded trading activity helped fill in rural populations along the floodplain. Contacts between people living both within and outside the Nile Valley intensified dramatically. But distances along the Nile were so large that significant regional differences emerged, with a boundary between Upper and Lower Egypt somewhere near modern Cairo. The increased volume of trade during late pre-Dynastic times is reflected in the importation of not only copper but also other exotic items that occur in profusion in sites of about 3500 B.C. Some of these objects are of unmistakable west Asian or Mesopotamian origin. The Naqada site, for example, yielded a cylinder seal of Mesopotamian form. Some pots bear depictions of Mesopotamian boat designs and of fabulous animals and creatures with intertwined necks and other motifs that derive from Asia.

Writing

The same trade brought another innovation: the art of writing, which became fully developed in Egypt in about 3100 B.C. Hieroglyphs (Greek for "sacred carving") are commonly thought to be a form of picture writing. In fact they constitute a script that combines pictographs (pictures) and phonetics (vocal sounds), and they were not only written on papyrus but also carved on public buildings or painted on clay or wood. Writing was probably first developed in Mesopotamia, and Egyptian priests developed their own script, which was easier to produce with papyrus-reed paper and ink than on clay. Doubtless, early hieroglyphs played a significant role in trade and record keeping, but they also may have evolved as a way of conveying the meanings of funerary rituals on painted pots deposited with the dead (Hassan, 1988).

3100 B.C.

Ultimately, Egyptian scribes developed a cursive (running-on) hieroglyphic script that was a form of handwriting and was much easier to use on documents and other, less formal communications. Only the consonants were written in all forms of hieroglyphs; the vowel sounds were omitted, although both were pronounced. With practice, reading this form of script is easy enough, and a smpl tst 'f ths srt shld shw ths qt wll (Figure 16.5) (Robinson, 1995).

The acquisition of writing, with all its organizational possibilities, was one of the catalysts for the unification of all Egypt into a single political entity.

A Scenario for Unification

Archaeology and myth combine for a hypothetical scenario of unification: By 3500 B.C., the kingdoms of Upper Egypt may have had direct contact with southern Arabia and Southwest Asia, bypassing Lower Egypt. Mesopotamian cylinder seals have come from Upper Egyptian sites, and gold was obtained from mines in the desert east of the Nile. Conflict ensued, with the politically most developed center, Nekhen, emerging victorious. The rulers of Nekhen finally embarked on a campaign of military conquest, which eventually engulfed all of Egypt between the Mediterranean and Aswân. By 3100 B.C., a semblance of political unity, commemorated by the Narmer palette, joined Upper and Lower Egypt in the symbolic linking of the gods Horus and Seth depicted in later Egyptian art. As these events unfolded, a new state came into being, founded not only on physical but also on a symbolic geography, a harmony achieved by balanced opposites, of which Horus and Seth are only one manifestation. For thousands of years,

Unification
c. 3100 B.C.

Hieroglyphs				
Cursive hand (hieratic script)				
Shorthand				
Translation	Amun	rôemt humankind	per-'o Pharaoh	hru day

FIGURE 16.5 Egyptian writing is referred to as hieroglyphs, the familiar symbols that appear in formal inscriptions and on tomb walls. In fact, Egyptian scribes also developed cursive hands used for everyday purposes. These examples show formal hieroglyphic script (top line) and below it both the cursive script and the scribe's shorthand, which was used for rapid writing.

the Egyptians were concerned with the potential of a world torn between potential chaos and order. They believed that disorder—disequilibrium—could be contained by the rule of kings and by the benign force of the power of the sun. Thus, the Egyptians' intellectual view of the universe coincided with the structure of political power.

Unification was the culmination of local social and political developments that resulted from centuries of gradual change in economic and social life. Pre-Dynastic villages were autonomous units, each with its local deities. During the fourth millennium B.C., the larger villages became the focal points of different territories, which in Dynastic times became the *nomes,* or provinces, through which the pharaohs administered Egypt. The nomarchs (provincial leaders) were responsible for the gradual coalescence of Egypt into larger political and social units. Their deeds are recorded on ceremonial palettes that were used for moistening eye powder. Some of these palettes show alliances of local leaders dismantling conquered villages. Others commemorate the administrative skills of leaders who had brought their villages through drought years by skillful management. The unification of Egypt was a gradual process of both voluntary and involuntary amalgamation. Voluntary unification resulted from common needs and economic advantage. Perhaps it was only in the final stages of unification that military force came into play to bring larger and larger political units under single rulers (Bard, 2000).

Intensification of Agriculture and Irrigation

Unification may have involved some intensification of agriculture as population densities rose; but as Karl Butzer (1976) has pointed out, the Egyptian technology for lifting water was so rudimentary that the early rulers were unable to organize any elaborate forms of irrigation. In all probability, most ancient Egyptian agriculture involved irrigation schemes on a modest scale that merely extended the distribution of seasonal floodwaters from natural flood basins. Still, even these efforts must have required a considerable degree of administrative organization. Also, with a centralized form of administration, the divine leader, the pharaoh himself, was responsible for the success of the harvest. Since the Nile flood fluctuated considerably in cycles of abundant and lean years, and the pharaohs could do little to control the success or failure of irrigation without much more elaborate technology than they possessed, their political position could, theoretically, be threatened by famine years: If the divine leader could not provide, who could? Perhaps a different leader would provide. Small wonder that some periods of political instability, which may have coincided with poor flood years, saw rapid successions of ineffective pharaohs, as was the case at the end of the Old Kingdom, c. 2180 B.C.

Butzer (1976) has pointed out that civilizations can be regarded as ecosystems that emerge in response to sets of ecological opportunities. Over time, a variety of social and environmental adjustments are inevitable, some of them successful, leading to population growth, and others unsuccessful, so that the population shrinks. These demographic adjustments are commonly associated with ups and downs of political power. The political structures of, say, ancient Egyptian civilization were not nearly as durable as the basic adaptive system they purported to control or the cultural identity of which they had once been a part. Butzer draws an analogy with the ecological concept of trophic levels among biotic communities, in which organisms such as herbivores and carnivores define successive tiers interlinked in a vertical chain. Likewise, he hypothesizes, an efficient social hierarchy comprises several levels arranged in what he calls a "low-angle pyramid, supported by a broad base of farmers and linked to the peak of the pyramid by a middle-level bureaucracy. The vertical structures channel food and information through the system, and an efficient energy flow allows each trophic level to flourish in a steady state" (p. 22). In this model, a flatter pyramid with little vertical structure would provide less information flow and would limit the potential productivity of the lower levels. Butzer's pyramid would allow growth at the lower levels, with new technologies or organizational devices favoring expanded energy generation. A steep, top-heavy pyramid laden with nobles and bureaucrats, however, places so much burden on the lowest levels that external and internal forces can undermine the stability of the society.

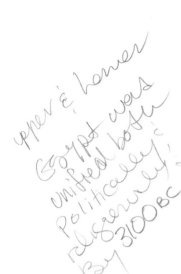
upper & lower Egypt were unified both politically & religiously by 3100 BC

This model, when applied to the long history of ancient Egyptian civilization, shows how the Egyptians persisted in adjusting to a floodplain environment for thousands of years. They overcame external and internal crises by reorganizing their state and economic structure. The key variables were the fluctuations of the Nile itself, occasional foreign intervention, the character of the pharaohs' leadership, and a progressively more out-of-touch society of elite nonproducers who persisted in exploiting the common farmer, a process that led to eventual social collapse. However, through all these variables, the essential components of the sociopolitical system survived more or less intact, right up to the nineteenth century A.D. Indeed, the visitor to rural Egypt can still see farming villages functioning much as they did in ancient Egyptian times.

🌀 Archaic Egypt and the Creation of the Great Culture (2920 to 2575 B.C.)

Egyptologists conventionally divide ancient Egyptian civilization into four broad periods: Archaic Egypt and the Old Kingdom, the Middle Kingdom, the New Kingdom, and the Late period. The first three were separated by two intermediate periods that were intervals of political change and instability (Table 16.2) (Aldred, 1998; Kemp, 1989; Shaw, 2000).

The Archaic period, comprising the first four and a half centuries of Egyptian civilization, was a long and complex period of consolidation, of subordinating powerful

Archaic period
2920–2575 B.C.

TABLE 16.2
Major subdivisions and developments of ancient Egyptian civilizations

Years B.C.	Period	Characteristics
30	Roman occupation	Egypt becomes an imperial province of Rome.
332 to 30	Ptolemaic period	The Ptolemies bring Greek influence to Egypt, beginning with the conquest of Egypt by Alexander the Great in 332 B.C.
1070 to 332	Late period	Gradual decline in pharaonic authority, culminating in Persian rule (525 to 404 and 343 to 332 B.C.).
1530 to 1070	New Kingdom	Great imperial period of Egyptian history, with pharaohs buried in the Valley of Kings; pharaohs include Rameses II, Seti I, and Tutankhamun, as well as Akhenaten, the heretic ruler.
1640 to 1530	Second Intermediate period	Hyksos rulers in the delta.
2040 to 1640	Middle Kingdom	Thebes achieves prominence, also the priesthood of Amun.
2180 to 2040	First Intermediate period	Political chaos and disunity.
2575 to 2180	Old Kingdom	Despotic pharaohs build the pyramids and favor conspicuous funerary monuments; institutions, economic strategies, and artistic traditions of ancient Egypt established.
3100 to 2575	Archaic period	Consolidation of the state (treated as part of the Old Kingdom in this book).
c. 3150	Unification of Egypt under Narmer (Menes)	

local chiefdoms into a unified whole (Wilkinson, 1999). Narmer and his successors assumed awesome responsibilities. They inherited all the powers of village shamans, or curers, and were thought to have complete authority over the Nile, its life-giving inundation and the fertility of the soil. Contending with the forces of evil, they were depicted smiting nomads from the desert east of the Nile and hostile Nubians from upstream. The pharaohs wore the regalia of pastoral chiefs, carrying the crook and the incense-gum-collecting flail of a shepherd. They developed the centralized bureaucracy that directed labor and collected taxes. Above all, they "invented" Egypt's pharaonic tradition, converting its ideology into architectural and artistic styles that survived for centuries. Royal tombs became statements on kingship. The early pharaohs and their high officials developed a mechanism of symbolic geography, a national framework of myth, which accommodated regional diversity, reflected in art and architecture. Just like the Mesoamerican rulers (Chapter 21), the pharaohs made a great play of their rare public appearances, developing spectacular settings for major ritual events and festivals.

At the center of the state lay the concept of a great king, a terrestrial ruler, who symbolized the triumph of order over universal chaos. The ideas and ideals that legitimized the rule of the pharaohs over their subjects survived the ups and downs of political history for 3000 years. In Egypt, the terms *father, king*, and *god* were metaphors for one another and for a form of political power based on the inequality considered part of a natural order established by the gods at the time of creation.

The early civilizations depended on the skillful administration of resources of all kinds. Power came not so much from landownership as from the control of agricultural surpluses and labor. The manipulation of these resources was for the benefit of a tiny elite, but the benefits spread to a significant sector of the general population. Rulers everywhere in the ancient world relied on a classic resource cycle: taxation, which brought in resources, and redistribution, which distributed them to large numbers of people working for the benefit of the state. Such resource cycles require precise record keeping and an army of officials to monitor every transaction. Two words sum up the passions of early bureaucracies: system and detail. In a preindustrial society like Egypt, where money was unknown, people bartered food and other commodities. The entire Egyptian government functioned on a system of rations and bartering. At the core of this nonmoney society, as in other early civilizations, was writing.

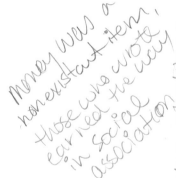

Most people in modern industrial societies can read and write. But in Egyptian society, those who could read and write were among the elite. To be a scribe ("writing man") was an honored calling. "Be a scribe. Your limbs will be sleek, your hands will grow soft. You will go forth in white clothes, honored, with courtiers saluting you," a young man is advised. The title of scribe was an essential part of a high Egyptian official's qualifications, writing being the accomplishment valued above all other crafts, even highly skilled ones. Writing was power, the key to controlling the labor of hundreds, if not thousands, of people.

Bureaucracy is sometimes a pejorative word in our society, but it was a valued institution in Egypt, where everything depended on the equitable and prompt distribution of food rations instead of wages. Scribes supervised every moment of the food cycle. They measured grain yields at the threshing floor, monitored the grain in transit to curb pilfering, and inventoried granaries—even the loaves turned out by bakers. They also collected taxation in kind, and in labor. Officialdom was essential to Egypt's long-term survival. High officials could raise armies and build temples. They were the instruments of cooperation, conservative, long-term planners who tried to mitigate the impact of an unpredictable river. Egyptian civilization survived because of this conservatism and the cohesion wrought by strongly centralized economic control.

This new administrative mechanism was put to an early test. Between 3000 and 2800 B.C., average Nile floods dropped 1 to 2 m (3 to 5 feet), to about 30 percent below normal. Judging from the historically documented inundation of 1877, which was 2.1 m (6.5 feet) below average, about a third of the valley would have remained dry. Simple irrigation and flood basin agriculture would have been no protection against such a disaster. During these two centuries, we know that desert nomads encroached on settled valley lands and that the pharaohs barely survived armed insurrection and civil unrest. But the state endured, probably because of decisive administration and the increasing government control of food surpluses.

We know little of the earliest pharaohs, except from their tombs in the Umm el-Qa'ab cemetery at Abydos. The First and Second Dynasty kings lay in mud-brick chambers built in large pits. Such sepulchers were a direct development from earlier graves, marked with a pair of freestanding columns carved with the king's name. A separate funerary palace closer to the floodplain consisted of a double enclosure with a freestanding building inside. Both the enclosure walls and the building were adorned with niches decorated with paintings and brightly colored matting. The entire structure was a formal setting for the receipt of tribute and other major ceremonial occasions when the king appeared in public. The royal tomb had already become a key symbol of kingship. Such symbols were magnified tenfold a generation later, with the appearance of the first pyramids.

Abydos
3150 B.C.

These were the centuries when the "Great Culture" of Egypt was born, a culture that originated in royal courts, from large-scale public works, and from carefully organized patronage of the arts and crafts. The Great Culture was a tradition that became part of the instruments of authority, a distinctive ideology that systematized religion and other cultural expressions over wide areas at the expense of local traditions. As the Great Culture expanded, so the "little culture" of provincial towns and villages shrank, even if local gods made their appearances at state ceremonies as symbols of unification.

🐾 The Old Kingdom and the Pyramids (c. 2575 to 2180 B.C.)

The Old Kingdom saw four dynasties of pharaohs governing Egypt from a royal capital at Memphis, near Cairo. By this time, Egyptian society had been shaped in the image of a state where the well-being of the common people depended on their ruler, who was supported by their labors. Some of the pharaohs had reputations as cruel despots, notably Khufu and Khafre, who built the pyramid-tombs of Giza, stretching the state's economic resources to the limit.

Old Kingdom
2575 to 2180 B.C.

The Archaic and Old Kingdom pharaohs used dramatic settings for their public appearances. A large open space, an elevated place shaded with a canopy where the king would be glimpsed, and a small palace for donning formal attire and resting—these were the ingredients of a setting for the pageantry accompanying the eternity of death, and for the vital Sed festival, the jubilee celebration of 30 years of royal rule. The first, and one of the most spectacular, setting for such a ceremony was the famous Step Pyramid of Djoser at Saqqara (see Site box, page 386).

Saqqara
2650 B.C.

Djoser and his predecessors were terrestrial monarchs, supreme rulers epitomizing the triumph of order over chaos. But a new image of kingship emerged some time after his death in 2649 B.C. The ruler was now absorbed into the mystic symbol of the sun. An increasingly powerful priesthood fused sun worship with the cult of the pharaoh. The sun god became a heavenly monarch, the pharaoh no longer a territorial conqueror but the deity's representative on earth. After death, the king assumed the identity of Osiris, the Lord of the Dead. According to Egyptian beliefs, the stars were divine beings and the ruler was destined to take his place among them. "The king goes to his double . . . a ladder is set up for him that he may ascend on it," says a spell in a royal Pyramid Text (Edwards, 1985, p. 12). (Pyramid Texts are texts inscribed in pyramid chambers.) Thus it was that the Old Kingdom pharaohs lavished enormous resources on the building of their sepulchers—at first earthen mounds, then pyramids that became symbolic ladders to heaven.

Egyptologist I. E. S. Edwards believes that the growing influence of the sun cult led to new conceptions of the afterlife that had the deceased ruler following the sun god across the sky. Thus, he needed a new way to climb to heaven, on the rays of the sun itself. "I have laid down for myself those rays of yours as a stairway under my feet on which I will ascend," the king tells the sun god Ra in one Fifth Dynasty Pyramid Text (Edwards, 1985). The pyramids were symbolic depictions in stone of the sun's rays

SITE

The Step Pyramid at Saqqara, Egypt

Like other early Old Kingdom kings, Third Dynasty pharaoh Djoser (2668–2649 B.C.) grappled with internal political problems. He managed to extend his rule as far upstream as Aswân and laid great emphasis on his role as king and supreme territorial claimant, a role he celebrated within a large enclosure dominated by a unique structure: the Step Pyramid at Saqqara opposite the royal capital at Memphis.

Djoser's vizier Imhotep devised the architecture of the Step Pyramid (Figure 16.6). The great architect drew his inspiration from earlier royal tombs, rectangular structures like those at Abydos, which were eternal mansions for dead monarchs. Such tumuli (mounds) had associations with the primordial earthen mound that formed an integral part of the Egyptian legend of the creation. Imhotep erected a stepped pyramid instead of a mound. It rose in six diminishing steps to over 60 m (372 feet) above the desert, the faces oriented to the cardinal points. The effect is like a giant double staircase rising toward heaven. A wall with a palacelike facade over 1.6 km (1 mile) in perimeter surrounded the entire mortuary complex. The court before the pyramid was a setting for royal appearances, complete with ceremonial territorial markers, a throne platform, and a token palace. On occasion, the pharaoh laid claim to his kingdom by striding around the limits of the court and its markers. The entire complex was an arena for the eternal pageantry of kingship on earth (Kemp, 1989).

The Step Pyramid was an area for the king's spirit, comprising six platforms, one atop the other. Each formed a bench, or *mastaba,* resembling earlier royal tombs, here built into a stepped pyramid. The substructure is a honeycomb of shafts and tunnels, many dug by tomb robbers, others containing large numbers of often exquisite stone vases. Some of them bear the names of earlier kings, as if Djoser incorporated them into his pyramid as an act of piety to his predecessors. Only a mummified left foot remains of the king himself. Other members of the royal family were buried in some of the shafts and tunnels. As the pyramid grew, so these burial chambers were sealed off. Finally, the builders dug a new entrance for Djoser's burial chamber on the north side. They sealed it with a 3-ton granite plug.

A thick stone wall surrounded the pyramid, forming a huge courtyard, 108 by 187 m (354 by 613 feet), with a main gateway at the southeastern corner. An entrance hall decorated with columns opened into a vestibule. The king's internal organs were buried in the so-called South Tomb facing the main pyramid on the south side of the enclosure. Thus, there were two sepulchers, one for the Two Lands, Upper and Lower Egypt.

• •

bursting through the clouds, a permanent stone stairway with the king's mortuary temple on the east side, the side of the rising sun (Lehner, 1997) (Figure 16.7).

The court cemeteries and pyramid complexes of the Old Kingdom pharaohs extend over a 35-km (22-mile) stretch of the western desert edge, most of it slightly north of Memphis. In about 2528 B.C., Khufu built the Great Pyramid of Giza, one of the spectacular wonders of ancient Africa and one of the Seven Wonders of the Ancient World. It covers 5.3 ha (13.1 acres) and is 146 m (481 feet) high. Well over 2 million limestone blocks, some weighing 15 tons each, went into its construction. A long causeway linked each pyramid in the Giza complex to a royal mortuary temple. These were austere buildings that housed statues of the king, best shown in the complex of Khafra, who built the second pyramid of Giza. Khafra's temple was crafted in limestone and granite. Ceiling-height louvers let in a diffused glow that shone on the royal figures within. Khafra himself sat on a royal throne, protected by the god Horus, who wraps his wings around the nape of the pharaoh's neck. The nearby sepulchers vested these temples with great authority, for they associated the ruler with what was, in effect, a powerful ancestor cult that linked them to their predecessors and to the gods.

We do not know why the pharaohs suddenly embarked on this orgy of pyramid construction, with all the accompanying demands that it made on the fledgling state.

Giza

2528 B.C.

The Step Pyramid was an elaborate formal setting for the display of kingship—and of the ruler himself—either to his courtiers or the populace at large. Here the ruler could be seen by large number of people, adorned in his ceremonial robes. The "appearance of the king" was an important occasion throughout Egyptian history.

FIGURE 16.6   The Step Pyramid of Djoser I at Saqqara. The stepped pyramid was part of an elaborate setting for public ceremonies symbolizing the king's role as supreme territorial ruler and claimant.

FIGURE 16.7   The pyramids of Giza. The culmination of royal pyramid building, these stupendous tombs formed part of a much larger mortuary complex of causeways, temples, and elite cemeteries.

Their construction, like other major Egyptian public works, was a triumph of bureaucratic organization, of organizing and transporting food and building materials. Officials marshaled skilled artisans and village laborers to quarry, dig, and drag stone into place. What is staggering is the efficient management overview, achieved without computers, deploying and supporting thousands of villagers for short periods of time, as they fulfilled their annual tax-by-labor obligations to the state.

Perhaps, as Kurt Mendelssohn (1974) has argued, the pyramids were built as a means of linking the people to their guardian, the king, and to the sun god, the source of human life and of bountiful harvests. The relationship between the king and his subjects was both one of mutual obligation and of spiritual fellowship. The pharaoh was a divine king, whose person was served by annual labor. In short, pyramid building created public works that helped to define the authority of the ruler and to make his subjects dependent on him. Every flood season, when agriculture was at a standstill, the pharaohs organized thousands of peasants into construction teams. The permanent (year-round) labor force comprised relatively few, mainly skilled artisans, the fruit of whose work was placed in position on the main structure once a year. As far as is known, the peasants were paid volunteers, whose loyalty to the divine pharaoh provided the motivation for the work.

Mendelssohn believes that the construction of the pyramids was a practical administrative device designed to organize and institutionalize the state by trading redistributed food for labor. As construction proceeded from one generation to the next, the villagers became dependent on the central administration for food for three months a year, food obtained from surpluses contributed by the villages themselves in the form of taxation. After a while, the pyramids had fulfilled their purpose, and the state-directed labor forces could be diverted to other, less conspicuous state works. A new form of state organization had been created, one that both fostered and exploited the interdependence of Egyptian villages (for a discussion, see Wenke, 1991b).

〰 The Egyptian State

Egypt was the first state of its size in history (Kemp, 1989). The pharaohs ruled by their own word, following no written laws, unlike the legislators of Mesopotamian city-states. The pharaoh had power over the Nile flood, rainfall, and all people, including foreigners. He was a god, respected by all people as a tangible divinity whose being was the personification of *Ma'at*, or "rightness." *Ma'at* was far more than just rightness; it was a "right order" and stood for order and justice. *Ma'at* was pharaonic status and eternity itself—the very embodiment of the Egyptian state. As the embodiment of *Ma'at*, the pharaoh pronounced the law, regulated by a massive background of precedent set by earlier pharaohs.

A massive hereditary bureaucracy effectively ruled the kingdom, with rows of officials forming veritable dynasties. Their records tell us that much official energy was devoted to tax collection, the supervision of harvests, and the administration of irrigation (Figure 16.8). An army of 20,000 men, many of them mercenaries, was maintained at the height of Egypt's prosperity. The Egyptian Empire was a literate one; that is, trained scribes were an integral part of the state government. Special schools trained writers for careers in the army, the palace, the treasury, and numerous other callings (Aldred, 1998; Kemp, 1989).

A vast gulf separated the person who could read and write from the uneducated peasant worker. The life of an Egyptian peasant, given good harvests, was easier than that of a Greek or a Syrian farmer, although the state required occasional bouts of forced labor to clear irrigation canals or to haul stone, both tasks being essential to maintain Egyptian agriculture. Minor craftsworkers and unskilled laborers lived more regimented lives, working on temples and pharaohs' tombs. Many were organized in shifts under foremen. There were strikes, and absenteeism was common. A scale of rations and daily work was imposed. Like many early states, however, Egypt depended on slave labor for some public works and much domestic service, but foreign serfs and war prisoners could wield much influence in public affairs. They were allowed to rent and cultivate land.

FIGURE 16.8 Estate workers engaged in agricultural tasks in their lord's fields. New Kingdom, tomb of Menna, scribe of the fields and estate inspector under Pharaoh Tutmosis of the Eighteenth Dynasty, Deir el-Medina, Thebes.

The Old Kingdom in Egypt was a time of powerful, confident rulers, of a virile state governed by a privileged class of royal relatives and high officials. Their talents created a civilization that was for the benefit of a tiny minority. It was for this privileged elite, headed by a divine king, that Egyptian merchants traded for the famed cedars of Lebanon, mined turquoise and copper in Sinai, and sought ivory, semiprecious stones, and mercenaries for Egypt's armies from Nubia.

ᵓᵐᵗ The First Intermediate Period and the Middle Kingdom (2180 to 1640 B.C.)

But the prosperity did not last long. The last great Old Kingdom pharaoh was Pepi II (2246 to 2184 B.C.), who reigned for a staggering 94 years, having ascended the throne as a 6-year-old. His successors never matched his authority. As the central power of the state declined, so local leaders (*nomarchs*) became more or less independent rulers within their own provinces. This decline in the monarchy coincided with a prolonged drought cycle that settled over northern Africa after 2180 B.C. The droughts of early dynastic times had taught the pharaohs the importance of centrally controlled agriculture. They had responded to new economic realities by expanding irrigation works, canals, and the agricultural development of the delta. In the short term, they were so successful that Egypt's population had risen to more than a million by 2250 B.C. But the intensification of agriculture made the Egyptians even more vulnerable, for when another lean cycle struck in that year, there were many more mouths to feed. There were repeated famines for more than 300 years. Contemporary writers refer to widespread plundering and anarchy, to drinking-water shortages and corpses rotting in the fields. "The Nile was empty and men crossed over on foot," laments a chronicler of the day, as the magical powers of short-lived pharaohs fell into disrepute (Kemp, 1989, p. 16). Egypt became a competing mosaic of small kingdoms, whose rulers ignored the steady procession of short-lived pharaohs in Memphis.

In about 2134 B.C., the city of Thebes in Upper Egypt became the center of rebel movements that eventually took over the country under Pharaoh Mentuhotep II

First Intermediate period
2180 to 2134 B.C.

Middle Kingdom
2134 to 1640 B.C.

in 2040 B.C. The Middle Kingdom pharaohs who followed were mostly energetic rulers who extended trading contacts throughout Southwest Asia and conquered the desert lands of Nubia south of the First Cataract (see Figure 16.1). The pharaohs became somewhat less despotic, considered themselves more like shepherds of the people, and had some concern for the common welfare. The Middle Kingdom has been described as the classic period of Egyptian civilization, centuries when the pharaohs became more human and more approachable than their Old Kingdom predecessors, who had cast themselves in the role of gods. During these centuries, Egypt's rulers strove to create a kingdom in the image of a bureaucratic utopia, a realm where there were logical, often mathematical, solutions to every economic problem. The experiment was successful for a while, but it faltered when Egypt's human and natural resources proved unequal to the task.

At the same time, trade relations with the eastern Mediterranean expanded dramatically. The pharaohs mined copper and gold in the Sinai and imported cedar from Lebanon. Objects bearing their inscriptions have been found as far afield as Byblos and the port of Ugarit on the northern Syrian coast. It was from such centers that objects from the Aegean islands and the Minoan towns on Crete reached the Nile (see Chapter 19). The government also tried to increase agricultural production. At the height of the Middle Kingdom, the pharaoh Senusret II began the development of the Fayyum Oasis about 80 km (50 miles) southwest of Memphis. He and his successors turned the marshy oasis into a vast network of fields and irrigation canals protected by large dikes, an unprecedented agricultural project that provided high crop yields for the state, even in drought years. This kind of organized irrigation was very different from the informal, village-based canals and drainage ditches that marked most earlier Egyptian agriculture. The Fayyum project was only one manifestation of a state concerned with remodeling a society with strong local roots into a closely regimented and centralized society and planted planned towns even in sparsely populated areas. The pharaohs strove for an organized oasis.

Kahun
c. 1890 B.C.

Enormous public works and royal mortuaries required small armies of workers, sometimes housed in special communities some distance from their place of work. The Middle Kingdom town at Kahun (known to the Egyptians as Hetep-Senusret (meaning "King Senusret is at peace") stood close to the entrance to the Fayyum, near the pyramid of Senusret II. Here lived the priests and workers responsible for the king's mortuary cult, as well as people engaged in other construction work and agriculture (Kemp, 1989). Kahun lay inside mud-brick walls, the interior laid out on a strict grid pattern of small houses and streets. Egyptologist Flinders Petrie (1890) uncovered intricately designed, fairly large houses with substantial granaries in which household activities revolved around an inner court and walled garden. Much smaller houses outnumbered these residences by about 20 to 1, and an estimated 3000 people lived within the tightly packed community. The town plan indicates a society with well-defined social classes, reflected in house design as well as occupation.

Papyri found during Petrie's excavations reveal the existence of a mayor, legal offices, and a prison. They also contain census data, including the household of a mortuary priest with only one son and daughter but many "serfs," some of them attached to his office, others domestic servants, "field laborers," cooks, tutors, and women who were "clothmakers" and gardeners. These groups of workers depended on the granaries of the larger houses for their rations, thus forming the economic teams that were so much a part of Egyptian society. Kahun's population also included scribes and soldiers, as well as numerous small households of half a dozen people or more, many of them relatives and widows with dependent children.

Kahun represents the ultimate in Egyptian bureaucracy, a town laid out by noble officials with little conception of the realities of society. The pharaohs organized Kahun at two levels: top officials and others. In fact, the papyri reveal a more complex reality, of individuals and households wrestling with the realities of debt and children, of sudden inheritances and caring for the elderly. These realities meant that, after the Middle Kingdom, the state gave up planning any form of community other than small workers' camps.

⌇ The Second Intermediate Period (1640 to 1530 B.C.)

The Middle Kingdom lasted until approximately 1640 B.C., when another period of political instability and economic disorder began. Disputes over the royal succession at Thebes led to a series of pharaohs who reigned for short periods. Pharaonic control of the Nile Valley as a whole weakened. By this time, large numbers of Asians lived in Egypt. They were cooks and brewers, seamstresses and merchants. Many of the finest Egyptian wine makers came from Syria. Others were nomadic herders who had moved into the delta to seek sanctuary from drought or to buy corn. Their chiefs were called *Hikau khasut*, "Princes of Desert Uplands," known as the *Hyksos*, a term referring not only to the chiefs but to all their people. By the seventeenth century B.C., the delta had come under the political control of a line of Hyksos kings, who had taken advantage of the weakness of the Thirteenth Dynasty pharaohs to seize power over Lower Egypt, ruling it from the town of Avaris. They assumed the titles, traditions, and religious beliefs of the pharaohs, acquiring such prestige that the rulers of Thebes paid them tribute, perhaps linking the royal houses through intermarriage.

The Second Intermediate period was a turning point in Egyptian history. The Hyksos brought new ideas to a conservative civilization that was slowly stagnating away from the mainstream of the Southwest Asian world. They introduced more sophisticated bronze technology and traded silver from Asian mines. Friezes in the palace at Avaris in the delta are painted in the Minoan style, as if Cretan merchants and artisans lived in their capital (Chapter 19). In their battles with the Thebans, the Hyksos brought new weaponry to the Nile: stronger bows, new forms of swords and daggers, and the horse-drawn chariot.

All these innovations kept Egypt up-to-date and ensured that subsequent pharaohs would play a leading role in the wider eastern Mediterranean world.

Second Intermediate period
1640 to 1530 B.C.

⌇ The New Kingdom (1530 to 1070 B.C.)

The New Kingdom began when a series of Theban rulers fought and won a war of independence from the Hyksos. It was Ahmose the Liberator who finally overcame the foreigners and established a firm hold on Egypt from the delta to Nubia. At the same time, Ahmose turned Egypt into an efficiently run military state, tolerating no rivals and rewarding his soldiers and mercenaries with grants of land, but retaining economic power and wealth in his own hands. Like Mentuhotep in the Middle Kingdom, Ahmose set the tone for an entire era, the greatest in Egyptian history. Now the pharaoh became a national hero, a military leader who sat on a throne midway between the Asian world in the north and the black Nubian kingdoms of the south. He was an imperial ruler, a skilled general, the leader of a great power. Egypt became a major player in the shifting sands of Southwest Asian politics, competing with two great states: Mitanni, to the east of the Euphrates, and Hatti, the kingdom of the Hittites in Anatolia (see Chapter 19). Each wanted to control the lucrative gold, copper, and pottery trade of the eastern Mediterranean for itself.

The pharaohs financed their state and their empire with Nubian gold, turning the lands upstream of the First Cataract into a lucrative colony. At the same time, the Egyptians expanded their trade routes down the Red Sea to the mysterious "Land of Punt," which probably lay between the Red Sea and the Middle Nile, on the north and northwest flanks of the Ethiopian highlands, in the modern eastern Sudan. A Punt expedition was a major undertaking, involving an overland journey from Koptos on the Nile to the Red Sea coast, then by ship southward through windy, often treacherous waters. In 1472 B.C., Queen Hatshepsut, the only female pharaoh, sent a royal trading party to Punt. Spectacular reliefs on her mortuary temple chronicle the successful voyage. Separate scenes depict the ships under sail, the arrival at Punt, the exchange of gifts with the lord of the land, and the loading of the ships "very heavily with the marvels of the land of Punt: with . . . good herbs of God's Land and heaps of nodules of myrrh" (Kemp, 1989, p. 213). The story ends with the triumphant return to the sun god Amun's sacred city: Thebes.

New Kingdom
1530 to 1070 B.C.

Thebes: The "Estate of Amun"

Thebes, the home of Amun, was known to the Egyptians as the "City," or the "Estate of Amun." The Temples of Amun at Karnak and Luxor, built mostly during the Eighteenth Dynasty (1550 to 1307 B.C.), were the heart of the sacred capital. The temples lay on the old city mound, surrounded by the buildings of the New Kingdom city. Karnak represented a major shift in public architecture. Earlier kings had built their most imposing monuments on the edges of the western desert. Local temples were usually modest mud-brick structures in the heart of a community. Karnak and its lesser equivalents were settings for public ceremonies and processions, as when the boatlike shrine of Amun was carried along carefully prepared parade routes. Religion now became public spectacle, a psychological way of influencing public opinion, more subtle, and probably more effective, than the bureaucratic regulation of earlier times.

Karnak and its equivalents were surrounded by white, painted mud-brick walls modeled like turreted battlements, which kept out most of the Theban populace. The great pylons marking the entrance bore brightly colored scenes of the king conquering his enemies in the presence of the gods (Figure 16.9). Karnak was a statement of raw imperial power, but was also the place where the gods found shelter and were nurtured by food offerings. Amun's temples owned cattle and mineral rights and maintained enormous grain stores. In short, as Barry Kemp (1989) points out, the gods were landed gentry, fed from vast temple estates cultivated by small-scale farmers who paid their rent in produce. The mortuary temple of Rameses II near Thebes had storerooms capable (theoretically) of feeding as many as 20,000 people. The wealth of the large temples and the authority of their gods were such that the temples were not only a major element in the New Kingdom economy but a significant factor in the affairs of state.

Amun-Ra was the "king of the gods," a solar deity portrayed in human form and the source of fecundity. He was the divine father figure who conceived the kings, then protected them in life and death. The great pageants at Thebes, the processions between the temples at Karnak and Luxor during the annual *Opet* festival, proclaimed to the populace that the king had renewed his divine *ka,* or spiritual essence, in the innermost shrine of Amun himself. The myths, rituals, and great temples all served to guarantee the continuity of proper rule, a concept absolutely central to Egyptian thinking. At the same time, the priesthood had little political power, for the ultimate authority lay in the hands of the king and his host of carefully trained scribes.

The "Estate of Amun" extended across the Nile to the western bank. Here, the pharaohs erected an elaborate city of the dead. At the beginning of the Eighteenth Dynasty, in about 1505 B.C., Pharaoh Amenhotep and his illustrious successors elected

FIGURE 16.9 The Temple of Amun at Karnak.

FIGURE 16.10 The mortuary temple of Queen Hepshepsut near the Valley of Kings.

to be buried in secret rock-cut tombs in the arid Valley of Kings on the west bank of the river opposite Thebes. The underground tombs evolved over the centuries to become models of the caverns of the underworld traversed by the night-sun. The royal mortuary temples lay on the plain nearby, surrounded by the tombs of queens, princes, and court officials (Figure 16.10) (see the box, "Mummies and Mummification").

Amarna and Akhenaten

Amun's power came through the age-old cult of Ra Herakhty, the primordial sun god of Heliopolis. His Great Disk, Aten, illuminated the worlds of the living and the dead. Amun was all-powerful until the pharaoh Akhenaten came to the throne in 1353 B.C. (Aldred, 1988; Van Dijk, 2000). The new ruler departed from religious orthodoxy in placing a greater emphasis on Aten and Aten alone, excluding all the old gods of the pantheon from their association with the sun. In effect, Akhenaten made Aten a divine pharaoh, the equivalent in heaven of the living king on earth. We do not know why Akhenaten altered the sacred canon, but the art of his day suggests he regarded himself and his family as the sole intermediaries between the people and the sun god. Akhenaten expected to be adored like a god (see Figure 1.19).

In the fifth year of his reign, the heretic pharaoh founded a brand-new capital at El-Amarna, on land associated with no established deity. El-Amarna was occupied for little more than a quarter century before being abandoned, leaving an Egyptian city of more than 20,000 inhabitants for archaeologists to investigate. The ceremonial precincts of El-Amarna centered on a processional way that linked the north (royal) city to the central city. The fortified royal palace at the north end was isolated from the rest of El-Amarna. Here, Akhenaten and his court resided in a self-sufficient, well-guarded community with its own warehouses. The pharaoh rode down the processional way on festival days, protected by his bodyguard as his subjects adulated him. The road ended at the Great Palace, a huge structure by the waterfront with a central courtyard where the king received emissaries and conducted many ceremonies, including the rewarding of high officials who were dependent on his largesse. The administrative functions of state were performed in offices attached to the palace. It was here that the "Bureau for the Correspondence of the Pharaoh" lay, the archive which housed the now-famous El-Amarna diplomatic tablets, which tell us much of

El-Amarna
1350 B.C.

Mummies and Mummification

Mummies: They have become lasting symbols of ancient Egyptian civilization and the subject of innumerable Hollywood movies. Who can forget actor Boris Karloff as a hyperactive Egyptian mummy come back to life?

The practice of mummification dates back to the early third millennium B.C. or even earlier (Ikram and Dodson, 1998). Hitherto, Egyptians had been buried in shallow pits in the desert sand. But when walled graves came into use, bodies soon rotted away, since they were no longer in contact with desiccating sand. The first attempts at mummification involved little more than bandaging the body with cloth stiffened with resin. About 2575 B.C., the embalmers began removing the abdominal organs, putting them in special canopic jars. They also discovered the properties of natron, a compound of sodium carbonate and sodium chloride, which dehydrated human and animal tissue.

By New Kingdom times, the process was highly sophisticated (Figure 16.11). Two or three days after a person died, the embalmers extracted the internal organs through a slit below the left ribs. They removed the liver, stomach, intestines, and lungs, leaving the heart, thought to be the center of human feelings, in place. Next, the embalmers took a bronze rod, inserted it into the left nostril and removed the brain through an enlarged opening made by smashing the fragile ethmoid bone. Resin, sawdust, or cloth was then poured or packed into the skull cavity. The body was sewn up, cleaned, and covered with natron to dehydrate it completely. Once completely dried out, the corpse was washed in Nile water and anointed with unguents to make it smooth and sweet-smelling. Laying the body on a lion-shaped funerary bed, the embalmers now bandaged it, using a strict protocol, which began with the fingers and limbs, the head being last. Numerous small amulets were placed between the layers of bandages, which were soaked with resin and other unguents. Finally, the fully bandaged and mummified body was placed in a coffin and returned to the family.

This elaborate procedure was extremely expensive and was reserved for royalty, high officials, and the very wealthy. Simpler techniques involved simply desiccating the body with natron and bandaging it with recycled household linens. The poorer Egyptians were often just stacked in remote caves without any formal grave goods or elaborate funerary rituals.

Through the process of mummification, the preserved body became identified with the body of the god Osiris, ruler of the underworld. At burial, the mummy began a second life, which began with a ritual known as the "Opening of the Mouth" ceremony, performed just before the body was laid in its tomb. Anubis, the keeper of the kingdom of the dead, would receive the deceased, who was now judged in the presence of Osiris. His or her heart was weighed on a balance against a feather, the symbol of *Ma'at* ("goodness"). If "justified," the dead person could now undertake the journey through the underworld. If the heart was too heavy, it was gobbled up by the waiting goddess Ammit, and the guilty person was consigned to lasting death.

FIGURE 16.11 The mummy of pharaoh Rameses II, conserved with state-of-the-art science.

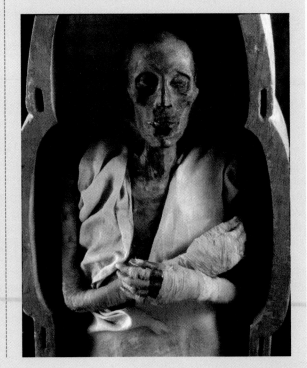

diplomatic relations between Egypt and other powers like the Hittites. The Great Temple of Aten stood nearby.

But El-Amarna's greatest significance lies in its unique archaeological evidence concerning New Kingdom Egyptian society. Most El-Amarna residents lived on two large housing tracts north and south of the central city, huddled in small houses along streets parallel to the river, intersected by smaller alleys. The larger flat-roofed dwellings stood in a small, walled compound among a maze of alleyways and garbage heaps. Each had a central living room with a low brick dais for receiving guests. Around the central space were reception rooms, bedrooms, and storage rooms. We know the names of only a few individual owners, among them Ra-nefer, a chief charioteer, who lived in a modest house, and Thutmose, a sculptor who carried out his work in small courtyards by his house, in an area of the town devoted to sculptors.

Papyri tell us how some prominent officials struggled to maintain a prosperous lifestyle, using income from their small country estates and donations from the king. Minor officials, domestic servants, merchants, fisherfolk, sailors, and farmers huddled in the crowded smaller houses. The inhabitants all had close ties to the countryside, to their home villages, often many kilometers away. Few Egyptians were true city dwellers. Egyptian cities were little more than large agglomerations of villages. Their inhabitants lived their lives in another world from that of the pharaoh, who dwelled in splendid isolation from the common people, surrounded by his relatives and bodyguards and appearing at regular intervals to receive the adoration of his subjects.

The Restoration of Amun

Religious fanatic, indolent madman, benevolent pacifist, or heretic—history's judgments on Akhenaten have rarely been favorable. He died in the seventeenth year of his reign, leaving a corrupt and chaotic kingdom behind him. His successor, Smenkhkare, a son of Amenhotep III, reigned for a mere three years and was succeeded in turn by 8-year-old Tutankhamun (1333 to 1323 B.C.), who achieved in death an immortality that transcends that of all other pharaohs, simply because Howard Carter and Lord Carnarvon discovered his intact tomb in the Valley of Kings (Figure 16.12) (Reeves, 1990).

Tutankhamun presided over a troubled country, abandoned to chaos by the alienated gods. The young king's powerful and experienced advisers took the course obvious to someone reared in the deeply religious Egyptian world. They propitiated the gods by restoring the old spiritual order, rebuilding temples, and reverting to the dynastic traditions of the early pharaohs. The cult of Amun was revived at Thebes; Amarna was abandoned. An able general named Horemhab campaigned in Syria, while Tutankhamun himself may have led a raiding party into Nubia in 1323 B.C., which resulted in a fatal arrow wound by his left ear. (The manner of his death is highly controversial.) His unexpected death caught the court by surprise. It was not until Horemhab assumed the throne in 1319 that the old ways were fully restored.

The Rameside pharaohs of the Nineteenth Dynasty (1307 to 1196 B.C.) who followed labored hard to elevate the kingdom to its former glory as an imperial power. Their wealth came from Nubian gold and far-flung trade, for Nubia was now an Egyptian dependency. Rameses II (1290 to 1224 B.C.) campaigned far into Syria until he met his match at the Battle of Kadesh, where the Hittites fought his army to a standstill. From that moment on, Egypt lost political influence in Southwest Asia and began a slow, at first barely perceptible, decline.

🐾 The Late Period (1070 to 332 B.C.)

With the death of Rameses III in 1070 B.C., Egypt entered a period of political weakness, when local rulers exercised varying control over the Nile. Nubian rulers threatened the pharaohs and actually ruled over Egypt for a short time in the eighth century B.C. The Assyrians were a constant hazard after 725 B.C. Their army occupied parts of the country and looted Thebes in 665. After the eclipse of Assyria, the Egyptians enjoyed a few centuries of independence before being conquered by the

Late period
1070 to 332 B.C.

(a)   (b)

FIGURE 16.12 Tutankhamun's tomb. Tutankhamun's jumbled possessions were so opulent that it has taken generations for us to appreciate their wealth and significance. The dead pharaoh traveled through the heavens in the sun god's bark. His many gold-leaf and inlaid figures and amulets ensured his well-being during the eternal journey. At the same time, his tomb provided for his material needs: clothing, perfume and cosmetics, personal jewelry, and chests to keep them in. There are chairs, stools, beds, and headrests, as well as weapons and hunting gear. Baskets and vases contained food and wine. Even the pharaoh's chariots lay in pieces inside the tomb. The tomb provides a fleeting portrait of the fabulous wealth of Egypt's court. (a) The antechamber with its jumble of furnishings. (b) The golden sarcophagus of the king.

Persians in 343 B.C. and by Alexander the Great in 332 B.C. The Ptolemies, pharaohs of Greek ancestry, succeeded Alexander. They ruled Egypt until Roman times. It was the Ptolemies who brought much of Egyptian lore and learning into the mainstream of emerging Greek civilization and ensured that the Land of the Pharaohs would make a critical contribution to Western civilization.

ᨀ Egypt and Africa

The ancient Greeks and Romans believed that Egypt was the fountain of all civilization. While archaeological discoveries have shown that urban civilization developed in both Egypt and Mesopotamia at much the same time, scholars still argue over the contribution of the ancient Egyptians to the roots of Western civilization. Most Egyptologists argue that civilization developed in isolation along the Nile, in a fertile, if unpredictable, river valley that was a world unto its own. They believe it became an integral part of a cosmopolitan eastern Mediterranean world, especially during the New Kingdom, when Egypt vied with Assyria and the Hittite kings for control of the eastern Mediterranean trade routes. Some African-American historians of the so-called Afrocentrism school disagree, for they believe that the institutions of urban Western civilization were born in tropical Africa and that ancient Egypt was a black African civilization. It was from the Nile, they argue, that the institutions of Western civilization were derived. These arguments, which first surfaced in the 1950s, have reached a high level of complexity in Martin Bernal's so-called Black Athena theory (1987), in which he presents historical, linguistic, and even archaeological evidence to place ancient Egypt at the core of Western civilization. Bernal's research has been severely criticized by Egyptologists, who have effectively demolished his arguments on the basis that they do not stand against scientific data. For example, Afrocentrists claim that the ancient Egyptians were black-skinned tropical Africans. In fact, both tomb paintings and biological data point to a generally Mediterranean population, but one that became increasingly cosmopolitan in later centuries as Egypt enjoyed closer contacts with other lands, including tropical Africa (Lefkowitz, 1996).

༃ Nubia: The Land of Kush

If ancient Egypt was indeed a civilization unto itself, what connections did it enjoy with the people of the Nile Valley living south of the First Cataract at Aswân? The arid country that lay upstream was Nubia, sometimes called the Land of Kush, famous to the ancient Egyptians for its gold, ivory, and slaves. As Nubian expert William Adams remarked, "For millennia Egypt treated [Nubia] as a kind of private game reserve for human and animal game" (1977, p. 3). Nubia straddled the Middle Nile, on a narrow strip of fertile land that extended far upstream into modern-day Sudan as far as the borders of highland Ethiopia. The most fertile valley lands lie along the Dongola Reach between the Third and Fourth Cataracts. It was here that some of the earliest complex Nubian societies developed, among groups that had been herders and farmers since before 4000 B.C. Even as early as 3500 B.C., what Adams calls the "shadow of Egypt" was falling across Nubia, whose raw materials attracted a civilization where wealth and divine kingship went together.

4000 B.C.

Old Kingdom pharaohs sent their armies to subdue Nubia and boasted of lucrative cattle raids. Egyptian prospectors journeyed far into the desert in search of fine rocks and semiprecious stones. The Middle Kingdom kings were more ambitious, for they discovered Nubian gold. In 1900 B.C., pharaoh Amenemhet fortified strategic reaches with ten strongholds, most of them at points where trade routes intersected with the river. This trade lay in the hands of the Nubian chieftains of Kerma, in the heart of the Dongola Reach, a small town with palaces and temples, fortified with elaborate defenses and four gates. Kerma's rulers enjoyed great wealth and were buried under large burial mounds surrounded by as many as 400 sacrificial victims (Figure 16.13). All this wealth came from trade connections with people living in the desert and farther upstream and with the Egyptians far downstream. But the New Kingdom pharaohs wanted this wealth for themselves; they marched on Kerma and the state of Kush in 1500 B.C., and made it a colony. Nubia now changed from a country of village farmers and chiefdoms into something resembling a vast plantation state, worked for the benefit of absentee landlords to provide commodities of all types at the cheapest possible cost (S. Smith, 1995).

1900 B.C.

Kerma
Kush
1500 B.C.

The economic and political shock waves that rolled over the eastern Mediterranean after 1200 B.C. (see Chapter 19) not only overthrew the Hittites and weakened Egypt but also loosened the pharaohs' hold on Nubia. After four centuries of confusion, Nubian civilization achieved new heights. The rulers of the new Kush espoused ancient Egyptian religious beliefs and assumed the powers and ideology of the pharaohs. Their wealth came from the Egyptian export trade, from gold, ivory, and many other commodities. They were buried under royal pyramids in large cemeteries, not only in Kush but, later, far upstream at Meroe. The list of Nubian kings begins in about 806 B.C. and ends in A.D. 320, a thousand years later.

1200 B.C.

806 B.C.

Between 730 and 663 B.C. Nubian monarchs ruled not only over Kush but also over Egypt itself. King Piye marched north in 730, honored the sun god Amun at Thebes, and then subdued rebellious rulers in the delta far downstream. Piye was content to rule Egypt from Kush, but his successors transferred their court to Thebes, as the servant became the master, the conquered the conquerors. The Nubian pharaohs did

Nubian pharaohs
730 to 663 B.C.

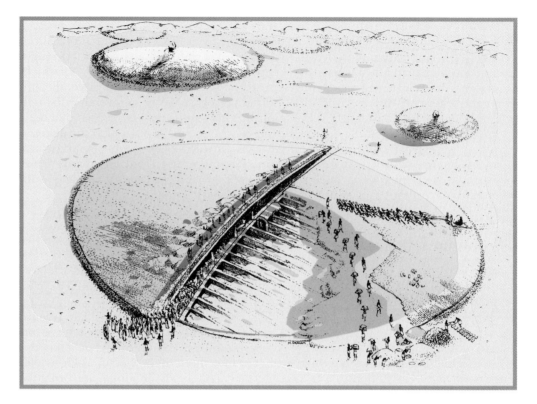

FIGURE 16.13 A royal tomb at Kerma—people rush to complete the mound as the burial takes place.

591 B.C.

much to restore art and religion, but they were inexperienced in foreign affairs, and this inexperience led to their downfall. In 663 B.C., King Assurbanipal of Assyria sacked Thebes, and the ruler of the day fled to the safety of Kush. In 591 B.C., an Egyptian army marched upstream and "waded in Kushite blood." Nubian king Aspelta fled some 500 km (300 miles) upstream to Meroe, where Nubian monarchs ruled in peace for more than 800 years.

〰 Meroe and Aksum

Meroe
593 B.C. to A.D. 350

The move to Meroe came when the focus of Nubian trade was shifting away from the eastern Mediterranean to the Red Sea and the Indian Ocean. This new commercial world linked the Red Sea, the Persian Gulf states, India, and ultimately Southeast Asia and China into a vast web (see Table 16.1). India, for example, had an insatiable demand for African ivory, favored over that of Indian elephants for making bridal ornaments. Cotton cloth, porcelain and china vessels, silk, and glass items came from India and farther east. Gold, spices, and even mangrove poles—all were staples of a trade that flowed along overland caravan routes and on the wings of the monsoon winds of the Indian Ocean. These predictable winds allowed sailing vessels to voyage from India to the Red Sea and East Africa and back in the course of a year.

The island of Socotra off northeast Africa (see the map in Figure 16.16) and the mysterious Land of Punt on the coast of the southern Red Sea were spice-rich lands where Africans rubbed shoulders with Arabians, Indians with Egyptians. Well-traveled trade routes linked Red Sea coasts with the Nile and the eastern Mediterranean coastline, traversed by laden asses and increasingly by camels, aptly named the "ships of the desert" by the Arabians, who first domesticated them as early as 2500 B.C. Centuries passed before desert nomads developed fighting saddles for their beasts, turning them from mere beasts of burden into a potent military weapon. By the third century B.C., camel breeders dominated the overland caravan trade and brought prosperity to Meroe.

Meroe lies on the east bank of the White Nile, some 200 km (124 miles) north of Khartoum, Sudan (Robertson, 1992; Shinnie, 1967). Its rulers administered a string of villages and towns along the river from lower Nubia to Sennar on the Blue Nile,

FIGURE 16.14 Royal pyramids at Meroe, Sudan.

controlling the gold, ivory, and slave trade with Egypt. The city also lay astride bustling caravan routes that linked the river with the Red Sea and extended far to the west, along the southern margins of the Sahara. Today, Meroe lies in a desert landscape, but in ancient times large herds of cattle, goats, and sheep grazed nearby (Figure 16.14). Centuries of overgrazing, combined with voracious charcoal burning to fuel iron-smelting furnaces, helped chronic drought turn the environment into an arid wilderness.

Some 24 kings and queens ruled over Meroe between 593 and 220 B.C. These black-skinned rulers were the descendants of the great pharaoh Piye and his successors. They preserved many of the conservative standards of ancient Egyptian civilization, but with a distinctive black African slant. For centuries, they administered a complex, exploitative economic enterprise for their own benefit, controlling trade through a network of carefully policed trade routes and by force. Most people lived at the subsistence level, for the international trade benefited only a minority. Ironworking was big business at Meroe, since iron ore was plentiful nearby.

Huge slag heaps overlook the temples and palaces of the city, accumulated over centuries of manufacture that began as early as the seventh century B.C. Iron-tipped tools and weapons gave Meroe's armies strategic advantages over their desert neighbors. Early scholars believed that Meroe's ironsmiths introduced the new technology to tropical Africa, but we now know that iron was introduced into the central Sahara and West Africa at about the same time as it was to Meroe itself. Meroe reached the height of its prosperity during the first century A.D., when it maintained regular trading contacts with the Roman Empire. A century later, the city was in decline and, between A.D. 325 and 350, was finally overthrown by the armies of King Ezana of Aksum in the nearby Ethiopian highlands.

Aksum was an African kingdom whose rulers adopted many ideas from south Arabia in the five centuries before Christ (Connah, 2001; Munro-Hay, 1991). Its highland homeland was fertile, although it had an unpredictable environment, and irrigated cereal crops, among them a native grass called *teff,* flourished, providing large food surpluses in good years. By the first century A.D., Aksum was a powerful kingdom in regular contact with Rome, handling all manner of exotic luxuries and commodities through its port at Adulis on the Red Sea. An eight-day journey took one inland to the town of Aksum, while another caravan route reached Aswân in Egypt in 30 days.

Aksum
A.D. 100 to 650

FIGURE 16.15 Royal stela at Aksum, Ethiopia, carved to depict a multistory building. (Copyright Werner Forman/Art Resource, NY.)

Adulis became so important that Aksum soon overshadowed Meroe as the Nile trade declined.

Aksum's rulers lived in imposing multistory palaces and were buried under tall columns up to 33 m (108 feet) high, carved to represent multistory buildings (Phillipson, 2000) (Figure 16.15). At about the time he overthrew Meroe, King Ezana abandoned the religion of his forefathers and adopted Christianity, which had reached his domains through Aksum's widespread trading connections.

Christianity flourishes in Ethiopia to this day, but Aksum faltered as Islam acquired increasing influence over the Red Sea trade in the seventh century A.D. At the height of its powers, Aksum was a potent symbol of a new, much more international world, which sprang from the ruins of the Roman Empire and linked Asia and Africa with lasting ties.

〰️ North Africa

The North African coast had long been a staging post for maritime traders from the eastern Mediterranean. During the first millennium B.C., the Phoenicians (see Chapter 19) set up port colonies (N. K. Sanders, 1985), among them the great city of Carthage. Carthage had become a dominant power by 400 B.C., but a series of devastating wars led to its destruction at the hands of Rome. The Romans realized the agricultural potential of the North African hinterland and turned their new colony into a vast grain combine. It was said that North African granaries fed Rome's masses for nine months a year, Egypt's for four.

400 B.C.

The Romans had little interest in the desert, although there were some indirect contacts with peoples living deep in the Sahara. It was the camel that opened up the desert, once camel breeders had developed a saddle for load carrying and riding over long distances. Soon after the time of Christ, camel routes linked the Nile with the central highlands of the desert and the same mountains with North Africa. There, the Romans used the camel for agriculture and for some cavalry operations. The real expansion of the Saharan caravan trade came in later centuries, especially after Islamic armies swept across North Africa in the seventh century A.D.

A.D. 700

Gold and salt—these were the commodities that fueled the Saharan caravan trade (Connah, 2001; Oliver, 2000). Salt deposits were plentiful in parts of the desert. Salt

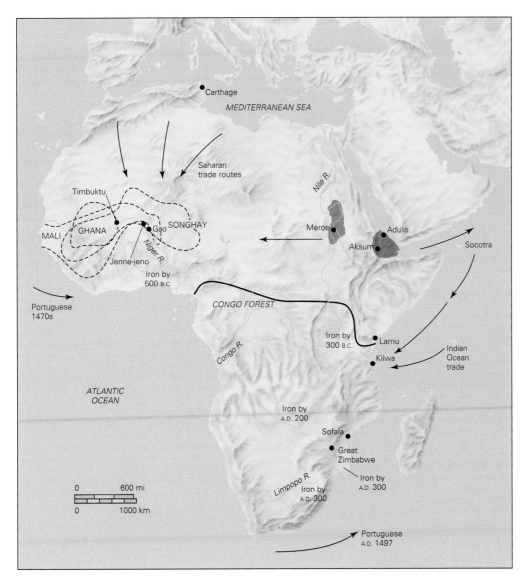

FIGURE 16.16 Map showing the extent of Bantu Africa and the indigenous states mentioned in the text.

was easily mined and carried on camelback to farmers south of the Sahara, who lacked this vital substance in their homeland. They craved salt and had gold dust to offer in exchange. So eager were some West Africans for salt that they would trade it for its equivalent weight in gold. The Saharan gold and salt trade soon grew into an elaborate network of local and long-distance connections that linked North Africa with the West African savanna and forest regions far to the south (Figure 16.16). Tropical foodstuffs and stimulants like the kola nut were in constant demand, as were woollen garments and leather goods from the north, as well as copper, slaves, and glassware. By the time Christopher Columbus landed in the Bahamas in 1492, two-thirds of Europe's gold was coming from West African sources.

🐾 Jenne-jeno and the Rise of African States

By 1000 B.C., small farming communities flourished throughout the West African savanna and in the forest regions of the south. Iron technology reached some of these villages by the sixth century B.C., at about the same time it arrived at distant Meroe (Phillipson, 1994). Iron axes and adzes improved the efficiency of forest clearance and agriculture, but it was the Saharan trade that offered new opportunities for ambitious African leaders. For example, Jenne-jeno in Mali's inland Niger Delta began as a small village of mixed farmers in the third century B.C. (McIntosh and McIntosh, 1980).

1000 B.C.

FIGURE 16.17
Excavations at Jenne-jeno, Mali, showing early house foundations.

The settlement was no more than a few acres in extent, but even at this early date, the inhabitants were obtaining iron ore, grindstones, and stone beads from outside their delta homeland. Most likely, they were bartering surplus grain, fish, and animal products in exchange.

Jenne-jeno
200 B.C. to A.D. 800 and later

During the next five centuries, Jenne-jeno grew rapidly, covering 25 ha (62 acres) by A.D. 300, and becoming a prosperous farming and fishing community of brush and mud houses (Figure 16.17). Two centuries later, Jenne-jeno's trading contacts had expanded considerably. Copper from Saharan sources appeared by A.D. 400, savanna or forest gold between 600 and 800, by which time the town covered 33 ha (82 acres) and boasted of a mud fortification wall 2 km (1.2 miles) in circumference and 3.6 m (11.8 feet) wide. Ten centuries after its founding, Jenne-jeno was a mature town, with numerous round houses up to 3.9 m (13 feet) in diameter, constructed of cylindrical bricks. This growth to maturity coincided with a gradual buildup in local and long-distance trade, as Jenne-jeno became a leading exchange point for Saharan copper and salt. Lying as it did at the extreme southwestern end of the Niger Delta, it was ideally placed to barter savanna gold, iron, and agricultural produce. Judging from the hierarchy of lesser contemporary settlements found nearby, the rulers of Jenne-jeno presided over a considerable area of the floodplain, a territory that may have extended at least 100 km (60 miles) downstream of the town. Their government provided a stable environment for a growing volume of trade with the Sahara.

Jenne-jeno was only one of many such growing communities and states south of the desert (Connah, 2001; Phillipson, 1994), all of them basing their prosperity on the gold trade with North Africa. The Saharan trade passed into Islamic hands at the end of the first millennium A.D., and Arab authors began describing the remarkable African kingdoms flourishing south of the desert. The geographer al-Bakri drew a vivid picture of the kingdom of Ghana, whose gold was well known in northern latitudes by the eleventh century. "It is said," he wrote, "that the king owns a nugget as large as a big stone" (Levetzion, 1973, p. 186).

Ghana

Ghana
c. A.D. 700 to 1100

The kingdom of Ghana straddled the northern borders of the gold-bearing river valleys of the upper Niger and Senegal (Levetzion, 1973). No one knows when it first came into being, but the kingdom was described by Arab writers in the eighth century A.D. The Ghanians' prosperity depended on the gold trade and the constant demand for ivory in the north. Kola nuts, slaves, and swords also crossed the desert, but gold, ivory, and salt were the foundations of their power. Islam was brought to Ghana sometime in the late first millennium A.D. and linked the kingdom more closely to the desert trade. The king of Ghana was a powerful ruler, who, wrote al-Bakri, "can put 200,000 men in the field, more than 40,000 of whom were bowmen" (Levetzion, 1973, p. 189).

Ghana was a prime target for Islamic reform movements, whose desert leaders longingly eyed the power and wealth of their southern neighbor. One such group, the Almoravids, attacked Ghana in approximately A.D. 1062, but it was 14 years before the invaders captured the Ghanaian capital. The power of Ghana was fatally weakened, and the kingdom disintegrated into a series of minor chiefdoms, somewhat, perhaps, as many early Egyptian polities had done in the centuries preceding unification in 3100 B.C.

Mali

The kingdom of Mali appeared two centuries later, after many tribal squabbles (Levetzion, 1973). A group of Kangaba people under the leadership of Sundiata came into prominence in approximately A.D. 1230 and annexed their neighbors' lands. Sundiata built his new capital at Mali on the Niger River. He founded a vast empire that a century later extended over most of sub-Saharan West Africa. The fame of the Mali kings spread throughout the Muslim world. Timbuktu became a widely known center of Islamic scholarship. Malian gold was valued everywhere. When the king of Mali went on a pilgrimage to Mecca in A.D. 1324, the price of gold in Egypt was reduced sharply by the king's liberal spending. Mali appeared on the earliest European maps of West Africa as the outside frontier of the literate world. It provided most of Europe's gold reserves and royal wealth.

Mali
c. A.D. 1230 to 1460

The key to Mali's prosperity and political stability was the unifying effect of Islam, which overcame much factionalism and many tribal rivalries. Mali's Islamic rulers governed with supreme powers granted by Allah and ruled their conquered provinces with carefully selected religious appointees, or even with astute slaves, chosen for their loyalty and political acumen. Islam provided a reservoir of thoroughly trained, literate administrators who believed that political stability resulted from efficient governance and sound trading practices.

Songhay

In approximately A.D. 1325, the greatest of the kings of Mali, Mansa Musa, brought the key trading center of Gao on the Niger under his sway. Gao was the capital of the Dia kings, who shook off Mali's yoke in approximately A.D. 1340 and founded the kingdom of Songhay. Their state prospered increasingly as Mali's power weakened and expired in A.D. 1460. The great chieftain Sonni Ali led the Songhay to new conquests between A.D. 1464 and 1492, expanding the frontiers of his empire deep into Mali country and far north into the Sahara. He monopolized much of the Saharan trade, seeking to impose law and order with his vast armies to increase the volume of trade that passed through Songhay hands. Sonni Ali was followed by other competent rulers who further expanded Songhay. Its collapse came in the sixteenth century.

Songhay
A.D. 1340 to 1550

〰️ Farmers and Traders in Eastern and Southern Africa

While cattle herders had settled in the East African highlands as early as 2000 B.C. (Chapter 11), the great savannas of eastern and southern Africa were still home to Stone Age hunter-gatherer groups. The spread of farming economies into the savanna coincided in part with the spread of iron technology and perhaps with the dispersal of Bantu languages over much of eastern, central, and southern Africa from a homeland in eastern West Africa (for a summary of recent research, see Robertson and Bradley, 2000).

2000 B.C.

300 B.C.

This complex series of local population movements is still little understood, but we know that iron-using farmers had settled in the East African lakes region (now Uganda and Tanzania) by 300 B.C. and that they lived in the Zambezi Valley soon after the time of Christ, moving across the Limpopo River into South Africa soon afterward. These savanna farmers used shifting agriculture and careful soil selection to produce a diet of sorghum, millet, and other cereal crops. They kept cattle and small stock, relying on hunting and foraging for much of their diet. Their architectural styles and pottery have a clear but indirect relationship to those of many present-day African groups (Phillipson, 1994).

Towns and Trade on the East African Coast

A.D. 500 to 1500

The same monsoon winds that linked the Red Sea with India also linked the East African coast between Somalia and Mozambique with a much wider commercial world (Oliver, 2000). As early as the first century A.D., traders from Arabia were coasting southward in search of gold, ivory, and other commodities, trading with small farming communities near the Red Sea shore. By the end of the first millennium, the coastal trade was under Islamic control, centered on small towns and strategic bays. Lamu in northern Kenya was one such port. So was Kilwa Island off the Tanzanian coast, a strategic transshipment point, where oceangoing dhows (sailing ships) loaded gold dust and ivory obtained from Sofala in southeast Africa (Figure 16.18). For more than 1000 years, a distinctive coastal civilization flourished along the East African coast, a cosmopolitan blend of African and Islamic culture based on "stone towns," compact trading settlements of rock and coral houses controlled by prominent merchant families.

Until the early nineteenth century, most contacts between the coast and the far interior were indirect, through local intermediaries. But the volume of gold, ivory, and copper that flowed to the coast was impressive. These commodities, in high demand overseas, were bartered for cheap baubles like glass beads and cotton cloth. Another popular item was Indian Ocean seashells, worn as ornaments, which assumed great prestige in the interior. When explorer David Livingstone passed through western Zambia in 1855, the going price for one circular *Conus* shell was a slave, for five a tusk of elephant ivory. They could be picked up by the dozen on coastal reefs. Just as in West Africa, a series of powerful African states took advantage of the coastal trade.

FIGURE 16.18
Architect Peter Garlake's reconstruction of the Sultan's Palace at Kilwa, on the East African coast.

Great Zimbabwe

Trading states first appear to the south of the Congo Forest in central Africa as early as the ninth century A.D., and especially south of the Zambezi River, where Shona-speaking peoples had settled at about the same time. The Shona were cattle-herding people living in a highland environment, where political power was measured by wealth on the hoof. Both agriculture and herding were high-risk enterprises in a landscape where rainfall was unpredictable, so Shona chiefs were quick to realize the potential of long-distance trade with the coast. They mined gold and hunted elephants, using their exports to acquire "exotic" commodities like cloth and glass beads, which they then used to acquire more grain and cattle.

By A.D. 1200, Shona society was acquiring some complexity, perhaps a mosaic of small chiefdoms, each having its own territory with sufficient range to graze cattle not only through the rainy season but through the dry months as well. One of them, Great Zimbabwe on the southern plateau, rose to prominence. Its rulers were able to maintain and raise armies and to intervene in the politics of their neighbors. For many generations, they exacted tribute not only from their own "core" area but also from surrounding chiefdoms. The size of the state fluctuated constantly, for vassal chiefs often acted with remarkable independence.

The gold trade with the Indian Ocean coast flourished because the Shona encouraged it. From the region known as Sofala, the tentacles of the gold and ivory trade extended far inland, up the Limpopo, Sabi, and Zambezi rivers to the plateau country of the interior. For centuries, this trade was at best sporadic and on a small scale. It was a long-distance trade that merged imperceptibly with the myriad bush paths that carried essential commodities and luxuries from one village to the next. The change came after the tenth century A.D. on the coast, and sometime later in the interior, when the international demand for gold and ivory skyrocketed. It can be no coincidence that the trade with Sofala picked up dramatically as the East African coastal towns enjoyed their greatest prosperity. The chiefs of Great Zimbabwe managed to dominate the trade between the southwestern goldfields and the coast.

The word *Zimbabwe* is either a contraction of the Shona words *dzimba dza mabwe,* "houses of stone," or, more likely, of *dzimba hoye,* "venerated houses," an expression used to describe chiefs' houses or graves. Judging from archaeological data, Great Zimbabwe served both these roles (Beach, 1993; Garlake, 1973). In about A.D. 1000, Shona groups, probably direct ancestors of the present-day inhabitants of the area, settled near Great Zimbabwe. One village lay on the western end of the low hill that now dominates the site, its cattle enclosures and millet gardens spread out over the valley below. These people and their neighbors lived in good farming and cattle country, where they were able to maintain large grain surpluses and to develop great wealth on the hoof, but theirs was not a vital gold-producing area.

At first, only a few families farmed and grazed their herds at the site. They built circular mud-and-stick thatched huts both on the hill and in the valley below. As time went on, they erected stone cattle enclosures, then more and more walls. They reinforced the walls of the larger huts and joined the large boulders atop the hill to form small enclosures, creating the first stages of a complex known to archaeologists as the Acropolis or Hill Ruin. By 1250, like their neighbors, the Great Zimbabwe chiefs presided over a sizable territory and measured their wealth in large herds. Perhaps it was the uncertainty of cereal agriculture and cattle herding that made trading with foreigners an attractive risk-management strategy—a way of cushioning themselves against the depredations of cattle disease, of drought, and even of marauding neighbors. Within a few generations, Great Zimbabwe became a sizable town, perhaps with as many as 18,000 people living in it and nearby. Great Zimbabwe was in part a military state, capable of raising armies from its herding population that could enforce tribute assessments and toll collections. At the same time, the chiefs could manipulate their cattle as a means of acquiring wives and, eventually, relatives and supporters. Great Zimbabwe's stone buildings, built of easily quarried granite slabs, sprawl over about 8 sq km (3 square miles). The Hill Ruin overlooks the valley, the summit a mass of weathered granite boulders linked by freestanding stone walls. These form a maze of large and small enclosures, accessible by a narrow stepped entrance on the north side

Great Zimbabwe
c. A.D. 950 to 1450

FIGURE 16.19 Interior of the Elliptical Building at Great Zimbabwe, showing the Conical Tower which dominates the interior and is thought to be a symbolic grain bin, an expression of chiefly power.

or via a secretive defile that squeezes between large boulders on its way up to the western enclosure on the summit.

The Hill Ruin looks down on the celebrated "Elliptical Building" or "Great Enclosure" that dominates the valley (Figure 16.19). Its oval-shaped freestanding outer wall is more than 244 m (800 feet) long and rises 9.7 m (32 feet) at its highest point. The Elliptical Building is a secluded place, divided by low stone walls into several enclosures. Substantially built mud huts once stood within them, for this was the residence of the chief. The valley between the Hill Ruin and the Elliptical Building is a jumble of stone-walled enclosures and large occupation sites; it was in some of these that the chief's many wives may have resided.

By the fifteenth century, Great Zimbabwe was the most powerful of some ten chiefdoms that flourished on the plateau. Each controlled a territory about 160 km (100 miles) across, sufficient land to allow not only shifting cultivation but also large-scale seasonal grazing of sizable cattle herds. Eventually, overgrazing, exhausted soils, and denuded woodland may have caused much of the population to move elsewhere. Great Zimbabwe was abandoned in about 1500, as the center of political power shifted northward, closer to the Zambezi River, a major trade route to the coast.

〰️ Europe and Africa

Even as Christopher Columbus landed in the Bahamas, Portuguese ships were coasting southward, seeking to outflank Islam by reaching the West African gold mines from the sea (Oliver, 2000). By 1470, they had rounded the bulge of Africa. In 1488, Bartholomeu Dias rounded the Cape of Good Hope. Nine years later, Vasco da Gama sailed up the East African coast and used the monsoon route to reach India. During the next four centuries, Africans were drawn increasingly into a much wider economic world fueled by insatiable demands for raw materials and, above all, slaves to work the sugar and cotton plantations of the New World. During these years of increasing economic dependence, Africans were aggressive in seizing new opportunities and in acquiring wealth and political prestige. It was they who controlled the sources of slaves, who mined for gold, and who organized the hunting of elephants. Increasingly, the

A.D. 1488

destiny of Africa became intertwined with the unfolding economic and political fortunes of a wider and ever more international and industrialized world.

Summary

Ancient Egyptian civilization arose out of complex processes of forced and voluntary integration along the Nile Valley. This process was accelerated by increasing trade contacts with Southwest Asia, culminating in the emergence of the ancient Egyptian state in about 3100 B.C.

Egyptologists conventionally subdivide ancient Egyptian civilization into four main periods: the Archaic and Old Kingdom, Middle Kingdom, New Kingdom, and the Late period, the first three of which were separated by brief intermediate periods of political chaos. The Old Kingdom was notable for its despotic pharaohs and its frenzy of pyramid construction, an activity that may be connected with pragmatic notions of fostering national unity. The Middle Kingdom saw a shift of political and religious power to Thebes and Upper Egypt. New Kingdom pharaohs made Egypt an imperial power with strong interests in Asia and Nubia. Ancient Egyptian civilization began to decline after 1000 B.C., and Egypt fell under Roman rule in 30 B.C.

Nubia, upstream of the First Cataract, was exploited by the Egyptians for centuries, but it came into its own as the pharaohs' power declined. Nubian kings from Kush actually ruled over Egypt in the eighth century B.C., but they were forced to retreat to Meroe, far upstream, two centuries later. Meroe became a center for the Red Sea and Indian Ocean trade, ruled by kings and queens who preserved Egyptian customs. It prospered until the fourth century A.D., when it was conquered and finally eclipsed by the kingdom of Aksum in the Ethiopian highlands.

The camel opened up the Sahara to regular gold and salt trade, fostering the development of powerful West African states such as Ghana, Mali, and Songhay. At the same time, expanding Indian Ocean trade nurtured a network of trading towns on the East African coast. During the fourteenth and fifteenth centuries A.D., Great Zimbabwe in southern Africa controlled much of the gold and ivory trade in southeastern Africa.

Guide to Further Reading

Adams, William. 1977. *Nubia: Corridor to Africa.* London: Alan Lane.
  A detailed synthesis of the archaeology of Nubia. Somewhat outdated but authoritative and well written.

Clayton, Peter A. 1994. *Chronicle of the Pharaohs.* London and New York: Thames & Hudson.
  A summary of all the Egyptian pharaohs, lavishly illustrated.

Connah, Graham. 2001. *African Civilizations,* 2nd ed. Cambridge: Cambridge. University Press.
  An excellent general account of early sub-Saharan African states for the beginning reader.

Kemp, Barry. 1989. *Ancient Egypt: The Anatomy of a Civilization.* London: Routledge.
  Quite simply, the best academic book on ancient Egyptian civilization ever written. Destined to become a classic for its elegant exposition and beautiful line drawings.

McIntosh, Susan K., ed. 1999. *Beyond Chiefdoms.* Cambridge: Cambridge University Press.
  Technical essays on the emergence of social complexity in tropical Africa. Strongly recommended for the more advanced reader who seeks thought-provoking analysis.

O'Connor, David. 1993. *Ancient Nubia: Egypt's Rival in Africa.* Philadelphia: University Museum.
  An up-to-date, authoritative account of Nubian archaeology and civilization for the general reader.

Oliver, Roland. 2000. *The African Experience,* 2nd ed. London: Weidenfeld & Nicholson.
  African history from human origins to modern times, synthesized for the general reader. An excellent overall discussion.

Phillipson, David. 1994. *African Archaeology,* 2nd ed. Cambridge: Cambridge University Press.
  A somewhat technical account of African archaeology from its beginnings to European contact.

EARLY STATES IN SOUTH AND SOUTHEAST ASIA

Elephants parade at Angkor Wat.

n 1950, the famed excavator Sir Mortimer Wheeler assembled a team of young archaeologists, students, and local laborers to work on a confusion of mud bricks that projected out of a weathered citadel mound at Mohenjodaro on the banks of the Indus River, in Pakistan. The laborers removed foot after foot of sand, the few bricks grew into many, "until the stark walls of a huge platform began to emerge from the hillside. The aspect was of a fortress, towering grim and forbidding above the plain" (Wheeler, 1968, p. 317).

Wheeler puzzled over the mass of brickwork. A grid of narrow passages, signs of a timber superstructure, a carefully designed platform with an approach way: The enormous structure looked less and less like a fortress, but what was it? Suddenly a light went on in his brain. The narrow passages were ducts for air to dry the floor of the timber barn that once housed the city's grain, accessible only from the site, away from the teeming streets. The "fortress" was the municipal granary. More recent excavations have thrown Wheeler's bold interpretation into doubt, but many details of the Harappan civilization of South Asia, one of the world's least known (see Table 15.1), came from his classic investigations of a half century ago.

South Asia lies within vast geographic barriers (Figure 17.1). To the north lie the Himalayas, a vast mountain chain extending more than 2000 km (1200 miles) from the Hindu Kush in the west to Assam in the east. High passes traverse the mountains into Afghanistan, central Asia, and Tibet, but the most accessible routes are the northwestern defiles into western Afghanistan, Iran, and Baluchistan. The Arabian Sea, the Indian Ocean, and the Bay of Bengal surround the Indian subcontinent, while tropical rain forests restrict access to the east.

A rim of mountainous terrain rings the north and northwest of South Asia, giving way in the west to the alluvial plains of the Indus River, which merge with the Thar Desert in the east, 150 m (500 feet) above the floodplain. The desert in turn yields to the central tableland, the Deccan Plateau, more fertile than the lowlands and once densely forested. North and east of the central tableland lies the Ganges basin, which extends into Bihar, Bengal, and Bangladesh. This vast alluvial corridor enjoys greater rainfall as one moves east, and it gives way to the dense tropical forests that continue into Southeast Asia. The Deccan Peninsula lies south of the higher terrain of the central tableland, higher on the west than in the east, which means rivers flow eastward and the coastal plain is wider on the Bay of Bengal side.

Hemmed in by mountains, oceans, and tropical rain forest, South Asia developed its own distinctive civilizations, marked by the ability to assimilate ideas from outside. The subcontinent itself always had, and still has, a distinctive cultural identity along with great local diversity created by the isolation caused by east-west flowing rivers, different ethnic origins, and linguistic differences (Allchin and Allchin, 1983).

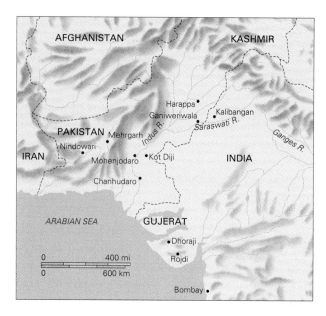

FIGURE 17.1   The Harappan civilization, showing sites mentioned in this chapter.

⁕ The Roots of South Asian Civilization

The Indus River, on the banks of which South Asian civilization began, rises in southern Tibet and then descends 1600 km (1000 miles) through Kashmir before flowing through the semi-arid Indus plains. Here, deep silt deposits provide soft, easily turned soils that can be cultivated on a large scale without metal tools. The Indus plains border on Baluchistan and eastern Afghanistan, forming a region with some environmental resemblances to the southern Mesopotamian plains and the neighboring Iranian Plateau. Like Mesopotamia, this is an area of climatic extremes: searingly hot summers and sometimes very cold winters. Farmers living in this harsh region obtain their water supplies from rivers and streams that rise in the mountains.

10,000 B.C.   Twelve thousand years ago, both borderland and plains were home to Stone Age hunter-gatherer groups that continued to flourish for many thousands of years. Despite now-refuted claims to the contrary, there is little evidence for agricultural communities in South Asia before the third millennium B.C., except in the northwest, where farming was probably introduced from the west. And even when agriculture took hold, as it did over wide areas between the fifth and third millennia B.C., hunting and gathering remained a viable lifeway for many South Asians, as it did into modern times. Most authorities on South Asian archaeology agree that humped cattle, buffalo, and pig were domesticated there from local wild populations (Sharma et al., 1980). Perhaps sheep and goats were also. The earliest dates for domesticated animals are in the period of 4500 to 4000 B.C., from sites near Quetta in Baluchistan and Rajasthan in northwest India. The farmers eventually domesticated not only indigenous Indian cultigens such as rice and dwarf wheat but also peas, barley, lentils, and other west Asian species; the dates of this early domestication are still unknown.

Mehrgarh   The best known early farming settlement is Mehrgarh, 200 km (125 miles) west of **6000 B.C.**   the Indus River, occupied by village farmers before 6000 B.C. (Jarrige, 1993). They grew west Asian wheat and used domesticated goats from the same region, as if the new economies had been introduced from the west, for Mehrgarh had cultural links with western and central Asia (Turkmenia). A thousand years later, the local people lived in sizable, permanent mud-brick houses. Their village lay astride a centuries-old trade route from the Indus Valley to the Iranian highlands. The Mehrgarh deposits contain copper artifacts and imported turquoise from Iran and shells from the distant Arabian coast, obtained, perhaps, by the export of cotton.

In the millennia before the emergence of urban civilization in India, dozens of regional variations of farming culture flourished throughout India and Pakistan; these peasant cultures are still little understood (Allchin and Allchin, 1983; Possehl, 1993).

The alluvial Indus plains were settled as early as the fourth millennium B.C. Scattered across a vast area of the plains are dozens of pre-Harappan settlements, many of them boasting fortifications, metallurgy, and planned streets, often grouped under the label Early Harappan. The Indus flooded between June and September. The farmers planted their wheat and barley as the floods receded, then harvested them the following spring, using the floodborne silts as a natural fertilizer. Over many centuries, the Indus Valley became an artificial environment, a maze of irrigation canals and floodworks, with human settlements built above the highest flood level but as close to the river as possible. Indus floods are sometimes violent and always unpredictable, so massive floodworks were sometimes needed. Many villages and small towns practiced intensive agriculture.

4000 B.C.

Typical of these settlements is Kot Diji, on the left bank of the Indus, approximately 33 km (20 miles) from the river (Mughal, 1974). In the early third millennium B.C., the inhabitants were forced to pile up boulders to protect themselves against the inundation. They finally erected a massive defensive wall that served as both a flood dike and a fortress. The stone and mud-brick houses of the village were clustered inside the wall. Nevertheless, Kot Diji was attacked and burned at least twice. The same fate must have awaited many other settlements that became involved in quarrels between ambitious local chieftains vying for the control of smaller communities and prime agricultural lands. The increased competition is hardly surprising, for between 3000 and 1500 B.C., farming had changed the natural ecology of the Indus Valley beyond all recognition (Kenoyer, 1997).

Kot Diji
3000 B.C.

Botanists have chronicled these ecological changes by using the minute pollen grains embedded in the Indus Valley soils. They found that the natural tree and grass cover on the floodplain increased between 2400 and 1000 B.C., perhaps as a result of a period of higher rainfall that lasted at least 2000 years. This thicker tree cover became established just as the farming population was taking advantage of good rains and expanding agricultural production. The pollen counts show not only more trees but also dramatic rises in the proportions of cereal grains and cultivated weeds at the expense of the natural vegetation. A complex multiplier effect then linked rapidly rising village populations with corresponding increases in agricultural production, leading to drastic consequences for the plains environment.

As the valley population rose, so did pressure on the land. The farmers cleared and burned off more and more riverine forest and grazed ever-growing herds of goats and sheep on watershed meadows. Acres of forest were burned to bake bricks for the houses of growing villages and newly founded cities. Mile after mile of the plains were denuded of natural vegetation, with disastrous consequences for erosion control and the floodplain environment. Deprived of natural controls, the rising floodwaters swept over the plains, carrying everything with them. Confronted with what may have seemed like the wrath of the gods, the people had only one defense: cooperative floodworks and irrigation agriculture that fed more mouths and provided at least a degree of security from the vagaries of the elements.

Until the early second millennium B.C., another river, known as the Saraswati, ran parallel to, and south of, the Indus River. The Saraswati dried up during the second millennium as a result of tectonic upheavals in the Himalayas that diverted the course of several of the rivers that merged to become the Saraswati. Archaeological surveys along the dried-up riverbed show that settlement along the river and its tributaries was very dense, to the point where the Saraswati may have been more important agriculturally than the Indus. Many unexcavated sites, including the major Harappan city of Ganweriwala, lie along its banks. Surviving in these harsh environments required intense cooperation at the community level. The obvious leaders of these new communal efforts were the chieftains, priests, and kin leaders, who acted as intermediaries between the people and the gods. By 2700 B.C., the most successful leaders of larger settlements presided over hierarchies of cities, towns, and villages.

〰 Highlands and Lowlands: The Kulli Complex

This scenario fits the few archaeological facts available from the lowlands. The early stages of the Harappan civilization date to between 3200 and 2600 B.C. The people lived in small villages covering only a few acres, and there are no signs of social ranking

Kulli complex

(Kenoyer, 1997). Their environment was like that of Mesopotamia, low-lying and hot, with fertile soils but no metals. Thus, its inhabitants could not flourish in isolation. Long before the rise of Harappan civilization in the valley, the peoples of the lowlands interacted constantly with their neighbors to the north and the west, especially in the highlands of southern Baluchistan, in western Pakistan. Metals, semiprecious stones, and timber came from the highlands, where people depended for their subsistence on dry agriculture and sheep herding. Over the millennia, the relationship between lowlands and highlands was fostered not only by regular exchanges of foods and other commodities but also by seasonal population movements that brought enormous herds of goats and sheep down from mountain summer pastures in Baluchistan to the lowlands during the harsh winters in the west. In a real sense, economic and social development in both regions occurred along parallel if somewhat diverse tracks, every region being dependent on its neighbors.

Nindowari
2600 to 2200 B.C.

In Baluchistan, a complex of large and small centers, subsumed under the Kulli complex, evolved during the third millennium B.C. The largest of these settlements was Nindowari, a major center dominated by a sizable monumental structure and massive public buildings. Nindowari was occupied between about 2600 and 2200 B.C. and was contemporary with mature Harappan civilization in the Indus lowlands. Harappan seals and other artifacts are found at Nindowari, and there are signs that Kulli communities were heavily involved in regular exchange with the lowlands to the east (Figure 17.2). Kulli also lay on the borders of eastern Iran, with its intricate exchange networks that reached far to the west toward Mesopotamia (see Chapter 15), but it is uncertain how many of its products flowed to the east. For centuries, the Kulli communities of the highlands were specialized partners of the Harappan civilization of the lowlands. One major commodity was cotton cloth. A South Asian–domesticated crop, cotton was probably first used as a fodder crop for cattle before people discovered that its fluffy white flower could be woven into fine cloth both for domestic use in a hot climate and for a hard-wearing fabric ideal for export. Such cloth first appears at the Harappan city of Mohenjodaro in the 3rd millennium B.C.

This symbiosis between Baluchistan and the Indus, among other regions, may have been a major catalyst in the rise of complex societies in both areas, a symbiosis that was vital not only in the Indus Valley but in distant Mesopotamia as well.

FIGURE 17.2 Mohenjodaro. Steatite seal bearing a mythical animal and eight symbols.

🐾 A Rapid Transition

Early Harappan society contrasted sharply with the complex, sometimes urban society that developed in the lowlands after about 2600 B.C. The transition from egalitarian to ranked society was an indigenous one that took place with what Gregory Possehl calls "a veritable paroxysm of change" (1986, p. 27). There was a short period of explosive growth over one or two centuries, ending about 2500 B.C. This span contrasts dramatically with the long period of increasing social, political, and economic complexity in Egypt and Mesopotamia.

Possehl (1999) believes that this growth may have coincided with a major shift in Sumerian trade patterns. As we saw in Chapter 15, the Sumerians obtained many exotic objects and basic raw materials from the Iranian Plateau before 2600 B.C. Judging from historical records, they experienced considerable frustration in their transactions with these exchange networks. After 2600 B.C., they reorganized their trade in luxuries and raw materials and then obtained many of their needs by sea from three foreign states: Dilmun, on the island of Bahrain in the Persian Gulf; Magan, a port farther east; and Meluhha, even farther away, where ivory, oils, furniture, gold, silver, and carnelian, among other commodities, were to be obtained (Rice, 1993). The Sumerians exchanged these goods for wool, cloth, leather, oil, cereals, and cedarwood. Possehl (1996) believes Meluhha to be the Indus Valley region.

2600 B.C.

In about 2350 B.C., King Sargon of Agade boasted that ships from all these locations were moored at his city. There are even records of villages of Meluhhans near Lagash and elsewhere in Mesopotamia. This was a highly organized mercantile trade conducted by specialized merchants, a trade quite different than that of the exchange networks in the highlands far inland. The sea trade increased the volume of Sumerian imports and exports dramatically. One shipment of 5900 kg (13,000 pounds) of copper is recorded, and the entire enterprise was very different from the basically noncommercial exchange systems of the Iranian Plateau. The trade was under Mesopotamian control, much of it conducted through Dilmun, and in Possehl's (1986) view, it had a major impact on the growth of Harappan civilization. Interestingly, its beginnings coincide with the growth of urban centers in both Mesopotamia and the Indus Valley (Edens, 1993).

A dramatic increase in long-distance trade may well have been the context in which Harappan civilization developed, trade that amplified the centuries-old symbiosis between highlands and lowlands to the northwest (Kenoyer, 1997). With the development of these coastal trading routes between the Persian Gulf and the South Asian peninsula, South Asia became part of what some archaeologists call an early world system, linking the eastern Mediterranean, parts of Eurasia, and western and southern Asia with loose and ever-changing economic ties. However, many scholars believe overseas trade was less important than is sometimes claimed and that Harappan civilization was an entirely indigenous development.

🐾 Mature Harappan Civilization

By 2600 B.C., the Indus people had mastered the basic problems of irrigation and flood control, partly by using millions of fired bricks made of river alluvium and baked with firewood cut from riverine forests. (For an up-to-date description of the Harappan civilization, see Mcintosh, 2002.) Mature Harappan civilization developed and flourished over a vast area of just under 1,294,900 sq km (580 square miles), a region considerably larger than modern Pakistan. The Indus and Saraswati valleys were the cultural focus of the Harappan civilization, but they were only one part of a much larger, very varied civilization, whose influences and ties extended over the lowlands of Punjab and Sind, from the highlands of Baluchistan to the deserts of Rajasthan, and from the Himalayan foothills almost to Bombay. The age-old relationship between highland Baluchistan and the Indus plains placed the Harappans within a larger cultural system, as did their maritime links with the Persian Gulf. But Possehl calls the Harappan civilization an "experiment in sociocultural organization which failed" (1993, p. 111). It was a large system, he says, but one that did not fully mature, with many settlements more village-like than citylike in the Western sense. Many communities were like large 'Ubaid settlements in southern Mesopotamia before urban civilization began.

Harappan civilization
2600 to 1700 B.C.

The Harappan civilization was different from that of the predominantly urban Sumerians in Mesopotamia, covering a core area of more than 777,000 sq km (300,000 square miles). Possehl makes an analogy with Egypt, where the Upper and Lower Nile were part of the same civilization, but there were always administrative, cultural, and social differences between the two regions. The same may have been true of the Harappan, with Mohenjodaro in Sind and Harappa in the Punjab, Ganweriwala on the Saraswati, and other sites in Gujarat and Sawashtra. These were major regional subdivisions of the Harappan civilization, linked by common symbolism and religious beliefs, the foundations of a cultural tradition that endured, although in modified form, for many centuries.

Harappa

Like the Sumerians, the Harappans adopted the city as a means of organizing and controlling their civilization. We know of at least five major Harappan cities: Harappa, after which the civilization is known; Mohenjodaro; Kalibangan; Chanhudaro; and Dhoraji in Gujarat (Meadows, 1991; Possehl, 1993). Harappa and Mohenjodaro were built on artificial mounds above the floods, at Herculean effort.

Mohenjodaro

Mohenjodaro is by far the largest of the Harappan cities, with six times the area of Harappa, and was rebuilt at least nine times, sometimes because of disastrous inundations. Widely accepted population estimates, based on the densities of modern, somewhat similar settlements, place some 35,000 to 40,000 people at Mohenjodaro, 23,500 at Harappa. The two cities are so similar that the same architect might have designed both of them.

A high citadel lies at the west end of each city, dominating the streets below. Here lived the rulers, protected by great fortifications and floodworks. Mohenjodaro's towering citadel rises 12 m (40 feet) above the plain and is protected by massive flood embankments and a vast perimeter wall with towers. The public buildings on the summit include a pillared hall almost 27 m (90 feet) square, perhaps the precinct where the rulers gave audience to petitioners and visiting officials. There are no spectacular temples or richly adorned shrines. Religious life was centered on a great lustral bath made of bitumen-sealed brickwork and fed by a well (Figure 17.3). An imposing colonnade surrounded the pool, which was approached by sets of steps at both ends. We cannot be sure of the exact use of the great bath, but *lustration* (ceremonial bathing) was an important part of later Indian religions. Perhaps the great bath was where the devout carried out their ceremonial bathing rituals.

The rulers of each city looked down on a complex network of at least partially planned streets (Figure 17.4). The more spacious dwellings, perhaps those of the nobility and the merchants, were laid out around a central courtyard where guests may have been received, food prepared, and servants probably worked. Staircases and thick

FIGURE 17.3 The great bath on the citadel at Mohenjodaro, Pakistan. Pedestals from now-vanished rooms surrounded the pool.

FIGURE 17.4 A street at Mohenjodaro with the citadel in the background.

ground walls indicate that some houses had two or even three stories. The larger residences had a well and contained rooms for bathing and toilets that may have been joined to an elaborate system of public drains. At both Harappa and Mohenjodaro, there were also groups of single-row tenements or workshops where the poorest people lived, many of them presumably laborers.

Some areas of Harappa and Mohenjodaro served as bazaars, complete with shops. Archaeologists have inventoried the finds from artisans' quarters where bead makers, coppersmiths, cotton weavers, and other specialists manufactured and sold their wares. The potters' workshops were filled with painted pots decorated with animal figures, as well as plain, ordinary wheel-made vessels that were manufactured not only in the cities but also in villages for hundreds of miles around. There were water jars and cooking bowls, storage pots, and drinking vessels. Metalworkers cast simple axes in open molds and manufactured chisels, knives, razors, spears, and fishhooks. Only a few expert artisans made more elaborate objects, such as small figurines (Figure 17.5), or a piece as complicated as a canopied cart. They would make a wax model of the cart and encase it in clay, which was fired to melt the wax. Then molten copper or bronze was poured into the mold. This "lost-wax" process is still used by Indian artists.

The technologies used in Harappan cities had been developed centuries earlier in small villages and transferred to the cities without change. One of the most developed manufactures was the seal, made from steatite and other soft rocks. Excavations of seal workshops have yielded not only finished specimens, hardened in a furnace, but also the blocks of steatite from which square seals were cut as intaglios. For hours, the seal makers would crouch over the tiny squares, expertly cutting representations of animals in profile. They reserved some of their best efforts for religious scenes. Indian archaeologists working at the Harappan town of Chanhudaro, south of Mohenjodaro, found a complete bead maker's shop that gave some idea of the labor needed to produce small ornaments. The bead makers prepared bars of agate and carnelian approximately 7.6 cm (3 inches) long that were then ground and polished into shorter perforated cylinders and strung in necklaces. To experience the bead-making process, the archaeologists took a Harappan stone-tipped drill and some abrasive powder from the workshop and attempted to drill through one of the bead blanks. It took them 20 minutes to drill a small pit in the end of the bead. At that rate, it would have taken 24 hours to drill a single bead!

FIGURE 17.5 Bronze figurine of a dancing girl from Mohenjodaro, Pakistan, 11 cm (4.3 inches) high.

Who Were the Harappans?

Three-quarters of a century of excavations have revealed a highly varied society that archaeologists have named the Harappan simply because they do not know what the Harappans called themselves. We do not even know the names of the rulers who controlled the major cities, like Harappa and Mohenjodaro, nor do we have insights into the intricate ties that linked city with town and major centers with minor hamlets. This civilization was different from that of the predominantly urban Sumerians in Mesopotamia. There were only three major cities the size of Uruk in an area of more than 770,000 sq km (300,000 square miles) (Possehl, 1980). It seems unlikely that there was the cultural and social uniformity found in Sumer.

There was constant interaction throughout this vast area, with abundant evidence that contemporary, relatively complex societies were developing elsewhere at the same time, developments known from sites like Kulli in Baluchistan (Possehl, 1993). The relationships between highland areas like Baluchistan, with their cold winters, and the lowlands led to complicated seasonal population shifts that brought highlanders and their herds to the Indus lowlands. This classic *transhumance* (seasonal movement) pattern may have placed the Harappans and their highland neighbors within the same larger cultural system.

The Harappan civilization was part of a vast network of regional interactions that functioned through trade routes that extended along the Arabian coast, into northern Afghanistan and Turkmenia, and onto the Iranian Plateau, through thousands of square miles of mountainous terrain rich in minerals and other natural resources. Regular caravan routes linked lowlands and highlands. These routes carried grain and textiles, carnelian beads, pearls, and sweet-smelling rosewood—luxuries exchanged for minerals and other raw materials. Deep-sea trading vessels cruised the shores of the Indian Ocean into the Persian Gulf (Edens, 1993). During the 1950s and 1960s, archaeologists uncovered a Harappan-style coastal town on the Gulf of Cambay. This settlement may have served as a river port, perhaps one of several on the Pakistani coast.

The anonymity of the Harappan leaders extends even to their appearance (Figure 17.6). These were no bombastic rulers boasting of their achievements on grandiose palace walls. Thus far, the evidence of archaeology reveals leadership by rulers, perhaps merchants, ritual specialists, or people who controlled key resources or large areas of land. They seem to have led unostentatious lives marked by a complete lack of priestly pomp or lavish public display. There is nothing of the ardent militarism of the Assyrian kings or of the slavish glorification of the pharaohs.

One reason we know so little about Harappan leaders is that their script has still not been deciphered (Parpola, 1994). Almost 400 different pictographic symbols have

FIGURE 17.6 Limestone sculpture of a bearded, thick-lipped man, perhaps a priest or ruler, from Mohenjodaro. Height: 19 cm (7.4 inches). He stares at the world through slitted eyes, as if withdrawn in meditation, perhaps detached from worldly affairs. He wears an embroidered robe that was once inlaid with metal. One shoulder is uncovered, a sign of reverence during the Buddha's lifetime more than 1000 years later. Perhaps the man was a priest or a priest-king.

been identified from their seals. Linguists do not even agree on the language in the script, let alone the ultimate identity of the Harappans. Some success has been achieved with computer-aided decipherment techniques, which have established the script as logosyllabic; that is, it is a mixture of sounds and concepts, just like Egyptian hieroglyphs. Some authorities believe the seals served not only as religious symbols but also as tags or labels written in Sumerian on bundles of merchandise sent to distant Sumer. Enough of the Indus script has been deciphered to show how many of the short seal inscriptions designate the names of individuals and their ranks. It seems, too, that some describe major figures of the Harappan cosmos and name the chiefs, as well as identifying scribes and leading artisans.

The writing system worked in conjunction with standardized weights and measures. The Harappan authorities developed a standard weight that was close to one-half of a modern ounce. Later, Indian societies used a unit known as the karsa for the same purpose. This weighed the equivalent of 32 rattis, seeds of the Gunja creeper, a measure that could fluctuate slightly from year to year. Four karsas weighed almost exactly the same as the basic Harappan unit of half a modern ounce. Similar devices could be found in nineteenth-century bazaars.

Everything points to some form of centralized government and a stratified society, with the focus of the civilization on agriculture and trade. Irrigation produced large surpluses of barley and wheat close to the cities, but many villagers away from the valley and river still practiced dry agriculture. Cotton and dates were also important crops in a society where the state may have controlled many acres of land and where every farmer turned over much of the household crop to the government. The entire agricultural enterprise was a much larger scale version of the communal village farming that had originally made colonization of the Indus Valley possible, but one that supported a hierarchical society.

Both Harappa and Mohenjodaro housed a comfortable and unpretentious middle class of merchants and petty officials who lived in stolid and standardized brick houses along the city streets. They wore finely woven, decorated cotton robes. Judging from clay figurines, the women wore short skirts and headdresses and perhaps longer robes. Dozens of shops sold wire neck bangles, necklaces, and pendants. Unfortunately, organic materials survive badly, but we can assume the Harappans made abundant use of wood and textiles.

The artisans—metalsmiths, potters, weavers, bead makers, seal carvers—formed another class of Harappan society, as did the minor bureaucrats and priests needed to administer the state. However, such people were a tiny minority compared with the vast mass of the populace: farmers, laborers, seafarers, and menial workers of every type. The commoners lived in small urban dwellings or, more often, in the countryside and wore the simplest cotton loincloths or robes. To judge from modern times, they had an extended family of several generations that provided a network of kinship ties and other benefits such as the communal ownership of property. Perhaps, too, the Harappan people were organized in a hierarchy of castes that restricted upward mobility and provided a wider identity outside the confines of the family.

Harappan Beliefs

Like the Sumerians, the Harappans lived in an environment that they modified for their own protection, one in which the annual floods meant a renewal of life and food for the coming year. Like the Mesopotamians, they seem to have believed that they lived in the valley to serve the gods, who caused crops to grow and soils to be fertile. We can speculate that the primeval roots of Indian religion may have been age-old fertility cults that served the same function as Inanna among the Sumerians and the mother goddess in many other Southwest Asian civilizations—an assurance that life would continue. The only clues we have to the origins of Indian religion come from minute seal impressions and small clay figurines from Harappan villages and cities that depict a female deity with conspicuous breasts and sexual organs. We do not know her name, but she probably embodied earth and life-giving nature for the Indus people.

A seal from Mohenjodaro bears a three-headed figure who sits in the yogic posture and wears a horned headdress. A tiger, an elephant, a rhinoceros, a water buffalo, and a deer surround him. Some Harappan experts think that the seal represents a forerunner of the great god Siva in his role of Lord of the Beasts. Many Harappan seals depict cattle, which may be symbols of Siva, who was worshiped in several forms. To judge from later beliefs, he may have had a dual role, serving as a fertility god as well as a tamer or destroyer of wild beasts (Miller, 1985). Siva gave life by planting the seed but could also destroy any creature, including a human being, at a flick of the finger. In part, he may have symbolized the unpredictable dangers of flood and famine that could threaten a village or a city. Harappa and Mohenjodaro have yielded dozens of carved phallic symbols and circular stones with round holes, which represent Siva's consort Devi's teeming womb. Perhaps these are simple prototypes of the Hindu *lingam* and *yoni* symbols that are found in the temples of Siva and Devi to this day. If the evidence of figurines and seals is to be believed, the symbolism of early Indus religion bears remarkable similarities to that of modern Hinduism. Many other elements of more modern South Asian religion may have flourished in Harappan society, among them the use of fire altars in homes, worship with fruit and flowers, meditation, and well-developed astronomical knowledge. These similarities highlight the deeply ingrained conservatism of South Asian society from the earliest moments of Harappan civilization and even further back in the past.

𓂃 South Asia After the Harappans

The Harappan civilization reached its peak in about 2000 B.C. Three centuries later, Harappa and Mohenjodaro were in decline and soon abandoned. Their populations dispersed into smaller settlements over an enormous area as the volume of long-distance trade declined dramatically, except perhaps in metals (Figure 17.7). The reasons for this change are still little understood, but it may have been due to a variety of factors, among them possible flooding along the Indus, shifts in patterns of Mesopotamian trade, and changes in subsistence farming (Ghosh, 1993). One fundamental cause may have been

FIGURE 17.7   Rojdi, Gujarat, India, a Harappan town dating to the period immediately following the abandonment of cities. Left, excavation of house walls. Right, artist's reconstruction of the same dwellings.

major geological disturbances near the source of the all-important Saraswati River, which caused it to dry up and some tributaries to divert to new courses, thereby catastrophically disrupting farming life along its banks (Possehl, 2000).

Other changes followed soon afterward. By 1500 B.C., rice cultivation had taken hold in the Ganges basin, opening up a new environment for farming where conditions were unsuitable for wheat and barley cultivation. At the same time, millets became important in the Gujarat region, some of them of African origin, crops that were especially suited to the more humid parts of southern India. The effect of these new crops may have been to widen the area where agriculture was practiced, thereby reducing the environmental circumscription that may have been one of the bases of Harappan civilization.

The rural components of Harappan culture continued to flourish in Gujarat and other areas for two centuries or more, until Aryan nomads arrived in the Indus Valley and the lowlands. By that time, the Harappans had passed on a priceless legacy of beliefs and philosophies that formed one of the mainstreams of all subsequent Indian history. No cities developed in South Asia east of the Indus region until long after the Harappan civilization went into decline (Allchin, 1995). As the highly developed socioeconomic system of the Indus broke down, urban life vanished, to emerge once again far to the east in the Ganges Valley many centuries later. At the same time, many well-developed, but still little-known, regional farming cultures flourished both inside the Indus region and beyond.

But the second millennium B.C. was a period of vital importance in South Asian history, for it was during these centuries, sometimes called the Vedic period, that Indo-Aryan–speaking people spread into the subcontinent, an event described in the *Samhita,* a compilation of the hymns (*vedas*) of the *Rigveda.* Many of the hymns were composed centuries earlier, then passed from generation to generation by word of

1500 B.C.

mouth. Many scholars argue that Indo-European–speaking peoples spread across the Iranian Plateau into South Asia during the second millennium B.C., where they intermarried with indigenous groups. Thus were born the Indo-Aryan, Sanskritic languages spoken throughout South Asia today. But another school of thought believes that there was no invasion, that Indo-Aryan developed indigenously in South Asia and was present there from a much earlier period (Mallory, 1988; Shaffer and Lichtenstein, 1995).

The process of conquest, assimilation, and acculturation may have begun in the northwest in the closing era of the Indus civilization and continued for as long as a thousand years. By 800 B.C., an indigenous iron technology was in full use throughout the subcontinent. Iron tools accelerated rice cultivation on the Ganges plain. Two centuries later 16 major kingdoms were concentrated around urban centers on the Ganges plain.

City life in the Ganges Valley marked the beginning of the classic period of South Asian civilization (Allchin, 1995). The new cities became economic powerhouses and centers of great intellectual and religious ferment. Brahmanism, a form of Hinduism that placed great emphasis on ritual and sacrifice, was the dominant religion during the early first millennium. But philosophers of the sixth century B.C., like Buddha and Makhali Gosala, challenged Brahmanism with revolutionary doctrines that militated against sacrifice. Buddhism, with its teachings of personal spiritual development, spread rapidly, becoming the dominant religion in the north within five centuries.

Meanwhile, outside powers eyed the fabled riches of the subcontinent. King Darius of Persia invaded the northwest in 516 B.C. and incorporated the Indus Valley into the Persian Empire. Two centuries later, Alexander the Great ventured to the Indus River and brought Greek culture to the area. The great ruler Chandragupta Maurya of Magadha benefited from the power vacuum following Alexander's conquests and carved out the Mauryan Empire, which extended from Nepal and the northwest deep into the Deccan (Figure 17.8). His grandson Asoka presided over the empire at its height between 269 and 232 B.C., seeking to unify its diverse people by a well-defined moral and ethical code based on Buddhist principles.

Mauryan Empire
269 to 232 B.C.

Magadha and other northern cities in Asoka's empire prospered greatly from overland trade routes leading northwest to Charsada, Taxila, and other frontier cities. Far to the east, the port of Tamluk at the mouth of the Ganges gave access to new and expanding marine trade routes to Southeast Asia. And, as the Mauryan Empire came to an end in 185 B.C., the monsoon winds of the Indian Ocean linked the South Asian coast with the Roman world and its insatiable demands for ivory, spices, and fine textiles from South Asian markets. Roman coins have come from ancient ports in the south, as well as from Arikamedu, a trading station on the east coast of the Deccan.

By Roman times, South Asia was part of a vast trading network that linked the Mediterranean world to all parts of the Indian Ocean and, indirectly, to new sources of raw materials many sea kilometers to the east.

FIGURE 17.8 Map of the extent of the Mauryan Empire.

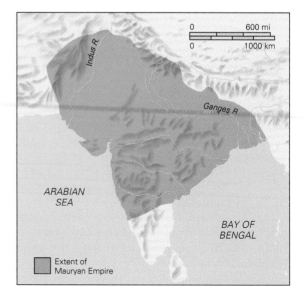

Southeast Asian States

Ten thousand years ago, the Southeast Asian mainland extended far offshore, most of it low-lying marshland intersected by several major river systems. The three major river systems of Southeast Asia are much reduced versions of earlier rivers, each with its own fertile delta (Figure 17.9). The Middle Thailand and Chao Phraya Delta forms one such system; the lower Mekong and Tonle Sap plains, the major concern of this discussion, a second; and the Red, Ma, and Ca rivers of Vietnam a third. The rivers flood seasonally, inundating large areas of farmland with shallow water where long-stalked, fast-growing rice can be grown. These three river valleys have been the homelands of complex societies for many centuries, fertile enclaves surrounded by higher ground where deciduous, drought-resistant forest and moist tropical forest flourish. Watered by monsoon cycles and marked by considerable local variations in climate and topography, parts of Southeast Asia supported high population densities only within the past 2000 years.

8000 B.C.

The staple crop in ancient Southeast Asia was rice, domesticated in China's Yangzi River valley before 6500 B.C. (see Chapter 12). Rice farming was well established in Southeast Asia by 2000 B.C., but agricultural populations were never large. Between 1500 and 500 B.C., Southeast Asia's egalitarian farming communities adopted bronze metallurgy and traded widely with one another. Both mining and smelting were important activities, probably during the agriculturally quiet dry season (Higham, 2000, 2002). The Ban Na Di site in northern Thailand contains an important cemetery, where the dead lay in orderly clusters, with clear evidence of social ranking within the village and of trade with other communities.

6500 B.C.

1500 to 500 B.C.

Ban Na Di

By 500 B.C., iron technology was in use, as local populations rose and settlements grew much larger, some of them with as many as 25,000 inhabitants. These were the centuries when Southeast Asians began to participate in maritime trade routes that linked the mainland and offshore islands, New Guinea and the Philippines, as well as India and China. As early as the fourth century B.C., carnelian beads and a carving of a lion found at Ban Don Ta Phet in central Thailand reveal trade links with India, and bronze bowls, traced from their alloys back to Southeast Asia, have been found in the Indian subcontinent.

A portrait of society at the time comes from the Noen U-Loke site in the Mun Valley of northeastern Thailand, where a sample of 126 graves dating from 400 B.C. to about A.D. 300 shows a dramatic increase in the amount of effort expended on burying the

Noen U-Loke

400 B.C. to A.D. 300

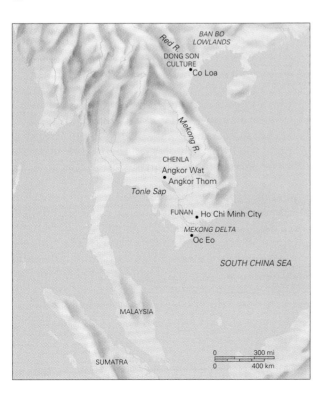

FIGURE 17.9 Southeast Asia, showing sites mentioned in the text.

dead. Some of the deceased were laid in graves filled with burnt rice; other graves were lined and capped with clay, like coffins. The graves lay in clusters of men, women, and children, presumably family groups. The contents of one cluster were almost all carnelian jewelry and rice, another was associated with spindle whorls, and a third with most of the clay-lined caskets. Three of them featured exceptionally wealthy males, adorned with bronze belts, bangles, ear disks, and other elaborate ornaments. These were not peaceful times, perhaps the product of an increasingly crowded landscape. One man lay prone with an iron arrowhead buried in his spine (Higham and Thosarat, 1998).

Throughout Southeast Asia, population densities and social complexity increased, as rich and warlike chiefdoms appeared at the end of the first millennium B.C. Expert seafarers and traders, they were active participants in a much larger world that linked the Han Empire of China with India and the mainland to islands far offshore.

This trend toward complexity and competition was an indigenous development, even if innovations from outside fueled political and social change. Iron metallurgy was grafted onto the existing bronze technology, but it is uncertain whether ironworking was an independent invention or perhaps an introduction from India, where forging (smelting in a small furnace) was used, or from China, where sophisticated casting methods involving molten iron at very high temperatures were developed. Larger communities developed, usually centers for craft production. In earlier times, rice cultivation had been concentrated in small stream valleys and along the margins of major river floodplains. Such dry rice farming was much less productive than wet cultivation in waterlogged fields (paddies), which produced much higher and more predictable crop yields. The appearance of larger settlements may have coincided with both intensive wet farming and the advent of plowing and double-cropping, which greatly increased food production and produced much larger crop surpluses.

A trend toward centralized governance developed, focused on large centers ruled by highly ranked lineages. Their power was underwritten by their control of food surpluses and rice lands, by their support of expert artisans, and by carefully managed exchange monopolies over high-status imports and exotic materials. The leaders of these societies wore fine ceremonial weapons and badges of rank, and they lived in finely decorated houses. Over a period of several centuries, far more complex societies developed, especially in fertile riverine areas, societies whose leaders controlled maritime and inland trade over large areas. The exposure to artifacts, technologies, and ideas from China and India increased alongside these major changes as powerful leaders surrounded themselves with all the panoply of public ceremony, ritual feasting, and ostentation.

Dong Son

Dong Son culture
1000 B.C. to A.D. 43

The best known of these societies is the Dong Son culture of Vietnam's Red River valley, where a moist climate allows two rice crops a year. The indigenous origins of the Dong Son culture go back to at least 1000 B.C., when bronze smiths were already at work in the valley. The intensification of bronze working required enormous quantities of metal and much larger food surpluses, obtained by extensive wet rice agriculture on the Red River Delta. Dong Son metalworkers were masters of their craft, casting elaborate, richly decorated artifacts and eventually adopting the iron technology of their Chinese neighbors to the north. Drums, in particular, became symbols of high social status in Dong Son society (Figure 17.10).

The Lac Lords, paramount chiefs, warriors, and keepers of the drums, ruled over this prosperous society. One of them ruled from Co Loa, founded by the third century B.C. Co Loa boasted of three sets of ramparts, their moats supplied with water from a tributary of the Red River. The fortifications enclosed an area of 600 ha (1482 acres). The Chinese Han knew of the Lac Lords as the most distant of "southern barbarians," and traded and fought with them for centuries. Finally, in A.D. 43, the warrior nobles of Dong Son succumbed to their powerful neighbors. Their domains became a Chinese protectorate, but Han records tell us they retained their traditional rights over land (Wheatley, 1979).

Trade and Kingdoms

By about A.D. 1, the sea-trading networks of Southeast Asia were part of a much larger commercial universe. Finds of sewn-plank boats dating to the third to fifth centuries A.D.

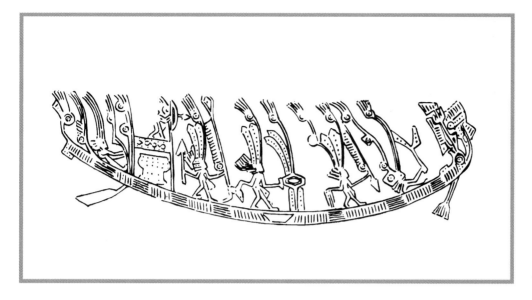

FIGURE 17.10 A Dong Son boat that formed part of the decoration on a bronze drum. A war prisoner and well-armed warriors ride in the craft, which carries a drum stored in a cabin with an archer perched on the roof.

testify to a long tradition of seafaring. Chinese records tell us that some oceangoing vessels were up to 50 m (164 feet) long and weighed as much as 500 tons. Striking evidence of the monsoon trade comes from the Sembiran site in Bali, where archaeologist A. W. Ardika has found Indian trade pottery from the southern Indian coast 4350 km (2700 miles) westward as the crow flies (Bellwood, 1997).

The traders themselves were an entirely maritime people of no particular nationality, called Mwani, or "barbarians," by the Chinese of the time. They spoke polyglot tongues and were of many lands, some Malays, some Indians—true wanderers who ventured as far east as the South China Sea. The Gulf of Tonkin and south China were served by Jiwet, Chinese mariners who brought luxuries to the coast, whence the goods were transported overland to the imperial capital (see Table 16.1).

That India had a profound influence on the development of Southeast Asian civilization is unquestionable (Chandler, 1983). During the late second century B.C., Indian emperor Asoka's edicts spread the teachings of Buddhism throughout the territory of the Mauryan Empire in South Asia. His inscriptions make it clear that the prosperity of Buddhism was closely connected to the dealings of prosperous merchants. The older religion, Brahmanism, had placed severe and authoritarian restraints on foreign voyages, but Buddhism and Jainism (a form of Hinduism) rejected the racist teachings espoused by the predecessor religion. Travel was encouraged, which was a catalyst for expanded trade. In another political development, the Roman emperor Vespasian had prohibited exporting metals from the Roman Empire in approximately A.D. 70, a move that turned Indian merchants' eyes to the southeast. Nomadic raids on Asian caravans had also closed the Siberian gold mines to them. Metals were not the only attraction; spices could be obtained in abundance. Trade was expanded entirely for commercial profit.

Southeast Asia was a vital part in the chain of trading ports that linked China to India and Asia to the Roman Empire. The maritime trade brought a vigorous exchange of ideas and new cultural influences. Inevitably, argues Sinologist Paul Wheatley (1975, 1983), Southeast Asian chieftains learned a new way of seeing society and the world, perhaps by assembling commodities for trade and acquiring organizational skills. The authority and powers needed to expand and maintain the commerce were not part of the kin-linked society in which the chieftains had lived all their lives. In time they became familiar with the Brahman and Buddhist conceptions of divine kingship. There was even a brahmanic rite by which chieftains could be inducted into the ruling class, a group whose authority was vested in an assumption of divine kingship.

Toward the end of the first millennium B.C., some Southeast Asian societies had become highly ranked, centralized kingdoms, presided over by an aristocratic class to whom formal display, feasting, and ritual were of paramount importance. They ruled by virtue of their close relationships with their ancestors. As in Maya society in

Mesoamerica (see Chapter 21), rank and ancestry were closely connected. The growing complexity of such societies came in part from the ability of their overlords to attract loyal followers and to organize people. In time, many such rulers aspired to even greater status. They tried to preside over far larger kingdoms carved out by force. When they prevailed, they ruled by sheer charisma, cementing their authority with the creation of magnificent palaces and temples that served as the focus for elaborate public ceremonials and prestigious displays.

These Southeast Asian kingdoms were in a constant state of political flux and without fixed boundaries. The currency of political life was external but always fluid. Alliances developed between neighboring rulers. Everything revolved around the principal overlord, whose ability to cement alliances and deal with potential enemies dictated his relationships with his rivals. Some experts use a Sanskrit word, *mandala*, an Indian political doctrine, to describe the relationships between these rulers, whose territories are thought of as circles. It is as if they were concertinas, which expanded and contracted as different polities interacted with one another. Each society focused on its own center and on its own religious ruler and his retinue. The personal and spiritual qualities of each leader were important variables in a complex, ever-changing political equation (Wolters, 1982).

Divine kingship revolutionized social and political organization in Southeast Asia. Kingdoms flourished in riverine and lowland areas, along the lower Mekong, and in the middle Mekong Valley, including the celebrated Tonle Sap plains, the homeland of Khmer-speaking peoples. (Khmer is an Austroasiatic language of considerable antiquity.) There were also kingdoms on the Khorat Plateau, along the central Vietnamese coastal plain, and in the Red River area, the latter under Chinese control. The Chinese called the lower Mekong region Funan, which meant "the port of a thousand rivers," but the term has little real historical meaning. According to Chinese records, the ports of the delta handled bronze, silver, gold, spices, and even horses brought by sea from central Asia. One such port was Oc Eo, linked to the coast by a canal, a large town excavated by French archaeologists. Another was Angkor Borei. Canals linked the two communities, drained water, and also carried trade goods. Populations were densely concentrated, land was acquired through territorial conquest, and marshes were drained for more farmland. Whether there was a single kingdom or a series of competing chiefdoms is a matter of debate. Chinese accounts of Funan extol its rich trade. They tell of a drainage and transport system that rapidly transformed much of the delta from barren swamps into rich agricultural land. The development of these fields took the communal efforts of hundreds of people living off the fish that teemed in the bayous of the delta. Most Funanese lived in large lake cities fortified with great earthworks and moats swarming with crocodiles. Each major settlement was a port connected to the ocean and its neighbors by a canal network.

Oc Eo
A.D. 300 to 600

The coastal region prospered greatly from the third to the sixth centuries A.D., thanks to its long traditions of indigenous metallurgy and other crafts and trading expertise. In the sixth century, many more Indian Brahmans arrived in the region. They brought the cult of the god Siva. He appeared in the temples in the form of a *linga*, a phallic emblem of masculine creative power. Where rulers were worshipers of Siva, the royal linga stood in a temple that symbolized the center of the capital.

The political situation along the lower Mekong was always volatile, especially since the kingdoms upstream had only indirect contact with foreign traders. Leaders inland responded by carving out new routes to the coast, bypassing the delta. In this, they were successful. By the sixth century A.D., the center of economic and political gravity had shifted to the middle Mekong and the Tonle Sap, an area the Chinese called Zhenla. Numerous rivers fed the Tonle Sap, the central basin of Cambodia, its fluctuating water levels supporting many acres of fertile soil. Most of the year, the basin is a shallow series of muddy pools some 66 km (40 miles) long, drained by the Tonle Sap, which runs into the Mekong. However, so much water floods into the Mekong Delta between August and October that the Tonle Sap's course is reversed and the pools become a vast lake, 133 to 167 km (80 to 100 miles) long, 25 to 50 km (15 to 30 miles) wide, and up to 16 m (50 feet) deep. Late in October, the water starts receding, trapping millions of fish in the muddy bayous. In the twelfth century A.D., the environment was so bountiful that it supported dense urban populations and generated large food surpluses, sufficient to support a glittering, wealthy civilization. At the time of Christ, the farmers of this favored region lived under local chiefs who controlled local reservoirs, water control being critically important for successful agriculture. Over the next few centuries, small kingdoms developed that maintained their independence or coalesced, depending on the abilities of individual overlords to assert their authority. Constant warfare and political maneuvering eventually led to the emergence of hereditary rulers and small states.

The Rise of the God-Kings

Competing Zhenla rulers acquired sufficient food surpluses to embark on ambitious conquests and, eventually, to develop a new political concept of divine kingship that united their far-flung domains in a common purpose: the glorification of the god-king on earth. Devotion to the Hindu creator Siva became a mechanism that provided divine justification for kingship, as well as a focus for the loyalty and devotion of a ruler's retinue, who would endow temples in return for royal favors.

Between the time of Christ and the end of the eighth century, centralization and high status were so unstable that they could fluctuate considerably within an individual's lifetime. Ambitious men would try and try again to raise themselves above others and their kingdoms to supreme rule. Throughout the centuries, these were never states in the Western sense of the word. Rather, the "concertina" effect of kingdom politics was constantly at work, with competing polities asserting independence at times, becoming tribute givers and vassals at others.

⚜ The Angkor State (A.D. 802 to 1430)

The overlords of the Tonle Sap all shared one ambition: to establish hegemony over as large an area as possible. The earlier kings were unable to hold the kingdom together until a dynamic Khmer monarch named Jayavarman II came to power in A.D. 802. He conquered his competitors and set up his new territories as tribute kingdoms, giving his loyal generals land grants. Jayavarman II is said to have merged the cult of the ancestors with that of Siva in the form of a linga to consolidate his new kingdom. A much later inscription tells us he called himself Supreme King. His subjects were taught to worship him as a god. All resources of an increasingly centralized government were devoted to the preservation of the cult of the god-king. Everyone, whether noble, high priest, or commoner, was expected to subordinate his or her ambitions to the need to perpetuate the existence of the king on earth and his identity with the god in this life and the next. This remarkable leader reigned for 45 years, the first of at least three dynasties of Khmer rulers, who often came to power after vicious fighting and presided over an ever-changing state that reached the height of its prosperity between A.D. 900 and 1200 (Higham, 2000).

Previous monarchs had encouraged the worship of Siva in the form of the phallic image, but now Jayavarman II presented himself as the reincarnation of Siva on earth. He was the *varman*, the protector, and his priests were the instruments of practical political power. The high priests were invariably energetic, imposing nobles who presided over a highly disciplined hierarchy of religious functionaries. The ruler himself headed a bureaucracy of high-status families, which included generals and administrators who settled land disputes. The bureaucracy supervised every aspect of Khmer life, from agriculture to warfare, tax collection, and the rituals of the state religion. As always with preindustrial civilizations, there was a close link between food surpluses and the control of the enormous labor forces needed to construct temples, reservoirs, and other public works. Most building activity probably took place during the dry months. The custom of building a new majestic and holy temple to house the royal linga of each king was the most important of all the religious rituals. As a result, many of the 30 monarchs who followed Jayavarman II left massive religious edifices to commemorate their reigns. These they built on artificial mounds in the center of their capitals, the hub of the Khmer universe, an area known today as Angkor. The Khmer's unique form of kingship produced, instead of an austere civilization like that of the Indus, a society that carried the cult of wealth, luxury, and divine monarchy to amazing lengths (Higham, 2000). This cult reached its apogee in the reign of Suryavarman II, who built the temple of Angkor Wat in the twelfth century (see Site box).

Angkor state
A.D. 802 to 1430

Angkor Wat
A.D. 1117

SITE

Angkor Wat, Cambodia

For four years after his succession in A.D. 1113, King Suryavarman II commenced building his masterpiece, an extraordinary shrine that is a spectacle of beauty, wonder, and magnificence, the largest religious building in the world. Angkor Wat (Figure 17.11) is 1500 m (5000 feet) by 1200 m (4000 feet) across. The central block measures 215 m by 186 m (717 feet by 620 feet) and rises more than 60 m (200 feet) above the forest. It dwarfs even the largest Sumerian ziggurat and makes Mohenjodaro's citadel look like a village shrine (Riboud, 1992).

Every detail of this extraordinary building reproduces part of the heavenly world in a terrestrial mode (Figure 17.12). The Khmer believed that the world consisted of a central continent known as Jambudvipa, with the cosmic mountain, Meru, rising from its center. The gods lived at the summit of Meru, represented at Angkor Wat by the highest tower. The remaining four towers depict Meru's lesser peaks; the enclosure wall depicts the mountain at the edge of the world, and the surrounding moat depicts the ocean beyond. Angkor Wat was the culminating attempt of the Khmer to reproduce a monument to the Hindu god Visnu, the preserver of the universe.

Angkor Wat's bas-reliefs show Suryavarman seated on a wooden throne wearing an elaborate crown and pectoral. He receives his high officials as they declare their loyalty. Next, the king progresses down a hillside on an elephant accompanied by the high priest and his generals. The court rides with him through a forest, with noble ladies in litters, everyone protected by heavily armed soldiers. Scattered throughout Angkor Wat are scenes of battles and bas-reliefs of celestial maidens. Naked to the waist, slender and sensuous, the dancers wear skirts of rich fabric. Their flowered background, the subtle rhythm of their gestures, their jeweled necklaces and diadems bring to light the

FIGURE 17.11 Angkor Wat, a representation of the Hindu universe.

Angkor Wat taxed the resources of the kingdom severely at a time of increased strife with neighboring powers. In 1181, another ruler, Jayavarman VII, who was a Buddhist, started building a huge new capital at Angkor Thom nearby. A dark and forbidding 12.8-km (8-mile) wall surrounds the capital. When visitors walked inside, they entered a symbolic Hindu world with the king's funerary temple, the Bayon, at the center

delights of paradise promised to the king after his death. Inscriptions also spell out the terrible punishments that awaited ill-doers.

Angkor Wat was constructed using a measurement of 0.435 m (1.43 feet), a Khmer unit of measurement known as a *hat*. The length and breadth of the central structure of the temple corresponded to 365.37 *hat*, while the axial distances of the great causeway correspond with the four great eras of Hindu time. Someone standing in front of the western entrance on the spring equinox was able to see the sun rising directly over the central lotus tower. During his lifetime, Suryavarman used Angkor Wat as the place where he, as a divine monarch, communicated with the gods. When he died, his remains were placed in the central tower, so that his soul entered his divine image and made contact with the royal ancestors. Here the immortal ruler became as one with Visnu, master of the universe.

FIGURE 17.12   The paved causeway at Angkor Wat approaches the temple through an entrance gallery with a tower. The causeway is 150 m (500 feet) long, flanked with balustrades adorned with mythical, multiheaded snakes. The gallery opens onto a cruciform terrace in front of a rectangular temple that rises in three imposing tiers to a central cluster of five towers. Each tower bears a lofty pinnacle that from afar looks like a giant lotus bud. The causeway leads across a huge moat, 180 m (600 feet) wide and enclosed by masonry walls 6.4 km (4 miles) in circumference. The engineers built the walls with a total error of less than 2 cm (an inch)! The moat is still a beautiful sight, with floating water lilies, wild orchids, and other shimmering blooms.

(Figure 17.13). The Grand Plaza of Angkor Thom was the scene of ceremonies and contests, of vast military reviews and massed bands.

Angkor Thom
A.D. 1181

It is said that a million people once lived in or near Angkor Thom. One temple dedicated to the king's father contained no fewer than 430 images, with more than 20,000 in gold, silver, bronze, and stone in the wider precincts. An inscription in the Ta Prohm

FIGURE 17.13   The "Face Tower" at the Bayon temple, Angkor Thom.

temple nearby, dedicated to the king's mother in the image of the Buddha's mother, records that 306,372 people from 13,500 villages worked for the shrine, consuming 38,000 tons of rice a year. An inscription in the nearby temple of Ta Prohm inventories a staff of 18 senior priests, 2740 minor functionaries, 615 female dancers, and a total of 66,625 "men and women who perform the service of the gods." All this royal construction was designed to make merit for the king and his followers. He also built fully staffed hospitals and pilgrims' shelters to gain further credit. The result of Jayavarman's building projects was a totally centripetal religious utopia in which every product, every person's labor, and every thought was directed toward embellishing the hub of the universe and the kings who enjoyed it (Wheatley, 1983).

The impression of prosperity and stability was illusory in a society where the ruler's power depended on the granting of favors, on his successful patronizing of the major aristocratic families. There was no stable bureaucracy with appointed officials to run the state. The king mediated with the gods for rain, settled disputes, and used the rich resources of the land to redistribute wealth among his subjects. He sat at the center of the circle represented by the *mandala,* its boundaries defined only by the loyalties of the aristocrats who ruled the outlying provinces. A Khmer king's hold on the reins of power depended on the control of the center, the Angkor. Thus, when the central administration was weak, the kingdom tended to break up into regional units.

By Jayavarman VII's death, Buddhism had gained a strong foothold, but religious dissension became common until Theravada, a form of low Buddhism preaching equality, became popular. Theravada did not deal with traditional ideas of kingship, so building activity slowed. Warfare was endemic. In 1430–31, the Thai sacked Angkor after a long siege, and the great state finally dissolved.

A.D. 1430–31

Late in the thirteenth century, the strategic trade routes through the Malay Straits came under Islamic control in a new chapter of international trade. Melaka became an important port and stronghold on the northern shore of the straits. The rest of the kingdoms and ports of the islands soon adopted the new religion, which preached a message of religious egalitarianism in the face of centuries of Indian statecraft based on notions of divine kingship. Within three centuries, the rulers of inland Java had adopted Islam, perhaps to maintain control over their subjects, who were welcoming the new beliefs with open arms. Islam and trade went hand in hand in island Southeast Asia, until the arrival of Portuguese gun-bearing sailing ships at Melaka in 1519.

A.D. 1519

The Khmer state is a classic example of how a combination of cultural processes and able individuals can lead to the appearance of powerful, yet volatile states. Yet these same states face constantly the problem of controlling not only the center but the periphery, especially in times of weak rule and menacing competition from outside.

Summary 🐾

State-organized societies on the Indian subcontinent developed from indigenous roots in about 2600 B.C. The Harappan civilization of the lowland Indus Valley developed as the result of a major shift in Sumerian long-distance trade patterns and long-term interactions between the Harappan culture of the lowlands and the Kulli complex of the Baluchistan highlands. Harappan civilization flourished along the Indus for about a thousand years. It was an urban society with many smaller satellite settlements, carefully planned and ruled by priest-kings who controlled both religious and economic life. After 1700 B.C., the major cities went into decline, but Harappan society flourished in rural settings for a considerable time. The center of economic and political gravity moved eastward to the Ganges River valley, culminating in the Mauryan Empire of the first millennium B.C.

Southeast Asian peoples had developed bronze working by at least 1500 B.C. The process of forming local states (*mandalas*) began around the same time, but the first historical records of complex states date to the third century A.D. Many such states developed in and around the central Mekong Valley and, later, in the central Cambodian basin. There, after A.D. 802, flourished the flamboyant Khmer civilization, a society based on divine kingship and strong notions of conformity. After six centuries of spectacular development, the Khmer civilization came in contact with expanding Islamic trade networks and new religious doctrines, which caused its partial demise.

Guide to Further Reading 🐾

South Asia

Allchin, Bridget, and Raymond Allchin. 1983. *The Rise of Civilization in India and Pakistan.* Cambridge: Cambridge University Press.
A summary account of the roots of the Indus civilization that is readable and well argued, but now somewhat outdated.

Allchin, Raymond. 1995. *The Archaeology of Historic South Asia.* Cambridge: Cambridge University Press.
A detailed synthesis of later South Asian civilization; for the advanced reader.

Mcintosh, Jane R. 2002. *A Peaceful Realm.* Boulder, CO: Westview Press.
Mcintosh has written a graceful and easy-to-read story of the Harappan civilization.

Possehl, Gregory, 1999. *Indus Age: The Beginnings.* Philadelphia: University of Pennsylvania Press.
The ultimate source on the Harappan by a world authority.

Southeast Asia

Chandler, David. 1983. *A History of Cambodia.* Boulder, CO: Westview Press.
A useful summary of the history of the region.

Giteau, M. 1966. *Khmer Sculpture and the Angkor Civilization.* London: Thames & Hudson.
A wonderful lay reader's guide to the elaborate artistry and architecture of the Khmer. Lavishly illustrated.

Higham, Charles. 2000. *The Civilization of Angkor.* London: Cassel.
Higham has written an authoritative summary of Angkor states.

———. 2002. *Early Cultures of Southeast Asia.* London and New York: Thames & Hudson.
A comprehensive account of mainland Southeast Asia that melds archaeological and historical evidence. Up-to-date and authoritative.

Rovedo, Vittorio. 2002. *Sacred Angkor.* London and New York: Thames & Hudson.
A study of the intricacies and meaning of Angkor art. Beautifully illustrated.

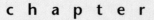

chapter

EARLY CHINESE
CIVILIZATION

The terra-cotta regiment of the Emperor Shihuangdi, 221 B.C.

The inscribed bone came from a curio shop—part of an ox shoulder blade that seemed out of place among precious jade and porcelain bowls. Archaeologist Tung Tso-pin was intrigued and wondered if the weathered bone was connected to the ancient, legendary Shang civilization. The Shang people had lived on the banks of the Huang Ho, their capital said to be near the town of Anyang. Even as early as the eleventh century, local scholars had collected exotic bronze vessels from the flat farmland where Shang kings once lived. Tung Tso-pin had visited Anyang in the late 1920s, just after the river had changed course nearby, exposing rich cultural debris—including more ox shoulder blades—in the banks. He dug several deep pits that contained carefully packed "archives" of oracle bones—ox shinbones and scapulae—and tortoiseshells, marked with inscriptions that gave historians a list of the Shang kings until their capital was destroyed by catastrophic floods. Excavations at Shang capitals have continued sporadically ever since, revealing a civilization known hitherto only from ancient legend. This chapter discusses the origins of ancient Chinese civilization, as we know it from archaeological and historical research (Table 18.1).

 The Origins of Chinese Civilization

By 4000 B.C., agriculture had taken such hold in China that population densities rose throughout the country (Barnes, 1993; Chang, 1986; Nelson, 1995). The farmers took more and more land into cultivation until there was little new acreage available for planting. Some pollen analyses from northern villages show how the trees that once surrounded many settlements were felled as the fields lapped right up to the houses. This population growth also coincided with an expansion of wet rice farming in lowland areas, on moist floodplains, and in lush water meadows where irrigation was easy (Figure 18.1). Those villages fortunate enough to possess lands that could be irrigated, especially in the Huang Ho and Yangzi valleys, soon turned into much more permanent settlements, often protected with earthen walls to guard against floods and marauding neighbors. Even these larger communities were part of a self-regulating folk society in which kinship loyalties and the extended family were all-important and old age was deeply revered. The family ancestors were the conduit to the gods who controlled the harmony of the world.

However, there are signs that a new order existed, for some settlements of the time contain elaborate burials adorned with jade ornaments and ceremonial weapons. Village artisans created fine clay vessels exclusively for the use of these privileged people. These were important leaders who are known to have raided their neighbors, for the corpses of their enemies have

TABLE 18.1

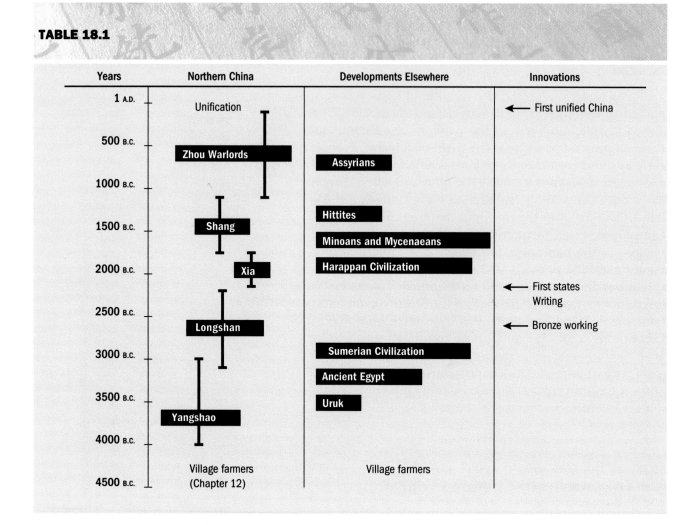

Years	Northern China	Developments Elsewhere	Innovations
1 A.D.	Unification		← First unified China
500 B.C.	Zhou Warlords	Assyrians	
1000 B.C.			
1500 B.C.	Shang	Hittites	
		Minoans and Mycenaeans	
2000 B.C.	Xia	Harappan Civilization	
2500 B.C.			← First states / Writing
	Longshan		← Bronze working
3000 B.C.		Sumerian Civilization	
3500 B.C.		Ancient Egypt	
		Uruk	
4000 B.C.	Yangshao		
4500 B.C.	Village farmers (Chapter 12)	Village farmers	

FIGURE 18.1 (a) Distribution of farming cultures that immediately preceded Shang civilization in northern China. Each shaded area represents a different regional culture (not described in detail in the text). (b) The approximate distribution of Shang civilization in about 1400 B.C. (Xiao-tun and other royal sites are close to Anyang).

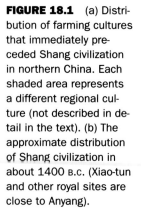
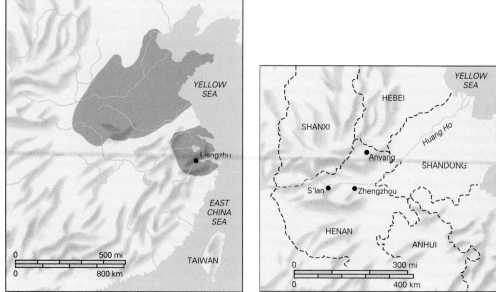

(a)　　　　(b)

been found deposited in village wells. In both the north and the south, a few peasant villages became important centers ruled by new generations of kin leaders who became the nobles of more sophisticated societies. They were probably expert warriors and were certainly people of great spiritual authority, experts in predicting the future and communicating with the ancestors.

These developments would never have been possible without the unswerving conservatism of the country farmer. The village crops might change from cereals to rice, the fertility of the soils depend on radically different rainfall patterns, and building materials alter from brick and tile to bamboo, but what never varied was the unquestioning acceptance by the peasants of an emerging social order that imposed an almost alien wealthy, privileged society. The viability of this aristocratic civilization depended on simple loyalties that persisted from the earliest centuries of farming life into modern times. Every Chinese noble, however unimportant, cashed in on this loyalty.

Longshan and Liangzhu

After about 4000 B.C., the several regional Longshan farming cultures of north and south China became interlinked in what Chang (1986) calls an "interaction sphere," that is, trading raw materials, luxury goods, and other commodities over long distances. (The generic, and inaccurate, term *Longshan* is often used to label these cultures.) This interdependence spurred similar developments in more complex social organization, as well as technological changes that spilled over from narrow territorial boundaries to affect much of China. These innovations included copper metallurgy, the construction of rammed-earth town walls, and the first widespread use of earthen fortifications. Powerful new rituals and beliefs emerged, among them a doctrine based on animals and birds and the use of divination to communicate with the ancestors (Nelson, 1995).

On the east coast, the Liangzhu culture of the Shanghai Delta region had developed by 3250 B.C., a society known largely from its prestigious burials. Liangzhu's expert potters were specialist artisans, some of the first in East Asia. Many of their finely made black polished wares were made not by hand but on a potter's wheel. The wealthiest members of society were buried in special burial precincts, their graves adorned with finely made jade ornaments (Huang, 1992). The bodies of sacrificial victims surround some of the elite. Liangzhu was a highly stratified society, one of the earliest in China where extreme wealth and an enormous social distance separated the rulers from the ruled. These many changes were the result of constant interaction among many different farming societies, a kind of relationship among complex chiefdoms that inevitably drew them into a larger system. This interaction and constant warfare developed after 4000 B.C., culminating in the emergence of Chinese civilization in about 2000 B.C. (Chang, 1986).

Perhaps the most significant of all Longshan innovations was the appearance of rectangular defensive enclosures. The walls are of a special Chinese construction known as *hang tu*, or "rammed earth," and are the earliest examples of this technique. Regular layers of loose earth, some 10 to 15 cm (4 to 6 inches) thick, were poured between parallel lines of timber shuttering—rather in the way that concrete is poured today. Then the workers compacted the layers by pounding them with long wooden poles, some 3 to 4 cm (1 to 1.5 inches) in diameter. Once that layer was finished, another would be poured on top and the process repeated until the desired height was reached. Longshan walls made in this way were up to 10 m (35 feet) thick and sometimes have survived to a height of several feet, the horizontal marks left by the timber shuttering clearly visible on their sides.

There is other evidence, too, that these were violent times. At one Longshan site a number of people had been thrown into two dry wells, some decapitated, others showing signs of struggle. If these people suffered a violent fate, there is evidence that they themselves inflicted similar suffering on others. Six skulls had been placed as a foundation deposit beneath one of the houses, all with signs of wounds or scalping. The archaeology of the Longshan culture suggests a pattern of warring elites, struggling to maintain their position or gain greater ascendancy over their neighbors. It

4000 B.C.

Longshan cultures
4000 B.C.

Liangzhu culture
3250 B.C.

also indicates that ritual vessels (first high-quality pottery, later copper or bronze) were the all-important mark of elite status. In this as in so many respects, Longshan directly anticipated the full civilization of the Shang Bronze Age.

Shoulder Blades and Oracles

When archaeologists dug into a walled site named Chengziyai by the Huang Ho in Shandong province in 1930–1931, they found not only the remains of a farming village but also dozens of cracked ox shoulder blades that they identified as oracle bones used in divination ceremonies (Figure 18.2) (Keightley, 1978). The cracks were made by applying hot metal to the bone and then were interpreted as messages from the ancestors. None of the Longshan bones bear written inscriptions, but the hundreds of shoulder blades found in pits near Anyang farther upstream are a mine of information about the origins of Chinese civilization, a unique written archive of official deliberations by the very first kings of northern China. One scholar has suggested that Chinese writing may have originated from the need to interpret the cracks on the bones, with the new writing symbols resembling persistent crack patterns, but there are incised potsherds in earlier Longshan and Liangzhu cultures that may represent earlier writing traditions (Postgate et al., 1995).

Clearly, some Chinese ideographs originated as pictograms, such as that for the hill, originally shown with three humps and now written as a horizontal line with three

FIGURE 18.2 Shang oracle bones. Priests read cracks in the surface of the ox bone caused by applying heat to the shoulder blade and thereby interpreted messages from the ancestors as sacred divinations.

vertical strokes. Perhaps as early as 2500 B.C., divination rituals were a vital part of village government. All official divinations were addressed to the royal ancestors, who acted as intermediaries between the living and the ultimate ancestor and supreme being, the ruler of heaven and the creator, Shang Di. This deity served as the ancestor not only of the royal line but also of the "multitude of the people." The king was the head of all family lines, which radiated from his person to the nobility and then to the common people. These actual and imputed kinship ties were the core of early Chinese civilization, for they obligated the peasants to provide food and labor for their rulers.

In addition to shoulder blades from oxen and water buffalo, the diviners used tortoiseshells for their ceremonies. The term *scapulimancy,* meaning "shoulder blade divination," refers to the bones used most frequently in the ceremonies. The bones and shells were smoothed and cleaned and perhaps soaked in liquid to be softened. Rows of hollows were then produced on the underside to make the substance thinner and the surface more susceptible to being cracked. When a question was posed, the diviner would apply a metal point to the base of the hollow, causing the surface to crack. The response of the ancestors was "read" from the fissures. A skillful diviner could control the extent and direction of the cracks. Thus, divination provided an authoritative priest with a useful and highly effective way of giving advice. A leader could regard disagreement as treason.

⁙⁙⁙ Xia and Shang

The obvious starting point in the study of Chinese civilization is Chinese legends, which tell us that the celebrated ruler Huang Di founded civilization in the north in 2698 B.C. This great legendary warlord set the tone for centuries of the repressive harsh government that was the hallmark of early Chinese civilization. About 2200 B.C., a Xia ruler named Yu the Great gained power through his military prowess and his knowledge of flood control, by which he could protect the valley people from catastrophic inundations.

2698 B.C.
Xia dynasty
2200 B.C.

What exactly do these legends mean? Who were the Xia and the Shang? In all probability they were dynasties of local rulers who achieved lasting prominence among their many neighbors after generations of bitter strife (Chang, 1980, 1986). Every chieftain lived in a walled town and enjoyed much the same level of material prosperity, but each ruler came from a different lineage and was related to his competitors by intricate and closely woven allegiances and kin ties. Each dynasty assumed political dominance in the north in turn, but for all these political changes, Shang civilization itself continued more or less untouched, a loosely unified confederacy of competing small kingdoms that quarreled and warred incessantly.

The archaeological record reveals that Shang-type remains are stratified on top of Longshan occupation levels at many places in northern China, and they represent a dramatic increase in the complexity of material culture and social organization (Chang, 1986). The same trends toward increasing complexity are thought to have occurred elsewhere in China at approximately the same time, for literate states may have emerged from a Longshan base in the south and the east as well. In form, they probably resembled the Shang closely, but few details of the others are known. It seems likely that the Shang dynasty was dominant from 1766 to 1122 B.C. but that other states continued to grow at the same time. The larger area of Chinese civilization ultimately extended from the north into the middle and lower courses of the Huang Ho and Yangze. In this account, we concentrate on northern Chinese civilization simply because more is known about the archaeology of the Shang than about that of any other early Chinese state.

Shang civilization
1766 to 1122 B.C.

Capitals and Sepulchers

The oracle bones and other historical sources provide only a sketchy outline of the early dynasties and the ways the Shang kings went about their business. The bones inform us that the rulers lived in at least seven capitals, situated near the middle

Ao
1557 B.C.

reaches of the Huang Ho in the modern provinces of Henan, Shandong, and Anhui (Keightley, 1999). The sites of all these towns are still uncertain, but in 1557 B.C., the Shang kings moved their capital to a place named Ao, which archaeologists have found under the modern industrial city of Zhengzhou, some 153 km (95 miles) south of Anyang close to the Huang Ho (Wheatley, 1971).

Unfortunately, the royal compound lies underneath the modern downtown area, so only limited excavations have been possible. However, the diggers have found traces of a vast precinct surrounded by an earthen wall more than 10 m (33 feet) high, enclosing an area of 5 sq km (2 square miles). It would have taken 10,000 workers laboring 330 days a year for no fewer than 18 years to erect the fortifications alone. This walled compound housed the rulers, the temples, and the nobles. Some foundations of their large houses and ancestral altars have come from excavations inside the compound. The residential quarters and craft workshops lay outside the Shang walls. These included two bronze factories, one of them covering more than an acre. The metalworkers lived in substantial houses near their furnaces. There were bone workshops, too, where animal and human bones were fashioned into arrowheads, pins, and awls. Zhengzhou's potters lived in a satellite village close to the kilns, where they fired hundreds of fine vessels. The excavations revealed dozens of unfired and incomplete vessels.

Anyang
1400 B.C.

The capital moved to the Anyang area in approximately 1400 B.C., where it remained until the fall of the Shang more than 250 years later. This new royal domain was known as Yin and may have encompassed a network of compounds, palaces, villages, and cemeteries extending over an area some 310 sq km (120 square miles) on the northern bank of the Huang Ho. The core of this "capital" was near the hamlet of Xiao-tun, 2.4 km (1.5 miles) northwest of the modern city of Anyang. Years of excavations at Xiao-tun have revealed 53 rectangular foundations of rammed earth up to 36 m (120 feet) long, 19.5 m (65 feet) wide, and as much as 1.5 m (5 feet) high, many of them of buildings associated with sacrificial burials of both animals and humans (Chang, 1980, 1986). One group of 15 foundations on the north side of the excavated area supported timber houses with mud and stick walls, devoid of sacrificial victims. These are believed to have been the royal residences that housed the extended noble families living in large halls and smaller rooms closed off with doors (Figure 18.3). Twenty-one massive foundations on an elevated area in the center of the excavations formed two rows of temples associated with a series of five ceremonial gates. The builders buried animals, humans, and even chariots in this vicinity, perhaps to dedicate the temples. Nearby were semisubterranean houses where the royal servants and artisans lived. The service areas included bronze foundries, workshops, and pottery kilns.

The Shang Royal Burials

The Shang rulers at first buried their dead in a cemetery just under 2 km (1.24 miles) northeast of Anyang. Eleven royal graves from this cemetery were excavated during the 1930s (Chang, 1986). Furnished on a lavish scale, they date to between 1500 and 1200 B.C. The best-known grave is in the shape of a crosslike pit approximately 9.9 m (33 feet) deep, with slightly sloping walls. Four ramps lead from the surface to each side of the pit (Chang, 1980). The coffin of the ruler, which was placed inside a wooden chamber

FIGURE 18.3
Reconstruction of a structure from the ceremonial area at Xiao-tun, Anyang, in Henan province. Throughout Chinese history, the nobility lived apart from commoners.

erected in the burial pit, was accompanied by superb bronze vessels and shell, bone, and stone ornaments. One ceremonial halberd has an engraved jade blade set in a bronze shaft adorned with dragons and inlaid with malachite. The rulers were accompanied in death by slaves and sacrificial victims buried both in the chamber itself and on the approach ramps. Many had been decapitated: Their bodies were found in one place and their heads in another.

The Shang kings surrounded their sepulchers with hundreds of lesser burials. No fewer than 1221 small graves have been dug up nearby, many of them burials of between 2 and 11 people in a single tomb. Some of the skeletons are associated with pottery, weapons, or bronze vessels, but most are devoid of all adornment. In 1976, archaeologists uncovered nearly 200 of these graves. Most of them contained decapitated, dismembered, or mutilated bodies. Some of the victims had been bound before death. These can only have been sacrificial offerings consecrated when the kings and their relatives died.

The Bronze Smiths

The Shang people are justly famous for their bronze work, best known to us from ceremonial artifacts found in royal tombs. This people's prestigious metal was not gold, which was in short supply, but bronze. Most Shang bronzes are food or drinking vessels; some are weapons, a few are musical instruments, and many are chariot and horse fittings. Bronze working was the guarded monopoly of the rulers, a complex art that the Chinese developed quite independently of the West before 2000 B.C. Their smiths produced some of the most sophisticated and elegant bronze objects ever crafted (Figure 18.4).

The Shang people discovered bronze working on their own, perhaps as a result of their long experience with kiln-fired pottery baked at high temperatures. They made the smaller objects, such as spearheads, arrowheads, and ax blades, by pouring a mixture of copper and tin into a single- or two-piece mold. Much more complex procedures had to be employed to manufacture large ceremonial vessels. These elaborate

FIGURE 18.4 Shang bronze vessel from approximately 1300 B.C. Such cast-bronze artifacts were highly prized by the nobility and accompanied them in death.

display pieces were copies of clay prototypes carefully sculpted around a baked-clay core and encased in a segmented mold. Once the clay version had been completed, the baked outer mold was removed, the model was broken away from the core, and, in the case of the two-piece mold, the two parts were reassembled to receive the molten bronze. This complex technique remained in use for at least five centuries. An alternative would have been the lost-wax process, in which a single-piece mold encases a wax mold that is heated and then poured out to be replaced with metal.

〰️ The Warlords

Every early Chinese ruler stayed in power by virtue of a strong army. Shang society was organized on what might be called military lines, so that the royal standing army could be supplemented with thousands of conscripts on very short notice. The kings were frequently at war, protecting their frontiers, suppressing rebellious rivals, or raiding for as many as 30,000 sacrificial victims at one time. In a sense, every early Chinese state was an armed garrison that could call on armies of more than 10,000 men. The secret was a sophisticated permanent military establishment and a kin organization through which people were obligated to serve the king when called upon. The same basic organization persisted long after the fall of the Shang dynasty in 1122 B.C.

The Anyang graves reveal that every foot soldier carried a set of weapons: a bow and arrows, halberd, shield, small knife, and sharpening stone. The bows were made of horn and ox sinew and were approximately a man's height. They propelled stone-, bone-, or bronze-tipped arrows equipped with feathers. The Shang soldiers used a small leather or basketry shield for chariot warfare and a longer one when they were on foot, both painted with tiger designs.

Most surviving Shang weapons come from sacrificial chariot burials, such as the one excavated near Anyang in 1973. The archaeologists uncovered not the wooden chariot itself but a cast of the wooden parts preserved in the soil (Figure 18.5). They brushed away the surrounding soil with great care until they reached the hardened

FIGURE 18.5 Chariot burial from the royal Shang tombs near Anyang. Casts of the wooden parts of the chariot were excavated by following discolorations made by the decaying wood in the ground.

SITE

The Burial Mound of Emperor Shihuangdi, China

King Zheng, the "Tiger of Qin," was the first sovereign emperor (Shihuangdi) of China. He became ruler of Qin at the age of 13 in 246 B.C., unifying China after a series of ruthless military campaigns in 221 B.C. Work may have begun on the emperor's tomb as early as 246 B.C., but it intensified with unification. The emperor considered himself unique, so his sepulcher was to be the largest ever built. Later court histories write of more than 700,000 conscripts, many of them convicts, who worked on the tomb, the capital, and the royal palace.

The great burial mound measures more than 335 m (1100 feet) on each side and rises 43 m (140 feet) above the surrounding countryside, 40 km (25 miles) east of Xianyang on the banks of the Wei River. Inside lies what is said to be a replica of the royal domains, with China's great rivers recreated in mercury flowing, by some mechanical device, into the ocean. The constellations of the heavens appear on the ceiling of the burial chamber, the earth's geography beneath. Scale models of palaces and pavilions contain the emperor's personal possessions, and models of courtiers attend him in death. Many concubines, also laborers who worked on the tomb, were sacrificed and buried inside the tumulus. While Han dynasty historians state that the mound was looted after the fall of the Qin line, Chinese archaeologists have detected unusually high concentrations of mercury in the soil chemistry of the mound and suspect Shihuangdi's grave goods may be intact. Chinese archaeologists decline to excavate the tomb, as they say they lack the resources and skills to dig it properly and conserve the contents. The mound once lay in the middle of a large funerary park surrounded by a 6.4-km (4-mile) outer wall.

In the 1970s, Chinese archaeologists excavated a regiment of terra-cotta soldiers to the side of the funerary mound—armed cavalrymen, kneeling archers, and their officers, perhaps a ceremonial guard assigned to protect the eastern side of the tomb (Figure 18.6). The molded figures were finished with individual hairstyles, mustaches, and other features and were fully armed. Other finds near the tumulus include two half-scale bronze chariots and their horses, as well as underground stables, some with mangers containing horses buried alive.

FIGURE 18.6 Shihuangdi's terra-cotta regiment as first exposed, guarding their master's tomb.

particles of fine sand that had replaced the wooden structure of the buried chariot. They were able to photograph not only the "ghost" of the chariot but also the skeletons of the two horses. The charioteer had been killed at the funeral and his body placed behind the vehicle. The yokes of the chariot rested on the horses' necks. Even the reins were marked by lines of bronze roundels in the grave. The charioteer had ridden on a wicker and leather car measuring between 0.9 to 1.2 m (3 to 4 feet) across and borne on a stout axle and two spoked wheels with large hubs adorned with bronze caps. In all probability, the nailless chariot had been held together with sinew lashings, adorned with bronze and turquoise ornaments, and perhaps painted in bright colors.

Zhou dynasty
1122 B.C.

The Shang dynasty fell about 1122 B.C. at the hands of the neighboring Zhou. The conquerors did not create a new civilization; rather, they took over the existing network of towns and officials and incorporated them into their own state organization. In this way they shifted the focus of political and economic power to the south and west, away from Anyang into the fertile Wei Valley near the modern city of S'ian. By this time, the influence of what may loosely be called Shang civilization extended far beyond the north, into the rice-growing areas of the south and along the eastern coasts. The Zhou divided their domains into various, almost independent provinces, which warred with one another for centuries. It was not until 221 B.C. that the great emperor Zheng (Shihuangdi) unified China into a single empire (Site box, page 439).

Unification
221 B.C.

By Roman times, Chinese civilization had been flourishing for more than 2000 years—a distinctive and highly nationalistic culture that differed sharply from its Western contemporaries in its ability to assimilate conquerors and the conquered into its own traditions. In contrast, the Roman Empire was built on the groaning backs of slaves and collapsed into the Dark Ages when attacked by barbarian nomads. The ability of the Chinese people simply to assimilate these same nomadic conquerors explains why the essential fabric of their civilization survives to this day.

Summary 🐾🐾🐾

Early Chinese civilization emerged independently of state-organized societies in the West. By 4000 B.C., population densities were rising in farming communities throughout China, and there are signs of social differentiation in village cemeteries.

Exchange networks already linked thousands of small communities by 4000 B.C., spurring social and technological changes that included copper metallurgy and the widespread use of earthen fortifications. A new cosmology based on animals and the use of divination to communicate with the dead came into widespread use.

The Shang civilization of the Huang Ho is the best-known early Chinese state, flourishing from 1766 to 1122 B.C. It was probably the dominant state among several throughout northern China. Shang society was organized along class lines, with the rulers and nobles living in segregated precincts and the mass of the people scattered in townships and villages in the surrounding countryside.

Shang civilization ended with the overthrow of the Shang dynasty by Zhou rulers, who reigned over a wide area of northern China from 1122 to 221 B.C. China was unified under the Emperor Zheng (Shihuangdi) in that year.

Guide to Further Reading 🐾🐾🐾

Barnes, Gina L. 1993. *China, Korea, and Japan.* London and New York: Thames & Hudson.
  A summary of the archaeology of three crucial regions of Asia for the general reader. Lavishly illustrated.

Chang Kwang-Chih. 1980. *The Shang Civilization.* New Haven, CT: Yale University Press.
  A detailed reconstruction of Shang civilization derived not only from archaeological data but also from a complicated palimpsest of legends, oracle bone inscriptions, and documentary records. An impressive, meticulous book that is a basic source on this remarkable society.

_____. 1986. *The Archaeology of Ancient China,* 4th ed. New Haven, CT: Yale University Press.

The fundamental account of prehistoric China for all serious students. Lavishly illustrated. Major emphasis on chronology and artifacts.

Nelson, Sarah. 1995. *The Archaeology of Northeast China: China Beyond the Great Wall.* London: Routledge.
    Describes important discoveries to the north and east of the best-known areas of Shang civilization.

Wheatley, Paul. 1971. *The Pivot of the Four Quarters.* Chicago: Aldine.
    A learned book that will daunt many casual readers but is a crucial source for understanding early Chinese civilization. Concentrates on the early Chinese city.

HITTITES, MINOANS, AND MYCENAEANS

Two boys boxing. Akrotiri, c. 1800 B.C.

"I have found the graves which, according to tradition, are those of Agamemnon, Cassandra, Eurymedon, and their companions." With this dramatic telegram to the king of Greece, archaeologist Heinrich Schliemann announced the discovery of the gold-smothered graves of Mycenae to an astounded world in 1876. Fresh from his triumphs at Troy, Schliemann had descended on Mycenae like a whirlwind, excavating in a circular area inside the main gate of what he thought was the Homeric hero Agamemnon's fortress. Within a few weeks, he and his wife uncovered 15 skeletons lying in five gold-smothered graves, a spectacular discovery that prompted his royal telegram. One of the bodies was so well preserved that some of the nonskeletal parts still remained, the gold ornaments in perfect condition. Schliemann commissioned an oil painting of the grave while a local druggist mixed alcohol and gum arabic in a frantic effort to preserve the burial. So much gold came from the excavations that Schliemann lit great watch fires to prevent looting. It was the first watch fire, he said, to shine out at Mycenae since Agamemnon's time.

Later research has shown that Schliemann was wrong in attributing the Mycenaean graves to Agamemnon and his family; nonetheless, they are eloquent testimony to the riches and power of the earliest mainland Greek civilization. We now explore the developments that led to Mycenae and its predecessors. This chapter covers an enormous area of the ancient world. It is concerned not only with the humble beginnings of the formation of states and complex societies in areas like Anatolia but also with the rapid growth of what we have called a nascent world system over the mainland of Southwest Asia and the entire eastern Mediterranean after about 2000 B.C. (Figure 19.1). (See Table 15.1.) The societies described in this chapter all played a part in a much larger development: the growth of a truly international economic system that extended from Spain in the west to the distant Indus Valley in the east and lasted in various forms into historical times.

Early Towns in Anatolia

Anatolia, with its rich obsidian and copper outcrops, was an early player in the great regional exchange networks that developed in Southwest Asia as early as 8000 B.C. (see Chapter 9). At first, there were few large communities, but those that did flourish controlled trade over a large area around them. Çatalhöyük in central Anatolia was one such community (Mellaart, 1967; Hodder, 1996). This complex settlement was organized by the creation of ritual and other mechanisms that attempted to retain the close kinship ties of village life while adapting to the new complexities of long-distance trading and

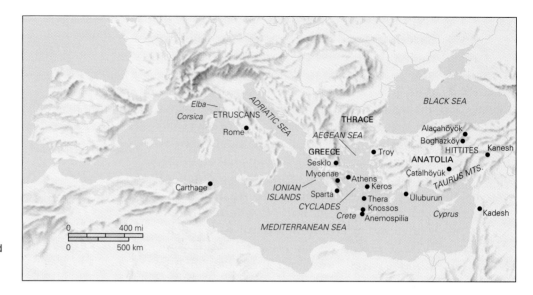

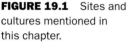
FIGURE 19.1 Sites and cultures mentioned in this chapter.

8000 B.C.

growing population. Unlike the system in Mesopotamia, where new mechanisms and organizations evolved to handle social change, the system at Çatalhöyük broke down: Anatolia's first and largest town was abandoned, and people went back to living in small villages.

The entire plateau of Anatolia seems to have experienced a subsequent gradual
3000 B.C.
population increase after 3000 B.C., as long-distance trading with Mesopotamia in minerals and other materials increased. The evidence for the concentration of power and wealth in major Anatolian settlements is found after 3000 B.C. in the walled fortresses of Hissarlik (Troy) and Kultepe (ancient Kanesh) (M. Larsen, 1976).

Hissarlik
Hissarlik was first occupied in about 3500 B.C., when a small fortress was built on
3500 B.C. and later
bedrock. Its foundations show that it contained a rectangular hall of a basic design that had been in use for centuries. The structure was to become the standard palace design of later centuries and perhaps a prototype for the classical Greek temple. In about 2300 B.C., a new settlement known to archaeologists as Troy II flourished at Hissarlik. This fortified town boasted more elaborate buildings and yielded valuable hoards of gold and bronze ornaments—a clear sign that the rulers of the settlement were supporting skilled craftspeople who designed and executed fine ornaments of rank.

Alaçahöyök
Thirteen royal tombs were found at the site of the town of Alaçahöyök in central
2000 B.C.
Anatolia, dating to about 2000 B.C. The tombs contained the bodies of men and their wives, accompanied by domestic vessels, weapons, and many metal items (Roaf, 1990). The ornaments included copper figurines with gold breasts and finely wrought cast-bronze stags inlaid with silver, which were perhaps mounted on the ends of poles (Figure 19.2).

Both the Alaçahöyök and the Hissarlik finds testify to the far-flung exchange networks that crisscrossed Anatolia by 2000 B.C. They were an emerging component in the nascent world system that brought copper, tin, and other raw materials from the highlands to the lowlands of Mesopotamia and textiles and other lowland products back in return. The coastal eastern Mediterranean and the island of Cyprus now emerged as major players in the new trade networks. Maritime trade, using simple coastal vessels, was assuming considerable importance along the Turkish coast and among the Aegean islands, where a trade in obsidian, timber, pottery, wine, and olive oil had begun centuries earlier.

Toward the end of the third millennium B.C., Indo-European–speaking peoples seem to have infiltrated Anatolia from the northwest, causing considerable political unrest. Despite such upheaval, the volume of trade between Anatolia and Mesopotamia reached new heights, as the two areas were becoming part of an ever more closely meshed economic system. By 1900 B.C., for example, there was a sizable Assyrian merchant colony outside the city of Kanesh, one of several trading centers (*karums*) that were staging posts for long-distance commerce in minerals and other commodities. The *karums* served as marketplaces and caravan termini, natural entrepôts where prices

FIGURE 19.2 Bronze stag from Alaçahöyök, Anatolia, inlaid with silver, and a figurine of a ruler. (Copyright The British Museum.)

for goods were carefully regulated. Local rulers levied taxes on the caravans, which brought Assyrian ideas to Anatolia and reinforced the economic and political power of the elite at both ends of the trade routes (M. Larsen, 1976).

ⵗⵗⵗ Balance of Power: The Hittites

All these developments came from ever-closer economic ties between different regions of Southwest Asia (M. Larsen, 1987). These ties were a sign of an economic interdependency that persisted regardless of political change or war. The desert caravans of black asses and the ships that plied Mediterranean waters resulted from a more durable international economic network system that transcended the boundaries of local societies and even entire civilizations. At the center of this economic system lay the strategic eastern Mediterranean coast, a coastline with few natural harbors but with trade routes to Mesopotamia, Anatolia, and the Nile.

During the second millennium B.C., the eastern Mediterranean coastlands formed a network of small and prosperous states. These kingdoms lived in the shadow of the great kingdoms that lay inland: Egypt to the south, Mitanni to the east of the Euphrates, and Hatti (the kingdom of the Hittites in Anatolia). Each of these three kingdoms controlled a large area of territory surrounded by a hinterland that lay more or less under their influence (Figure 19.3). The three states competed directly in the coastal zone, and they had complex dealings on all frontiers. Mitanni, for example, tried to prevent the city-state of Assur in northern Mesopotamia from going its own way, and the famous El-Amarna tablets, an archive of Egyptian diplomatic correspondence, tell of shifting allegiances among the city-states of the coast. By this time, the eastern Mediterranean shore was a land of many cities, a regular military and diplomatic battlefield for its powerful neighbors.

The Hittites were the newest, and perhaps the most able, diplomatic players. Originally the rulers of Kanesh, they expanded their domains and seized control of the rest of Anatolia just before 1650 B.C. (MacQueen, 1996). A foreign minority, the Hittites rose to political power by judiciously melding conquest and astute political maneuvering, quickly becoming acculturated into their new milieu while preserving their traditional values and outlook on life. The king was not deified until after his death, if then.

Hittite civilization
1650–1200 B.C.

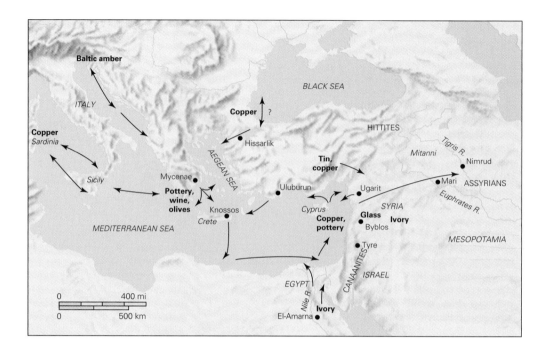

FIGURE 19.3 The balance of power in Southwest Asia in the second millennium B.C.: Egypt, Mitanni, and the Hittite Empire, showing major trade routes.

His duties were well defined: to ensure the state's welfare, wage war, and act as high priest under clearly defined circumstances. A hierarchy of officials supported the king, ruling an empire based on a rigid feudal system of landownership and governance. Hittite kings exercised enormous political influence in Southwest Asia from their capital at Boghazkoy, with its 6.5 km (4 miles) of city walls.

Boghazkoy

In the fifteenth century B.C., Syria had been a province of the Egyptian Empire. The Hittites pressed the Egyptians hard on both diplomatic and military fronts until the Great King of Hatti, Suppiluliumas I (1375 to 1335 B.C.), could claim Lebanon as his frontier. In 1286, the conflict culminated in the indecisive Battle of Kadesh between the forces of Pharaoh Rameses II and the Hittite ruler Muwatallis. Egypt was exhausted by this effort, and diplomatic archives in Akkadian cuneiform contain records of the peace treaty of about 1269 between the Hittite and Egyptian kings, which confined Egyptian interests to southern Palestine. The same treaty is also recorded on the walls of the temple of Karnak at Thebes. The grandiose public architecture of the period commonly depicted Egyptians and Hittites locked in battle with state-of-the-art weaponry. This included light two-wheeled chariots manned by archers and new siege machinery for use against the many walled cities in the disputed areas.

All of this diplomatic and military activity on the part of the great kingdoms was aimed at control of the lucrative gold, copper, and pottery trade of the eastern Mediterranean. This trade, in the hands of eastern Mediterranean and Mycenaean traders, has been vividly illustrated by investigations of a Bronze Age shipwreck off the southern Turkish coast. The advantage of shipwrecks from the archaeological point of view is that they provide sealed capsules of maritime trade frozen at a moment in time.

Uluburun

1305 B.C.

The famous Uluburun ship, excavated by Çemal Pulak from the waters near Kas off southern Turkey, was shipwrecked in the fourteenth century B.C. The ship carried over 350 copper ingots, each weighing about 27 kg (60 pounds), a load of 10 tons, enough to equip a small army with weapons and armor (Figure 19.4). A ton of resin traveled in two-handled jars made by people living in the Syria region; it was used, so Egyptian records tell us, as incense for Egyptian rituals. There were dozens of blue glass disks, ingots being sent to Egypt from Tyre. The cargo also included hardwood, Baltic amber, tortoiseshells, elephant tusks and hippopotamus teeth, ostrich eggs, jars of olives, and even large jars holding stacked Canaanite and Mycenaean pottery. Judging from a gold scarab found on board, at least one of the crew members was Egyptian. The Uluburun ship's cargo contained items from Africa, Egypt, the eastern Mediterranean coast, the Greek mainland and the Aegean, and Cyprus, and even copper from Sardinia (see a general description in Fagan, 1996a).

FIGURE 19.4 Excavations on the Bronze Age shipwreck at Uluburun, near Kas, southern Turkey. Note copper ingots in the foreground.

The cargo is a dramatic reflection of the truly international nature of eastern Mediterranean trade in the second millennium B.C., when the Hittites were at the height of their power. The great powers of the day competed savagely for control of the eastern Mediterranean shore, for it lay at the very center of an interlocking maze of trade routes.

This maritime trade was still expanding in Hittite times. It played a major role in the diffusion of iron tools and weapons over the eastern Mediterranean. Iron was first smelted in the middle of the first millennium B.C., perhaps in the highlands immediately south of the Black Sea. The new metal had many advantages, for its tough, sharp edges were invaluable for military purposes and in farming and carpentry as well. Iron was plentiful, unlike the tin used to alloy bronze. Iron tools soon became commonplace over a wide area of Europe and Southwest Asia, although it was some time before domestic artifacts such as axes and hoes were made with the new technology (Wertime and Muhly, 1980).

By 1200 B.C., Hatti was in trouble. The Hittites had prospered by virtue of their well-organized professional army, long a stabilizing influence in the eastern Mediterranean. They were expert diplomats who controlled what is now northern Syria through their rule over two great cities: Carchemish on the Euphrates and Alalakh of Mukish in the west. There were also treaty relationships with other powerful neighbors, including Ugarit (Ras Shamra) on the northern coast of the eastern Mediterranean. Ugarit was a cosmopolitan city ruled by a monarch who was almost like a merchant prince. He controlled vast supplies of gold and a fleet of more than 150 ships, some of considerable size. These ventured as far afield as Cyprus and the Nile, the former being a center of exchange with the Aegean. Ugarit was vital to the Hittites, for they depended on its ships and never became a maritime power.

Both the lack of maritime power and a rigid feudal system contributed to Hatti's undoing. A major drought around 1300 B.C. may also have caused widespread suffering and population movements in the entire eastern Mediterranean region (Butzer, 1995). About 1200 B.C., repeated migrations of foreigners flowed into Anatolia from the northwest, whence the Hittites had come only four centuries earlier (Drews, 1993). These population movements came to a head when the Phrygian peoples from Thrace ravaged the plateau as far south as the Taurus Mountains. The central Hittite government collapsed, partly because of attacks from outside but also because powerful vassals threw off their allegiance to the king. The rulers appealed to Ugarit and other maritime neighbors for assistance, but none was forthcoming. Anatolia dissolved into dozens of small city-states, each striving to maintain its independence. Only a few Hittite communities survived in small states in northern Syria until they were engulfed in the vast Persian Empire of the first millennium B.C.

〰 The Sea Peoples and the Rise of Israel

The situation in the eastern Mediterranean was explosive, for the withdrawal of the great powers left a political vacuum that could not be filled by local rulers, who depended heavily on mercenary armies. With the collapse of the Mycenaean trade at about the same time, there was a general weakening of authority (Drews, 1993). Highly centralized palace bureaucracies ruled the imperial powers and petty kingships that

1200 B.C.

made up the eastern Mediterranean world of 1200 B.C. The systems they controlled were very specialized, allowing for significant economies of operation and dense population concentrations. This very specialization made the entire system vulnerable to the effects of local upheavals, for a collapse in one area—say, the Hittite Empire—reverberated through the entire system. The exact causes of the almost dominolike collapse of Hittite and Mycenaean civilization, and of the weakening of the Egyptian Empire, are still a mystery, but may be connected to severe droughts, among other factors. The abrupt collapse of trade weakened the urban elites and the foundations of their power (Whitelaw and Coote, 1987).

The same interdependencies also affected the nomads and peasants who lived in the hinterlands of eastern Mediterranean cities, both on the coast and inland. The cuneiform tablets from the city of Mari, at the head of a powerful state on the Euphrates centuries earlier, provide compelling evidence of the intricate relationships between the cities and those who herded their flocks on the outskirts (Dalley, 1984). These groups were also dependent on the international trade, but as the trade declined, they became increasingly politically independent during the period of destruction, a "dark age" that lasted more than 300 years. This was a time of piracy and widespread suffering, much of it at the hands of warlike bands known to archaeologists as the Sea Peoples (N. K. Sanders, 1985).

In the eastern Mediterranean, many rural groups moved to the highlands inland during these centuries, relying more heavily on pastoralism and agriculture as their dependence on the trading centers diminished. Village communities, nomadic herders, and even bandits lived in proximity outside the reach of state power. In this milieu, a loose federation of highland villages, small towns, pastoral nomad groups, and former bandits formed to preserve and defend their sovereignty from outside

Israel
c. 1000 B.C.

states. This federation became the state of Israel, which acquired its own monarchy after 1000 B.C. and protected itself with a network of walled cities (Silberman, 1992; Whitelaw and Coote, 1987). By this time, eastern Mediterranean trade was recovering. The hillside federation expanded into lowland territory, circumscribed by the sea and the desert and by the still powerful Egyptian and Mesopotamian civilizations on either side.

〰 The Phoenicians

Phoenicians
c. 1100 to 800 B.C.

The general economic recovery of the first millennium B.C. was in large part attributable to the Phoenicians. They had first come into prominence in the eastern Mediterranean by acting as middlemen in the growing trade in raw materials and manufactured goods (Aubet, 1993; Moscati, 1988). Their ships were soon carrying Lebanese cedarwood to Cyprus and the Nile. North of Israel, powerful Phoenician cities like Tyre, Sidon, and Byblos now expanded this trade. Their ships took over the copper and iron ore trade of the Mediterranean. Their trading networks later extended as far as Carthage in North Africa and to the copper and tin mines of Spain, and Phoenician merchants made enormous profits from purple dye extracted from seashells and much used for expensive fabrics.

By 800 B.C., Phoenician merchants were everywhere in the Mediterranean, witness the recent discovery of two Phoenician cargo ships of 750 B.C. in depths of over 300 m (1000 feet) on the seabed between Phoenicia and Carthage in 2000. The vessels were heavily laden with cargos of wine amphorae. A century later, the great Phoenician cities were forced to acknowledge Assyrian rule and to pay tribute to foreign masters. Magnificent Phoenician ivories came from the royal palaces at Nimrud on the Tigris, perhaps tribute or plunder from military campaigns. Israel, too, was absorbed into the Assyrian Empire in the eighth century B.C. as the eastern Mediterranean coast came under the sway of alien empires for many centuries, right into modern times.

〽 The Aegean and Greece

Even as early as 10,000 B.C., seagoing ships were plying the waters of the Aegean, trading obsidian from the islands to mainland Greece. Seagoing trade got under way in earnest after 4000 B.C., as long-distance exchange networks expanded rapidly. In a real sense, the history of early Aegean and Greek civilizations is the story of the growth of international trade in eastern Mediterranean waters.

10,000 B.C.

4000 B.C.

Farming settlements had developed in parts of mainland Greece and the Aegean as early as 7000 B.C. More intensive settlement of western Greece, the islands, and Crete did not occur until much later. The Sesklo village in Thessaly was occupied by about 5500 B.C. and is typical of northern Greek sites of the time (Dickinson, 1994). The people lived in stone and mud houses connected by courtyards and passages. Their mixed farming economy depended heavily on cereal cultivation. Somewhat similar villages are found on Crete, where farming settlement dates back to at least 6000 B.C.

There were radical changes in the settlement pattern after 2500 B.C., when villages were established in the Cyclades, throughout Crete, and on the Ionian islands of the west. In contrast, northern Greece seems to have lagged behind. The reason may have been agriculture, for southern Greece and the islands are ideal environments for the cultivation of olives and vines, with cereal crops interspersed between them (Broodbank, 2001; Renfrew, 1972). There was a veritable explosion in village crafts as well, in the manufacture of fine painted pottery, marble vessels, and magnificent stone figures (Figure 19.5). Stone vases and fine seals were made by Cretan workers; the seals were used to mark the ownership of prized possessions or pots full of oil or other commodities. By 2500 B.C., the peoples of the Aegean and Greece were smelting copper and making bronze artifacts as well as ornaments in gold and silver. These included exquisite gold and silver drinking cups and the elaborate ornaments found at Troy II, which included more than 8700 gold beads, wire ornaments, chain links, and objects of fine gold sheet. The achievements of the Aegean metallurgists resulted in part from the rapid expansion of trading throughout the Aegean, far into Anatolia, and to Cyprus, with its rich copper outcrops (Dickinson, 1994; Manning, 1995).

2500 B.C.

The Aegean is well endowed with comfortable ports and alternative trading routes that provide easy communication from island to island for most of the year. Even relatively primitive vessels could coast from one end of the Aegean to the other in easy stages. Sailing vessels appear on Cretan seals dating to approximately 2000 B.C. The Aegean trade flourished on olive oil and wine, metal tools and ores, marble vessels and figurines, and pottery. The success of the trade led to a constant infusion of new products and ideas into Greece and the Aegean. By 2500 B.C., numerous small towns housed farmers, traders, and skilled craftsworkers on the mainland and the islands (Renfrew, 1991).

The beginnings of town life created considerable cultural diversity in the Aegean, a diversity fostered by constant trading connections and an increased complexity in social and political organization. Nowhere is this diversity better documented than on Crete, where a brilliant civilization flourished in towns and palaces throughout the island. In contrast, mainland Greece lagged somewhat behind, its many small towns having only occasional contact with the Aegean islands and Crete.

FIGURE 19.5   Harper in marble, executed by an artisan on the island of Keros in the Aegean.

ᨐ The Minoans

Minoan civilization
2000–1450 B.C.

The development of the Minoan civilization of Crete was almost certainly the result of many local factors, among them the intensive cultivation of the olive and the grapevine. Minoan development is best documented at Knossos in northern Crete (Figure 19.6) (Cadogan, 1976; Warren, 1984). The first prehistoric inhabitants of Knossos settled there in about 6100 B.C. No fewer than 7 m (23 feet) of early farming occupation underlie the Minoan civilization. The first Knossos settlement was founded at approximately the same time that Çatalhöyük was first occupied in Anatolia. The Knossos farmers lived in sun-dried mud-brick huts of a rectangular ground plan that provided for storage bins and sleeping platforms. By 3730 B.C., signs of long-distance trading increase in the form of exotic imports such as stone bowls. The first palace at Knossos was built by about 1930 B.C.; it is a large building with many rooms grouped around a rectangular central court.

Knossos
1930–1450 B.C.

At least nine periods of Minoan civilization have been distinguished by pottery styles found at the later levels of the Knossos site. Even during the earlier periods of the civilization, the Minoans traded regularly with Egypt, for their pottery and metal objects have been found in burials there. About 1700 B.C., an earthquake destroyed the earlier palaces.

The high point of Minoan civilization followed that destruction, occurring between 1700 and 1450 B.C., when the Palace of Knossos reached its greatest size. This remarkable structure, said to be the home of the legendary Cretan King Minos, was made mainly of mud brick and timber beams, with occasional limestone blocks and wood columns. Some buildings had two stories; the plaster walls and floors were decorated initially with geometric designs and, after 1700 B.C., with vivid scenes or individual pictures of varying size. Sometimes the decorations were executed in relief; in other cases, colors were applied to the damp plaster. Artistic themes included formal landscapes, dolphins and other sea creatures, and scenes of Minoan life (Figure 19.7). The most remarkable art depicted dances and religious ceremonies, including acrobats leaping

FIGURE 19.6   General view of the Palace of Knossos, Crete.

vigorously along the backs of bulls. Figurines of priestesses also survive (Figure 19.8). Writer Mary Renault (1963) has vividly reconstructed Cretan society at Knossos in novels that bring Minoan culture to life.

At the height of its prosperity, Crete was self-supporting in food and basic raw materials, exporting foodstuffs, cloth, and painted pottery all over the eastern Mediterranean. The Cretans were renowned mariners. Their large ships transported gold, silver, obsidian, ivory, and ornaments from central Europe, the Aegean, and Southwest Asia; and ostrich eggs were probably traded from North Africa.

Minoan religious practices differed from those of Egypt and other Southwest Asian civilizations in that they were centered on palaces, caves, and shrines, where, apparently, people offered sacrifices to individuals who metamorphosed themselves into deities. Greek archaeologist Nanno Marinatos (1993) believes that the ruling class had an investment in portraying themselves in divine forms, to the point where the imagery

FIGURE 19.7   The throne room of the Palace of Knossos, Crete.

FIGURE 19.8 A Minoan priestess with flounced dress, carrying snakes.

of gods and rulers fused into one. She argues, however, that there were no supreme Minoan rulers or divine kings in the sense of an Egyptian pharaoh or an Assyrian despot, all-conquering in war, and that the palaces were the backbone of religious life. Secular prestige may have been gained through religious office.

At times, the Minoans resorted to human sacrifice and, perhaps, cannibalism. British archaeologist Peter Warren (1984) excavated a house on the north side of Knossos. This fine building had collapsed in the great earthquake of 1450 B.C. The first-floor ceiling had fallen into the basement, taking a magnificent set of ritual vessels with it. The basement fill also contained the scattered bones of two children in perfect health. A microscopic examination of the limb bones showed that knives had been used to remove flesh from the bone.

Warren believes that this may be evidence not only of human sacrifice but perhaps of ritual cannibalism as well, possibly related to a fertility rite associated with the Cretan Zeus and the Earth Mother. In another spectacular and controversial find, Greek archaeologists Yanni Sakellarakis and Efi Sapouna Sakellaraki (1981) uncovered a shrine at Anemospilia, in the mountains south of Knossos, where, they claim, an earthquake interrupted a human sacrifice, the collapsed roof killing the priest and his attendant and leaving the crouched body of the young male victim lying on a sacrificial table.

Santorini eruption
?1688 B.C.

A major event during the later stages of the Minoan civilization was the massive volcanic explosion on the island of Santorini (Thera), a Minoan outpost 113 km (70 miles) from Crete, probably during the late seventeenth century B.C. (Manning, 1988). The eruption probably caused destruction on the north coast of the Minoan kingdom, but Knossos continued to flourish long afterward. The Thera eruption is equated by some people with the eternal legend of Atlantis, the mysterious continent said to have sunk to the ocean bottom after a holocaust thousands of years ago (Doumas, 1983).

The Thera eruption may have accelerated the decline of Minoan civilization, which was already showing signs of weakness. In about 1400 B.C., many Minoan sites were destroyed and abandoned. Warrior farmers, perhaps from mainland Greece, established sway over the empire and decorated the walls of Knossos with military scenes. Seventy-five years later, the palace was finally destroyed by fire, thought to have been the work of Mycenaeans who razed it. By this time, the center of the Aegean world had shifted to the Greek mainland, where Mycenae reached the height of its power.

A generation ago, British archaeologist Colin Renfrew (1972) emphasized an interlinked series of factors to explain the rise of the Minoan palaces. These included intensification of agriculture, growth of foreign trade, and increased craft specialization. Renfrew argued that these factors interacted with each other by the process of "positive feedback" to magnify and accelerate the scale of change (what he called the "multiplier effect") and to result in the formation of palace-based states. Some parts of Renfrew's model, however, are now generally discounted. It implies, for instance, a steady evolution of complex society on Crete during the early Minoan period, which the available evidence does not support.

Renfrew also ascribed an important role to grapevines and olives. These are not grown on the same land as cereals and therefore do not compete with them. Renfrew proposed that the introduction of domesticated vines and olives in the early Bronze Age allowed a substantial expansion in the amount of land under cultivation and helped to power the emergence of a complex society. Some archaeologists and paleobotanists have recently questioned this view, pointing out that the available evidence for cultivated vines and olives does not show their presence much before the late Bronze Age. It is difficult to date their introduction with confidence from the scanty preserved remains, however, and some element of agricultural change would have been essential to support the larger population of palace-period Crete. Furthermore, elaborate drinking vessels appeared in Crete during the early Bronze Age and may indicate that the Cretans were already drinking wine at that period. But there is no firm evidence of extensive agricultural expansion on Crete during the early Bronze Age. Agricultural change, rather than being the driving force of Cretan state formation, was probably just one of several associated factors, along with social and ideological developments.

As agricultural economies became more diversified and goods and commodities could be exchanged both locally and over longer distances, a far-reaching economic interdependence resulted. Eventually, it led to redistribution systems that were organized and controlled by the inhabitants of Minoan palaces and elsewhere in the Aegean where there were major centers of olive production. The redistribution networks carried metal objects and other luxury products the length and breadth of the Aegean. Interest in long-distance trading brought about some cultural homogeneity from trade, gift exchange, and perhaps piracy. The skills of craftsworkers were highly valued in village and palace alike. Specialized artisans practiced their crafts in the major palaces; they lived well, in stone buildings with well-designed drainage systems, and had wooden furniture.

Renfrew (1972) describes both the Minoan society and that of its successors, the Mycenaeans of the Greek mainland, as civilizations. He points to their sophisticated art and metalwork, to the complex palaces organized around specialized craftsworkers, and to their development of redistribution networks for foods. The Minoans and the Mycenaeans did not build vast temples like those at Tikal in Guatemala (see Chapter 21) or in Egypt. They also did not live in cities. Palaces and elaborate tombs were the major monuments. Renfrew looks for the origins of Minoan and Mycenaean civilizations within Greece and the Aegean and considers them the result of local social change and material progress.

🐾 The Mycenaeans

The landscape of mainland Greece makes it ideal territory for the development of autonomous small-scale kingdoms. Mountains break the terrain into fertile coastal plains, each of which could naturally form the focus of a separate state. These kingdoms

FIGURE 19.9 Mycenae from the air. The Lion Gate is at right.

first become visible at the beginning of the late Bronze Age, when the elites who governed them began to engage in long-distance trade with the hinterland of Europe and to proclaim their wealth and power through the richness of their grave goods.

Mycenaean civilization
1600–1150 B.C.

The Mycenaean civilization, centered on the fertile plain of Argos on the Greek mainland, began to flourish about 1600 B.C. (Taylour, 1990). The chieftains who ruled over the walled fortress of Mycenae (Figure 19.9) were buried in spectacular graves that contained weapons adorned with copper and gold as well as fine gold face masks modeled in the likeness of their owners (Figure 19.10). Their wealth and economic power came from their trading contacts and from their warrior skills (Figure 19.11). The kings were skilled charioteers and horsemen whose material culture and lifeway are immortalized in the Homeric epics. These epics, however, were written many centuries after the Mycenaeans themselves had become folk memories (Fagles, 1990).

Mycenaean commerce took over where the Minoans left off, although many Greek cargos were carried in ships of other nations. Much of the rulers' prestige was based on their contacts in the metal trade. As the Uluburun ship shows, minerals were in constant demand in the central and eastern Mediterranean, especially tin for alloying copper to make bronze. Both copper and tin were abundant in central Cyprus and Anatolia, and the Mycenaeans developed the necessary contacts to obtain regular supplies.

The Mycenaeans also prized Baltic amber, a yellow-brown fossil resin that, when rubbed, seems to be "electric." Occasional pieces of this precious substance reached Mycenae, and amber has been found in the royal graves there. Just how extensive the Mycenaeans' trading activities in Europe were has been much debated. They may well have been minimal (see Harding, 1984).

So complex did their trading transactions become that the Mycenaeans found it necessary to establish a writing system. They refined one that had been developed by the Minoans. The Mycenaeans used a form of script written in the Greek language, known now as Linear B (Robinson, 1995). Eighty-nine characters make up Linear B, 48 of which can be traced back to Minoan writing, Linear A. Linear A probably originated in the simple pictographic script of the earliest Minoans (Figure 19.12). The terms *Linear A* and *Linear B* were coined by Sir Arthur Evans (1921) when he first studied Minoan writing in the early twentieth century. Linear B was in more widespread use than A, partly because the Mycenaeans exerted greater political and economic power than the Cretans (Chadwick, 1976).

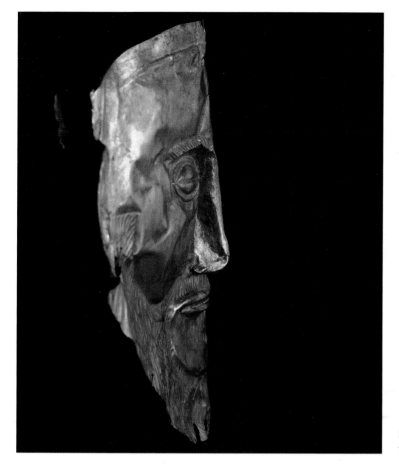

FIGURE 19.10 Gold mask of a bearded man, from Shaft Grave V at Mycenae, 1600 B.C.

Mycenae was a major partner in eastern Mediterranean trade until about 1150 B.C., when a combination of internal bickering and decline in agricultural yields led to its collapse (see Site box). In the same century, the Phrygians of the northeast overthrew the Hittite kingdom in Anatolia. This incursion into the Mediterranean world was caused by unsettled political conditions in Europe, at least partly the result of population pressures and tribal warfare (see Chapter 20).

FIGURE 19.11
Impression of a warrior wielding an ax against an enemy with a dagger, from an engraved ring, shaft graves, Mycenae.

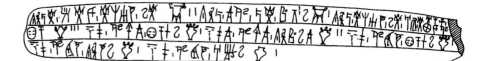

FIGURE 19.12 Mycenaean script. Above, a tablet from the Palace of Nestor at Pylos in western Greece, bearing an inventory of goblets and cauldrons. Below, a specimen listing: "Larger sized goblet with three handles 2."

dipae   mezoe   tiriowee   2

(larger-sized goblet with three handles 2)

〰 Greek City-States After Mycenae

After Mycenae fell in 1150 B.C., small-town merchants on the Greek mainland continued to trade, monopolizing commerce in the Aegean and Black seas. By the eighth and seventh centuries B.C., trade had revived. Small colonies of Greek settlers lived on the northern and western shores of the Black Sea and along the north coast of Anatolia and developed trade in gold, copper, iron, salt, and other commodities (Bonzek, 1985). Other Greeks voyaged westward and settled in southern France; they soon had a brisk trade in wine and other goods with central Europe (Ridgeway, 1992).

In Greece, mountain ranges separate many fertile agricultural areas. Traders and seafarers of the Aegean islands and the Greek mainland therefore formed a network of small city-states that competed with one another for trade and political power (Morris, 1994). The concept of the *city-state* was the major organizing principle in the Greek world. Typically, it consisted of the city itself (usually fortified, since the city-states were often at war with each other) and the surrounding rural hinterland, dotted with farmsteads and villages. Many such city-states were small both in extent and in population; some could field only a few hundred men of military age. On the other hand, there were those that could afford to build grandiose temples and public buildings—not palaces for the wealthy but monuments to the prestige of their own city. This is a trend seen most obviously in fifth-century Athens, when the resources of the Athenian Empire were poured into the reconstruction of the Acropolis and above all the Parthenon, with its gold and ivory statue of the patron goddess of the city-state, Athena (see Figure 19.14, page 458).

Greek states unified only in times of grave political stress, as when Persian kings sought to add Greece to their possessions. Darius's defeat at Marathon (490 B.C.) and Xerxes' ten years later in a naval battle at Salamis ensured the security of Greece and made classical Greek civilization possible. Athens was foremost among the Greek states, becoming head of a league of maritime cities that was soon turned into an empire (Bury and Meiggs, 1976; Morris, 1987). This was the Athens that attracted wealthy immigrants, built the Parthenon, and boasted of Aeschylus, Sophocles, and other mighty playwrights. Classical Greek civilization flourished for 50 glorious years.

490 B.C.

However, throughout the brilliant decades of Athenian supremacy, bickering with Sparta in the Peloponnesus never abated. A deep animosity between the two cities had its roots in radically different social systems. Sparta's government was based on military discipline and a rigid class structure. Athenians enjoyed a more mobile society and a democratic government.

431 to 404 B.C.

The long rivalry culminated in the disastrous Peloponnesian War, 431 to 404 B.C., which left Sparta a dominant political force on the mainland, but was followed by disarray. Greece soon fell under the sway of Philip of Macedon, whose rule between 359 and 336 B.C. began to develop political unity. His son, Alexander the Great, then

SITE

The Mycenaean Shrine at Phylakopi, Melos Island, Greece

The small Mycenaean town of Phylakopi on the island of Melos in the Aegean Sea was home to an estimated 1400 to 2100 people between 1390 and 1090 B.C. The settlement was a maze of small stone houses, narrow alleyways, and courtyards. Colin Renfrew (1985) excavated the site using a 10-m (33-foot) grid that allowed him to record architectural changes and stratigraphy with great precision. This excavation method, combined with meticulous studies of the Mycenaean pottery, provided very precise contexts for the finds and enabled Renfrew to identify an important shrine in the town.

He first suspected a shrine when he recovered broken animal and human figurines in his trenches. Slow-moving excavation over the floors of the putative shrine rooms revealed stone platforms and exotic objects like seal stones. But the evidence for religious activity was modest at best, until the excavators uncovered a side chamber and a wall niche in the westernmost shrine room. This contained a pedastalled vase, the fragments of an ox-like figure, other figurines, and a remarkable female figurine, which stood upright in the room.

"The Lady of Phylakopi," as Renfrew named her, had a conical stem painted like a long skirt, a bulbous body with small breasts, a painted brown chin, staring eyes, and eyebrows and hair outlined in brown. Another complete female figurine stood to one side.

The figurines could have come from a storeroom, so Renfrew studied the design of the chambers. He found that the builders had laid them out in such a way that the symmetrically placed platforms were the focus of attention. The objects displayed on them would have caught attention at once. Furthermore, the "shrines" yielded conch-shell trumpets, identical to those blown by priestesses on seals from Crete. Perforated tortoiseshell fragments were the remains of lyre bodies. The fine pottery found inside the two shrines was of much better quality than that from elsewhere on the site (Figure 19.13).

The precise contexts of these finds allowed Renfrew to conclude that he had found the town shrine, which is duplicated, at least superficially, at other sites on Crete and the Greek mainland.

FIGURE 19.13 Reconstruction of the shrine at Phylakopi, Melos.

FIGURE 19.14 The Parthenon, Athens, one of the glories of classical Greece.

embarked on a campaign of imperial conquest that took him from Macedon into Persia and then to Mesopotamia. Alexander was welcomed as a hero and a god in Egypt, where he paused long enough to sacrifice to the local deities and have himself proclaimed pharaoh. His continued quests took him as far east as the Indus Valley and back to Babylon, where he died of fever in 323 B.C. By the time of his death, Alexander had united an enormous area of the ancient world under at least nominal Macedonian rule. His extraordinary empire fell apart within a generation, but his conquests paved the way for the uniform government of Imperial Rome.

323 B.C.

∰ The Etruscans and the Romans

During the first millennium B.C., the Mediterranean world was linked from one end to the other by highly intricate mercantile ties. Phoenicians and Greeks controlled much of this trade in metals and other essentials, as well as exotic luxuries. The trade extended into temperate Europe and throughout the Italian peninsula, helping set the stage for large-scale Etruscan and Roman urban civilization in later centuries.

The Etruscans

By approximately 1000 B.C., some Urnfield people (named after their habit of burying cremated ashes in clay urns) from central Europe (see Chapter 20) had settled south of the Alps in the Po Valley (Wells, 1981). They developed a skilled bronze-working tradition in which products were traded far into central Europe and throughout Italy. This people evolved into the Villanovan culture, which appeared in the ninth century B.C. and was soon in touch with Greek colonies in southern Italy and perhaps with the Phoenicians (Spivey and Stoddart, 1990). Ironworking was introduced to the Villanovans in approximately the ninth century B.C. Iron tools and extensive trading contacts won the Villanovans political control over much of northern and western Italy. They established colonies on the islands of Elba and Corsica. Several centuries of trade and other contacts culminated in the literate Etruscan civilization (Pallottino, 1978).

Villanovan culture
850 B.C.

Etruscan civilization

Like classical Greece, Etruscan civilization, with its city-states, was more a unity of cultural tradition and trade than a political reality. The Etruscans traded widely in the central Mediterranean and with warrior peoples in central Europe. Etruscan culture was derived from the Villanovan culture, but it owed much to eastern immigrants and trading contacts that brought Southwest Asian influence to Italian towns. The political units of Etruscan territory were city-states with much independence, each with substantial public buildings and fortifications. Their decentralized political organization made them vulnerable to foreign raiders. Warrior bands from central Europe overran some Etruscan city-states in the centuries after 450 B.C., at which time Etruscan prosperity began to crumble.

450 B.C.

By the time of Etruscan decline, however, the Mediterranean was a civilized lake. Phoenician colonists had founded Carthage and other cities in North Africa and Spain and controlled the western Mediterranean. The rulers of Greece and Egypt, and later Philip of Macedon, controlled the east, and the Etruscans were in control of most of Italy and many central European trade routes.

The Romans

The Etruscans had been the first people to fortify the seven famed hills of Rome. In 509 B.C., the native Romans evicted this foreign dynasty of rulers and began to develop their own distinctive city-state. The next few centuries saw the emergence of Rome from a cluster of simple villages by the Tiber River to the leadership of the Mediterranean and far beyond. The Romans inherited the mantle of classical Greece and added their own distinctive culture to this foundation. They then carried Greco-Roman civilization to many parts of the world that were still inhabited by preliterate peasant societies. Roman legions campaigned not only in Egypt, Mesopotamia, and southern Arabia but also in central and western Europe and in Britain. But for the Romans, the administrative and linguistic face of Europe would be very different today (Cornell, 1995; Holloway, 1994).

Rome
753 B.C.

By 295 B.C., the power of Rome dominated the whole of Italy. At this time, Rome was a form of democracy, governed by a delicate balance of aristocratic and popular authority. This type of governance was appropriate for a large city-state but was hopelessly inadequate for the complexities of a huge empire. Eventually, civil strife led to autocratic rule of the empire under the emperors, the first of whom was Julius Caesar, familiar to every student of Roman history for his epic conquest of Gaul (France). (His great-nephew, Augustus, was the first ruler actually to claim the title of emperor.)

295 B.C.

After two vicious wars with their rich rival Carthage, the Romans achieved mastery over the western Mediterranean by 200 B.C., and by 50 B.C., much of Asia was under uneasy Roman domination. The Romans lacked the mechanisms to administer their empire successfully until Emperor Augustus reorganized the civil service and established the *Pax Romana* ("Roman peace") over his vast domains. There ensued a period of great material prosperity and political stability, at the price of political freedom of speech.

200 to 50 B.C.

The stresses that led to the collapse of the Roman Empire first began to appear on the European frontiers in the second and third centuries A.D. Roman power began to decline as ambition and sophistication grew among the Iron Age tribes living on the edges of Roman territory. The "barbarians" on the fringes of the empire were mainly peasant farmers who had obtained iron by trading and intermarriage with La Tène peoples (see Chapter 20). Many served as mercenaries in the Roman armies, acquiring wealth and sophistication and, perhaps most important of all, an insight into Roman military tactics.

Shortage of farmland and increasing disrespect for Rome caused many Germanic tribes to raid Rome's European provinces. The raids were so successful that the imperial armies were constantly campaigning in the north. In A.D. 395, after Emperor Theodosius died, the Roman Empire was split into eastern and western divisions. Large invasions from northern Europe ensued. Fifteen years later, Germanic tribes from central Europe sacked Rome itself; then the European provinces were completely overrun by warrior peoples. Other Germanic groups disturbed North Africa and crossed much of Asia Minor but left little lasting mark on history there.

A.D. 395

What was the legacy of Rome? Its material legacy can be seen in the road system, which still provides a basis for many of Europe's and Southwest Asia's communications, and in the towns, like London, which are still flourishing modern cities. In cultural terms, its principal legacy was the legal system, which lies at the core of most Western law codes. Roman literature and art dominated European culture for centuries after the Renaissance. Their spoken and written language, Latin, survived for centuries as the language of the educated person and as the principal means of business communication between nations. Latin lies at the base of many modern European languages and was only recently abandoned as the liturgical language of the Roman Catholic church. The Romans and their culture are the foundation of Western civilization.

Summary 〰️

Small towns became growing economic centers in parts of Anatolia as early as 3600 B.C. Communities like Çatalhöyük failed to develop the necessary administrative and social mechanisms to cope with the increased complexity of the settlement and its trading activities. The town failed, and Anatolians of the fifth millennium B.C. reverted to village life. Small fortified villages flourished in the fourth millennium B.C. One of them, Troy I, dates to just after 3000 B.C. Troy II, founded in about 2300 B.C., was a fortified town with more elaborate architecture and fine gold and bronze metallurgy. By this time, the Anatolians were trading widely over the highlands and into the Aegean, and chieftaincies were scattered over mineral-rich areas. About 1900 B.C., the Assyrians set up a trading colony at Kanesh in central Anatolia.

The Hittites assumed power in Anatolia in about 1650 B.C. They held a vital place in the history of their time, for they played the Assyrians off against the Egyptians. Hittite power was based on diplomatic and trading skills until about 1200 B.C., when international trade in the eastern Mediterranean collapsed and a period of confusion, partly the work of the Sea Peoples, ensued. The state of Israel was born during this interregnum, among agricultural and herding peoples in the highlands behind the eastern Mediterranean coast.

Farming settlements developed in Greece and the Aegean islands before 5000 B.C. There were radical changes in the late second millennium B.C., when the cultivation of the olive and the grapevine became widespread and the trading of minerals, stoneware, and other products expanded rapidly. Numerous small towns flourished throughout the Aegean and eastern Greece by 2500 B.C., linked by regular trading routes. The Minoan civilization of Crete developed in about 2000 B.C. and lasted until approximately 1450 B.C. The great volcanic explosion of its satellite island, Thera, in the seventeenth century B.C. may have weakened Minoan power for a while.

After 1400 B.C., the center of civilization passed to the mainland, where the Mycenaeans flourished until 1150 B.C. Mycenaean civilization collapsed as a result of internal dissension and possibly the exhaustion of agricultural land. Trading activities continued to expand in the Aegean after the decline of Mycenae. Small city-states flourished, unifying only in the face of a common danger, such as the Persian invasions of the fifth century B.C.

The Athenians enjoyed a long period of supremacy among city-states, the period of classical Greek civilization in the fifth century B.C. Alexander the Great built an enormous empire across Southwest Asia, of which Greece was part, in the late fourth century B.C. The Roman Empire, which followed, marks the entry of the entire Mediterranean area into historic times. Developed from Villanovan and Etruscan roots in Italy, Imperial Roman power was based on the ruins of Alexander's empire.

Guide to Further Reading 〰️

Dickinson, Oliver. 1994. *The Aegean Bronze Age.* Cambridge: Cambridge University Press.
    A definitive summary of the subject addressed to more specialist readers.

Doumas, Christos. 1983. *Thera: Pompeii of the Aegean.* London: Thames & Hudson.
    Lavishly illustrated survey of Thera's spectacular Akrotiri site.

MacQueen, J. G. 1996. *The Hittites,* 3d ed. London: Thames & Hudson.
    A general account of Hittite civilization. Lavishly illustrated.

Scarre, Chris. 1995. *Chronicle of the Roman Emperors.* London: Thames & Hudson.
   A description of the early history of Rome and the careers of all its emperors. Well illustrated and an ideal reference book.

Spivey, N., and S. Stoddart. 1990. *Etruscan Italy: An Archaeological History.* London: Batsford.
   An excellent summary of Etruscan civilization for general readers.

Whitelaw, Keith W., and Robert B. Coote. 1987. *The Emergence of Early Israel.* Sheffield, England: Almond Press.
   A closely argued account of the rise of Israel, based on prehistoric archaeology and ecology. Provocative and convincing.

EUROPE BEFORE THE ROMANS

Fortified Iron Age camp, Biskupin, central Europe

n the year 1667, a country squire named John Aubrey galloped into the village of Avebury in southern England during a fox hunt. He was "wonderfully surprized" to find it surrounded by a large ditch and bank and with circles of massive stones. Aubrey had visited the mysterious stone circles at Stonehenge when he was 8 years old and had long been a casual antiquary. None other than King Charles II encouraged him to survey the ancient earthworks and circles, a task that took Aubrey many years. His great work, *Monumenta Britannica*, which included his survey maps, was unfinished at the time of his death in 1697 and was not published until 1980. But archaeologists have long known what he thought of the people who built these ancient shrines: "The inhabitants were almost as savage as the Beasts, whose skins were their only rayment.... They were two or three degrees I suppose less savage than the Americans.... The Romans subdued and civilized them."

No modern-day archaeologist would agree with Aubrey's characterization, for science has shown that both the Native Americans and the late prehistoric Europeans were much more sophisticated than Julius Caesar and other Roman authors would have us believe. By the time Roman legions campaigned north of the Alps, the society of temperate Europe enjoyed a level of complexity that has fascinated archaeologists for generations (Figure 20.1). How, then, did such complexity arise? Did it develop as a result of indigenous cultural evolution or because of a diffusion of people and ideas from Southwest Asia (see Table 15.1)?

For years, V. Gordon Childe (1952) and others argued that the constant demands by Southwest Asian societies for copper, tin, and other metals led to cultural development in the backwater that was temperate Europe. However, this traditional viewpoint has been challenged by calibrated radiocarbon chronologies that place the appearance of copper working in the Balkans earlier than in Greece or the Aegean. Many people now believe that Europeans were just as innovative as their eastern neighbors (Champion et al., 1984; Cunliffe, 1994).

Early Copper Working

Colin Renfrew (1978) and Ruth Tringham (1971) have argued that the farmers of southeastern Europe developed copper smelting independently, partly because they already used improved pottery-firing techniques that were very suitable for copper smelting. Witness the finds at the Varna Cemetery near the Black Sea in Bulgaria.

At the Varna Cemetery, more than 130 richly decorated graves have yielded dozens of fine copper and gold tools and ornaments (Figure 20.2). Colin Renfrew has described the

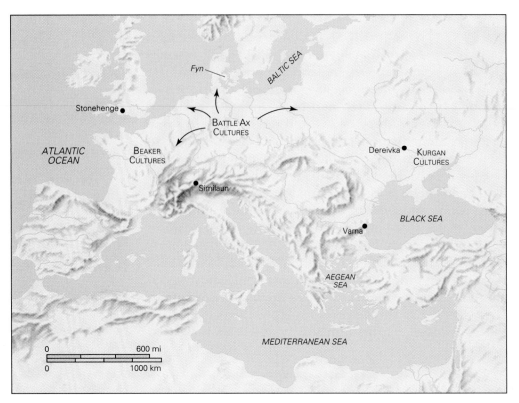

FIGURE 20.1 Europe, 3500 to 2500 B.C. While extreme western and northwestern Europe remained the territory of stone-using farmers, copper working spread in central Europe and bronze came into use in Southwest Asia and peripheral regions. The building of communal tombs was widespread in the west, but more mobile lifeways developed in central Europe and on the eastern steppes. This new pattern expanded into surrounding areas.

FIGURE 20.2 Goldwork from Varna, Bulgaria.

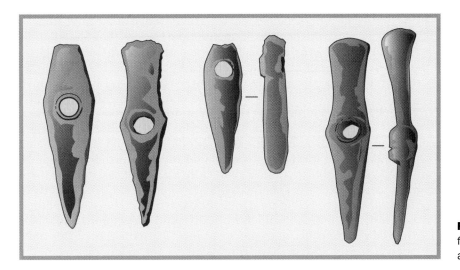

FIGURE 20.3 Simple copper ax heads from the Czech Republic (one-third actual size).

Varna finds as "the earliest major assemblage of gold artifacts to be unearthed any-where in the world" (1978, p. 212), for they date to approximately 4600 to 4200 B.C. Both the copper and the gold are of Balkan origin; indeed, both metals were being worked there earlier than they were in Southwest Asia. (Such a statement reflects find-ings thus far; it does not preclude future discoveries of earlier metals in Southwest Asia.) The Balkan copper industry was quite sophisticated and was organized to serve trading networks over a wide area. In places, fissures mark the places where early min-ers followed ore veins deep into the ground. One mine in Bulgaria has ancient shafts more than 10 m (33 feet) deep. These copper mines are the earliest so far discovered and show that metallurgy developed rapidly into a considerable industry in the Balkans during the fifth millennium B.C.

Varna
4600 to 4200 B.C.

The Varna burials provide striking evidence for differential wealth; some of the graves are richly decorated with gold ornaments, whereas others contain few artifacts. Unfortunately, the settlement associated with the Varna Cemetery has yet to be found, but Renfrew believes that the users of the burial ground were part of a chiefdom in which the leaders used gold and copper ornaments to fulfill the social need for con-spicuous display. As he points out, the problem with explaining the rise of metallurgy is not a technical but a social one, that is, defining the social conditions under which metal objects first came into widespread use. The earliest copper axes had few practi-cal advantages over stone axes (Figure 20.3). Both copper and gold were used mainly for ornamental purposes. Perhaps it was no coincidence that the first metallurgists in temperate Europe developed a wide range of ornaments, luxury items traded through exchange networks that accelerated the spread of copper working to other parts of temperate Europe.

🐾 Battle Axes and Beakers

The technology of copper working is really an outgrowth of that used for pottery manufacture and probably arose after many experiments with fire, clay, and stone. The beginnings of copper metallurgy in temperate Europe were probably almost imper-ceptible, since only a handful of simple hammered copper artifacts date to as early as 4000 B.C. At least two possible areas of indigenous copper working have been identified in southern Europe, both near copper outcrops. One is in southern Spain (Iberia) and the other in northern Italy. In both regions, the copper workers started smelting by about 3000 B.C. Britain is also rich in copper ores, and the metal was exploited early there, too. Wherever it developed, coppersmithing was probably a seasonal or at best a part-time occupation, and it was not until much later that tougher bronze artifacts came into daily use in the field and the chase.

Copper
4000 B.C.

3000 B.C.

The archaeological record of the period between 3500 and 2000 B.C. is incredibly complicated, but we can discern two broad groupings of societies, the so-called Battle Ax and Beaker peoples, who ultimately mingled.

Kurgan culture
3200 B.C.

In eastern Europe, settled farming societies had lived on the edge of the huge Russian steppe for hundreds of years. Like the peoples of Anatolia and Greece, they had sporadic contacts with the nomads who roamed the plains to the east; about these dealings we know little. In the southern Russian region, a widespread population of copper-using agriculturalists lived in rectangular thatched huts, cultivated many crops, and also tamed domestic animals, possibly including the horse. This loosely defined Kurgan culture, which was part of the Battle Ax culture, was remarkable for its burial customs, each corpse being deposited under a small mound. The Kurgans used wheeled vehicles and made the copper or stone battle ax a very important part of their armory. The wheeled cart and the battle ax had spread widely over central and parts of northern Europe by 3000 B.C. (Piggott, 1992). The globular pots associated with these artifacts, many of them bearing characteristic cord-impressed decorations, have been found at hundreds of sites. The same artifacts have often been found in megalithic tombs. These new cultural traits were absorbed into the millennia-old European cultural tradition, and many experts feel that the Indo-European language spread into Europe at about this time. (Indo-European speech is thought to have originated in the region between the Carpathian and Caucasus mountains. The entire Indo-European controversy is complex and outside the scope of this book. Interested readers should consult Mallory, 1988, and Renfrew, 1987.)

It was at about this time that new house forms appeared in the European temperate zones. Smaller timber dwellings, just large enough to house a single family, replaced the Bandkeramik longhouse (see Chapter 10). With their battle axes, warriors were buried under small mounds, a reflection of new cultural traditions that were to persist in Europe for thousands of years. The warrior leaders who descended from Bronze Age chieftains were the German tribespeople whom the Romans encountered on the frontiers of their European empire.

2700 B.C.

Beakers

Between 2700 and 2000 B.C., a series of highly characteristic artifacts came into fashion over a large region of Europe: coastal Spain, southern France, Sardinia, northern Italy, east and central Europe, the Low Countries, and Britain (R. Harrison, 1980). These included finely made bell-shaped beakers found in hundreds of graves and burial mounds (Figure 20.4). Archaeologists such as V. Gordon Childe (1936) thought in terms of tribes of "Beaker Folk" who spread the length and breadth of Europe, bringing a new culture and copper working with them. It seems more likely that these vessels spread widely not as a result of itinerant merchants or great population movements but simply because beakers, as well as other trinkets such as metal brooches, became prized status symbols throughout Europe. They may also have been traded for what

FIGURE 20.4 Beaker vessels and other artifacts, including arrowheads, from various localities in south-central Britain.

SITE

Ötzi the Iceman, Similaun Glacier, Italian Alps

A combination of high winds and extreme cold dried out and preserved the body of a prehistoric European found in 1991 high on the Similaun glacier in the Italian Alps (Spindler, 1994). The Similaun corpse has been radiocarbon-dated to between 3350 and 3300 B.C.

The man's body lay in a crouched position, as if he had taken shelter in bad weather when lost. Experts believe the man was in his earlier 40s and was either hunting or looking for minerals like copper, which are plentiful in the Alps. Others believe he was a shepherd on his way to summer pastures. The controversies continue to unfold. His corpse and possessions are yielding a mine of information to modern-day archaeological detectives. Judging from an ember for starting a fire that he carried with him, which was from a tree species that grows to the south of the mountains, he came from that direction, perhaps from the fertile Venosta Valley in northern Italy. A single grain of wheat adhering to his clothing suggests that he was in contact with the valley within a few days of his death. The man carried a copper ax with a wooden shaft, a leather quiver with 14 bone- and wood-pointed arrows, and replacement heads and a puttylike substance for mounting them. He wore leather boots lined with hay for warmth, a stone necklace, and leather and fur garments, as well as a grass cloak of a type still worn by some peasants in the Alps a century ago (Figure 20.5). His knee and back bore small tattoos.

The latest techniques of medical science have established that his stomach was empty and that he had not eaten within eight hours of his death. The Ice Man had not been in perfect health. His lungs were black with soot, perhaps from living in smoke-filled huts. His bones carry 17 Harris lines, layers of bony material which form at times of stunted growth due to malnutrition. Experts estimate he suffered such episodes in his ninth, fifteenth, and sixteenth years, perhaps as a result of winter hunger. The dead man's hair yielded large amounts of copper dust, and there are high arsenic concentrations in his system, as if he had been involved in processing malachite, a copper carbonate commonplace in the Alps.

The Ice Man had been in a fight before his death. An arrowhead is buried deep in his left shoulder, and there is a dagger wound in one of his hands as he parried an attack (Gostner and Vigl, 2002). Maybe he was killed where he fell, or perhaps he ran away wounded, then collapsed, helpless, and died of hyperthermia. We will probably never know.

FIGURE 20.5 Reconstruction of the appearance of the Ice Man from Similaun, Italy. He wears a fur cap, an outer cape with coat underneath, leggings, and shoes. Two birch-bark containers and a backpack lie at his feet. He carries a stringless bow.

they contained—perhaps beer or mead—and may have become valued heirlooms, priceless grave furniture, or artifacts exchanged as bride wealth (goods given by the bridegroom's family to the bride's father) or displayed at tribal gatherings.

Plow

2200 B.C.

Beakers were only one of several innovations that were changing the face of European society. Another was the plow, which came into widespread use about 2200 B.C., opening the way for the cultivation of heavier soils and much larger acreages.

We know something of the appearance of Bronze Age people from the remarkable discovery of the "Iceman" in the Italian Alps (see Site box, page 467).

〰 The European Bronze Age

In the Aegean there was steady development from this early threshold of metalworking toward complex state organizations, but Europe remained settled by small village societies. The temperate zones were densely occupied and exploited, and vast acreages of forest had been cleared and brought under cultivation by 2000 B.C. The villagers managed woodland carefully, engaged in hunting to supplement their diet, and mined both hard ax stone and soft copper ore. They also panned for gold. Every community used basic metal technologies and had access to boats or wheeled transport. European village society was stable and self-sufficient, with thousands of communities connected by ties of kin and family and by long-established paths that led from valley to valley along the hill ridges. Above all, European society enjoyed reliable food supplies that helped bind the communities together.

The European Bronze Age began not as a result of dramatic events and military conquest, nor because of some startling invention (Coles, 1982; Coles and Harding, 1979). It was merely a gradual and inevitable quickening of responses to a number of new opportunities (Harding, 2000). Many of these changes were in material culture and settlement patterns. A series of landscape surveys in southern Britain, for example, has revealed vast networks of fields and land boundaries joining river valleys, ridges, and watersheds into a managed landscape in which different communities owned closely defined agricultural land. One Dorsetshire, England, Bronze Age agricultural system encompassed 200 ha (494 acres), with settlements of four to five huts linked to enclosures with narrow herd paths. There were fields, hoe plots, stock corrals, and homesteads, all joined in single managed agricultural units. By 900 B.C., Bronze Age food production was sophisticated. It relied heavily on plow agriculture and field fallowing as well as manuring, and it was based on the rotation of many different cereal and root crops.

From about 2000 B.C., metallurgy was a growth industry throughout temperate Europe. A series of local bronze industries developed in different parts of Europe, bringing with them a whole range of related activities: the trading of ores and finished artifacts from major mining centers and the barter of both prosaic and prestigious artifacts and ornaments over considerable distances. For the first time, a major European industry was practiced in areas where supplies of raw materials were scarce. For instance, Bronze Age communities in Scandinavia, which had no metals, went to considerable trouble to acquire metal ore and finished tools both from tribes in Britain and from central European sources. European smiths produced some of the finest bronze artifacts made in the ancient world: axes and adzes, battle axes, daggers, swords, spearheads, shields, and an enormous range of brooches and pins. They also made delicate, prestigious gold ornaments that were highly prized and buried with important chieftains.

For all of these metallurgical innovations, the basic tenor of agricultural life remained unchanged, except for a gradual evolution in the structure of European society: the emergence of social ranking. Just what form this ranking took is a matter of lively controversy since it is reflected only in a differentiation of grave goods between a few individuals and the rest of society. In Denmark, for example, excavations on the island of Fyn have revealed rich Bronze Age burials and a nearby settlement with a wealth of gold and bronze. These are clear evidence that a powerful community was located there having extensive trading connections with metal-rich regions to the south. The evidence from Bronze Age graves across Europe shows that rich and poor

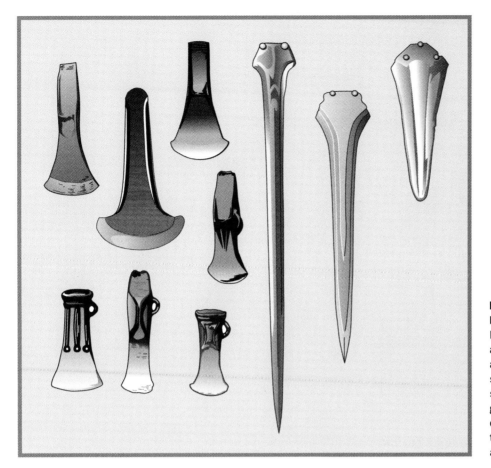

FIGURE 20.6 Copper and bronze implements from Britain. Left, simple flat axes and flanged and socketed axes (one-third actual size). Right, dagger and sword blades (one-fourth actual size). Although both copper and gold were used for ornaments, copper also formed effective utilitarian agricultural implements and weapons.

were buried side by side, the former with substantial quantities of valuable metal artifacts that were thus lost to the people burying them. This can only mean that some members of society, perhaps important traders and more influential kin leaders, aggrandized wealth and power at the expense of others and became a new elite in European society (Gilman, 1995; Sherratt, 1994b).

Although one day the first occurrence of bronze may be shown to date to about 4000 B.C. in southeastern Europe, the earliest widespread use of tin-copper alloys occurred in approximately 2500 B.C., in what is now the Czech Republic (Coles and Harding, 1979). The new bronze implements, with their tougher working edges (Figure 20.6), were initially in short supply, but their use spread gradually as new trade routes were opened across central and western Europe. The earliest bronze working was centered in Unetice (Figure 20.7), where there was an industry manufacturing axes, knife blades, halberds, and many types of ornaments (Piggott, 1965). The bronze workers themselves obviously belonged to cultural traditions long established in the area, for their burial customs were identical to those of earlier centuries. Some believe that the art of alloying tin with copper, as well as casting techniques, came to Europe from Syria. Most people now argue, however, that bronze working developed independently in Europe, in that the calibrated carbon-14 dates from the Unetice industry are earlier than those for the Southwest Asian prototypes from which the other school of thought assumes the Unetice industry to have evolved.

Bronze working soon appeared in southern Germany and Switzerland as well, where deposits of copper and tin were to be found. Other places with copper outcrops also were soon using the new methods, including Brittany, the British Isles, and northern Italy, all more remote from the initial centers of bronze working. The period between approximately 1700 and 1300 B.C. was one of rapid technological progress and considerable social change, generated in large part by the reinforcing effects on the local bronze-working centers of the persistent demand for critical raw materials and finished tools.

2500 B.C.

Unetice

1700 to 1300 B.C.

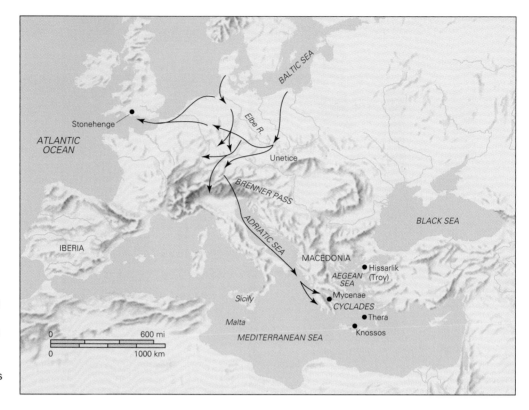

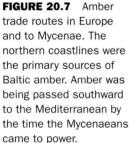

FIGURE 20.7 Amber trade routes in Europe and to Mycenae. The northern coastlines were the primary sources of Baltic amber. Amber was being passed southward to the Mediterranean by the time the Mycenaeans came to power.

By this time, European trading networks carried far more than bronze artifacts and metal ores. The amber trade went from the shores of the Baltic to the Mediterranean, following well-established routes (see Figure 20.7) (Harding, 1984). Seashells, perhaps faience (glass) beads, and other exotic luxuries were dispersed northward into the temperate zones in exchange for raw materials. Some centers of bronze production became major places for redistributing other goods as well. The salt miners of Austria were also very active in the long-distance trade.

During the second millennium B.C., even societies remote from metal outcrops were engaged in metallurgy. Many more copper and bronze artifacts became available for domestic consumption. Central European smiths introduced some new tool forms, including socketed axes and varied woodworking tools. More farmers were using the ard (a scraping plow drawn by oxen), which had been in use since at least 2500 B.C. The ard was a significant innovation, for it allowed deeper plowing, more advanced agricultural methods, and higher crop productivity. More intensive farming techniques were vital to feed the many new mouths, and prime farmland was harder to find than ever before. The surplus food and energy from improved agriculture were not devoted to generating additional surpluses and extra production but in some societies were channeled into erecting majestic religious monuments, of which Stonehenge in southern Britain is probably the most celebrated (Figure 20.8).

Stonehenge
2950 to 1500 B.C.

Shrouded in fantasy and speculation, and associated by many people with the ancient Druids' cult, Stonehenge is in fact a fantastically old religious temple (Chippindale, 1994). It began as a simple circle of ritual pits in about 2950 B.C. and went through vigorous reconstructions, reaching the zenith of its expansion in about 2900 B.C. That Stonehenge was associated with some form of astronomical activity seems unquestionable, although the details are much debated. Doubtless, special priests were needed to maintain this and other major shrines and to perform the rituals in their precincts. Religious activity was supported by the food surplus, not by the increased productivity in agriculture, trade, and craft specialization that generated spectacular social evolution in Southwest Asia. Thus, during the third and part of the second millennium B.C., little social evolution went on in Europe; political power and wealth belonged to chieftains and warriors rather than to divine kings and a hierarchical society.

FIGURE 20.8
Stonehenge, England, from the air, with the surrounding ditch clearly visible.

Bronze Age Warriors

European societies eventually became more socially ranked. As trade intensified, local monopolies over salt and other supplies came to be concentrated in the hands of comparatively few individuals. Population growth and perhaps some climatic deterioration put new pressure on agricultural land (Figure 20.9). All of this may have led to considerable political instability in Europe and to alliances of small tribes under the rule of powerful and ambitious chieftains, themselves once minor village leaders. Some warrior groups even began to strike at the edge of the Mediterranean world, raiding Mycenae and the Hittite Empire.

One powerful group of warrior peoples in west Hungary is known to archaeologists as the Urnfield people because of their burial customs: Their dead were cremated and their ashes deposited in urns; huge cemeteries of urn burials are associated with fortified villages, sometimes built near lakes. Urnfield people began to make full use of horse-drawn vehicles and new weaponry. Skilled bronze smiths produced sheet-metal helmets, shields, and bronze body armor for a warrior elite. These fighters used the slashing sword, a devastating weapon far more effective than the cutting swords of earlier times.

Urnfield people

The emergence of warrior elites was accompanied by a quickening of trade, reflected in a remarkable standardization of weapons and burial customs throughout much of central and western Europe (Figure 20.10). Within a couple of centuries, characteristic slashing swords and other central European tools had been deposited in cemeteries in Italy, the Balkans, and the Aegean. The exploitation of copper mines such as those in Austria's Tyrol was intensified. There, bands of miners used bronze-tipped picks to dig deep into the ground for copper ore. Their efforts increased the supplies of copper and tin available to central Europe (Coles and Harding, 1979). Urnfield weaponry and burial rites spread from Hungary throughout central and parts of western Europe.

Between 1800 and 1200 B.C., the population movements associated with central European peoples introduced a more consolidated system of agriculture to much of

1800 to 1200 B.C.

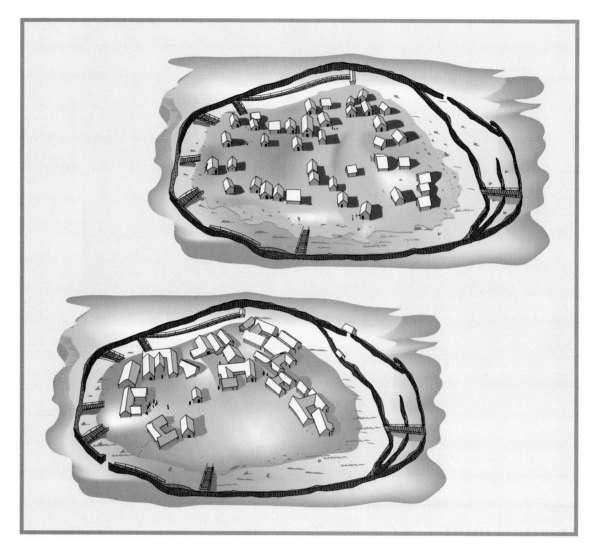

FIGURE 20.9 Bronze Age lakeside settlement at Wasserburg-Buchau, Federsee, Germany. The village was set in marshy ground and first occupied in about 1100 B.C., at a time when climatic change may have put pressure on good agricultural land. Fortified settlements may have been a response to territorial disputes. Top, the village was oval, and was surrounded by a wooden palisade, with 38 log-cabinlike structures inside. Bottom, somewhat later, the village was rebuilt with large rectangular buildings, some joined to make H-shaped or L-shaped houses. The settlement was eventually destroyed by fire.

Europe, which allowed the exploitation of much heavier soils as well as stock breeding (Sherratt, 1994a). For the first time, stock were fully integrated into the food-producing economy and cattle were used for meat, milk, and draft work; sheep were bred as much for wool as for their flesh. At the same time, improved technology in new implements of tillage was fully exploited to achieve a truly effective economic symbiosis between flora and fauna, carefully balancing forest clearance with cultivation and pasturage.

〰 The Scythians and Other Steppe Peoples

The vast rolling grasslands and steppes from China to Ukraine were not settled by farming peoples until they had a culture enabling them to survive in an environment with extreme contrasts of climate and relatively infertile soils. The carrying capacity of the land is such that only a vast territory can support herds of domestic stock. The

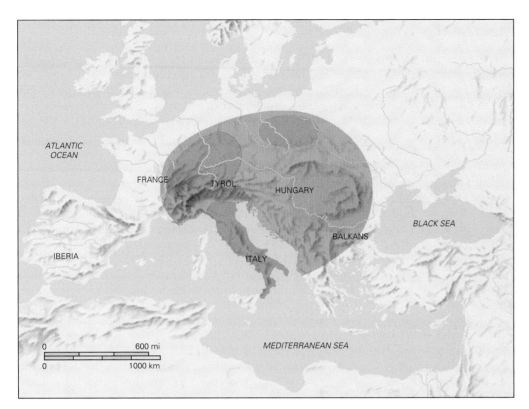

FIGURE 20.10
Approximate distribution of Urnfield cultures in Europe.

prehistory of this huge area is obscure until the first millennium B.C., when the Scythians (from an area in southeast Europe) and other steppe peoples first appeared in the historical record. No one should doubt, however, the importance of nomads in the prehistory of Europe in earlier millennia (Phillips, 1972). The Kurgan people and other possible Indo-European speakers were familiar with the vast open spaces of the steppes.

As early as 4000 B.C., people living at the Dereivka site on Ukraine's Dnieper River were riding horses with rope bits. Their successors roamed the steppes for centuries before the Scythians came out of history's shadows, living in stout felt tents and subsisting mostly on horse's milk and cheese as well as on food from hunting and fishing. The nomadic life, though, leaves few traces in the archaeological record, except when permafrost has preserved burials in a refrigerated state.

Dereivka
4000 B.C.

We are fortunate in having extensive data about the vigorous society of nomad peoples from the spectacular frozen tombs of Siberia. Russian archaeologist Sergei Rudenko (1970) has excavated several nomad burial mounds erected in 400 B.C. at Pazyryk in northeast Siberia. The chiefs of Pazyryk were elaborately tattooed, wore woollen and leather clothes, and employed skillful artists to adorn their horse trappings and harnesses with exuberant and elaborate stylized animal art. A powerful chief was accompanied to the next world by his wife and servants, horses and chariots, and many of his smaller possessions. The Pazyryk burials contain fragments of woven rugs, the earliest examples of such art in the world.

Pazyryk
400 B.C.

The steppe peoples lived to the north of the well-traveled trade routes of Greek merchants, but their territory was constantly being explored and sometimes colonized by farmers whose lands were becoming overpopulated or overgrazed. Enormous areas of steppe were needed to support even a small band of horse riders, for just a slight increase in population could drastically affect the food supplies of the original inhabitants. The result was constant displacement of populations as the nomads sought to expand their shrinking territory to accommodate their own population pressures. The nomads menaced the northern frontiers of the Mediterranean world throughout classical and more recent times.

🐾 The First Ironworking

Late Bronze Age Europeans were effective farmers, traders, and metallurgists capable of exploiting Europe's forested environment far more efficiently than their predecessors could. They lived amid a complicated network of trade that carried not only metals but also salt, grain, gold, pottery, and many other commodities. Their economic organization probably included community smiths, specialists supported by the village, but still no centralized state system of the Southwest Asian type.

Iron

1000 B.C.

These exchange networks facilitated the spread of ironworking techniques across Europe with considerable rapidity after 1000 B.C. In widespread use for both weapons and utilitarian objects by 700 B.C., ironworking is much more difficult than bronze working, for the technology is harder to acquire and takes much longer; however, once it is learned, the advantages of the new metal are obvious. Because the ore is found more widely, the metal is much cheaper and can be used for weapons and utilitarian artifacts as well. These would include axes, hoes, and plowshares, all of which contributed much to agricultural efficiency, higher crop yields, and greater food surpluses. The population increases and intensified trading activities of the centuries immediately preceding the Roman Empire are partly attributed to the success of iron technology in changing European agriculture and craftsmanship (Collis, 1997).

As iron technology spread north of the Alps, new societies arose whose leaders exploited the metal's artistic and economic potentials. The tribal chieftaincy was the structure of government; the most coherent broader political unit was a loose confederacy of tribes formed in time of war or temporarily under the aegis of a charismatic chieftain. Despite the onslaught of Roman colonization and exploitation, culture beyond the frontiers retained its essentially central European cast, an indigenous slant to cultural traditions that began when farming did (Wells, 1981).

Hascherkeller

1000 to 800 B.C.

For all the technological changes, farming life continued much as before. Peter Wells (1984) has excavated an Iron Age farming community near Hascherkeller in lower Bavaria, Germany (Figure 20.11), where he found three enclosed farmsteads. The farmstead complexes included dwellings, barns, sheds, and workshops; between 15 and 30 people lived in each settlement. Occupied between 1000 and 800 B.C., these farmsteads were self-sufficient communities without iron tools. They traded foodstuffs

FIGURE 20.11

Distribution of the Hallstatt Iron Age cultures (shaded area) in Europe during the eighth to fifth centuries B.C.

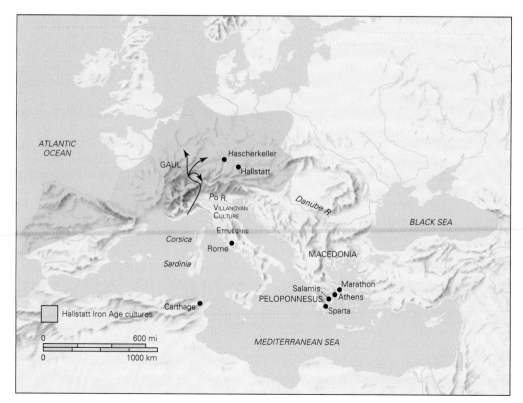

FIGURE 20.12 Bronze ritual cart from a Hallstatt grave in Austria, approximately 0.3 m (1 foot) long. Copper and bronze were still important ornamental metals.

for such items as imported bronze scraps, beads, and graphite, the latter used for pottery decoration. Hascherkeller was apparently without iron, which was still a new metal.

༝༐ The Hallstatt Culture

One strong culture was the Hallstatt, named after a site near Salzburg, Austria (see Figure 20.11) (James, 1992; Wells, 1981). Hallstatt culture began in the eighth and seventh centuries B.C. and owed much to Urnfield practices; the skillful bronze working of earlier times was still practiced, and bronze was still the dominant metal for horse trappings, weapons, and ornaments. Chiefs were buried, some in wagons, in large mounds within wooden chambers (Figure 20.12).

Hallstatt culture
c. 750 B.C.

    The Hallstatt people and their culture spread throughout former Urnfield territories as far north as Belgium and the Netherlands and into France and parts of Spain. Many Hallstatt sites are notable for their fortifications. The Hallstatt people traded with the Mediterranean along well-traveled routes up the Rhone River and through the Alps into central Europe. A significant import was the serving vessel for wine; containers of Mediterranean wine were carried far into central Europe as Hallstatt chieftains discovered wine drinking.

༝༐ La Tène Culture

By the last quarter of the fifth century B.C., a new and highly distinctive technology, La Tène, had developed in the Rhine and Danube valleys (James, 1992; Megaw and Megaw, 1989). An aristocratic clique of chieftains in the Danube Valley enjoyed implements and

La Tène culture
late 4th century B.C.
and later

FIGURE 20.13   Iron Age (Celtic) helmet from the bed of the Thames River in London, 20.5 cm (8.07 inches) at the base. La Tène artistry and bronze and iron technology reached a high state of development in Britain. (Copyright The British Museum.)

weapons elaborately worked in bronze and gold. Much of their sophisticated art had roots in the classical Greek and Mediterranean traditions, for La Tène craftsworkers were quick to adopt new motifs and ideas from the centers of higher civilization to the south. La Tène people spoke Celtic, a language that spread widely through Europe from perhaps as early as the ninth century B.C. Greek and Roman writers referred to these people as *Celts,* a term that has survived in their linguistic label.

La Tène technology was a specific adaptation of ironworking to woodland Europe. The culture extended north into the Low Countries and Britain in the fourth century B.C. (Figure 20.13). La Tène art is deservedly famous, and the hill forts and defensive settlements of this Iron Age culture are widespread in western Europe. The superior military tactics of La Tène people introduced the Romans to the short sword, for Celts sacked Rome in about 390 B.C. The last three centuries before Christ saw considerable change in Europe, with the appearance of coinage, the development of small autonomous states, and the foundation of large settlements known to archaeologists and historians as *oppida,* the Latin word for "towns." Many were fortified and somewhat similar to later towns in medieval Europe. La Tène peoples survived long after France and southern Britain had been conquered by Rome in 55 B.C. (Cunliffe, 1974).

390 B.C.

55 B.C.

Much territory in the temperate zones came under the domination of Rome, an uneasy frontier province that eventually crumbled before the inexorable pressure of the warlike tribes on its boundaries. The illiterate peoples who eventually sacked Rome and ravaged its provinces were the descendants of prehistoric Europeans whose cultural traditions had been evolving ever since the first farming cultures had developed north of the Mediterranean basin.

Summary 〰〰〰

Copper working developed in southeastern Europe by about 4600 B.C., and soon afterward in Spain and northern Italy. The new technology flourished because of a demand for fine metal ornaments. It was a logical outgrowth of earlier stone and ceramic technologies. Its more widespread use coincides with the spread of Beaker and Battle Ax artifacts throughout much of Europe. Bronze working began at an unknown date but was widespread in what is now the Czech Republic by 2000 B.C., as part of the Unetice culture. The trading networks of earlier times expanded to meet the increased indigenous demand for metal artifacts during a period of rapid technological change after 1700 B.C. Some wealthy chieftaincies developed in the temperate zones.

About 1800 B.C., new Urnfield burial customs and more advanced bronze-working techniques spread over much of central and western Europe. These were associated with an intensification of trading activity and greater social ranking, which resulted in an elite warrior class. After 1000 B.C., ironworking techniques spread into temperate Europe and diffused through the Hallstatt and La Tène cultural traditions during the first millennium B.C.

Guide to Further Reading

Champion, Timothy G., et al., eds. 1984. *Prehistoric Europe.* New York: Academic Press.
    A textbook on European prehistory from the earliest times to the expansion of the Roman Empire. Major emphasis on subsistence, trade, and social organization.

Coles, J. M., and A. F. Harding. 1979. *The Bronze Age in Europe.* London: Methuen.
    An authoritative account of the complexities of the European Bronze Age that covers the topic far more fully than we can in this book.

Collis, John. 1997. *The European Iron Age.* London: Routledge.
    A useful introduction to European ironworking cultures.

Cunliffe, Barry, ed. 1994. *The Oxford Illustrated Prehistory of Europe.* Oxford: Oxford University Press.
    This edited volume contains excellent and provocative chapters on later European prehistory.

James, Simon. 1992. *The World of the Celts.* London and New York: Thames & Hudson.
    A beautifully written description of the Celtic world for the general reader. Superb illustrations.

Piggott, Stuart. 1965. *Ancient Europe.* Chicago: Aldine.
    Somewhat outdated. An account of prehistoric Europe that is closer to Childe (1936) than to current evolutionary thinking but is still authoritative, with excellent illustrations.

NATIVE AMERICAN CIVILIZATIONS

2000 B.C. TO A.D. 1534

When yet all was in darkness, when yet no sun had shone and no dawn had broken—it is said—the gods gathered themselves together and took counsel among themselves there in Teotihuacán. They spoke, they said among themselves: "Come hither, O gods! Who will carry the burden? Who will take it upon himself to be the sun, to bring the dawn? . . ."

From an Aztec legend of the Creation, quoted from Anderson and Dibble,

The Florentine Codex (1978)

One of the remarkable phenomena of the human past is the way in which cultural developments unfolded along broadly parallel lines in many parts of the world. Part V describes the brilliant diversity of state-organized societies that flourished in the Americas over a period of more than 3500 years and ends with the arrival of the Spanish conquistadors in Mexico and Peru in the early sixteenth century A.D.

The theoretical literature surrounding the development of states and civilizations in the Americas is as voluminous as that for the Old World. Interested readers are referred to Chapter 14 for general theoretical background relevant to state origins throughout the world.

period
already
covered

period
covered
in this part

partial
coverage

| 5 mya | 2.5 mya | 1 mya | 100,000 B.P. | 10,000 B.C. | A.D. 1 | A.D. 1500 |

MESOAMERICAN CIVILIZATIONS

Maya Lord Shield Jaguar of Yaxchilán, Mexico holds a torch as his wife, Lady Xok, draws blood from her tongue, A.D. 709.

By any standards, New York lawyer-turned-traveler John Lloyd Stephens was a remarkable man. In 1839, he and Scottish artist Frederick Catherwood journeyed deep into the Mesoamerican rain forest, following rumors of vanished civilizations and great ruins masked by primordial jungle. They came first to the tiny modern village of Copán, where "around them lay the dark outlines of ruins shrouded by the brooding forest. The only sound that disturbed the quiet of this buried city was the noise of monkeys moving around among the tops of the trees" (Stephens, 1841, p. 48). While Catherwood drew the intricate hieroglyphs he had found on the Mayan stelae, Stephens tried to buy the ancient city of Copán for 50 dollars so that he could transport it block by block to New York. The deal fell through when he found he could not float the antiquities downstream. Stephens and Catherwood visited Palenque, Uxmal, Chichén Itzá, and other sites. They were the first to recognize the Maya as the builders of these great sites: "These cities . . . are not the works of people who have passed away . . . but of the same great race . . . which still clings around their ruins," Stephens wrote (1841, p. 222). All subsequent research into the Maya and into ancient Mesoamerican civilization has been based on his work. Today, Maya civilization, with its intricate, recently deciphered glyphs and spectacular cities, ranks among the most fascinating in the world. As we shall see in this chapter (Table 21.1), its origins lie deep in prehistory.

 Village Farming

Like other tropical cultivators, the Maya used ancient slash-and-burn farming methods to grow maize and beans (Coe, 2002). Come late fall, the farmer would cut down a patch of forest on well-drained land during the last of the dry season, then burn off the wood and brush. This was a critical time in the farming year, when the air was thick with wood smoke and dust. Great clouds of gray smoke billowed into the washed-out blue sky as the afternoon wind blew fine ash and soot over everything. As the burn subsided, the ash and charcoal fell on the soil. The farmers and their families worked the natural fertilizer into the earth, then planted maize seed in holes poked into the soft ground with a stick. Timing was everything, for planting had to coincide with the first rain showers. Such cleared gardens, called *milpa*, remain fertile for only about two years. The farmer must then move on to a new plot and begin again, leaving the original *milpa* to lie fallow for between four and seven years. When the Maya were purely village farmers, their settlements lay amidst patchwork quilts of newly cleared plots and regenerating land, surrounded by thick

TABLE 21.1

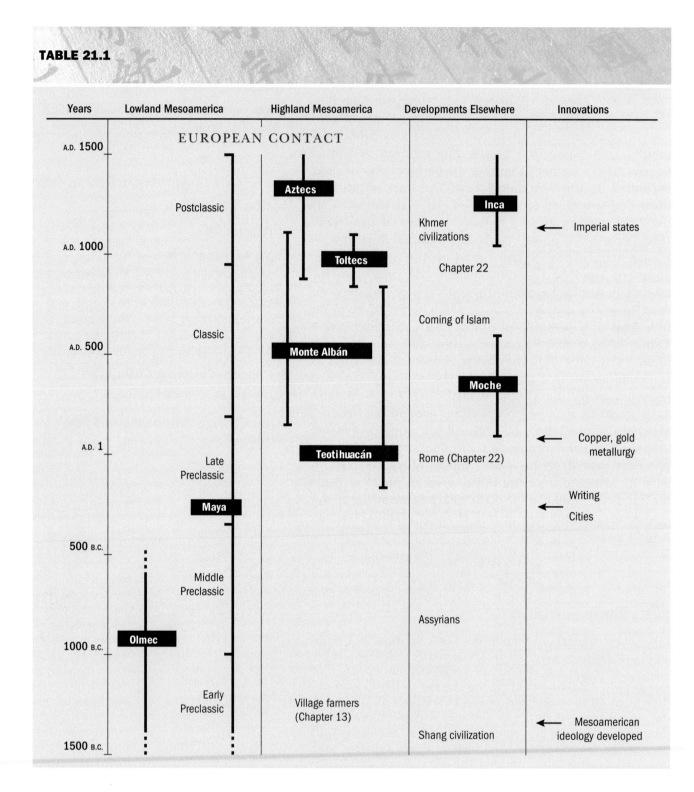

Years	Lowland Mesoamerica	Highland Mesoamerica	Developments Elsewhere	Innovations
		EUROPEAN CONTACT		
A.D. 1500		Aztecs		
	Postclassic		Inca	
A.D. 1000		Toltecs	Khmer civilizations	← Imperial states
			Chapter 22	
A.D. 500	Classic	Monte Albán	Coming of Islam	
			Moche	
A.D. 1		Teotihuacán	Rome (Chapter 22)	← Copper, gold metallurgy
	Late Preclassic			
	Maya			← Writing / Cities
500 B.C.				
	Middle Preclassic			
			Assyrians	
1000 B.C.	Olmec			
	Early Preclassic	Village farmers (Chapter 13)		← Mesoamerican ideology developed
1500 B.C.			Shang civilization	

forest that separated them from their neighbors. But as the farming population rose, expanding communities gradually ate up virgin land.

Slash-and-burn cultivation worked well enough when the Maya farming population was small, but the crop yields were never sufficient to support large settlements. Nor could the stocks of surplus grain feed more than a handful of nonfarmers, such as stone ax makers or priests. However, until the last few centuries before Christ, this simple farming system was the staple of an increasingly complex village society that flourished in a hot, low-lying environment with poor, shallow soils.

In 1972, geographer Albert Siemans and archaeologist Dennis Puleston used aerial photographs to study extensive tracts of wetlands in Mexico's southern Campeche (Adams et al., 1981; Fedick, 1996; Flannery, 1982). They identified irregular grids of gray lines in ladder, lattice, and curvilinear patterns, which turned out to be long-forgotten raised field systems. Most of them were narrow, rectangular plots elevated above the low-lying seasonally inundated land bordering rivers. The Siemans and Puleston research seemed to explain how village farmers had managed to build flourishing cities. The Maya started draining and canalizing swamps at least 2000 years ago, turning agriculturally useless land into highly productive acreage as long as there was ample groundwater. They also began cultivating steep hillsides. The stone-walled terraces rise in serried rows, thereby trapping silt that would otherwise cascade down dry hillsides during torrential rainstorms. Like the heavily cultivated wetlands, the terrace systems were a sign of intensive farming that made use of every patch of fertile land. Some estimates placed the Maya population at between 8 million and 10 million people in A.D. 800, a staggeringly high density for a tropical environment with such low natural carrying capacity.

There are no easy answers to how the Maya managed to support so many nonfarmers in a lowland tropical environment with only moderately fertile soils. Almost certainly, their agricultural systems were under severe stress as urban and rural populations rose during the first millennium A.D.

The Mesoamerican highlands (Figure 21.1) are highly diverse agricultural environments, as we have seen in the Tehuacán Valley (see Chapter 13). The earliest farming villages in the Valley of Oaxaca were concentrated in the valley floors, where water is within easy reach of the surface. Modern farmers choose similar villages for simple "pot" irrigation, where they plant their maize and other crops near small shallow wells. They simply dip pots into the wells and pour water from the shallow water table on the surrounding plants (Flannery, 1976). Flannery has argued that the Oaxacans used the same technique in prehistoric times, for it does not require large numbers of people. In time, as population densities rose, the Oaxacans were able to build on their simple and highly effective farming techniques, expanding onto slopes and into more arid lands with great success. Eventually, the economic power generated by these rising populations gave highland areas like this a decided edge in cultural evolution.

A similar diversity of agricultural techniques is found in the Valley of Mexico, where slash-and-burn methods, dry farming, and irrigation agriculture were all in use. The

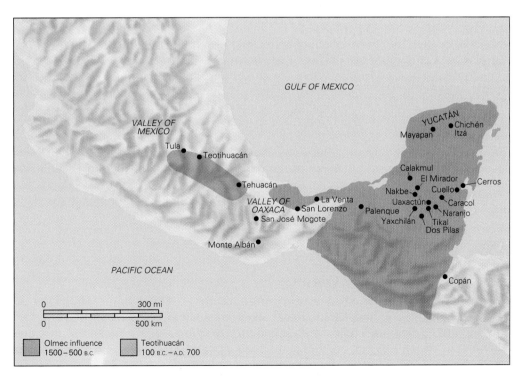

FIGURE 21.1

Mesoamerican archaeological sites mentioned in this chapter. Approximate distributions of two cultural traditions are shown.

farmers used both floodwaters and canals to bring water to dry gardens. The most famous of all raised-field techniques, however, is the *chinampa*, or "floating garden," method, a highly intensive and productive agricultural system based on the reclaiming of swamps. The farmers piled up natural vegetation and lake mud to form huge grids of naturally irrigated gardens. The *chinampas* were used very systematically to grow a variety of crops, so timed that different crops came into harvest throughout the year (Sanders et al., 1970). This system is amazingly productive and is estimated to have supported approximately 100,000 people from 10,117 ha (25,000 acres) in 1519, the date of Spanish contact. Each *chinampa* produced large food surpluses that could be used to feed thousands of nonagricultural workers and specialists. William Sanders and his colleagues (1970) have argued that these *chinampas* could actually have supported approximately 180,000 people. That this highly effective agricultural system was the basis of early civilization and urban life in the Valley of Mexico is beyond question.

The agricultural system of the Valley of Mexico may seem complicated, but it supported and was part of a far more elaborate system of food marketing that provided not only tribute for taxes but also opportunities for the trading of special foodstuffs from one area of the highlands to another. The highland peoples relied on elaborate markets that were strictly regulated by the state and conducted on a barter system. The Valley of Mexico was an economic unit before Teotihuacán made it a political one as well. It was the great agricultural productivity of the valley and the sophisticated market economy of the emerging city that made the prodigious social and religious as well as material developments of later centuries possible. This economic system fostered the development of specialist crafts that were sold in the city markets and exported over wide areas.

𝖜 Preclassic Peoples in Mesoamerica

Early Preclassic

Early Preclassic
1500 to 1000 B.C.

Many centuries elapsed between the beginnings of village life and that of Mesoamerican civilization. By 2000 B.C., sedentary farming villages were common in most of Mesoamerica (Weaver, 1991). The first signs of political and social complexity appear in many regions of Mesoamerica between about 1500 and 1000 B.C., during the early part of an era named the Preclassic or Formative by archaeologists, a period that lasted to as late as A.D. 250 in some areas. In many regions, small but often powerful chiefdoms appeared, headed by a chief and an elite. The elite dominated economic, political, and religious life and ruled over large general populations. A similar pattern of emerging social and political complexity has been documented in Mesopotamia, Egypt, China, and other areas where early state-organized societies evolved.

Cuello
1200 B.C. to A.D. 400

In Mesoamerica, as elsewhere, the new chiefdoms can be identified by differences in house designs, by the appearance of small shrines, by social rankings detectable through grave goods, and by prestigious as opposed to more utilitarian artifacts. This process is well documented at Cuello, in lowland northern Belize, which is radiocarbon-dated to between about 1200 B.C. and A.D. 400 (Hammond, 1991). The inhabitants of this site were maize farmers, who also relied heavily on wild plant foods; their meat came from wild deer and turtles and domestic dogs, killed and eaten after their first year of growth.

There was no one region where this emerging sociopolitical complexity occurred first. Rather, it was a development that took place more or less simultaneously in many regions of Mesoamerica, each region interacting with others (Sharer and Grove, 1989). The most famous of these societies is that of the Olmec.

Middle Preclassic: The Olmec

Middle Preclassic
1000 to 400 B.C.

Olmec civilization
1500 to 500 B.C.

The Olmec people lived on the Mexican southern Gulf Coast from about 1500 to 500 B.C. (I. Bernal, 1969; Coe and Diehl, 1980). Their homeland is low-lying, tropical, and humid, with fertile soils. The swamps, lakes, and rivers are rich in fish, birds, and other animals. It was in this region that the Olmec created a highly distinctive art style, executed in sculpture and in relief. The artists concentrated on natural and supernatural beings, the dominant motif being the "were-jaguar," or humanlike jaguar. Many jaguars were given infantile faces, drooping lips, and large, swollen eyes, a style also applied to human figures, some of which resemble snarling demons. Olmec contributions to Mesoamerican art and religion were enormously significant. For years, scholars have believed that elements of their art style and imagery were diffused southward to Guatemala and El Salvador and northward into the Valley of Mexico.

San Lorenzo.   The origins of the Olmec are a complete mystery, but the culture probably had strong local roots. The earliest traces of Olmec occupation are best documented at San Lorenzo in the Mexican state of Veracruz, where Olmec people lived on a platform in the midst of frequently inundated woodland plains. Around their platform, they erected ridges and mounds, on which they built pyramids and possibly ball courts and placed elaborate monumental carvings overlooking the site. The earliest occupation of San Lorenzo shows few Olmec features, but by 1250 B.C., the inhabitants were beginning to build some raised fields, a task that required organized labor forces. By that time, too, distinctive Olmec sculpture began to appear. A century later, magnificent monumental carvings adorned San Lorenzo (Figure 21.2), distinctive and often mutilated by the Olmec themselves, perhaps when rulers died.

San Lorenzo
1250 to 900 B.C.

The population of San Lorenzo may have numbered 2500 people (Coe and Diehl, 1980). The inhabitants enjoyed extensive trade, especially in obsidian and other semiprecious materials obtained from many parts of Mesoamerica. San Lorenzo fell into decline after 900 B.C. and was surpassed by La Venta, the most famous Olmec site, nearer the Gulf of Mexico.

La Venta.   The La Venta ceremonial center was built on a small island in the middle of a swamp (Drucker, 1959). A rectangular earth mound, 120 m (393 feet) long by 70 m (229 feet) wide and 32 m (105 feet) high, dominates the island. Long, low mounds surround a rectangular plaza in front of the large mound, faced by walls and terraced mounds at the other end of the plaza (Figure 21.3). Vast monumental stone sculptures and altars litter the site, including some Olmec heads bearing expressions of contempt

La Venta
800 to 400 B.C.

FIGURE 21.2 Monumental Olmec head from San Lorenzo.

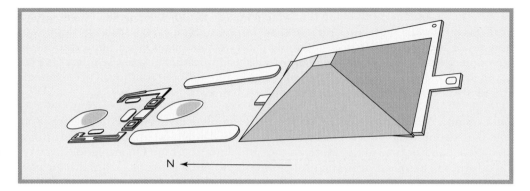

FIGURE 21.3 La Venta, Site 4: Layout of the major structures.

and savagery (Figure 21.4). Caches of jade objects, figurines, and a dull green rock (serpentine) are common, too. Every stone for sculptures and temples had to be brought from at least 96 km (60 miles) away, a vast undertaking, for some sculptured blocks weigh more than 40 tons. The people traded ceremonial jade and serpentine from as far away as Costa Rica. La Venta flourished for approximately 400 years from 800 B.C. After approximately 400 B.C., the site was probably destroyed; we deduce this occurrence from signs that many of its finest monuments were intentionally defaced.

San Lorenzo and La Venta, with their relatively small populations, are manifestations of a much more complex social and political order, not in the fashion of a state-organized society, as earlier scholars suggested, but a series of chiefdoms with powerful leaders who maintained contacts with other such societies in the lowlands and perhaps farther afield (Diehl, 1989). For years, scholars thought of the Olmec as the "mother culture" of Mesoamerican civilization. Increasingly, however, this theory is being questioned (Sharer and Grove, 1989).

Arthur Demarest (1989) points out that Olmec society changed over the centuries. At first, during the early Preclassic, it was a set of chiefdoms along the Gulf Coast of Veracruz and Tabasco that may have exercised some influence over adjacent areas of Chiapas and central Mexico. Later, during the middle Preclassic, Olmec society flourished during a period when art motifs, religious symbols, and ritual beliefs were shared by developing chiefdoms in many regions through the regular contacts between elites and day-to-day trade from region to region (for ancient Mexican religion, see Miller and Taube, 1993). It was what Demarest calls a "lattice of Middle Formative interaction" over many centuries that produced the complex and sophisticated traditions of

FIGURE 21.4 Olmec altar from La Venta, Mexico. A sculpted ruler emerges from a symbolic cave.

Mesoamerican civilization that were to follow. Another archaeologist, Kent Reilly (1991), has coined the term "Formative Ceremonial Complex" to describe the Olmec phenomenon. He believes that Olmec kingship was antecedent to, and basically similar to, that of the lowland Maya.

Late Preclassic

The trajectory of rapid cultural change continued in many regions during the late Preclassic (300 B.C. to A.D. 250). This was the period when a common religious system and ideology began to unify large areas of Mesoamerica. The leaders of the new orders validated their rule with elaborate public ceremonies in spectacular ceremonial centers, dedicated to potent and widely recognized deities. Distinctive art and architecture went with the new religion, the practice of which required precise measurements of calendar years and of longer cycles of time. Writing and mathematical calculations were developed to affirm religious practices, a unifying political force in the sense that they welded scattered village communities into larger political units. By the time the Classic Mesoamerican civilizations arose, dynasties of elites had been ruling parts of Mesoamerica along well-established lines for nearly 1000 years (Sabloff, 1989; Sharer, 1995).

🙵 The Rise of Complex Society in Oaxaca

The Preclassic cultures of the Valley of Oaxaca have been studied intensively by Kent Flannery, Joyce Marcus, and their students, using highly sophisticated systems approaches to document changing settlement patterns and economic and demographic trends (Marcus and Flannery, 1996). Something like 90 percent of the Preclassic Oaxaca villages were little more than hamlets of 50 to 60 people, and the remainder were much larger settlements of 1000 to 1200, with populations of priests and craftspeople.

The evolution of larger settlements in Oaxaca and elsewhere was closely connected with the development of long-distance trade in obsidian and other luxuries such as seashells and stingray spines from the Gulf of Mexico. The simple barter networks for obsidian of earlier times evolved into sophisticated regional trading organizations in which village leaders controlled monopolies over sources of obsidian and its distribution. Magnetite mirrors, seashells, feathers, and ceramics were all traded in the highlands, and from the highlands to the lowlands as well. Olmec pottery and other ritual objects began to appear in highland settlements between 1150 and 650 B.C., many of them bearing the distinctive were-jaguar motif of the lowlands, which had an important place in Olmec cosmology.

To Joyce Marcus and Kent Flannery (1996), the defining moment in the Valley of Oaxaca was between 1200 and 1150 B.C., during the so-called San José phase, named after a large site, San José Mogote. They draw analogies between what happened in Oaxaca and a model for the emergence of ranked societies in Southeast Asian villages developed by anthropologist Jonathan Friedman (1979).

San José Mogote
1200 to 1150 B.C.

Friedman describes egalitarian villages composed of lineages of equal prestige, each community associated with a *nat,* or village spirit, the remote ancestor of all lineages who owns the village land. Originally, according to this model, all lineages share equal responsibility in sponsoring feasts and other community activities, but in time, one harder-working lineage acquires enough resources to become the permanent sponsor. Public opinion supports this move, for this particular lineage is seen as having an especially close association with the *nat*—indeed, as being directly descended from it. The leader of this lineage eventually becomes a hereditary ruler, who serves as a mediator between the community and the supernatural. Eventually, individual villages lose autonomy and become part of larger regional entities as the new rulers enter into alliances with neighbors and become associated with the highest ranks of celestial spirits, who control much larger areas.

Marcus and Flannery (1996) point out that what appear to be images of celestial ancestors of human lineages were carved on pottery from San José Mogote and contemporary villages (Figure 21.5, left). They believe that these images reflect an ancient belief in the power of Earth and Sky, which could express anger in the forms of

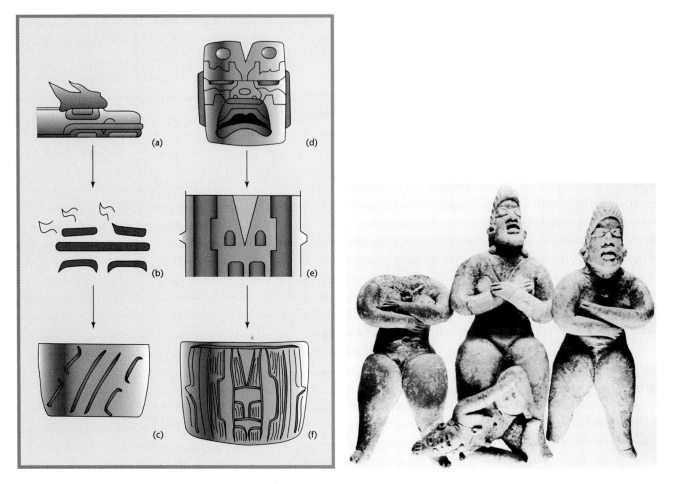

FIGURE 21.5 Social ranking appears in the Valley of Oaxaca. Left, evolution of stylized lightning and earthquake motifs in pottery of the San José phase: Panels (a) to (c) show lightning as a realistic "fire serpent" and its stylization into a symbol found on a carved vessel; panels (d) to (f) show earthquake as a realistic "cleft-head" mask and a similar stylistic progression to a carved and incised vessel. Right, ritual scene composed of four clay figurines from San José Mogote, which may represent the burial of a high-status individual with three retainers; buried under an early Preclassic house at San José Mogote. Height of largest figurine: 16 cm (6 inches).

earthquakes and lightning. Judging from male burials, Earth and Sky appear to be associated with male descent groups in some villages of the San José phase, some even with infant graves, as if such association and status were inherited. In burials and middens at San José Mogote itself, different residential areas appear to be associated with Earth and Sky. Finds of *mat* motifs on San José pottery, as well as on models of four-footed stools, later to become symbols of rulership, appear to confirm the appearance of social ranking and status by 1150 B.C.

Public buildings now appear in villages such as San José Mogote. Many of them were oriented 8 degrees west of north; they were built on adobe and earth platforms. Conch shell trumpets and turtle shell drums from the Gulf of Mexico are associated with these buildings, as are clay figurines of dancers wearing costumes and masks (Figure 21.5, right). There were marine fish spines, too, probably used in personal bloodletting ceremonies that were still practiced even in Aztec times. The Spanish described how Aztec nobles would gash themselves with knives or with the spines of fish or stingrays in acts of mutilation before the gods, penances required of the devout (Saunders, 1989). The diffusion of common art styles throughout Mesoamerica may have resulted both because of an increased need for religious rituals to bring the various elements of society together and because a new Oaxacan elite, aspiring to the status of their chiefly neighbors, took to the new beliefs in slavish conformity.

𖤲 Monte Albán

By 400 B.C., there were at least seven small polities in the Valley of Oaxaca, of which the one centered at the growing city of Monte Albán soon became dominant. Although massive population growth and increased economic power were among the interacting factors that aided in the rise of Monte Albán, its special terrain may have been vital in its ascendancy (Blanton and others, 1999; Marcus and Flannery, 1996).

Richard Blanton has surveyed more than 2000 terraces on the slopes of Monte Albán, terraces used for agriculture and housing areas. Monte Albán commanded the best terrain in the valley, sloping land that was organized for agriculture and dense settlement by a population of several thousand people, far larger than that of most major settlements in Mesoamerica at the time. Even as early as 400 B.C., some of the terraces were in use by a highly organized population whose leaders resided in a ceremonial and civic center built on the summit of the Monte Albán ridge. Although the large-scale buildings of later times have contoured the summit beyond recognition, it is clear that the first leaders to live there undertook major public works, many of them wood and thatch buildings that had incised sculptures of what may be dead and tortured enemies set into the walls.

Monte Albán went on to develop into a vast ceremonial center with splendid public architecture; its settlement area included public buildings, terraces, and housing zones that extended over approximately 40 sq km (15 square miles) (Figure 21.6). The more than 2000 terraces held one or two houses, and small ravines were dammed to pond valuable water supplies. Perhaps 16,500 people lived at Monte Albán itself between A.D. 200 and 700. Many very large villages and smaller hamlets lay within easy distance of the city; the entire Valley of Oaxaca had about 115,000 inhabitants (Marcus and Flannery, 1996). The enormous platforms on the ridge of Monte Albán supported complex layouts of temples and pyramid-temples, palaces, patios, and tombs. A hereditary elite seems to have ruled Monte Albán, the leaders of a state that had emerged in the Valley of Oaxaca by A.D. 200. Their religious power was based on ancestor worship, a pantheon of at least 39 gods, grouped around major themes of ritual life. The rain god and lightning were associated with the jaguar motif; another group of deities was linked with the maize god, Pitao Cozabi. Nearly all these gods were still worshiped at the time of Spanish contact, although Monte Albán itself was abandoned after A.D. 700, at approximately the same time as another great ceremonial center, Teotihuacán in the Valley of Mexico, began to decline.

Monte Albán
400 B.C. to A.D. 700

FIGURE 21.6 Monte Albán, Valley of Oaxaca, a major Mesoamerican city that was a rival to Teotihuacán in the middle of the first millennium A.D.

ᨡ Teotihuacán

We have already referred to the Valley of Mexico as an economic unit, a network of markets that probably flourished long before large states came into being in the highlands. Perhaps the sequence of events that led to the founding of such polities, especially Teotihuacán, began with the buildup of agricultural populations in diverse environments such as the Valley of Oaxaca in the first and second millennia B.C. This population growth led to the development of more intensive agricultural methods, including both irrigation and *chinampa* systems. At the same time, different areas were linked by increasingly sophisticated trading networks and by an emerging market economy, perhaps with some specialized merchants.

Religious activity was stimulated by the introduction of beliefs and sacred objects from the lowlands. Trade in exotic luxuries increased as ceremonial centers and stratified societies were founded. By 200 B.C., the effects of increased religious activity, intensified trading, and the production of huge food surpluses from the diverse environment had led to the founding of at least two major cities in the Valley of Mexico. One of these, Teotihuacán, reached an enormous size and enjoyed vast political, economic, and religious power in the centuries that followed. In the Valley of Oaxaca, Monte Albán achieved a similar dominance. The two great states probably maintained an uneasy alliance through regular diplomatic exchanges (Marcus and Flannery, 1996).

Teotihuacán
200 B.C. to A.D. 750

Teotihuacán lies northeast of Mexico City and is now one of the great archaeological tourist attractions of the world. It was one of the dominant political and cultural centers of all Mesoamerica in approximately A.D. 500, the culmination of centuries of vigorous cultural development in the Valley of Mexico (Berrin and Pasztory, 1994; Millon, Drewitt, and Cowgill, 1974; Pasztory, 1997; Storey, 1992). The first buildings appeared at Teotihuacán in approximately 200 B.C., making up a handful of villages, at least one of which may have specialized in obsidian manufacture. By 100 B.C., Teotihuacán had begun to expand rapidly, and the scattered villages became a settlement covering more than 9 sq km (3.5 square miles). Much of this early settlement is covered by the vast structures of later times. It is estimated that 600 people inhabited this early town. There were several public buildings.

René Millon (1996), who carried out a systematic survey of Teotihuacán, found that by A.D. 150, the city extended over 13 sq km (5 square miles) and housed more than 20,000 people. Obsidian trade and manufacture were expanding fast. There were two major religious complexes for which, among other structures, the Pyramids of the Sun and of the Moon were first built at this time.

Between A.D. 150 and 600, Teotihuacán exploded in size. Anyone traversing the Valley of Mexico had to pass through the city, with its diverse population of priests, merchants, craftspeople, and other specialists. The rulers of the city erected hundreds of standardized apartment complexes and continued a master plan that laid out the city on a north-south axis, centered on the Street of the Dead (Figure 21.7), with another great avenue oriented east-west. The city consisted of avenues and plazas, markets, temples, palaces, apartment buildings, and complex drainage and agricultural works. The entire city was dominated by the Pyramid of the Sun, a vast structure of earth, adobe, and piled rubble. The pyramid, faced with stone, is 64 m (210 feet) high and 1098 m (650 feet) square. A wooden temple probably sat on the summit of the terraced pyramid. The long Street of the Dead passes the west face of the pyramid, leading to the Pyramid of the Moon, the second largest structure at the site. The avenue is lined with civic, palace, and religious buildings, and the side streets lead to residential areas. A large palace and temple complex dedicated to the Plumed Serpent (Quetzalcoatl), with platform and stairways around the central court, lies south of the middle of Teotihuacán, across from a central marketplace. More than 200 burials of retainers lie inside (Figures 21.8a and b).

The Street of the Dead and the pyramids lie amid a sprawling mass of small houses. Priests and craftsworkers lived in dwellings around small courtyards; the less privileged lived in large compounds of rooms connected by narrow alleyways and patios. By any standard, Teotihuacán was a city, and it once housed up to 120,000 people. Although some farmers probably lived within the city, we know that rural villages flourished nearby. These were compact, expertly planned, and administered by city rulers.

FIGURE 21.7
Teotihuacán, looking
down from the Pyramid of
the Moon along the
Street of the Dead.

The comprehensive settlement-pattern data from the Millon survey enable us to say
something about the structure of Teotihuacán society. Farmers living in the city and in
satellite villages produced the food surpluses that supported the city. Tribute from
neighboring states also helped feed the city, and control of large areas of the plateau
ensured that adequate food supplies would come to Teotihuacán's huge market. It is
not known how significant *chinampa* agriculture was for Teotihuacán, but irrigation
farming was a key element in subsistence. Craftspeople accounted for perhaps 25 percent of the urban population; they lived in compounds of apartments near the more
than 500 workshops, which produced everything from obsidian tools to clay vessels.

Merchants were probably a major class in the city, as were civil servants, who carried
out the routine administration of Teotihuacán. There were even foreign quarters, one of
which housed Oaxacans and another people from Vera Cruz in the lowlands (Paddock,
1983; Price et al., 2000). The elite included priests, warriors, and secular leaders, who
controlled the vast city and its many dealings through a strict class society. Religious
beliefs continued the rituals of earlier times, but it appears that cannibalism and human
sacrifice became increasingly prominent in later centuries as the leaders of the city
became more and more militaristic, a trend that was to continue into Aztec times.

Teotihuacán ruled the Valley of Mexico and parts of Puebla, but its influence
through alliance, tribute, and warfare, as well as trading, extended over a far larger
area of Mesoamerica. As in later times, the rulers of Teotihuacán probably controlled
some highly strategic and economically significant zones, but there were large areas
where their influence was minimal. In the final analysis, Teotihuacán was probably a
huge city-state bound to other city-states by uneasy alliances and tribute exchanges.

By A.D. 600, a secular ruler probably governed Teotihuacán, probably a divine king
of some kind. A class of nobles controlled the kinship groups that organized the bulk
of the city's huge population. In approximately A.D. 650, Teotihuacán was deliberately
burned down, perhaps as a result of internal revolt and outside intervention (Millon,
1988). The very success of Teotihuacán may have accelerated its downfall. The new
orders of society and politics spawned by the city may have been copied by other leaders, perhaps more aggressive and less tradition-bound than those of the mother city.
No one knows exactly why this great city collapsed so suddenly. Its rapid development
may have resulted in serious internal weaknesses that made Teotihuacán vulnerable to
easy overthrow. A drought may also have weakened the city and provided an opportunity for jealous rivals to attempt an attack. Whatever the precise cause, by A.D. 700 the
city's population scattered into a few villages. Much of the formerly urban population

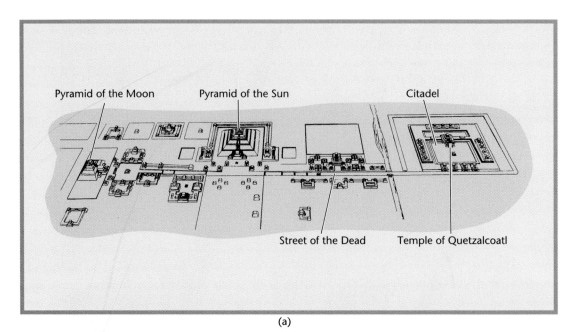

(a)

(b)

FIGURE 21.8 (a) Plan of the major public buildings at Teotihuacán. (b) Facade of the Temple of Quetzalcoatl at Teotihuacán, Mexico, showing a head of the rain god Tlaloc.

settled in neighboring regions, which thereby reaped the benefit of Teotihuacán's misfortunes.

Whatever the cause of Teotihuacán's collapse, its heyday marks the moment when one can begin to think of the Mesoamerican world in more than purely local, and even regional, terms. Teotihuacán's political and social influence was considerable, and its traders ventured to many parts of the highlands and lowlands. For example, the ways in which Maya kings went to war were profoundly affected by the military practices and war-making rituals of Teotihuacán. The greatest legacy of Teotihuacán was not merely its cosmology, ideology, and trade networks but a new interconnectedness between the many societies of prehistoric Mesoamerica.

Joyce Marcus (1976) points to the remarkable similarity in the ways in which Mesoamerican states rose, reached their peak, and then collapsed. She notes a consistent scenario in both the lowlands and the highlands, not only in Maya civilization but at Monte Albán and Teotihuacán and in the Toltec and Aztec civilizations in the highlands: First, a new city-state—say, Maya Tikal or Teotihuacán—expanded its territory through diplomacy, political marriages, and military conquest. This new city-state reached its maximum territorial limits early in its history. Then, once some provinces had reached a significant level of cultural complexity and development, they broke away from their nominal master and became independent polities. Far from being weakened, the core city-state still prospered, investing its energy and resources in its own local area rather than in expansion. But sometimes the old provinces, now independent states, would ally themselves against their former overlord and conquer it, so that it then became a subordinate center. This cycle of rise, expansion on the margins, fissioning, and then decline repeated itself again and again, to the point where it can be considered a consistent pattern of Mesoamerican civilization.

𝔐 Maya Civilization

The Maya civilization is the best known of all early American civilizations, one that has excited the imagination of scholars for more than a century. It took shape in lowland rain forest areas that provided a highly varied environment in which people grew maize and other crops and harvested trees, such as the ramon.

Maya civilization
300 B.C. to A.D. 1519

Maya Origins

Although the ultimate roots of Maya culture go back far into the Preclassic period, considerable debate surrounds the origins of Maya civilization, partly because until recently virtually nothing was known about Maya subsistence patterns (Coe, 1999). Perhaps the initial Maya settlement was dispersed, with villages scattered throughout the rain forest, in situations that seemed to militate against political or economic unity. The people flourished in a fundamentally empty landscape where there was plenty of room for slash-and-burn agriculture and little incentive for cooperation. Their predecessors were hunter-gathers, small groups occupying tiny campsites, who made no pottery. One such Archaic camp is known from the Colha site in Belize, in a level overlaid by farming occupation that dates to later than 900 B.C. (Hester et al., 1982). Early farming settlement at Cuello dates to the late second millennium B.C. (Hammond, 1991). It is not known whether the Colha and Cuello sites represent the changeover from hunting and gathering to farming in this part of the lowlands, but a date of around 1500 to 1200 B.C. would not be unexpected.

The earliest certain Maya communities come from the middle Preclassic (1000 to 400 B.C.). During this period, large numbers of farmers moved into the lowlands, bringing with them settled village life, the use of fine clay vessels, and domesticated plants. The Maya were well established in the Yucatán by 800 B.C., and they were constructing massive pyramids at several sites in the central Petén by 600 B.C. No one has yet accounted for this rapid buildup, but there are reasons to suspect that it was connected with a growing demand for such lowland products as honey and salt by elites elsewhere. A growing volume of long-distance exchange contributed, then, to an efflorescence of indigenous lowland civilization within a few centuries.

At the same time, ancestral burial within platforms and the cores of other structures took hold as a persistent pattern of interment, as opposed to merely burying people under their houses. This changeover represented the sanctification of an ancestral place, where ancestors were venerated, as a basis for reckoning genealogy and claiming ownership of places. In other words, ancestor veneration was a way of structuring the inheritance of property and resources from one generation to the next (see a discussion in McAnany, 1995).

Between 600 and 400 B.C., the middle Preclassic inhabitants of Nakbe were constructing elaborate complexes of finely finished stone buildings that stood on huge platforms (Coe, 1999). Within a few centuries they began erecting carved stelae that are thought to depict the center's rulers. Certainly by late Preclassic times, the lords of Nakbe were commissioning for their pyramids beautiful masonry and plaster masks of the gods and ancestors. These facades seem to relate directly to the emerging notion

Nakbe
600 to 400 B.C.

of divine kingship, *Ch'ul Ahau*, in Maya civilization, a form of kingship that between 600 and 100 B.C. developed rapidly out of some earlier form of central authority (Freidel and Schele, 1988). Another site of the same general antiquity, Uaxactún, has yielded images of kings with deity masks wearing the Jester God crown of kingship.

El Mirador
150 B.C. to A.D. 50

By far the largest Preclassic Maya center is El Mirador, which was built between about 150 B.C. and A.D. 50. El Mirador covered about 16 sq km (6 square miles) lying on low, undulating land; parts of the area were flooded during the rainy season. The scale of El Mirador is vast, and it bears all the complicated iconography associated with Maya kingship. Archaeologists from Brigham Young University have uncovered more than 200 structures; among them are great complexes of pyramids, plazas, causeways, and buildings (Matheny, 1986; Sabloff, 1990).

The Danta Pyramid at the east end of the site dominates El Mirador. It rises from a natural hill more than 70 m (210 feet) high. The western face of the hill is sculpted into large platforms that are surmounted by buildings and temples. A little over 2 km (1 mile) west rises the Tigre complex, a pyramid 55 m (182 feet) high surrounded by a plaza, a small temple, and several smaller buildings (Figure 21.9). The Tigre complex covers about 58,000 sq m (624,000 square feet)—an area a little larger than the base of Teotihuacán's Pyramid of the Sun. Three buildings, the largest in the center, are on a truncated landing on the pyramid. This "triad" theme is also found at later sites, such as Tikal.

FIGURE 21.9

(a) El Mirador, Petén: Reconstruction of the Tigre complex of buildings and platforms. The entire complex dates to the Preclassic period, c. 100 B.C. to A.D. 50. (b) Archaeologists at work on the Tigre Temple, El Mirador. The building and mask date to the late Preclassic period.

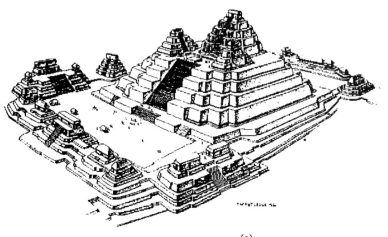

(a)

(b)

El Mirador is unique because it was not altered in any significant way after the Preclassic period. As excavations proceed, it should be possible to compare Preclassic with Classic occupation and to study the evolution of Maya architecture, city planning, and social and political organization. El Mirador is yielding some of the earliest examples of Maya writing. They appear on an inscribed pot fragment, and some symbols are inscribed on the Tigre sculpture.

El Mirador itself was an elaborate city and was probably controlled by a highly organized elite. They used artisans, priests, architects, and engineers, as well as traders and thousands of unskilled villagers. This stupendous city flourished successfully for centuries before it suddenly collapsed in the early Christian era. The dynamics of this collapse are little understood but are mirrored by other Preclassic Maya communities, where the institution of kingship arose and was then apparently abandoned. The volatility of many centers may have been connected to endemic warfare, but despite this constant change, many centers, among them Tikal and Uaxactún, developed continuously into Classic times.

In 50 B.C., the small late Preclassic town of Cerros on the eastern coast of the Yucatán housed fisherfolk and traders. Within two generations, this tiny community transformed itself into a large center. The village disappeared under plazas and temples, deliberately abandoned in favor of houses erected around the new sacred center. The unknown leaders of Cerros built their new temple according to pyramid designs that had developed among earlier peoples like the Olmec, designs that invoked a symbolic landscape in which religious activity took place (Schele and Freidel, 1990). Everyone in the community shared in the communal labor of building the sacred mountain, a gateway to the Otherworld that was very important in Maya religion. It was a symbolic act that acknowledged the arrival of kingship in the community. The first temple at Cerros was followed by later shrines, the settings for the ritual bloodlettings and sacrifices that served to legitimize the roles of the emerging nobility and of the leader. Kingship flourished at Cerros for a short time and then collapsed, for reasons that are still a mystery. Perhaps there were problems in transferring power from one generation to the next, or perhaps the experiment simply failed, as it did in other Maya communities of the day. In any event, the great temples fell into disuse, but people still lived around the ruined structures, living off fishing and trade.

Cerros
50 B.C.

Kingship: Sacred Space and Time

The leaders of Cerros and other Preclassic Maya communities are now anonymous. They left no record of their names or personal histories. Their only legacy to their successors was a distinctive architectural heritage that stressed social ranking and the use of large-scale structures to perpetuate royal dynasties. The rituals performed by these shaman-lords took place on the pyramids and in the plazas of the great Maya centers, which were symbolic replicas of the sacred landscape created by the gods at the beginning of the world. The architecture of the great ritual structures replicated forests, mountains, and caves as stelae, pyramids, and temple openings. The rituals were powerful, so powerful that the places where they were conducted became more and more sacred as successive rulers built new temples on the same spots. Generations of rulers replicated the iconography and sculpture of earlier buildings, elaborating on them to produce the sacred settings within which the strategies of political competition between neighbors were carried out (Miller and Taube, 1993).

Maya civilization was also embedded in a matrix of unfolding cyclic time. Maya priests used the movements of planets and stars to mark the passage of time. They tried to understand the cycles of the cosmos, deciding which days were propitious for ritual, trade, royal marriages, war, and so on. Religious events were regulated according to a sacred year (*tzolkin*) with 13 months of 20 days each (see Figures 21.10a and b). The 260 days of the sacred year were unrelated to any astronomical phenomenon, being closely tied to ritual and divination. The length of this year was arbitrary and had probably been established by long tradition. Tzolkins were, however, closely intermeshed with a secular year (*haab*) of 365 days, an astronomical calendar based on the solar cycle. The *haab* was used to regulate state affairs, but the connections between sacred and secular years were of great significance in Maya life. Every 52 years, a complete

(a)

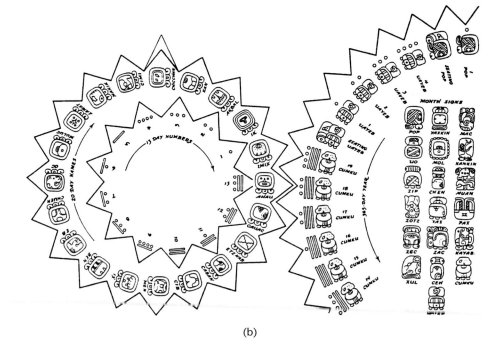

FIGURE 21.10 The Maya calendar. (a) A Venus calendar depicted on stone tablets with glyphs, mythological figures, warriors, and gods. (b) The Maya calendar comprised two interlocking cycles. The left wheel is the 260-day *tzolkin*, the sacred calendar with 13 numbers (inner wheel) and 20 day names (outer wheel). The right-hand wheel is the *haab*, or secular cycle, with 20 months of 18 days each.

(b)

cycle of all the variations of the day and month names of the two calendars occurred, an occasion for intense religious activity.

The calendar was vital to Maya life, for the complex geography of sacred time helped determine political strategies and social moves. The records kept by Maya scribes in hieroglyphic codices (books) were incredibly intricate records of divine actions on each day of the cyclic calendar (Figure 21.10a). Each day had a character, a distinctive identity in the *tzolkin* and *haab*, and a position in all the permutations of cyclic time (Figure 21.10b). Each Maya king developed a relationship to this constantly moving time scale. Some events, like planting and harvest, were regular events on the calendar. Others, like dates of accession, important victories, and royal deaths and births, left their marks on the calendar, sometimes as days that assumed great significance in the history of an individual dynasty. Maya rulers linked their actions to those of the gods and the ancestors, sometimes legitimizing their descent by claiming that it reenacted mythical events. Maya history was linked to the present and the Otherworld, to the legendary Olmec civilization of the past. Society was embedded in a matrix of sacred place and time (Schele and Freidel, 1990; Schele, Freidel, and Parker, 1993).

The Maya developed a hieroglyphic script for calculating calendars and regulating religious observances (Coe, 1992). The script was also much used to record genealogies, king lists, conquests, and dynastic histories. The symbols are fantastically grotesque, consisting mostly of humans, monsters, or god's heads (Figure 21.11). After more than a decade of intensive research, over half the extant Classic inscriptions have been deciphered. In its emphasis on religious and cosmological matters, Maya writing is closest to ancient Egyptian script in terms of its role in society.

These hieroglyphic records were of cardinal importance in Maya life, for the institution of kingship was based on the principle that the royal crown passed from father to son, or brother to brother to son, in a line that led back to a founding ancestor. From there, families and clans were carefully ranked by their distance from the central royal descent line. This system of family ranking and allegiance was the basis of political power, a system that worked well but that depended on a careful documentation of genealogies.

The Maya prized social status above almost everything else, as we can see at the great center of Copán, a major frontier capital of the Maya world at the edge of the Central American chiefdoms. Its pyramids, temples, and stelae are a remarkable record of Maya kings exercising political and social power. Although cosmology was a feature of Copán's building designs, the main function of the civic structures there, as elsewhere, was to commemorate major events in the lives of kings and the political histories of

FIGURE 21.11 Maya glyphs. Left, the Leiden Plate, a jade plaque that shows a Maya lord trampling a captive underfoot. Right, the reverse side shows the Long Count (the Maya count of years) date in glyphs: 8.14.3.1.12, a day in the year A.D. 320. Height: 21.6 cm (8.5 inches).

kingdoms. Each building was dedicated by the king who built it in the context of a specific event, everything from a royal accession to an important victory or a new alliance. Among its many buildings, Copán features a ball court, a stadium used for an elaborate ceremonial contest in which sacrificial victims and kings descended through a symbolic "abyss" into the Otherworld. The players wore protective padding and used a rubber ball, which perhaps they aimed at markers—sometimes stone rings or macaw heads high on the side walls. We do not know the rules of this ball game, but the games were associated with human sacrifice and much pomp and circumstance.

By combining archaeological excavation at Copán with historical art interpretation and text translations, scholars have been able to trace a lineage of nobles who specialized in hieroglyphic writing, a skill that gave them special prestige (Fash, 1991). Members of another noble rank, the *sahalob* (vassals), served as expert administrators and received many privileges for their skill. Status was inherited and was one way in which the legitimacy of society as a whole was maintained.

Copán is just one of many sites where archaeologists have documented the complicated political and social history of Maya civilization. The public monuments erected by the Classic Maya emphasize not only the king's role as shaman, as the intermediary with the Otherworld, but also his position as family patriarch. Genealogical texts on stelae legitimized his descent, his close relationship to his often long-deceased parents. Maya kings used both the awesome regalia of their office and elaborate rituals to stress their close identity with mythical ancestral gods. This was a way in which the kings asserted their kin relationship to and political authority over subordinate leaders and every member of society.

The king believed himself to have a divine covenant with the gods and ancestors, a covenant that was reinforced again and again in elaborate private and public rituals. The ruler was often depicted as the World Tree, the conduit by which humans communicated with the Otherworld. Trees were the living environment of Maya life and a metaphor for human power. So the kings of the Maya were a forest of symbolic human World Trees within a natural forested landscape.

The Maya calendar ensured a constant round of ceremonies and rituals at the great ceremonial centers erected by the labor of hundreds of people, farmers who also fed the kings, priests, and artisans. Yet the Maya worldview created serious and binding obligations among the king and his nobility and all the people, reflected in the king's responsibilities in gathering and redistributing commodities of all kinds and in implementing agricultural schemes that turned swamps into organized, productive landscapes. The lives of Maya rulers and all their subjects were interconnected in vital, dynamic ways. The king was state shaman, the individual who enriched everyone's life in spiritual and ceremonial ways. His success in organizing trade and agriculture gave all levels of society access to goods and commodities. The great ceremonial centers built by Maya leaders created a setting in which elaborate rituals and ceremonies took on intense significance. The "histories written and pictured by the kings on the tree stones standing before human-made mountains gave form to time and space in both the material and spiritual worlds" (Schele and Freidel, 1990, p. 319).

Political Organization

Maya civilization was far from uniform. It appears to have been a mosaic of political units, large and small, and it is difficult to be specific about the political relationships among Maya settlements, divided as the people were into many small and multicenter polities. One possible approach is through the identification of "emblem glyphs," titles that were carried by kings and their highest nobility in the major kingdoms. The emblem glyph of Palenque was *Ch'ul Bac Ahaw* ("Holy Bone Lord"), and that of Tikal was *Mutul* ("tied bundle" or "tied flower"), depicting a man's hair topknot seen from the rear. The emblem glyphs can be taken as statements of political affiliation with particular kingdoms, for subordinate centers would sometimes use their overlord's glyph. They would identify political control over a territory by stating that events occurred *u cab* ("in the land of") (Culbert, 1991).

Many Mayanists have thought of Maya civilization in terms of small competing kingdoms. But Joyce Marcus (1993) has studied Maya political territoriality using a combination of epigraphy (the study of inscriptions), iconography, and settlement patterns, assuming that site emblem glyphs and their distributions would reflect the structure and ranking of ceremonial centers. She has developed a general scenario for Maya political history and organization that envisages four major city-states during the Classic period, rather than dozens of smaller polities, as follows: Between A.D. 292 and 434, there were no regional capitals, no well-defined hierarchy of settlement, and different monument styles in the various regions of the Maya homeland. Most centers were, on average, about 27 km (18 miles) apart, apparently autonomous and competitive and of roughly equal rank. Tikal and Uaxactún appear to have been the earliest dominant centers. By A.D. 514 to 534, a standardized symbolic system was being used at monuments at even the most dispersed Maya centers. There were now four regional capitals, each with its own emblem glyph and each ruling over a well-defined hierarchy of lesser settlements, an arrangement suggesting a form of pyramidical state dominated by a few ruling dynasties. A hieroglyphic text of A.D. 731 from Copán, perhaps a biased source, lists these four capitals: Tikal, Palenque, Calakmul, and Copán.

A.D. 292 to 434

Marcus believes that the Maya capitals enjoyed some form of military alliance between A.D. 672 and 751. The ruler of each communicated with his neighbors of equal rank, a situation reflected by the adoption of a uniform lunar calendar and a homogeneous style and iconography of monuments. Within each region, the ruler achieved integration by strategic marriage alliances with ruling families from lesser, dependent centers—between, for example, Palenque and nearby Yaxchilán. But these arrangements did not last long. After A.D. 830 to 909, over 60 percent of all monuments were erected at what had previously been lesser centers, as if the authority of the original capitals had been replaced by more appropriate mechanisms for governing smaller, more dispersed populations. This changeover coincides with the so-called Maya collapse (see next section).

The Marcus scenario was developed at a time when Maya glyphs were less well understood than they are today and may not reflect true political reality. There were other major centers than the great four, some of which have only been excavated in recent years. Caracol in Belize is a case in point. Another important Maya center, it started as a few hamlets in 900 B.C., but became a growing city by the first century A.D. (Chase and Chase, 1996a). Caracol's rulers engaged in widespread trading in jadeite and other materials. During the sixth century, Caracol embarked on military campaigns throughout the southern lowlands. Lord Yahaw Te K'inich ("Lord Water") defeated Tikal in A.D. 562. The city was now a major political player. Its rulers developed strategic alliances with other states, among them Calakmul to the north. Caracol's population swelled from about 19,000 to more than 120,000, larger than either Calakmul or Tikal, the people fed by elaborate complexes of terraced fields and reservoirs. This was a period of major building activity, including roads that connected the city to outlying settlements and allowed rapid deployment of the army. Caracol was a prosperous state, apparently marked by much closer social integration than other polities such as Tikal. There is clear evidence of a flourishing middle class, who enjoyed many luxury goods, found in their burials (Chase and Chase, 1996b). The city began to lose population after A.D. 800. Much of Caracol was burned a century later as the fabric of the state collapsed.

Caracol
900 B.C. to A.D. 800

There were many elements common to all Maya polities, among them the calendar and the hieroglyphic script, essential to the regulation of religious life and the worship of the gods. Architectural and artistic styles in ceramics and small artifacts varied from center to center as each developed its own characteristics and cultural traditions (Coe, 1999). Religion unified the Maya more than political or economic interests, in much the same way, perhaps, as the spread of Islam unified diverse cultures.

The political mechanisms used by the Maya included warfare, which had strong ritual overtones and was probably very destructive. It may have been aimed more at economic hegemony than territorial expansion. Much art and many inscriptions concentrate on the ceremonial and ideological aspects of war—the capture and sacrifice of prisoners as a way of validating political authority (Schele and Miller, 1992). Whether this was the primary purpose of going to war is uncertain. However, judging from emblem glyphs, most wars were between immediate neighbors, the capture and sacrifice of a ruler sometimes leading to the dominance of one capital by another for generations but at other times apparently having little effect. The inscriptions tell us that visits by rulers or their representatives to other capitals were important occurrences, usually to commemorate significant political events such as an accession or when a ruler designated his heir (Schele and Mathews, 1991). At the core of all these diplomatic and military maneuvers were ongoing rivalries between powerful noble families, which endured over many centuries. For example, the Jaguar Claw clan seems to have risen to prominence at Preclassic El Mirador, then spread its influence to Tikal, Caracol, and ultimately to Dos Pilas. Much Maya warfare was more between factions of powerful clans than between different clans.

Classic and Late Classic Maya Political History

With this general scenario in mind, one can lay out the beginnings of a narrative of Maya political history from as early as the third century A.D. (Coe, 1999; Sabloff and Henderson, 1993; Schele and Freidel, 1990; Sharer, 1995). With constant new discoveries and decipherments, the snapshots given here, based on individual site histories, are, necessarily, an incomplete picture.

Tikal and Uaxactun.   Cerros and El Mirador were major centers during the late Preclassic, but even as they prospered, new centers were emerging a short distance away. Tikal and Uaxactún were growing during the late Preclassic and stepped into the political vacuum left by the decline of El Mirador. The two centers were less than 20 km (12 miles) apart, too close for bitter rivals to coexist. Tikal rose in a strategic position atop some low hills, where extensive chert deposits occur. Nearby seasonal swamps may have provided a basis for intensive agriculture and some protection against sudden attack. The growing settlement also sat astride a critical river portage between water systems that carried trade goods from east to west across the Maya lowlands. Important trade routes to highland cities like Teotihuacán also passed through Tikal. At the same time, Tikal had powerful supernatural associations as the current seat of one of the oldest royal dynasties in the region.

Tikal
1st century A.D. to
A.D. 800

Tikal had expanded greatly during the first century as large public buildings rose on the foundations of earlier, more humble structures (P. Harrison, 1999). Clearly, the intent was to rival, and outdo, El Mirador's splendor. During this century an elite emerged at Tikal, people represented by the burial of a noblewoman under a shrine and tomb paintings of richly decorated nobles. One burial contained a headless and thighless corpse tied up in a bundle, with a green fucsite portrait head that had once been the chest pectoral of the deceased. The human face on the pectoral wears the Jester God headdress that kings wore for centuries afterward. Uaxactún just to the north underwent a similar transition during the same century. Here, Preclassic temples bear stucco masks and facades that depict the Maya world and the king who built the structures. At both Tikal and Uaxactún, Maya kings memorialized themselves on their temples, but the two centers were political and economic equals during this century (Figure 21.12).

Tikal's inscriptions are the chronicle of a remarkable dynasty that ruled one of the four Maya capitals from the early Classic until the ninth century A.D. The earliest recorded monarch is Yax Ch'aktel Xok ("First Scaffold Shark"), who is thought to have reigned around A.D. 200, although the city had a long, and much earlier history. During his reign, strong influences from Teotihuacán on the highlands appear, shown by pottery styles and green obsidian from the city's closely controlled sources. This strong influence on political, military, and religious affairs at Tikal continued until A.D. 550.

Yak Ch'aktel Xok was not the earliest king, but was the one who served as founding ancestor for the great royal clan of Tikal that ruled in coming centuries. Tikal's hieroglyphic texts identify 31 rulers (18 known by name) after the founder, the earliest dating to A.D. 292, the last known one to A.D. 869, making for 669 years of recorded history. Uaxactún also fostered a powerful royal dynasty, whose monuments, like those of the Tikal kings, soon depicted rulers with sacrificial victims cowering at their feet, noble victims taken in hand-to-hand combat for later sacrifice in public rituals. These portraits signal a crucial development in Maya history: the increasing role of warfare and campaigns of deliberate conquest.

FIGURE 21.12
Reconstruction of the central precincts of Tikal.

Between A.D. 320 and 378, Great-Jaguar Claw, the ninth successor of Yax-Moch-Xoc, sat on the throne of Tikal, at a time when rivalries with nearby Uaxactún came to a head. He died in 378, at a time when a warrior named Fire-Born arrived, a warrior from the "west," presumably Teotihuacán. The connection between Great-Jaguar Claw's death and Fire-Born's arrival is unclear, but it was the former who defeated the armies of Uaxactún on January 16, 378. His army ignored long-established rules of combat and sacked Uaxactún, setting up Fire-Born as the founder of a new dynasty (see a discussion, including unpublished primary references, in Harrison, 1999). The war was associated with new rituals first developed at Teotihuacán in the highlands, and it linked the god Tlaloc and the planet Venus. Tikal's military expansion took place with assistance from Teotihuacán during a period of regular trading contacts between the great highland city and many Maya centers, marked by many finds of the distinctive green obsidian mined by the great city. The same contacts may have brought new philosophies of war and conquest and the rituals associated with them. These rituals were to become part of the Mesoamerican religious tradition for many centuries (Figure 21.13).

Tikal's royal dynasty prospered in the coming centuries. It eventually headed a multicenter polity, extending its influence by conquest and long-distance trade and by judicious political marriages that gave neighboring rulers maternal kin ties to the center. At the height of its powers, Tikal's territory may have supported an estimated population of as many as 300,000 people, the city and its immediate hinterland perhaps 200,000; however, these are perhaps high estimates.

In about A.D. 557, Tikal went into decline after its defeat by the lord of a new rising state, Caracol, then prospered anew during the late Classic.

Calakmul and Caracol.   Caracol, which lies in south-central Belize, 70 km (43 miles) southeast of Tikal, controlled important crystalline rock supplies and was an important rival. Its imposing ceremonial core covered at least 2.25 sq km (0.9 square mile) during the seventh century, when between 30,000 and 50,000 people lived there, and as many as 100,000 in the surrounding countryside (see the summary in Sharer, 1995). Caracol commenced hostilities against Tikal in A.D. 557, soon after Tikal had captured and executed a prominent lord. The Caracol ruler, Lord Water, defeated Tikal, apparently capturing the city's then-ruler, Double Bird. Tikal now became a tribute dependency of Caracol, which grew in size and prestige as its vassal declined. Lord Water's successors dominated Tikal for at least 150 years and embarked on ambitious conquests against neighboring Calakmul and Naranjo. But eventually Caracol paid the price for its military adventures, only to rise again during the late Classic.

Uaxactún
1st century A.D. to A.D. 800

FIGURE 21.13 Lord Stormy Sky of Tikal is depicted on Stela 31 at Tikal, together with his parentage. The lord died on February 19, 456.

Calakmul
1st century A.D. to
A.D. 820

The ever-shifting diplomatic and military landscape in the lowlands involved dozens of city-states and cities, large and small, whose relationships with the major centers and lesser kingdoms are a tangle of claims, counterclaims, and archaeological data. In addition to Caracol, both Tikal and Calakmul, also in the southern lowlands, were rival regional capitals during the early Classic. At its height, Calakmul had a ceremonial precinct covering about 2 sq km (0.7 square mile) and a surrounding residential area over 20 sq km (7.7 square miles) in extent. At least 50,000 people lived in the urban core of a great city and important rival of Tikal between at least A.D. 514 and 814 (Folan et al., 1995).

Like Tikal, Calakmul sat astride an important overland trade route. The rivalry between the two cities may have been both a power play and a struggle for dominance of long-distance exchange. There may have been family ties between the two cities. The rivalry was intense, culminating in warfare and constant shifts in allegiance between Tikal, Calakmul, and Caracol, which are virtually impossible to decipher today.

FIGURE 21.14
Palenque, with the Temple of the Inscriptions at left, the palace at right.

Tikal had few allies in its immediate vicinity but maintained friendlier relations with two more distant city-states—Palenque and Copán.

Palenque.   The city of Palenque, another Maya capital, but in the western lowlands, is remarkable not only for its fine buildings but also for its rulers' obsession with their ancestry (see the summary in Sharer, 1995) (Figure 21.14). Two Palenque rulers, Pacal the Great ("Shield") and his oldest son, Chan-Bahlum ("Snake-Jaguar"), who ruled in the seventh century A.D., stand out for their vision and wisdom. Palenque's dynastic history began on March 11, 431, when Bahlum-Kuk ("Jaguar-Quetzal") became ruler, and lasted until sometime after 799. The experts have used the rich inscriptions left by Pacal and others to reconstruct a dynasty of no fewer than 12 kings, with, however, what Schele and Freidel (1990) call some "minor sidesteps." These sidesteps accounted for the obsession with history that was so remarkable in Pacal and Chan-Bahlum's day.

Succession was through the male line, yet Pacal inherited the throne from his mother, Lady Zac-Kuk, who served for a time as ruler (Figure 21.15). She must have been a remarkable woman, although we know nothing of her. Pacal claimed the throne as her son and, in so doing, had to change the genealogical rules so that he could override the age-old rule of descent through the father and claim succession. In short, he, and later his son, orchestrated orthodox belief with clever fictions. First, they declared Lady Zac-Kuk to be equivalent to the first mother of gods and kings at the beginning of the present creation. This mother deity was the mother of the three major gods of Maya religion. Next, Pacal and Chan-Bahlum claimed that Pacal had been born on the very day of the calendar that coincided with that of the goddess's birth. Thus, both Pacal and the goddess were of the same divine substance. Pacal inherited the throne from his mother because this was what had happened at the beginning of creation: Authority had been transmitted through both males and females.

Palenque
Before A.D. 431 to 800

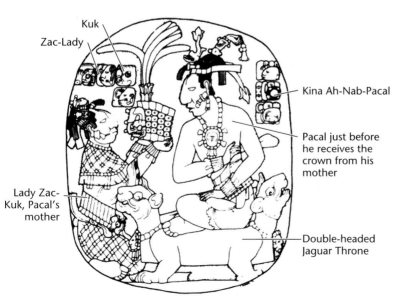

Kuk

Zac-Lady

Kina Ah-Nab-Pacal

Pacal just before he receives the crown from his mother

Lady Zac-Kuk, Pacal's mother

Double-headed Jaguar Throne

FIGURE 21.15   Pacal the Great (A.D. 603 to 683), ruler of Palenque, reigned for 67 years. This oval tablet commemorates his receipt of the crown from his mother, Lady Zac-Kuk. By using the name of a Maya goddess to refer to his mother, Pacal declared her to be the equivalent of a mother of the gods, making him divine offspring. (After Schele and Freidel, 1990.)

FIGURE 21.16 A Maya frieze from Bonampak, showing a lord and executed prisoners.

It may have helped that Pacal ascended to the throne at the age of 12, while his mother was still alive, and that she lived for another 25 years. The real power may have been in her hands for all those years, for it was only after her death in 640 that Pacal commissioned major inscriptions that justified his own rule.

Toward the end of his long reign, which lasted 67 years, Pacal built the Temple of the Inscriptions, a masterpiece of Maya architecture under which his tomb lies. His artists carved the images of his direct ancestors around his coffin deep under the temple; on this sarcophagus his strategy of dynastic legitimization was recorded (Schele and Freidel, 1990). Chan-Bahlum continued his father's preoccupation with dynastic succession. Both rulers made Palenque a major power that dominated the southwestern lowlands during their lifetimes, between A.D. 603 and 702, but the dynasty survived for only another century or so after Chan-Bahlum's death (Figure 21.16).

Copán
A.D. 435 to 800

Copán. Copán in Honduras is adorned with pyramids and plazas covering 12 ha (30 acres), rising from the vast open spaces of the Great and Middle Plazas to an elaborate complex of raised enclosed courtyards, pyramids, and temples known to archaeologists as the Acropolis (Figure 21.17). Here successive rulers built their architectural

FIGURE 21.17 Artist Tatiana Proskouriakoff's reconstruction of the central precincts at Copán.

SITE

Architecture as a Political Statement: The Hieroglyphic Stairway at Copán, Honduras

Today's Maya archaeologist works closely with epigraphers, using carefully deciphered glyphs and inscriptions to reconstruct complex architectural events, as well as the ritual or political motives behind them. William and Barbara Fash (1991) combined both lines of evidence to reconstruct the Hieroglyphic Stairway at Copán, erected by the ruler Smoke Shell in A.D. 755 on one of the city's most sacred precincts.

In the 1930s, archaeologists of the Carnegie Institution restored much of the ruined stairway, replacing the glyph blocks in approximate order. They were unable to read the inscriptions, which made the task difficult. In 1986, a team of archaeologists and epigraphers headed by the Fashes set out to restore and conserve the building while establishing the true meaning of the stairway. Using meticulous excavation, the archaeologists recovered thousands of tenoned mosaic fragments from the structure, which were drawn and photographed, then pieced together in a precise reconstruction of the building. They recovered a powerful political statement (Figure 21.18).

More than 2200 glyphs ascend the sides of the stairway and provide an elegant statement of the Maya kings' supernatural path. William Fash believes the building was an attempt by Smoke Shell to relegitimize the conquered dynasty of earlier times. Portraits on the stairs depict Copán's lords as warriors carrying shields, with inscriptions recounting their deeds. A figure, perhaps Smoke Shell himself, stands where an altar forms the base of the stairway, in the form of an inverted head of the rain god Tlaloc. Tlaloc seems to be belching forth the inscriptions, his lower jaw forming the top of the stairs. Inside his head lay an offering of

decorated flints in the form of portraits and artifacts perhaps used by Smoke Shell himself in the sacrificial and bloodletting ceremonies that dedicated the stairway. Unfortunately, the stairway was shoddily, and hastily, built. It soon collapsed, at a time when Copán was rapidly losing its political authority.

FIGURE 21.18 Artist Tatiana Proskouriakoff's reconstruction of the Hieroglyphic Stairway at Copán.

statements atop those of their predecessors in an archaeological jigsaw puzzle of the first magnitude.

The earliest inscription at the site dates to December 11, 435, and was the work of ruler Yax-Ku'k-Mo' ("Blue Quetzal Macaw"), although there may have been earlier rulers. For four centuries, Blue Quetzal Macaw's successors formed a powerful dynasty at Copán and became a major force in the Maya world. At one point, Copán ruled over neighboring Quirigua. More than 10,000 people lived in the surrounding valley. However, on May 3, 738, the subordinate ruler of Quirigua turned on his master and captured and sacrificed him. But Copán seems to have maintained a measure of independence and survived. In 749, a new ruler, Smoke Shell, ascended to the throne of the once-great city. He embarked on an ambitious campaign of rehabilitation, even marrying a princess from distant Palenque. He also embarked on a building frenzy, which culminated in the Temple of the Hieroglyphic Stairway, built in 755 and one of the oldest and most sacred of Copán's precincts (see Site box). Smoke Shell's son from his Palenque marriage, Yax-Pac ("First Dawn"), ruled during troubled times, with internal factionalism on the rise. By this time, the city was top-heavy with privilege-hungry nobles and rife with political intrigue. Collapse was imminent.

The diplomatic and military landscape was constantly changing, as alliances were formed and just as rapidly collapsed again. During the very late Classic, after A.D. 771, a new political pattern emerged, indicative of changed conditions and stressful times. Carved inscriptions began to appear in the houses of local nobles at Copán and other sites, as if the rulers were now granting the privilege of using inscriptions to important individuals, perhaps as a way of gaining their continued support in times of trouble. This proliferation of inscriptions in the Petén and elsewhere may also reflect minor nobles' taking advantage of confused times and a disintegrating political authority claiming their own brief independence. The confusion accelerated. By A.D. 800, Maya populations were declining sharply, and both monument carving and major construction soon came to an end.

The central institution of Maya civilization was kingship, for it was the concept that unified society as a whole. Maya kings lived and carried out their deeds in the context of a history they recorded in building projects at Copán, Palenque, Tikal, and elsewhere. Maya elites lived out their lives in the context of the kings who ruled them, and in turn, thousands of commoners lived their lives with respect to the nobility (Figure 21.13 on page 502). We are only beginning to understand the tapestry of their history.

〽️ The Ninth-Century Collapse

Maya civilization reached its peak after A.D. 600 (Figure 21.19). Then, at the end of the eighth century, the great ceremonial centers of the Petén and the southern lowlands were abandoned, the Long Court calendar was discontinued, and the structure of religious life and the state decayed. Within a century, huge sections of the southern lowlands were abandoned, never to be reoccupied (Webster, 2002). At Tikal, perhaps the greatest Maya center, the elite vanished and the population declined to a third of its earlier level. The nonelite survivors clustered in the remains of great masonry structures

FIGURE 21.19
Distribution of Classic Maya, Toltec, and Aztec civilizations. (The Toltec and Aztec areas overlap.)

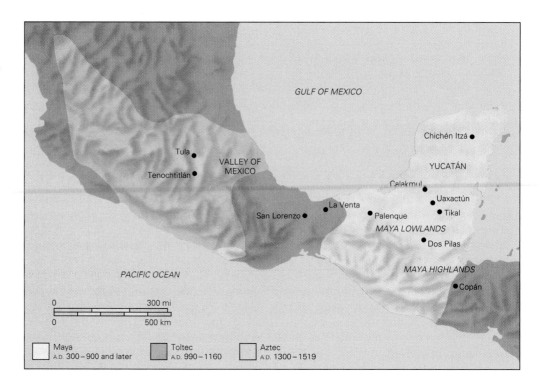

GULF OF MEXICO

Chichén Itzá ●

Tula ●
VALLEY OF MEXICO
Tenochtitlán ●

YUCATÁN

Calakmul ●
● Uaxactún

San Lorenzo ●
La Venta ●
Palenque ●
● Tikal

MAYA LOWLANDS

● Dos Pilas

PACIFIC OCEAN

MAYA HIGHLANDS

● Copán

| 0 | 300 mi |
| 0 | 500 km |

| | Maya | | Toltec | | Aztec |
| | A.D. 300–900 and later | | A.D. 990–1160 | | A.D. 1300–1519 |

and tried to retain a semblance of their earlier life. Within a century, even they were gone. All this is not to say that Maya civilization vanished completely, for new centers may have emerged in neighboring areas, taking in some of the displaced population. Maya civilization continued to flourish in the northern Yucatán (Sabloff and Freidel, 1984).

Everyone studying this ninth-century collapse agrees that a multiplicity of factors—some ecological, some political and social—led to catastrophe in the southern lowlands. The theories of a generation ago argued that the collapse of Teotihuacán gave the Maya a chance to enlarge their managerial functions in Mesoamerican trade. According to these theories, the elite became increasingly involved in warfare and competition between regions. The late Classic saw a frenzy of public building and increased pressure on the people, the source of both food and labor for prestige projects. Agricultural productivity fell, disease may have reached epidemic proportions, and population densities plummeted, so that recovery was impossible. There is some evidence of disease, stature decline, and malnutrition, but the evidence is incomplete (Wright and White, 1996).

More recently, endemic warfare has been invoked as a powerful factor in the collapse. At Dos Pilas in northern Guatemala, 105 km (65 miles) from Tikal, and founded by a renegade noble from Tikal in A.D. 645, Arthur Demarest uncovered evidence of civil war and prolonged conflict. Dos Pilas's later rulers embarked on campaigns of expansion that enlarged their territory to more than 3884 sq km (1500 square miles) by the mid-eighth century. Dos Pilas now controlled major jade and obsidian routes. Its lords lavished wealth on ornate palaces and a pyramid topped by three temples. Demarest and Juan Antonio Valdés dug deep under a small temple behind a stela that commemorated "Ruler 2," who reigned between 698 and 726, and uncovered the ruler's burial chamber. He wore a shell mosaic headdress adorned with monster faces, a heavy jade necklace, and jade bracelets. At his waist hung a stingray spine, once used for genital bloodletting. Hieroglyphs associated with the grave tell of the lord's carefully contrived diplomatic marriages with neighbors and of his delicate political marriages and his military campaigns.

Dos Pilas
A.D. 645 to 761

Dos Pilas flourished until A.D. 761. By then, its rulers had overextended themselves, despite frantic efforts to maintain their domains. In that year, nearby Tamrindo attacked its former sovereign and killed "Ruler 4," despite desperate resistance by the Dos Pilas inhabitants. The invaders tore down the royal palace and robbed temple facades to build rough defensive walls with wooden palisades to surround the central precinct. Here, the people clustered in a small village of crude huts while the nobles fled and built a new center at Aguateca. The new center lay atop a steep cliff above a deep chasm, protected on three sides by natural features, as well as by massive defense walls. The Aguatecans held out for another half century, despite repeated attacks. In the early ninth century A.D., Demarest believes, intensive warfare drove these survivors of Dos Pilas into fortified towns and villages, where they erected defensive walls even around large tracts of agricultural land. Local conditions may have become so insecure that farmers were limited to defended acreage, so that crop yields may have been affected dramatically. In a last desperate stand, the remaining Aguatecans dug three moats, one 140.2 m (460 feet) long, across a peninsula in Lake Petexbatun, creating an island fortress. The bedrock from the canals became defensive walls and a walled wharf for a canoe landing. The outpost did not last long, for the inhabitants abandoned it in the 800s (Demerast, 1997).

The various collapse theories have been subjected to exhaustive analysis by research that involves both simulation studies and examinations of trading patterns and demographic and ecological stresses that could have affected population densities. Patrick Culbert has examined population densities and the potential for agricultural production in the southern lowlands (Culbert and Rice, 1990). He has shown that population densities rose to as many as 200 persons per sq km (518 per square mile) during the late Classic over an area so large that it was impossible for people to adapt to bad times by moving to new land or emigrating. He believes that the magnitude of the population loss during the two centuries after 800 was such that social malfunction alone cannot account for it. Failure of the agricultural base must have been an important component in the collapse equation at the local level.

Maya agriculture became increasingly intense as populations rose, and both terrace and raised-field systems covered large areas in many parts of the lowlands. At some of the larger sites, like Tikal, the people may have been transporting great quantities of food-stuffs from distances of between 50 and 100 km (31 and 62 miles) away. In the short term, the intensification strategies worked, but they carried the seeds of collapse. The risks of climatic change, plant disease, erosion, and long-term declines in soil fertility are always present in such enterprises. To continue functioning efficiently, the newly intensified systems would have had to be managed constantly. Just the repair of field systems after floods and rains would have required watchful effort on a large scale. There are no signs that the Maya made any social changes that enabled them to achieve such a level of management, especially when so many people were engaged in public construction projects and apparently in military activity (perhaps the Maya were under pressure from the north).

Long-term environmental degradation was an important element in the scenario, where short-term gains in productivity were followed by catastrophic declines. For example, as populations rose, fallow cycles may have been shortened, so that there was increased competition between crop plants and weeds; this is a problem that can be solved only by constant weeding, a very labor-intensive activity. Shortened fallow cycles also lead to lower levels of plant nutrients and declining crop yields, and we do not know whether the Maya tried to counteract these trends by systematic mulching or by planting soil-restoring crops. The problem of erosion may have been even more acute. There are signs that the people lost much soil to runoff in the lowlands, for they did not build the terraces needed in time to retain the soil. Some of this erosion may have resulted from extensive deforestation. At the same time, severe drought cycles played havoc with subsistence agriculture in an environment with only moderately fertile soils and already overly dense populations, phenomena now well documented in Mesoamerican lake sediments (Hodell et al., 1995, 2001). Such droughts may, indeed, have been the trigger that brought about the collapse in the southern lowlands.

Long-term field surveys of Copán and its hinterland have documented dramatic population changes during the collapse period (Freter, 1994). Between A.D. 550 and 700 the Copán city-state expanded rapidly, with most of the population concentrated in the core and the immediate periphery. There was only a small, scattered rural population. Between 700 and 850, the Copán Valley reached its greatest sociopolitical complexity, with a rapid population increase to between 18,000 and 20,000 people. These figures, calculated from site size, suggest that the local population was doubling every 80 to 100 years, with about 80 percent of the people living within the core and the immediate periphery. Rural settlement expanded outward along the valley floor, but it was still relatively scattered. But now people were farming foothill areas, as the population density of the urban core reached over 8000 people per sq kilometer (0.3 square mile) and the periphery housing about 500 people per sq km (0.3 square mile). Eighty-two percent of the population lived in relatively humble dwellings, an indication of the extreme stratification of Copán society.

Copán's ruling dynasty ended in 810, just as serious urban depopulation began. The urban core and the periphery zones lost about half their population after 850, while the rural population increased by almost 20 percent. Small regional settlements replaced the scattered villages of earlier times, in response to cumulative deforestation, the overexploitation of even marginal agricultural soils, and uncontrolled soil erosion near the capital. By 1150, the Copán Valley population had fallen to between 5000 and 8000 people.

The expanding Maya population was dependent on an agricultural system that made no allowance for long-term problems. Eventually, the system could produce no further riches, could not expand, and could only decline—with catastrophic results. But it would be a mistake to think of the Maya "collapse" as a universal phenomenon. Rather, the collapse of the ninth century was a marked episode in a long series of periodic flowerings and collapses characteristic of Maya civilization—indeed, of Mesoamerican civilization generally.

〰️ The Toltecs

Although by A.D. 900 the Classic period had ended, Maya religious and social orders continued in northern Yucatán. The continuity of the ancient Mesoamerican tradition survived unscathed. Basic economic patterns and technological traditions were

FIGURE 21.20   A monolithic statue at Tula, capital of the Toltecs.

retained, although religious and ideological patterns and priorities were disarranged. New ceremonial centers were built, but war and violence became primary as militaristic rulers achieved dominance in Mesoamerica (Davies, 1977, 1980).

We have mentioned the unsettled Postclassic political conditions caused by population movements and tribal warfare. Many groups of invaders vied for political power in central Mexico until the Toltecs achieved dominance in the tenth century. The oral legends of the Aztec rulers, who followed the Toltecs, describe how the Toltecs came into Mesoamerica from the northwest frontiers beyond the civilized world. They settled at Tula, 57 km (37 miles) south of the Valley of Mexico, where they built a ceremonial center dedicated to their serpent god, Quetzalcoatl (Figure 21.20) (Diehl, 1984; Healan, 1989). Tula is notable for its animal sculpture and pottery styles, but it did not have a long life, for in approximately A.D. 1160 some newcomers with a less developed religious organization arrived from the north and destroyed the temples.

Chichén Itzá in northern Yucatán was an important Maya ceremonial center in Postclassic times (Figure 21.21). In the ninth century A.D., Chichén Itzá came under Toltec influence (Weaver, 1991). The extent of this influence is much debated, but it probably represented a fresh political order, a complex mixing of Mexican and Maya factions among the elite. The new leaders developed new artistic and political styles that separated political functions from the personality of an individual ruler. The Chichén Toltecs developed a flexibility and a resilience that enabled them to be far more adaptive to changing political conditions than their southern neighbors had been.

The leaders of Chichén Itzá developed a truly regional state. They controlled the two great resources of the northern Yucatán: a well-organized population and massive salt fields along the coast. The site was abandoned in the thirteenth century, but the city of Mayapán, a walled settlement clustered around a ceremonial center, rose to

Toltec civilization
A.D. 900 to 1200

Tula

Chichén Itzá
A.D. 1100

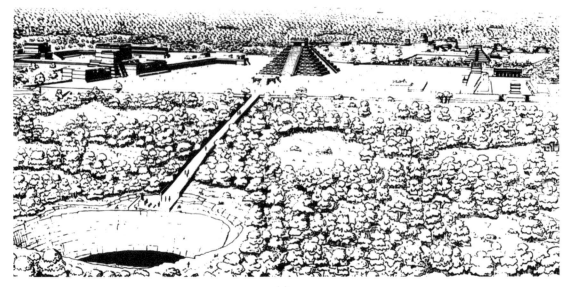

(a)

(b)

FIGURE 21.21 Chichén Itzá. (a) Reconstructed view of the site and the Sacred Cenote, a limestone sinkhole where sacrificial offerings were made. (b) The Castillo, the largest building at the site.

prominence elsewhere in northern Yucatán. At least 12,000 people lived in this Maya city, which was ruled by the Cocom family. Maya civilization enjoyed a resurgence in this area, although Mayapán declined during the civil wars of the fifteenth century. A century later, the Spanish found Yucatán ruled by numerous petty chiefs.

The militaristic Toltecs were the leading military and political force in Mesoamerica for such a short time that their influence evaporated rapidly when Tula was destroyed. Another period of political chaos in the Valley of Mexico ensued as more nomadic groups from the north (Chichimecs) maneuvered for political power (Davies, 1980).

〰 Aztec Civilization and the Spanish Conquest

When the first Spanish conquistadors arrived in highland Mexico in 1519, they were astounded by the rich civilization they found. The capital city of Tenochtitlán was the headquarters of a series of militaristic Aztec kings who ruled over a wide area by religious decree, constant human sacrifice, and bloodthirsty campaigning. Within a few years of Spanish contact, Aztec civilization literally ceased to exist. Tenochtitlán was reduced to rubble after a siege that lasted 91 days (Clendinnen, 1991).

Aztec civilization
12th century A.D. to 1521

The Aztecs were one of several nomadic, semicivilized Chichimeca groups who settled in the Valley of Mexico after the fall of Tula (M. Smith, 1996; Townsend, 1992). They arrived during the early twelfth century, a politically weak but aggressive group that barely retained its own identity. After years of military harassment, the Aztecs fled into the swamps of Lake Texcoco in about 1325. There they founded a small hamlet named Tenochtitlán (now under Mexico City). Less than two centuries later, this village had become the largest city in pre-Columbian America (Conrad and Demarest, 1984).

At first, the Aztecs lived peaceably with their neighbors, and Tenochtitlán flourished as an important market center. By judicious diplomacy, discreet military alliance, and well-timed royal marriages, the Aztecs quietly advanced their cause until they were a force to be reckoned with in local politics. Then, in the early fifteenth century, they abruptly changed their foreign policy and embarked on a ruthless campaign of long-term military and economic conquest. Soon they controlled a loosely connected network of minor states and cities that extended across Mesoamerica. The real leader behind this change was a general named Tlacaelel, who was adviser to a series of aggressive Aztec rulers. It was he who encouraged the use of terror and human sacrifice as a means of controlling conquered territory. The rich tribute from conquered states and cities made Tenochtitlán the center of the Mesoamerican world, the hub of a political and economic confederacy that extended from near the Pacific Ocean to the Gulf of Mexico and from northern Mexico as far south as Guatemala.

The Aztec Empire was far from a monolithic and highly centralized state, like that of Imperial Rome (M. Smith, 1996). It was a mosaic of ever-changing alliances, cemented by an elaborate tribute-gathering machine. The state itself was controlled by a tiny group of rulers, the lord of Tenochtitlán being principal among them. Everything was run for the benefit of a growing elite, who maintained their power by ruthless and efficient taxation campaigns, political marriages, and the constant threat of military force. Tribute was assessed on conquered cities and taken in many forms, as raw materials like gold dust or tropical bird feathers for ceremonial mantles and headdresses (see Figure 21.22). Fine ornaments, even capes, were assessed from communities specializing in such products. Twenty-six cities did nothing but provide firewood for one royal palace alone. Metal artifacts were major tribute items, for they played a telling role in the Aztec and the earlier Mesoamerican states. Expert smiths made musical instruments like bells, and they alloyed copper to bring out shimmering gold and silver hues. Both color and sound were central parts of Mesoamerican ideology, commemorating the sun and the moon, the sounds of rain, thunder, and rattlesnakes, helping to bring symbolic order to the world.

Both settlement data and other archaeological data suggest that the Aztec Empire was less centralized, both as a society and as an economy, than its great predecessor, Teotihuacán (Berdan et al., 1996). To what extent it had originated through decision making at the top, as opposed to market dynamics such as supply and demand, is still unknown. For example, pottery distributions show that political considerations such as alliances were more important than proximity to major markets in determining access to certain types of clay serving vessels. And both archaeology and ethnohistorical studies of market locations hint that imperial rulers located markets and decided the craft specializations within them to the advantage of their own cities and at the expense of subordinate communities. There is clear evidence of major changes in standards of living under imperial Aztec rule. For example, in the western Morelos area of central Mexico, agricultural and textile production increased under Aztec rule, while living standards declined.

Under the highly visible and much touted imperial veneer lay a complex foundation of small kingdoms, towns, and villages, all integrated into local economies. Many

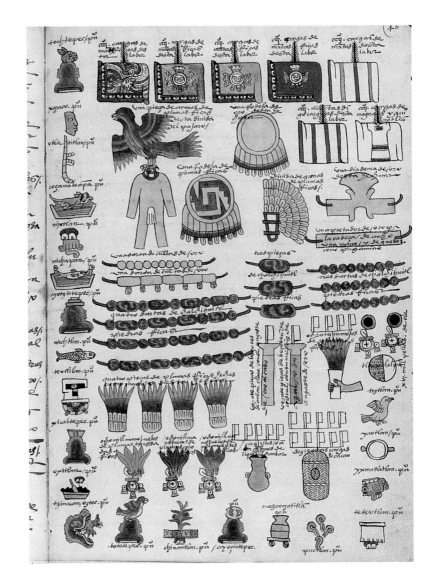

FIGURE 21.22 A tribute list from the Codex Mendoza, one of the few surviving Aztec codices. The list records tributes owed by the conquered province of Tochtepec, including feathered masks, warriors' regalia, and dried fish.

of them had existed before the Aztec, or even earlier, civilizations came into being, and they continued after the Spanish Conquest. At the same time, the economic and political patterns of the empire were highly variable, both regionally and socially, in everything from land tenure to craft specialization, from patterns of urbanization to merchants and markets. This intricate social mosaic, only now being revealed by a new generation of archaeological research, lay behind a facade of seeming political and economic uniformity and centralization (M. Smith, 1996).

Tenochtitlán

A.D. 1325 to 1521

Tenochtitlán, a city of more than 200,000 people, was a spectacular sight in the sixteenth century, with markets where more than 60,000 people are said to have assembled every day (Figure 21.23) (Diaz, 1963; J. B. Morris, 1962). The market sold every form of foodstuff and provided every luxury and service. The principal streets of Tenochtitlán were of beaten earth, and there were at least 40 pyramids adorned with fine decorated stonework (Moctezuma, 1988). Tenochtitlán was certainly larger, and probably cleaner, than many European cities of the time.

Large residential areas surrounded the central precincts, and houses with *chinampa* gardens lay on the outskirts of the city. Six major canals ran through Tenochtitlán, and three causeways connected the city with the shore. At least 200,000 canoes provided convenient transport for the people of the city, which was divided into 60 or 70 well-organized wards. Tenochtitlán was a magnificent city set in a green swath of country in the middle of a clear lake, with a superb backdrop of snowcapped volcanoes.

Aztec society was moving closer and closer to a rigid, highly stratified class system at the time of Spanish contact. No ordinary person was allowed to enter a waiting room

FIGURE 21.23 A reconstruction drawing of the central precincts at Tenochtitlán, with the Temple of Huitzilopochtli and Tlaloc at the left.

in the palace used by nobles. The king was revered as a semigod and had virtually despotic powers. He was elected from a limited class group of *pipiltin,* or nobles. There were full-time professional merchants, called *pochteca,* and also a class of warriors whose ranks were determined by the number of people they had killed in battle. Groups of lineages called *calpulli* ("big house") were the most significant factor in most people's religious, social, and political life. Many of these groups coincided with the wards in the city. The great mass of the people were free people, or *macehualtin;* serfs, landless peasants, and slaves made up the bottom strata of society. (For a discussion of women in Aztec society, see Brumfiel, 1991.)

Much of Aztec society's efforts went toward placating the formidable war and rain gods, Huitzilopochtli and Tlaloc, whose benevolence was ensured by constant human sacrifices. These sacrifices reached their peak at the end of each 52-year cycle, like those of the Maya, when the continuity of the world would be secured by bloodthirsty rites (Figure 21.24).

FIGURE 21.24 Aztec human sacrifice. Priests ripped out the still-beating hearts of sacrificial victims and rolled their corpses down the temple steps.

By the time of the Spanish Conquest in 1519, Aztec society seems to have been in a state of frenetic and bloody terrorism that flourished at the behest of arrogant imperial rulers. The Aztecs had learned the fine art of terror as a political instrument and regularly staged elaborate public displays in Tenochtitlán to which subject leaders were invited. The Spaniards estimated that at least 20,000 people were sacrificed to the gods throughout the Aztec Empire each year. This figure may be an exaggeration, but there is no doubt that a considerable number of prisoners of war and slaves perished by having their hearts ripped out in the presence of the gods. Indeed, the finest death for an Aztec warrior was to perish under the sacrificial knife after honorable capture in battle. Such a fate was known as the "flowery death."

The Aztecs have acquired a formidable reputation from historians—and, it must be confessed, from some archaeologists—because of their penchant for human sacrifice and cannibalism. That they were addicted to human sacrifice is certain; the cannibalism is less well documented. Some believe that the Aztec nobles ate human flesh to compensate for a lack of meat in their diet, but the beans they ate as a staple were more than sufficient as a source of protein. It seems more likely that the Aztec nobles and priests engaged in occasional ritual cannibalism as part of their intensely symbolic religious beliefs (Townsend, 1992). Human sacrifice was also an instrument for social control and intimidation, especially of prospective conquests.

By the time the Spaniards arrived in the Mexican lowlands, Aztec civilization was in danger of being torn apart. The society was becoming top-heavy with nobles because they were allowed to marry from the people and their children automatically became aristocrats. The demands for tribute both from subject states and from the free people of the city became ever larger and more exacting. There may well have been intense philosophical disagreements between the militant priests and warriors, who increasingly encouraged conquest and human sacrifice, and those more sophisticated and educated Aztecs who believed in a gentler, less aggressive world. It is fascinating to speculate what would have happened had Hernán Cortés not landed in Mexico. Given the past history of Mexico, it seems likely that Aztec civilization would have collapsed suddenly, to be replaced in due time by another society much like it. In truth, Aztec civilization had reached a point of complexity that was beyond the capacity of its rulers to control and administer, a complexity that Old World civilizations had brought under control, and we can be certain that the Aztecs' successors would have eventually done so as well.

The Aztecs were the most important political entity in Mesoamerica when the Spaniards first explored the Americas. From coastal villagers in the lowlands, the explorers heard stories of the fabled rich kingdoms in the high interior. Soon the conquistadors pressed inland. Hernán Cortés was the first Spaniard to come into contact with the Aztecs, now ruled by Moctezuma II, a despotic ruler who had assassinated most of his predecessor's counselors and had had himself deified. Moctezuma's reign was disturbed by constant omens of impending doom and predictions that the god Quetzalcoatl would reclaim his homeland (Dibble and Anderson, 1978). The king was deeply alarmed by the reports of Spanish ships on the coast. There were, then, considerable psychological stresses on Moctezuma and his followers before the Spaniards arrived (Clendinnen, 1991).

A.D. 1519

It took Cortés two tough years to reduce the Aztecs to slaves and their marvelous capital to rubble. A handful of explorers on imported horses, armed with a few muskets and cannons, were able to overthrow one of the most powerful tribute states in the history of America. Without question, Cortés's task was made easier by both rebellious subjects of the Aztecs and the extraordinary tensions the Aztecs had placed on themselves. Cortés also unwittingly introduced smallpox, which decimated his adversaries.

A.D. 1680

By 1680, the Indian population of the Aztec heartland had been reduced from approximately 1.2 million to some 70,000—a decimation resulting from war, slavery, disease, overwork and exploitation, famine, and malnutrition. Mesoamerica as a whole lost between 85 and 95 percent of its indigenous population during that 160-year period. Only a few fragments of the fabulous Mesoamerican cultural tradition survived into modern times, and the Native American population faced a new and uncertain chapter in its long history.

Summary ﹉﹉

The Preclassic period of Mesoamerican prehistory lasted from approximately 2000 B.C. to A.D. 250, a period of major cultural change in both lowlands and highlands. Sedentary villages traded with each other in raw materials and exotic objects. These exchange networks became increasingly complex and eventually came under the monopolistic control of larger villages. Increasing social complexity went hand in hand with the appearance of the first public buildings and the evidence of social stratification. These developments are well chronicled in the Valley of Oaxaca and in the Olmec culture of the lowlands, which flourished from approximately 1500 to 500 B.C. Olmec art styles and religious beliefs were among those that spread widely over lowlands and highlands during the late Preclassic period.

Preclassic cultural developments culminated in the highlands in a number of great cities, among them Monte Albán and Teotihuacán. Teotihuacán had collapsed by approximately A.D. 700, probably as a result of warfare with other rival states in the highlands.

Religious ideologies, ritual organization, and extensive trading networks were key factors in the development of Maya society in the lowlands after 1000 B.C. Classic Maya civilization flourished from A.D. 250 to 900 and consisted of an ever-changing patchwork of competing states. Maya glyphs show that Maya civilization was far from uniform. Religious beliefs rather than political or economic interests unified the Maya. Until about A.D. 600, the largest states were in northeast Petén, with a multicenter polity headed by the "Sky" rulers of Tikal. Maya civilization reached its height in the southern lowlands after the seventh century, collapsing suddenly in the Yucatán after A.D. 900. The reasons for the collapse are still uncertain, but environmental degradation, pressure on the labor force, and food shortages were doubtless among them.

Teotihuacán's collapse in the highlands resulted in a political vacuum for some centuries, which was eventually filled by the Toltecs and then the Aztecs, whose civilization was dominant in the Valley of Mexico at the time of the Spanish Conquest in A.D. 1519.

Guide to Further Reading ﹉﹉

Clendinnen, Inga. 1991. *The Aztecs: An Interpretation.* Cambridge: Cambridge University Press.
A wonderfully articulate and sophisticated analysis of Aztec civilization and its institutions. Truly engrossing.

Coe, Michael. 1999. *The Maya,* 6th ed. London and New York: Thames & Hudson.
A well-established synthesis of Maya civilization that is both readable and authoritative.

———. 2002. *Mexico,* 5th ed. London and New York: Thames & Hudson.
Coe's general summary of Mexico's archaeology is a classic.

Harrison, Peter D. 1999. *The Lords of Tikal: Rulers of an Ancient Maya City.* London and New York: Thames & Hudson.
This admirable synthesis of Tikal gives telling insights into the intricacies of Maya architecture, archaeology, art, and politics impossible to achieve within the brief compass of this chapter.

Marcus, Joyce, and Kent Flannery. 1996. *Zapotec Civilization.* London and New York: Thames & Hudson.
Lavishly illustrated general summary of the rise of Zapotec civilization in the Valley of Oaxaca.

Sabloff, Jeremy A. 1989. *The Cities of Ancient Mexico.* London and New York: Thames & Hudson.
A straightforward account of major Mesoamerican centers and cities. For a general audience.

Schele, Linda, and David Freidel. 1990. *A Forest of Kings.* New York: Morrow.
A popular account of Maya history as known from glyphs. Entertaining, provocative, and challenging, but should be checked critically against other sources.

Sharer, Robert. 1995. *The Ancient Maya.* Stanford, CA: Stanford University Press.
A magisterial study of Maya civilization for the advanced reader. Definitive.

Townsend, Richard F. 1992. *The Aztecs.* London and New York: Thames & Hudson.
A straightforward description of Aztec civilization for the general reader. Richly illustrated and authoritative.

Webster, David. 2002. *The Fall of the Ancient Maya.* London and New York: Thames & Hudson.
A comprehensive analysis of the Classic Maya collapse aimed at a general audience.

chapter

ANDEAN STATES

Portrait vase depicting a Moche lord.

The year was 1911. American explorer Hiram Bingham was high in the Andes, struggling along precipitous, densely forested paths, slipping ankle-deep in mud at every corner. He and his men climbed in places on all fours, high above the tumbling Urubamba River. Suddenly he emerged into the open, high atop a mountain ridge. Bingham climbed a granite stairway leading to a plaza with two temples. He wandered through "a maze of beautiful granite houses . . . covered with trees and moss and the growth of centuries." He wandered for hours among "walls of white granite . . . carefully cut and exquisitely fitted together" (Bingham, 1963, p. 267). This was Machu Picchu, an Inca settlement in such a remote, inaccessible setting that Bingham claimed it was the "lost city of the Incas." For three years, Bingham worked at Machu Picchu, clearing, excavating, and mapping houses and temples.

Machu Picchu is one of the most spectacular archaeological sites in the world, but it was never a lost city, for the local farmers were well aware of its existence. What makes it so dramatic is its mountain setting, its testimony to the incredible skill of the Andeans in mastering climatic extremes.

In its late-fifteenth-century heyday, the vast Inca Empire, known as Tawantinsuyu ("The Land of the Four Quarters"), extended from high-altitude mountain valleys in the Andes, through dry highland plains, to foothills, tropical rain forests, and coastal deserts, some of the driest landscape on earth (Figure 22.1). (For the chronology of later Andean archaeology, see Table 22.1).

Over many centuries, two "poles" of Andean civilization developed: one along the north coast of what is now Peru, the other in the south-central Andes. Only the Inca succeeded in joining the two into one vast empire.

The northern pole was centered on the bleak and effectively rainless Peruvian desert plain, which extends south nearly 550 km (350 miles) along the coast as far as Collasuyu, reaching a width of up to 100 km (62 miles) in the area of the Lambayeque River. Some 40 rivers and streams fueled by mountain runoff flow across the plain, but they can be used for irrigation only in areas where the surrounding desert is low enough. Four such locations were the most densely settled in ancient times. The two largest were centered on the north coast, in the Chicama-Moche area and in the Motupe-Lambayeque-Jequetepeque region. Local topography allowed farmers to link their field systems to canals, which brought water from several rivers, permitting far higher population densities.

The southern pole embraced the altiplano (high-altitude grasslands) and the Lake Titicaca basin, highland Bolivia, and parts of Argentina and northern Chile in the south-central Andes. Much of the altiplano was too dry and cold to sustain dense human populations. The northern end of the Lake Titicaca basin was somewhat warmer and better watered, so

TABLE 22.1

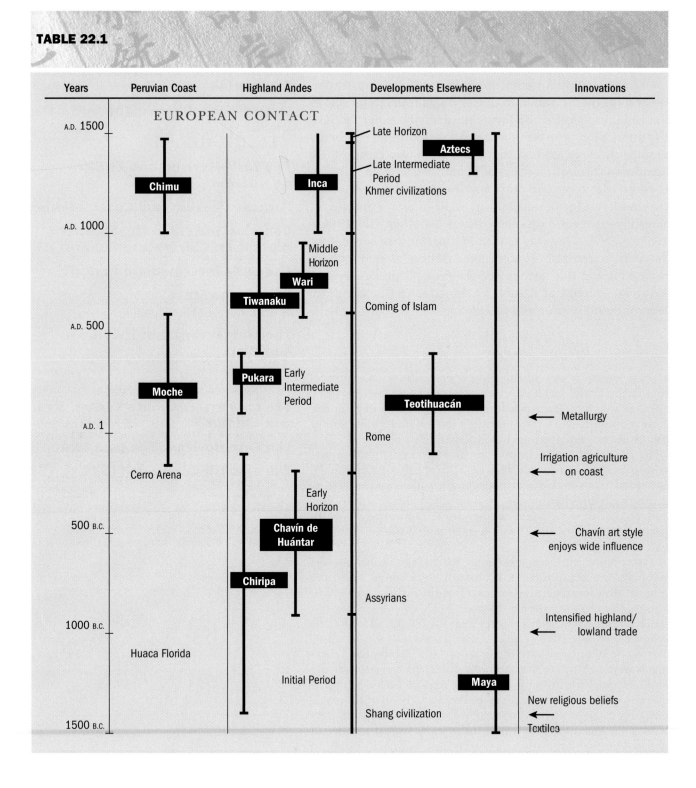

Years	Peruvian Coast	Highland Andes	Developments Elsewhere	Innovations
A.D. 1500	EUROPEAN CONTACT		Late Horizon	
	Chimu	Inca	Aztecs	
			Late Intermediate Period	
			Khmer civilizations	
A.D. 1000				
		Middle Horizon		
		Wari		
		Tiwanaku	Coming of Islam	
A.D. 500				
		Pukara — Early Intermediate Period		
	Moche		Teotihuacán	
A.D. 1				← Metallurgy
	Cerro Arena		Rome	Irrigation agriculture ← on coast
		Early Horizon		
500 B.C.		Chavín de Huántar		← Chavín art style enjoys wide influence
		Chiripa		
			Assyrians	
1000 B.C.				Intensified highland/ ← lowland trade
	Huaca Florida			
		Initial Period	Maya	New religious beliefs ←
1500 B.C.			Shang civilization	Textiles

that both alpaca and llama herding and potato and quinoa agriculture were possible. This was where the powerful Tiwanaku state flourished in the first millennium A.D. The puna grasslands of the higher altiplano were used to graze alpaca and llama, the economic exploitation of the plains varying with the altitude. The civilizations of the southern highlands traded regularly with the southern coast, bounded in the north by the Ica River, in the south by the Moquegua Valley.

Andean civilization pursued many different pathways, which came together in a remarkable mosaic of states and empires, in large part as a result of widely held

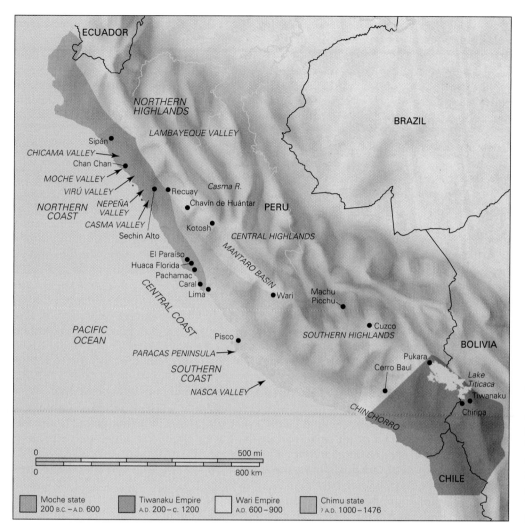

FIGURE 22.1
Archaeological sites mentioned in this chapter. Approximate distributions of various traditions are also shown. Some sites in coastal river valleys are omitted from the map. Their general location is clear from the text.

spiritual beliefs and of constant interchange between the coast and the highlands and between neighboring valleys and large population centers. Tawantinsuyu itself was a unique political synthesis sewn together by the Inca lords of the Andes in the centuries just before European contact. It was the culmination of centuries of increasing social complexity throughout the Andean area. How did such complex states arise in this landscape of extraordinary contrasts?

The Maritime Foundations of Andean Civilization

The rugged central Andean mountains are second only to the Himalayas in height, but only 10 percent of their rainfall descends the Pacific watershed. The foothill slopes and plains at the western foot of the mountains are mantled by one of the world's driest deserts, which extends virtually from the equator to 30° south, much of it along the Peruvian coast. At the opposite extreme, the richest fishery in the Americas hugs the Pacific shore, yielding millions of small schooling fish such as anchovies. These easily netted shoals support millions of people today, and they supported dense prehistoric populations. In contrast, the cultivation of this dry landscape requires controlling the runoff from the Andes with large irrigation systems that use long canals built by the co-ordinated labors of hundreds of people. Only 10 percent of this desert can be farmed, so its inhabitants rely heavily on the incredible bounty of the Pacific. Surprisingly, perhaps, this apparently inhospitable desert was a major center of complex early states that traded with neighbors in the highlands and built large ceremonial centers.

The mechanisms by which complex states arose on the Peruvian coast are still little understood, partly because research has tended to concentrate on larger, more spectacular sites (Haas et al., 1987; Moseley, 1975; D. J. Wilson, 1983). Such research tells us little about the relative size of different communities or about population densities, which are critical measures of an evolving state society. It is only recently that large-scale river valley surveys have collected such data, research like Gordon Willey's (1963) classic work on the Virú and Donald Proulx's (1985) fieldwork in the Nepeña Valley. These investigations have shown that there were major changes in site clustering through time, especially after the introduction of maize agriculture and irrigation to the coast after 2500 B.C.

Archaeologist Michael Moseley (1975) proposed a hypothesis he called the "maritime foundations of Andean civilization." He argued that the unique maritime resources of the Pacific Coast provided sufficient calories to support rapidly growing sedentary populations, which clustered in large communities. In addition, the same food source produced sufficient surplus to free up time and people to erect large public monuments and temples, work organized by the leaders of newly complex coastal societies. This scenario runs contrary to conventional archaeological thinking, which regards agriculture as the economic basis for state-organized societies. In the Andes, argued Moseley, it was fishing. For thousands of years, coastal populations rose, and their rise preadapted them to later circumstances, in which they adopted large-scale irrigation and maize agriculture.

Moseley implies that mollusks and large fish were vital resources on the coast, but marine biologists drew his attention to the incredible potential of anchoveta and other small schooling fish. Anchoveta can be easily netted throughout the year from small canoes. The fish offer predictable food supplies that can be dried or ground into fine meal. Such harvests would provide an abundance of protein. Judging from modern yields, if prehistoric coastal populations had lived at 60 percent of the carrying capacity of the fisheries and eaten nothing but small fish, the coast could have supported more than 6.5 million people. That is not to say that it did, but the figures make the point that the exploitation of small fish would have provided a more than adequate economic base for the emergence of complex societies on the coast. It is interesting that small mesh nets and floats have come from earlier South American coastal sites such as Paloma (see Chapter 13).

Several critiques of the maritime foundations hypothesis have appeared, all of them based on the assumption that large coastal settlements could not have been supported by maritime resources alone (see, for example, Raymond 1981, and D. J. Wilson, 1981, 1983). Most of these critiques have tended to ignore the potential of anchovetas. Another argument revolves around the famous El Niño phenomenon, the periodic changes in Pacific currents that reduce the fisheries to a shadow of their normal selves for several years at a time. In fact, as Moseley (1985) points out, El Niño brings unfamiliar, but edible, fish species to the coast as well as torrential rainfall that has the potential to disrupt irrigation systems with catastrophic results, some of which are now being identified in the archaeological record. Overall, the maritime foundations hypothesis has stood the test of time well, provided it is seen as a component in a much broader evolutionary process that also took place inland, in the highlands, and in areas where the width of the coastal shelf precluded extensive anchoveta fishing.

Richard Burger (1985) argues that changing dietary patterns in the highlands, where agriculture became increasingly important, would have created a demand among farmers for lowland products: salt, fish, and seaweed. Seaweed is rich in marine iodine and may have been an important medicine in the highlands, used to combat endemic goiter and other conditions. By the same token, carbohydrate foods like oca, ullucu, and white potatoes that could not be grown on the coast have been found in preceramic sites in the Ancón-Chillón area of the Pacific lowlands. Thus, the formation of states in both lowlands and highlands may have been fostered by continuous, often highly localized interchange between coast and interior.

Michael Moseley believes that this reliance on maritime resources led to the formation of large, densely concentrated populations whose leaders were able to organize the labor forces needed not only for building large ceremonial centers but also for transforming river valleys with sizable irrigation schemes. In this scenario, irrigation farming was in the hands of a well-defined group of authority figures who took advantage of the existing simple technology and local populations to create new economies.

This transformation, based as it was on trade, maize agriculture, and a maritime diet, acted as a "kick" for radical changes in Andean society (Moseley, 1985). But the transformation was based on ancient fishing traditions, which can be documented thousands of years earlier at early coastal villages.

Moseley's key point is that Andean civilization evolved in many ways, in many ecological zones, from highland, tropical rain forest, and lowland strategies of great antiquity, some dating to the earliest millennia of human settlement. Thus, the maritime foundations hypothesis may help explain the development of states on the Peruvian coast, but it cannot account for parallel developments elsewhere in South America.

🐾 Coastal Foundations: The Initial Period

Until comparatively recently, agriculture remained a secondary activity in the lowlands. Nevertheless, sedentary villages of several hundred people flourished along the north coast between 2500 and 1800 B.C., among them Huaca Prieta, whose inhabitants were remarkably skillful cotton weavers. This "Initial Period" of Andean civilization was a critical millennium, for new concerns both with the cosmos and with religion permeated the Andes. The new beliefs manifested themselves in a wave of monumental construction in both lowlands and highlands. The Initial Period saw the development of distinctive coastal and highland societies at either end of the Andean world: on the north coast and on the shores of Lake Titicaca far to the south. At the same time, textiles, like those found in the Paracas cemeteries (see pages 527–529) assumed great importance in Andean life.

Huaca Prieta
2500 to 1800 B.C.

Caral

We do not know when the first, more complex societies developed along the coast, but recent discoveries near Lima show that it was well before 2000 B.C. By 2600 B.C., a large kingdom ruled by a center named Caral developed in the hot Supe Valley, about 193 km (120 miles) north of modern-day Lima (Shady Solis, Haas, and Creamer, 2001). There were as many as 17 centers in the Supe region, supported by cultivating guavas, beans, peppers, and fruit grown with skilled irrigation agriculture. The farmers also grew cotton, but not maize and potatoes, the two later staples of Andean life. The kingdom may have prospered by growing and trading cotton for net manufacture. Certainly, much of its subsistence came from anchovies, which occur in desiccated feces from the site.

Caral
2600 to c. 2000 B.C.

Caral is dominated by six large stone platforms with structures atop them built of quarried stone and filled in with cobbles from the nearby river (Figure 22.2). The largest is 152 m by 137 m (500 feet by 450 feet) and 18 m (60 feet) high. There are three sunken plazas and eight sectors containing different types of dwellings—apartment

FIGURE 22.2 View of Caral in the Supe Valley, the earliest Andean center, showing the terraced mounds that once surrounded the central plaza. (Jonathan Haas, The Field Museum, Chicago.)

complexes, modest houses, and grand, stone-walled residences. Fortunately for science, the platform builders had carried their loads of cobbles in bags woven from reeds, which were added to the fill, carriers and all. Radiocarbon dates from the netting date the construction to about 2627 B.C., a task carried out in two efficiently organized stages.

Clearly, a small and authoritative elite governed this important kingdom, but we still know almost nothing about them or about the ways in which they commanded the loyalty of the hundreds, if not thousands, of people who built their imposing centers. Caral was abandoned for unknown reasons between 2000 and 1500 B.C., just as other kingdoms came into prominence along the coast to the north. This remarkable site, called by some a city, was the largest settlement in the Americas in its day, a full millennium and a half before Teotihuacán in Mexico. It rose in the Supe Valley at the time when the Egyptian pharaohs were building pyramids on the other side of the world.

Initial Period Centers

A set of interacting chiefdoms emerged along the northern and central parts of the coast after 1800 B.C. Political units centered on the Moche, Casma, Chillón, and other river valleys where irrigation agriculture developed. Centuries before, when pottery was unknown on the coast but cotton had already been widely cultivated, communication networks had arisen that linked not only neighboring coastal river valleys but lowlands and highlands as well. These trade routes, which straddled all manner of environmental zones, helped spread technology, ideology, pottery making, and architectural styles over large areas, creating a superficial sense of unity that was reflected in the widespread use of common art motifs.

During the Initial Period, coastal ceremonial buildings were greatly elaborated and new architectural devices were adopted (Haas, 2001; Haas et al., 1987). Among them was a distinctive U-shaped platform often associated with elaborate adobe friezes. **El Paraíso**, built close to the mouth of the Chillón River in about 1800 B.C., is the oldest of these U-shaped ceremonial complexes and the closest one to the Pacific (Figure 22.3) (Quilter, 1985). This vast site consists of at least six huge square buildings constructed of roughly shaped stone blocks cemented with unfired clay. The people painted the polished clay-faced outer walls in brilliant hues. Each complex consisted of a square building surrounded by tiers of platforms reached by stone and clay staircases. The largest is more than 250 m (830 feet) long and 50 m (166 feet) wide, standing more than 10 m (30 feet) above the plain. The rooms were apparently covered with matting roofs supported by willow posts. Perhaps as many as 100,000 tons of rock excavated from the nearby hills were needed to build the El Paraíso buildings. There are few signs of occupation around them, however, as if they were shrines and public

**El Paraíso
1800 B.C.**

FIGURE 22.3
El Paraíso, a major ceremonial center on the coast dating to about 1800 B.C. This was one of the first U-shaped sacred buildings constructed in the Andean region.

precincts rather than residential quarters. The two largest mounds of collapsed masonry lie parallel to one another, defining a vast, elongated patio covering more than 2.5 ha (6 acres). The same arrangement is found in the great Río Rímac complex of Huaca Florida, built in about 1700 B.C.

Huaca Florida is an imposing mound of boulders and adobe lying approximately 13 km (8 miles) inland of El Paraíso (Patterson, 1985). Built somewhat later, in about 1700 B.C., and on an even larger scale, the great platform is more than 252 m (840 feet) long and 54 m (180 feet) wide, and towers 30 m (100 feet) above the valley. A rectangular court lies close to the north side of the platform, but here the landscape is revealing, for Huaca Florida lies in the midst of an artificial environment created by irrigation. The focus of human settlement had moved inland, and the subsistence base had changed from fishing to large-scale irrigation agriculture.

Huaca Florida
1700 B.C.

What is most surprising about these huge structures is that people from dozens of scattered villages erected them. For reasons not yet understood, these people united in a building project that channeled most of their surplus energies into a vast monumental center, a place where few people lived but where everyone apparently congregated for major public ceremonies. The people themselves lived lives of seeming simplicity. They owned only simple stone and wooden artifacts and wore cotton clothing decorated with basic geometric patterns and stylized animal-like motifs. They buried their dead in several layers of garments, nets, or looped sacks. Why should such a village society build such enormous structures, and who were the leaders who organized these massive public works?

People who subsisted on a fish-meal diet from the incredibly rich fisheries close offshore and who traded extensively with communities inland built El Paraíso. Its U-shaped layout coincides with the florescence of similarly shaped ceremonial centers in the interior at a time when coastal people began to consume much larger amounts of root crops, to make pottery, and to shift their settlements inland to river valleys. Some scholars believe that this move coincided with the introduction of large-scale canal irrigation (Moseley, 1985). Perhaps the spread of U-shaped ceremonial centers reflects a radical restructuring of society that coincided with a major economic change. Moseley argues that the introduction of irrigation technology required a major reorganization of labor that coincided with the appearance of new artistic traditions and architectural devices.

In many parts of the Americas, the ritual manipulation of smoke and water served as a way of bridging stratified layers of air, earth, and bodies of water (Sullivan, 1989). Thus, it is argued, the early ceremonial centers of the coast and the highlands reflect an ancient tradition of using these substances to maintain communication with the cosmos. Burnt offerings are found at some Andean sites, among them Kotosh in the mountain foothills. Water flowed through masonry channels at many highland sites and also at the famous ritual center at Chavín de Huántar. There, galleries and ritual waterways flowed through the ceremonial platform and beneath a circular sunken court, connections that allowed the water to resonate under the ground so that the temple "roared." The vast, open courts of coastal U-shaped ceremonial complexes may have housed sacred orchards and gardens irrigated with specially manipulated water supplies. These ritual waterways were to reach their greatest elaboration thousands of years later in the coastal state of Chimu and the great imperial Inca capital at Cuzco (Donnan, 1985).

Water and irrigation assumed major roles in Andean civilization. Irrigation dates back far earlier than Huaca Florida, for the first farmers had probably made some limited use of canals to water their riverside gardens. However, the new works were on a far larger scale, spurred by the availability of an army of workers fed by abundant Pacific fish; by the presence of gentle, cultivable slopes inland; and by the expertise of the local people in farming cotton, gourds, and many lesser crops such as squashes and beans. Huaca Florida's leaders organized the reclamation of the desert by building canals along the steeper areas of the coastal valleys, where the gradients made the diversion of river water an easy task.

At first the members of each individual family may have worked together to irrigate the family's own sloping gardens, but gradually each community grew so much that essential irrigation works could be handled only by cooperative effort. Perhaps organized irrigation began as many minor cooperative works between individual families and neighboring villages. These simple projects eventually evolved over many centuries into elaborate public works that embraced entire inland valleys and were controlled by a corporate authority that held a monopoly over both the water and the land it irrigated. The process of organization was the result of many complex factors, among them population growth and the emergence of increasing numbers of non-farming society members, such as priests and artisans, whose food needs had to be met by other people.

Sechin Alto
1400 B.C.

By 1400 B.C., the inhabitants of the Casma Valley on the coast were building the huge stone-faced 40-m (130-foot) high platform of Sechin Alto. This mound, nearly 300 m (1000 feet) long and over 250 m (800 feet) wide, formed the base of a huge U-shaped ceremonial center with sunken courts, plazas, and flanking mounds. A vast sprawl of houses and platforms lies around this largest of all early ceremonial structures on the coast. Only parts of the site have been excavated, including a small building, erected in about 1300 B.C., surrounded by a mosaic of carved monoliths depicting a procession of armed men with dismembered human remains (Figure 22.4). The shrines at Sechin employ one of the persistent themes of ceremonial architecture in the Andes and on the coast: that of artificially raising or lowering sacred spaces relative to one another (Moseley, 1985).

On the coast, early ceremonial sites feature rectangular platform mounds fronting on a circular sunken court that is usually housed in a rectangular forecourt (Donnan, 1985). This form of architecture had appeared by at least 2000 B.C. People entered the forecourt of the sacred complex at ground level, descended into the sunken court, and then climbed the temple platform.

In social and political terms, the Initial Period remains somewhat of a mystery. There are few signs in burial rituals of any social ranking or personal wealth. Leadership and

FIGURE 22.4 Figure from Cerro Sechin.

the power of making decisions were probably not inherited and may have been regularly rotated from one person to the next. The many ceremonial centers suggest that different kin groups commemorated their identities by erecting their own shrines, perhaps competitively. There were probably some larger polities extending over several river valleys, one centered in the Casma Valley and three others along nearby parts of the coast, but no one knows who held sway over each of these political units (Pozorski and Pozorski, 1987).

🐾 The Early Horizon and Chavín de Huántar

In 1943, archaeologist Julio Tello identified a distinctive art style in stone, ceramics, and precious metals over a wide area of highland Peru, a style he named Chavín after a famous prehistoric ceremonial center at Chavín de Huántar in central Peru. Tello's research led to a long-held belief among Peruvianists that the widespread Chavín art style was a "mother culture" for all later Andean civilizations, somewhat equivalent to the Olmec phenomenon in Mesoamerican prehistory (Pozorski and Pozorski, 1987). This became a distinctive "Early Horizon" in Peruvian prehistory, dating to about 900 B.C., when there was a great expansion of indigenous religious belief by conquest, trade, and colonization—when civilization began.

Early Horizon
900 to 200 B.C.

Chavín de Huántar testifies to an elaborate, well-developed iconography (Burger, 1992a). The temple area is terraced, with an impressive truncated pyramid on the uppermost level (Figure 22.5a). The 10-m (32-foot) high pyramid appears solid but is in fact hollow, a honeycomb of stone passages and rooms. Special rectangular tubes ventilate the galleries. The temple housed a remarkable carving of a jaguarlike human with hair in the form of serpents, the famous "Lanzón," which may have served as an axis joining the heavens, the earth, and the underworld (Figure 22.5b). The deity seems to be acting as an arbiter of balance and order (Burger, 1992b). The entire center was a place of mediation with the heavens and the underworld. Chavín's priests and religious functionaries served as intermediaries between the living and the supernatural. In this shamanlike role, they transformed themselves into supernatural jaguars and crested eagles.

Chavín de Huántar
850 to 200 B.C.

Chavín art reflects these transformations. Jaguar motifs predominate; humans, gods, and animals have jaguarlike fangs or limbs; snakes flow from the bodies of many figures (Figure 22.5c). The art is both grotesque and slightly sinister. Many figures were carved in stone, others in clay or bone, their nostrils dripping with mucus from ingesting hallucinogenic substances. The rituals at Chavín de Huántar included shamanistic transformations and involved both music and elaborate costumes as priests in jaguar and other animal costumes proceeded up the stairway leading to the summit of the temple. The principal god may have been a nature deity associated with thunder and other powerful meteorological phenomena of the nearby high mountains.

Conceivably, theorizes Burger, Chavín de Huántar was a four-stage artificial mountain where rituals surrounded the circulation of water. In these beliefs, the earth floated on a vast ocean. From there, water circulated through mountains to the Milky Way in the heavens, where it became rain to water crops before flowing back into the ocean. Peruvian archaeologist Luis Lumbreras has replicated the deep roaring sound of water flowing through the elaborate stone-lined tunnels and canals of the great shrine. He believes that the roar of the water would have echoed through the temple during the rainy season and created a symbolic link between the rain-giving mountains, the temple, and the layers of the cosmos (Burger, 1992b).

With its tangled animal and human motifs, Chavín art has all the flamboyance and exotic touches of the tropical forest. The animals depicted—cayman, jaguar, and snake—are all forest animals. The art may have originated in the tropical forests to the east of the Andes, but the Early Horizon Chavín temple has a U-shape with a sunken central plaza, an architectural design documented centuries earlier at other coastal and highland sites (Burger, 1985; Pozorski and Pozorski, 1987).

Chavín de Huántar is far more than just a temple. Richard Burger (1992a) has excavated areas outside the well-known ceremonial precincts and established that the site was occupied residentially between about 850 and 200 B.C. At first, the population was

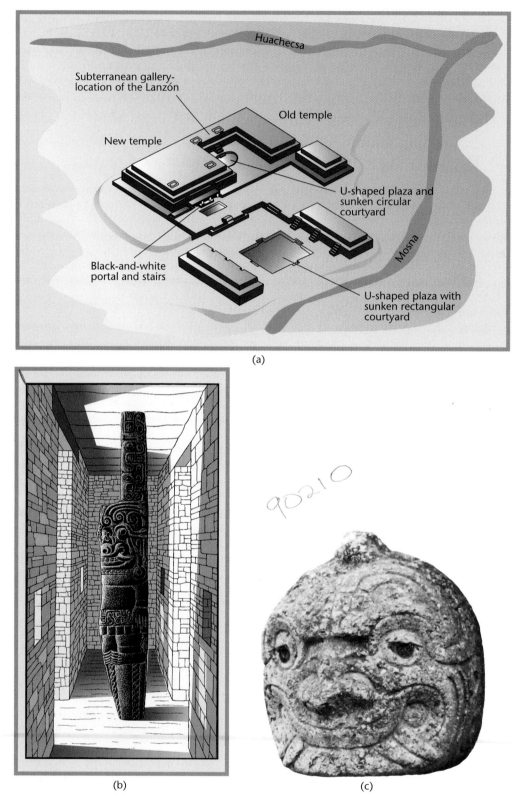

FIGURE 22.5 Chavín de Huántar. (a) Plan of the ceremonial center showing major architectural features. (b) The "Lanzón" god carved on a pillar set in the midst of the temple interior. (c) A Chavín wall insert approximately 20 cm (7.8 inches) high, showing feline features. Stone inserts such as these are common on the walls of the ceremonial buildings.

(a)

(b)

(c)

small, perhaps few more than 100 people. It seems to have expanded considerably by the fourth century B.C., at which point as many as 2000 to 3000 people may have been living near the temple precincts. Chavín de Huántar was certainly a large center, probably an influential place within its local area, and one of the largest settlements in Peru at the time of its occupation. It failed to expand into a fully developed urban center, however, and the nascent civilization that worshiped there collapsed, leaving nothing more than a small town and a persistent art style and iconography.

The Chavín style may have influenced artistic traditions over a wide area of Peru. Perhaps the religious beliefs behind the motifs were more significant than the art itself. Settlements like Chavín de Huántar were important ceremonial centers that unified surrounding farming villages in a common religious belief, but Chavín de Huántar was not unique. There were many other, often much earlier, centers with the same general architectural and iconographic style.

For example, from about 2000 to 200 B.C., the small ceremonial center at Huaricoto in the highlands, only 55 km (34 miles) from Chavín de Huántar, was the home of a religious ideology (Burger and Salazar-Burger, 1985). The "Kotosh religious tradition" practiced here is known to us by sacrificial hearths on which ceremonial offerings were burned. These included animal bones and grain. The ritual hearth was sunk into the floor with a ventilator leading to the outside. Once the sacrifice was complete, the hearth was filled in. At first, the rituals were performed in the open, but larger superstructures surrounded the hearths by the late Initial Period. The rituals may have been performed sporadically at certain times of the year, with the audience watching in the open. The Kotosh religious tradition appears to have flourished over an area of at least 250 km (155 miles) north to south in the highlands in the region where the Chavín cult, with its wild and extravagant animal motifs, was to gain strength.

Huaricoto
2000 to 200 B.C.

Many scholars have assumed that the so-called Early Horizon associated with Chavín was a period of the unification and coalescence of early Peruvian culture under a single theology, but in reality the situation was more complicated than that. Chavín itself was a late manifestation of a primeval Andean architectural style, a coalescence of traits and ideas from both the coast and the forest that formed a flamboyant culture in a local area of the highlands. The Early Horizon itself, rather than being a catalytic time of unification, may well have been a long period of the disruption of age-old communication networks and well-established small polities on the coast. For instance, foreigners from the highlands invaded the coastal Casma. The newcomers forged the coastal valley and neighboring highlands into a single political unit for the first time in prehistory. This development was the precursor of far larger states. Perhaps it is better to refer to the Early Horizon as the Early Period, a prolonged time of cultural change and political adjustment.

🐾 Paracas: Textiles and Coastal Prehistory

Initial Period and Early Horizon sites are remarkable for their fine textiles. Few ancient societies rivaled the textile artistry of the coastal Peruvians. They lived in an environment in which both animal and plant (especially cotton) fibers were plentiful, and they were able to create fine, complex fabrics adorned with colorful, intricate patterns (Figure 22.6). The textiles have survived remarkably well in the dry coastal environment, in very large cemeteries where the dead were wrapped in fabric burial shrouds. The most spectacular textile finds come from very large cemeteries of mummified individuals on the sandy, desolate Paracas Peninsula south of the modern town of Pisco, and also from the Chinchorro culture of southern Peru and northern Chile. (For south coast sites and cultures, see Silverman, 1996.)

Paracas

The Paracas bodies lie in bottle-shaped chambers or stone-lined subterranean vaults with wooden roofs, approximately 5 m (16 feet) high and 4 m (13 feet) across, and cut through sand into soft rock. The sepulchers were divided into small chambers where dozens of mummy bundles were placed. The Andeans did not practice mummification in the formal ancient Egyptian sense; they simply took advantage of the exceptionally dry climate. Each corpse was disemboweled and then allowed to dry out in the hot sand in a fetal position, with the knees at the chin. Eventually, the bodies were wrapped in brightly colored cotton, wool, or both. Sometimes the dead wore decorated mantles, shirts, turbans, or loincloths tailored to the size of the mummy bundle rather than the living person. Occasionally, the mourners attached small ornaments to the mummies or buried tools, food, or even pet monkeys or parrots with the deceased.

From these mummies, we learn the most minute details of Peruvian textiles, for the wrapping cloths are often almost perfectly preserved. The earliest textiles preserved on the coast date to approximately 4500 B.C., soon after cotton was first cultivated. The

FIGURE 22.6   A border motif from a Paracas mantle showing an anthropomorphic figure wearing a tunic and skirt similar to those found on Paracas mummy bundles.

weavers were expert dyers and used more than 190 hues from plant dyes. The earliest dye in common use was blue, followed by red, and then a multitude of bright colors. Decorative motifs included simple checkerboards, filled squares, and stylized depictions of birds, felines, and other animals. The oldest textiles had rather coarse and uneven yarns produced by the twisting of untreated yarn. After 2000 B.C., however, the weavers began to use delicate wood-and-thorn spindles mounted in a special pottery, gourd, or wooden cup that minimized vibration. Thus they could produce much finer cloth.

Most of the textiles found in coastal tombs were made on backstrap looms just like those still in use in Peru today (Figure 22.7). Two sticks carry the lengthwise threads, the upper one suspended from a post and the lower tied to a belt around the weaver's back. As the work proceeds, the fabric is unrolled from the upper bar and the finished

FIGURE 22.7   Andean backstrap loom.

cloth is rolled onto the lower stick. The yarn is wound with a figure-eight motion between the two stakes and is laced fast to the loom sticks so that the edges of the fabric are uniformly finished off. The disadvantage of this type of loom is that the width of the cloth is limited by the span of the weaver's arms. The weavers sometimes combine several backstrap looms to create wider cloths.

🐾 Complex Society in the Southern Highlands: Chiripa and Pukara

As Chavín de Huántar rose to prominence in the northern highlands, a separate Early Horizon tradition of complex society developed around Lake Titicaca far to the south (Stanish, 2002). The plains landscape of the basin was gradually transformed by ever more intensive agriculture and herding.

Chiripa (1400 to 100 B.C.).   Chiripa, on the southern shore of Lake Titicaca, was a fishing and fowling settlement where farming and herding were integrated into much earlier hunter-gatherer traditions. Chiripa itself remained a small village until about 1000 B.C., when a platform mound was built in the community, then modified many times over the centuries. The platform itself was stone-faced, with a sunken square court surrounded by rectangular buildings on the platform summit.

Chiripa
1400 to 100 B.C.

Between 600 and 100 B.C., the Chiripa platform was enlarged until it measured 55 m (180 feet) square and 6 m (20 feet) high. The stone-faced sunken court was now 23 m (75 feet) square and 1.5 m (5 feet) deep. Carved stone plaques set into the walls depicted serpents, animals, and humans in the earliest appearance of a stone-carving tradition that persisted along the shores of the lake for many centuries. Sixteen rectangular buildings surrounded the court. Many features of the Chiripa shrine—especially the stepped doorways, sunken courts, and nichelike windows—are ancestral to the later Tiwanaku architectural tradition, which used the same devices for its ceremonial architecture. The religious beliefs associated with this architecture have been grouped under the "Yaya-Mama religious tradition," which flourished for many centuries.

Pukara (400 B.C. to A.D. 100).   Pukara, 75 km (47 miles) northwest of Lake Titicaca, was a major center, with a large residential area and an imposing ceremonial complex on a stone-faced terrace, complete with rectangular sunken court and one-room structures on three sides. Pukara's elite lived on nearby terraces, the entire settlement being large enough to be classified as a protocity. Such a dense population could be achieved only by a major investment in agriculture, including many acres of raised fields and large shallow ponds, known as *cochas*, which filled seasonally and where crops were planted at water's edge as the pond dried up.

Pukara
400 B.C to A.D. 100

Judging from the distribution of Pukara pottery styles, the kingdom's power was confined to the northern Titicaca basin, but ceramics and other artifacts from as far afield as the northern coast reflect widespread trade connections. Tiwanaku, then a smaller center than in later centuries, presided over the southern shores of the lake between 400 B.C. and A.D. 100. There is no evidence that Pukara incorporated its southern neighbor.

By 1200 B.C., ceramics, woven textiles, and irrigation agriculture had spread from the Titicaca region to the southern coast, where human populations were much smaller.

From the Initial Period onward, the Andean region witnessed an extraordinary array of state-organized societies that displayed a remarkable diversity of culture, art, organization, and religious belief. At the same time, there were broad similarities in cosmology and culture that distinguished these societies from states elsewhere in the prehistoric world.

🐾 The Early Intermediate Period

A series of brilliant states flourished on the coast and in the highlands during the Early Intermediate Period: Moche on the northern coast, Nasca in the south, and Recuay and Pukara in the highlands, to mention only a few.

Cerro Arena
200 B.C.

By 200 B.C., some settlements, such as Cerro Arena in the Moche Valley, covered more than a square kilometer. Excavations there during the 1970s revealed more than 2000 separate structures, some with as many as 20 rooms. A small group of 25 finely finished houses may have formed the administrative and residential quarters of Cerro Arena. There were considerable variations between these quarters and the humbler dwellings that surrounded them, as if Cerro Arena society was more complex than that of earlier settlements. This and other large settlements were supported by irrigation systems that required much labor to construct and maintain, as well as strict water controls.

Most of the cultivated land lay along the terraced edges of the valley, where the soils were better drained and easily planted with simple wooden digging sticks, just as they are to this day. Even today the local people divert the seasonal river water into side canals by building dams of stakes and boulders in the streams. There is no reason to suppose that the same simple but effective technique was not used in antiquity. The ancient irrigation canals wound along the sides of the valley, a series of narrow channels approximately 1.2 m (4 feet) wide, set in loops and S-shaped curves, watering plots approximately 21 m (70 feet) square. The surplus flowed off into the Pacific.

!!!!! The Moche State

Moche state
200 B.C. to A.D. 700

By 200 B.C., the Moche state had begun in northern coastal Peru; it flourished for 800 years. Its origins lay in the Chicama and Moche valleys, with great ceremonial centers and huge irrigation works (Donnan and McClelland, 1979). Information about the Moche people of 2000 years ago comes not only from irrigation systems and spectacular monuments but also from hundreds of finely modeled clay pots and human burials preserved in the dry desert sand of the Moche cemeteries. Unfortunately, these burials are a prime target of commercial grave robbers. Many Moche cemeteries look like battlefields after heavy bombardment, for their pots fetch astronomical prices in the international art market.

Sipán
A.D. 400

The spectacular discovery of undisturbed Moche tombs near the village of Sipán, about 680 km (420 miles) northwest of Lima, has revolutionized our knowledge of Moche's elite (Alva and Donnan, 1993) (see Site box). Peruvian archaeologist Walter Alva excavated three unlooted royal burials. The first contained a plank coffin that held the extended skeleton of a man in his late 30s or early 40s lying on his back with his arms along his sides. He wore gold nose and ear ornaments, gold and turquoise bead bracelets, and copper sandals. A ceremonial rattle, crescent-shaped knives, scepters, spears, and exotic seashells surrounded the body (Figure 22.8).

Comparing the objects found in the Sipán tombs with people depicted in Moche art, Christopher Donnan (Alva and Donnan, 1993) has identified the man as a warrior-priest. Such individuals are depicted on Moche pots presiding over sacrifices of prisoners of war (Figure 22.9). Apparently, Moche warriors went to war specifically to take captives. They would strip them of their armor and weapons and lead them in front of the warrior-priest. Then the prisoner's throat was cut, the warrior-priest and others drinking the blood of the slain victim while the corpse was dismembered. On pot after pot, the warrior-priest wears a crescent-shaped headdress atop a conical helmet, exactly the regalia found in the Sipán tombs. Such men were a priesthood of nobles living in different parts of the kingdom who enacted the sacrifice ceremony at prescribed times.

When warrior-priests died, they were buried at the place where they had performed the ritual, wearing the formal regalia and the objects they had used in the ceremony. Their successors assumed their roles, wearing new sets of the same costumes and artifacts, not only perpetuating the official religion but also ensuring work for the dozens of skilled artisans who manufactured precious artifacts for the nobility. Alva has unearthed two earlier burials, one of them an older man with a gold funerary mask, a magnificent necklace of golden spiders atop their webs, and a gilded copper crab effigy of a deity more than 0.6 m (2 feet) tall that had once been mounted on a fabric banner.

What little we know about the Moche state comes mainly from undisturbed burials and from museum studies of looted pots (Quilter, 2002). They show that Moche society consisted of farmers and fisherfolk as well as skilled artisans and priests, who

SITE

The Lords of Sipán, Peru

The discovery of the undisturbed Moche burials at Sipán, on Peru's northern coast, ranks as one of the greatest archaeological discoveries of all time (Alva and Donnan, 1989). Peruvian archaeologist Walter Alva spent months painstakingly excavating the royal tombs, using conservation laboratories in Peru and Europe. The result is a triumph of scientific archaeology.

Tomb I held the body of a warrior-priest in his late 30s or early 40s. The mourners had built a brick burial chamber deep in the pyramid (Figure 22.8), building the sepulcher like a room with solid mud-brick benches along the sides and at the head end. They set hundreds of clay pots in small niches in the benches. Priests dressed the dead lord in his full regalia, including a golden mask, and wrapped his corpse and regalia in textile shrouds. Then they placed him in a plank coffin and set it in the center of the burial chamber, the lid secured with copper straps. They laid out more ceramics, mainly fine spouted bottles, at the foot and head of the coffin. Next, someone sacrificed two llamas and placed them on either side of the foot of the coffin. At some point, the priests also sat the body of a 9- or 10-year-old child in poor health at the head of the warrior-priest.

Five cane coffins were then lowered into the grave, each containing the body of an adult. The two male dead, perhaps bodyguards or members of the lord's entourage, were each laid on top of one of the llamas. One was a strongly built male, over 35 years old, adorned with copper ornaments and laid out with a war club. The other bore a beaded pectoral and was between 35 and 45 years old. Two of the three women's coffins lay at the head of the royal casket; in the third, at the foot of the coffin, the woman had been turned on her side. Interestingly, the women's disarticulated and jumbled bones suggest they were not sacrificial victims, for they had died long before the lord and were partly decomposed at the time of their burial. Perhaps they had been wives, concubines, or servants. Once the coffins had been positioned, a low beam roof was set in place, too low for someone to stand inside the chamber. Then the tomb was covered, a footless male victim being laid out in the fill. Finally, a seated body with crossed legs watched over the burial chamber from a small niche in the south wall, about 1 m (3 ft) above the roof.

FIGURE 22.8   Burial chamber of a Lord of Sipán

FIGURE 22.9 Using a rotating stand, photographers have "unrolled" both Maya and Moche pots, allowing researchers to view complete scenes painted on them as friezes. This scene from an unrolled Moche pot is an excellent example. Prisoners of war arrive at a ceremonial center for arraignment and sacrifice.

are depicted on pots with felinelike fangs set in their mouths and wearing puma skin headdresses. A few expert craft potters created superb modeled vessels with striking portraits of handsome, arrogant men who can only have been the leaders of Moche society (Figure 22.10a). The potters modeled warriors, too, complete with shields and war clubs, well-padded helmets, and colorful cotton uniforms. Moche burials show that some members of society were much richer than others, lying in graves filled with as many as 50 vessels or with weapons or staffs of rank. We do not know exactly how Moche society was organized, but we can assume that the ruler wielded authority over a hierarchical state of warrior-priests, doctors, artisans, and the mass of the agricultural population. For instance, there was at least one Moche-style settlement in each subordinate valley.

Fortunately, the Moche artists and artisans gave us some more intimate glances at their society than did those of many civilizations (Figure 22.10b). Their paintings show the ruler with a fine feather headdress seated on a pyramid as a line of naked prisoners parades before him. A decapitated sacrifice at the base of one painting reminds us that human sacrifice may have been the fate of some prisoners of war. We see Moche soldiers in battle, charging their opponents with raised clubs. The defenders raise their feather-decked shields in defiance as the battle is fought to the death. The potters modeled maize-beer-befuddled drunks being supported by their solicitous friends, women with owl features, women giving birth with the midwife in attendance, and wives carrying babies on their backs in shawls and in wooden cradles suspended by nets. The women carried out all domestic activities, and the men were warriors, farmers, and fishermen. We see the men on a seal hunt, clubbing young seals on the rocky coast as their prey scurry in every direction. A clay llama strains reluctantly under its load, and a mouse eats a maize cob.

The pots also depict vividly what the Moche people wore. The men worked in short loincloths or cotton breeches and short, sleeveless shirts underneath tunics that ended above the knee and were fastened around the waist with colorful woven belts. More socially prominent people wore large mantles and headdresses made from puma heads or feathers from highland jungles. Nearly everyone donned some form of headgear: Brightly decorated cotton turbans wound around small caps and held in place with fabric chin straps were in common use. A small cloth protected the back of the neck from the burning sun. Moche women dressed in loose tunics that reached the knee, and they went bareheaded or draped a piece of cloth around their heads. Many men painted their lower legs and feet in bright colors and tattooed or daubed their

(a)   (b)

FIGURE 22.10   Moche vessels. (a) Portrait vase, of a Moche man, approximately 29 cm (11.4 inches) high. (b) A depiction of an owl-woman healer.

faces with lines and other motifs. They often wore disk or crescent nose ornaments and cylindrical bar earrings, sometimes modeled in gold. Their necks bore large collars of stone beads or precious metal, and bracelets covered their arms and legs. Many people wore fiber sandals to protect their feet from the hot sand.

By this time, the coastal people were expert metalworkers (Benson, 1979). They had discovered the properties of gold ore, and they extracted it by panning in streambeds rather than by mining. Soon they had developed ways of hammering it into fine sheets and had learned how to emboss it to make raised designs (Figure 22.11). They had also worked out the technique of annealing, making it possible to soften the metal and then hammer it into more elaborate forms, and they joined sheets with fine solder. The smiths used gold as a setting for turquoise and shell ornaments and as crafted crowns, circlets, necklaces, pins, and tweezers. Gold was in such short supply in prehistoric times that the metalworkers became expert at depletion gilding, an annealing technique that oxidizes the metal in an alloy of copper and gold to give the finished product a goldlike appearance even when the gold content is as low as 12 percent by weight. Many of the large gold objects, such as animals and plate decorations seized from the Inca by Francisco Pizarro's soldiers, were made of an elaborate alloy of some gold, silver, and copper.

The greatest efforts of the Moche people were devoted not to irrigation systems or elaborate burials but to the erection of vast monumental platforms and temples on the southern edge of the cultivated land in the Moche Valley, approximately 6.45 km (4 miles) southeast of the modern city of Trujillo. They used tax labor to build a huge adobe temple platform rising 23 m (76 feet) above the plain at the foot of a conical hill named Cerro Blanco. The Spaniards called this complex Huaca de la Luna, the Temple of the Moon. Huaca del Sol (the Temple of the Sun), standing close by to the west, is a confused mass of mud brick that once consisted of a ramp that gave access to

Cerro Blanco
A.D. 600

FIGURE 22.11 A golden ear ornament worn by a Lord of Sipán, inlaid with turquoise. The warrior at center wears a ceremonial headdress and an owl's head necklace. He is accompanied by two attendants. (Courtesy of UCLA Fowler Museum of Cultural History.)

five temple platforms, the highest, to the south, towering 41 m (135 feet) above the ground (Figure 22.12). The sides of the pyramid were steeply terraced and have been badly damaged by erosion and looters. Both platforms once supported courts, corridors, and room complexes, perhaps roofed with matting. Huaca del Sol may have been a palace, for there are deep rubbish heaps on the summit of the platform. In contrast, Huaca de la Luna is spotlessly clean, its temple buildings painted with brightly colored murals.

The Moche kingdom was a multivalley state that may have consisted of a series of satellite centers that ruled over individual valleys but owed allegiance to the great centers of the Moche Valley. At one time, the Moche presided over the coast as far south as the Nepeña Valley. Where possible, the Moche extended their ambitious irrigation

FIGURE 22.12 Huaca del Sol.

systems to link several neighboring river valleys and then constructed lesser copies of their capital as a basis for the secure administration of their new domains. Their traders were in contact with the north and with the Nasca people on the southern coast as well (Proulx, 1985).

Like all Andean coastal societies, the Moche lived at the mercy of droughts and El Niños. Michael Moseley (2000) believes that a series of natural disasters struck Moche domains in the late sixth century. The first may have been a devastating drought cycle between A.D. 564 and 594, identified from the growth rings deep in mountain glaciers between Cuzco and Lake Titicaca. Crop yields in some valleys may have fallen as much as 20 percent. Sometime between 650 and 700, a great earthquake struck the Andes, choking rivers with debris from landslides. Silt-laden floodwaters may have blocked irrigation canals, preventing water from reaching the nearby fields. The silt flowed into the ocean and was washed ashore, then blown inland by the prevailing winds to form huge sand dunes. Dense sandstorms may have blanketed entire villages and many acres of irrigated land.

An El Niño flooded the imperial capital itself just before A.D. 600. The city was repaired, and then was overwhelmed by coastal dunes that buried most of it, except the great huacas, under fine sand. The same El Niño devastated the coastal fisheries. Anchovies vanished from the inshore waters and torrential rains flooded the arid coastal plains, turning them into swamps and sweeping away entire villages and carefully maintained irrigation schemes. At this point, the southern Moche domains broke off from the state. The great lords abandoned Huaca del Sol and moved northward to Pampa Grande in the Lambayeque Valley, more than 50 km (30 miles) from the Pacific and close to where the rivers debouched from the mountain foothills and intensive irrigation maximized water supplies. But only half a century later, another El Niño descended on the coast with catastrophic effects, and Moche civilization collapsed (Chapdelaine, 2000).

||||| The Middle Horizon: Tiwanaku and Wari

The Middle Horizon flourished between A.D. 600 and 1000 in the southern highlands. This period saw the beginnings of monumental building at a highland site—Tiwanaku—that would influence much of the Peruvian world (Kolata, 1993, 2002).

Middle Horizon
A.D. 600 to 1000

Tiwanaku

Between A.D. 600 and 1000, the wealthiest highland districts lay at the southern end of the central Andes, in the high, flat country surrounding Lake Titicaca. This was fine llama country. The local people maintained enormous herds of these beasts of burden and were also expert irrigation farmers. The altiplano supported the densest population in the highlands, and almost inevitably, the Titicaca region became an economic and demographic pole of the prosperous northern coast. By A.D. 450, Tiwanaku, on the southern side of the lake, was becoming a major population center as well as an economic and religious focus for the region (Kolata, 2002). The arid lands on which the site lies were irrigated and supported a population of perhaps 20,000 around the monumental structures near the center of the site. By A.D. 600, Tiwanaku was acquiring much of its prosperity from trade around the lake's southern shores. Copper working probably developed independently of the well-established copper technology on the northern coast.

Tiwanaku
c. A.D. 450 to 1200

Tiwanaku was not only an economic force but a religious one as well. The great sunken court of Kalasasaya is dominated by a large earth platform faced with stones (Figure 22.13a). Nearby, a rectangular enclosure is bounded with a row of upright stones, and there is a gateway carved with an anthropomorphic god, sometimes called Viracocha (Figure 22.13b). Smaller buildings, enclosures, and huge statues are also near the ceremonial structures. One recently excavated temple contained the skeleton of a young warrior, perhaps a captive, sacrificed in A.D. 600.

The striking Tiwanaku art style is related to earlier iconography found at Pukara. Like the Chavín tradition, this tradition probably represents a powerful iconography.

(a)

FIGURE 22.13
Tiwanaku. (a) A great sunken court. (b) Gateway of the Sun, made from one block of lava. The central figure is known as the Gateway God; notice its jaguar mouth and serpent-ray headdress. The running figures flanking the god often are called messengers.

(b)

Tiwanaku's art motifs include pumas and condors, as well as anthropomorphic gods attended by lesser deities or messengers. They occur over much of southern Peru, as well as in Bolivia, the southern Andes, and perhaps as far afield as northwest Argentina. So powerful was the iconography of—and presumably the political and economic forces behind—Tiwanaku that there was a serious political vacuum in the south after A.D. 1200, when Tiwanaku inexplicably collapsed into obscurity.

Tiwanaku obtained much of its food from large community-based raised-field systems developed on the low-lying pampas (plains) and surrounded with irrigation canals. The water in the canals provided excellent protection for potatoes and other growing plants against harsh winter frosts, which decimated crops on higher ground. The same fields were highly fertile, the soils enriched by muck from the surrounding canals. In recent years, archaeologists have worked closely with development agencies to reintroduce the ancient agricultural expertise to local villages, with marked success (Erickson, 1992; Kolata, 1993).

Wari

Wari, in the Ayacucho Valley, is a highland urban and ceremonial center that stands on a hill (Isbell and Schreiber, 1978). It is associated with huge stone walls and many dwellings that cover several square miles. The Wari art styles also show some Pukara influence, especially in anthropomorphic feline, eagle, and serpent beings depicted on ceramic vessels. Like their southern neighbors, the Wari people seem to have revered a Viracocha-like being. By A.D. 800, their domains extended from Moche country in the Lambayeque Valley on the northern coast to south of Nasca territory, down the Moquequa Valley of the south-central Andes and into the highlands south of Cuzco. They were expert traders, who probably expanded their domain through conquest, commercial enterprise, and perhaps religious conversion. Storehouses and roads were probably maintained by the state. As with the Inca of later centuries, the state controlled food supplies and labor (Schreiber, 1987).

Wari
A.D. 800

The Cerro Baul site in the Moquequa Valley was a fortified settlement placed by the Wari on an impregnable mesa, with only a single, heavily defended trail giving access to the flat summit, where the inhabitants constructed complexes of rectangular structures, courts, patios, and occasional D-shaped buildings. Cerro Baul is a powerful Wari presence in a foreign valley, perhaps sited there to exploit local sources of copper, lapis lazuli, or obsidian (Moseley et al., 1991).

Wari itself was abandoned in the ninth century A.D., but its art styles persisted on the coast for at least two more centuries. Both Wari and Tiwanaku were a turning point in Peruvian prehistory, a stage when small regional states became integrated into much larger political units. This unification may have been achieved by conquest and other coercive means, but the iconography shared by many coastal and highland Peruvians at the time must have been a powerful catalyst for closer political unity. There was constant and often intensive interaction between two poles of Andean civilization in the highlands and the lowlands, each with quite different food resources and products. This interaction, long a feature of Andean life, was to intensify in the centuries that lay ahead.

These two great polities collapsed toward the end of the first millennium, leaving a vast political vacuum of small competing states that was filled by the Inca after a period of conflict and warfare.

፤ The Late Intermediate Period: Sicán and Chimor

The highland states traded regularly with several emerging polities on the coast, each of them founded on extensive irrigation systems. The decline of Moche in the Lambayeque Valley had left somewhat of a vacuum, filled by the Sicán culture after A.D. 700. Sicán reached its peak between A.D. 900 and 1100, centered in the Lambayeque Valley and remarkable for its magnificent gold work. In Sicán society, metals of all kinds served as markers of social status and wealth and as a prestigious medium of political, social, and religious expression, since people's access to artifacts and ornaments in different ores was carefully limited according to rank. Sicán lords encouraged intensive metal production, as well as seagoing trade in copper and other metals far to the north along the Ecuadorian coast. At the same time, they supervised massive irrigation works from major centers like Tucumé in the Leche Valley (Heyerdahl, 1996). Intervalley canals, requiring constant cooperation between lords in neighboring centers, sometimes linked these various cities. If oral traditions are to be believed, many of these lords were related to one another and had common ancestors.

Sicán culture
A.D. 900–1100

Tucumé
A.D. 1000

Between A.D. 1050 and 1100, an El Niño caused widespread flooding and disruption. The royal precincts at Sicán itself were burned as political power shifted west to the El Purgatorio region. In 1375, an expanding Chimu state overthrew Sicán and absorbed its domains into a new empire.

The Moche Valley had long been densely cultivated, but the Chimu people now embarked on much more ambitious irrigation schemes. They built large storage reservoirs and terraced hundreds of miles of hillside to control the flow of water down steep slopes. One channel extended nearly 32 km (20 miles), from the Chicama Valley to the capital, Chan Chan, and was designed to supplement the relatively limited water

FIGURE 22.14 Chan Chan. Oblique air photograph of a walled enclosure, or compound.

supplies that came from the nearby Moche Valley (Figure 22.14). Even in periods of extreme drought these canals carried water from the deep-cut riverbed to terraces long distances away. Thus, the Chimu created thousands of hectares of new fields and used water from great distances to harvest two or three crops a year from plots where only one crop had been possible before, and that at the time of the annual flood. So effective were these irrigation techniques that the Chimu controlled more than 12 river valleys with at least 50,590 cultivable ha (125,000 acres), all of them farmed with hoes or digging sticks. Today, the local farmers water their maize crops approximately every ten days, and this probably was the practice in Chimu times as well.

Chimu state (Chimor)
A.D. 1375 to 1475

According to seventeenth-century Spanish chroniclers, the Chimu always maintained that their domains had originally been ruled over by petty chiefs, but when the Inca conquered them between 1462 and 1470, they were led by a ruler named Michancamán, who governed through a network of hereditary local nobility. His courtiers held specific ranks, such as "Blower of the Shell Trumpet"; "Master of the Litter and Thrones"; and "Preparer of the Way," the official who scattered powdered shell dust wherever the ruler was about to walk. An archaeologist working at Chan Chan in 1969–1970 found a layer of powdered shell dust on a bench in a forecourt, perhaps evidence that the Preparer of the Way had been at work. Loyal local leaders ruled the various provinces of the kingdom. They enjoyed not only tribute privileges but also rights to crops and land and to agricultural labor by commoners. Perhaps the most privileged members of society were the Oquetlupec, herb curers paid by the state to look after the sick. This was a hierarchical, highly organized society with strict social classes of nobles and commoners. Perhaps to enforce the social hierarchy, the legal system was very strict (Rowe, 1948).

Chan Chan
A.D. 1400

The focus of the Chimu state was Chan Chan, a huge complex of walled compounds lying near the Pacific at the mouth of the Moche Valley. Chan Chan covers nearly 10 sq km (4 square miles), the central part consisting of nine large enclosures laid out in a sort of broken rectangle. Each enclosure probably functioned as the palace of the current ruler of Chan Chan, who probably built himself a new headquarters near those of his predecessors (Moseley and Day, 1982). The adobe walls of these compounds once stood as high as 9.9 m (33 feet) and covered areas as large as 200 by 600 m (670 by 2000 feet). The walls were constructed not to defend the rulers but to provide physical and ritual isolation, as well as privacy and some shelter from the ocean winds. Each enclosure had its own water supply, a burial platform, and lavishly decorated residential rooms roofed with cane frames covered with earth and grass. The same enclosure that served as a palace during life became the ruler's burial place in death. The common people lived in tracts of small adobe and reed-mat houses on the western side of the city. Similar dwellings can be seen on the coast to this day.

Oral traditions tell us that the Chimu rulers practiced the institution of split inheritance, whereby each ruler inherited no material possessions to finance his reign. Split inheritance, described on page 540, was to play a major role in Inca civilization. Chimu rulers had access to and control of a huge labor pool. To expand and maintain irrigation works, they employed laborers who also served in military levies to acquire new lands and expand the tax base (Pozorski, 1987).

These rulers soon learned the value of officially maintained roadways that enabled them to move their armies from one place to the next with rapid dispatch. They constructed roads that connected each valley in their domain with the capital. The rural routes were little more than tracks between low adobe walls or widely spaced posts, mostly following centuries-old paths through the fields. In the densely populated valleys, Chimu roads were between 4.5 m and 7.5 m (15 feet and 25 feet) across. In some places, the roadway widened dramatically to 24 m (80 feet) or more. These were the roads that carried gold ornaments and fine hammered vessels to Chan Chan and textiles and fine black-painted vessels throughout the empire. The traveler would occasionally encounter heavily laden llamas carrying goods to market, but most loads were carried on people's backs, for the Chimu never developed the wheeled cart. All revenues and tribute passed along the official roadways, as did newly conquered peoples being resettled in some area far from their original homeland. This draconian resettlement tactic was so successful that the Inca adopted it. The ruler would then install his own appointee in the new lands, in a compound palace that was a smaller version of Chan Chan itself.

The Chimu Empire extended far south, at least to the Casma Valley and perhaps reaching to the vicinity of modern Lima, for the main focus of civilization lay on the northern Peruvian shore, where the soils were fertile and large-scale irrigation was a practical reality. Chimu armies fought with powerful neighbors to the south, among them the chief of Pachacamac, who controlled some narrow valleys south of Lima. Pachacamac had long been a venerated shrine and already boasted a terraced temple covering 0.3 ha (0.6 acre). Pachacamac has been a grave robbers' paradise for centuries. Later, the Inca built a vast Temple of the Sun at Pachacamac, an irregular trapezoid in a commanding position on a rocky hill.

For all its wide-ranging military activities and material wealth, the Chimu Empire was very vulnerable to attack from outside. The massive irrigation works of the northern river valleys were easily disrupted by an aggressive conqueror, for no leader, however powerful, could hope to fortify the entire frontier of the empire. We know little of the defenses, except for Paramonga in the Fortaleza Valley, a massive terraced structure built of rectangular adobes that overlooks the probable southern limits of Chimu territory. The Chimu were also vulnerable to prolonged drought, for the storage capacity of their great irrigation works was sufficient to carry them over only one or two lean seasons. Perhaps, too, the irrigated desert soils became too saline for agriculture, so that crop yields fell drastically when population densities were rising sharply. Since the Chimu depended on a highly specialized agricultural system, once that system was disrupted—whether naturally or artificially—military conquest and control of the irrigation network were easy, especially for aggressive and skillful conquerors such as the Inca, who conquered the Chimu in the 1460s.

☙ The Late Horizon: The Inca State

The Late Horizon of Peruvian archaeology was also the shortest, dating from A.D. 1476 to 1534. It is the period of the Inca Empire, when those mighty Andean rulers held sway over an enormous area of highland and lowland country (Rowe, 1946; Stanish, 2001).

The Inca were born into an intensely competitive world, their homeland lying to the northwest of the Titicaca basin in the area around Cuzco (Conrad and Demarest, 1984). They were a small-scale farming society living in small villages and organized in kin groups known as *ayllu,* groups claiming a common ancestry and also owning land in common (Hastorf, 1992). The Inca were a self-sufficient people, and their *ayllu* leaders contributed labor to one another as a means of organizing and distributing labor reciprocally. The ancestors protected the *ayllu* and legitimized its landownership. It was small wonder that the Inca always took good care of their ancestral mummies.

Late Horizon
A.D. 1476 to 1534

The bodies of the dead, their tombs, and their fetishes, as well as numerous other sacred places and phenomena, were known as *huaca.*

The later Inca rulers clothed their origins in a glorious panoply of heroic deeds. It is likely, however, that the Inca had originally been a fractious, constantly quarreling petty chiefdom. The chronicles of early conquest reflect the constant bickering of village headmen, and the earliest Inca rulers were probably petty war leaders (*sinchi*), elected officials whose success was measured by their victories and booty. To stay in office, they had to be politically and militarily adept so that they could both defeat and appease their many potential rivals. The official Inca histories speak of at least eight Inca rulers between 1200 and 1438, but these genealogies are hardly reliable (Rowe, 1946). They probably depict little more than legendary figures. During the fourteenth century, a number of small tribal groups in the southern highlands began to develop a more powerful military confederacy, but the Inca flourished in this competitive atmosphere because their leaders were expert politicians as well as warriors. A leader named Viracocha Inca rose to power at the beginning of the fifteenth century. Unlike his raiding predecessors, however, he turned to permanent conquest and soon presided over a small kingdom centered in Cuzco. Viracocha Inca became the living god, in the first of a series of constant religious changes that kept the new kingdom under tight control. At about the same time, a new religious cult emerged, that of Inti, a celestial divine ancestor who was part of the sky god. (We say "part" because Inti was more of a cluster of solar aspects than the sun god.)

Inca civilization
A.D. 1476 to 1534

Around 1438, a brilliant warrior named Cusi Inca Yupanqui was crowned Inca (the term *Inca* can refer to both the ruler and the people) after a memorable victory over the neighboring Chanca tribe. He immediately took the name Pachakuti ("He Who Remakes the World") and set about transforming the Inca state. In particular, he and his henchmen developed a form of royal ancestor cult. This in itself was not especially significant, since Pachakuti was simply reworking an age-old Andean tradition, but the law of split inheritance that went along with it had a lasting and profound significance. A dead ruler was mummified. His palace, servants, and possessions were still considered his property and were maintained by all his male descendants except his successor, normally one of his sons. The deceased was not considered dead, however. His mummy attended great ceremonies and would even visit the houses of the living (Figure 22.15). Those entrusted to look after the king ate and talked with him, just as if he were still alive. This element of continuity made the royal mummies some of the holiest artifacts in the empire. Dead rulers were living sons of Inti, visible links with the gods, the very embodiment of the Inca state and of the fertility of nature.

FIGURE 22.15 An Inca royal mummy as depicted by seventeenth-century native chronicler Felipe Guaman Poma de Ayala.

Meanwhile, the ascending ruler was rich in prestige but poor in possessions. The new king had to acquire wealth so he could both live in royal splendor and provide for his mummy in the future—and the only wealth in the highland kingdom was taxable labor. Therefore, every adult male in Inca country had to render a certain amount of labor to the state each year after providing for the basic subsistence needs of his own *ayllu*. This *mit'a* system repaired bridges and roads, cultivated state-owned lands, manned the armies, and carried out public works. It was a reciprocal system. The state, or those benefiting from the work, had to feed and entertain those doing it. Since the Inca rulers needed land to provide food for those who worked for them and the earlier kings owned most of the land near Cuzco, the only way a new ruler could obtain his own royal estates was by expansion into new territory. This expansion could not take the form of temporary raids. The conquest had to be permanent, the conquered territory had to be controlled and taxed, and the ruler's subjects had to be convinced of the value of a policy of long-term conquest.

A highly complicated set of benefits, economic incentives, rewards, and justifications fueled and nourished the Inca conquests. Inca rulers turned into brilliant propagandists, reminding everyone that they were gods and that the welfare of all depended on the prosperity of all rulers, past and present, and on constant military conquest. There were initial economic advantages, too, in the form of better protection against famine. Also, the rulers were careful to reward prowess in battle. Nobles were promoted to new posts and awarded insignia that brought their lifestyle ever closer to that of the king, and even a brave regular warrior could become a member of the secondary nobility.

The successful ideology of the Inca provided them with a crucial advantage over their neighbors, and within a decade of Pachakuti's accession they were masters of the southern highlands. Their army had become an invincible juggernaut, and in less than a century the tiny kingdom taken over by Pachakuti had become a vast empire. Topa Inca (1471–1493) extended the Inca Empire into Ecuador, northern Argentina, parts of Bolivia, and Chile. His armies also conquered the Chimu state, whose water supplies Topa Inca already controlled. The best Chimu craftsworkers were carried off to work for the court of the Inca. Another king, Wayna Capac, ruled for 32 years after Topa Inca and pushed the empire deeper into Ecuador (for a different view of Inca development, see Bauer, 1992).

The Inca rulers developed an efficient administrative system to run their empire, one based firmly on the precedents of earlier societies. Tawantinsuyu ("The Land of the Four Quarters") was divided into four large provinces known as *suyu* (quarters), each subdivided into smaller provinces, some of them coinciding with older conquered kingdoms (D'Altroy, 1992; Hyslop, 1990; Patterson, 1992). A leading member of a local family, known as a *curaca*, usually ruled conquered peoples in the Inca Empire. These hereditary chiefs were a form of secondary non-Inca nobility who governed a taxpaying population of 100 people or more, but all the really important government posts were held by Inca nobles. The Inca rulers realized, however, that the essence of efficient government in such varied topography was efficient communications, so the road builders commandeered a vast network of age-old highways from the states they conquered (Figure 22.16). They linked them in a coordinated system with regular rest houses so that they could move armies, trade goods, and send messengers from one end of the kingdom to the other in short order (Hyslop, 1984).

The Inca passion for organization impinged on everyone's life. Their society was organized into 12 age divisions for the purposes of census and tax assessment, divisions based on both physical changes like puberty and major social events like marriage. The most important stage was adulthood, which lasted as long as one could do a day's work. All the census and other data of the empire were recorded not on tablets but on knotted strings. These *quipu* were a complex and sophisticated record-keeping system that seems to have been so efficient that it more than made up for the lack of writing (Ascher and Ascher, 1981). They also were a powerful instrument for codifying laws and providing data for the inspectors, who regularly visited each household to check that everyone was engaged in productive work and living in sanitary conditions.

At the time of the Spanish Conquest, the Inca controlled the lives of as many as 6 million people, most of them living in small villages dispersed around religious and

FIGURE 22.16 An Inca mountain road and agricultural terracing.

political centers (D'Altroy, 1992). It was here that Inca artisans labored, producing major works of art in gold and silver. Brightly painted Inca pottery is found throughout the empire; it is decorated with black, white, and red geometric designs. Despite the widespread distribution of Inca pots and artifacts, however, regional pottery styles flourished because the village potters, many of whom were conquered subjects, continued the cultural traditions of earlier centuries. Inca political and religious power was based on major ritual centers like Cuzco in the Andes, where the ceremonial precincts were built of carefully fitted stones (Figure 22.17) (Gasparini and Margolies, 1980).

FIGURE 22.17 Inca masonry at the fortress of Sacsahuaman near Cuzco, Peru.

The Inca ruler held court in Cuzco, surrounded by plotting factions and ever-changing political tides. One villain was the very institution of split inheritance that fueled Inca military conquest. Every ruler faced increasingly complex governance problems as a result. The need for more and more conquests caused great military, economic, and administrative stress. The logistics of long-distance military campaigns were horrendous, and the soldiers had to be fed from state-owned land, not royal estates. Moreover, although their tactics were well adapted to open country, where they were invincible, the rulers eventually had to start fighting in forested country, where the armies fared badly. Meanwhile, the empire had grown so large that communication became an increasingly lengthy process, compounded by the great diversity of the people living within the Inca domain. Also, the increasing number of high-ranking nobles devoted to the interests of dead rulers led to chronic factionalism in Cuzco. Under its glittering facade, Tawantinsuyu was becoming politically unstable. In the end, the Inca Empire was overthrown not by Peruvians but by a tiny band of foreigners with firearms who could exploit the inherent vulnerability of such a conforming hierarchical society.

〰 The Spanish Conquest (1532 to 1534)

This vulnerability came home to roost in 1532, when a small party of rapacious Spanish conquistadors landed in northern Peru (Hemming, 1970). When Francisco Pizarro arrived, the Inca state was in some political chaos, its people already decimated by smallpox and other diseases introduced by the first conquistadors. Inca Wayna Capac had died in an epidemic in A.D. 1525. The empire was plunged into a civil war between his son Huascar and another son, Atahuallpa, half brother to Huascar. Atahuallpa eventually prevailed, but as he moved south from Ecuador to consolidate his territory, he learned that the Spanish adventurer Francisco Pizarro had landed in Peru.

A.D. 1532

The Spaniards had vowed to make Peru part of Spain and were bent on plunder and conquest. Pizarro arrived in the guise of a diplomat, captured Atahuallpa by treachery, collected a huge quantity of gold in ransom, and then brutally murdered him. A year later, the Spaniards captured the Inca capital with a tiny army. They took over the state bureaucracy and appointed a puppet ruler, Manco Inca, but many Inca groups continued their traditional lifeways in isolated locations like Machu Picchu high in the Andes (Figure 22.18). Three years later, Manco Inca turned on his masters in a bloody

FIGURE 22.18 Machu Picchu. Forgotten for nearly 400 years after the Spanish Conquest, Machu Picchu was rediscovered by the American explorer Hiram Bingham in 1911.

FIGURE 22.19 A silver, long-haired Inca llama; the figure epitomizes late Andean artistry in sheet metal. Tragically, few such artworks survived the depredations of the Spanish Conquest.

revolt. Its suppression finally destroyed the greatest of the Peruvian empires (Figure 22.19). The Spanish conquest of Mexico and Peru saw the last major confrontation between the forces of an expanding Europe that was emerging from centuries of feudalism and complex non-Western societies that were still living with the full legacy of prehistoric times.

The four and one-half centuries since the Spanish conquests of Mexico and Peru have seen European settlement in all corners of the globe, the emergence of the industrial state, and the acting out of the last, tragic chapter of human prehistory: the clash between the Western and non-Western worlds (Wolf, 1984).

Summary 🐾🐾🐾

The earliest complex societies of coastal Peru may have developed as a result of the intensive exploitation of maritime resources, especially small fish easily netted from canoes. In time, abundant food surpluses, growing population densities, and larger settlements may have preadapted coastal people to intensive irrigation agriculture. These societies were organized in increasingly complex ways. During the so-called Initial Period of Peruvian prehistory, large monumental structures appeared, many of them U-shaped, just before and during the transition toward greater dependence on maize agriculture. This was also a period of continuous interaction and extensive trade between the coast and the highlands.

This florescence of social complexity, new art traditions, and monumental architecture coincided with the emergence of several small polities in river valleys on the coast. The culmination of this trend is seen in various local traditions, among them the famous Chavín style. Chavín de Huántar, once thought to have been the source of Peruvian civilization, is now known to be a late manifestation of cultural trends that began as early as 2000 B.C. After the Early Horizon ended, in about 200 B.C., a series of coastal kingdoms of the so-called Middle Horizon developed between 200 B.C. and A.D. 600 and lasted until about A.D. 1000, the political and economic influence of which spread beyond their immediate valley homelands. These states included Moche and Nasca, remarkable for their fine pottery styles and expert alloy and gold metallurgy. They flourished in the first millennium A.D.

About A.D. 1375, Chimu, with its great capital at Chan Chan on the northern coast, dominated a wide area of the lowlands. Its compounds reflect a stratified state with many expert craftspeople and a complex material culture. During the Late Horizon of

Peruvian prehistory (A.D. 1400 to 1534), there was unification of the highlands and the lowlands under the Inca Empire, which may have emerged as early as A.D. 1200 and lasted until the Spanish Conquest in 1532–1534. The Inca rulers were masters of bureaucracy and military organization. They governed a highly structured state—one, however, that was so weakened by civil war and disease that it fell easily to the conquistador Francisco Pizarro and his small army of adventurers.

Guide to Further Reading ﹏﹏

Alva, Walter, and Christopher Donnan. 1993. *Royal Tombs of Sipán.* Los Angeles: Fowler Museum of Cultural History, University of California.
A magnificently illustrated and definitive account of one of the most important archaeological discoveries of the twentieth century.

Conrad, Geoffrey W., and Arthur A. Demarest. 1984. *Religion and Empire: The Dynamics of Aztec and Inca Expansionism.* Cambridge: Cambridge University Press.
A clear and succinct analysis of two imperial preindustrial civilizations. A sophisticated, well-argued book. Strongly recommended.

Haas, Jonathan, S. Pozorski, and T. Pozorski, eds. 1987. *The Origins and Development of the Andean State.* Cambridge: Cambridge University Press.
A useful series of essays on the complex processes of state formation in the Andean region. Not for beginners.

Hemming, John. 1970. *The Conquest of the Incas.* New York: Harcourt, Brace, Jovanovich.
Hemming's gripping account of the Spanish Conquest is a standard work and very readable.

Moseley, Michael E. 1975. *The Maritime Foundations of Andean Civilization.* Menlo Park, CA: Cummings.
A short essay that argues that the foundations of Peruvian civilization lay on the coast in subsistence patterns that relied heavily on maritime resources. Controversial, but convincing for the most part.

_____. 2000. *The Incas and Their Ancestors,* 2nd ed. London and New York: Thames & Hudson.
A definitive account of Andean prehistory and complex societies for the general reader. Lavishly illustrated.

Rowe, John H. 1946. *Inca Culture at the Time of the Spanish Conquest.* Vol. 2. *Handbook of South American Indians.* Washington, DC: Smithsonian Institution.
The classic account of Inca culture, reconstructed from historical documents and limited archaeological investigations.

GLOSSARY OF CULTURES AND SITES

These brief descriptions give some background on the major prehistoric sites and cultures mentioned in the text; they are not meant to be precise definitions. Please note that major civilizations, like, for example, Sumerian civilization, or well-known subdivisions of said societies (i.e., the Egyptian New Kingdom) are not included here, as they are self-evident. Ask your instructor for more information and references on cultures and sites here if you need them. Sites mentioned in passing in the text are not included in this list.

Abu Hureyra, Syria   Hunter-gatherer, then early farming settlement in Syria's Euphrates Valley, occupied between about 10,500 and 6000 B.C.

Abu Simbel, Egypt   Ancient Egyptian temple erected by Rameses II in Nubia, c. 1250 B.C. The site with its seated figures of the pharaoh was moved to higher ground to prevent its flooding by Lake Nasser in 1968 at a cost of $40 million.

Abydos, Egypt   Site of many early ancient Egyptian burials including King Scorpion, c. 3150 B.C.

Acheulian   A widespread early Stone Age culture named after the town of St. Acheul in northern France. The Acheulian flourished in Africa, western Europe, and southern Asia from before a million years ago until less than 100,000 years before present. The Acheulians made many types of stone artifacts, including multipurpose butchering hand.

Adena, Ohio   A distinctive burial cult and village culture in the Ohio Valley of the Midwest. It flourished between about 500 B.C. and A.D. 400 and was remarkable for its long-distance trading and distinctive burial cults, expressed in large earthworks and mounds.

Afontova Gora-Oshurkovo Tradition   A poorly defined Siberian late Ice Age cultural tradition that flourished around 19,000 B.C.

'Ain Ghazal, Jordan   An early farming village in the Jordan Valley, occupied c. 7500 B.C. It is remarkable for its clay female figurines, perhaps evidence of an early fertility cult.

Akrotiri, Greece   A Bronze Age village on Santorini Island in the Aegean Sea, destroyed by a huge volcanic explosion in about 1450 B.C.

Aksum, Ethiopia   A city and state that flourished off the Red Sea and Indian Ocean trade during the first millennium A.D. Famous for its tall royal burial markers.

Alaçahöyök, Turkey   A major city in central Anatolia, famous for its royal burials, c. 2000 B.C.

Ali Kosh, Iran   Early farming site on the Deh Luran plain in Iran, where evidence for cereal cultivation was found with flotation techniques. The site dates to as early as 7500 B.C.

Allia Bay, Kenya   Site on Lake Turkana in northern Kenya that yielded a 4.10-million-year-old hominid: *Australopithecus anamensis*.

Ambrona, Spain   See **Torralba**.

Anangula, Alaska   A fishing and sea mammal hunting community in the Aleutian Islands, dating to c. 6700 B.C.

Angkor Thom, Cambodia   Khmer capital city, shrine, and temple complex built by King Jayavarman VII, c. A.D. 1181.

Angkor Wat, Cambodia   An elaborate mortuary temple built by Khmer King Suryavarman II in the twelfth century A.D. as a reproduction of the Hindu universe.

Anyang, China   The capital of Shang civilization after 1400 B.C.

Ao, China   Major early Shang capital with massive fortifications, c. 1557 B.C.

Apple Creek, Illinois   An Archaic site where people engaged in intensive collecting of wild vegetable foods after 3000 B.C. They concentrated on hickory nuts, acorns, and other common species.

Aramis, Ethiopia   Early hominid site dating to c. 4.5 million years ago.

Archaic   Term used to describe a broad spectrum hunter-gatherer tradition that flourished in many forms over North America (and other parts of the Americas), c. 9500 B.C. to A.D. 1000.

Arctic Small Tool tradition, Alaska   A distinctive small tool stone technology that appeared in Alaska, c. 2300 B.C. and remained in use until 1500 B.C.

Asana, Peru   A site with a corral containing llama dung, southwest of Lake Titicaca, c. 2000 B.C.

Avaris, Egypt   A palace and trading site in Lower Egypt celebrated for its Minoan (Cretan) wall paintings, evidence of trade between Egypt and Crete in about 1500 B.C.

Avebury, England   A spectacular stone circle and accompanying sacred landscape, built c. 2500 B.C.

Bandkeramik complex, Europe   An early farming complex that spread across Europe around 5300 B.C.

Ban Mae Tha, Thailand   The site of three humanly manufactured artifacts, dating to c. 700,000 years ago.

Ban Na Di, Thailand   Site of a major cemetery where the dead lay in clusters, denoting social ranking. First millennium B.C.

Benin, Nigeria   A West African state ruled from the city of Benin from before A.D. 1400 to modern times.

Bluff Cave, Australia (also **ORS 7**)   Sites in south-central Tasmania occupied as early as 28,500 B.C.

Bobongara, New Guinea   A location that yielded stone axes, dating to c. 38,000 B.C.

Boghazkoy, Turkey   Capital of the Hittite Empire during the second millennium B.C.

Bouri, Ethiopia   Important *Homo erectus* location, dating to between 1 mya and 800,000 B.P.

Boxgrove, England   *Homo erectus* site in southern England; contains evidence of big-game hunting.

Broken Mammoth, Alaska   Early human settlement in Alaska's Tenana River dating to 11,700 B.C.

Cahokia, Illinois   Mississippian ceremonial center at the height of its power in A.D. 1050 to 1250.

Calakmul, Mexico   A large Maya city, one of the great city-states, first century A.D. to A.D. 820.

Caracol, Belize   A major Maya center that began as a small hamlet and dominated a wide area of the lowlands in the sixth century A.D.

Caral, Peru   The earliest large center in Peru, dating to c. 2600 to after 2000 B.C. A center for cotton agriculture and trade.

Casas Grandes, Mexico   A major farming and trading settlement in northern Mexico, which traded extensively with the Southwest, c. 1400 B.C.

Çatalhöyük, Turkey   Large farming village and obsidian trading center dating to c. 6000 B.C.

Caverna da Pedra Pintada, Brazil   A cave containing evidence of human occupation in a forested environment, c. 9000 B.C.

Çayönü, Turkey   Early farming village in eastern Turkey, dating to c. 9500 to 6500 B.C.

Cerro Arena, Peru   A large settlement in the Moche Valley of Peru's north coast, perhaps a founder community of the Moche state.

Cerro Blanco, Peru   Capital of the Moche state, c. A.D. 600, marked by two spectacular adobe pyramids.

Cerro Juanaqueña, Mexico   An early maize-farming settlement of about 1150 B.C., comprising about 135 pithouses.

Cerro Palenque, Honduras   Terminal Classic Maya center dating to after A.D. 900.

Cerros, Mexico   A small Maya community of 50 B.C., where kingship emerged briefly.

Chaco Canyon, New Mexico   Anasazi people built a series of "Great Houses," multiroom pueblos, in this canyon between A.D. 950 and 1175. The canyon was first occupied c. A.D. 490.

Chan Chan, Peru   Capital of the Chimu state, A.D. 1375 to 1475.

Chauvet, Grotte de, France   Cave in southeastern France famous for its rock art, dating to c. 31,000 to 24,000 years ago.

Chavín de Huántar, Peru   An important ceremonial center and place of pilgrimage in the Andean foothills, c. 850 to 200 B.C.

Chesowanya, Kenya   Purported location for the use of fire, 1.6 mya.

Chichén Itzá, Mexico   A Postclassic Maya ceremonial center in the northern Yucatán dating to c. A.D. 1100.

Chilca, Peru   A coastal site with a strong maritime adaptation, as well as simple agriculture, dating to 3800 to 2650 B.C.

Chinchorro culture, Chile   A coastal forager culture in northern Chile, famous for its mummies, dating to c. 2500 B.C.

Chiripa, Peru   A fishing and fowling settlement south of Lake Titicaca, which was at first a village, then a small center, 1400 to 100 B.C.

Choga Mami, Iraq   A large farming village near Samarra in central Iraq that practiced simple irrigation, c. 6000 B.C.

Clovis   Paleo-Indian culture that flourished in North America, and perhaps further afield, about 11,200 to 10,900 B.C.

Cochise culture, western United States   A widespread desert hunter-gatherer culture that flourished for thousands of years after 10,000 B.C. and endured, albeit in modified form, into historic times.

Copán, Honduras   A Classic Maya city, A.D. 435 to 900.

Coxcatlán, Mexico   A Tehuacán Valley rock shelter that yielded some of the earliest maize cobs known in the Americas. Occupied by hunter-gatherers as early as 10,000 B.C.

Cro-Magnon, France   A rock shelter near Les Eyzies in the Dordogne, which gave the name Cro-Magnons to the first modern human in western Europe. Cro-Magnon burials were found there.

Cuello, Belize   Early Maya village and long-lived ceremonial center, c. 1200 B.C. to A.D. 400.

Dalton tradition, North America   Long-lived Archaic cultural tradition mainly in the southern United States, 9950 to 7900 B.C.

Dapenkeng culture, Taiwan   A rice farming culture of people who lived close to lakes and rivers, c. 5000 B.C.

Dereivka, Ukraine   A settlement of 4000 B.C., which has yielded clear evidence of horse domestication and riding.

Devil's Lair, Australia   Long-occupied Australian rock shelter, 30,500 B.C. and later.

Diospolis Parva, Egypt   A pre-Dynastic cemetery site, c. 3500 B.C., famous for Petrie's sequence dating.

Dmanisi, Georgia   Important fossil location that has yielded *Homo erectus* fragments dating to c. 1.7 mya.

Dolní Vestonice, Czech Republic   Late Ice Age hunting camp, dating to c. 24,000 B.C.

Dong Son culture, Vietnam   A bronzeworking and trading society centered on Vietnam's Red River valley, 1000 B.C. to A.D. 43.

Dos Pilas, Guatemala   Maya center of A.D. 645 to 761 that controlled major trade routes.

Dry Creek I, Alaska   A Paleo-arctic site in the Nenana Valley dating to c. 11,500 B.C.

D'uktai, Russia   A late Ice Age cave on Siberia's Lena River, occupied as early as 16,000 B.C.

Eastern Gravettian tradition   A widespread late Ice Age hunter-gatherer cultural tradition that flourished in central and eastern Europe, also into Eurasia, c. 28,000 to 8000 B.C.

Easton Down, England A Stone Age communal burial mound, built in about 3200 B.C. See also **Avebury, England.**

El-Amarna, Egypt Capital of the pharaoh Akhenaten, downstream of Thebes, and famous for its diplomatic archives, c. 1350 B.C.

Eland's Bay, South Africa A location celebrated for its chronicle of different subsistence activities between 11,000 and 6000 B.C.

El Mirador, Guatemala A huge late Preclassic Maya city, built between 150 B.C. and A.D. 50.

El Paraíso, Peru A large U-shaped ceremonial center on Peru's north coast, c. 1800 B.C.

Epidauros, Greece Greek amphitheater first dedicated in the fifth century B.C. and subsequently restored by the Romans.

Eridu, Iraq An early city in the Mesopotamia delta that boasted of a major temple as early as 4500 B.C. One of the earliest cities in the world.

Ertebølle culture, northern Europe A coastal hunter-gatherer culture of 4600 to 3200 B.C., marked by a broad spectrum exploitation of many food resources.

Fayyum, Egypt Site of a series of early agricultural settlements, dating to c. 4350 B.C. The Fayyum Depression, west of the Nile River, was also a major center of irrigation agriculture for Middle and New Kingdom Egypt.

Flag Fen, England A Late Bronze Age field system and ceremonial center in eastern England dating to c. 1350 B.C. and, later, famous for its wooden artifacts and timber posts and trackways.

Folsom Paleo-Indian culture that flourished on the North American Plains after 9000 B.C.

Franchthi Cave, Greece A long-occupied cave site with evidence of agriculture by 6000 B.C., also of offshore seafaring to the Aegean islands.

Ganj Dareh, Iran Seasonal hunting camp, then a farming village, first occupied before 10,000 B.C.

Garnsey, New Mexico A bison kill site of the fifteenth century A.D.

Gatecliff Rock Shelter, Nevada A deep rock shelter seasonally occupied from at least 6000 B.C. to modern times.

Giza, Egypt The Pyramids at Giza were built in the desert near Cairo during Egypt's Old Kingdom, around 2550 B.C. The Great Pyramid, built in 2528 B.C., is 146.6 m (481 feet) high and covers 21 ha (13.1 acres).

Godin Tepe, Iran A trading settlement dating to c. 4000 B.C.

Gona, Ethiopia Site of the earliest human-made artifacts, dating to about 2.6 mya.

Gournia, Crete A small Minoan town, c. 1500 B.C.

Gran Dolina, Spain Important site for *Homo erectus* fossils dating to c. 800,000 years ago.

Grasshopper Pueblo, Arizona An important Pueblo site occupied in the fourteenth and fifteenth centuries A.D.

Great Zimbabwe, Zimbabwe A complex of stone buildings in Central Africa associated with Shona chieftains and cattle groups dating to between A.D. 850 and 1450.

Grotta dell'Uzzo, Italy A cave on the northwest coast of Sicily occupied by farmers between 6000 and 5800 B.C.

Grotte de Chauvet, France A magnificent painted cave in southeastern France, visited sporadically for ritual purposes between about 31,000 and 24,000 B.C.

Gwisho Hot Springs, Zambia Hunter-gatherer camp celebrated for its fine preservation, occupied c. 1000 B.C.

Haçilar, Turkey Farming village in central Turkey first occupied before 8000 B.C.

Hadar, Ethiopia A region of Ethiopia where hominid fossils dating to as early as 4 million years ago have been found.

Halafian, Iraq A widely traded form of painted pottery in northern Iraq, c. 6000 B.C.

Hallan Çemi Tepesi, Turkey Early pig-herding settlement in eastern Turkey, before 9500 B.C.

Hallstatt culture, Austria An ironworking culture of the eighth century B.C., known mainly from cemeteries.

Harappa, Pakistan A city based in the Indus Valley that flourished from before 2500 to 1500 B.C.

Hascherkeller, Germany A farming community of 1000 to 800 B.C., with iron tools.

Hassuna, Iraq Type site for a widespread form of pottery, c. 6000 B.C., used extensively over northern Iraq.

Head-Smashed-In, Canada Bison kill site in western Canada used by Plains hunters for over 5000 years and intensively after A.D. 150 as a mass killing site.

Hemudu culture, China A widespread rice farming culture south of Shanghai, dating to as early as 7000 B.C.

Hissarlik, Turkey The site of Homeric Troy in northwestern Turkey, which was an important Bronze Age city during the second millennium B.C.

Hogup Cave, Utah A dry cave in the Great Basin occupied from c. 9000 B.C. until recent times, famous for its excellent dry preservation of organic artifacts such as fiber sandals.

Hohokam, Arizona A Southwestern cultural tradition that originated as early as 300 B.C. and lasted until A.D. 1500. The Hohokam people were farmers who occupied much of what is now Arizona. Their cultural heirs are the Pima and Tohono O'odham Indians of today.

Hopewell, Ohio Between A.D. 1 and 600, the "Hopewell Interaction Sphere" flourished in the Midwest. Hopewell religious cults and distinctive burial customs were associated with an art tradition that spread far and wide through long-distance trading connections.

Huaca Florida, Peru A major center on the north coast, built c. 1700 B.C.

Huaca Prieta, Peru A sedentary village on Peru's north coast, dating to 2500 to 1800 B.C., with extensive cotton cultivation and fine textiles.

Huaricoto, Peru Center for a distinctive religious ideology known to archaeologists as the Kotosh religious tradition, 2000 to 200 B.C.

Jarmo, Iran   Compact farming settlement of 7500 B.C. that practiced both cereal agriculture and animal husbandry.

Jenne-jeno, Mali   A farming and trading community at the southern edge of the Sahara Desert, 200 B.C. to later than A.D. 850. Jenne-jeno played a major role in the formation of West African states.

Jericho, Jordan   Long-lived city, with roots in early farming towns dating to the eighth millennium B.C.

Jiahu, China   Early rice farming site in the Huai Valley of northern China, dating to 6500 to 5500 B.C.

Jomon tradition, Japan   A Japanese cultural tradition dating from c. 10,500 B.C. until about 300 B.C., remarkable for its early manufacturing of pottery and complex hunter-gatherer culture and, later, agriculture.

Kabwe (Broken Hill), Zambia   Site of an archaic-looking and robust *Homo sapiens* skull, dating to c. 100,000 years ago.

Kahun, Egypt   Middle Kingdom town built to service the mortuary complex of King Senusret II, c. 1890 B.C.

Kanesh, Turkey   An important Hittite trading town of 1900 B.C., famous for its Assyrian colony outside the community.

Karanovo culture, southeastern Europe   An early farming culture that developed before 5500 B.C. in the Balkans. Marked by long-term occupation of mound sites.

Karnak, Egypt   Site of the temple of the ancient Egyptian sun god Amun, which reached the height of its glory in the New Kingdom c. 1500 B.C.

Kebaran culture, Israel   A hunter-gatherer culture of 13,000 to 11,000 B.C., marked by great mobility and exploitation of contrasting environments.

Kerma, Sudan   Capital of the Kingdom of Kush, at the height of its power c. 1500 B.C.

Khirbat Hamra Ifdan, Jordan   Copper production and mining center in Jordan's Faynan district, 2700 to 2200 B.C.

Khok Phanom Di, Thailand   A village and burial ground dating to 2000 to 1400 B.C.

Khorsabad, Iraq   Palace of Assyrian King Sargon, eighth century B.C.

Kilu, Solomon Islands   A rock shelter containing human occupation dating to between 26,000 and 18,000 B.C., the earliest settlement of an offshore Pacific island.

Klasies River Cave, South Africa   A Middle Stone Age cave, occupied c. 120,000 to 100,000 years ago, which yielded fossil and cultural evidence for very early modern humans.

Knossos, Crete   Palace and shrine complex in northern Crete that started life as a small village in about 6000 B.C. and became the major center of Minoan civilization. It was abandoned in the late second millennium B.C.

Kongemose culture, northern Europe   A Mesolithic hunter-gatherer culture base on the shores of the Baltic Sea, dating to 5700 and 4600 B.C. and marked by increasing social complexity.

Koobi Fora, Kenya   A location on the eastern shores of Lake Turkana in northern Kenya, where the earliest traces of human culture have been found, dating to more than 2.5 million years ago.

Koonalda, Australia   South Australian cave occupied as early as 22,000 B.C. until 13,000 B.C.

Kostenki, Ukraine   A plains hunter-gatherer site on the Eurasian steppe-tundra of c. 22,000 B.C.

Koster, Illinois   From before 7000 B.C. until less than 1000 years ago, hunter-gatherers and later farmers settled at this location on the Illinois River to exploit the fertile river bottom. The site is unusual for its long stratigraphic sequence of Archaic and Woodland settlements and abundant food remains.

Kot Diji, Pakistan   Fortified farming village in the Indus Valley, c. 3000 B.C.

Kourion, Cyprus   A small Roman port in southwestern Cyprus in the eastern Mediterranean overwhelmed by a great earthquake early on the morning of July 21, A.D. 365. Excavations at the village have revealed many details of a long-forgotten disaster.

Kuk, New Guinea   Highland site that has yielded early evidence of root cultivation, c. 7000 B.C.

Kulli complex, Pakistan   A complex of smaller and larger centers in Baluchistan that traded in cotton. c. 2600 to 2200 B.C.

Kurgan culture, Russia   Widespread copper-using culture of 3200 B.C. that may have domesticated horses.

Kush, Kingdom of, Sudan   A major African kingdom that traded with Egypt. At the height of its powers c. 1500 B.C.

Kutikina Cave, Australia   Tasmanian cave occupied from 18,000 to 12,000 B.C. during the late Ice Age.

Laetoli, Tanzania   This East African site yielded the earliest hominid footprints, potassium-argon dated to more than 3.5 million years ago.

Lant'ien, China   600,000-year-old site that yielded hominid fragments, probably of *Homo erectus*.

Lapita cultural complex, southwestern Pacific   An early maritime culture in the southwestern Pacific, centered on the Bismarck Archipelago off New Guinea, remarkable for its long-distance voyaging and trade, 1600 to 1000 B.C. and later.

Lascaux Cave, France   A painted cave of the Magdalenian culture of southwestern France dating to about 17,000 years ago.

La Tène culture, Europe   A highly distinctive Celtic culture with sophisticated art and metallurgy, dating to after the late fourth century B.C.

Laugerie Haute, France   A large rock shelter with extensive Cro-Magnon occupation, especially after 20,000 B.C. A place where reindeer were hunted.

La Venta, Mexico   Major center of the Olmec civilization, 800 to 400 B.C.

Lene Hara, East Timor   A small cave containing evidence of human occupation, c. 29,000 B.C.

Liangzhu culture, China   A farming culture of the Shanghai Delta region, known for its prestigious burials, c. 3250 B.C.

Lokalelei, Kenya   A site on Lake Turkana in northern Kenya where human-made tools date to about 2.34 mya.

Longgupo, China A location where a hominid jaw, two stone tools, and numerous animal bones may date to c. 2 million years ago.

Long Rongrien, Thailand A 37,000-year-old site containing human artifacts that may have been manufactured by modern humans. This is the earliest such record in the region.

Longshanoid (Longshan) cultures, China Complex farming cultures that flourished throughout much of northern China 4000 B.C. and later. The term subsumes much local cultural variation.

Lovelock Cave, Nevada A desert site in the far western United States, occupied as early as 7000 B.C. Located near a desert marsh, it has yielded minute details of prehistoric desert adaptations over a long period.

Maadi, Egypt An important trading center in the Nile Delta, c. 3650 B.C.

Machu Picchu, Peru Spectacular Inca town high in the Andes that was occupied over a long period of Inca civilization.

Magdalenian culture The apogee of late Ice Age hunter-gatherers in western and central Europe, c. 16,000 to 13,000 B.C.

Maglemose culture, northern Europe A Mesolithic, predominantly shoreline culture of 7500 to 5700 B.C. that focused on fishing and fowling.

Maiden Castle, England An Iron Age hill fort in southern England attacked by the Romans in A.D. 43.

Malaia Suja, Russia A late Ice Age hunter-gatherer site of 32,500 B.C., west of Lake Baikal, one of the earliest human occupations in western Siberia.

Mal'ta, Russia Late Ice Age site by Lake Baikal, Siberia, occupied from 24,000 to 18,000 B.C.

Meadowcroft, Pennsylvania Long-occupied rock shelter containing evidence of human occupation that may be as early as 14,000 B.C.

Meer, Belgium Stone Age site of 7000 B.C., famous for its stone tool research.

Mehrgarh, Pakistan An early farming village west of the Indus Valley, dating to c. 6000 B.C.

Merimde Beni Salama, Egypt An early agricultural settlement in the Nile Delta, dating to c. 3900 B.C.

Meroe, Sudan A major caravan city from 593 B.C. to A.D. 350. Also a major ironworking center.

Mesa Verde, Colorado An area famous for its Anasazi pueblos, notably the Cliff Palace, which reached its heyday in the twelfth century A.D.

Mezhirich, Ukraine A settlement of mammoth-bone framed houses near the Dnepr River, occupied by Stone Age big-game hunters about 15,000 B.C.

Minoan civilization, Crete Bronze Age civilization based on trading of olive oil and wine, c. 2000 to 1450 B.C.

Mississippian A widespread cultural tradition in the southeastern United States from the tenth to fifteenth centuries A.D. and more recently.

Moche civilization A coastal state in northern coastal Peru that reached its height after A.D. 400.

Modjokerto, Indonesia *Homo erectus* site dating to 1.8 million years ago.

Modoc Rock Shelter, Wisconsin Occupied between 8000 and 2000 B.C., Modoc developed into an important base camp for people exploiting fish and nut harvests.

Mohenjodaro, Pakistan A major city of the Harappan civilization after 1700 B.C.

Monte Albán, Mexico Ancient Zapotec capital of the Valley of Oaxaca, Mexico, in its heyday in the late to mid-first millennium A.D.

Monte Verde, Chile Early human settlement in South America dating to between 11,800 and 12,000 B.C.

Moundville, Alabama Mississippian ceremonial center of the early first millennium A.D.

Mousterian culture The material culture associated with Neanderthal groups in Europe that appeared about 100,000 years ago and endured until about 30,000 years before present.

Nabta Playa, Egypt A desert site near the west bank of the Nile that has yielded domesticated barley dating to c. 6000 B.C.

Nakbe, Guatemala A major middle Preclassic Maya center that flourished between 600 and 400 B.C.

Naqada, Egypt A pre-Dynastic kingdom and town, c. 4000 B.C.

Naranjo, Guatemala Maya center dating to c. A.D. 900. See also **Tikal, Guatemala.**

Nariokatome, Kenya Site of the earliest known *Homo erectus* find, dating to c. 1.6 mya.

Narmada, India A *Homo erectus* location dating to c. 230,000 years ago, one of the oldest.

Natufian culture, Israel A complex hunter-gatherer culture of 11,000 to 8500 B.C. that focused on intensive exploitation of plant foods and enjoyed more sedentary settlement.

Neanderthal, Germany Cave that yielded the first Neanderthal skull (named after the site) in 1856.

Nekhen, Egypt A pre-Dynastic kingdom in Upper Egypt, c. 3800 B.C., whose rulers played a major role in the unification of Egypt, 3100 B.C.

Nelson's Bay, South Africa Late Stone Age coastal cave in southeastern Africa, occupied as early as 13,000 B.C. until later than 5000 B.C.

Netiv Hagdud, Israel A small village, occupied in about 10,000 B.C., whose inhabitants practiced a simple form of cultivation.

Nevado Ampato, Peru Site of an Inca ceremonial burial, c. A.D. 1490.

Niah Cave, Borneo A deep cave with human occupation going back at least 40,000 years, possibly the work of modern humans.

Niaux, France A superb painted Cro-Magnon cave, dating to about 10,800 B.C.

Nimrud, Iraq Assyrian city, the biblical Calah. See also **Khorsabad, Iraq.**

Nindowari, Pakistan A major center of the Kulli complex, c. 2500 B.C.

Nineveh, Iraq Assyrian capital, famous for the palace of King Assurbanipal in the seventh century B.C. See also **Khorsabad, Iraq.**

Nippur, Iraq A Sumerian city in southern Iraq, c. 2800 B.C., celebrated in archaeological circles for its clay tablet archives.

Noen U-Loke, Thailand A large settlement with a cemetery that contains unrivaled evidence for emerging social ranking and the appearance of ironworking, dating to 400 B.C. to A.D. 300.

Norton tradition, Alaska A Bering Strait–centered sea mammal hunting tradition that flourished about 25,000 years ago.

Oc Eo, Vietnam Major trading city in the Mekong Delta, c. A.D. 300 to 600.

Olduvai Gorge, Tanzania Stratified lake beds with associated artifact scatters and kill sites, also early hominids; dating from slightly before 1.75 million years ago up to 100,000 years before present.

Olmec Olmec culture flourished in lowland Mexico from around 1200 B.C. to 500 B.C. Olmec people traded widely, had a distinctive art tradition that depicted humanlike jaguars and both natural and supernatural beings, and developed many of the basic patterns that were to sustain the Maya and other Mesoamerican civilizations such as Teotihuacán.

Olsen-Chubbuck, Colorado An 8000-year-old bison kill site on the North American Plains that revealed many details of Paleo-Indian hunting and butchering techniques.

Olympia, Greece Site of the Olympic Games in the northern Peloponnese c. 400 B.C.

Omo Kibish, Ethiopia A 130,000-year-old site that yielded modern looking *Homo sapiens* remains.

Palenque, Mexico Classic Maya city and ceremonial center that reached its height in the mid-first millennium A.D.

Paleoarctic A term used to describe Paleo-Indian cultures in the far north, c. 9000 B.C. and earlier.

Paleo-Indian A generic term used by American archaeologists to describe the earliest cultural traditions of the New World.

Paloma, Peru A large fishing and gathering settlement on Peru's central coast, dating to before 5500 B.C.

Panalauca, Peru A cave site occupied in about 2500 B.C. and containing evidence of exploitation of young camelids.

Paracas, Peru Cemeteries on the dry Peruvian south coast used by ancient Andeans between 600 and 150 B.C.

Parmerpar Meethaner, Australia Tasmanian rock shelter in southwestern Tasmania dating to about 32,000 B.C.

Pazyryk, Russia Horsemen's burials of 400 B.C. that preserve many organic remains and details of nomadic life in the region at the time.

Pecos, New Mexico An Anasazi pueblo in the American Southwest that was occupied for much of the past 2000 years and provided the first stratigraphic sequence for southwestern prehistory as a result of A. V. Kidder's excavations.

Peiligang culture, China A farming culture of central and northern China marked by semisubterranean houses and dating to between 6300 and 5000 B.C.

Pengtoushan, China Middle Yangzi Valley rice farming site dating to between 6500 and 5800 B.C.

Poverty Point, Louisiana A widespread Archaic trading culture centered on the Mississippi floodplain, dating to between 2200 and 600 B.C., known after the site of that name.

Pueblo Bonito, New Mexico Ancestral Pueblo "Great House," first constructed about A.D. 850 and in its heyday in the twelfth century A.D.

Pukara, Peru A major center northwest of Lake Titicaca, 400 B.C. to A.D. 100.

Purritjarra Rock Shelter, Australia Rock shelter occupied from at least 25,000 to about 4000 B.C.

Qadan culture, Egypt A Nile Valley–based hunter-gatherer culture marked by intensive exploitation of fish and plant foods, 10,000 B.C. and later.

Qafzeh, Israel A rock shelter that has yielded Neanderthal burials, thermoluminescence-dated to about 100,000 years ago.

St Césaire, France A rock shelter dating to 34,000 B.C., where Neanderthals made blade tools.

San Andrés, Mexico A lowland farming village that has yielded evidence of maize cultivation, c. 5100 B.C.

Sand Canyon, Colorado Anasazi pueblo in the Four Corners region of the American Southwest, occupied in the twelfth century A.D. See also **Mesa Verde, Colorado.**

San José Mogote, Mexico A large village with a ceremonial center in the Valley of Oaxaca, 1200 and 1150 B.C.

San Lorenzo, Mexico Important Olmec center, c. 1250 to 900 B.C., with spectacular monumental sculpture.

San Marcos, Mexico A Tehuacán Valley cave that has produced maize cobs dating to at least 3600 B.C.

Saqqara, Egypt Site of King Djoser's Step Pyramid, c. 2649 B.C., and a major burial area for Egyptian rulers and nobility.

Schoningen, Germany Site where 400,000-year-old wooden spears were discovered, probably manufactured by *Homo erectus*.

Sechin Alto, Peru A major ceremonial center of 1400 B.C. in the Casma Valley, remarkable for its carved monoliths of armed men.

Shang Civilization Early Chinese civilization that flourished from as early as 2700 B.C. when the Xia dynasty arose in the north. The Shang dynasty rose to power around 1766 B.C. and ruled until 1122 B.C. Its rulers occupied a series of capitals near the Yellow River, the most famous being Anyang, occupied around 1400 B.C.

Shari-i-Shokhta, Iran A trading city near Lake Helmand in eastern Iran that flourished off the turquoise and lapis lazuli trade after 2800 B.C.

Shugnou, Russia   The highest known late Ice Age site in the world, dating to c. 18,000 to 13,000 B.C.

Sicán culture, Peru   Successor culture to the Moche state, centered on the Lambayeque Valley of the north coast, A.D. 900 to 1100. Famous for its goldwork.

Sima de Los Huesos, Spain   Northern Spanish cave that has yielded to remains of over 30 archaic *Homo sapiens* individuals, dating to c. 300,000 years ago.

Similaun, Italy   The Similaun glacier, high in the European Alps, yielded the well-preserved corpse of a Bronze Age man, dating to about 3350 to 3300 B.C.

Sipán, Peru   Site of four spectacularly adorned warrior-priest graves of the Moche civilization, c. A.D. 400.

Snaketown, Arizona   A Hohokam pueblo in Arizona, occupied about 850 to 500 years ago and famous for its ball court and platform mounds. The Snaketown people probably maintained trading contacts with Mexican communities to the south.

Sounion, Greece   Classical Greek temple of the fifth century B.C., dedicated to the sea god Poseidon.

Spirit Cave, Thailand   A hunter-gatherer site occupied c. 9000 B.C., marked by intensive exploitation of plant foods.

Star Carr, England   A postglacial hunting site in northeast England dating to about 9200 B.C., remarkable for the bone and wooden artifacts recovered from a small birchbark platform at the edge of a small lake.

Stonehenge, England   Stone circles in southern Britain that formed a sacred precinct as early as 2950 B.C. and remained in use until about 1500 B.C. Some authorities believe Stonehenge was an astronomical observatory, but this viewpoint is controversial. See also **Avebury, England.**

Studenoe-2, Russia   Early microblade site near Lake Baikal, dated to c. 15,800 B.C.

Sumerians   Creators of the civilization that flourished in southern Iraq between about 2900 and 2200 B.C. Sumerians lived in small city-states that perennially quarreled with one another. They depended on irrigation agriculture.

Susa, Iran   A city-state in Khuzistan that traded extensively with Mesopotamian city-states. Precursor of the Elamite state.

Swan Point, Alaska   See **Broken Mammoth.**

Swartkrans, South Africa   Important location for Australopithecine finds, also for the reported use of fire, 1.6 mya.

Tehuacán Valley, Mexico   A valley in which evidence for a gradual shift from hunting and gathering to deliberate cultivation of squashes and other minor crops, then maize, has been documented. Tehuacán was occupied as early as 10,000 B.C., with maize agriculture appearing before 2700 B.C.

Tell al 'Ouelli, Iraq   A large 'Ubaid community dating to 5800 B.C., with substantial buildings.

Telloh, Iraq   Sumerian city where the civilization of that name was first recognized in the 1870s. See also **Eridu, Iraq.**

Tenochtitlán, Mexico   The spectacular capital of the Aztec civilization in the Valley of Mexico, founded in A.D. 1325 and destroyed by Spanish conquistador Hernan Cortés in 1521.

Teotihuacán, Mexico   A vast pre-Columbian city in highland Mexico that flourished from as early as 200 B.C. until it declined before A.D. 750. Teotihuacán maintained extensive political and trade contacts with lowland Mexico and is famed for its enormous public buildings and pyramids.

Tepe Yahya, Iran   A major trading city on the Iranian Plateau associated with the steatite trade, c. 3400 B.C. and later.

Thule   A sea-mammal-hunting tradition that emerged in the far north in the first millennium B.C. and spread eastward into the Canadian arctic, c. A.D. 1000.

Tikal, Guatemala   Classic Maya city in the Guatemalan lowlands that reached its height in about A.D. 600.

Tiwanaku, Bolivia   An Andean state and major ceremonial complex near Lake Titicaca at the height of its powers during the first millennium A.D.

Toro-Menalla, Chad   Location where a cranium of *Sahelanthropus tchadensis* was found and provisionally dated to 6 to 7 mya.

Torralba, Spain   An elephant butchering site dating to c. 300,000 years ago, and attributed to archaic *Homo sapiens*.

Tripolye culture, eastern Europe   A farming culture of 4000 B.C. that flourished on the eastern European plains.

Tucumé, Peru   A center of the Sicán kingdom, engaged in extensive trading activity, c. A.D. 1000.

Tula, Mexico   Capital of Toltec civilization, c. A.D. 1100.

Uaxactún, Guatemala   A Maya city conquered by Tikal, A.D. 378.

'Ubaid culture, Iraq   The earliest known farming culture of southern Iraq, found at the base of numerous ancient cities there; c. 5800 B.C.

Ubeidiya, Israel   A hominid site dating to c. 1.4 mya, with fragmentary human remains.

Uluburun, Turkey   Spectacular Bronze Age shipwreck dating to 1305 B.C. with cargo from all over the eastern Mediterranean.

Unetice, Czech Republic   Early bronze-working culture of 2500 B.C., perhaps a center of independent European bronze working.

Ur, Iraq   Biblical city in southern Iraq that grew from a tiny farming hamlet founded as early as 4700 B.C. Known for its Early Dynastic Sumerian burials, where a ruler's entire retinue committed institutionalized suicide. See also **Eridu, Iraq.**

Uruk, Iraq   The earliest city in southern Iraq, a complex settlement before 4600 B.C.

Uxmal, Mexico   Late Classic Maya city and ceremonial center in the northern Yucatán.

Varna, Bulgaria   A cemetery of 4600 to 4200 B.C., famous for its gold and metallurgy.

Villanovan culture, Italy   Predecessor culture to Etruscan civilization in northern Italy, famed for their bronze working and, later, their iron technology.

Wadi Kubbaniya, Egypt   A hunter-gatherer site by the banks of the Nile River, occupied between 17,000 and 15,000 B.C.

Walker Road, Alaska Paleoarctic site in the Nenana Valley, dating to between 11,400 and 11,100 B.C.

Wari, Peru A ceremonial center in the Ayacucho Valley that developed a large empire, c. A.D. 800.

Warreen, Australia Tasmanian cave visited as early as 33,000 B.C. by wallaby hunters.

Xianrendong, China A site in the Yangzi Valley inhabited by foragers for wild rice; they may have started domesticating rice between 9200 and 7550 B.C.

Yangshao culture, China A widespread early cereal farming culture centered around the Haunghe River in northern China, c. 4800 to 3200 B.C.

Yayoi period, Japan The period immediately preceding the unification of Japan into a single kingdom, c. A.D. 600.

Zawi Chemi Shanidar, Iran Hunting camp in the Zagros Mountains for wild goats and sheep, c. 10,500 B.C.

Zhoukoudian Cave, China World-famous location where numerous *Homo erectus* fossils have been found, dating to between 460,000 and 230,000 years ago.

BIBLIOGRAPHY OF WORLD PREHISTORY

The literature of world prehistory proliferates more and more every year, to the point that it is now beyond the ability of any one scholar to keep abreast of it. This bibliography is not intended as a comprehensive reference guide to the subject. Rather, it is a compilation of most of the sources used to write this book and a cross section of the most important monographs and papers relating to all parts of the world. Readers interested in probing more deeply into the literature should pursue the references given in the publications listed here or consult a specialist.

Adams, R. E. W., et al. 1981. "Radar Mapping, Archaeology, and Ancient Maya Land Use." *Science* 213:1457–1463.

Adams, Robert M. 1966. *The Evolution of Urban Society.* Chicago: Aldine.

———. 1981. *Heartland of Cities.* Chicago: University of Chicago Press.

———. 2001. "Complexity in Archaic States." *Journal of Anthropological Archaeology* 20 (3):345–360.

Adams, Robert M., and Hans J. Nissen. 1972. *The Uruk Landscape.* Chicago: University of Chicago Press.

Adams, William Y. 1977. *Nubia: Corridor to Africa.* London: Allen Lane.

Adler, Michael A., ed. 1996. *The Prehistoric Pueblo World, A.D. 1150–1350.* Tucson: University of Arizona Press.

Adovasio, J. M. 2002. *The First Americans.* New York: Random House.

———, et al. 1981. *Meadowcroft Rockshelter and the Archaeology of the Cross Creek Drainage.* Pittsburgh: University of Pittsburgh Press.

Adovasio, J. M., et al. 1996. "Upper Palaeolithic Fibre Technology: Interlaced Woven Finds from Pavlov I, Czech Republic, c. 26,000 years ago." *Antiquity* 70:526–534.

Adovasio, J. M., et al. 1998. "Two Decades of Debate on Meadowcroft Rockshelter." *North American Archaeologist* 19 (4):317–341.

Aiello, L. C., and M. C. Dean. 1990. *An Introduction to Human Evolutionary Anatomy.* London: Academic Press.

Aiello, L. C., and Robin Dunbar. 1993. "Neocortex Size, Group Size, and Cognition." *Current Anthropology* 36:199–221.

Aiello, L. C., and P. Wheeler. 1995. "The Expensive Tissue Hypothesis." *Current Anthropology* 36:184–193.

Aikens, C. Melvin. 1970. *Hogup Cave.* Salt Lake City: University of Utah Press.

Aldenderfer, Mark. 1995. *Montane Foragers: Asana and the South-Central Andean Archaic.* Iowa City: University of Iowa Press.

Aldred, Cyril. 1988. *Akhenaten,* 2nd ed. London: Thames & Hudson.

———. 1998. *The Egyptians,* 3rd ed. New York: Thames & Hudson.

Algaze, Guillermo. 1993. "Expansionary Dynamics of Some Early Pristine States." *American Anthropologist* 95 (2): 304–337.

Allan, William. 1965. *The African Husbandman.* Edinburgh: Oliver & Boyd.

Allchin, Bridget, and Raymond Allchin. 1983. *The Rise of Civilization in India and Pakistan.* Cambridge: Cambridge University Press.

Allchin, Raymond. 1995. *The Archaeology of Early Historic South Asia.* Cambridge: Cambridge University Press.

Allen, J. 1994. "Radiocarbon Determinations, Luminescence Dating, and Australian Archaeology." *Antiquity* 68:339–343.

———, J. Golson, and Rhys Jones, eds. 1977. *Sunda and Sahul: Prehistoric Studies in Southeast Asia, Melanesia, and Australia.* New York: Academic Press.

Allen, J., C. Gosden, and J. P. White. 1989. "Pleistocene New Ireland." *Antiquity* 63 (240):548–561.

Allen, J., and J. S. Holloway. 1995. "The Continuity of Pleistocene Radiocarbon Determinations in Australia." *Antiquity* 69:101–112.

Allen, J., and James O'Connell, eds. 1996. "Transitions: Pleistocene to Holocene in Australia and Papua New Guinea." *Antiquity* 69 (265), Special Volume.

Allen, J., and J. P. White. 1989. "The Lapita Homeland: Some New Data and an Interpretation." *Journal of the Polynesian Society* 93:129–146.

Allen, Melinda. 1995. "Style and Function in East Polynesian Fishhooks." *Antiquity* 70:97–111.

Alva, Walter, and Christopher Donnan. 1993. *Royal Tombs of Sipán.* Los Angeles: Fowler Museum of Cultural History, UCLA.

Ambrose, Stanley H. 1984. "The Introduction of Pastoral Adaptations to the Highlands of East Africa." In *From Hunters to Farmers.* J. Desmond Clark and Steven A. Brandt, eds. Pp. 212–239. Berkeley: University of California Press.

———. 2001. "Paleolithic Technology and Human Evolution." *Science* 291:1748–1753.

Ames, K. M., and Herbert D. Maschner. 1999. *Peoples of the Northwest Coast: Their Archaeology and Prehistory.* London and New York: Thames & Hudson.

Anawak, Jack. 1994. "Inuit Perceptions of the Past." In *Who Needs the Past?* 2nd ed. R. Layton, ed. Pp. 45–50. London: Routledge.

Anderson, Arthur O., and Charles Dibble, eds. 1978. *The Florentine Codex.* Salt Lake City: University of Utah Press.

Anderson, Atholl. 1991. "The Chronology of Colonization in New Zealand." *Antiquity* 65:767–795.

———. 1992. *Prodigious Birds: Moas and Moa-Hunting in Prehistoric New Zealand.* Cambridge: Cambridge University Press.

———, and M. McGlone. 1991. "Living on the Edge: Prehistoric Land and People in New Zealand." In *The Native Lands: Prehistory and Environmental Change in Australia and the Southwest Pacific.* J. Dodson, ed. Pp. 199–241. Sydney, Australia: Longman Cheshire.

Anderson, D. G. 1994. *The Savannah River Chiefdoms: Political Change in the Late Prehistoric Southeast.* Tuscaloosa: University of Alabama Press.

———. 1997. "The Role of Cahokia in the Evolution of Southeastern Mississippian Society." In *Cahokia: Domination and Ideology in the Mississippian World.* Timothy R. Pauketat and Thomas E. Emerson, eds. Pp. 248–268. Lincoln: University of Nebraska Press.

———, and J. Christopher Gillam. 2000. "Paleoindian Colonization of the Americas: Implications from an Examination of Physiography, Demography, and Artifact Distribution." *American Antiquity* 65 (1):43–66.

Anderson, D. G., and Kenneth E. Sassaman, eds. 1996. *The Paleoindian and Early Archaic Southeast.* Tuscaloosa: University of Alabama Press.

Anderson, Douglas. 1990. *Long Rongrien.* Philadelphia: University of Pennsylvania Museum.

Arnold, Jeanne, ed. 2001. *The Origins of the Pacific Coast Chiefdom.* Salt Lake City: University of Utah Press.

Arsuaga, Juan-Luis, et al. 1993. "Three New Human Skulls from the Sima de los Huevos Middle Pleistocene Site in Sierra de Atapuerca, Spain." *Nature* 362:534–539.

Ascher, Marcia, and Robert Ascher. 1981. *The Code of the Quipu.* Ann Arbor: University of Michigan Press.

Asfaw, Berhane, et al. 1999. "*Australopithecus garhi:* A New Species of Early Hominid from Ethiopia." *Science* 284:629–634.

Asfaw, Berhane, et al. 2002. "Remains of *Homo erectus* from Bouri, Middle Awash, Ethiopia." *Nature* 416:173–320.

Aubet, Maria Eugenia. 1993. *The Phoenicians and the West: Politics, Colonies and Trade.* Cambridge: Cambridge University Press.

Aurenche, O., and S. Kozlowski. 1999. *La naissance au néolithique au Proche Orient, ou le paradis perdu.* Paris: Editions Errance.

Avise, J. C. 1994. *Molecular Markers, Natural History, and Evolution.* London: Chapman & Hall.

Bahn, Paul, ed. 1996. *The Cambridge Illustrated History of Archaeology.* Cambridge: Cambridge University Press.

———, ed. 2001. *The Penguin Archaeology Guide.* London: Penguin.

Bahn, P., and J. R. Flenley. 1992. *Easter Island, Earth Island.* London and New York: Thames & Hudson.

Bahn, P., and Jan Vertut. 1988. *Images of the Ice Age.* New York: Viking Press.

Bard, Kathryn A. 1994. "The Egyptian Predynastic: A Review of the Evidence." *Journal of World Prehistory* 21 (3):265–288.

———. 2000. "The Emergence of the Egyptian State (c. 3200–2686 B.C.)." In *The Oxford History of Ancient Egypt.* Ian Shaw, ed. Pp. 61–88. Oxford: Oxford University Press.

Barker, Graeme. 1985. *Prehistoric Farming in Europe.* Cambridge: Cambridge University Press.

Barnard, Alan. 1992. *Hunters and Herders of Southern Africa.* Cambridge: Cambridge University Press.

Barnes, Gina L. 1993. *China, Korea, and Japan.* London and New York: Thames & Hudson.

Bar-Yosef, O. 1986. "The Walls of Jericho." *Current Anthropology* 27 (2):157–162.

———. 1987. "Late Pleistocene Adaptations in the Levant." In *The Pleistocene Old World: Regional Perspectives.* Olga Soffer, ed. Pp. 219–236. New York: Plenum Press.

———. 1999. "Lower Palaeolithic Sites in South Western Asia. *Anthropologie* 37:51–69.

———, and A. Belfer-Cohen. 1989. "The Origins of Sedentism and Farming Communities in the Levant." *Journal of World Prehistory* 3 (4):447–498.

Bar-Yosef, O., and B. Vandermeersch. 1993. "Modern Humans in the Levant." *Scientific American* 268:113–121.

Bar-Yosef, Ofer, et al. 1991. "Netiv Hagdud: An Early Neolithic Village Site in the Jordan Valley." *Journal of Field Archaeology* 18:405–424.

Basgall, Mark. 1987. "Resource Intensification Among Hunter-Gatherers: Acorn Economies in Prehistoric California." *Research in Economic Anthropology* 9:21–52.

Bauer, Brian S. 1992. *The Development of the Inca State.* Norman: University of Oklahoma Press.

Baugh, T. G., and J. E. Ericson, eds. 1994. *Prehistoric Exchange Systems in North America.* New York: Plenum Press.

Bayman, James. 2002. "The Hohokam of Southwest North America." *Journal of World Prehistory* 15 (3):257–311.

Beach, David. 1993. *The Shona.* Oxford: Blackwell.

Beadle, George. 1981. "The Ancestor of Corn." *Scientific American* 242 (1):96–103.

Beaglehole, J. C. 1974. *Captain James Cook: A Life.* Palo Alto, CA: Stanford University Press.

Bellwood, Peter. 1970. "Fortifications and Economy in Prehistoric New Zealand." *Proceedings of the Prehistoric Society* 37 (1):56–95.

———. 1987. *The Polynesians.* London: Thames & Hudson.

———. 1997. *The History of the Indo-Malaysian Archipelago,* 2nd ed. Honolulu: University of Hawaii Press.

———. 2001. "Early Agriculturalist Population Diasporas? Farming, Languages, and Genes." *Annual Review of Anthropology* 30:181–207.

———, and J. Koon. 1989. "Lapita Colonists Leave Boats Unburned." *Antiquity* 63 (240):613–622.

Beltran, Antonio, ed. 1999. *Cave of Altamira.* New York: Harry Abrams.

Ben-Amos, P. 1980. *The Art of Benin.* London: Thames & Hudson.

Bender, Barbara. 1985. "Emergent Tribal Formations in the American Midcontinent." *American Antiquity* 50 (1): 52–62.

Benefit, B. R., and M. L. McCrossin. 1995. "Miocene Hominoids and Human Origins." *Annual Review of Anthropology* 24:68–78.

Benfer, Robert. 1982. "The Lomas Site of Paloma (5000 to 7500 B.P.), Chilca Valley, Peru." In *Andean Archaeology.* Ramerio Matos, ed. Pp. 27–54. New York: Academic Press.

Benson, Elizabeth. 1979. *Pre-Columbian Metallurgy of South America.* Washington, DC: Dumbarton Oaks.

Berdan, Francis, et al. 1996. *Aztec Imperial Strategies.* Washington DC: Dumbarton Oaks.

Bernal, Ignacio. 1969. *The Olmec World.* Berkeley: University of California Press.

Bernal, Martin. 1987. *The Afroasiatic Roots of Classical Civilization.* New Brunswick, NJ: Rutgers University Press.

Berrin, Kathleen, and R. Pasztory, eds. 1994. *Teotihuacán.* London: Thames & Hudson.

Bettinger, Robert L. 2001. "Holocene Hunter-Gatherers." In *Archaeology at the Millennium.* Gary M. Feinman and T. Douglas Price, eds. Pp. 137–198. New York: Kluwer Academic.

Bever, Michael R. 2001. "An Overview of Alaskan Late Pleistocene Archaeology: Historical Themes and Current Perspectives." *Journal of World Prehistory* 15 (2): 125–191.

Binford, Lewis R. 2001a. *Constructing Frames and Reference: An Analytical Method for Archaeological Theory Building Using Ethnographic and Environmental Data Sets.* Berkeley: University of California Press.

_____. 2001b. *In Pursuit of the Past,* 2nd ed. Berkeley: University of California Press.

_____, and Sally Binford. 1966. "A Preliminary Analysis of Functional Variability in the Mousterian of Levallois Facies." *American Anthropologist* 68 (2):238–295.

Bingham, Hiram. 1963. *Lost City of the Incas.* New York: Atheneum. (Reprint edition.)

Birdsell, J. 1977. "The Recalibration of a Paradigm for the First Peopling of Greater Australia." In *Sunda and Sahul.* J. Allen, J. Golson, and R. Jones, eds. Pp. 113–167. Orlando, FL: Academic Press.

Birley, Robin. 1977. *Vindolanda.* London: Thames & Hudson.

Björck, S., et al. 1996. "Synchronized Territorial-Atmospheric Deglacial Records Around the North Atlantic," *Science* 274:1155–1160.

Blanton, Richard E. 1978. *Monte Albán: Settlement Patterns at the Ancient Zapotec Capital.* New York: Academic Press.

_____, et al. 1999. *Ancient Oaxaca.* Cambridge: Cambridge University Press.

Blumenschine, Robert, and John Cavallo. 1992. "Scavenging and Human Evolution." *Scientific American* 257 (10):90–96.

Blumer, M. A. 1991. "Independent Invention and Recent Genetic Evidence on Plant Domestication." *Economic Botany* 46:98–111.

Blust, Robert. 1995. "The Prehistory of the Austronesian-Speaking Peoples: A View from Language." *Journal of World Prehistory* 9 (4):453–510.

Boesch, Christophe, and Michael Tomasello. 1998. "Chimpanzee and Human Cultures." *Current Anthropology* 39 (5):591–614.

Bogucki, Peter, ed. 1993. *Case Studies in European Prehistory.* Boca Raton, FL: CRC Press.

Bogucki, Peter, and Ryszard Grygiel. 1986. "Early Farmers of the North European Plain." *Scientific American* 248 (4):105–115.

Bonsall, Clive, ed. 1989. *The Mesolithic in Europe.* Edinburgh: Edinburgh University Press.

Bonzek, Jan, ed. 1985. *The Aegean, Anatolia, and Europe in the 2nd Millennium B.C.* New York: Academic Press.

Bordes, François. 1968. *The Old Stone Age.* New York: McGraw-Hill.

Boserup, Ester. 1965. *The Conditions of Agricultural Growth: The Economics of Agrarian Change Under Population Pressure.* Chicago: Aldine.

Boule, Marcellin, and H. Vallois. 1957. *Fossil Men.* London: Thames & Hudson.

Bower, John R. F. 1984. "Settlement Behavior of Pastoral Cultures in East Africa." In *From Hunters to Farmers.* J. Desmond Clark and Steven A. Brandt, eds. Pp. 252–259. Berkeley: University of California Press.

Bowler, J. M., et al. 1970. "Pleistocene Human Remains from Australia: A Living Site and Human Cremation from Lake Mungo, Western New South Wales." *World Archaeology* 2:39–60.

Bowman, A. K., and G. Woolf, eds. 1994. *Literacy and Power in the Ancient World.* Cambridge: Cambridge University Press.

Boyer, Pascal. 1994. *The Naturalness of Religious Ideas: A Cognitive Theory of Religion.* Berkeley: University of California Press.

Braidwood, R. J., and L. S. Braidwood, eds. 1983. *Prehistoric Archaeology Along the Zagros Flanks.* Chicago: Oriental Institute.

Braidwood, R. J., and H. Cambel. 1980. *Prehistoric Research in Southeastern Anatolia.* Istanbul: Edebıyat Facultesi Basimevi.

Brain, Jeffrey P., and Philip Phillips. 1995. *Shell Gorgets: Styles of the Late Prehistoric and Protohistoric Southeast.* Cambridge, MA: Peabody Museum, Harvard University.

Brauer, Günter. 1992. "Africa's Place in the Evolution of *Homo sapiens.*" In *Continuity or Replacement: Controversies in Homo sapiens Evolution.* Günter Brauer and F. H. Smith, eds. Pp. 83–98. Rotterdam: Balkema.

Braun, David. 1989. "Coevolution of Sedentism, Pottery Technology, and Horticulture in the Central Midwest,

200 B.C.–A.D. 600." In *Emergent Horticultural Economies of the Eastern Woodlands*. W. F. Keegan, ed. Pp. 153–182. Carbondale: Southern Illinois University Press.

Breuil, Henri. 1952. *Four Hundred Centuries of Cave Art*. Montignac, France: Centre d'Etudes et de Documentation.

Broodbank, Cyprian. 2001. *An Island Archaeology of the Early Cyclades*. Cambridge: Cambridge University Press.

Broughton, Jack M., and James O'Connell. 1999. "On Evolutionary Ecology: Selectionist Archaeology and Behavioral Archaeology." *American Antiquity* 64 (1): 153–165.

Brown J., and J. Phillips, eds. 1983. *Late Archaic Hunter-Gatherers in the Midwest*. New York: Academic Press.

Brumfiel, Elizabeth. 1983. "Aztec State Making: Ecology, Structure, and the Origin of the State." *American Anthropologist* 85 (2):261–284.

_____. 1991. "Weaving and Cooking: Women's Production in Aztec Mexico." In *Engendering Archaeology*. Margaret Conkey and Joan Gero, eds. Pp. 224–247. Oxford: Blackwell.

_____. 1992. "Distinguished Lecture in Archaeology: Breaking and Entering the Ecosystem." *American Anthropologist* 94 (3):551–567.

_____, and John Fox, eds. 1994. *Factional Competition and Political Development in the New World*. Cambridge: Cambridge University Press.

Brunet, Michel, et al. 1995. "The First Australopithecine 2500 km West of the Rift Valley, Chad." *Nature* 378:273–275.

Brunet, Michel, et al. 2002. "A New Hominid from the Upper Miocene of Chad, Central Africa." *Nature* 418:145–151.

Bunn, Henry. 1994. "Early Pleistocene Hominid Foraging Strategies Along the Ancestral Omo River at Koobi Fora, Kenya." *Journal of Human Evolution* 27:247–266.

_____, and J. Kroll. 1986. "Systematic Butchery by Plio/Pleistocene Hominids at Olduvai Gorge, Tanzania." *Current Anthropology* 27 (5):431–451.

Bunn, Henry, et al. 1980. "FxJj50: An Early Pleistocene Site in Northern Kenya." *World Archaeology* 12 (2):109–136.

Burger, Richard L. 1985. "Prehistoric Stylistic Change and Cultural Development at Huaricoto, Peru." *National Geographic Research* 1 (4):505–534.

_____. 1992a. *Chavín and the Origins of Andean Civilization*. London and New York: Thames & Hudson.

_____. 1992b. "The Sacred Center of Chavín de Huantar." In *The Ancient Americas: Art from Sacred Landscapes*. Richard F. Townsend, ed. Pp. 265–277. Chicago: Art Institute of Chicago.

Burger, Richard L., and Lucy Salazar-Burger. 1985. "The Early Ceremonial Center of Huaricoto." In *Early Ceremonial Architecture in the Andes*. Christopher Donnan, ed. Pp. 111–138. Washington, DC: Dumbarton Oaks.

Burger, Richard L., and Nikolaas van der Merwe. 1990. "Maize and the Origin of Highland Chavín Civilization." *American Anthropologist* 92 (1):85–92.

Burmeister, S. 2000. "Archaeology and Migration: Approaches to an Archaeological Proof of Migration." *Current Anthropology* 41:539–568.

Bury, J. B., and Russell Meiggs. 1976. *A History of Greece*, 4th ed. London: Macmillan.

Butzer, Karl. 1974. *Environment and Archaeology*. Chicago: Aldine.

_____. 1976. *Early Hydraulic Civilization in Egypt*. Chicago: University of Chicago Press.

_____. 1982. *Archaeology as Human Ecology*. Cambridge: Cambridge University Press.

_____. 1995. "Environmental Change in the Near East and Human Impact on the Land." In *Civilizations of the Ancient Near East*. J. M. Sasson, ed. Pp. 123–151. New York: Scribners.

_____, and LL. Glynn Isaac, eds. 1975. *After the Australopithecines*. Chicago: Aldine.

Byrd, B. F. 1989. "The Natufian: Settlement Variability and Economic Adaptation in the Levant at the End of the Pleistocene." *Journal of World Prehistory* 3 (2):159–198.

Cadogan, Gerald. 1976. *Palaces of Minoan Crete*. London: Barrie & Jenkins.

Cahen, David, and Francis van Noten. 1981. *The Hunter-Gatherers of Meer*. Tervuren, Belgium: Musée Royal de L'Afrique Centrale.

Canby, Thomas. 1979. "The Search for the First Americans." *National Geographic,* September: 330–363.

Caneva, I., M. Frangipane, and A. Palmiere 1987. "Predynastic Egypt: New Data from Maadi." *African Archaeological Review* 5:105–114.

Cann, Rebecca L. 2001. "Genetic Clues to Dispersal in Human Populations: Retracing the Past from the Present." *Science* 291:1742–1748.

_____, O. Rickards, and J. K. Lum. 1995. "Mitochondrial DNA and Human Evolution: Our One Lucky Mother." In *Origins of Anatomically Modern Humans*. M. H. Nitecki and V. Nitecki, eds. Pp. 135–148. New York: Plenum Press.

Carneiro, Robert L. 1970. "A Theory of the Origin of the State." *Science* 169:733–738.

_____. 1994. "War and Peace: Alternating Realities in Human History." In *Studying War: Anthropological Perspective*. S. P. Reyna and R. E. Downs, eds. Pp. 3–28. Amsterdam: Gordon and Breach.

Carter, Elizabeth F., and Mathew Stolper. 1984. *Elam: Surveys of Political History and Archaeology*. Berkeley: University of California Press.

Caton-Thompson, G., and E. W. Gardner. 1934. *The Desert Fayum*, 2 vols. London: Royal Anthropological Institute.

Cavalli-Sforza, L. L., and F. Cavalli-Sforza. 1995. *The Great Human Diasporas*. Reading, MA: Helix Books.

Chadwick, John. 1976. *The Mycenaean World*. Cambridge: Cambridge University Press.

Champion, Timothy G., et al. 1984. *Prehistoric Europe*. New York: Academic Press.

Chandler, David. 1983. *A History of Cambodia*. Boulder, CO: Westview Press.

Chang, Kwang-Chih. 1980. *Shang Civilization*. New Haven, CT: Yale University Press.

_____. 1986. *The Archaeology of Ancient China*, 4th ed. New Haven, CT: Yale University Press.

Chapdelaine, Claude. 2000. "Struggling for Survival: The Urban Class of the Moche Site, North Coast of Peru." In *Environmental Disaster and the Archaeology of Human Response*. Garth Bawden and Richard Martin Reycraft, eds. Pp. 121–142. Albuquerque: Maxwell Museum of Anthropology.

Chapman, Jefferson. 1994. *Tellico Archaeology*, 2nd ed. Knoxville: University of Tennessee Press.

Chase, Arlen F., and Diane Z. Chase. 1996a. "A Mighty Maya Nation." *Archaeology* 49 (5):67–72.

_____. 1996b. "More than Kin and King." *Current Anthropology* 37 (5):803–829.

Chauvet, Jean-Marie, Eliette Deschamps, and Christian Hillaire. 1996. *Dawn of Art: The Chauvet Cave*. New York: Abrams.

Childe, V. G. 1936. *Man Makes Himself*. London: Watts.

_____. 1952. *New Light on the Most Ancient East*. London: Routledge & Kegan Paul.

Chippindale, Christopher. 1994. *Stonehenge Complete*, 2nd ed. London: Thames & Hudson.

Chun, Tang, and Gai Pei. 1986. "Upper Palaeolithic Cultural Traditions in North China." *Advances in World Archaeology* 5:339–364.

Clark, G. R., A. J. Andrews, and T. Vunidilo, eds. 2001. *The Archaeology of Lapita Dispersal in Oceania*. Canberra: Australian National University, Pandaus Press.

Clark, J., and W. Parry. 1990. "Craft Specialization and Cultural Complexity." *Research in Economic Anthropology* 12:289–346.

Clark, J. D., and Steven A. Brandt, eds. 1984. *From Hunters to Farmers*. Berkeley: University of California Press.

_____. 1971. "A Re-examination of the Evidence for Agricultural Origins in the Nile Valley." *Proceedings of the Prehistoric Society* 37 (2):34–79.

_____. 1984. "Prehistoric Cultural Continuity and Economic Change in the Central Sudan in the Early Holocene." In *From Hunters to Farmers*. J. Desmond Clark and Steven A. Brandt, eds. Pp. 113–126. Berkeley: University of California Press.

Clark, J. Desmond, and J. W. K. Harris. 1985. "Fire and Its Roles in Early Hominid Lifeways." *African Archaeological Review* 3:3–28.

Clark, J. G. D. 1954. *Star Carr*. Cambridge: Cambridge University Press.

_____. 1958. "Blade and Trapeze Industries of the European Stone Age." *Proceedings of the Prehistoric Society* 24:24–42.

_____. 1975. *The Earlier Stone Age Settlement of Scandinavia*. Cambridge: Cambridge University Press.

_____. 1977. *World Prehistory: A New Outline*, 3rd ed. Cambridge: Cambridge University Press.

Clay, R. Berle. 1998. "The Essential Features of Adena Ritual and Their Implications." *Southeastern Archaeology* 17 (1):1–21.

Clayton, Peter A. 1994. *Chronicle of the Pharaohs*. London and New York: Thames & Hudson.

Clendinnen, Inga. 1991. *The Aztecs: An Interpretation*. Cambridge: Cambridge University Press.

Clottes, Jean. 1995. *Les Cavernes de Niaux: Art Préhistorique en Ariège*. Paris: Seuil.

_____. 1998. *The Shamans of Prehistory: Trance and Magic in the Painted Caves*. New York: Abrams.

Clutton-Brock, Juliet, ed. 1989. *The Walking Larder*. London: Unwin Hyman.

Cobb, C. R., and P. H. Garrow. 1996. "Woodstock Culture and the Question of Mississippian Emergence." *American Antiquity* 61:21–37.

Coe, M. D. 1992. *Breaking the Maya Code*. London and New York: Thames & Hudson.

_____. 1999. *The Maya*, 6th ed. London and New York: Thames & Hudson.

_____. 2002. *Mexico*, 5th ed. London and New York: Thames & Hudson.

_____, and Richard Diehl. 1980. *In the Land of the Olmec*. 2 vols. Austin: University of Texas Press.

Cohen, Mark. 1977. *The Food Crisis in Prehistory*. New Haven, CT: Yale University Press.

_____. 1988. *Health and the Rise of Civilization*. New Haven, CT: Yale University Press.

Coles, B., and J. M. Coles. 1989. *People of the Wetlands*. London and New York: Thames & Hudson.

Coles, J. M. 1982. "The Bronze Age in North West Europe: Problems and Advances." *Advances in World Archaeology* 1:266–321.

_____, and A. F. Harding. 1979. *The Bronze Age in Europe*. London: Methuen.

Collis, John. 1997. *The European Iron Age*. London: Routledge.

Conkey, Margaret, and Joan Gero, eds. 1991. *Engendering Archaeology*. Oxford: Blackwell.

Connah, Graham. 2001. *African Civilizations*, 2nd ed. Cambridge: Cambridge University Press.

Conrad, Geoffrey W., and Arthur A. Demarest. 1984. *Religion and Empire: The Dynamics of Aztec and Inca Expansionism*. Cambridge: Cambridge University Press.

Cordell, Linda. 1997. *Prehistory of the Southwest*, 2nd ed. New York: Academic Press.

Cornell, T. J. 1995. *The Beginnings of Rome*. London: Routledge.

Cosgrove, R. 1995. "Late Pleistocene Behaviorial Variation and Time Trends: The Case from Tasmania." *Archaeology in Oceania* 30 (3):83–104.

_____, J. Allen, and B. Marshall. 1990. "Pleistocene Occupation of Tasmania." *Antiquity* 64 (242):59–78.

Courand, Claude. 1985. *L'Art Azilien.* Paris: Gallia Préhistoire.

Covey, Curt. 1984. "The Earth's Orbit and the Ice Ages." *Scientific American* 280 (2):58–77.

Crawford, Gary. 1992. "Prehistoric Plant Domestication in East Asia." In *The Origins of Agriculture.* Wesley Cowan and Patty Jo Watson, eds. Pp. 7–38. Washington, DC: Smithsonian Institution Press.

Crawford, Harriett. 1991. *Sumer and the Sumerians.* Cambridge: Cambridge University Press.

Crawford, Michael H. 2001. *The Origins of Native Americans: Evidence from Anthropological Genetics.* Cambridge: Cambridge University Press.

Croes, Dale, and S. Hackenberger. 1988. "Hoko River Archaeological Complex: Modelling Prehistoric Northwest Coast Economic Evolution." *Research in Economic Anthropology,* Supplement 3:19–85.

Crown, Patricia L. 1990. "The Hohokam of the American Southwest." *Journal of World Prehistory* 4 (2):223–255.

_____, and W. James Judge, eds. 1991. *Chaco and Hohokam: Regional Systems in the American Southwest.* Santa Fe, NM: School of American Research Press.

Culbert, T. Patrick, ed. 1991. *Classic Maya Political History.* Cambridge and Santa Fe, NM: Cambridge University Press and School of American Research.

Culbert, Patrick T., and Don S. Rice, eds. 1990. *Precolumbian Population History in the Maya Lowlands.* Albuquerque: University of New Mexico Press.

Cullen, Tracy, ed. 2001. *Aegean Prehistory: A Review.* Boston: Archaeological Institute of America.

Cunliffe, Barry. 1974. *Iron Age Communities in Britain.* London: Routledge & Kegan Paul.

_____, ed. 1994. *The Oxford Illustrated Prehistory of Europe.* Oxford: Oxford University Press.

Curtis, John, ed. 1993. *Early Mesopotamia and Iran: Contact and Conflict 3500–1600 B.C.* London: British Museum Press.

D'Acevedo, Warren. 1986. *The Great Basin.* Vol. 5. *Handbook of North American Indians.* Washington, DC: Smithsonian Institution Press.

Dalley, Stephanie. 1984. *Mari and Karana: Two Old Babylonian Cities.* London: Longmans.

D'Altroy, B. 1992. *Provincial Power in the Inka Empire.* Washington, DC: Smithsonian Institution Press.

Dancey, W. S. 1996. "Putting an End to Ohio Hopewell." In *A View from the Core: A Synthesis of Ohio Hopewell Archaeology.* Paul Pacheco, ed. Pp. 395–405. Columbus: Ohio Archaeological Council.

_____, and Paul J. Pacheco, eds. 1997. *Ohio Hopewell Community Organization.* Kent, OH: Kent State University Press.

Daniel, Glyn E. 1973. *Megaliths in History.* London: Thames & Hudson.

Dart, Raymond A. 1925. "*Australopithecus africanus:* The Man-Ape of Southern Africa." *Nature* 115:195.

Davidson, Janet. 1987. *The Prehistory of New Zealand.* Auckland: Longman Paul.

Davies, Nigel. 1977. *The Toltecs.* Norman: University of Oklahoma Press.

_____. 1980. *The Toltec Heritage.* Norman: University of Oklahoma Press.

Davis, Richard S. 1987. "Regional Perspectives on the Soviet Central Asian Paleolithic." In *The Pleistocene Old World: Regional Perspectives.* Olga Soffer, ed. Pp. 121–134. New York: Plenum Press.

Deacon, Hilary. 1979. "Excavations at Boomplas Cave: A Sequence Through the Upper Pleistocene and Holocene in South Africa." *World Archaeology* 10:241–257.

_____. 1992. "Southern Africa and Modern Human Origins." *Philosophical Transactions of the Royal Society, Series B,* 337:177–183.

_____, and Jeanette Deacon. 1999. *Human Beginnings in South Africa: Uncovering the Secrets of the Stone Age.* Walnut Creek, CA: Altamira Press.

Deacon, Hilary, and V. B. Geleijinse. 1988. "The Stratigraphy and Sedimentology of the Main Site Sequence, Klasies River, South Africa." *South African Archaeological Bulletin* 43:5–14.

De Heinzelin, Jean, et al. 1999. "Environment and Behavior of 2.5-Million-Year-Old Bouri Hominids." *Science* 284:625–629.

Demarest, Arthur. 1989. "The Olmec and the Rise of Civilization in Eastern Mesoamerica." In *Regional Perspectives on the Olmec.* Robert Sharer and David Grove, eds. Pp. 303–344. Cambridge: Cambridge University Press.

_____. 1997. "The Vanderbilt Petexbatun Project." *Ancient Mesoamerica* 8 (2):217.

Demoule, Jean-Paul, and Catherine Perlès. 1993. "The Greek Neolithic: A New Review." *Journal of World Prehistory* 7 (4):355–416.

Dennell, Robin C. 1983. *European Economic Prehistory: A New Approach.* New York: Academic Press.

d'Errico, Francesco. 1995. "A New Model and Its Implications for the Origin of Writing: La Marche Antler Revised." *Cambridge Archaeological Journal* 5 (2):163–206.

Diaz, Bernal. 1963. *The True History of the Conquest of New Spain.* Trans. J. M. Cohen. Baltimore: Pelican.

Dibble, Charles E., and Arthur J. O. Anderson. 1978. *Florentine Codex.* Vol. 14. Salt Lake City: University of Utah Press.

Dickinson, Oliver. 1994. *The Aegean Bronze Age.* Cambridge: Cambridge University Press.

Diehl, Richard. 1984. *Tula.* London: Thames & Hudson.

_____. 1989. "Olmec Archaeology: What We Know and What We Wish We Knew." In *Regional Perspectives on the Olmec.* Robert Sharer and David Grove, eds. Pp. 17–32. Cambridge: Cambridge University Press.

Dillehay, Tom. 1989, 1997. *Monte Verde: A Late Pleistocene Settlement in Chile.* 2 vols. Blue Ridge Summit, PA: Smithsonian Institution Press.

_____. 2000. *First Settlement of America: A New Prehistory.* New York: Basic Books.

_____, and David J. Meltzer, eds. 1991. *The First Americans: Search and Research.* Boca Raton, FL: CRC Press.

Doebley, John, et al. 1999. "Limits of Selection During Maize Domestication." *Nature* 398:236–241.

Dolukhanov, P. M., et al. 2002. "Colonization of Northern Eurasia by Modern Humans: Radiocarbon Chronology and Environment." *Journal of Archaeological Science* 29 (6):593–606.

Dominguez-Rodrigo, Manuel. 2002. "Hunting and Scavenging by Early Humans: The State of the Debate." *Journal of World Prehistory* 16 (1):1–54.

Donnan, Christopher B., ed. 1985. *Early Ceremonial Architecture in the Andes*. Washington, DC: Dumbarton Oaks.

_____, and Donna McClelland. 1979. *The Burial Theme in Moche Iconography*. Washington, DC: Dumbarton Oaks.

Dorn, R. I., M. Nobbs, and T. A. Cahill. 1988. "Cation-Ratio Dating of Rock Engravings." *Antiquity* 62 (237):681–689.

Dortch, Charles, and Duncan Merrilees. 1973. "Human Occupation of Devil's Lair, Western Australia, During the Pleistocene." *Archaeology and Physical Anthropology in Oceania* 8:89–115.

Doumas, Christos. 1983. *Thera: Pompeii of the Aegean*. London: Thames & Hudson.

Drews, R. 1993. *The End of the Bronze Age: Changes in Warfare and the Catastrophe ca. 1200 B.C.* Princeton, NJ: Princeton University Press.

Drucker, Phillip. 1959. *La Venta, Tabasco: A Study of Olmec Ceramics and Art*. Washington, DC: Smithsonian Institution Press.

Dumond, Don. 1987. *The Eskimos and Aleuts*. London: Thames & Hudson.

Dumond, Don E., and Richard L. Bland. 1995. "Holocene Prehistory of the Northernmost North Pacific." *Journal of World Prehistory* 9 (4):401–452.

Dunbar, R. I. M. 1991. "Functional Significance of Social Grooming in Primates." *Folia Primatologica* 57:121–131.

_____. 1992. "Neocortex Size as a Constraint on Group Size in Primates." *Journal of Human Evolution* 20:469–493.

Earle, Timothy. 1978. *Economic and Social Organization of a Complex Chiefdom: The Halelea District, Kaua'i, Hawaii*. Ann Arbor: Museum of Anthropology, University of Michigan.

Edens, Christopher. 1992. "Dynamics of Trade in the Ancient Mesopotamian World System." *American Anthropologist* 94 (1):118–139.

_____. 1993. "Indus-Arabian Interaction During the Bronze Age: A Review of Evidence." In *Harappan Civilization*, 2nd ed. Gregory Possehl, ed. Pp. 335–363. New Delhi: Oxford and IBH.

Edwards, I. E. S. 1985. *The Pyramids of Egypt*. Baltimore: Pelican.

Eisenberg, J. F. 1981. *The Mammalian Radiation*. London: Athlone.

Emerson, T. E. 1997. *Cahokia and the Ideology of Power*. University of Alabama Press, Tuscaloosa, AL.

Engel, Frederick. 1963. *A Preceramic Settlement on the Central Coast of Peru: Asia, Unit 1*. Philadelphia: American Philosophical Society.

Erickson, Clark L. 1992. "Applied Archaeology and Rural Development: Archaeology's Potential Contribution to the Future." *Journal of the Steward Anthropological Society* 20 (1–2):1–16.

Ericson, J. E., and T. G. Baugh, eds. 1993. *The American Southwest and Mesoamerica*. New York: Plenum Press.

Erlandson, John. 1994. *The Early Hunter-Gatherers of the California Coast*. New York: Plenum Press.

_____. 2001. "The Archaeology of Aquatic Adaptations: Paradigms for a New Millennium." *Journal of Archaeological Research* 9 (4):281–350.

Ervard, Wolfgang, et al. 2002. "Molecular Evolution of FOXP2: Speech and Language." *Nature* 418:869–872.

Eubanks, Mary W. 2001. "The Origin of Maize: Evidence for *Tripsacum* Ancestry." *Plant Breeding Reviews* 20:15–66.

Evans, Arthur J. 1921. *The Palace of Minos at Knossos*. 4 vols. Oxford: Clarendon.

Fagan, Brian M. 1979. *Return to Babylon*. Boston: Little, Brown.

_____. 1985. *The Adventure of Archaeology*. Washington, DC: National Geographic Society.

_____. 1990. *The Journey from Eden*. New York: Thames & Hudson.

_____. 1996a. *Time Detectives*. New York: Touchstone Books.

_____, ed. 1996b. *The Oxford Companion to Archaeology*. New York: Oxford University Press.

_____, ed. 1997. *Eyewitness to Discovery*. New York: Oxford University Press.

_____. 1999. *Floods, Famines, and Emperors: El Niño and the Fate of Civilizations*. New York: Basic Books.

_____. 2000a. *In the Beginning*, 10th ed. Upper Saddle River, NJ: Prentice Hall.

_____. 2000b. *Ancient North America*, 3rd ed. New York: Thames & Hudson.

_____. 2004. *The Rape of the Nile*, 3rd ed. Boulder, CO: Westview Press.

_____, and F. van Noten. 1971. *The Hunter-Gatherers of Gwisho*. Tervuren, Belgium: Musée Royal de l'Afrique Centrale.

Fagles, Robert. 1990. *The Iliad*. New York: Viking.

Fairbanks, Richard G. 1989. "A 17,000-Year Glacio-Eustatic Sea Level Record: Influence of Glacial Melting Rates on the Younger Dryas Event and Deep Sea Circulation." *Nature* 342:637–642.

Farnsworth, Paul, et al. 1985. "A Re-evaluation of the Isotopic and Archaeological Reconstruction of Diet in the Tehuacán Valley." *American Antiquity* 50 (1):102–116.

Fash, William. 1991. *Scribes, Warriors, and Kings*. London and New York: Thames & Hudson.

Feddon, Robin. 1975. *Egypt: Land of the Valley*. London: Faber and Faber.

Feder, Kenneth L. 1998. *Frauds, Myths, and Mysteries*. Mountain View, CA: Mayfield.

Fedick, Scott, ed. 1996. *The Managed Mosaic*. Salt Lake City: University of Utah Press.

Feinman, Gary, and Linda Manzanilla, eds. 2002. *Cultural Evolution: Contemporary Viewpoints*. New York: Kluwer Plenum.

Fiedel, Stuart J. 1992. *Prehistory of the Americas*, 2nd ed. Cambridge: Cambridge University Press.

_____. 1999. "Older Than We Thought: Implications of Corrected Dates for Paleoindians." *American Antiquity* 64 (1):95–115.

_____. 2000. "The Peopling of the New World: Present Evidence, New Theories, and Future Directions." *Journal of Archaeological Research* 8 (1):39–103.

Finney, Ben R. 1994. *Voyage of Rediscovery*. Berkeley: University of California Press.

Flannery, Kent V. 1965. "The Ecology of Early Food Production in Mesopotamia." *Science* 147:1247–1256.

_____. 1968. "Archaeological Systems Theory and Early Mesoamerica." In *Anthropological Archaeology in the Americas*. Betty Meggers, ed. Pp. 67–87. Washington, DC: Anthropological Society of Washington.

_____. 1972. "The Cultural Evolution of Civilizations." *Annual Review of Ecology and Systematics* 4:399–426.

_____, ed. 1976. *The Early Mesoamerican Village*. New York: Academic Press.

_____, ed. 1982. *Maya Subsistence*. New York: Academic Press.

_____. 1983. "Settlement, Subsistence, and Social Organization of the Proto-Otomangans." In *The Cloud People*. Kent V. Flannery and Joyce Marcus, eds. Pp. 32–36. New York: Academic Press.

_____. 1986. *Guilá Naquitz*. Orlando, FL: Academic Press.

_____. 1999. "Process and Agency in Early State Formation" *Cambridge Archaeological Journal* 9:3–21.

Fleagle, J. 1988. *Primate Evolution and Adaptation*. London: Academic Press.

Flood, J. 1983. *The Archaeology of the Dreamtime*. London: Collins.

Folan, William J., Joyce Marcus, and W. Frank Miller. 1995. "Verification of a Maya Settlement Model Through Remote Sensing." *Cambridge Archaeological Journal* 5 (2):277–281.

Foley, Robert. 1984a. "Early Man and the Red Queen." In *Hominid Evolution and Community Ecology*. Robert Foley, ed. Pp. 85–110. London: Academic Press.

_____, ed. 1984b. *Hominid Evolution and Community Ecology: Prehistoric Human Adaptation in Biological Perspective*. London: Academic Press.

_____. 1984c. "Putting People into Perspective." In *Hominid Evolution and Community Ecology*. Robert Foley, ed. Pp. 1–24. London: Academic Press.

_____. 1987a. *Another Unique Species: Patterns in Human Evolutionary Ecology*. London: Longmans.

_____. 1987b. "Hominid Species and Stone-Tool Assemblages: How Are They Related?" *Antiquity* 61:380–392.

_____. 1995. *Humans Before Humanity*. Oxford: Blackwell.

Forest, J. D. 1986. "Tell el-Ouelli: Preliminary Report on the 4th Season." *Iraq* 44 (1–2):55–60.

Fowler, Melvin L. 1958. *Modoc Rockshelter*. Springfield: Illinois State Museum.

_____. 1997. *The Cahokia Atlas: A Historical Atlas of Cahokia Archaeology*, rev. ed. Urbana: Illinois Transportation Archaeology Research Program.

Frankel, David. 1991. *Remains to Be Seen: Archaeological Insights into Australian Prehistory*. Melbourne: Longman Cheshire.

Frayer, D. W., et al. 1994. "Getting It Straight." *American Anthropologist* 96:424–438.

Freidel, David, and Linda Schele. 1988. "Symbol and Power: A History of the Lowland Maya Cosmogram." In *Maya Iconography*. Elizabeth Benson and Gillett Griffin, eds. Princeton, NJ: Princeton University Press.

Freter, AnnCorinne. 1994. "The Classic Maya Collapse at Copán, Honduras: An Analysis of Maya Rural Settlement." In *Archaeological Views from the Countryside*. G. M. Schwartz and S. E. Falconer, eds. Pp. 160–176. Washington, DC: Smithsonian Institution Press.

Friedman, Jonathan. 1979. *System, Structure, and Contradiction: The Evolution of "Asiatic" Social Formations*. Cambridge: Cambridge University Press.

Frison, George C. 1992. *Prehistoric Hunters of the High Plains*, 2nd ed. New York: Academic Press.

Gabunia, Leo, and others. 2000. "Earliest Pleistocene Hominid Cranial Remains from Dmanisi, Republic of Georgia: Taxonomy, Geological Setting and Age." *Science* 283 (5468):1019–1025.

Galinat, Walter C. 1985. "Domestication and Diffusion of Maize." In *Prehistoric Food Production in North America*. Richard I. Ford, ed. Pp. 245–278. Ann Arbor: University of Michigan Museum of Anthropology.

Gamble, Clive. 1986. "The Mesolithic Sandwich." In *Hunters in Transition*. Marek Zvelebil, ed. Pp. 33–42. Cambridge: Cambridge University Press.

_____. 1993. *Timewalkers: The Prehistory of Global Colonisation*. Stroud, England: Alan Sutton.

_____. 1999. *The Palaeolithic Societies of Europe*. Cambridge: Cambridge University Press.

Gardner, R. Allen, and Beatrice A. Gardner. 1969. "Teaching Sign Language to a Chimpanzee." *Science* 163:664–672.

Garlake, Peter. 1973. *Great Zimbabwe*. New York: McGraw-Hill.

Garrod, D. A. E., and Dorothea Bate. 1937. *The Stone Age of Mount Carmel*. Cambridge: Cambridge University Press.

Gasparini, Graziano, and Luise Margolies. 1980. *Inca Architecture*. Bloomington: Indiana University Press.

Gebauer, A., and T. D. Price. 1992. "Introduction." In *Transitions to Agriculture in Prehistory*. A. Gebauer and T. D. Price, eds. Pp. i–xx. Madison, WI: Prehistory Press.

Geneste, J.-M., and H. Plisson. 1993. "Hunting Technologies and Human Behavior: Lithic Analysis of Solutrean Shouldered Points." In *Before Lascaux: The Complex Record of the Early Upper Palaeolithic*. H. Knecht, A. Pike-Tay, and R. White, eds. Pp. 117–135. Boca Raton, FL: CRC Press.

Geotcheus, V. G., et al. 1994. "Window on the Bering Land Bridge: A 17,000-Year-Old Paleosurface on the Seward Peninsula, Alaska." *Current Research in the Pleistocene* 11:131–132.

Ghosh, A. 1993. "Deurbanization of the Harappan Civilization." In *Harappan Civilization*, 2nd ed. Gregory Possehl, ed. Pp. 381–383. New Delhi: Oxford and IBH.

Gibson, J. L. 2001. *The Ancient Mounds of Poverty Point: Place of Rings.* Gainesville: University Presses of Florida.

Gilman, A. 1995. "Prehistoric European Chiefdoms: Rethinking 'Germanic' Societies." In *Foundations of Social Inequality.* T. D. Price and G. M. Feinman, eds. Pp. 235–251. New York: Plenum Press.

Goebel, T. 1999. "Pleistocene Colonization of Siberia and Peopling of the Americas: An Ecological Approach." *Evolutionary Anthropology* 8 (6):208–227.

_____, and S. Slobodin. 1999. "The Colonization of Western Beringia: Technology, Ecology, and Adaptations." In *Ice Age Humans of North America.* R. Bonnichsen and K. L. Turnmier, eds. Pp. 104–155. Corvallis: Oregon State University Press.

Goebel, T., and M. Akensenov. 1996. "Accelerator Radiocarbon Dating of the Initial Upper Palaeolithic in Southeast Siberia." *Antiquity* 69:115–123.

Goebel, T., et al. 2000. "Studenoe-2 and the Origin of Microblade Technology in Transbakal Siberia." *Antiquity* 74:567–575.

Golla, Victor. 2000. "Language Families of North America." In *America Past, America Present: Genes and Languages in the Americas and Beyond.* Colin Renfrew, ed. Pp. 59–72. Cambridge: McDonald Institute for Archaeological Research.

Golson, Jack. 1977. "No Room at the Top: Agricultural Intensification in the New Guinea Highlands." In *Sunda and Sahul.* J. Allen, J. Golson, and Rhys Jones, eds. Pp. 602–638. New York: Academic Press.

_____, and D. S. Gardiner. 1990. "Agriculture and Sociopolitical Organization in New Guinea Highlands Prehistory." *Annual Review of Anthropology* 19:393–417.

Goodall, Jane. 1986. *The Chimpanzees of Gombe.* Cambridge, MA: Harvard University Press.

Gosden, C. 1995. "Aboriculture and Agriculture in Coastal Papua New Guinea." *Antiquity* 69:807–817.

_____, et al. 1989. "Lapita Sites of the Bismarck Archipelago." *Antiquity* 63 (240):561–586.

Gostner, P., and Egarter Vigl. 2002. "Insight: Report of Radiological-Forensic Findings on the Ice Man." *Journal of Archaeological Science* 29:323–326.

Gould, Richard A. 1977. *Puntutjarpa Rockshelter and Australian Desert Culture.* New York: American Museum of Natural History.

Gowlett, John. 1978. "Culture and Conceptualization: The Oldowan-Acheulian Gradient." In *Stone Age Prehistory.* G. N. Bailey and P. Callow, eds. Pp. 243–260. Cambridge: Cambridge University Press.

_____. 1984. "Mental Abilities of Early Man: A Look at Some Hard Evidence." In *Hominid Evolution and Community Ecology.* Robert Foley, ed. Pp. 167–192. London: Academic Press.

Grayson, Donald K. 1983. *The Establishment of Human Antiquity.* Orlando, FL: Academic Press.

_____. 1993. *A Natural History of the Great Basin.* Washington, DC: Smithsonian Institution Press.

_____. 2001. "The Archaeological Record of Human Impacts on Human Populations." *Journal of World Prehistory* 15 (1):1–68.

Greber, N'omi, and Katherine C. Ruhl. 1989. *The Hopewell Site: A Contemporary Analysis Based on the Work of Charles C. Willoughby.* Boulder, CO: Westview Press.

Greenberg, Joseph. 1987. *Language in the Americas.* Palo Alto, CA: Stanford University Press.

Griffin, J. B. 1967. "Eastern North American Prehistory: A Summary." *Science* 156:175–191.

Groube, L., et al. 1986. "40,000-Year-Old Human Occupation Site at Huon Peninsula, Papua, New Guinea." *Nature* 324:453–455.

Gumerman, George, ed. 1990. *Exploring the Hohokam.* Albuquerque: University of New Mexico Press.

Gutin, J. 1995. "Remains in Spain Now Reign as Oldest Europeans." *Science* 269:12–13.

Haas, Jonathan, ed. 2001. *From Leaders to Rulers.* New York: Plenum/Kluwer.

_____, et al., eds. 1987. *The Origins and Development of the Andean State.* Cambridge: Cambridge University Press.

Hahn, J. 1993. "Aurignacian Art in Central Europe." In *Before Lascaux: The Complex Record of the Upper Palaeolithic.* H. Knecht, A. Pike-Tay, and R. White, eds. Pp. 229–241. Boca Raton, FL: CRC Press.

Hammond, Norman, ed. 1991. *Cuello: An Early Maya Community in Belize.* Cambridge: Cambridge University Press.

Hard, Robert J., and John R. Roney. 1998. "A Massive Terraced Village Complex in Chihuahua, Mexico, 3000 Years Before Present." *Science* 279:1661–1664.

Harding, A. F. 1984. *The Mycenaeans and Europe.* New York: Academic Press.

_____. 2000. *European Society in the Bronze Age.* Cambridge: Cambridge University Press.

Harlan, J. R. 1992. *Crops and Man,* 2nd ed. Madison, WI: American Society for Agronomy.

_____. 1998. *The Living Fields: Our Agricultural Heritage.* Cambridge: Cambridge University Press.

_____, et al., eds. 1976. *Origins of African Plant Domestication.* The Hague: Mouton.

Harris, D., and G. Hillman, eds. 1989. *Foraging and Farming.* London: Unwin Hyman.

Harris, David R., ed. 1980. *Human Ecology in Savanna Environments.* New York: Academic Press.

Harrison, Peter D. 1999. *The Lords of Tikal: Rulers of an Ancient Maya City.* London and New York: Thames & Hudson.

Harrison, Richard J. 1980. *The Beaker Folk.* London: Thames & Hudson.

Hassan, Fekri. 1981. *Demographic Archaeology*. Orlando, FL: Academic Press.

_____. 1986. "Desert Environment and Origins of Agriculture in Egypt." *Norwegian Archaeological Review* 19 (2):63–76.

_____. 1988. "The Pre-Dynastic of Egypt." *Journal of World Prehistory* 2 (2):135–186.

Hastorf, Christine A. 1992. *Agriculture and the Onset of Political Inequality Before the Inka*. Cambridge: Cambridge University Press.

_____. 1999. "The Cultural Life of Early Domestic Plant Use." *Antiquity* 72: 773–782.

Hather, J. G. 1994. *Tropical Archaeobotany*. London: Routledge.

_____, and P. V. Kirch. 1991. "Prehistoric Sweet Potato (*Ipomoea batatas*) from Mangaia Island, Central Polynesia." *Antiquity* 65:887–893.

Haury, Emil. 1976. *Hohokam, Desert Farmers and Craftsmen: Excavations at Snaketown*. Tucson: University of Arizona Press.

_____. 1985. *Mogollon Culture in the Forestdale Valley, East-Central Arizona*. Tucson: University of Arizona Press.

Hayden, Brian. 1981. "Research and Development in the Stone Age: Technological Transitions Among Hunter-Gatherers." *Current Anthropology* 22 (5):519–548.

_____. 1990. "Nimrods, Piscators, Pluckers, and Planters: The Emergence of Food Production." *Journal of Anthropological Archaeology* 9:31–69.

Haynes, C. Vance. 1982. "Were Clovis Progenitors in Beringia?" In *Paleoecology of Beringia*. David M. Hopkins et al., eds. Pp. 383–398. New York: Academic Press.

Haynes, Gary. 2002. *The Early Settlement of North America: The Clovis Era*. Cambridge: Cambridge University Press.

Healan, Dan, 1989. *Tula of the Toltecs*. Iowa City: University of Iowa Press.

Hemming, John. 1970. *The Conquest of the Incas*. New York: Harcourt Brace Jovanovich.

Henry, Donald O. 1989. *From Foraging to Agriculture*. Philadelphia: University of Pennsylvania Press.

Hester, T. R., et al. 1982. *Archaeology at Colha, Belize: The 1981 Interim Report*. San Antonio, TX: Center for Archaeological Research.

Heun, M. R., et al. 1997. "Site of Einkorn Wheat Domestication Identified by DNA Fingerprinting." *Science* 278:1312–1314.

Heyerdahl, Thor. 1996. *Tucumé*. London and New York: Thames & Hudson.

Higham, Charles F. W. 1993. "The Transition to Rice Cultivation in Southeast Asia." In *Transitions to Agriculture in Prehistory*. Douglas Price and Birgitte Gebauer, eds. Pp. 210–231. Madison, WI: Prehistory Press.

_____. 1994. *Khok Phanom Di: Prehistoric Adaptation to the World's Richest Habitat*. New York: Harcourt.

_____. 2000. *The Civilization of Angkor*. London: Cassel.

_____. 2002. *Early Cultures of Mainland Southeast Asia*. London and New York: Thames & Hudson.

_____, and Ian Glover. 1996. "New Evidence for Early Rice Cultivation in South, Southeast, and East Asia." In *The Origins and Spread of Agriculture and Pastoralism in Eurasia*. D. R. Harris, ed. Pp. 413–441. London: University College London Press.

Higham, Charles F. W., and Tracey L.-D. Lu. 1998. "The Origins and Dispersal of Rice Cultivation." *Antiquity* 72 (278):867–877.

Higham, Charles F. W., and Rachanie Thoserat. 1998. *Prehistoric Thailand*. Bangkok: River Books.

Hillman, G. C., and M. S. Davis. 1990. "Measured Domestication Rates in Wild Wheats and Barley Under Primitive Cultivation, and Their Archaeological Implications." *Journal of World Prehistory* 4 (2):157–222.

Hiscock, Peter. 1994. "Technological Responses to Risk in Holocene Australia." *Journal of World Prehistory* 8 (3):267–292.

Ho, Ping-Ti. 1984. "The Paleoenvironment of North China—A Review Article." *Journal of Asian Studies* 43 (4):723–733.

Hodder, Ian, ed. 1990. *The Domestication of Europe*. Oxford: Blackwell.

_____. 1996. *On the Surface: Çatalhöyük 1993–95*. Cambridge: McDonald Institute for Archaeological Research.

_____. 1999. *The Archaeological Process: An Introduction*. Oxford: Blackwell.

Hodell, David A., et al. 1995. "Possible Role of Climate in the Collapse of Classic Maya Civilization." *Nature* 375:391–347.

Hodell, David A., et al. 2001. "Solar Forcing of Drought Frequency in the Maya Lowlands." *Science* 292:1367–1370.

Hoffecker, John F. 2002. *Desolate Landscapes*. New Brunswick, NJ: Rutgers University Press.

_____, et al. 1993. "The Colonization of Beringia and the Peopling of the New World." *Science* 259:46–53.

Hoffman, Michael A. 1979. *Egypt Before the Pharaohs*. New York: Knopf.

_____, et al. 1982. *The Predynastic of Hierakonpolis*. Cairo: Egyptian Studies Association.

Hofman, Jack L., and Russell W. Graham. 1998. "The Paleo-Indian Cultures of the Great Plains." In *Archaeology on the Great Plains*. W. Raymond Wood, ed. Pp. 87–139. Lawrence: University Press of Kansas.

Hole, Frank. 1994. "Environmental Instabilities and Urban Origins." In *Chiefdoms and Early States in the Near East: The Organizational Dynamics of Complexity*. G. Stein and M. S. Rothman, eds. Pp. 121–143. Madison, WI: Prehistory Press.

_____, Kent V. Flannery, and J. A. Neely. 1969. *The Prehistory and Human Ecology of the Deh Luran Plain*. Ann Arbor: University of Michigan Museum of Anthropology.

Holloway, R. Ross. 1994. *The Archaeology of Early Rome and Latium*. London: Routledge.

Hope, Geoff, and Jack Golson. 1995. "Late Quaternary Change in the Mountains of New Guinea." *Antiquity* 69:818–830.

Hopkins, David M., et al., eds. 1982. *Paleoecology of Beringia*. New York: Academic Press.

Howell, F. Clark. 1966. "Observations on the Earlier Phases of the European Lower Palaeolithic." *American Anthropologist* 68 (2):111–140.

———. 1999. "Paleo-Demes, Species Clades, and Extinctions in the Pleistocene Hominin Record." *Journal of Anthropological Research* 55:191–243.

———, and J. Desmond Clark. 1963. "Acheulian Hunter-Gatherers of Sub-Saharan Africa." *Viking Fund Publications in Anthropology* 36:458–533.

Howell, John M. 1987. "Early Farming in Northwestern Europe." *Scientific American* 237 (11):118–126.

Huang, Tsui-mei. 1992. "Liangzhu—A Late Neolithic Jade-Yielding Culture in Southeastern Coastal China." *Antiquity* 66:75–83.

Huot, Jean-Louis. 1989. " 'Ubaidian Villages of Lower Mesopotamia." In *Upon These Foundations: The 'Ubaid Period*. E. F. Henrickson and I. Thueson, eds. Copenhagen: National Museum of Denmark.

Hyslop, John. 1984. *The Inca Road System*. New York: Academic Press.

———. 1990. *Inka Settlement Patterns*. Austin: University of Texas Press.

———, et al. 1987. *Huaca Prieta*. New York: American Museum of Natural History.

Ikram, Salima, and Aidan Dodson. 1998. *The Mummy in Ancient Egypt*. London and New York: Thames & Hudson.

Irwin, G. 1992. *The Prehistoric Exploration and Colonisation of the Pacific*. Cambridge: Cambridge University Press.

———, S. Brickler, and P. Quirke. 1990. "Pacific Voyaging by Canoe and Computer." *Antiquity* 64 (242):34–50.

Isaac, Glynn. 1984. "The Archaeology of Human Origins: Studies of the Lower Palaeolithic in East Africa, 1971–1981." *Advances in World Archaeology* 3:1–89.

———, and J. W. K. Harris. 1978. "Archaeology." In *The Fossil Hominids and an Introduction to Their Context, 1968–1974*. Vol. 1. *Koobi Fora Research Project*. M. D. Leakey and Richard E. Leakey, eds. Pp. 47–76. Oxford: Clarendon Press.

Isbell, William, and Katharina J. Schreiber. 1978. "Was Huari a State?" *American Antiquity* 43:372–389.

Jacobsen, Thomas W., and W. R. Farrand. 1987. *Franchthi Cave and Paralia*. Bloomington: Indiana University Press.

James, Simon. 1992. *The World of the Celts*. London and New York: Thames & Hudson.

Jarrige, Jean-François. 1993. "Excavations at Mehrgarh: Their Significance for Understanding the Background of the Harappan Civilization." In *Harappan Civilization*, 2nd ed. Gregory Possehl, ed. Pp. 79–84. New Delhi: Oxford and IBH.

Jeffries, R. W. 1987. *The Archaeology of Carrier Mills*. Carbondale: Southern Illinois University Press.

Jennings, Jesse D. 1957. *Danger Cave*. Salt Lake City: University of Utah Press.

Jochim, Michael. 1976. *Hunter-Gatherer Subsistence and Settlement*. New York: Academic Press.

———. 1983. "Paleolithic Cave Art in Ecological Perspective." In *Hunter-Gatherer Economy in Prehistory*. G. N. Bailey, ed. Pp. 212–219. Cambridge: Cambridge University Press.

Johanson, Donald C., and Maitland A. Edey. 1981. *Lucy: The Beginnings of Humankind*. New York: Simon & Schuster.

Johanson, Donald C., and Tim White. 1979. "A Systematic Assessment of Early African Hominids." *Science* 202:321–330.

Johanson, Donald C., et al. 1987. "New Partial Skeleton of *Homo habilis* from Olduvai Gorge, Tanzania." *Nature* 327:205–211.

Jones, J. S., and S. Rouhani. 1986. "How Small Was the Bottleneck?" *Nature* 319:449–450.

Jones, M., and T. Brown. 2000. "Agricultural Origins: The Evidence of Modern and Ancient DNA." *Holocene* 10 (6):775–72.

Jones, Rhys. 1989. "East of Wallace's Line: Issues and Problems in the Colonization of the Australian Continent." In *The Human Revolution*. Paul Mellars and Christopher Stringer, eds. Pp. 743–782. Edinburgh: Edinburgh University Press.

———. 1995. "Tasmanian Archaeology: Establishing the Sequences." *Annual Review of Anthropology* 24:423–446.

Kaufman, Terrence, and Victor Golla. 2000. "Language Groupings in the New World: Their Reliability and Usability in Cross-Disciplinary Studies." In *America Past, America Present: Genes and Languages in the Americas and Beyond*. Colin Renfrew, ed. Pp. 57–67. Cambridge: McDonald Institute for Archaeological Research.

Keightley, David N. 1978. *Sources of Shang History: The Oracle Bone Inscriptions of Bronze Age China*. Berkeley: University of California Press.

———. 1999. "The Shang." In *The Cambridge History of Ancient China*. Michael Lowe, ed. Pp. 123–164. Cambridge: Cambridge University Press.

Keller, Ferdinand. 1866. *The Lake Dwellings of Switzerland and Other Parts of Europe*. London: Longmans Green.

Kemp, Barry. 1989. *Ancient Egypt: The Anatomy of a Civilization*. London: Routledge.

Kennedy, Paul. 1987. *Rise and Fall of the Great Powers*. New York: Vintage Books.

Kenoyer, J. M. 1997. "Trade and Technology of the Indus Valley: New Insights from Harappa, Pakistan." *World Archaeology* 29 (2):262–280.

Kenyon, Kathleen. 1981. *Excavations at Jericho*. Vol. 3. Jerusalem: British School of Archaeology.

Kershaw, Peter. 1995. "Environmental Change in Greater Australia." *Antiquity* 69:656–675.

Keys, David. 1999. *Catastrophe*. London: Century.

Kidder, Alfred V. 1927. *An Introduction to the Study of Southwestern Archaeology*. New Haven, CT: Yale University Press.

Killion, Thomas W., ed. 1992. *Gardens of Prehistory*. Birmingham: University of Alabama Press.

Kimball, William H., and others. 1994. "The First Skull and Other New Discoveries of *Australopithecus afarensis* at Hadar, Ethiopia." *Nature* 368:449–451.

Kinnes, Ian. 1982. "Les Fouaillages and Megalithic Origins." *Antiquity* 56:24–30.

Kirch, Patrick V. 1982. "Advances in Polynesian Prehistory: Three Decades in Review." *Advances in World Archaeology* 2:52–102.

———. 1984. *The Evolution of the Polynesian Chiefdoms.* Cambridge: Cambridge University Press.

———. 1985. *Feathered Gods and Fishhooks.* Honolulu: University of Hawaii Press.

———. 1988. "The Talepakemalai Lapita Site and Oceanic Prehistory." *National Geographic Research* 4 (3):328–342.

———. 1996. "Microcosmic Histories: Island Perspectives on 'Global' Change." *American Anthropologist* 98 (3):254–271.

———. 2000. *On the Road of the Winds: An Archaeological History of the Pacific Islands Before European Contact.* Berkeley: University of California Press.

———, and T. L. Hunt, eds. 1996. *Historical Ecology in the Pacific Islands: Prehistoric Environmental and Landscape Change.* New Haven, CT: Yale University Press.

Kirch, Patrick V., and Marshall Sahlins. 1992. *Anahulu: The Anthropology of History in the Kingdom of Hawaii.* Chicago: University of Chicago Press.

Klein, Richard. 1979. "Stone Age Exploitation of Animals in Southern Africa." *American Scientist* 67:23–32.

Klein, Richard G. 1999. *The Human Career,* 2nd ed. Chicago: University of Chicago Press.

———. 2001. "Fully Modern Humans." In *Archaeology at the Millennium: A Sourcebook.* Gary M. Feinman and T. Douglas Price, eds. Pp. 109–136. New York: Kluwer Academic/Plenum.

Knecht, H., et al., eds. 1993. *Before Lascaux: The Complex Record of the Early Upper Palaeolithic.* Boca Raton, FL: CRC Press.

Knight, V. J. 1986. "The Institutional Organization of Mississippian Religion." *American Antiquity* 61:675–687.

———, and Vincas Steponaitis, eds. 1998. *Archaeology of the Moundville Chiefdom.* Washington, DC: Smithsonian Institution Press.

Kohl, P. 1978. "The Balance of Trade in Southwestern Asia in the Mid-Third Millennium B.C." *Current Anthropology* 19:463–492.

Kolata, Alan L. 1993. *Tiwanaku.* Oxford: Blackwell.

———. 2002. *Tiwanaku and Its Hinterland, Archaeology and Paleoecology of an Andean Civilization: Urban and Rural Archaeology.* Washington, DC: Smithsonian Institution Press.

Kozlowski, S. 1999. *The Eastern Wing of the Fertile Crescent.* Oxford: BAR International Series 760.

Kramer, Samuel. 1963. *The Sumerians.* Chicago: University of Chicago Press.

Kurtén, Björn. 1968. *Pleistocene Mammals in Europe.* Chicago: Aldine.

———, and E. Anderson. 1980. *Pleistocene Mammals of North America.* New York: Columbia University Press.

Kuzmin, Yaroslav V., and Kenneth B. Tankersley. 1996. "The Colonization of Eastern Siberia: An Evaluation of the Paleolithic Age Radiocarbon Dates." *Journal of Archaeological Science* 32:577–585.

Laitman, Jeffrey T. 1984. "The Anatomy of Human Speech." *Natural History* 93 (9):20–27.

———, J. S. Reidenberg, D. R. Freidland, and P. J. Gannon. 1991. "What Sayeth Thou Neanderthal? A Look at the Evolution of Their Vocal Tract and Speech." *American Journal of Physical Anthropology* 12:109.

Lamberg-Karlovsky, C. C. 1973. "Urban Interactions on the Iranian Plateau: Excavations at Tepe Yahya, 1967–1973." *Proceedings of the British Academy* 59:5–43.

———. 1978. "The Proto-Elamites and the Iranian Plateau." *Antiquity* 52:114–120.

———, and T. Bealc, eds. 1986. *Excavations at Tepe Yahya, Iran: The Early Periods.* Cambridge, MA: Harvard University Press.

Larichev, Vitaliy. 1988. "The Upper Paleolithic of Northern Asia." *Journal of World Prehistory* 2 (4):359–396.

———, et al. 1987. "Lower and Middle Paleolithic of Northern Asia: Achievements, Problems, and Perspectives." *Journal of World Prehistory* 1 (4):415–464.

Larick, Roy, and Russell Ciochon. 1996. "The First Asians." *Archaeology* 49 (1):51–53.

Larsen, Clark Spencer. 1995. "Biological Changes in Human Populations with Agriculture." *Annual Review of Anthropology* 24:185–213.

Larsen, Mogens. 1976. *The Old Assyrian City-State and Its Colonies.* Copenhagen: Akademisk Forlag.

———. 1987. "Commercial Networks in the Ancient Near East." In *Centre and Periphery in the Ancient World.* Michael Rowlands, Mogens Larsen, and Kristian Kristiansen, eds. Pp. 47–56. Cambridge: Cambridge University Press.

———. 1995. *The Conquest of Assyria.* London: Routledge.

Layton, R., ed. 1994. *Who Needs the Past?* 2nd ed. London: Routledge.

Leakey, L. S. B. 1951. *Olduvai Gorge, 1931–1951.* Cambridge: Cambridge University Press.

Leakey, M. D. 1971. *Olduvai Gorge.* Vol. 3. Cambridge: Cambridge University Press.

———, and J. D. Harris. 1990. *Laetoli: A Pliocene Site in Northern Tanzania.* Oxford: Oxford University Press.

Leakey, M. G., and others. 1995. "New Four Million Year Old Hominid Species from Kanapooi and Allia Bay, Kenya." *Nature* 376:565–571.

Lee, Richard B. 1979. *The !Kung San.* Cambridge: Cambridge University Press.

———, and Irven DeVore, eds. 1976. *Kalahari Hunter-Gatherers.* Cambridge: Cambridge University Press.

Lefkowitz, Mary. 1996. *Not Out of Africa.* New York: Basic Books.

Legge, A. J., and Peter Rowley-Conwy. 1987. "Gazelle Hunting in Stone Age Syria." *Scientific American* 238 (8):88–95.

Lehner, Mark. 1997. *The Complete Pyramids.* London and New York: Thames & Hudson.

Lekson, Stephen H. 1999. *The Chaco Meridian: Centers of Political Power in the Ancient Southwest.* Walnut Creek, CA: AltaMira Press.

Leroi-Gourhan, André. 1965. *Treasures of Palaeolithic Art.* New York: Abrams.

_____. 1984. *The Dawn of European Art: An Introduction to Palaeolithic Cave Painting.* Cambridge: Cambridge University Press.

Levetzion, Nehemiah. 1973. *Ancient Ghana and Mali.* London: Methuen.

Levy, Thomas E., et al. 2002. "Early Bronze Age Metallurgy: A Newly Discovered Copper Manufactory in Southern Jordan." *Antiquity* 76:425–437.

Lewin, Roger. 1987. *Bones of Contention.* New York: Simon & Schuster.

_____. 1993. *The Origins of Modern Humans.* New York: Scientific American Library.

_____. 1998. *Principles of Human Evolution,* rev. ed. Cambridge: Blackwell.

Lewis-Williams, David. 1981. *Believing and Seeing: Symbolic Meanings in Southern San Rock Art.* New York: Academic Press.

_____. 1995. "Modelling the Production and Consumption of Rock Art." *South African Archaeological Bulletin* 50 (162):143–154.

_____. 2002. *The Mind in the Cave: Consciousness and the Origins of Art.* London and New York: Thames & Hudson.

Lieberman, Philip. 1991. *Uniquely Human: The Evolution of Speech, Thought, and Selfless Behavior.* Cambridge, MA: Harvard University Press.

Liverani, M., ed. 1993. *Akkad: The First World Empire.* Padua, Italy: Sargon.

Lloyd, Seton. 1983. *The Archaeology of Mesopotamia,* 2nd ed. London: Thames & Hudson.

Lourandos, Henry. 1987. "Pleistocene Australia: Peopling a Continent." In *The Pleistocene Old World: Regional Perspectives.* Olga Soffer, ed. Pp. 147–166. New York: Plenum Press.

_____, ed. 1997. *Continent of Hunter-Gatherers: New Perspectives in Australian Prehistory.* Cambridge: Cambridge University Press.

McAnany, Patricia. 1995. *Living with the Ancestors: Kinship and Kingship in Ancient Maya Society.* Austin: University of Texas Press.

McCollum, Melissa A. 1999. "The Robust Australopithecine Face: A Morphogenetic Perspective." *Science* 284:301–305.

McCorriston, Joy, and Frank Hole. 1991. "The Ecology of Seasonal Stress and the Origins of Agriculture in the Near East." *American Anthropologist* 93:46–69.

McGhee, Robert. 1984. "Contact Between Native North Americans and the Medieval Norse: A Review of Evidence." *American Antiquity* 49 (2):4–26.

_____. 1996. *Ancient People of the Arctic.* Vancouver: University of British Columbia Press and the Canadian Museum of Civilization.

Mcintosh, Jane R. 2002. *A Peaceful Realm.* Boulder, CO: Westview Press.

McIntosh, Susan K., ed. 1999. *Beyond Chiefdoms.* Cambridge: Cambridge University Press.

_____, and R. J. McIntosh. 1980. *Prehistoric Investigations at Jenne-jeno, Mali.* Oxford: British Archaeological Reports.

_____. 1988. "From Stone to Metal: New Perspectives on the Later Prehistory of West Africa." *Journal of World Prehistory* 2 (1):89–131.

MacNeish, Richard, ed. 1970. *The Prehistory of the Tehuacán Valley.* Austin: University of Texas Press.

_____. 1978. *The Science of Archaeology.* North Scituate, MA: Duxbury Press.

_____, and Mary W. Eubanks. 2000. "Comparative Analysis of the Río Balsas and Tehuacán Models for the Origin of Maize." *American Antiquity* 11 (1):3–20.

MacNeish, Richard, and J. Libby, eds. 1995. *Origins of Rice Agriculture: The Preliminary Report of the Sino-American Jiangxi (PRC) Project.* El Paso: University of Texas Publications in Anthropology 13.

MacQueen, J. G. 1996. *The Hittites,* 3rd ed. London: Thames & Hudson.

Maisels, Charles. 1993. *The Emergence of Civilization: From Hunting and Gathering to Agriculture, Cities and the State in the Near East.* London: Routledge.

_____. 2001. *Early Civilizations of the Old World: The Formative Histories of Egypt, the Levant, Mesopotamia, India, and China.* London: Routledge.

Malinowski, Bronislaw. 1922. *Argonauts of the Western Pacific.* London: Routledge & Kegan Paul.

Mallory, J. P. 1988. *In Search of the Indo-Europeans.* New York: Thames & Hudson.

Malone, Caroline. 1989. *Avebury.* London: English Heritage.

Manning, Stuart. 1988. "The Bronze Age Eruption of Thera." *Journal of Mediterranean Archaeology* 1 (1):17–82.

_____. 1995. *Absolute Chronology of the Aegean Early Bronze Age.* Sheffield, England: Sheffield Academic Press.

Marcus, Joyce. 1976. *Emblem and State in the Classic Maya Lowlands.* Washington, DC: Dumbarton Oaks.

_____. 1993. *Mesoamerican Writing Systems: Propaganda, Myth, and History in Four Ancient Civilizations.* Princeton, NJ: Princeton University Press.

_____, and Kent V. Flannery. 1996. *The Zapotec Civilization.* London and New York: Thames & Hudson.

Marinatos, Nanno. 1993. *Minoan Religion.* Columbia: University of South Carolina Press.

Marks, Anthony E. 1983. "The Middle to Upper Palaeolithic Transition in the Levant." *Advances in World Prehistory* 2:51–98.

Marshack, Alexander. 1972. *The Roots of Civilization.* New York: McGraw-Hill.

Martin, Paul, and Richard Klein, eds. 1984. *A Pleistocene Revolution.* Tucson: University of Arizona Press.

Matheny, Ray. 1986. "Early States of the Maya Lowlands During the Late Preclassic Period." In *City-States of the Maya: Art and Architecture.* Elizabeth P. Benson, ed. Pp. 1–44. Denver: Rocky Mountain Institute of Pre-Columbian Studies.

Matson, R. G. 1991. *The Origins of Southwestern Agriculture.* Tucson: University of Arizona Press.

Maxwell, Moreau S. 1985. *Prehistory of the Eastern Arctic.* New York: Academic Press.

Meadows, Richard H. 1989. "Osteological Evidence for the Process of Animal Domestication." In *The Walking Larder.* Juliet Clutton-Brock, ed. Pp. 80–90. London: Unwin Hyman.

_____, ed. 1991. *Harappa Excavations 1986–1990.* Madison, WI: Prehistory Press.

Megaw, R., and J. V. S. Megaw. 1989. *Celtic Art from Its Beginnings to the Book of Kells.* London and New York: Thames & Hudson.

Mellaart, James. 1967. *Çatal Hüyük.* New York: McGraw-Hill.

_____. 1975. *The Neolithic of the Near East.* London: Thames & Hudson.

Mellars, Paul. 1985. "The Ecological Basis of Social Complexity in the Upper Palaeolithic of Southwestern France." In *Prehistoric Hunter-Gatherers: The Emergence of Cultural Complexity.* T. Douglas Price and James Brown, eds. Pp. 271–297. Orlando, FL: Academic Press.

_____. 1993. "Archaeology and the Population-Dispersal Hypothesis of Modern Human Origins in Europe." In *The Origin of Modern Humans and the Impact of Chronometric Dating.* M. J. Aitken, C. B. Stringer, and P. A. Mellars, eds. Pp. 196–216. Princeton, NJ: Princeton University Press.

_____. 1996. *The Neanderthal Legacy.* Princeton, NJ: Princeton University Press.

_____. 1998. "The Fate of the Neanderthals." *Science* 395:539–560.

_____, and Petra Dark. 1998. *Star Carr in Context.* Cambridge: McDonald Institute for Archaeological Research.

Meltzer, David. 1988. "Late Pleistocene Adaptations in Eastern North America." *Journal of World Prehistory* 2 (1):1–52.

_____. 1995. "Clocking the First Americans." *Annual Review of Anthropology* 24:21–45.

_____, James Adovasio, and Tom Dillehay. 1994. "On a Pleistocene Human Occupation at Pedra Furada, Brazil." *Antiquity* 68 (261):695–714.

Mendelssohn, Kurt. 1974. *The Riddle of the Pyramids.* New York: Praeger.

Mercader, Julio, Melissa Panger, and Christophe Boesch. 2002. "Excavation of a Chimpanzee Stone Tool Site in the African Rainforest." *Science* 296:1452–1455.

Midant-Reynes, Béatrice. 2000. "The Naqada Period (c. 4000 to 3200 B.C.)" In *The Oxford History of Ancient Egypt.* Ian Shaw, ed. Pp. 44–60. Oxford: Oxford University Press.

Milisauskas, S., and J. Kruk. 1989. "Neolithic Economy in Central Europe." *Journal of World Prehistory* 2 (3): 403–446.

Miller, Daniel. 1985. "Ideology and the Harappan Civilization." *Journal of Anthropological Archaeology* 4:1–38.

Miller, Mary, and Karl Taube. 1993. *The Gods and Symbols of Ancient Mexico and the Maya.* London and New York: Thames & Hudson.

Millon, R. 1988. "The Last Days of Teotihuacán." In *The Collapse of Ancient States and Civilizations.* Norman Yoffee and George Cowgill, eds. Pp. 102–164. Tucson: University of Arizona Press.

_____. 1996. "State and Society at Teotihuacán, Mexico." *Annual Review of Anthropology* 26:129–161.

_____, R. Bruce Drewitt, and George Cowgill. 1974. *Urbanization at Teotihuacán, Mexico.* Austin: University of Texas Press.

Milner, George R. 1998. *The Cahokia Chiefdom.* Washington, DC: Smithsonian Institution Press.

Mithen, Steven. 1996. *The Prehistory of the Mind.* London: Thames & Hudson.

Mochanov, Yuri A. 1978. "Stratigraphy and Chronology of the Paleolithic of Northeast Asia." In *Early Man in America from a Circum-Pacific Perspective.* Alan L. Bryan, ed. Pp. 67–68. Edmonton: University of Alberta.

Moctezuma, Eduardo Matos. 1988. *The Great Temple of the Aztecs.* New York: Thames & Hudson.

Molleson, Theya. 1994. "The Eloquent Bones of Abu Hureyra." *Scientific American* 271 (2):70–75.

Moore, A. M. T., and Gordon Hillman. 1992. "The Pleistocene to Holocene Transition and Human Economy in Southwest Asia: The Impact of the Younger Dryas." *American Antiquity* 57 (3):482–494.

Moore, Andrew T. 1985. "The Development of Neolithic Societies in the Near East." *Advances in World Archaeology* 4:1–70.

_____, et al. 2000. *Village on the Euphrates.* New York: Oxford University Press.

Moorey, P. R. S. 1994. *Ancient Mesopotamian Materials and Industries: The Archaeological Evidence.* Oxford: Clarendon Press.

Morlan, Richard. 1983. "Pre-Clovis Occupation North of the Ice Sheets." In *Early Man in the New World.* Richard Shutler, ed. Pp. 47–64. Beverly Hills: Sage Publications.

Morris, I., ed. 1987. *Burial and Ancient Society. The Rise of the Greek City-State.* Cambridge: Cambridge University Press.

_____, 1994. *Classical Greece: Ancient Histories and Modern Archaeologies.* Cambridge: Cambridge University Press.

Morris, J. Bayard, ed. 1962. *Five Letters of Cortés to the Emperor, 1519–1526.* New York: Norton.

Morse, Dan, and P. A. Morse. 1983. *Archaeology of the Central Mississippi Valley.* New York: Academic Press.

Morwood, M. J., et al. 1999. "Fission Track Age of Stone Tools and Fossils on the East Indonesian Island of Flores." *Nature* 392:173–176.

Moscati, Sabatino. 1988. *The Phoenicians*. Milan: Bompiani.

Moseley, Michael. 1975. *The Maritime Foundations of Andean Civilization*. Menlo Park, CA: Cummings.

_____. 1985. "The Exploration and Explanation of Early Monumental Architecture in the Andes." In *Early Ceremonial Architecture in the Andes*. Christopher Donnan, ed. Pp. 28–58. Washington, DC: Dumbarton Oaks.

_____. 2000. *The Incas and Their Ancestors*, 2nd ed. London and New York: Thames & Hudson.

_____, and Kent C. Day, eds. 1982. *Chan Chan: Andean Desert City*. Albuquerque: University of New Mexico Press.

Moseley, Michael E., et al. 1991. "Colonies and Conquest: Tiahuanaco and Huari in Moquequa." In *Huari Administrative Structure*. William H. Isbell and Gordon F. McEwen, eds. Pp. 121–146. Washington, DC: Dumbarton Oaks.

Mughal, R. M. 1974. "New Evidence of the Early Harappan Culture from Jalipur, Pakistan." *Archaeology* 27 (2):106–113.

Muller, Jon D. 1989. "The Southern Cult." In *The Southeastern Ceremonial Complex: Artifacts and Analysis*. Patricia Galloway, ed. Pp. 11–26. Lincoln: University of Nebraska Press.

Mulvaney, John, and Johan Kamminga. 1999. *The Prehistory of Australia*. Washington, DC: Smithsonian Institution Press.

Munro-Hay, Stuart. 1991. *Aksum: An African Civilization of Late Antiquity*. Edinburgh: Edinburgh University Press.

Murowchick, R., ed. 1994. *Cradles of Civilization. China, Ancient Culture, Modern Land*. Norman: University of Oklahoma Press.

Murray, Tim, ed. 1998. *The Archaeology of Aboriginal Australia*. Sydney: Allan Unwin.

Muzzolini, Alfred. 1995. *Les Images Rupestres du Sahara*. Toulouse: Author.

Nelson, Sarah. 1993. *The Archaeology of Korea*. Cambridge: Cambridge University Press.

_____. 1995. *The Archaeology of Northeast China: Beyond the Great Wall*. London: Routledge.

Nichols, D. L., and T. H. Charlton, eds. 1995. *The Archaeology of City-States: Cross Cultural Approaches*. Washington, DC: Smithsonian Institution Press.

Nissen, Hans J. 1988. *The Early History of the Near East 9000–2000 B.C.* Chicago: University of Chicago Press.

_____, et al. 1993. *Archaic Bookkeeping. Early Writing and Techniques of Economic Administration in the Ancient Near East*. Chicago: University of Chicago Press.

Nitecki, Matthew H., and Doris V. Nitecki, eds. 1994. *Origins of Anatomically Modern Humans*. New York: Plenum Press.

Oates, Joan. 1973. "The Background and Development of Early Farming Communities in Mesopotamia and the Zagros." *Proceedings of the Prehistoric Society* 39:147–181.

O'Connor, David. 1993. *Ancient Nubia: Egypt's Rival in Africa*. Philadelphia: University Museum.

O'Connor, Sue, Matthew Spriggs, and Peter Veth. 2002. "Excavation at Lene Hara Cave Establishes Occupation in East Timor at Least 30,000 to 35,000 Years Ago." *Antiquity* 76:45–50.

O'Connor, Sue, and Peter Veth, eds. 2000. *East of Wallace's Line. Studies of Past and Present Maritime Cultures and the Importance of Chronology*. Rotterdam: Balkema.

Oliver, Douglas. 1977. *Ancient Tahitian Society*. Honolulu: University of Hawaii Press.

Oliver, Roland. 2000. *The African Experience*. London: Weidenfeld & Nicholson.

Özdogan, M., and N. Basgelen, eds. 1999. *Neolithic in Turkey: New Discoveries*. Istanbul: Arkeoloji ve Sanat Yayinlari.

Paddock, John. 1983. "The Oaxaca Barrio at Teotihuacán." In *The Cloud People*. Kent Flannery and Joyce Marcus, eds. Pp. 170–175. New York: Academic Press.

Pallottino, Massimo. 1978. *The Etruscans*. Harmondsworth, England: Penguin.

Parkington, John. 1987. "Prehistory and Paleoenvironments at the Pleistocene-Holocene Boundary in the Western Cape." In *The Pleistocene Old World: Regional Perspectives*. Olga Soffer, ed. Pp. 349–364. New York: Plenum Press.

Parpola, Asko. 1994. *Deciphering the Indus Script*. Cambridge: Cambridge University Press.

Pasztory, Esther. 1997. *Teotihuacán: An Experiment in Living*. Norman: University of Oklahoma Press.

Patterson, Thomas C. 1985. "The Huaca La Florida, Rímac Valley, Peru." In *Early Ceremonial Architecture in the Andes*. Christopher Donnan, ed. Pp. 59–70. Washington, DC: Dumbarton Oaks.

_____. 1992. *The Inca Empire*. London: Berg.

Pauketat, T. R. 1994. *The Ascent of Chiefs: Cahokia and Mississippian Politics in Native North America*. Tuscaloosa: University of Alabama Press.

_____. 1998. "Refiguring the Archaeology of Greater Cahokia." *Journal of Archaeological Research* 6 (1):45–89.

_____, and Thomas E. Emerson. 1997. *Cahokia: Domination and Ideology in the Mississippian World*. Lincoln: University of Nebraska Press.

Pavlides, C., and C. Gosden. 1994. "35,000-Year-Old Sites in the Rainforests of West New Britain, Papua New Guinea." *Antiquity* 68:604–610.

Pearson, Richard J., et al., eds. 1986. *Windows on the Japanese Past: Studies in Archaeology and Prehistory*. Ann Arbor: Center for Japanese Studies, University of Michigan.

Perlès, Catherine. 2001. *The Early Neolithic in Greece*. Cambridge: Cambridge University Press.

Petit, J. R., and others. 1999. "Climate and Atmospheric History of the Past 420,000 Years from the Vostok Ice Core, Antarctica." *Nature* 399:429–436.

Petrie, W. M. Flinders. 1890. *Kahun, Gurob, and Hawara*. London: Egypt Exploration Society.

Phillips, E. D. 1972. "The Scythian Domination in Western Asia." *World Archaeology* 4:129–138.

Phillipson, D. W. 1994. *African Prehistory*, 2nd ed. Cambridge: Cambridge University Press.

_____, ed. 2000. *Archaeology at Aksum, Ethiopia, 1993–97*. London: Society of Antiquaries.

Piggott, Stuart. 1965. *Ancient Europe*. Chicago: Aldine.

_____. 1992. *Wagon, Chariot, and Carriage*. London and New York: Thames & Hudson.

Pilbeam, David. 1986. "Distinguished Lecture: Hominoid Evolution and Hominoid Origins." *American Anthropologist* 88 (2):295–312.

Pinker, Stephen. 1994. *The Language Instinct*. Cambridge, MA: MIT Press.

Piperno, Dolores R., and Deborah M. Pearsall. 1998. *The Origins of Agriculture in the Lowland Neotropics*. San Diego, CA: Academic Press.

Plog, Fred. 1997. *Ancient Peoples of the American Southwest*. London and New York: Thames & Hudson.

Plomley, N. J. B. 1969. *An Annotated Bibliography of the Tasmanian Aborigines*. London: Royal Anthropological Institute.

Pollock, Susan. 1992. "Bureaucrats and Managers, Peasants and Pastoralists, Imperialists and Traders: Research on the Uruk and Jemdet Nasr Periods in Mesopotamia." *Journal of World Prehistory* 6:297–336.

_____. 1999. *Ancient Mesopotamia*. Cambridge: Cambridge University Press.

Pope, Geoffrey G. 1984. "The Antiquity and Paleoenvironment of the Asian Hominidae." In *The Evolution of the East Asian Environment*. R. O. I. Whyte, ed. Pp. 922–947. Hong Kong: Center of Asian Studies, University of Hong Kong.

_____. 1989. "Bamboo and Human Evolution." *Natural History* 10 (89):49–56.

_____, et al. 1986. "Earliest Radiometrically Dated Artifacts from Southeast Asia." *Current Anthropology* 27 (3):275–279.

Pope, Kevin, et al. 2001. "Origin and Environmental Setting of Ancient Agriculture in the Lowlands of Mesoamerica." *Science* 292:1370–1073.

Porch, Nick, and Jim Allen. 1995. "Tasmania: Archaeological and Palaeoecological Perspectives." *Antiquity* 69:714–732.

Possehl, Gregory L. 1980. *Indus Civilization in Saurashta*. Delhi: B. R.

_____. 1986. *Kulli*. Durham: University of North Carolina Press.

_____. 1993. *Harappan Civilization*, 2nd ed. New Delhi: Oxford and IBH.

_____. 1996. "Meluhha." In *The Indian Ocean in Antiquity*. Julian Reade, ed. Pp. 133–208. London: Kegan Paul International.

_____. 1999. *Indus Age: The Beginnings*. Delhi: Oxford University Press.

_____. 2000. "The Drying Up of the Sarasvati: Environmental Disruption in South Asian Prehistory." In *Environmental Disaster and the Archaeology of Human Response*. Garth Bawden and Richard Martin Reycraft, eds. Pp. 63–74. Albuquerque: Maxwell Museum of Anthropology.

_____, and M. H. Raval. 1989. *Harappan Civilization and Rojdi*. New Delhi: Oxford and IBH.

Postgate, Nicholas. 1993. *Early Mesopotamia: Economy and Society at the Dawn of History*. London: Kegan Paul.

_____. 1994. "How Many Sumerians per Hectare?—Probing the Anatomy of an Early City." *Cambridge Archaeological Journal* 4:47–65.

_____, et al. 1995. "The Evidence for Early Writing: Utilitarian or Ceremonial?" *Antiquity* 69:459–480.

Potts, D. T. 1999. *The Archaeology of Elam*. Cambridge: Cambridge University Press.

Potts, Richard. 1984a. "Home Bases and Early Hominids." *American Scientist* 72:338–347.

_____. 1984b. "Hominid Hunters? Problems of Identifying the Earliest Hunter-Gatherers." In *Hominid Evolution and Community Ecology*. Robert Foley, ed. Pp. 129–166. London: Academic Press.

_____. 1996. *Humanity's Descent: The Consequences of Ecological Instability*. New York: William Morrow.

Powers, William R., and Thomas D. Hamilton. 1978. "Dry Creek: A Late Pleistocene Human Occupation in Central Alaska." In *Early Man in America from a Circum-Pacific Perspective*. Alan L. Bryan, ed. Pp. 72–78. Edmonton: University of Alberta.

Powledge, Tabitha M., and Mark Rose. 1996. "The Great DNA Hunt." *Archaeology* 49 (5):36–44.

Pozorski, Thomas. 1987. "Changing Priorities Within the Chimu State: The Role of Irrigation Agriculture." In *The Origins and Development of the Andean State*. Jonathan Haas et al., eds. Pp. 111–120. Cambridge: Cambridge University Press.

_____, and Sheila Pozorski. 1987. "Chavín, the Early Horizon, and the Initial Period." In *The Origins and Development of the Andean State*. Jonathan Haas et al., eds. Pp. 36–46. Cambridge: Cambridge University Press.

Price, T. Douglas. 1983. "The European Mesolithic." *American Antiquity* 48:761–778.

_____. 1985. "Foragers of Southern Scandinavia." In *Prehistoric Hunter-Gatherers: The Emergence of Cultural Complexity*. T. Douglas Price and James Brown, eds. Pp. 212–236. New York: Academic Press.

_____. 1987. "The Mesolithic of Western Europe." *Journal of World Prehistory* 1 (3):225–305.

_____, ed. 2000. *Europe's First Farmers*. Cambridge: Cambridge University Press.

_____, and James Brown, eds. 1985. *Prehistoric Hunter-Gatherers: The Emergence of Cultural Complexity*. New York: Academic Press.

Price, T. Douglas, Linda Manzanilla, and William D. Middleton. 2000. "Immigration and the Ancient City of Teotihuacán in Mexico: A Study Using Strontium Isotope Ratios in Human Bone and Teeth." *Journal of Archaeological Science* 27 (10):903–913.

Price, T. D., et al. 2001. "Prehistoric Human Migration in the *Linearbandkeramik* of Central Europe." *Antiquity* 75:593–603.

Pringle, Heather. 1997. "Ice Age Communities May Be Earliest Known Net Hunters. *Science* 277:1203–1204.

_____. 1998. "New Women of the Ice Age." *Discover,* April: 62–69.

Proulx, Donald. 1985. "An Analysis of the Early Cultural Sequence in the Nepeña Valley, Peru." *Research Report of Department of Anthropology, University of Massachusetts, Amherst,* No. 25.

Quilter, Jeffrey. 1985. "Architecture and Chronology at El Paraíso, Peru." *Journal of Field Archaeology* 12 (3):274–298.

_____. 2002. "Moche Politics, Religion, and Warfare." *Journal of World Prehistory* 16 (2):145–195.

Ramenofsky, Ann. 1987. *Vectors of Death.* Albuquerque: University of New Mexico Press.

Rathje, William. 1971. "The Origin and Development of Classic Maya Civilization." *American Antiquity* 36:249–270.

Ravensloot, J. C. 1988. *Mortuary Practices and Social Differentiation at Casas Grandes, Chihuahua, Mexico.* Tucson: University of Arizona Press.

Raymond, J. Scott. 1981. "The Maritime Foundations of Andean Civilization: A Reconsideration of the Evidence." *American Antiquity* 46:806–820.

Reanier, Richard E. 1995. "The Antiquity of Paleo-Indian Materials in Northern Alaska." *Arctic Anthropology* 32 (1):31–50.

Redman, Charles L. 1978. *The Rise of Civilization: From Early Farmers to Urban Society in the Ancient Near East.* San Francisco: Freeman.

Reeves, Nicholas. 1990. *The Complete Tutankhamun.* New York: Thames & Hudson.

Reilly, Kent. 1991. "Olmec Iconographic Influences on the Symbols of Maya Rulership: An Examination of Possible Sources." In *Sixth Palenque Round Table, 1986.* Virginia M. Fields, ed. Pp. 151–174. Norman: University of Oklahoma Press.

Renault, Mary. 1963. *The King Must Die.* New York: Random House.

Renfrew, Colin. 1972. *The Emergence of Civilization.* London: Methuen.

_____. 1978. "Varna and the Social Context of Early Metallurgy." *Antiquity* 52:199–203.

_____. 1983. "The Social Archaeology of Megaliths." *Scientific American* 249:152–163.

_____. 1985. *The Archaeology of Cult: The Sanctuary at Phylakopi.* London: British School of Archaeology in Athens and Thames & Hudson.

_____. 1987. *The Archaeology of Language.* London: Cape.

_____. 1991. *The Cycladic Spirit.* Cambridge: Cambridge University Press.

_____, ed. 2000. *America Past, America Present: Genes and Languages in the Americas and Beyond.* Cambridge: McDonald Institute for Archaeological Research.

_____, and Paul Bahn. 2000. *Archaeology: A Handbook of Ideas and Methods,* 3rd ed. New York: Thames & Hudson.

Reynolds, Robert. 1986. "Computer Simulation." In *Guilá Naquitz.* Kent Flannery, ed. Pp. 263–289. Orlando, FL: Academic Press.

Reynolds, T. E. G., and G. L. Barnes. 1984. "The Japanese Palaeolithic: A Review." *Proceedings of the Prehistoric Society* 50:49–62.

Riboud, Marc. 1992. *Angkor.* London and New York: Thames & Hudson.

Rice, Michael. 1993. *The Archaeology of the Arabian Gulf.* London: Routledge.

Rick, John. 1980. *Prehistoric Hunters of the High Andes.* New York: Academic Press.

Ridgeway, David. 1992. *The First Western Greeks.* Cambridge: Cambridge University Press.

Rightmire, Philip. 1990. *The Evolution of Homo erectus.* Cambridge: Cambridge University Press.

Rizkana, I., and J. Seeher. 1984. "New Light on the Relation of Maadi to the Upper Egyptian Cultural Sequence." *Mitteilungen des Deutschen Archaologischen Instituts Abteilung Kairo* 40:237–252.

Roaf, M. 1990. *Cultural Atlas of Mesopotamia and the Ancient Near East.* Oxford: Facts on File.

Roberts, Mark, and Simon Parfitt. 1999. *A Middle Pleistocene Hominid Site at Eartham Quarry, Boxgrove, West Sussex.* London: English Heritage.

Roberts, Neil. 1998. *The Holocene: An Environmental History,* 2nd ed. Oxford: Blackwell.

Roberts, R. G., Rhys Jones, and M. A. Smith. 1994. "Beyond the Radiocarbon Barrier in Australia." *Antiquity* 68:611–616.

Robertson, John H. 1992. "History and Archaeology at Meroe." In *An African Commitment: Papers in Honour of Peter Lewis Shinnie.* Judy Sterner and Nicholas David, eds. Pp. 35–50. Calgary, Alberta: University of Calgary Press.

_____, and Rebecca Bradley. 2000. "A New Paradigm: The African Early Iron Age Without Bantu Migration." *History in Africa* 27:287–323.

Robinson, Andrew. 1995. *The Story of Writing.* London and New York: Thames & Hudson.

Rocek, Thomas R. 1995. "Sedentarization and Agricultural Dependence: Perspectives from the Pithouse-to-Pueblo Transition in the American Southwest." *American Antiquity* 60 (2):218–239.

Roche, H., and others. 1999. "Early Hominid Stone Tool Production and Technical Skill 2.34 Myr Ago in West Turkana, Kenya." *Nature* 399:57–60.

Roebroeks, W., and T. van Kolfschoten. 1994. "The Earliest Occupation of Europe: A Short Chronology." *Antiquity* 68:489–503.

_____, Roebroeks, W., et al., eds. 2000. *Hunters of the Golden Age.* Leiden: University of Leiden Press.

Rogers, A. R., and L. B. Jorde. 1995. "Genetic Evidence on Modern Human Origins," *Human Biology* 67:1–36.

Rolland, Nicholas, and Harold L. Dibble. 1990. "A New Synthesis of Middle Paleolithic Variability." *American Antiquity* 55 (3):480–499.

Roosevelt, Anna. 1996. "Paleo-Indian Cave Dwellers in the Amazon: The Peopling of the Americas." *Science* 275:373–374.

Rosenberg, Michael, et al. 1998. "Hallan Çemi, Pig Husbandry, and Post-Pleistocene Adaptations along the Tauros-Zagros Arc (Turkey)." *Paléorient* 24 (1):25–41.

Roth, Barbara, and Kevin Wellman. 2001. "New Insights into the Early Agricultural Period in the Tucson Basin: Excavations at the Valley Farms Site (AZ AA:12:736)." *Kiva* 67 (1):59–80.

Rovedo, Vittorio. 2002. *Sacred Angkor.* London and New York: Thames & Hudson.

Rowe, John H. 1946. *Inca Culture at the Time of the Spanish Conquest.* Vol. 2. *Handbook of South American Indians.* Washington, DC: Smithsonian Institution.

_____. 1948. "The Kingdom of Chimor." *Acta Americana* 6:26–59.

Rowley-Conwy, Peter. 1986. "Between Cave Painters and Crop Planters: Aspects of the Temperate European Mesolithic." In *Hunters in Transition.* Marek Zvelebil, ed. Pp. 17–32. Cambridge: Cambridge University Press.

Rudenko, Sergei. 1970. *The Frozen Tombs of Siberia: The Pazyryk Burials of Iron Age Horsemen.* Trans. M. W. Thompson. Berkeley: University of California Press.

Ruspoli, Mario, and Yves Coppens. 1987. *The Cave of Lascaux: The Final Photographs.* New York: Harry Abrams.

Russell, John Malcolm. 1991. *Sennacherib's Palace Without Rival at Nineveh.* Chicago: University of Chicago Press.

Ryan, William, and Walter Pitman. 1999. *Noah's Flood: The New Scientific Discoveries About the Event That Changed History.* New York: Simon & Schuster.

Sabloff, Jeremy A. 1989. *The Cities of Ancient Mexico.* New York: Thames & Hudson.

_____. 1990. *The New Archaeology and the Ancient Maya.* New York: Scientific American Library.

_____, and David A. Freidel. 1984. *Cozumel: Late Maya Settlement Patterns.* New York: Academic Press.

Sabloff, Jeremy A., and John S. Henderson, eds. 1993. *Lowland Maya Civilization in the Eighth Century A.D.* Washington, DC: Dumbarton Oaks.

Sabloff, Jeremy A., and C. C. Lamberg-Karlovsky, eds. 1975. *Ancient Civilization and Trade.* Albuquerque: University of New Mexico Press.

Sage, R. A. 1995. "Was Low Atmospheric CO_2 During the Pleistocene a Limiting Factor for the Origin of Agriculture?" *Global Change Biology.* 1:93–106.

Sakellarakis, Y., and Efi Sapouna-Sakellaraki. 1981. "Drama of Death in a Minoan Temple." *National Geographic,* May: 205–223.

Sanders, N. K. 1985. *The Sea People,* 2nd ed. London: Thames & Hudson.

Sanders, William T., Jeffrey R. Parsons, and Robert S. Santley. 1979. *The Basin of Mexico: Ecological Processes in the Evolution of a Civilization.* New York: Academic Press.

Sanders, William T., et al. 1970. *The Natural Environment: Contemporary Occupation and Sixteenth Century Population of the Valley: Teotihuacán Valley Project Final Report.* University Park: Pennsylvania State University Press.

Sanlaville, Pierre. 1989. "Considérations sur L'Évolution de la Basse Mésopotamie au Cours des Derniers Millénaires." *Paléorient* 15 (2):5–27.

Sarich, Vincent. 1983. "Retrospective on Hominoid Macromolecular Systematics." In *New Interpretations of Ape and Human Ancestry.* R. L. Ciochon and R. S. Corrucini, eds. Pp. 137–150. New York: Plenum Press.

Sassaman, Kenneth E., and David G. Anderson, eds. 1996. *Archaeology of the Mid-Holocene Southeast.* Pp. 259–287. Gainesville: University Presses of Florida.

Saunders, Nicholas. 1989. *People of the Jaguar.* London: Souvenir Press.

Savage-Rumbaugh, E. S., and D. M. Rumbaugh. 1993. "The Emergence of Language." In *Tools, Language, and Cognition in Human Evolution.* K. R. Gibson and T. Ingold, eds. Pp. 86–108. Cambridge: Cambridge University Press.

Scarre, Chris. 1995. *Chronicle of the Roman Emperors.* London: Thames & Hudson.

_____, and Brian Fagan. 2003. *Ancient Civilizations,* 2nd ed. Upper Saddle River, NJ: Prentice Hall.

Schaafsma, Curtis F., and Carroll L. Riley, eds. 2001. *The Casas Grandes World.* Salt Lake City: University of Utah Press.

Schele, Linda, and David Freidel. 1990. *A Forest of Kings.* New York: William Morrow.

Schele, Linda, David Freidel, and Joy Parker. 1993. *Maya Cosmos.* New York: Morrow.

Schele, Linda, and Peter Mathews. 1991. "Royal Visits and Other Intersite Relationships Among the Classic Maya." In *Classic Maya Political History.* Patrick Culbert, ed. Pp. 226–252. Cambridge: Cambridge University Press.

Schele, Linda, and E. Miller. 1992. *The Blood of Kings.* London and New York: Thames & Hudson.

Schick, Kathy D. 1994. "The Movius Line Reconsidered: Perspectives on the Earlier Paleolithic of Eastern Asia." In *Integrative Paths to the Past: Paleoanthropological Advances in Honor of F. Clark Howell.* Robert S. Corruccini and Russel L. Ciochon, eds. Englewood Cliffs, NJ: Prentice Hall.

_____, and Nicholas Toth. 2001. "Palaeoanthropology at the Millennium." In *Archaeology at the Millennium: A Sourcebook.* Gary M. Feinman and T. Douglas Price, eds. Pp. 39–108. New York: Plenum/Kluwer.

Schick, Kathy, and others. 1999. "Continuing Investigations into the Stone Tool-Making and Tool-Using Capabilities of a Bonobo (*Pan paniscus*)." *Journal of Archaeological Science* 26:821–832.

Schledermann, Peter. 1990. *Crossroads to Greenland.* Calgary, Alberta: Arctic Institute of North America.

Schmandt-Besserat, D. 1992. *Before Writing.* 2 vols. Austin: University of Texas Press.

Schmidt, Peter, ed. 1996. *The Culture and Technology of African Iron Production.* Gainesville: University Presses of Florida.

Schreiber, Katharina J. 1987. "Conquest and Consolidation: A Comparison of the Wari and Inka Occupation of a Highland Peruvian Valley." *American Antiquity* 52 (2):266–284.

Schwartz, G. M., and S. E. Falconer, eds. 1994. *Archaeological Views from the Countryside.* Washington, DC: Smithsonian Institution Press.

Scudder, Thayer. 1962. *The Ecology of the Gwembe Tonga.* Manchester, England: Manchester University Press.

_____. 1971. *Gathering Among African Woodland Savannah Cultivators.* Lusaka: University of Zambia.

Sebastian, Lynn. 1992. *The Chaco Anasazi: Sociopolitical Evolution in the Prehistoric Southwest.* Cambridge: Cambridge University Press.

Semaw, S., et al. 1997. "2.5-Million-Year-Old Stone Tools from Gona, Ethiopia." *Nature* 385:333–336.

Sept, J. M. 1994. "Beyond Bones: Archaeological Sites, Early Hominid Subsistence, and the Costs and Benefits of Exploiting Wild Plant Foods in East African Riverine Landscapes." *Journal of Human Evolution* 27:295–320.

Service, Elman. 1962. *Primitive Social Organization.* New York: Random House.

Shackleton, N. J., and N. D. Opdyke. 1973. "Oxygen Isotope and Paleomagnetic Stratigraphy of Equatorial Pacific Ocean Core V28–238." *Quarternary Research* 3:38–55.

Shady Solis, Ruth, Jonathan Haas, and Winifred Creamer. 2001. "Dating Caral, a Prehispanic Site in the Supe Valley on the Central Coast of Peru." *Science* 292:723–726.

Shaffer, Jim G., and Diane A. Lichtenstein. 1995. "The Concepts of 'Cultural Tradition' and 'Paleoethnicity' in South Asian Archaeology." In *The Indo-Aryans of Ancient South Asia.* George Erdosy, ed. Pp. 126–154. Berlin and New York: de Gruyter.

Sharer, Robert. 1995. *The Ancient Maya,* 5th ed. Stanford, CA: Stanford University Press.

Sharer, Robert, and Wendy Ashmore. 2001. *Archaeology: Discovering the Past,* 3rd ed. New York: McGraw-Hill.

Sharer, Robert, and David Grove, eds. 1989. *Regional Perspectives on the Olmec.* Cambridge: Cambridge University Press.

Sharma, G. R., et al. 1980. *Beginning of Agriculture.* Allahabad, India: University of Allahabad.

Shaw, Ian, ed. 2000. *The Oxford History of Ancient Egypt.* Oxford: Oxford University Press.

Shawcross, Kathleen. 1967. "Fern Root and Eighteenth-Century Maori Food Production in Agricultural Areas." *Journal of the Polynesian Society* 76:330–352.

Shennan, Stephen J. 1993. "Settlement and Social Change in Central Europe." *Journal of World Prehistory* 7 (2):121–162.

Sherratt, Andrew G. 1994a. "The Transformation of Early Agrarian Europe: The Later Neolithic and Copper Ages." In *The Oxford Illustrated Prehistory of Europe.* Barry Cunliffe, ed. Pp. 244–276. Oxford: Oxford University Press.

_____. 1994b. "The Emergence of Elites: Earlier Bronze Age Europe." In *The Oxford Illustrated Prehistory of Europe.* Barry Cunliffe, ed. Pp. 244–276. Oxford: Oxford University Press.

Shinnie, Peter. 1967. *Meroe.* London: Thames & Hudson.

Shipman, Pat. 1984. "Scavenger Hunt." *Natural History* 93 (4):20–28.

_____, and J. Rose. 1983. "Evidence of Butchery and Hominid Activities at Torralba and Ambrona." *Journal of Archaeological Science* 10 (5):475–482.

Shutler, Richard, ed. *Early Man in the New World.* Beverly Hills: Sage Publications.

Silberman, N. A. 1992. "Who Were the Israelites?" *Archaeology* 45 (2):22–30.

Silverman, Helene. 1996. "The Formative Period on the South Coast of Peru: A Critical Review." *Journal of World Prehistory* 10 (2):95–146.

Simons, Elwyn. 1992. "The Fossil History of Primates." In *The Cambridge Encyclopedia of Human Evolution.* J. S. Jones, R. Martin, and D. Pilbeam, eds. Pp. 124–128. Cambridge: Cambridge University Press.

Sinapoli, Carla. 2001. "Empires." In *Archaeology at the Millennium: A Sourcebook.* Gary M. Feinman and T. Douglas Price, eds. Pp. 439–474. New York: Kluwer/Plenum.

Smith, Andrew B. 1992. *Pastoralism in Africa.* Johannesburg: Witwatersrand University Press.

Smith, Bruce D. 1986. "The Archaeology of the Southeastern United States: From Dalton to De Soto, 10,500–500 B.P." *Advances in World Archaeology* 5:1–92.

_____. 1992. *Rivers of Change.* Washington, DC: Smithsonian Institution Press.

_____. 1997. "The Initial Domestication of *Cucurbita pepo* in the Americas as of 10,000 Years Ago." *Science* 276:930–934.

_____. 1998. *The Emergence of Agriculture,* 2nd ed. New York: Freeman.

_____. 1999. "Between Foraging and Farming." *Science* 279:1651–1652.

_____. 2001. "The Transition to Food Production." In *Archaeology at the Millennium: A Sourcebook.* Gary M. Feinman and T. Douglas Price, eds. Pp. 199–229. New York: Kluwer/Plenum.

Smith, M. T. 1987. *Archaeology of Aboriginal Culture Change in the Interior Southeast.* Gainesville: University of Florida Presses.

Smith, Michael. 1996. *The Aztecs.* Oxford: Oxford University Press.

Smith, P. E. L. 1978. "An Interim Report on Ganj Dareh Tepe, Iran." *American Journal of Archaeology* 82:538–540.

Smith, Stuart T. 1995. *Askut in Nubia.* London: Routledge.

Snow, Dean. 1980. *Archaeology of New England.* New York: Academic Press.

Soffer, Olga. 1985. *The Upper Palaeolithic of the Central Russian Plains.* New York: Academic Press.

_____, et al. 1998. "Perishable Technologies and the Genesis of the Eastern Gravettian." *Anthropologie* 36 (1):43–68.

Solomon, A. 1997. "The Myth of Ritual Origins? Ethnography, Mythology and Interpretation of San Rock Art." *South African Archaeological Bulletin* 52:2–13.

Sparkes, Brian. 1994. "Classical Greek Attitudes to the Past." In *Who Needs the Past?* 2nd ed. R. Layton, ed. Pp. 119–130. London: Routledge.

Speth, John. 1983. *Bone Kills and Bison Counts: Decision Making by Ancient Hunters.* Chicago: University of Chicago Press.

Spindler, Konrad. 1994. *The Man in the Ice.* New York: Crown.

Spivey, N., and S. Stoddart. 1990. *Etruscan Italy: An Archaeological History.* London: Batsford.

Spooner, Brian, ed. 1972. *Population Growth: An Anthropological Perspective.* Cambridge, MA: MIT Press.

Spriggs, Matthew. 1989. "Dating the Island Southeast Asian Neolithic." *Antiquity* 63 (240):587–613.

_____, and Atholl Anderson. 1993. "Late Colonization of Eastern Polynesia." *Antiquity* 67:200–217.

Stahl, Ann Bower. 1984. "Hominid Dietary Selection Before Fire." *Current Anthropology* 25 (2):151–168.

Stanford, Craig B. 1998. "The Social Behavior of Chimpanzees and Bonobos." *Current Anthropology* 39 (4):399–420.

Stanish, Charles. 2001. "Regional Research on the Inca." *Journal of Archaeological Research* 9 (3):213–241.

_____. 2002. *Ancient Titicaca.* Berkeley: University of California Press.

Starling, N. J. 1985. "Colonization and Success: The Earlier Neolithic of Central Europe." *Proceedings of the Prehistoric Society* 51:41–57.

Stein, Gil. 2001. "Ancient State Societies in the Old World." In *Archaeology at the Millennium: A Sourcebook.* Gary M. Feinman and T. Douglas Price, eds. Pp. 353–379. New York: Kluwer Academic/Plenum.

_____, and M. S. Rothman, eds. 1994. *Chiefdoms and Early States in the Near East.* Madison, WI: Prehistory Press.

Steinkeller, P. 1989. *Sales Documents of the Ur III Period.* Stuttgart: Steiner Verlag.

Stephens, John Lloyd. 1841. *Incidents of Travel in Central America, Chiapas, and Yucatan.* New York: Harpers.

Steward, Julian. 1970. *A Theory of Culture Change.* Urbana: University of Illinois Press.

_____, et al. 1955. *Irrigation Civilizations: A Comparative Study.* Washington, DC: Pan American Union.

Storey, Rebecca. 1992. *Life and Death in the Ancient City of Teotihuacán.* Birmingham: University of Alabama Press.

Straus, L. G. 1993. "Upper Palaeolithic Hunting Tactics and Weapons in Western Europe." In *Hunting and Animal Exploitation in the Later Palaeolithic and Mesolithic of Eurasia.* G. L. Peterkin, H. M. Bickler, and P. Mellars, eds. Washington, DC: American Anthropological Association Archaeological Papers, 4:83–93.

_____, et al., eds. 1996. *Humans at the End of the Ice Age.* New York: Plenum Press.

Stringer, C. B. 1984. "The Origin of Anatomically Modern Humans in Western Europe." In *The Origins of Modern Humans.* Fred Smith and Frank Spencer, eds. Pp. 51–136. New York: Liss.

_____, and Clive Gamble. 1993. *The Search for the Neanderthals.* London: Thames & Hudson.

Stringer, C. B., and R. McKie. 1996. *African Exodus.* New York: Henry Holt.

Struever, Stuart, and Felicia Antonelli Holton. 1979. *Koster: Americans in Search of Their Past.* New York: Anchor Press/Doubleday.

Stuiver, Minze, et al., eds. 1998. "Radiocarbon Calibration Issue." *Radiocarbon* 40(3).

Sullivan, Lawrence. 1989. *Icanchu's Drum.* New York: Free Press.

Suwa, Gen., et al. 1997. "The First Skull of *Australopithecus boisei.*" *Nature* 378:489–492.

Swanton, John R. 1911. *Indian Tribes of the Lower Mississippi and Adjacent Coast of the Gulf of Mexico.* Washington, DC: Bureau of American Ethnology Bulletin 43.

Swisher, Carl, et al. 1994. "Age of the Earliest Known Hominids in Java, Indonesia." *Science* 263:1118–1121.

Tainter, Joseph. 1988. *The Collapse of Civilizations.* Cambridge: Cambridge University Press.

Tankersley, K. B. 1994. "Was Clovis a Colonizing Population in Eastern North America?" In *The First Discovery of America.* W. S. Dancey, ed. Pp. 95–116. Columbus: Ohio Archaeological Council.

Tattersall, Ian. 1996. *The Fossil Trail: How We Know What We Think We Know About Human Evolution.* New York: Oxford University Press.

Taylour, Lord William. 1990. *The Mycenaeans,* 2nd ed. London: Thames & Hudson.

Tedlock, Dennis. 1996. *Popul Vuh.* New York: Simon & Schuster.

Telegin, D. J. 1987. "Neolithic Cultures of the Ukraine and Adjacent Areas and Their Chronology." *Journal of World Prehistory* 1 (3):307–331.

Terrell, John. 1988. *Prehistory in the Pacific Islands.* Cambridge: Cambridge University Press.

Thieme, H. 1997. "Lower Palaeolithic Hunting Spears from Germany." *Nature* 385:807–810.

Thomas, David. 2003. *Archaeology: Down to Earth,* 3rd ed. New York: Holt, Rinehart & Winston.

_____, and Robert Bettinger. 1983. *The Archaeology of the Monitor Valley.* New York: American Museum of Natural History.

Thomas, Julian. 1987. "Relations of Production and Social Change in the Neolithic of Northwestern Europe." *Man* 22 (3):405–430.

_____. 1999. *Understanding the Neolithic,* 2nd ed. London: Routledge.

Thorne, Alan, et al. 1999. "Australia's Earliest Human Remains: Age of the Lake Mungo 3 Skeleton." *Journal of Human Evolution* 36:591–612.

Thorpe, I. J. 1996. *The Origins of Agriculture in Europe.* London: Routledge.

Tobias, P. V. 1991. *Olduvai Gorge.* Vol. 4. *Homo habilis.* Cambridge: Cambridge University Press.

Torrance, Robin. 1986. *Production and Exchange.* Cambridge: Cambridge University Press.

Torroni, Antonio. 2000. "Mitochondrial DNA and the Origin of Native Americans." In *America Past, America Present: Genes and Languages in the Americas and Beyond.* Colin Renfrew, ed. Pp. 77–87. Cambridge: McDonald Institute for Archaeological Research.

Tosi, Maurizo, ed. 1983. *Prehistoric Sistan I.* Rome: ISMEO.

Toth, Nicholas. 1985. "The Oldowan Reconsidered: A Close Look at Early Stone Artifacts." *Journal of Archaeological Science* 12:101–120.

_____, and K. D. Schick. 1993. *Making Silent Stones Speak: Human Evolution and the Dawn of Technology.* New York: Simon & Schuster.

Townsend, Richard F. 1992. *The Aztecs.* London and New York: Thames & Hudson.

Traill, David A. 1995. *Schliemann of Troy.* New York: St Martin's Press.

Trigger, Bruce G. 1989. *A History of Archaeological Thought.* Cambridge: Cambridge University Press.

_____. 1991. "Distinguished Lecture in Archaeology: Constraint and Freedom." *American Anthropologist* 93 (3):551–569.

Tringham, Ruth. 1971. *Hunters, Fishers, and Farmers of Eastern Europe: 6000–3000 B.C.* London: Hutchinson University Library.

_____, et al. 1980. "The Early Agricultural Site of Selevac, Yugoslavia." *Archaeology* 33 (2):24–32.

Trinkaus, Erik. 1983. *The Shanidar Neanderthals.* New York: Academic Press.

_____, and Pat Shipman. 1992. *The Neanderthals: Changing the Image of Mankind.* New York: Knopf.

Turner, Christy. 1984. "Advances in the Dental Search for Native American Origins." *Acta Anthropogenetica* 8:23–78.

Underhill, Anne P. 1997. "Current Isssues in Chinese Neolithic Archaeology." *Journal of World Prehistory* 11 (2):103–160.

Van Andel, H. Tjeerd, and Curtis Runnels. 1995. "The Earliest Farmers in Europe." *Antiquity* 69:481–500.

Van Dijk, Jacobus. 2000. "The Amarna Period and the Later New Kingdom." In *The Oxford History of Ancient Egypt.* Ian Shaw, ed. Pp. 272–313. Oxford: Oxford University Press.

Van Tilburg, J. A. 1994. *Easter Island: Archaeology, Ecology and Culture.* London: British Museum.

Verner, Miraslov. 2001. *The Pyramids: Their Archaeology and History.* Translated by Steven Randall. London: Atlantic.

Vinnecombe, Patricia. 1976. *People of the Eland.* Pietermaritzburg: Natal University Press.

Vrba, Elizabeth S., et al., eds. 1995. *Paleoclimate and Evolution, with Emphasis on Human Evolution.* New Haven, CT: Yale University Press.

Walker, Alan. 1981. "Dietary Hypotheses and Human Evolution." *Philosophical Transactions of the Royal Society of London* 292:56–64.

_____, and R. E. Leakey, 1993. *The Nariokotome Homo erectus Skeleton.* Cambridge: Cambridge University Press.

Warren, Peter. 1984. "Knossos: New Excavations and Discoveries." *Archaeology* 37 (4):48–57.

Weaver, Muriel Porter. 1991. *The Aztecs, Maya, and Their Predecessors,* 3rd ed. New York: Academic Press.

Webb, W. S. 1974. *Indian Knoll,* rev. ed. Knoxville: University of Tennessee Press.

Webster, David, 2002. *The Fall of the Ancient Maya.* London and New York: Thames & Hudson.

Weiss, Harvey, ed. 1986. *The Origins of Cities in Dry-Farming Syria and Mesopotamia in the Third Millennium B.C.* Guilford, CT: Four Quarters.

_____. 2000. "Beyond the Younger Dryas: Collapse as Adaptation to Abrupt Climate Change in Ancient West Asia and the Eastern Mediterranean." In *Environmental Disaster and the Archaeology of Human Response.* Garth Bawden and Richard Martin Reycraft, eds. Pp. 75–98. Albuquerque: Maxwell Museum of Anthropology.

Wells, Peter. 1981. *Culture Contact and Culture Change.* Cambridge: Cambridge University Press.

_____. 1984. "Early Iron Age Community in Central Europe." *Scientific American* 249 (6):68–93.

Wendorf, Fred, Romuald Schild, and Angela E. Close. 1980. *Loaves and Fishes: The Prehistory of Wadi Kubbaniya.* Dallas, TX: Department of Anthropology, Southern Methodist University.

Wendorf, Fred, et al., eds. 1984. *Cattle Keepers of the Eastern Sahara: The Neolithic of Bir Kiseiba.* Dallas: Southern Methodist University Press.

Wenke, R. J. 1991a. *Patterns in Prehistory.* New York: Oxford University Press.

_____. 1991b. "The Evolution of Early Egyptian Civilization: Issues and Evidence." *Journal of World Prehistory* 5 (3):279–329.

_____, J. E. Long, and Paul E. Buck. 1988. "Epipaleolithic and Neolithic Settlement in the Fayyum Oasis of Egypt." *Journal of Field Archaeology* 15 (1):29–51.

Wertime, Theodore A., and James D. Muhly, eds. 1980. *The Coming of the Age of Iron.* New Haven, CT: Yale University Press.

West, Richard H., ed. 1996. *American Beginnings.* Chicago. University of Chicago Press.

Whalen, Michael, and Paul Minnis. 1996. "Ball Courts and Political Centralization in the Casas Grandes Region." *American Antiquity* 61 (4):732–746.

_____, eds. 2001. *Casas Grandes and Its Hinterland: Prehistoric Regional Organization in Northwest Mexico.* Tucson: University of Arizona Press.

Wheat, Joe Ben. 1972. *The Olsen-Chubbock Site.* Washington, DC: Society for American Archaeology.

Wheatley, Paul. 1971. *The Pivot of the Four Quarters.* Chicago: Aldine.

_____. 1975. "Satyarta in Suvarnadvípa: From Reciprocity to Redistribution in Ancient Southeast Asia." In *Ancient Civilization and Trade*. Jeremy A. Sabloff and C. C. Lamberg-Karlovsky, eds. Pp. 227–284. Albuquerque: University of New Mexico Press.

_____. 1979. "Urban Genesis in Mainland Southeast Asia." In *Early Southeast Asia*. R. B. Smith and W. Watson, eds. Pp. 288–303. Oxford: Oxford University Press.

_____. 1983. *Nagara and Commandery*. Chicago: University of Chicago, Department of Geography Research Unit, Research Papers 207–208.

Wheeler, Mortimer. 1968. *The Indus Civilization*, 3rd ed. Cambridge: Cambridge University Press.

White, J. P., J. Allen, and J. Specht. 1988. "The Lapita Homeland Project." *Australian Natural History* 22 (9):410–416.

White, J. Peter, and James O'Connell. 1982. *A Prehistory of Australia, New Guinea, and Sahul*. Sydney: Academic Press.

White, Randall. 1982. "Rethinking the Middle/Upper Paleolithic Transition." *Current Anthropology* 23 (2):169–191.

_____. 1986. *Dark Caves and Bright Visions*. New York: American Museum of Natural History.

White, T. D., and others. 1994. "*Australopithecus ramidus*, a New Species of Early Hominid from Aramis, Ethiopia." *Nature* 371:306–312.

Whitelaw, K. W., and R. B. Coote. 1987. *The Emergence of Israel in Historical Perspective*. Sheffield, England: Almond Press.

Whittle, Alisdair. 1993. "The Neolithic of the Avebury Area: Sequence, Environment, Settlement, and Monuments." *Oxford Journal of Archaeology* 12 (1):29–53.

_____. 1996. *Europe in the Neolithic: The Creation of New Worlds*. Cambridge: Cambridge University Press.

_____, et al. 1993. "A Neolithic Downland Monument in Its Environment: Excavations at the Easton Down Long Barrow, Bishops Canning, North Wiltshire." *Proceedings of the Prehistoric Society* 59:197–239.

Wickler, Stephen, and Matthew Spriggs. 1988. "Pleistocene Occupation of the Solomons." *Antiquity* 62 (237):703–707.

Wilkinson, Toby A. H. 1999. *Early Dynastic Egypt*. London: Routledge.

Willey, Gordon R. 1963. *The Archaeology of the Virú Valley, Peru*. Cambridge, MA: Peabody Museum.

_____. 1971. *South America*. Vol. 2. *An Introduction to American Archaeology*. Englewood Cliffs, NJ: Prentice Hall.

Williams, Nancy M., and Daymbalipu Mununggurr. 1994. "Understanding Yolngu Signs of the Past." In *Who Needs the Past?* 2nd ed. R. Layton, ed. Pp. 74–83. London: Routledge.

Wills, S. H. 1989. *Early Prehistoric Agriculture in the American Southwest*. Santa Fe, NM: School of American Research.

Wilson, David J. 1981. "Of Maize and Men: A Critique of the Maritime Hypothesis of State Origins on the Coast of Peru." *American Anthropologist* 83:931–940.

_____. 1983. "The Origins and Development of Complex Prehispanic Society in the Lower Santa Valley, Peru: Implications for Theories of State Origins." *Journal of Anthropological Archaeology* 2:209–276.

Wilson, Hugh. 1988. "Quinoa Biosystematics. I. Domesticated Populations." *Economic Botany* 42:461–477.

Winters, Howard. 1967. *The Riverton Culture*. Springfield: Illinois State Museum.

Wiseman, David J. 1985. *Nebuchadnezzar and Babylon*. Oxford: Oxford University Press.

Wittfogel, Karl W. 1957. *Oriental Despotism: A Comparative Study of Total Power*. New Haven, CT: Yale University Press.

Wolf, Eric. 1984. *Europe and the People Without History*. Berkeley: University of California Press.

Wolpoff, M. H., et al. 1984. "Modern *Homo sapiens* Origins: A General Theory of Hominid Evolution Involving the Fossil Evidence from East Asia." In *Origins of Modern Humans: A World Survey of the Fossil Evidence*. F. H. Smith and F. Spencer, eds. Pp. 411–483. New York: Liss.

Wolters, O. W. 1982. *History, Culture and Region in Southeast Asian Perspectives*. Singapore: Institute of Southeast Asian Studies.

Wood, Bernard, and Mark Collard. 1999. "The Human Genus." *Science* 284:65–71.

Wood, W. Raymond, ed. 1998. *Archaeology on the Great Plains*. Lawrence: University Press of Kansas.

Woolley, Leonard. 1934. *Ur Excavations*. Vol. 2. *The Royal Cemetery*. London: British Museum.

Wright, Henry T. 1984. "Prestate Political Formations." In *On the Evolution of Complex Societies: Essays in Honor of Harry Hoijer*. W. Sanders et al., eds. Pp. 41–77. Malibu, CA: Undena Press.

_____. 1993. "Environmental Determinism in Near Eastern Prehistory." *Current Anthropology* 34:458–469.

Wright, Lori E., and Christine D. White. 1996. "Human Biology in the Classic Maya Collapse: Evidence from Paleopathology and Paleodiet." *Journal of World Prehistory* 10 (2):147–199.

Wymer, Dee Anne. 1996. "The Ohio Hopewell Econiche: Human-Land Interaction in the Core Area." In *A View from the Core*. Paul J. Pacheco, ed. Pp. 36–53. Columbus: Ohio Archaeological Council.

Wynn, T. 1991. "Tools, Grammar, and the Archaeology of Cognition." *Cambridge Archaeological Journal* 1:191–206.

Yamei, Hon, et al. 2000. "Mid-Pleistocene Acheulian-like Stone Technology of the Bose Basin, South China." *Science* 287:1622–1626.

Yen, D. E. 1995. "The Development of Sahul Agriculture with Australia as a Bystander." *Antiquity* 69:831–847.

Yerkes, Richard. 1988. "The Woodland and Mississippian Traditions in the Prehistory of Midwestern North America." *Journal of World Prehistory* 2 (3):307–358.

Yesner, David K. 1987. "Life in the Garden of Eden: Causes and Consequence of the Adoption of Marine Diets by Human Societies." In *Food and Evolution*. Marvin Harris and Eric B. Ross, eds. Pp. 111–131. Philadelphia: Temple University Press.

Yoffee, Norman. 1990. "Too Many Chiefs? Or Safe Texts for the 90s." In *Archaeological Theory—Who Sets the Agenda?* Andrew Sherratt and Norman Yoffee, eds. Pp. 60–78. Cambridge: Cambridge University Press.

_____. 1995. "Political Economy in Early Mesopotamian States." *Annual Review of Anthropology* 24:281–311.

Yoffee, Norman, and George Cowgill, eds. 1988. *The Collapse of Ancient States and Civilizations.* Tucson: University of Arizona Press.

Zbenovich, Vladimir G. 1996. "The Tripolye Culture: Centenary of Research." *Journal of World Prehistory* 10 (2):199–241.

Zeder, Melinda A. 1994. "After the Revolution: Post-Neolithic Subsistence in Northern Mesopotamia." *American Anthropologist* 96 (1):97–126.

_____, and Brian Hesse. 2000. "The Initial Domestication of Goats (*Capra hircus*) in the Zagros Mountains 10,000 Years Ago." *Science* 287:2254–2257.

Zeder, Melinda A., et al. 2002. *Documenting Domestication: New Genetic and Archaeological Paradigms.* Washington, DC: Smithsonian Institution Press.

Zohary, D., and Marie Hopf. 1988. *Domestication of Plants in the Old World.* Oxford: Clarendon Press.

Zvelebil, Marek, ed. 1986. *Hunters in Transition.* Cambridge: Cambridge University Press.

_____. 1994. "Plant Use in the Mesolithic and the Transition to Farming." *Proceedings of the Prehistoric Society* 60:35–74.

_____, and Paul M. Dolukhanov. 1991. "The Transition to Farming in Eastern and Northern Europe." *Journal of World Prehistory* 5 (3):233–278.

Zvelebil, Marek, and Peter Rowley-Conwy, eds. 1984. "Transition to Farming in Northern Europe: A Hunter-Gatherer Perspective." *Norwegian Archaeological Records* 17:104–128.

CREDITS

Institute of Human Origins, Arizona State University: *v*. Brian M. Fagan/Leslie Newhart: *xxv*.

Chapter 1: English Heritage Photo Library: *2*. Adriel Heisey Photography: *6*. Vindolanda Trust: *9 (top)*. Geoff Tompkinson/Aspect Picture LTD/Aspect Picture Library Ltd: *9 (bottom)*. © Copyright The British Museum: *10*. M. Shostak/Anthro-Photo File: *15*. Renfrew and Bahn, *Archaeology: Theories, Methods and Practice*. Copyright 2000. Reprinted with permission: *19*.

Chapter 2: Neg./Transparency no. 4936(7). Photo by D. Finnin/C. Chesek. Courtesy Dept. of Library Services, American Museum of Natural History: *30*. Redrawn from *The Ascent of Man* by David Pilbeam, Macmillan Publishing Co., Inc.: *36 (bottom)*. Redrawn from Prudence Napier, *Monkeys and Apes*, Grosset & Dunlap, Inc.: *38*. Tim D. White/Brill Atlanta: *44*. Institute of Human Origins, Arizona State University: *45*. John Reader/Science Photo Library/Photo Researchers, Inc: *47*. John Reader/Science Photo Library/Photo Researchers, Inc.: *48*. Original housed in National Museum of Kenya, Nairobi. © 1994 David L. Brill Atlanta: *49*. Institute of Human Origins, Arizona State University: *52*. Kathy Schick and Nicholas Toth: *55*. Peter Davey/Bruce Coleman Inc.: *59*. Institute of Human Origins, Arizona State University: *61 (bottom)*. Photo Researchers, Inc.: *67*.

Chapter 3: Brill Atlanta: *70*. Original housed in National Museum of Kenya, Nairobi. © 1994 David L. Brill Atlanta: *76 (bottom)*. Courtesy Dept. of Library Services, American Museum of Natural History: *78*. American Museum of Natural History: *81 (left)*. Annie Reynold/Getty Images, Inc.—Photodisc: *82*. Javier Trueba/Madrid Scientific Films: *84 (left and right)*. From John Gowlett in Robert Foley, *Hominid Evolution and Community Ecology*. Copyright © 1984. Reprinted with the permission of Academic Press: *86*. Reprinted by permission of Royal Anthropological Institute of Great Britain: *88 (top)*. Reprinted by permission of Professor J. Desmond Clark: *88 (bottom)*. From Robert Foley, *Hominid Evolution and Community Ecology*. Copyright © 1984. Reprinted with the permission of Academic Press: *89*. Howell F. Clark: *91 (top)*. Courtesy Dept. of Library Services, American Museum of Natural History: *93*. From *Mankind in the Making, 2nd edition* by W. W. Howells, copyright © 1959 by William Howells. Used by permission of Doubleday, a division of Random House, Inc.: *95*. Jacques Bordaz, *Tools of the Old and New Stone Age*. American Museum of Natural History: *98*. Eric Higgs and John Coles, *The Archaeology of Early Man* (London: Faber and Faber). Reprinted by permission: *99*. Kenneth Garrett/National Geographic Image Collection: *104*.

Chapter 4: Fanny Broadcast/Getty Images, Inc—Liaison: *112*. After Karl Butzer, *Environment and Archaeology, 3/e* Copyright 1974. Reprinted by permission of Dr. Karl Butzer: *116*. Chris Stringer: *117*. Nationalmuseet Danske Afdeling: *119*. Ministere de la Culture et de la Communication. Direction Regionale des affaires Culturelles de Rhone—Alpes. Service Regional de l'Archeologie: *127*. Ulmer Museum: *128 (left and right)*. American Museum of Natural History: *129 (left)*. Peter H. Buckley/Pearson Education/PH College: *130 (top)*. Neg. No. 39686. Photo, Kirschner. Courtesy Dept. of Library Services, American Museum of Natural History: *130 (bottom)*. Robert Frerck/Getty Images Inc.—Stone Allstock: *131*. Tom McHugh/Photo Researchers, Inc.: *132*. Alexander Marshack: *133*. Clive Gamble and Chris Stringer, *The Search for the Neanderthals*. Copyright © 1990. Reprinted by permission of Thames and Hudson: *134 (top)*. Jack Unruh, National Geographic Society: *134 (bottom)*. Courtesy *Antiquity* and Dr. James Adovasio, Archaeology Unit, Mercyhurst College: *135*. Sisse Brimberg/NGS Image Collection: *137*. C. B. M. McBurney, "Early Man in the Soviet Union." © The British Academy 1976. Reproduced by permission from *Proceedings of the British Academy, Vol. LXI* (1975): *139*.

Chapter 5: Head-Smashed-In Buffalo Jump Interpretive Center: *142*. Brian Fagan, *The Great Journey*. Copyright 1987, London: Thames & Hudson. Reprinted by permission: *150*. Tom Dillehay: *153*. National Archives and Records Administration: *155*. Anna C. Roosevelt: *157*. Denver Museum of Nature & Science: *160*. Joe Ben Wheat photo, University of Colorado Museum: *161*. From *Prehistory of North America* by Jesse D. Jennings. Copyright © 1989 by Jesse D. Jennings. Reprinted by permission of Mayfield Publishing Company: *162*. Utah Museum of Natural History: *163*. Courtesy, Frank H. McClung Museum, The University of Tennessee. Painting by Greg Harlin: *164*. National Anthropological Archives: *169*.

Chapter 6: David Lewis-Williams/Rock Art Research Unit: *172*. David Lewis-Williams, Rock Art Research Unit: *178*. Art Wolfe/Getty Images Inc.—Stone Allstock: *179*. Corbis Digital Stock: *180 (top)*. "Late Ice Age Southeast Asia," *Nature* 324. Copyright 1986. Reprinted by permission: *180 (bottom)*. "Waisted Stone Axe from the Huan Peninsula, New Guinea," *Nature* 324. Copyright 1986. Reprinted by permission: *182 (top)*. Dr. Stephen Wickler: *182 (bottom)*. Paul S. C. Tacon: *184 (bottom)*. Paul S. C. Tacon: *185*. Richard Cosgrove: *186*. Robert Edwards: *187*.

Chapter 7: Peter Howorth/Santa Barbara Museum of Natural History: *190*. Stark Museum of Art: *196 (bottom)*. Robert Flaherty/National Archives of Canada: *197*. Courtesy Jacques Bordaz: *199*. Dale Croes: *200*. Nationalmuseet Danske Afdeling: *206*. O Bar-Josef and A. Belfer-Cohen, "The Origins of Sedentism and Farming Communities in the Levant," *Journal of World Prehistory* 3(4): *460*. Reprinted with the permission of Kluwer Academic/Plenum Publishers: *209*. Donald O. Henry, *Foraging to Agriculture: The Levant at the End of the Ice Age*. Copyright © 1989. Reprinted by permission of the University of Pennsylvania Press: *210 (top)*. Dorothy Garrod, *The Stone Age of Mount Carmel, Vol. 1*. Copyright 1937. Reprinted by permission of Thames & Hudson: *210 (bottom)*.

Chapter 8: The Viesti Collection, Inc.: *214*. Cheryl Sheridan/Odyssey Productions, Inc.: *216*. Bruce D. Smith, *The Origins of Agriculture*. Copyright 1984, New York: Scientific American Library. Reprinted by permission of the author: *222*. M.&E. Bernheim/Woodfin Camp & Associates: *224 (top)*. Mark Boulton/Photo Researchers, Inc.: *224 (bottom)*. Reprinted by permission of Dr. Gordon Hillman: *228-29*. Reprinted by permission of Dr. Gordon Hillman: *230*. Photos by Tyler Dingee, Courtesy Museum of New Mexico, Neg. Nos. 44191, 73453, 73449: *232 (all three photos)*.

Chapter 9: Photograph from The Arthur Sackler Gallery, Washington, D.C. and reproduced with the permission of the Jordan Department of Antiquities: *234*. Andrew Moore: *239 (top and bottom)*. The Granger Collection: *240*. Archaeological Museum: *241 (top)*. Peter Dorrell and Stuart Laidlaw/Institute of Archaeology, University College, London: *241 (bottom)*. © 2001 The Natural History Museum, London: *242*. James Mellaart, *Catal Hoyuk*. Copyright 1967 (London: Thames & Hudson): *246 (top)*. Catalhoyuk Research Project: *246 (bottom)*. James Mellaart, *Catal Hoyuk*. Copyright 1967 (London: Thames & Hudson): *247*.

Chapter 10: Cheryl Hogue/Britstock: *250*. Derek Roe, *Prehistory*. Copyright 1970 University of California Press. Reprinted by permission. Also reproduced with permission of Palgrave Macmillan: *257*. Grahame Clark, *World Prehistory, 3/e*, p. 140. Copyright © 1977.

INDEX

SINGLE PC LICENSE AGREEMENT AND LIMITED WARRANTY

READ THIS LICENSE CAREFULLY BEFORE OPENING THIS PACKAGE. BY OPENING THIS PACKAGE, YOU ARE AGREEING TO THE TERMS AND CONDITIONS OF THIS LICENSE. IF YOU DO NOT AGREE, DO NOT OPEN THE PACKAGE. PROMPTLY RETURN THE UNOPENED PACKAGE AND ALL ACCOMPANYING ITEMS TO THE PLACE YOU OBTAINED THEM.

1. GRANT OF LICENSE and OWNERSHIP: The enclosed computer programs and data ("Software") are licensed, not sold, to you by Prentice-Hall, Inc. ("We" or the "Company") and in consideration of your purchase or adoption of the accompanying Company textbooks and/or other materials, and your agreement to these terms. We reserve any rights not granted to you. You own only the disk(s) but we and/or our licensors own the Software itself. This license allows you to use and display your copy of the Software on a single computer (i.e., with a single CPU) at a single location for academic use only, so long as you comply with the terms of this Agreement. You may make one copy for backup, or transfer your copy to another CPU, provided that the Software is usable on only one computer.

2. RESTRICTIONS: You may not transfer or distribute the Software or documentation to anyone else. Except for backup, you may not copy the documentation or the Software. You may not network the Software or otherwise use it on more than one computer or computer terminal at the same time. You may not reverse engineer, disassemble, decompile, modify, adapt, translate, or create derivative works based on the Software or the Documentation. You may be held legally responsible for any copying or copyright infringement which is caused by your failure to abide by the terms of these restrictions.

3. TERMINATION: This license is effective until terminated. This license will terminate automatically without notice from the Company if you fail to comply with any provisions or limitations of this license. Upon termination, you shall destroy the Documentation and all copies of the Software. All provisions of this Agreement as to limitation and disclaimer of warranties, limitation of liability, remedies or damages, and our ownership rights shall survive termination.

4. LIMITED WARRANTY AND DISCLAIMER OF WARRANTY: Company warrants that for a period of 60 days from the date you purchase this SOFTWARE (or purchase or adopt the accompanying textbook), the Software, when properly installed and used in accordance with the Documentation, will operate in substantial conformity with the description of the Software set forth in the Documentation, and that for a period of 30 days the disk(s) on which the Software is delivered shall be free from defects in materials and workmanship under normal use. The Company does not warrant that the Software will meet your requirements or that the operation of the Software will be uninterrupted or error-free. Your only remedy and the Company's only obligation under these limited warranties is, at the Company's option, return of the disk for a refund of any amounts paid for it by you or replacement of the disk. THIS LIMITED WARRANTY IS THE ONLY WARRANTY PROVIDED BY THE COMPANY AND ITS LICENSORS, AND THE COMPANY AND ITS LICENSORS DISCLAIM ALL OTHER WARRANTIES, EXPRESS OR IMPLIED, INCLUDING WITHOUT LIMITATION, THE IMPLIED WARRANTIES OF MERCHANTABILITY AND FITNESS FOR A PARTICULAR PURPOSE. THE COMPANY DOES NOT WARRANT, GUARANTEE OR MAKE ANY REPRESENTATION REGARDING THE ACCURACY, RELIABILITY, CURRENTNESS, USE, OR RESULTS OF USE, OF THE SOFTWARE.

5. LIMITATION OF REMEDIES AND DAMAGES: IN NO EVENT, SHALL THE COMPANY OR ITS EMPLOYEES, AGENTS, LICENSORS, OR CONTRACTORS BE LIABLE FOR ANY INCIDENTAL, INDIRECT, SPECIAL, OR CONSEQUENTIAL DAMAGES ARISING OUT OF OR IN CONNECTION WITH THIS LICENSE OR THE SOFTWARE, INCLUDING FOR LOSS OF USE, LOSS OF DATA, LOSS OF INCOME OR PROFIT, OR OTHER LOSSES, SUSTAINED AS A RESULT OF INJURY TO ANY PERSON, OR LOSS OF OR DAMAGE TO PROPERTY, OR CLAIMS OF THIRD PARTIES, EVEN IF THE COMPANY OR AN AUTHORIZED REPRESENTATIVE OF THE COMPANY HAS BEEN ADVISED OF THE POSSIBILITY OF SUCH DAMAGES. IN NO EVENT SHALL THE LIABILITY OF THE COMPANY FOR DAMAGES WITH RESPECT TO THE SOFTWARE EXCEED THE AMOUNTS ACTUALLY PAID BY YOU, IF ANY, FOR THE SOFTWARE OR THE ACCOMPANYING TEXTBOOK. BECAUSE SOME JURISDICTIONS DO NOT ALLOW THE LIMITATION OF LIABILITY IN CERTAIN CIRCUMSTANCES, THE ABOVE LIMITATIONS MAY NOT ALWAYS APPLY TO YOU.

6. GENERAL: THIS AGREEMENT SHALL BE CONSTRUED IN ACCORDANCE WITH THE LAWS OF THE UNITED STATES OF AMERICA AND THE STATE OF NEW YORK, APPLICABLE TO CONTRACTS MADE IN NEW YORK, AND SHALL BENEFIT THE COMPANY, ITS AFFILIATES AND ASSIGNEES. THIS AGREEMENT IS THE COMPLETE AND EXCLUSIVE STATEMENT OF THE AGREEMENT BETWEEN YOU AND THE COMPANY AND SUPERSEDES ALL PROPOSALS OR PRIOR AGREEMENTS, ORAL OR WRITTEN, AND ANY OTHER COMMUNICATIONS BETWEEN YOU AND THE COMPANY OR ANY REPRESENTATIVE OF THE COMPANY RELATING TO THE SUBJECT MATTER OF THIS AGREEMENT. If you are a U.S. Government user, this Software is licensed with "restricted rights" as set forth in subparagraphs (a)-(d) of the Commercial Computer-Restricted Rights clause at FAR 52.227-19 or in subparagraphs (c)(1)(ii) of the Rights in Technical Data and Computer Software clause at DFARS 252.227-7013, and similar clauses, as applicable.

Should you have any questions concerning this agreement please contact in writing: Legal Department, Prentice Hall, One Lake Street, Upper Saddle River, NJ 07458. If you need assistance with technical difficulties, call: 1-800-677-6337. If you wish to contact the Company for any reason, please contact in writing: Social Sciences Media Editor, Prentice Hall, One Lake Street, Upper Saddle River, NJ 07458.